Evidence in Negligence Cases

Tenth Edition

PLI Press's
Litigation Library

Complex Litigation, by James L. Stengel and Andrew M. Calamari (H1-3007)

Evidence in Negligence Cases (10th ed.), by Thomas A. Moore (H1-3011)

Federal Bail and Detention Handbook, by Hon. John L. Weinberg (C6-1182)

Federal Rules of Evidence At a Glance/Trial Objections At a Glance (2d ed.), by Kent Sinclair (H1-3010)

How to Handle an Appeal (4th ed.), by Herbert Monte Levy (H1-2894)

Sack on Defamation: Libel, Slander, and Related Problems (3d ed.), by Hon. Robert D. Sack (G1-1293)

Sinclair on Federal Civil Practice (3d ed.), by Kent Sinclair (H6-1538)

Trial Handbook (2d ed.), by Kent Sinclair (H6-1540)

Winning Strategies and Techniques for Civil Litigators, by James E. Lyons, editor and contributor (H3-3004)

PLI course handbooks on litigation law topics are also available. Please request a catalog.

PLI Press
810 Seventh Avenue
New York, New York 10019
(800) 260-4754
Fax: (800) 321-0093
Internet: www.pli.edu

Evidence in Negligence Cases

Tenth Edition

Thomas A. Moore

Incorporating Release No. 2
November 1999
H9-8002

Practising Law Institute
New York City

H1-3011

"This publication is designed to provide accurate and authoritative information in regard to the subject matter covered. It is sold with the understanding that the publisher is not engaged in rendering legal, accounting or other professional service. If legal advice or other expert assistance is required, the services of a competent professional person should be sought."

—from Declaration of Principles jointly adopted by Committee of American Bar Association and Committee of Publishers and Associations

Library of Congress Catalog Card Number: 97-211038

ISBN: 0-87224-107-6

Dedication

The first eight editions of *Evidence in Negligence Cases* were authored by the late Charles Kramer, lawyer, scholar, and teacher, to whose memory this tenth edition is dedicated.

THOMAS A. MOORE

About the Author

THOMAS A. MOORE is the senior partner and trial lawyer in the New York City law firm of Kramer, Dillof, Tessel, Duffy & Moore. He is a member of the New York State Trial Lawyers Association and American Trial Lawyers Association. Mr. Moore is also a member of the Inner Circle of Advocates, a Fellow of the International Academy of Trial Lawyers, and a member of the American Board of Trial Advocates. He writes a regular column on medical malpractice for *The New York Law Journal*. In addition to *Evidence in Negligence Cases,* he is the author of *Medical Malpractice* (PLI) and has contributed to the book *Best of Trial*, published by ATLA. To date, Mr. Moore has had sixty-three jury verdicts of $1 million or more, all in personal injury cases for plaintiffs injured through negligence or medical malpractice.

Table of Chapters

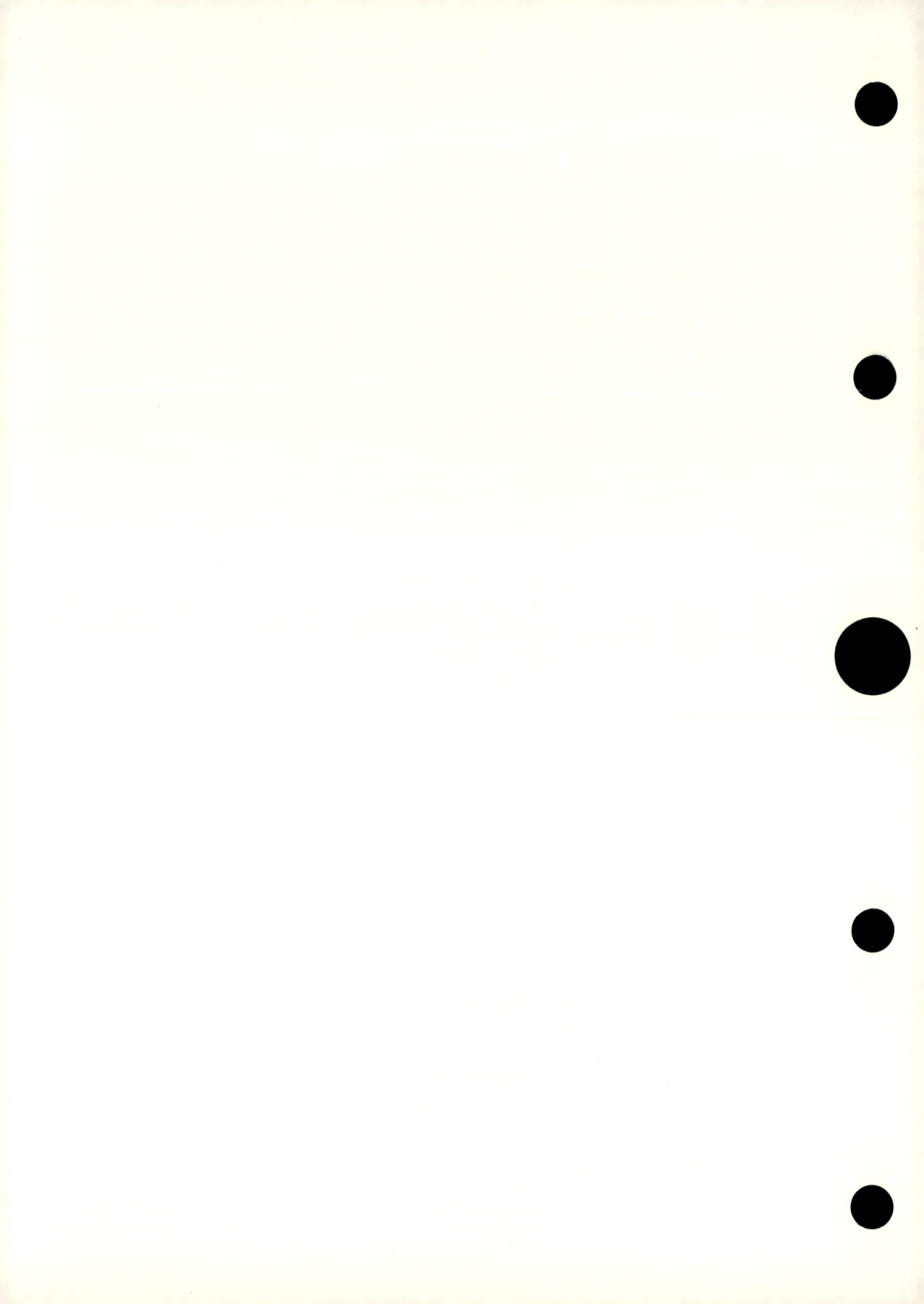

Table of Contents

Part One: Preparation for the Trial

Chapter 1: The Preliminary Investigation

Chapter 2: The Pleadings and Auxiliary Documents

Part Two: The Course of the Trial

Chapter 7: Recoverable Damages and Complicated Judgments

Chapter 8: The Court's Charge to the Jury

Chapter 9: The Summation

Part Three: The Testimony of Witnesses and Demonstrative Evidence

Chapter 10: Presenting Witnesses

Chapter 13: Using Expert Witnesses to Establish the Direct Case

Chapter 14: Impeaching and Rehabilitating a Witness with Prior Statements

Chapter 15: Cross-Examination

Chapter 16: Demonstrative Evidence

Part Four: The Substitutes for Testimony

Chapter 17: Hearsay

Chapter 18: Depositions

Chapter 19: Judicial Notice

Chapter 20: Res Ipsa Loquitur

Chapter 21: Presumptions

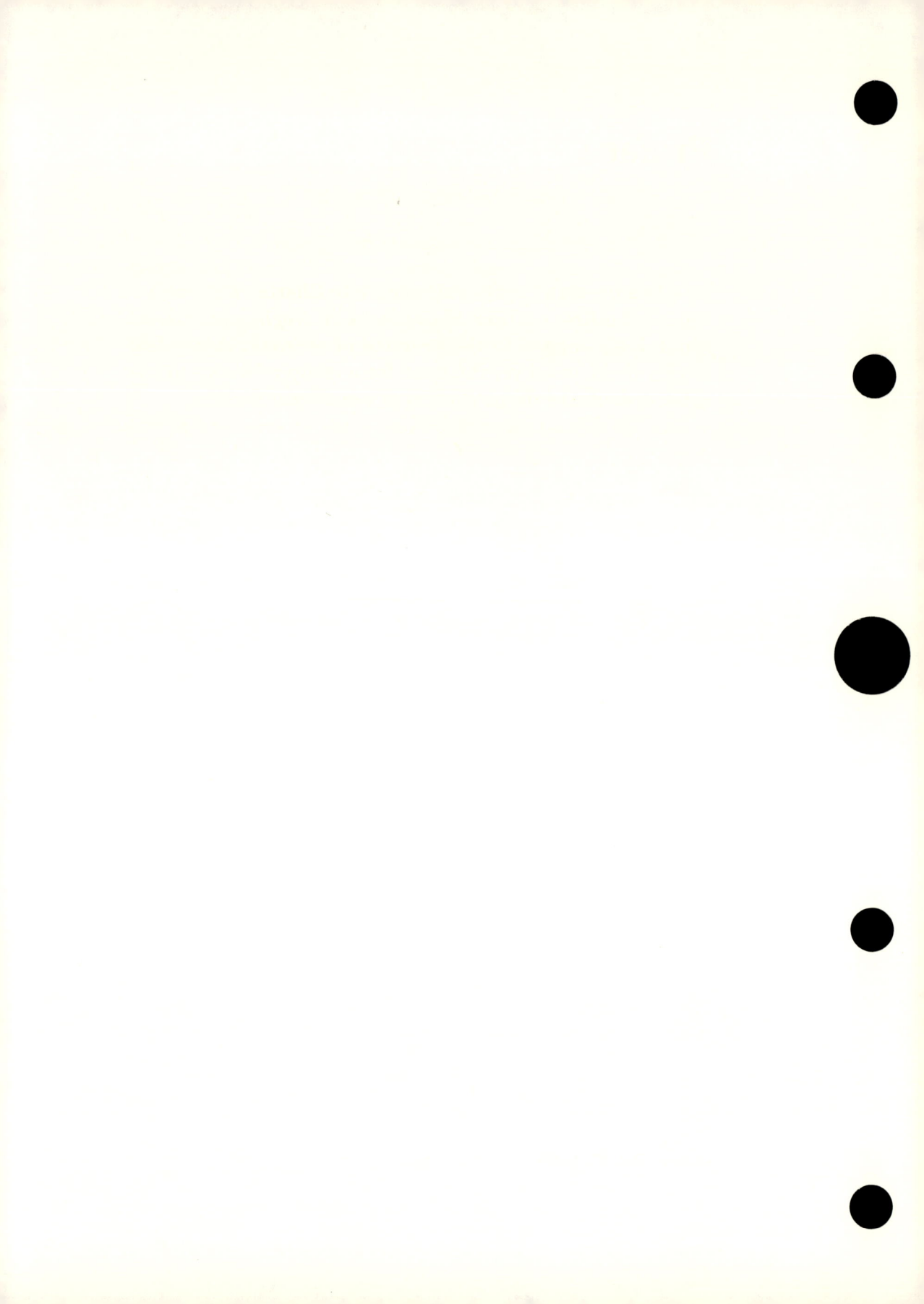

Preface

It is twenty-eight years since the late Charles Kramer authored the first edition of *Evidence in Negligence Cases*. Much has changed in the practice of personal injury law during those years yet the need for a ready reference to the rules of evidence in the context of a civil trial remains.

The Tenth Edition of this book is my attempt to fill that need.

THOMAS A. MOORE

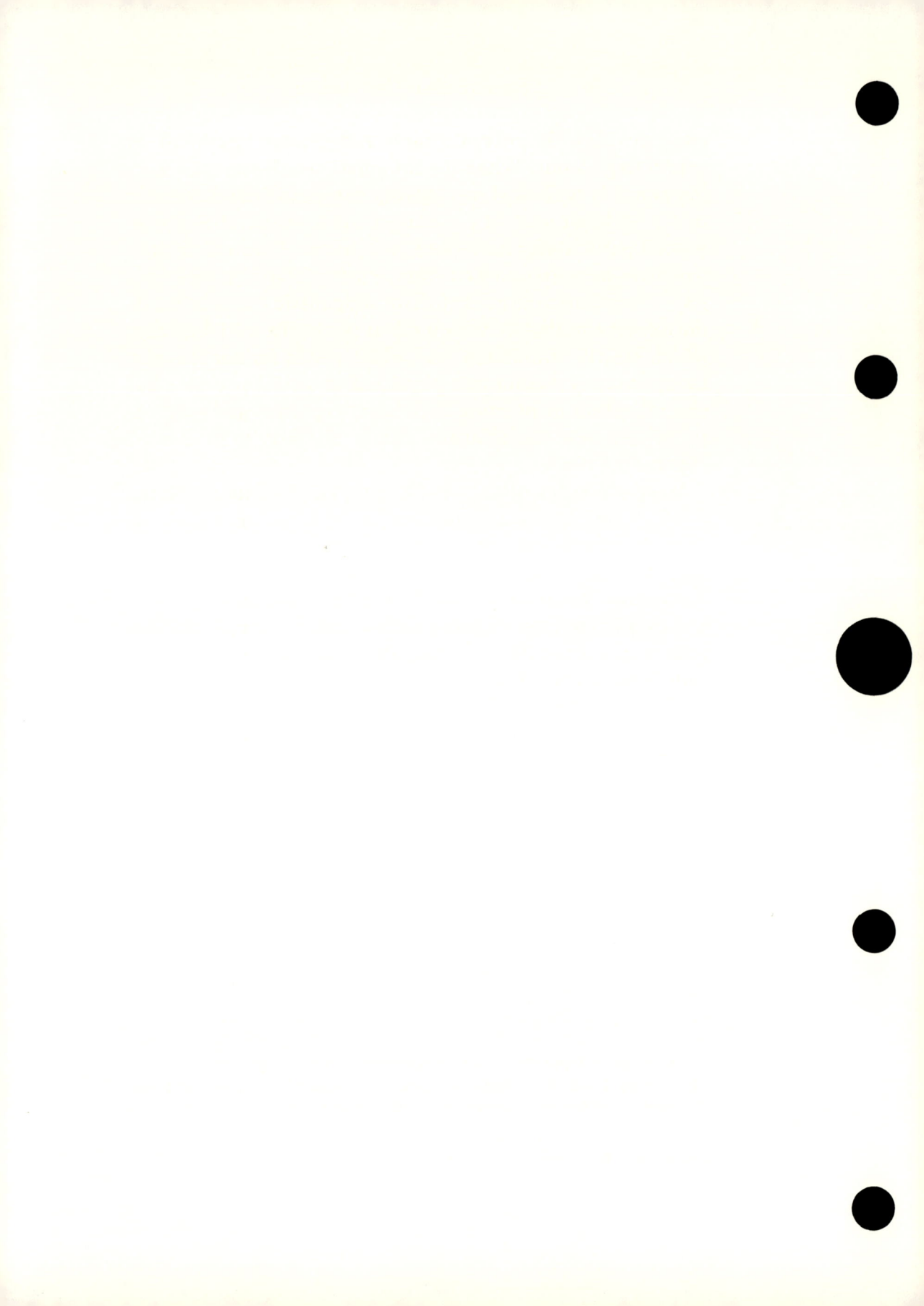

THE PREPARATION FOR THE TRIAL

I

The trial attorney spends far more time preparing for the trial than performing in it, and this preparation begins years before the trial. Thorough preparation often obviates the need for a trial. Therefore, Part One consists of two long chapters. Chapter 1 explains the preliminary investigation of the case and includes obtaining the necessary evidence, planning the case, specific preparation for the trial, and avoiding common errors. This chapter contains more than two dozen forms to assist the attorney. Chapter 2 explains the pleadings and auxiliary documents. These writings include the notice of claim, the complaint, the answer, the bill of particulars, the discovery order, and the marked pleadings. The trial attorney formulates these documents on the basis of his preliminary investigation. The succeeding parts of the book will deal with the course of the trial, the testimony of the witnesses, and the substitutes for testimony.

The Preliminary Investigation 1

Although it should be self-evident that the trial lawyer's success depends on adequate preparation, the headstrong litigator often arrives at the trial having failed to organize his or her evidence into a coherent presentation. As a result, the attorney may lose momentum at a critical phase of the trial and be unable to recover it. Although the attorney's skill and eloquence are important, even the most capable attorney cannot avoid the tedium of preparing the case. Instead, he or she must gather evidence, formulate theories, substantiate claims, and plan a lucid presentation for the trial. Preparation is indispensable to obtaining a favorable verdict or settlement.

This preparation includes both compiling the evidence and marshaling the evidence, i.e., assembling the evidence in the proper order to support the contentions of the client's case. In fact, the trial attorney marshals the evidence four times: when drafting the pleadings, before starting the trial, during the opening statement, and during the summation. Therefore, this book includes internal office forms to assist the attorney in compiling and marshaling the evidence.

Some readers may form the opinion that the author has written his book for plaintiff's attorneys, but that opinion will be incorrect. Since the plaintiff has the initiative, coherence requires us to begin most subjects with the actions of the plaintiff's attorney. Moreover, one explanation may be applicable to both sides of the suit, and the defense attorney must know his or her opponent's burden and details of the plaintiff's claim in preparing a defense.

Part one of the book consists of this chapter, the preliminary investigation, and chapter 2, the pleadings and auxiliary documents. Chapter 1 provides an introduction to preparing to try an action for negligence. Section 1.1 of this chapter explains obtaining the necessary evidence; section 1.2 discusses planning to try the case; section 1.3 explains preparing for the trial, and section 1.4 dispels common misunderstandings. The second and third sections may appear to be premature, but the author wishes the reader to have certain basic ideas consciously in mind as he or she begins the book or the investigation. In particular, the attorney should ask whether he or she can elicit admissible evidence to establish the client's case.

1.1 OBTAINING THE NECESSARY EVIDENCE

The trial attorney has the duty to marshal the evidence upon which the client's case depends. Having done so, the attorney will evaluate the claim, formulate a strategy, and anticipate the adversary's arguments. Meanwhile, obtaining the necessary evidence entails interviewing the client, obtaining medical records, collecting other reports, ascertaining the witnesses and the parties, obtaining another party's rules and regulations, taking photographs, conducting an inspection, establishing grounds for impeachment, securing expert testimony, and contacting the opposing party's attorney.

1.1.1 Interviewing the Client

The attorney should approach the interview with the client as a probing examination of the proposed claim: the attorney must develop the relevant facts and expose unethical[1] or conflicting claims. When the information to be elicited from the client is technical or medical, someone knowledgeable in that subject should conduct the interview. This procedure is particularly important in an action for medical malpractice because an attorney who is also a nurse or a physician can conduct informal diagnostic triage; that is, the expert can decide which claim is clearly well founded, which clearly unfounded, and which needs further thought. Every attorney cannot be a physician or a civil engineer, but specialization in practice does beget expertise and efficiency. In any case, the attorney should be ready to turn to an expert for advice.

Meanwhile, the client should complete four forms during the first visit to the attorney's office if the client's case appears to be at all meritorious: a fact sheet, a questionnaire on client's medical history, a retainer agreement, and an authorization for medical records. The first form (example 1-1) is a simple form for an automobile accident: completing this form will accelerate both the interview and any investigation. The second form is a questionnaire on the client's medical history (example 1-2). The third form is the mandatory retainer agreement for a contingent fee in a negligence case[2] (example 1-3). The fourth form is the client's authorization for the attorney to obtain the client's medical records (example 1-4); this form should be notarized and is appropriate if the client was injured or if his or her medical condition will be an issue.

---

1. For an excellent exposition of the American Bar Association's model ethical codes for lawyers and judges, *see* MCMULLEN, MARINO ON THE MULTISTATE PROFESSIONAL RESPONSIBILITY EXAM (1989).
2. Section 474-a of the Judiciary Law makes special provision for lower contingent fees in an action for medical malpractice.

1.1.2 Obtaining Medical Records

After the attorney has interviewed the client, the attorney should begin collecting the evidence to support or dispute the claim. In nearly every action for negligence, someone's medical records will be relevant, and in an action for medical malpractice, the primary sources of documentary evidence are the plaintiff's medical records, including hospital records, the doctor's office records, and the client's previous medical history. Both parties' attorneys will want to obtain copies of all x-rays, sonograms, ultrasound pictures, magnetic resonance imagings, electronic fetal monitoring tapes, and any other products of diagnostic devices that produce tangible and reproducible images.[3] Such records are particularly useful when they support an action alleging a physician's failure to diagnose a condition and they can provide a basis for alternative theories even when they are not supportive. Example 1-4A is a brief memorandum from the Medical Records Review Service, Inc. This memorandum illustrates how medical records beyond the obvious ones may be relevant. In this case, the records from the pharmacy where the decedent brought his prescriptions revealed other treating physicians—and, therefore, other ailments—of which the attorney was unaware.

The attorney usually obtains such records pursuant to an authorization signed by the patient, dated, notarized, and sent to the custodian of the records at the appropriate institution. New York prescribes a maximum charge of seventy-

---

3. Besides consulting an expert, the attorney should study the medicine in any one of several books for attorneys or in a continuing education course. Several lawyers' organizations offer such courses, but more courses are available through continuing education programs for nurses. For example, the Center for Continuing Education in Nursing and Health Care of Pace University, Pleasantville, N.Y., offers such courses as electronic fetal monitoring, interpretation of common laboratory tests, and even a mock trial of a medical malpractice case.

five cents per page for such records.[4] When the attorney encounters a recalcitrant party, i.e., one who either refuses to produce the records or who repeatedly produces illegible copies, the attorney should make a motion to compel production or to strike the opponent's pleading. Example 1-5 is an order to show cause, with the supporting petition to compel such a party to produce the client's records.

1.1.3 Collecting Reports

In an action for medical malpractice, the plaintiff's medical records are the primary sources of documentary evidence, but, in other actions for negligence, accident reports are major sources of evidence. Depending on the circumstances, a number of governmental agencies and private organizations may have filed such reports. The common types include the reports of police or fire departments, such federal agencies as the FAA, and ambulance or paramedical teams. In addition, insurance claims are a fertile source of documents concerning the insured's accidents.

When examining the reports, the attorney should be alert for recurring events, i.e., anything that would indicate a habit of negligence or that would impute knowledge of the hazard to one of the parties. In particular, previous accidents under similar circumstances could be relevant in an action against a municipality, and a record of adverse reactions to a certain drug would be valuable in a products liability action against a manufacturer of pharmaceuticals. In other actions for products liability, the attorney should try to discover engineering safety reports, internal memoranda, and correspondence concerning possible defects. The builder may have performed engineering safety tests during the planning and construction of the building. Manufacturers of

---

4. N.Y. PUB. HEALTH LAW § 17; Casillo v. St. John's Episcopal Hospital, 580 N.Y.S.2d 992 (Sup. Ct., N.Y., 1992), and Matter of Milagros Crystal Sup. Ct., N.Y., N.Y.L.J., May 19, 1992, p. 22.

automobiles even videotape their safety tests; for example, Ford had taped the safety tests that showed that certain Pinto models exploded when hit in the rear.

A police accident report for car crashes (example 1-6), the form for requesting a copy of the accident report (example 1-7), and the form for a no-fault insurance claim (example 1-7A) are reproduced at the end of the chapter. Since many institutions, e.g., universities, require people to submit questionnaires on their health, such documents will provide information on the party's health before the event. Therefore, example 1-7B is a letter of instruction from a college, and example 1-7C is such a questionnaire. The Consumer Produce Safety Commission is an especially valuable source of information on products and prior accidents. Therefore, example 1-7D is the Association of Trial Lawyers of America's supplement, "How to Use The Consumer Product Safety Commission," and example 1-7E is A.T.L.A.'s form for reporting incidents to the commission.

1.1.4 Ascertaining the Witnesses and the Parties

Utilizing the information gathered from the interview with the client and from the medical and accident records, the attorney should compile lists of the witnesses and the potential parties. Those lists will enable the attorney to acquire additional evidence and to assess the case. For example, when the evidence does not point to one clearly liable defendant but to a group of defendants (as is often the case in an action for medical malpractice), a list of potential defendants will assist the plaintiff's attorney in employing res ipsa loquitur to meet her client's burden of proof. A similar list will assist the defendant's attorney in formulating claims for indemnity or contribution. The attorneys for both parties will want to interview all the prospective witnesses.

There is, of course, no particular form for compiling a list of witnesses. However, to promote the orderly dispatch of business, the attorney should adopt some form and compile such lists. Example 1-8 is merely a tentative example.

As we have already observed, one of the first steps in preparing a case for trial is determining who the witnesses are and what they have to say. However, the attorney may be unable to determine the identity of all the witnesses because the opposing party controls this information. Hence, in every case each party serves upon opposing counsel a notice to produce the names and addresses of witnesses to the event.[5] A party's failure to comply with that notice often will result in precluding that witness's testimony at the trial,[6] or, if the attorney made a good-faith effort to comply, and the attorney's failure was neither willful nor contumacious, the trial court can be more liberal in its ruling.[7] Example 1-9 is a notice to produce the names and addresses of witnesses.

1.1.5 Obtaining Rules and Regulations

One party may obtain another party's rules and regulations with the intent of using those rules as evidence of the standard of care applicable to the latter. The procedure for obtaining these documents is a notice of discovery and inspection. The same notice may demand the identity of any eye witnesses (some of whom may become parties) and a demand for any accident reports. The Notice of Discovery and Inspection (example 1-10) seeks the rules and regulations of a defendant hospital's department of obstetrics and gynecology as well as the names, addresses, and places of employment of the witnesses.

After the hospital complies with the notice, the plaintiff's attorney may have additional names for her list of prospective witnesses. She will certainly have the text of the rules and regulations which the institution had imposed on itself

---

5. Fouchet v. Manhattan Ford-Lincoln Mercury, Inc., 141 Misc. 2d 204, 532 N.Y.S.2d 969 (Civ. Ct., N.Y., 1988).
6. Smith v. Saviolis, 136 A.D.2d 621, 523 N.Y.S.2d 868 (2d Dep't 1989).
7. Bermudez v. Laminates Unlimited, 134 A.D.2d 314, 520 N.Y.S.2d 791 (2d Dep't 1987); DeJesus v. Finnigen, 137 A.D.2d 649, 524 N.Y.S.2d 740 (2d Dep't 1988).

on the date of the accident. Example 1-10A is an extract of just a few pages from a hospital's policies and procedures for its department of anesthesiology.

1.1.6 Taking Photographs

When the plaintiff has suffered visible injuries, the plaintiff's attorney should arrange immediately for photographs of these injuries. Such photographs will preserve the disfigurement in its most vivid state and will be demonstrative evidence on the issue of damages. Without being prejudicial, a photo of the disfigurement, scarring, and subsequent corrective procedures can still elicit a strong emotional response from the jury.

In addition, enlarged photographs of the scene of the accident, aerial photographs in particular, may help the jury to visualize a complicated chain of events. Other demonstrative aids, such as floor plans, diagrams, and blueprints, may also assist the jury in comprehending an accident.

Although the defendant's attorney may be unable to take photographs of the plaintiff's injuries, the attorney may compile the other exhibits and may force the plaintiff to produce any photographs. Moreover, the defendant's attorney must act quickly since the scene of the accident will change with time, and the defendant's attorney may be weeks or months behind her opponent. If there is even a hint of a suit against a client, the attorney should order photographs immediately. An attorney of my acquaintance once observed another attorney taking photographs of the intersection that was the scene of an auto accident, but a third party had already cut down the high weeds which may have contributed to the accident. Fortunately, in some localities, photographic services respond to radio calls of emergencies, take photographs of the scene, and then sell the photographs to the parties. Example 1-11 provides a representative Diagram of Accident.

1.1.7 Conducting an Inspection

When the action involves a device, such as an automobile, that either caused or was a factor in the accident, the prudent attorney will demand to inspect the device. The attorney, an investigator, or an expert should also inspect any premises involved. The inspection will give the attorney a more accurate sense of the event than he or she could obtain from documents.

Be sure to have the inspection conducted by an appropriate expert who will be available to testify. Take measurements and photographs. If someone has already destroyed the device, prepare a charge of spoliation of evidence.

1.1.8 Preparing for Impeachment

While preparing the case, the trial attorney should seize any opportunity to gather materials for impeaching the adverse party's witnesses. (The attorney's preliminary investigation will have alerted her to the prospective witnesses.) In particular, by checking the records of the department of motor vehicles, the National Crime Information Center, and the Central Insurance Bureau, the attorney may determine whether a party or a witness has a criminal record or a history of litigation. The attorney should obtain a copy of any summons that resulted from the incident leading to the lawsuit, and she should ascertain how the opposing party pleaded to that summons. In addition, adverse information in the client's own records or in the client's plea can create a disadvantage that will need to be overcome.

The problem for an attorney is obtaining easy access to these databases. The author was therefore pleased to receive a brochure from a company which sells computer software for obtaining access to public databases. This software supposedly can generate reports which include a party's name, date of birth, current and previous addresses, driver's license and vehicle information, national criminal and driver's histories, bankruptcies, judgments, liens, real property, corporate affiliations, U.C.C. filings, telephone listings, relatives, etc. However, when contacted, the vendor declined to be included in this book for fear of attracting customers who are not lawyers, private detectives, and the like. Thus, the best that the author can advise is that you watch your mail.

In any case, example 1-12 is an illustration of one of the requests listed above: the form for the department of motor vehicles. The attorney should send his or her own cover letter with this form, and the form should be notarized.

1.1.9 Securing Expert Testimony

Frequently, the attorney should consult an expert and review the evidence with him. In an action for medical malpractice, a physician who will testify at the trial may examine the plaintiff and provide a written report to the attorney who requested the examination. If the report is favorable to the attorney's client and if the attorney intends to call the expert to testify, the attorney must serve the report on the attorney for the opposing party. The attorney should also ask a medical expert to review the plaintiff's medical history and records. In an action for negligence other than malpractice, a medical examination and an expert review may still be appropriate. Moreover, additional experts should review the circumstances surrounding the incident, examine the devices and premises involved, and calculate the plaintiff's economic damages.

Example 1-13 is a cover letter which the attorney might send to a physician with the plaintiff's medical records when soliciting the physician's opinion on the basis of those records or when preparing the physician to examine the plaintiff. (Chapter 2 contains an example of the physician's report to the attorney.) Note that the attorney must send the medical records to the physician and that these records must already be organized. Some specialized law firms organize and summarize the records themselves. However, there are companies in the business of obtaining, organizing, and summarizing medical records. Such a company does not issue a medical opinion, but the company's summary will point out gaps and contradictions in the records and may explain the medical processes. Some companies also will recruit an expert witness to review the records or to testify. Therefore, we have included a sample form for employing a medical records review service (example 1-14),[8] the index of the medical records from a medical malpractice case (example 1-15), and two pages from the summary (example 1-16). This case involved claims of a negligent diagnosis and a consequent but unnecessary amputation.[9] Page xi included particularly pertinent comments for the advocate's notice.

Of course, all experts are not medical experts. Therefore, also included (example 1-17) is the cover letter from an economist who was to testify regarding the plaintiff's lost future earnings. The economist attached twelve pages of tables and graphs to this letter.

1.1.10 Contacting the Opposing Party's Attorney

The trial attorney should contact the opposing party's attorney to discuss the dispute. Establishing civil relations with the adversary can expedite discovery, avoid unnecessary motions, and facilitate negotiations. The attorney for either party may take the initiative in establishing this contact, and neither attorney should consider civility to be a sign of weakness. Reproduced at the end of the chapter is a sample letter responding to various demands for discovery (exam-

---

8. Form provided courtesy of Medical Records Review Service, Inc., 1420 Woodland Avenue, Suite #1, Des Moines, Iowa 50309.
9. This summary provided courtesy of Edward Fogarty, Esq. of Omaha, Nebraska. The parties settled the case during mediation.

ple 1-18): the attorney would amend this sample by including the relevant details, e.g., the names of the employees and the list of authorizations. The actual authorizations and bills would accompany the letters.

1.1.11 Conclusion

As a practical matter, the attorney cannot obtain every item we have discussed before the plaintiff starts the suit. However, we have included all these items so that the attorney will understand what he or she is trying to do. Before serving the complaint, the plaintiff''s attorney must obtain and marshal all the evidence he or she can, e.g., an expert's opinion based on the medical records, and the attorney must estimate the evidence which can be obtained when the client's rights to discovery expand with the initiation of the suit. Similarly, the defendant's attorney must investigate the case quickly before serving the answer or the demand for a bill of particulars.

1.2 PLANNING THE CASE

After collecting the evidence necessary to initiate or oppose the action, the trial attorney prepares the pleadings, takes depositions, makes motions, and marshals the evidence. The attorney should formulate the client's position on the facts, as well as the attorney's own legal theories and causes of action or defenses.

1.2.1 The Pleadings

The plaintiff begins an action by serving a summons and complaint. The latter must set forth the elements of a cause of action in sufficient detail to apprise the defendant of the claim and its material elements. The defendant, in turn, serves an answer containing his responses to the allegations in the complaint. The answer must address each allegation individually and may also set forth the defendant's defenses, affirmative defenses, or counterclaims if any.

After the parties have served the complaint and the answer, either party may demand a bill of particulars from the other. Specifically, the defendant may demand a bill of particulars regarding any allegation, and the plaintiff may demand a bill of particulars for any affirmative defense or counterclaim. The party supplying the bill of particulars sets forth in more detail the allegations made in the pleading.

Nothing about these pleadings should be conceptually difficult. Their form is the current expression of a system that is traceable for two and one-half millenia. Our notions of advocacy originated in the Athens of two-thousand-five-hundred years ago. At that time, there was not a clear distinction between political and legal debate. There were formal pleadings as well as procedures for discovery and ascertaining particulars. However, in most civil cases, each party made one speech; a clerk read the affidavits of the witnesses when the advocates directed him, then hundreds of jurors voted without deliberating.[10] The flowering of Greek rhetoric was the result of the attempts of Greek citizens to cope with such a system. Contemporary philosophers, such as Aristotle, defined rhetoric as the discovery of all available means of persuasion, and they composed lists of topoi

---

10. S.C. Todd, THE SHAPE OF ATHENIAN LAW (New York: Oxford Univ. Press, 1993), pp. 127-130.

to aid invention, e.g., past, present, and future, or cause and effect.[11] Pleadings passed through oral and written phases in Roman Law, then pleadings in England went from being oral in French to written in Latin to written in English during the eighteenth century.

Common law pleading now both restricts and assists the lawyer by providing mandatory topoi, principally the elements of the cause of action. The advocate generates proof by applying reasoning to the evidence. Thus, the facts, the testimony, the steps in the reasoning, and the allegations form what one lawyer has called a pyramid of justification.[12] At the apex of the pyramid is the proposition that the defendant is liable to the plaintiff for the cause of action.

Before drafting the complaint, the plaintiff's attorney must marshal the evidence to ensure that he or she can support the allegations. Therefore, the attorney must compose an outline such as the one in example 1-19. When evaluating the plaintiff's claim, the defendant's attorney must compose the same outline. Note that this outline should be more specific than the allegations in the complaint.

An additional source of guidance is the work of other attorneys in similar cases. *Cases & Points* contains the documents filed in appeals of judgments in New York. However, the Association of Trial Lawyers of America functions as a national clearing house of such information. A.T.L.A.'s services include lists of members who have handled similar cases, abstracts of cases, citations to references, and databases on experts, recoveries, depositions, protective orders, standards and regulations, and products. In addition, A.T.L.A.'s publications contain advertisements of documents from particular cases (example 1-19A), summaries of

---

11. ARISTOTLE, RHETORICA, Bk I, c. 2, para. 1, and Bk II, c. 23, para. 24. Aristotle separated deliberative, forensic, and epideictic oratory. See generally CORBETT, CLASSICAL RHETORIC FOR THE MODERN STUDENT (1965).
12. MCMULLEN, ESSAY WRITING CLINIC WORKBOOK (New York: Marino Bar Review Course, 1978), p. 12.

sets of cases (example 1-19B), and requests for information on similar cases (example 1-19C).

1.2.2 The Examination Before Trial

Often, the critical element of preparation is the taking of depositions at the examination before trial. This proceeding sets the boundaries for the subsequent trial for it establishes the positions of the parties and their witnesses. If a witness's testimony at the trial deviates from his or her deposition, the opposing party's attorney will subject the witness to devastating impeachment for a prior inconsistent statement. With that possibility in mind, the trial attorney must consider whose deposition to take. The attorney must also remember that he or she probably cannot lead a witness into the same traps at the second cross-examination. As a general rule, the trial attorney should examine all the parties and, if the action was brought in federal court, the experts as well. The attorney may also subpoena nonparty witnesses expected to testify at the trial, examine their records, and take their depositions.

Once the attorney has decided whom to examine, questions must be drafted to elicit the specific responses the attorney desires. Those questions should focus on the issues raised by the pleadings. If the attorney's own client or witness will be examined, then the attorney should prepare questions to rehabilitate the witness or to clarify the witness' testimony. Thorough interviews will help the attorney to anticipate the impeachment or the confusion.

The attorney should arrive at the examination before trial prepared to try the case; that is, know the facts, understand the legal theories, and possess or have demanded the documents. When dealing with documents, especially medical records (which are easily and frequently altered), the attorney should demand any originals in the opposing party's possession, and the attorney should have a forensic examiner available to examine the documents for tampering.

The attorney who demands the examination usually provides the facility, one that is large enough and free from distractions. Therefore, the attorney's office is not necessarily the best place. Our firm rents rooms for this purpose on another floor of the Woolworth Building, and the New York County Lawyers' Association, which is two blocks away, offers conference rooms for modest fees.[13]

Although the examination is oral, several documents are necessary for arranging the examination and for deriving the benefits therefrom. Naturally, the attorney demanding the examination must notify the parties and the other witnesses, and this notice should specify the documents which these witnesses must produce. Since the defendant has the right to begin the examination, example 1-20 is a defendant's attorney's notice to the plaintif. Example 1-21 is a plaintiff's attorney's notice to the defendant. This document is entitled "Combined Demand and Notice of EBT" because it serves four purposes. First, the notice demands that the defendant appear for the examination. Second, the notice demands that the defendant produce various items, e.g., insurance policies, the identities and addresses of witnesses, the origi-

---

13. Simply as an example, these are the rates:

Room Rental Rates	Seating Capacity	Rental Charge Per Session Not-For-Profit	For-Profit
Meeting Room 1	10-14	$100	$150
Meeting Rooms 2 & 4	10-14	$100	$150
Meeting Rooms 5 & 6	20-25	$150	$200
Hearing Room	30-40	$175	$250
Board Room	35-45	$200	$275
President's Conference Room	10	$150	$250
Auditorium	70-180	$325	$425
Lounge	50-70	$225	$325

Each session is four hours.

nal medical records for an expert's scrutiny (i.e., not photostatic copies), and any photographs, films, or video tapes. Third, the notice demands a bill of particulars regarding affirmative defenses, and fourth, the notice contains a warning that the authorizations for the plaintiff's medical records do not include the rights either to interview anyone or to release those records.

Having arranged the examination, the attorney must prepare to conduct the examination: he or she must be familiar with the applicable law, the facts, the documents, and the relevant specialties, e.g., civil engineering or medicine. In a particular case, the attorney might hire an expert to examine the original documents for fabrications or additions, but, in every instance, the attorney must formulate questions to reveal the weaknesses in the opponent's case. The report from the medical records review service, for example, may assist the attorney by pointing out the gaps and inconsistencies in the medical records. Once again, however, specialization begets competence, and the attorney should acquire standard references for evaluating the cases in her field. For example, a firm specializing in obstetrical cases might compile an EBT Briefing Book from such sources as continuing education courses. The outline in example 1-22 is the summary of the table of contents of such a loose-leaf binder, and the actual contents include such details as the changes in the normal ranges of laboratory tests when a woman is pregnant.

The examination before trial begins with the attorneys stipulating to the ground rules: usually that the parties reserve for the trial the right to object to the content, as opposed to the form, of questions or to object to testimony. One of the attorneys should dictate the stipulations into the transcript (example 1-23).

Whether or not the attorney who conducted the examination will present the case to the jury, he or she should immediately draft a memorandum of what has transpired. This memorandum is incidentally a summary but is principally a survey of how the case is developing. Thus, the attorney should include who testified, an evaluation of the witness's qualifications, effectiveness as a witness, the important propositions he or she supported or contradicted, what the witness did not say, how the witness could be attacked or defended, and whether to use the witness at the trial. Example 1-24 is the entire memorandum of the plaintiff's attorney who examined the defendant, a doctor.

The attorney will insert this memorandum in the file of the case accompanied by the list of important questions the attorney composed before the examination. Moreover, the attorney should revise the outlines composed in order to draft the pleadings, as well as adding any additional defendants to the case and demanding any additional evidence which may have been revealed during depositions. (Refer to example 1-19.)

1.2.3 The Pre-Trial Motions

Pre-trial motions are available for various purposes, e.g., dismissing a cause of action or an affirmative defense. However, this is a book on evidence, so we will provide one example of a notice for discovery and inspection (example 1-24A) and two examples of motions regarding the production of evidence.

The trial attorney should go out of his or her way to cooperate with opposing counsel. Nevertheless, there are times to be adamant. One of those times arrives when the opposing counsel simply will not schedule his or her client's examination before trial. Therefore, example 1-25 is a motion to strike the defendants' answer for failure to submit to examination. Another time to be adamant arrives when the opposing party refuses to comply with the demand for discovery made pursuant to the examination before trial. Therefore, example 1-26 is a motion to compel discovery and, if the defendants fail to comply, to strike their answers.

In this case, the defendants had refused to produce their office records, an intake form, their curricula vitae, telephone logs, and logs for the emergency room. (The moving attorney would append several exhibits to these papers: the summons, complaint, and proof of service; the bill of particulars, and three letters.) Either the notice or one of these motions should induce the defendants to produce their office records (example 1-26A), their intake forms (example 1-26B), their curricula vitae (example 1-26C), or the log from the emergency room (example 1-26D).

1.3 PREPARING FOR THE TRIAL

1.3.1 Focusing on the Issues

The attorney must prepare to present his or her client's evidence in a simple and fluid manner, and that goal requires the attorney to focus on the contested issues. Any digression could confuse or mislead the jury. In order to prevail on the contested issues, the attorney must first determine which facts or theories are disputed, then marshal sufficient evidence to support the client's position, meet the burden of proof, and persuade the jury.

By this time, the plaintiff's attorney will have received the defendant's answer, served his or her own client's bill of particulars, conducted the examination before trial, and completed discovery. Therefore, the attorney should be in no doubt regarding the issues, either the stock issues represented by the allegations, e.g., negligence, or the precise ultimate issues, e.g., whether the witness could see the accident from the place where he was standing. (The real clash between the parties may be far down the pyramid of justification.) In order to focus on the issues, the attorney should draft opposing outlines. Turn a yellow legal pad sideways, then divide the page into three vertical columns.

If you are the plaintiff's attorney, use the first column to outline the plaintiff's arguments and evidence. In the second column, record the defendant's probable responses (arguments and evidence) directly next to the relevant entries in the plaintiff's case. (We are not discussing order of proof.) This refutation may consist of objections, impeachment, arguments, or contradictory evidence. In the third column, record the plaintiff's rebuttal of the defendant's refutation. The defendant's attorney should compose a similar outline for any affirmative defense and duplicate the plaintiff's outline with a fourth column for the defendant's surrebuttal.

1.3.2 Presenting the Witnesses

The attorney should organize the client's witnesses into their most effective order of appearance. Attorneys generally agree that the weakest witnesses should appear in the middle of the order so that the jury will not focus on their testimony. In any case, the attorney must call each witness for a specific reason, i.e., to prove a particular fact in issue. In some cases, a chronological order may be best, but the attorney should arrange the witnesses in a particular sequence for some expository reason. For example, the plaintiff in an action for medical malpractice often calls the defendant doctor as the plaintiff's first witness in order to fix the defendant's positions on the issues at the beginning of the trial.

Moreover, the attorney should draft questions to avoid evidentiary objections, and should review those questions with the witness to ensure that they will elicit the desired testimony (this precaution promotes clarity for the jury).

To facilitate presenting the witnesses in their proper order, the trial attorney should compile a list of witnesses in order, and should record under each witness's name his identity, the purpose or substance of his or her testimony, any problems, and their solutions. If the attorney anticipates an objection to the testimony, he or she should record that item and the justification for the admission. Finally, the attorney should indicate any documents the witness will introduce. The defendant's attorney must anticipate the order of the opponent's witnesses which may affect the order of the defendant's witnesses.

The order of the witnesses in this list (example 1-27) is generally chronological, but the auto mechanic and the plaintiff himself are the exceptions. Although the list seems long, the final version would be longer because it would include more detail regarding the testimony and the documents. This detail would help the attorney to select the witnesses to call. All of the medical witnesses probably would not be called for two reasons: their testimony would be redundant, and their fees would be considerable. The attorney's selection would be based on the content of each witness's testimony and his effectiveness as a witness.

1.3.3 Preparing the Witnesses

Preparing the witness is the key to an effective direct examination and to an ineffective cross-examination. Therefore, the attorney must devote time and effort to the task. First, the attorney should ask the witness to review his or her previous testimony and written statements. To avoid impeachment of the witness, the attorney must ensure that the previous testimony agrees with that to be presented at the trial; hence, the attorney should discovery and seek a rationale for any apparent discrepancies in advance of the trial. Second, the attorney should examine the documents and the prospective testimony that are relevant to the witness's testimony which come from other sources. Third, the attorney should disclose the questions that the witness will be asked on direct examination in an effort to will avoid unsettling surprises, awkward exchanges, or rambling during the witness's testimony at the trial. Fourth, the attorney should anticipate the questions that the opposing party's attorney will ask the witness during cross-examination. The attorney then should formulate any objections to the questions and prepare the witness for the generally unpleasant and sometimes harrowing experience of cross-examination.

Finally, the attorney must ensure that the witness is familiar with the documents that the attorney intends to introduce during the direct examination. When a foundation is necessary to introduce a document, a witness must be available to identify and to describe the document. Hence, the attorney should refresh the witness's recollection before he or she testifies in order to avoid performing this clumsy and time-consuming task at the trial.

To prepare the witness thoroughly, schedule a practice session. The attorney who will try the case should conduct the direct examination while another attorney makes objections and conducts the cross-examination. (A solo practitioner may find that a friend will play this role in return for a similar favor.) The caveat is that the timid witness who needs the practice the most may be frightened away by the experience.

1.3.4 Rehabilitating the Witness

The attorney should anticipate that the opposing party's attorney will attempt to impeach the witness. Hence, the attorney should prepare questions to rehabilitate the witness during the redirect examination. Those questions should clarify aspects of the witness's direct examination that may have been weakened through impeachment or should contest new issues that the opponent raised during cross-examination. Another method of rehabilitation is to call a rebuttal witness to corroborate the original witness's testimony; however, the rebuttal witness is limited to the issues raised by the cross-examination.

1.3.5 Making Objections

Throughout the trial, the attorney must be prepared to object when the opposing party's attorney offers evidence that is not properly admissible. In order to make intelligent objections, however, the attorney needs a working knowledge of the documents and the prospective testimony. For example, he or she should be able to identify the inadmissible parts of the documents that are critical to the opposing party's case. Furthermore, the attorney should construct the opponent's case as if it were his or her own. This exercise will most clearly reveal the weaknesses and problems which the opponent fears and will prepare the attorney to exploit them.

During the trial, the attorney making the objection must state the grounds for it specifically. If the objection is controversial or the law unclear, the presiding judge may direct each side to submit a memorandum of law in support of its position. In any case, the attorney should incorporate the adversary's likely response into his or her own argument supporting the objection. The attorney offering the evidence, of course, should anticipate the objection and formulate in advance an argument in favor of admissibility.

1.3.6 Preparing to Cross-examine the Opponent's Witnesses

The Constitution guarantees each party the right to cross-examine thoroughly the opposing party's witnesses. Naturally, the attorney must anticipate which witnesses the opposing party will present. If someone has testified at the examination before trial or has produced a written statement, the attorney must read that transcript or document and draft questions in anticipation of similar testimony at the trial. Specifically, the attorney must identify the subject and purposes of the cross-examination and formulate questions accordingly. The attorney may attack the witness's memory, knowledge, or understanding of the subject matter. When unable to attack the witness's testimony directly, the attorney may attack the witness's credibility by showing that the witness had made a prior inconsistent statement, is biased, has been convicted of a crime, has committed an immoral, criminal, or vicious act, or has a bad reputation for truth and veracity.

Do not trust either your memory or your ability to cross-examine a witness extemporaneously. Make a list of your opponent's order of proof similar to the list of your own order of proof. As part of this process, record specific purposes for cross-examination, i.e., that the witness could not have heard the sound, and specific questions to elicit this damaging information.[14]

1.3.7 Requesting a Charge

After the summations by the attorneys for the parties, the trial judge has the duty to charge the jury. The attorneys may request the court, however, to charge the jury in particular ways, and the court will rule on the requested charges and inform the attorneys how it intends to charge the jury before the attorneys deliver their summations. In preparing for the trial, therefore, the attorney should prepare appropriate requests to charge. At the end of the trial, the attorney must also be ready to object to elements of the court's actual charge that the attorney considers improper for the attorney's failure to object before the jury retires waives the client's right to appeal the verdict on the grounds that the charge was improper.

---

14. The classic introductory text is still WELLMAN, THE ART OF CROSS-EXAMINATION, 4th ed. (1936).

1.3.8 Composing the Closing Argument and the Opening Statement

In preparing for the trial, the attorney's major penultimate task is composing the closing argument, and the ultimate task is composing the opening statement. The attorney should have prepared his or her own and the opponent's cases so well that a tentative version of the closing argument can be written before the trial begins. Naturally, the attorney must adapt the actual summation to the events of the trial, and should speak from a written or mental outline, not a text. The attorney can prepare the opening statement with more confidence, and, therefore, can practice the speech until it appears to be spontaneous. The attorney should write this introduction last, not first, because he or she will have the best grasp of the case at the end of preparation. Remember, however, that the attorney's closing argument is frankly persuasive while the opening statement must be persuasion disguised as exposition or narration.

1.4 COMMON MISUNDERSTANDINGS AND ERRORS

As a final check on his or her preparation, the trial attorney should examine the case to ensure against committing any common but egregious error, e.g., relying on testimony from a witness who is incompetent to give it. At the examination before trial, did he or she elicit direct evidence with leading questions? If the attorney detects such an error, the plan for the trial must be revised. We have listed a few such errors below.

1.4.1 Asking Improper Hypothetical Questions

One common error is the asking of an improper hypothetical question. A proper hypothetical question, which attorneys frequently ask of expert witnesses, must rest on facts already in the record; consequently, the trial court will sustain an objection if the examining attorney has asked a hypothetical question that does not have a proper foundation in the evidence.

1.4.2 Eliciting Expert Testimony from a Lay Witness

Another common error is the attempt to elicit an expert opinion from a lay witness. The jury draws the conclusions from the facts so the trial court will not admit an opinion from a lay witness unless the subject is within common observation and understanding, e.g., size, age, and health.

1.4.3 Using Impeachment as Evidence-in-Chief

Evidence that impeaches a witness's credibility or discredits his or her version of the incident does not constitute evidence-in-chief for the impeaching party and may not, therefore, be used to establish that party's cause of action or affirmative defense. An exception to this rule arises when the witness is also a party and has made an admission against interest. (See the chapter on hearsay.)

1.4.4 Relying Excessively on Notes

Notes are necessary. However, an alarming error in trial technique is the excessive reliance on notes while examining witnesses. Notes become a distracting crutch when the attorney uses them as a substitute for knowledge. The trial attorney should prepare the questions so well and have so firm a grasp of the facts that the examination can be conducted with minimal notes. Notes should be used sparingly and for specific details. An attorney cannot conduct a facile and lucid examination that will persuade the jury while fumbling through a stack of papers. In fact, the attorney's use of minimal notes is a sign that he or she has constructed such extensive and intelligent notes they are no longer needed: preparation has made the attorney an expert.

1.4.5 Violating Miscellaneous Rules of Thumb

Three important rules of thumb are applications of common sense:

1. Do not ask leading questions on direct examination.
2. Do not argue with the witness.
3. Do not give the witness an opportunity to justify a damaging answer.

Asking leading questions on direct examination is impermissible, of course, unless the witness is the defendant, and violating this rule will elicit an instantaneous objection from even the most inexperienced adversary. Arguing with the witness only makes the attorney appear petty, incompetent, or a bully, none of which will persuade the jury. Finally, allowing a witness to justify damaging answers defeats the purpose of cross-examination, which is to undermine the witness's testimony. Instead, during cross-examination, the attorney should ask leading questions that will elicit answers that are damaging to the opposing party.

1.5 CONCLUSION

Chapter 1 has focused on the preparation for the trial because preparation is indispensable to successful litigation.

Moreover, the effort necessary to obtain the evidence and to arrange it into a coherent presentation is considerable. Such preparation requires keen attention and diligent application; it cannot be extemporized. Thus, this chapter lays a foundation for the legal issues explained in the remainder of the book. An attorney who is thoroughly prepared to try the case will be better able to address even a surprising evidentiary issue because he or she will not be distracted by a multitude of other issues.

EXAMPLE 1-1: FACT SHEET FOR NEGLIGENCE CASES

NAME: Tel. (Home & Business)

ADDRESS:

AGE:

MARITAL STATUS (Husband's name):

INFANT (date of birth):

OCCUPATION: WAGES:

NAME AND ADDRESS OF EMPLOYER OR SCHOOL:

PRIOR MEDICAL HISTORY OR ACCIDENTS:

DESCRIBE FULLY HOW ACCIDENT OCCURRED:

DATE OF ACCIDENT (day of week) TIME:

PLACE: WEATHER:

WAS A POLICEMAN AT SCENE OF ACCIDENT?

DESCRIBE INJURIES, HOSPITALIZATION, TREATMENT
(Dr.'s name & address):

REFERRED BY:

DEFENDANT(S) (name and address)

IF MOTOR VEHICLE (defendant's plate number & type of vehicle)

IF PLAINTIFF'S AUTO (state model)

Collision Insurance? Medical Payments?

Property Damage, if any:

IF PREMISES INVOLVED (describe defects)

How long defective?

Any actual notice? When: To Whom:

WITNESSES:

REMARKS:

EXAMPLE 1-2: MEDICAL HISTORY QUESTIONNAIRE

MEDICAL RECORDS REVIEW SERVICE INC.

THERESA T. THOMAN

LORNA MORELLI-LOFTIN, RN, LNC

1420 Woodland Avenue
Suite #1
Des Moines, Iowa
50309-3204

phone 515•244•MRRS
(6777)
1•800•984•MRRS

fax 515•244•1131

mrrsinc@netins.net

MEDICAL HISTORY QUESTIONNAIRE ©

General Information:

Full name:

Date of birth:

Maiden name:

Former married name(s):

Social Security number:

Current address:

Additional addresses past 10 years:

Current employer: Occupation:

Date of hire:

Job description:

Names/addresses/dates of hire of previous employers:

Medical Information: (Please include **each** medical providers' full name, address, telephone number & approximate dates of treatment):

Family physician:

List all daily medications (prescription & non-prescription):

Medical Records Review Service, Inc.
1420 Woodland Ave #1, Des Moines, IA 50309-3204/1-800-984-6777

Medical History Questionnaire © (cont)
Page 2

Pharmacy: (give dosage taken)

1. Prescription Drugs:

2. Over-the-counter medications:

3. Nutritional, vitamin, herbal supplements:

Brief history of illness or injury in question:

Physician/hospital who initially diagnosed/treated condition:

Additional physician(s)/hospitals treating this condition:

Consulting physicians:

Physical therapist(s):

Occupational or other therapist(s):

Psychologist(s):

Medical Records Review Service, Inc.
1420 Woodland Ave #1, Des Moines, IA 50309-3204/1-800-984-6777

Medical History Questionnaire © (cont)
Page 3

Psychiatrist(s):

Counselors, social worker(s), rehabilitation specialist(s):

Pain management physician or clinic:

Have you ever had a similar condition or injury?:

If yes, please describe each incident:

For each prior condition or injury, please identify each treating and/or consulting physician, therapist, counselor (same as above):

For each prior condition or injury, please briefly describe outcome(s):

Have you ever used, abused or been addicted to alcohol, prescription or non-prescription drug(s)?:

If yes, please advise each substance:

Medical Records Review Service, Inc.
1420 Woodland Ave #1, Des Moines, IA 50309-3204/1-800-984-6777

Medical History Questionnaire © (cont)
Page 4

Have you ever been treated for substance abuse?:

If yes, please provide the name(s) of all providers who treated you and identify the name(s) of facilities that provided in- and/or out-patient care:

Have you ever had surgery?

If yes, please list each procedure and the approximate date of surgery:

Please indicate for each procedure if they were in- or out-patient procedures:

Did you fully recover from each of these procedures?:

If no, please explain:

Have you continued to receive follow-up care for any of these conditions?:

If yes, please explain:

Have you ever served in any branch of the US Military?:

Medical Records Review Service, Inc.
1420 Woodland Ave #1, Des Moines, IA 50309-3204/1-800-984-6777

Medical History Questionnaire © (cont)
Page 5

If yes, please advise the branch, the dates of service and the names of all bases at which you were stationed?:

Did you ever receive medical care, other than routine, during your military service?:

If yes, please explain:

Have you ever been confined at a hospital for treatment of a mental or nervous condition?:

If yes, please identify the facility and provide a brief explanation:

Have you ever reported a work-related injury?:

If yes, please provide details of each incident:

For each incident, please advise if you were evaluated and/or treated by the company doctor or nurse?:

Medical Records Review Service, Inc.
1420 Woodland Ave #1, Des Moines, IA 50309-3204/1-800-984-6777

Medical History Questionnaire © (cont)
Page 6

For each incident, were you referred to an outside provider for consultation and/or treatment?:

If yes, please identify each provider, the approximate dates of treatment, a brief description of the treatment and the outcome of each injury:

Have you ever been involved in an auto accident?:

If yes, please provide details, including the approximate date(s):

Please also identify each provider who treated you?

Are your parents living?

If not, please advise age at time of death, as well as cause of death?

How many siblings in your family?

Medical Records Review Service, Inc.
1420 Woodland Ave #1, Des Moines, IA 50309-3204/1-800-984-6777

Medical History Questionnaire © (cont)
Page 7

Please describe general health of both your parents and each of your siblings.

Is there any past medical history in your family of hereditary diseases such as diabetes, hypertension, cancer, respiratory conditions, blood disorders or any other disease or condition?

And, if so, please advise the nature of each condition or disease and the relative who had the condition?

EXAMPLE 1-3: RETAINER AGREEMENT

Blumbergs Law Products C 540—Contingent Retainer—Straight 33⅓ Percent—1st and 2nd Dept., App. Div. 9-78

JULIUS BLUMBERG, INC., PUBLISHER, NYC 10013

To..

....

Retainer

The Undersigned, residing at..

hereby retains you to prosecute or adjust a claim for damages arising from—personal injuries sustained by..................

....

loss of services of..

property damage to..

on the..............*day of*..............................*19*........ *through the negligence of*..................................

....

or other persons, and the undersigned hereby gives you the exclusive right to take all legal steps to enforce the said claim and hereby further agrees not to settle this action in any manner without your written consent.

In consideration of the services rendered and to be rendered by you, the undersigned hereby agrees to pay you and you are authorized to retain out of any moneys that may come into your hand by reason of the above claim:

Thirty three and one-third (33-1/3) percent. of the sum recovered, whether recovered by suit, settlement or otherwise.

Such percentage shall be computed on the net sum recovered after deducting from the amount recovered expenses and disbursements for expert testimony and investigative or other services properly chargeable to the enforcement of the claim or prosecution of the action. In computing the fee, the costs as taxed, including interest upon a judgment, shall be deemed part of the amount recovered. For the following or similar items there shall be no deduction in computing such percentages: liens, assignments or claims in favor of hospitals, for medical care and treatment by doctors and nurses, or self-insurers or insurance carriers.

Dated..............................*, 19*........ ....*(L.S.)*

Witness.............................. ....*(L.S.)*

Signatures

EXAMPLE 1-4: AUTHORIZATION FOR MEDICAL RECORDS

TO: ______________________________

____

____

You are hereby authorized to furnish to ____________________

______________________________, copies of hospital/medical

records pertaining to:

Dated: ____

STATE OF NEW YORK)
ss.:
COUNTY OF NEW YORK)

On the day of 19 before me personally came and appeared __________________________ to me known and known to me to be the individual described in and who executed the foregoing instrument, and who duly acknowledged to me that he or she executed the same.

____

NOTARY

EXAMPLE 1-4A: MEMRANDUM FROM MRRS, INC.

THE IMPORTANCE OF RETRIEVING COMPREHENSIVE MEDICAL RECORDS

We are often asked to identify the single most difficult obstacle to overcome in potential medical malpractice case reviews. Our response is receiving comprehensive records which are needed to be able to perform the in-depth review. The term "comprehensive" as it applies to records means all "pertinent" records pursuant to the case at issue. Every case is different, so a little common sense must be applied on a per case basis to be able to identify the various provider records which will need to be retrieved in a specific case.

For example, a 49 year old male presented to a rural emergency room with chest pain. The ER doctor examined the patient and diagnosed an upper respiratory infection. A prescription for an oral antibiotic was given, as well as an expectorant. He was told to see his family doctor if his symptoms worsened or did not improve in 3-5 days. The patient was discharged home. About 7 hours later, an ambulance was called to his home and the rescue squad arrived and found the patient had died. He was taken back to the same ER where he was pronounced dead. The autopsy revealed the patient has suffered a massive coronary.

Comprehensive records in this case would include both sets of the ER records, the ambulance records and a copy of the final Autopsy Report. In order to properly review this case, 5-10 years of the patient's pre-existing baseline health records should also be retrieved from his family physician and pharmacy, if he was taking any daily prescription medications. Further, if the patient had previously been seen by an internist and/or cardiologist, those records should also be retrieved.

Additional information about the patient's past medical history would need to be obtained

Medical Records Review Service, Inc
1420 Woodland Ave #1/Des Moines,IA 50309-3204/1-800-984-6777

to determine if there may be other records germane to the potential case at issue. If the attorney discovers the patient underwent triple by-pass surgery in 1995, the identities of all treating physicians and hospitals will need to be obtained and all of these records would also need to be retrieved.

The attorney also learns the patient underwent a spinal fusion secondary to a 1987 MVA. Should those records be retrieved? Not likely, although if the issue of patient compliance is raised during the course of the review, the attorney may want to order "abstracted" or partial hospital records as well as pre- and post-operative records from the neurosurgeon. If the patient was likely non-compliant then, he may not have been compliant after his by-pass and contributed to his own death.

Once all providers have been identified and records ordered, each set must be thoroughly read to determine if the records produced are comprehensive. For example, the family doctor's records noted this patient was referred for a treadmill EKG, so be certain the corresponding report has been received. If pharmacy records reveal the names of 4 other doctors who were not previously known, there may be other missing provider records. The attorney will need to ask the family if and why the patient was seen by these other providers and decide if they are needed. When in doubt...order!

In potential medical malpractice cases, comprehensive records must be retrieved and reviewed. If an attorney bases his/her decision to go forward on incomplete records, it is often a decision he/she may later regret.

EXAMPLE 1-5: ORDER TO SHOW CAUSE WITH PETITION

At an I.A.S. Part of the Supreme Court of the State of New York, held in and for the County of New York, at the Courthouse located at 60 Center Street, New York, New York, 10007, on the day of , 199 .

P R E S E N T :

HONORABLE

JUSTICE.

---X

In the Matter of the Claim of JANE SMITH,

Petitioner,

-against-

<u>ORDER TO SHOW CAUSE</u> **

GENERAL HOSPITAL and ST. PATRICK'S MEDICAL CENTER,

Respondents.

--X

Upon reading and filing the annexed Petition of **THOMAS A. MOORE, ESQ.** dated ________________, with exhibits annexed and upon all the pleadings and proceedings heretofore had therein, it is

NOW, on the Petition of **KRAMER, DILLOF, TESSEL, DUFFY & MOORE, ESQS.**, attorneys for petitioners,

ORDERED, that the respondents **GENERAL HOSPITAL and ST. PATRICK'S MEDICAL CENTER** are required to show cause at an I.A.S. Part ____________, Justice __________________ thereof, at the Supreme Court of the State of New York, County of New York , at the Courthouse located at 60 Centre Street, New York, New York 10007, on the _________**day of**_______________**, 199** at 9:30 o'clock in the forenoon of that day or as soon thereafter as counsel may be heard why an Order should not be made and entered;

Why respondents should not be compelled to locate, copy and forward to petitioner's counsel a copy of the medical records of **JANE SMITH** within five days of the service of an Order of this Court, and for such other and further relief as to this Court may seem just and proper.

NO PRIOR APPLICATION FOR RECORDS HAS BEEN MADE.

Due and sufficient cause appearing therefore, let service by________________________ of a copy of this Order and papers upon which it was granted on respondents: **GENERAL HOSPITAL, 504 Elmford Avenue, New York, New York and ST. PATRICK'S MEDICAL CENTER, 321 East River Street, New York, New York** by delivery ______________________________________on or before the_________ day of ________________________ 199 , be deemed due and sufficient service.

E N T E R :

____

J.S.C.

****Please note that certain counties allow this relief to be requested in ordinary petition form.**

SUPREME COURT OF THE STATE OF NEW YORK
COUNTY OF NEW YORK
---x
In the Matter of the Claim of JANE SMITH,

Petitioner,

-against- PETITION

GENERAL HOSPITAL and ST. PATRICK'S MEDICAL CENTER,

Respondents.
---x

THOMAS A. MOORE, ESQ., an attorney duly admitted to practice law before the Courts of the State of New York, and a member of the firm of KRAMER, DILLOF, TESSEL, DUFFY & MOORE, ESQS., attorneys for the petitioner herein, hereby affirms the following to be true under the penalties of perjury:

I am fully familiar with the facts and circumstances underlying the within application by virtue of a file maintained in our office.

This petition is submitted in support of the Order to Show Cause why respondents should not be compelled to locate, copy and forward to petitioners counsel a copy of the medical records of JANE SMITH within five days of the service of an Order of this Court, and for such other and further relief as to this Court may seem just and proper.

NO PRIOR APPLICATION FOR RECORDS HAS BEEN MADE.

Although this seems at first not to be dire timing - it is. Records must be obtained and reviewed by both an attorney and a physician before this firm can assess whether a lawsuit should be brought.

This office is investigating an action for severe and serious personal injuries sustained by JANE SMITH which accrued during her admission to GENERAL HOSPITAL in of 199 and as an outpatient in ST. PATRICK'S MEDICAL CENTER. In order to properly investigate the matter, assess whether there is indeed a meritorious action and name the proper party defendants, we **must** obtain a complete and legible copy of the admission of , 199 ; Admitting history and physical, pathology report, all CT scans reports and copy of discharge summary along with a complete copy of outpatient records from GENERAL HOSPITAL. From ST. PATRICK'S MEDICAL CENTER a complete and legible copy of the outpatient records from 19 to present.

On , 199 and , 199 , we contacted ________________ (a medical records retrieval company) who wrote to and called the respondents and requested that they forward to us a copy of these records. Duly executed authorizations were sent at that time and we agreed to pay the cost of duplicating these records (copy of our authorizations and letters from that company annexed hereto). To date, we have not heard from the respondent.

Again, because we are under time constraints (statute of limitations expires in of 199), we respectfully request that the Court order these records be provided as soon as possible - that is, within five days of service of an Order so directing.

WHEREFORE, it is respectfully requested that the petition be granted to the extent indicated herein.

Dated: New York, New York
, 199

____
THOMAS A. MOORE

VERIFICATION

STATE OF NEW YORK)
:SS:
COUNTY OF NEW YORK)

THOMAS A. MOORE, an attorney duly admitted to practice in the Courts of New York State, a member of the firm **KRAMER, DILLOF, TESSEL, DUFFY & MOORE**, attorneys for the petitioner in the within action, hereby affirms under penalty of perjury:

That he has read the within petition and knows the contents thereof, and that the same is true to his own knowledge, except as to the matters therein stated to be alleged upon information and belief, and that as to those matters he believes it to be true.

That the sources of his information and knowledge are investigations and records in the file.

That the reason this verification is made by affirmant and not by the plaintiff is that the plaintiff is not within the County where the attorney has his office.

____

THOMAS A. MOORE

Sworn to before me this
day of 199.

____
Notary Public

EXAMPLE 1-6: POLICE ACCIDENT REPORT

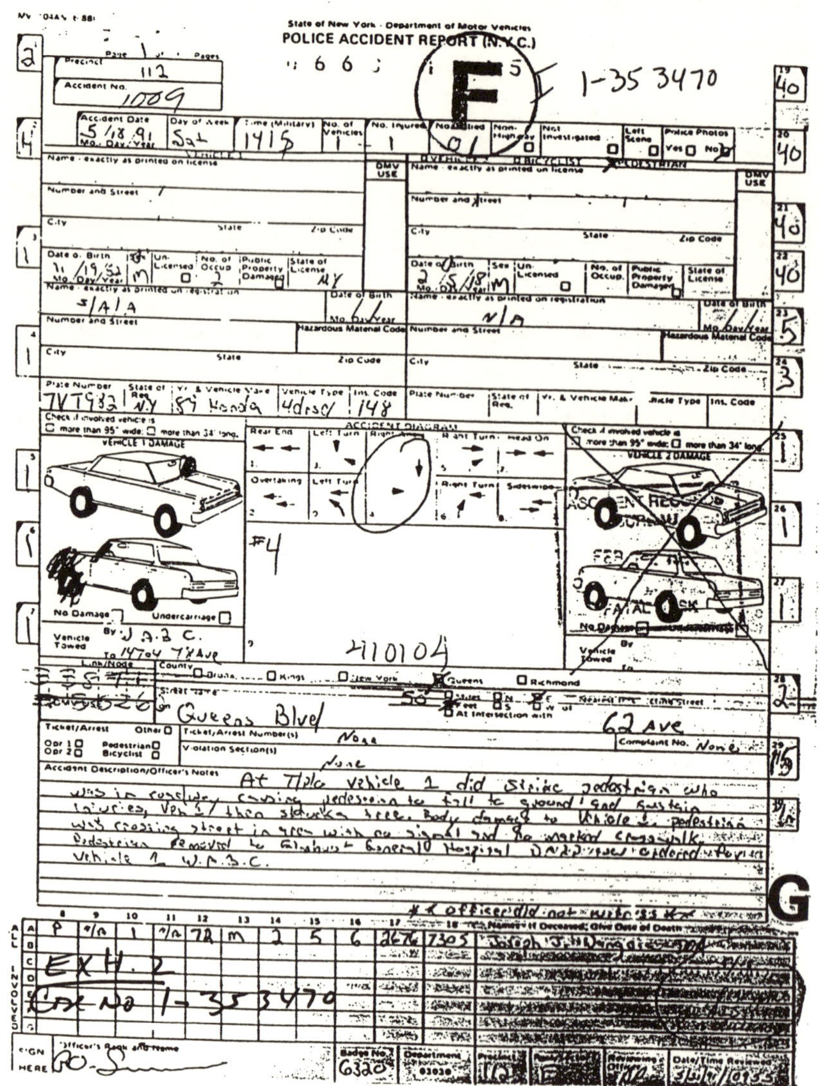

State of New York · Department of Motor Vehicles

POLICE ACCIDENT REPORT (N.Y.C.)

F 1-35 3470

Page 1 of 1 Pages

Precinct 112

Accident No. 1009

Accident Date 5/18/91 | Day of Week Sat | Time (Military) 1415 | No. of Vehicles 1 | No. Injured 1 | No. Killed 01 | Non-Highway | Not Investigated | Left Scene | Police Photos Yes No

VEHICLE 1 — Name - exactly as printed on license; Number and Street; City, State, Zip Code; Date of Birth 11/19/52; Sex M; Unlicensed; No. of Occup. 2; Public Property Damaged; State of License NY

Name - exactly as printed on registration S/A/A; Date of Birth; Number and Street; Hazardous Material Code; City, State, Zip Code

Plate Number 7VT982 | State of Reg. NY | Yr. & Vehicle Make 85 Honda | Vehicle Type 4drsd | Ins. Code 148

VEHICLE 2 / BICYCLIST / PEDESTRIAN — Name - exactly as printed on license; Number and Street; City, State, Zip Code; Date of Birth 2/5/18; Sex M; Unlicensed; No. of Occup.; Public Property Damaged; State of License

Name - exactly as printed on registration N/A; Date of Birth; Number and Street; Hazardous Material Code; City, State, Zip Code

Plate Number | State of Reg. | Yr. & Vehicle Make | Vehicle Type | Ins. Code

ACCIDENT DIAGRAM: Rear End; Left Turn; Right Angle; Right Turn; Head On; Overtaking; Left Turn; Right Turn; Sideswipe — #4 — 410104

VEHICLE 1 DAMAGE — No Damage; Undercarriage

VEHICLE 2 DAMAGE — No Damage; Undercarriage

Vehicle Towed By J.A.B.C. To 147-04 7X Ave

County: Bronx, Kings, New York, Queens [X], Richmond

On Queens Blvd — 50 Feet E of 62 Ave

Ticket/Arrest: Opr 1, Opr 2, Pedestrian, Bicyclist, Other — Ticket/Arrest Number(s) None — Violation Section(s) None — Complaint No. None

Accident Description/Officer's Notes: At T/P/O vehicle 1 did strike pedestrian who was in roadway causing pedestrian to fall to ground and sustain injuries, veh 1 then struck a tree. Body damage to vehicle 1. Pedestrian was crossing street in area with no signal and no marked crosswalk. Pedestrian removed to Elmhurst General Hospital [illegible] vehicle 1 W.A.B.C.

** officer did not witness **

	8	9	10	11	12	13	14	15	16	17	18 Names - If Deceased, Give Date of Death
A	P	n/a	1	n/a	72	M	2	5	6	2676	7305 Joseph J. [illegible]
B											
C											

EXH. 2 — Case No 1-353470

Sign Here — Officer's Rank and Name — P.O. [signature] | Badge No. 6320 | Department 03030 | Precinct 112 | Reviewing Officer | Date/Time Reviewed

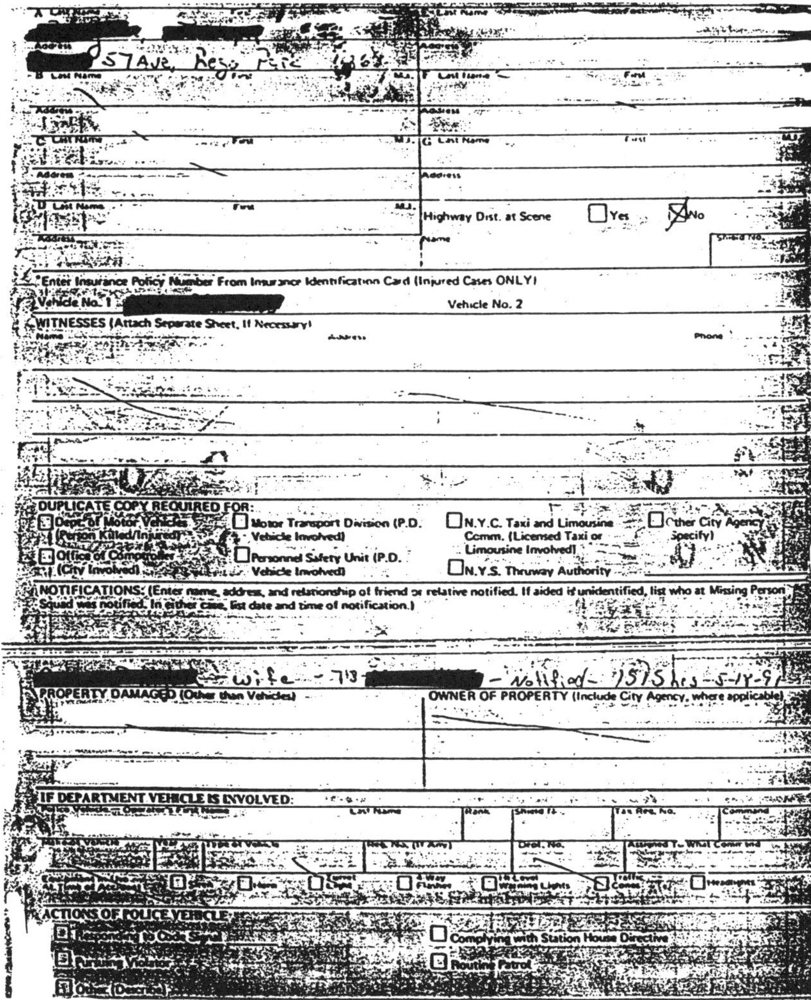

A Last Name | First | M.I. | E Last Name | First | M.I.

Address: 57 Ave, Rego Park

B Last Name | First | M.I. | F Last Name | First

Address | Address

C Last Name | First | M.I. | G Last Name | First | M.I.

Address | Address

D Last Name | First | M.I. | Highway Dist. at Scene ☐ Yes ☒ No

Address | Name | Shield No.

*Enter Insurance Policy Number From Insurance Identification Card (Injured Cases ONLY)

Vehicle No. 1 | Vehicle No. 2

WITNESSES (Attach Separate Sheet, If Necessary)

Name | Address | Phone

DUPLICATE COPY REQUIRED FOR:

☐ Dept. of Motor Vehicles (Person Killed/Injured)
☐ Office of Comptroller (City Involved)
☐ Motor Transport Division (P.D. Vehicle Involved)
☐ Personnel Safety Unit (P.D. Vehicle Involved)
☐ N.Y.C. Taxi and Limousine Comm. (Licensed Taxi or Limousine Involved)
☐ N.Y.S. Thruway Authority
☐ Other City Agency (Specify)

NOTIFICATIONS: (Enter name, address, and relationship of friend or relative notified. If aided is unidentified, list who at Missing Person Squad was notified. In either case, list date and time of notification.)

wife - 718 - Notified - 1515 hrs - 5-18-91

PROPERTY DAMAGED (Other than Vehicles) | OWNER OF PROPERTY (Include City Agency, where applicable)

IF DEPARTMENT VEHICLE IS INVOLVED:

Police Vehicle — Operator's First Name | Last Name | Rank | Shield No. | Tax Reg. No. | Command

Vehicle | Year | Type of Vehicle | Reg. No. (If Any) | Dept. No. | Assigned To What Command

Equipment In Use At Time of Accident: ☐ Siren ☐ Horn ☐ Turret Light ☐ 4 Way Flashers ☐ Hi Level Warning Lights ☐ Traffic Cones ☐ Headlights

ACTIONS OF POLICE VEHICLE:

☐ Responding to Code Signal
☐ Pursuing Violator
☐ Other (Describe)
☐ Complying with Station House Directive
☐ Routine Patrol

EXAMPLE 1-7: REQUEST FOR COPY OF AIDED/ ACCIDENT REPORT

REQUEST FOR COPY OF AIDED / ACCIDENT RECORD
PD 301-161 (Rev. 3-95)-H1

DO NOT DETACH - SUBMIT IN DUPLICATE

FOR EACH RECORD DESIRED, A SEPARATE APPLICATION IS REQUIRED
A SEARCH AND SERVICE FEE OF **$10.00** MUST ACCOMPANY EACH APPLICATION.
DO NOT SEND CASH

FOR USE BY AIDED UNIT ONLY

CHECK RECORD DESIRED

☐ AIDED REPORT (PD 304-152)

☐ POLICE ACCIDENT REPORT (MV-104 AN)

☐ MOTOR VEHICLE ACCIDENT AND MECHANISM REPORT (PD 301-151) WITNESS STATEMENT - VEHICLE ACCIDENT (PD 301-061)

NAME AND ADDRESS OF PERSON TO WHOM RECORD IS TO BE MAILED SHALL BE PRINTED OR TYPED IN THIS SPACE BY APPLICANT

Check One
☐ Mail-in
☐ In person request

INSTRUCTIONS FOR MAIL-IN REQUESTS

1. Information MUST be typed or printed. Incomplete information may result in the return of your application.
2. Include check or money order for **$10.00** payable to NYC Police Dept. THIS FEE IS NOT REFUNDABLE. DO NOT SEND CASH
3. Enclose a stamped, self-addressed envelope.
4. MAIL TO:

A) Aided Reports (PD 304-152)	New York City Police Department P.O. Box 2525 New York, N.Y. 10272-0525 Att.: Aided Unit
B) Police Accident Report (MV-104AN)	Precinct of Occurrence Call 212-374-5000 For Precinct Mailing Address (30 Days Maximum) Request for Police Accident Reports Beyond 30 Days Should Be Directed To The N.Y.S. Dept. of Motor Vehicles
C) Motor Vehicle Accident And Mechanism Report (PD 301-151) Witness Statement-vehicle Accident (PD 301-061)	New York City Police Department Highway Unit #3 198-13 Grand Central Parkway Queens, N.Y. 11423 Att.: A.I.S.

NOTE: Sections 2 and 4 MUST be completed in all cases or your request will be returned. Completion of the additional sections will help to insure a thorough search.

IF A MOTOR VEHICLE WAS INVOLVED, CHECK HERE ☐ IF NO MOTOR VEHICLE WAS INVOLVED, CHECK HERE ☐

1. License Plate Number(s) if known: Plate 1 | Plate 2 | Plate 3 | Plate 4
2. Date of Occurrence
3. Name(s) of All Injured [Include Year of Birth and Sex]
4. Place of Occurrence [Include Nearest Intersecting Street]
5. Precinct of Occurrence
6. Acc./Aided Report No.
7. Operator(s) of Vehicle(s)—Where Applicable
8. Owner(s) of Vehicle(s)—Where Applicable
9. Aided/Accident Information Reported To: Rank | Name | Shield No. | Precinct

EXAMPLE 1-7A: NO-FAULT INSURANCE CLAIM

ALLSTATE INSURANCE COMPANY
NEW YORK MOTOR VEHICLE NO-FAULT INSURANCE LAW
APPLICATION FOR MOTOR VEHICLE NO-FAULT BENEFITS

Market Claim Office
99 Sunnyside Blvd
Woodbury, NY 11797
(516) 682-7000

DATE : 10/10/97 POLICY NO : [redacted]
POLHLD:.
ACCIDENT DATE : 07/29/97 FILE NO : [redacted]

ESTATE OF

NY 11572

DESK : 2CY VF2

TO ENABLE US TO DETERMINE IF YOU ARE ENTITLED TO BENEFITS UNDER THE NEW YORK COMPREHENSIVE AUTOMOBILE INSURANCE REPARATIONS ACT, PLEASE COMPLETE THIS FORM AND RETURN IT PROMPTLY.

IMPORTANT
1. To be eligible for benefits you must complete and sign this Application.
2. You must also sign any attached Authorization(s).
3. Return promptly with copies of any bills you have received to date.

1. Your Name — 2. Phone No. Home Business

3. Your Address (No., Street, City or Town and Zip Code) — 4. Date of Birth — 5. Social Security No.

6. Date and Time of Accident: A.M. P.M. — 7. Place of Accident (Street, City or Town and State)

8. Brief Description of Accident

9. Describe Your Injury:

10. Identity of Vehicle You Occupied or Operated at the Time of the Accident
Owner's Name Make Year

11. Were you the driver of the Motor Vehicle? Yes ☐ No ☐
Were you a passenger in the Motor Vehicle? Yes ☐ No ☐
Were you a pedestrian? Yes ☐ No ☐
Were you a member of Our Policyholders household? Yes ☐ No ☐
Do you or a relative with whom you reside own a Motor Vehicle? Yes ☐ No ☐

This vehicle was:
☐ A bus or school bus ☐ An automobile
☐ A truck ☐ A motorcycle

Written proof of claim for other necessary expenses must be submitted as soon as reasonably practicable but, in no event, later than 90 days after services are rendered.

12. Were you treated by a doctor(s) or other person(s) furnishing health services? Yes ☐ No ☐
Names and Addresses of such doctor(s) or Person(s): ______

13. If you were treated at a hospital(s) were you an out-patient? ☐ In-patient? ☐ Date of Admission ______
Hospital's name and Address: ______

14. Amount of health bills to date: $
15. Will you have more health treatment? Yes ☐ No ☐
16. At the time of your accident were you in the course of your employment? Yes ☐ No ☐

17. Did you lose time from work? Yes ☐ No ☐ If yes, how much time?
18. Were you receiving unemployment benefits at the time of the accident? Yes ☐ No ☐
19. What are your Average Weekly Earnings? $ ____________

20. If you lost time: Date disability from work began:
Have you returned to work? Yes ☐ No ☐
If yes, date returned to work ____________
Number of days you work per week
Number of hours you work per day ____________

21. List names and addresses of your Employer and other Employers for one year prior to accident date and give occupation and dates of employment:

Employer and Address	Occupation	From	To
Employer and Address	Occupation	From	To
Employer and Address	Occupation	From	To

22. As a result of your injury have you had any other expenses? Yes ☐ No ☐
If Yes, attach explanation and amounts of such expenses.

23. Due to this accident have you received or are you eligible for payments under any of the following:
New York State disability Yes ☐ No ☐ Workmen's compensation Yes ☐ No ☐

The applicant authorizes the insurer to submit any and all of these forms to another party or insurer if such is necessary to perfect its rights of recovery provided for under the No-Fault Law.

"ANY PERSON WHO KNOWINGLY AND WITH INTENT TO DEFRAUD ANY INSURANCE COMPANY OR OTHER PERSON FILES AN APPLICATION FOR INSURANCE CONTAINING ANY MATERIALLY FALSE INFORMATION, OR CONCEALS FOR THE PURPOSE OF MISLEADING, INFORMATION CONCERNING ANY FACT MATERIAL THERETO, AND ANY PERSON WHO KNOWINGLY MAKES OR KNOWINGLY ASSISTS, ABETS, SOLICITS OR CONSPIRES WITH ANOTHER TO MAKE A FALSE REPORT OF THE THEFT, DESTRUCTION, DAMAGE OR CONVERSION OF ANY MOTOR VEHICLE TO A LAW ENFORCEMENT AGENCY, THE DEPARTMENT OF MOTOR VEHICLES OR AN INSURANCE COMPANY COMMITS A FRAUDULENT INSURANCE ACT, WHICH IS A CRIME, AND SHALL ALSO BE SUBJECT TO A CIVIL PENALTY NOT TO EXCEED FIVE THOUSAND DOLLARS AND THE VALUE OF THE SUBJECT MOTOR VEHICLE OR STATED CLAIM FOR EACH VIOLATION."

Signature ____________ Date ____________

C1363CNY-2 NF-2A

DO NOT DETACH

AUTHORIZATION FOR RELEASE OF WORK AND OTHER LOSS INFORMATION

This authorization or photocopy hereof, will authorize you to furnish all information you may have regarding my wages, salary or other loss while employed by you. You are authorized to provide this information in accordance with the NEW YORK COMPREHENSIVE MOTOR VEHICLE INSURANCE REPARATIONS ACT (NO-FAULT LAW).

NAME (PRINT OR TYPE) ____________ Social Security No. ____________

Signature ____________ Date ____________

C1363ANY-2

DO NOT DETACH

AUTHORIZATION FOR RELEASE OF HEALTH SERVICE OR TREATMENT INFORMATION

This authorization or photocopy hereof, will authorize you to furnish all information you may have regarding my condition while under youR observation or treatment, including the history obtained, X-ray and physical findings, diagnosis and prognosis. You are authorized to provide this information in accordance with the NEW YORK COMPREHENSIVE MOTOR VEHICLE INSURANCE REPARATIONS ACT(NO-FAULT LAW).

NAME (PRINT OR TYPE) ____________

Signature ____________ Date ____________

(If a minor, parent or guardian shall sign and indicate capacity and relationship)

C1363BNY-2

NOTICE AND PROOF OF CLAIM FOR DISABILITY BENEFITS

CLAIMANT: READ THE FOLLOWING INSTRUCTIONS CAREFULLY

1. USE THIS FORM ONLY IF YOU BECOME SICK OR DISABLED **WHILE EMPLOYED** OR IF YOU BECOME SICK OR DISABLED **WITHIN FOUR (4) WEEKS AFTER TERMINATION OF EMPLOYMENT**. USE **GREEN** CLAIM FORM **DB-300** IF YOU **BECOME** SICK OR DISABLED AFTER HAVING BEEN **UNEMPLOYED MORE THAN FOUR (4) WEEKS.**
2. YOU MUST COMPLETE ALL ITEMS OF PART A - THE **"CLAIMANT'S STATEMENT."** BE ACCURATE. CHECK ALL DATES.
3. BE SURE TO DATE AND SIGN YOUR CLAIM (SEE ITEM 12). IF YOU CANNOT SIGN THIS CLAIM FORM, YOUR REPRESENTATIVE MAY SIGN IN YOUR BEHALF. IN THAT EVENT, THE NAME, ADDRESS AND REPRESENTATIVE'S RELATIONSHIP TO YOU SHOULD BE NOTED UNDER THE SIGNATURE.
4. **DO NOT MAIL THIS CLAIM UNLESS YOUR HEALTH CARE PROVIDER COMPLETES AND SIGNS PART B - THE "HEALTH CARE PROVIDER'S STATEMENT."**
5. YOUR COMPLETED CLAIM SHOULD BE MAILED WITHIN THIRTY (30) DAYS AFTER YOU BECOME SICK OR DISABLED TO YOUR LAST EMPLOYER OR **YOUR LAST EMPLOYER'S INSURANCE COMPANY**.
6. MAKE A COPY OF THIS COMPLETED FORM FOR YOUR RECORDS BEFORE YOU SUBMIT IT.

Any person who knowingly and with intent to defraud any insurance company or other person files an application for insurance containing any materially false information, or conceals for the purpose of misleading, information concerning any fact material thereto, and any person who knowingly makes or knowingly assists, abets, solicits or conspires with another to make a false report of the theft, destruction, damage or conversion of any motor vehicle to a law enforcement agency, the Department of Motor Vehicles or an insurance company commits a fraudulent insurance act, which is a crime, and shall also be subject to a civil penalty not to exceed five thousand dollars and the value of the subject motor vehicle or stated claim for each violation.

PART A — CLAIMANT'S STATEMENT (Please Print or Type) ANSWER ALL QUESTIONS

2. My Social Security Number is: [ ][ ][ ] [ ][ ] [ ][ ][ ][ ]

1. My name is .... First .... Middle .... Last

3. Address .... Number .... Street .... City or Town .... State .... Zip Code .... Apt. No.

Tel. No. .... 4. My age is .... 5. Married (Check one) [ ] YES [ ] NO

6. My disability is (If injury, also state how, when and where it occurred) ....

7. I became disabled on .... Mo .... Day .... Year .... a. I worked on that day [ ] YES [ ] NO

b. I have since worked for wages or profit [ ] YES [ ] NO If "Yes," give dates ....

8. Give name of last employer. If more than one employer during last eight (8) weeks, name all employers.

Employer s			Dates of Employment						Average Weekly Wages (Include Bonuses, Tips, Commissions, Reasonable Value of Board, Rent, etc.)
			From			Through			
Business Name	Business Address	Telephone No	Mo	Day	Yr	Mo	Day	Yr.	

9. My job is or was .... Occupation .... Name of Union and Local No., If Member

10. For the period of disability covered by this claim
   a. Are you receiving wages, salary or separation pay: .... [ ] YES [ ] NO
   b. Are you receiving or claiming:
      (1) Workers' Compensation for work-connected disability .... [ ] YES [ ] NO
      (2) Damages for personal injury .... [ ] YES [ ] NO
      (3) Unemployment Insurance Benefits .... [ ] YES [ ] NO
      (4) Disability Benefits under the Federal Social Security Act .... [ ] YES [ ] NO

   If "Yes" is checked in any of the items a, b(1), b(2), b(3) or b(4), fill in the following:
   I have [ ] Received or [ ] Claimed from .... For the Period .... Date To .... Date

11. I have received disability benefits for another period or periods of disability within the 52 weeks immediately before my present disability began .... [ ] YES [ ] NO
   If Yes, fill in the following: I have been paid by .... From .... To ....

12. I have read the instructions above. I hereby claim Disability Benefits and certify that for the period covered by this claim I was disabled; and that the foregoing statements, including any accompanying statements, are to the best of my knowledge true and complete.

SIGN HERE → Claim signed on .... Date .... Claimant's Signature

If signed by other than claimant, print below: name, address, and relationship of representative.

NOTICE AND PROOF OF CLAIM FOR DISABILITY BENEFITS

IMPORTANT: USE THIS FORM ONLY WHEN THE CLAIMANT BECOMES SICK OR DISABLED **WHILE EMPLOYED** OR BECOMES SICK OR DISABLED **WITHIN FOUR (4) WEEKS AFTER TERMINATION OF EMPLOYMENT**. OTHERWISE USE GREEN CLAIM FORM DB-300.

PART B — DOCTOR'S STATEMENT (Please Print or Type)

The doctor's statement must be filled in completely. For Item 7-d, give approximate date. Make some estimate. Delay in the payment of Disability Benefits may be prevented. If disability is caused by or arising in connection with pregnancy, enter estimated delivery date under "Remarks."

1. Claimant's Name .... (First / Middle / Last) 2. Age ..... 3. ☐ Male ☐ Female

4. Diagnosis/Analysis: ....
   a. Claimant's Symptoms: ....
   ....
   ....
   b. Objective Findings: ....
   ....

5. Claimant Hospitalized? ☐ YES ☐ NO From .... To ....

6. Operation Indicated? ☐ YES ☐ NO a. Type .... b. Date ....

7. Enter Dates for the Following:

	Mo.	Day	Year
a. Date of your first treatment for this disability			
b. Date of your most recent treatment for this disability			
c. Date Claimant was unable to work because of this disability			
d. Date Claimant will be able to perform usual work			

(Even if considerable question exists, estimate date. Avoid use of terms such as unknown or undetermined.)

8. In your opinion, is this disability the result of injury arising out of and in the course of employment or occupational disease? ☐ YES ☐ NO
   If yes, has Form C-4/48 been filed with the Workers' Compensation Board? ☐ YES ☐ NO

Remarks (Attach additional sheet, if necessary): ....

---

9. I affirm that I am a .... (Physician, Podiatrist, Chiropractor, Dentist) Licensed in the State of .... License No. ....

Doctor's Signature .... Date ....

Doctor's Name *(Please Print)* .... Tel. No. ....

Office Address .... (Number / Street / City or Town / State / Zip Code)

Approval ______________________________

EXAMPLE 1-7B: LETTER OF INSTRUCTION

Bridgewater State College
Bridgewater, Massachusetts 02325

Dear Parents:

The following letter has been included in your son's/daughter's Orientation Folder. Please be informed that students without complete Health Records will not be allowed to move into the Residence Halls or register for second semester classes.

Dear Student:

Health Services congratulates you on your acceptance to Bridgewater State College.

So that your entry to college is as smooth as possible, this letter reviews the health requirements.

With your acceptance letter you should have received a ***Report of Medical History*** which must be completed and returned to Health Services by ***July 15.***

In addition, you will receive in June a brochure describing the BSC insurance plan and waiver card. If you already have a comparable insurance plan, you must return the signed waiver card. If a waiver card is not received by the College, you will be billed for the insurance.

Enjoy your summer and orientation programs. If you have any questions regarding your health requirements, don't hesitate to call Health Services at (508) 697-1252.

Sincerely,

Janice A. Murphy

Janice A. Murphy, Director
Health Services

EXAMPLE 1-7C: MEDICAL HISTORY

Medical History - USAV National Development Camps - 1997

Name ______________________ Camp # ________

Address ______________________ City ______________________

State ________ Zip ________ Phone ________ - ____________

Birth Date ________ Age ______ Sex ______ Height ______ Weight ______

Your health insurance company is?______________________ Policy # ______________

Is your insurance sufficient to cover your participation in this program? Yes ______ No ______

Emergency contact: Name ______________________ Day # ____________ Night # ____________

For Minors: Do you authorize camp personnel to obtain emergency medical/dental care for your son/daughter **(who is under age 18)**?

Yes ______ No ______ Signed (parent or guardian): ______________________

Health History

	Yes	No	Date	Please elaborate (especially on those conditions that might be aggravated)
Allergies	___	___	___	___
Asthma	___	___	___	___
Congenital Probs	___	___	___	___
Diabetes	___	___	___	___
Epilepsy	___	___	___	___
Heart	___	___	___	___
Ankle Injuries	___	___	___	___
knee Injuries	___	___	___	___
Back Injuries	___	___	___	___
Head/Nk Injuries	___	___	___	___
Shoulder Injuries	___	___	___	___
Elbow Injuries	___	___	___	___
Wrist Injuries	___	___	___	___
Hand/Finger	___	___	___	___
Other Injuries	___	___	___	___

Immunizations (Please state month and year): Tetanus ____________ Polio ____________ Measles (Rubella) ____________

Is there any Psycho-Social or physical condition for which the camper is currently under professional care? Yes ______ No ______

Explain: ______________________

Are you currently taking any medication? Yes ______ No ______ If so, please name the drug(s), dosage and frequency needed:

____

List any known drug allergies: ______________________

Please elaborate on any medical conditions we should be aware of: ______________________

____

Comments: ______________________

PLEASE COMPLETE THIS LINE 1- 2 DAYS BEFORE CAMP BEGINS

Please list any injuries or illnesses you have suffered within the last month: ______________________

____

Signed: ______________________ Date: ____________
Information provider

EXAMPLE 1-7D: HOW TO USE THE CONSUMER PRODUCT SAFETY COMMISSION

Supplement to TRIAL

How To Use The Consumer Product Safety Commission

What is the Consumer Product Safety Commission?
The Consumer Product Safety Commission is the Federal government agency responsible for protecting the public from unreasonable risks of injury associated with roughly 15,000 types of consumer products.

What information can you obtain from the Commission?
The Consumer Product Safety Act (CPSA) directs the Commission to collect, investigate, analyze and distribute information related to the causes and prevention of death, injury, and illness associated with consumer products. The Commission collects and disseminates information from the following sources:

The National Electronic Injury Surveillance System (NEISS). NEISS is a network of 91 hospital emergency rooms which report information about injuries which are treated at their facilities and which are associated with consumer products. The 91 participating hospitals are a probability sample of hospitals with emergency rooms in the United States and its territories. Consequently, the information reported through NEISS can be used by the Commission to make statistically valid national estimates of the frequency and severity of injuries associated with specific categories of consumer products.

Each report of an injury sent to the Commission through NEISS includes information about the particular type of product associated with the injury, the age and sex of the accident victim, the body part injury, and whether hospital treatment was required. Additionally, each report includes a short narrative account of the injury.

The information collected through NEISS can be used to generate computer print-outs of all reports of injuries associated with a given product during a specified period of time. Generally, the information does not identify manufacturers or brand names.

Other sources. The Commission receives information about injuries and potential injuries associated with consumer products from calls to its toll-free hot-line and correspondence from consumers. The Commission has a separate toll-free hot-line to receive information from professionals, including attending physicians, attorneys, and insurance companies. That number is (800) 638-8095.

Additionally, the Commission contracts with news clipping services to review newspapers and other periodicals and extract articles about deaths, injuries, or risks of injury associated with consumer products. Although these sources do not provide a statistical sample of product-related incidents, they can alert the Commission to dangerous products and new or developing hazards associated with consumer products.

Death certificates. The Commission purchases copies of certain death certificates issued by the 50 states, the District of Columbia, and New York City, in which the cause of death is a product subject to the jurisdiction of the Commission or which indicate consumer product involvement, such as deaths resulting from high-voltage electrical shocks, burns, and falls.

Medical Examiner Reports. The Commission collects reports from a network of participating medical examiners and coroners in all 50 states. The reporting system includes contracts with approximately 50 medical examiners covering large population areas and informal relationships with more than 2,000 other medical examiners and coroners. The Commission sends a newsletter to each participating medical examiner and coroner six times a year.

In-depth reports of injuries. In some cases, the Commission staff may need more detailed information about the facts concerning an injury associated with a consumer product than is provided in the brief narrative transmitted with a NEISS report, consumer complaint, death certificate, news report, trade complaint or other source. Using the information obtained through these sources, the

Commission staff may conduct on-site investigations or telephone interviews. These in-depth investigations provide additional details about the extent of the injury, the product involved, or the interaction of the product, the accident victim, and the environment. The Commission conducts more than 4,000 of these follow-up investigations each year.

How you can obtain information from the Commission:

Generic information. If you need information about a category or type of consumer product without reference to any specific manufacturer, call the Commission's National Injury Information Clearinghouse at (301) 504-0424 or write to the National Injury Information Clearinghouse, Consumer Product Safety Commission, Washington, D.C., 20207. Your request for information about products which are not identified by manufacturer can usually be filled within a few days.

Brand-specific information. Always make a written request under provisions of the Freedom of Information (FOI) Act for any information about injuries associated with a product which is identified by brand or manufacturer. Address your request to:

Todd A. Stevenson
Freedom of Information Officer
Office of the Secretary
Consumer Product Safety Commission
Washington, D.C. 20207

Upon receipt of your request, the FOI Officer will obtain all responsive documents from the Commission staff. To comply with provisions of section 6(b) of the Consumer Product Safety Act (15 U.S.C. 2055 (b)), the FOI Officer will then notify the manufacturer of the product in question of your request, transmit the responsive documents to that firm, and provide the firm a period of 23 days to comment on the accuracy of the information which the Commission proposes to release in response to your request.

When the FOI Officer transmits the responsive documents to the firm for its comments, he or she will advise you that those documents have been sent to the identified manufacturer. If you are in discovery, you can request that the opposing party produce the documents the Commission has sent it for review and comment.

The identified manufacturer of the product which is the subject of your request has the right to comment on the accuracy of the information which the Commission proposes to release and to object to release of some or all of that information. If the staff decides to release the information, the Commission must provide the firm ten working days' advance notice of the release, and the firm may initiate suit to enjoin release of the information.

If you are in litigation and subpoena documents from the Commission, it will submit to the Court which issued the subpoena the responsive information under seal together with an explanation that the Commission has not yet complied with all requirements of section 6 (b). The Court can then decide if it should provide you with the requested information.

Certified documents. If you intend to introduce any of the documents you receive from the Commission into evidence, request the FOI Office to have those documents certified by the Secretary of the Commission. Where appropriate, the Secretary will execute a certificate pursuant to Rule 44 of the Federal Rules of Civil Procedure that each document in the official records of the Commission is kept in the normal course of business.

How you can inform the Commission about a dangerous product:
To inform the Commission about a dangerous or unsafe product, call the Commission's toll-free number for professionals: (800) 638-8095. If you prefer to speak with one of the Commission's attorneys, call or write the Director of the Division of Administrative Litigation, Office of Compliance and Enforcement, Washington, D.C. (301) 504-0626.

Additionally, you can send information to the CPSC through the agency's Internet address: info@cpsc.gov.

You may also mail it, or fax the relevant information to the Commission at (800) 638-8095.

EXAMPLE 1-7E: PRODUCT-RELATED INJURY/ INCIDENT REPORT

Product-Related Injury/Incident Report

Return this report form to the Consumer Product Safety Commission, Division of Hazard and Injury Data Systems, EPDS, Washington, DC 20202, tel. (800) 638-8095, fax (800) 809-0924.

---

1. Date of incident/injury:
2. Description of injuries, if any: ____________________
3. Type of consumer product(s) involved: ____________________
4. Brief description of incident sequence, including age and sex of the victim(s): ____________________
5. Location of incident: City ____________ State ____________ Zip ____________

If available, please provide additional product information:

6. Manufacturer, model, brand name, and/or serial number of product(s): ____________________
7. Is product available for examination? ❑ Yes ❑ No ❑ Don't know
   If yes, where? ____________________

---

8. Contact information: Please include the name, address, and telephone number of any state/local personnel who investigated the incident.
   Name ____________ Telephone ____________
   Address ____________________
   City ____________ State ____________ Zip ____________

---

9. Reporter:
   Name ____________ Telephone ____________
   Address ____________________
   City ____________ State ____________ Zip ____________
   May we release your name to the public with this report? ❑ You may release my name ❑ Do not release my name

---

For CPSC use only: Date: ____________ Received by: ____________ rev: 940921 TC 27

5

EXAMPLE 1-8: LIST OF PROSPECTIVE WITNESSES

PROSPECTIVE WITNESSES' NAME, ADDRESS, TELEPHONE	SOURCE OF IDENTITY	ROLE OR POSSIBLE TESTIMONY
1. STERLING SHER-MAN 993 W. State St. Lamoni, N.Y. (914) XXX-XXXX	Client's son	Passenger in client's car; traffic light
2. HOLLI HYSETT 26-92 Leon Drive Jamaica, N.Y. (718) XXX-XXXX	Client and police report	Driver of other car
3. KALANI MAHI 36927 McDole Ave. Peoria, Illinois (XXX) XXX-XXXX	Identified self to client	Tourist standing on corner; light red for H.H.
4. JODY BROWN SIMMONS, M.D. 17 Graceland Way Lamoni, N.Y. (914) XXX-XXXX	Client	Personal physician; no previous fractures or neuro. injuries
5. CHAD MC DOLE 106th Precinct Jamaica, N.Y. (718) XXX-XXXX	Police accident report	Called to scene, position of cars

EXAMPLE 1-9: THE DEMAND TO PRODUCE THE NAMES AND ADDRESSES OF WITNESSES

SUPREME COURT OF THE STATE OF NEW YORK
COUNTY OF

---x

Plaintiff — COMBINED NOTICE FOR DISCOVERY

- against -

Defendants.

---x

PLEASE TAKE NOTICE, that pursuant to Article 31, Civil Practice Law and Rules, the undersigned requests discovery of the following items, or a statement that you do not at present know the information requested (or that documents requested are not within your possession or control), and further requests that you furnish same at the office of the undersigned within thirty (30) days after service hereof;

PLEASE TAKE FURTHER NOTICE, that these are continuing requests and that all information or documents responsive hereto should be furnished within thirty (30) days after such information first becomes known to you or such documents first come into your possession or control.

<u>WITNESSES</u>

1. Please furnish the name and address, if known, of each person whom you know or believe to have witnessed the occur-

rence of the injuries alleged in the complaint.

2. Please furnish the name and address, if known, of each person whom you know or believe to have witnessed (1) the nature and/or duration of any alleged condition which allegedly caused the injuries alleged in the complaint or (2) the acts or omissions that allegedly are the basis of the claimed negligence and malpractice.

3. Please furnish the name and address, if known, of each person whom you know or believe to be a witness to whether the defendants received actual notice of any condition which allegedly caused the injuries.

4. Please furnish (a) the name, address, and qualification of each expert witness whom you expect to call at trial, (b) state in reasonable detail the subject matter and substance of the facts and opinions on which each expert is expected to testify, and (c) set forth a summary of the grounds for each such opinion.

5. If any sum has been paid or promised to plaintiff(s) by any person claimed to be liable for the injuries (or damages) alleged in the complaint within the meaning of Gen. Ob. L 15-108, or if any cost, expense, loss of earnings, or other economic loss was or will be with reasonable certainty replaced or indemnified, in whole or in part, by collateral source within the meaning of CPLR 4545, please set forth (a) the name and address of the person, corporation, insurance company, or other entity making such payment or promise or providing such collateral source, and (b) state the amount(s)

which have been or will be with reasonable certainty received by plaintiff(s).

6. Please furnish the name, if known, or a description sufficient to reasonably identify, each defendant or employee of a defendant herein, whom you know or believe to have given any written or oral statement concerning the occurrence of the injuries (or damages) alleged in the complaint or concerning any defendant's responsibility therefor.

Dated: New York, New York
19

Yours, etc.,

Attorney for Defendant

TO: By:

EXAMPLE 1-10: NOTICE OF DISCOVERY AND INSPECTION

SUPREME COURT OF THE STATE OF NEW YORK
COUNTY OF NEW YORK
--X
JANE SMITH,

Index No.:

Plaintiffs,

-against-

NOTICE OF DISCOVERY
& INSPECTION

GENERAL HOSPITAL and ST. PATRICK'S MEDICAL CENTER,

Defendants.
--X
SIRS:

PLEASE TAKE NOTICE, that pursuant to CPLR 3120, the CPLR, plaintiff, Jane Smith, demands that General Hospital produce at the office of the undersigned, no later than thirty days from the date of this notice, the following items for discovery and inspection, copying and examination:

1. A copy of the Rules and Regulations pertaining to the Department of Obstetrics and Gynecology which were in effect during , 19 .

2. The full names, addresses, place of employment of any eye witnesses to the incident which occured on , 19 .

That, in lieu of the foregoing, said defendant may submit copies by mailing them to the office of the undersigned on or before the date they are to be produced.

PLEASE TAKE FURTHER NOTICE, that the foregoing is a continuing demand and that if any of the above items are obtained after the date of this demand, they are to be furnished to the undersigned pursuant to this demand.

Dated: New York, New York
, 19 .

Yours, etc.

KRAMER, DILLOF, TESSEL, DUFFY & MOORE
Attorney for Plaintiff
233 Broadway
New York, NY 10279
(212)267-4177

TO: **SMYTH & JONNES**
Attorney for Defendants
998 Seventh Avenue
New York, New Y ork 10987
(212) 990-3576

EXAMPLE 1-10A: POLICIES AND PROCEDURES FOR DEPARTMENT OF ANESTHESIOLOGY

WINTHROP-UNIVERSITY HOSPITAL

MINEOLA, LONG ISLAND, NEW YORK 11501 • (516) 663-0333

Formerly Nassau Hospital-Established 1896

POLICIES & PROCEDURES

Anesthesiology Department

Winthrop-University Hospital

Issued:	2/2/79
Effective:	2/2/79
Revised:	11/3/80
Revised:	Approved by Medical Bord Meeting of March 17, 1981
Revised:	7/83
Revised:	10/86
Revised:	1989

A major teaching affiliate, State University of New York, Stony Brook School of Medicine

TABLE OF CONTENTS

WINTHROP-UNIVERSITY HOSPITAL
MINEOLA, LONG ISLAND, NEW YORK 11501 • (516) 663-0333
Formerly Nassau Hospital-Established 1896

PATIENT SAFETY UNDER ANESTHESIA

I. All anesthesia care shall be provided in accordance with accepted standards of practice and shall ensure the safety of the patient during the anesthetic period.

a) An anesthetist shall be continously present in the operating room throughout the administration and the conduct of all general anesthetics, regional anesthetics, and monitored anesthesia care unless there is a documented hazard to the anesthetist in which case some provision is made for monitoring the patient.

b) Provisions shall be specified to ensure that the patient is attended by the anesthetist during the emergence from anesthesia, at least until the patient is under the care of qualified post anesthesia care staff or as necessary to meet the patient's needs.

c) During the administration and conduct of all anesthesia except locals and epidurals unless medically indicated, the patient's oxygenation shall be continuously monitored to ensure adequate oxygen concentration in the inspired gas and the blood through the use of a pulse oximeter. During every administration of general anesthesia using an anesthesia machine, the concentration of oxygen in the patient's breathing system shall

A major teaching affiliate, State University of New York, Stony Brook School of Medicine

WINTHROP-UNIVERSITY HOSPITAL

Patient Safety Under Anesthesia con't:

be measured by an oxygen analyzer with a low oxygen concentration limit alarm.

d) The patient's ventilation shall be continuously monitored during the conduct of all anesthesia. During regional anesthesia monitored anesthesia care and general anesthesia with a mask, the adequacy of ventilation shall be evaluated through the continual observation of the patient's qualitative clinical signs. For every patient receiving general anesthesia with an endotracheal tube, the quantitative carbon dioxide content of expired gases shall be monitored through the use of end-tidal carbon dioxide analysis. In cases when ventilation is controlled by a mechanical ventilator, there shall be in continuous use an alarm that is capable of detecting disconnection of components of the breathing system.

e) The patient's circulatory functions shall be continuously monitored during all anesthetics except locals unless medically indicated. This shall include the continuous display of the patient's electrocardiogram from the beginning of anesthesia until preparing to leave the anesthetizing location and the evaluation of the patient's blood pressure and heart rate at least every five minutes. For patients receiving general anesthesia, each patient's circulatory functions shall be continually evaluated through the use of a pulse oximeter.

f) During every administration of anesthesia, there shall be immediately available a means to continuously measure the patient's temperature.

3

WINTHROP-UNIVERSITY HOSPITAL

Patient Safety Under Anesthesia con't:

II. An intra-operative anesthesia record shall document all pertinent events that took place during the induction of, maintenance of, and emergence from anesthesia, including any intra-operative abnormalities or complications, blood pressure, pulse, the dosage and duration of all anesthetic agents, other drugs, intravenous fluids, and blood and blood components and the general condition of the patient.

III. Post-anesthetic follow-up evaluation and report by the individual who administers the anesthesia that is written within three to 48 hours after surgery and shall note the presence or absence of anesthesia related abnormalities or complications, and shall evaluate the patient for proper anesthesia recovery and shall document the general condition of the patient.

November 18, 1988

RS/mam

WINTHROP-UNIVERSITY HOSPITAL
MINEOLA, L.I., N.Y.

MEMORANDUM

TO: ALL MEMBERS DEPARTMENT OF ANESTHESIA

FROM: Roger Shammas, M.D.
Chairman

DATE: Jan. 13,1989

RE: ALARMS ON MONITORS

During the course of anesthesia the Pulse Tone and the alarm sounds are to be kept on at all times and not turned off on the Poet Monitors.
The same applies to respirators and blood pressure machines.

RS/mam

EXAMPLE 1-11: DIAGRAM OF ACCIDENT

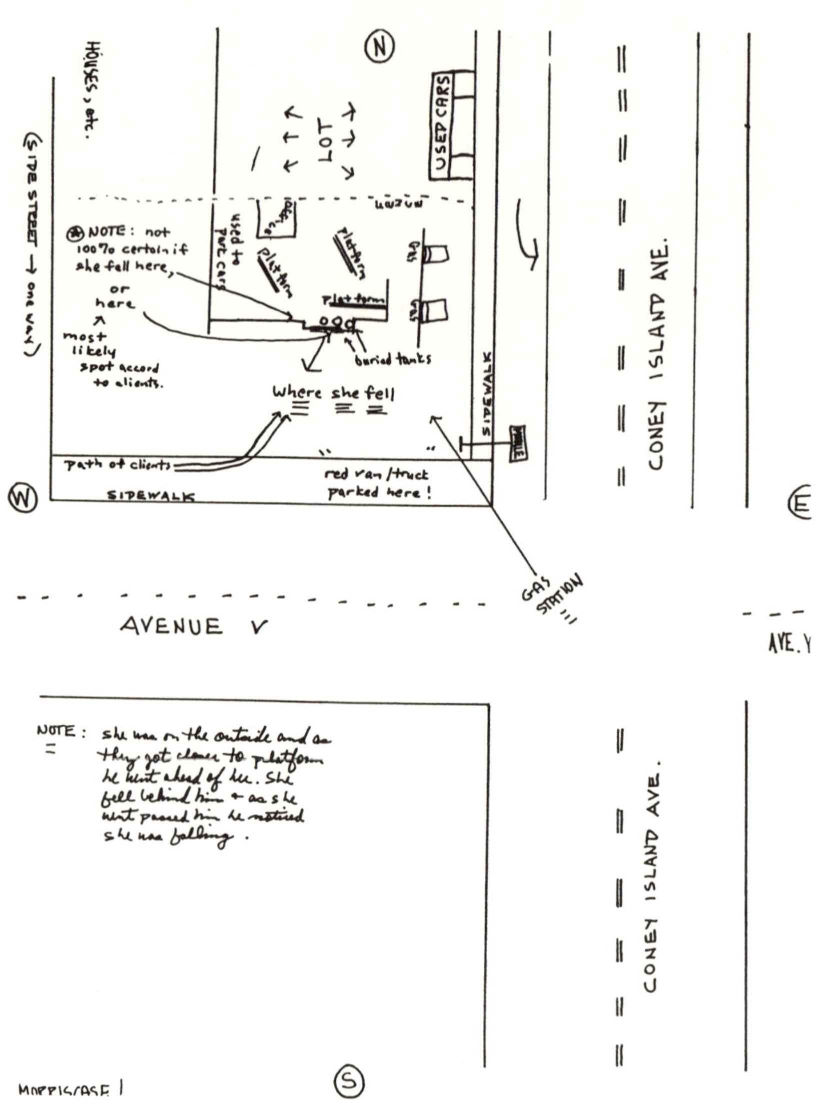

EXAMPLE 1-12: AUTHORIZATION FOR RECORDS

TO: State of New York Department of Motor Vehicles

The Governor Nelson A. Rockefeller Empire State Plaza

Albany, New York 12228

AUTHORIZATION FOR THE RECORDS OF

Jane Smith

I am involved in litigation against certain parties and am required by law to furnish their attorneys and/or their insurance companies with an authorization permitting you to provide them with a copy of your records pertaining to me. Accordingly, you are hereby authorized to furnish to:

a copy of my records, **with the following express provisos:**

1. You are to send a copy of whatever you give the above-named person(s) to my own attorneys, **KRAMER, DILLOF, TESSEL, DUFFY & MOORE**, 233 Broadway, New York, New York 10279-0137 [212/267-4177], who will pay you the reasonable cost of reproduction

2. You are **not authorized** to discuss me or my care and treatment with the above litigants, their attorneys or any representative therof

DATED: ________________ X ____________________________

Jane Smith

STATE OF NEW YORK)
COUNTY OF)ss

Before me this ______ day of ______________, 19 ___ came the above-named who is known to me to be the person who signed the within document

____

NOTARY PUBLIC

EXAMPLE 1-13: COVER LETTER TO A MEDICAL EXPERT

LAW OFFICES

KRAMER, DILLOF, TESSEL, DUFFY & MOORE

233 BROADWAY

NEW YORK, N.Y. 10279-0137

(212) 267-4177

FAX (212) 233-8525

CHARLES KRAMER (1918-1988)
THOMAS A. MOORE
JAMES R. DUFFY
JUDITH A. LIVINGSTON
THOMAS J. PRINCIPE

JO ANNE KEOGH
OFFICE MANAGER

MATTHEW GAIER
JOHN P. KOESTER
MITCHELL R. ORACH
ANDREW S. TARGUM
WILLIAM T. BURDO
MARY JO BROUSSARD

HENRY H. DILLOF
NORMAN BARD
STANLEY TESSEL
WILLIAM R. DILLOF
OF COUNSEL

March 11, 1996

, M.D.
East th Street
New York, New York 10021

Re: ________________, infant

Dear Dr. :

I am an associate at the law firm of Kramer Dillof Tessel Duffy & Moore and at Mr. Thomas Moore's instruction I am forwarding you the action of , an infant born at Medical Center on , 19 . The central in this action revolves around a botched, traumatic forceps delivery resulting in hematoma/fracture of the infant's skull. For your review, I have enclosed the following records:

1. Dr. 's office records on Mother.

2. Mother's chart at Medical Center.

3. External fetal monitor strips as to Mother.

4. Baby's chart at Medical Center.

Please review such records and issue a report to our office as to your findings.

Thank you for your time and effort in this matter.

Sincerely,

CR/mj - Encs.

EXAMPLE 1-14: CLIENT QUESTIONNAIRE

Medical Records Review Service, Inc.
1420 Woodland Ave #1, Des Moines, IA 50309-3204/1-800-984-6777

CLIENT QUESTIONNAIRE©

Date__________________

Attorney's
Name____

Firm Name____

Address____State & Zip__________

Telephone____________________FAX_______________ e-mail_____________________

Plaintiff / Defense Case (circle one): Type of Lawsuit__________________________

Dates of statutes:____

Date Case was filed_________________________________Case No____________________

Plaintiff(s) Name(s)____
Name of
Injured Party__________________________ Soc Sec #_______________ DOB_________

Defendant(s) Name(s)____

Deadline for MRRS, Inc.____

Brief facts of the case:____

____

____

____

____

____

____

____

If MRRS is to obtain medical records, please attach the Medical History Questionnaire ©.

Type of Review: Quick Look________, Summary: Level I_____, Level II_____, Level III_____

EXAMPLE 1-15: INDEX OF MEDICAL RECORDS AND BIBLIOGRAPHY

Medical Records Review Service, Inc
1420 Woodland Ave #1/Des Moines,IA 50309-3204/1-800-984-6777

INDEX

[redacted] MEDICAL RECORDS

Medical Records Review Service, Inc
1420 Woodland Ave #1/Des Moines,IA 50309-3204/1-800-984-6777

Medical Records Review Service, Inc
1420 Woodland Ave #1/Des Moines,IA 50309-3204/1-800-984-6777

C:\WP51\CASES\[redacted]\Index

EXAMPLE 1-16: SUMMARY OF MEDICAL RECORDS

Medical Records Review Service, Inc
1420 Woodland Ave #1/Des Moines,IA 50309-3204/1-800-984-6777

SUMMARY OF MEDICAL RECORDS FOR [redacted]

4/16/83	ER/[redacted] Hosp; police found in street with superficial laceration R ear & large swollen area R-side of face; pt smells of ETOH & somewhat uncooperative; cleansed wound & skull x-rays taken w/no fxs; pt refused sutures or further treatment.
4/19/83	OV/Dr. [redacted] (type of dr?); cc: displaced fx of zygomatic arch (cheek bone); OP surgery for repair of fx.
4/22/83	OP Report/[redacted] Hosp/Dr. [redacted], surgeon; repair of cheek bone fx.
4/26/83	OV/Dr. [redacted]; follow up post-op for cheek repair; sutures removed; wound healing.
8/1/83	ER/[redacted] Hosp; police bring pt to ER after pt was hit on head w/iron; dizzy; no loss of consciousness; Exam: laceration L forehead; 2 x 2 cm contusion on head; Plan: sutures; follow/up w/ Dr. [redacted].
10/1/83	Admit/thru [redacted] Hosp ER; 1 cm stab wound upper L quadrant of abdomen; discharged 10/2/83 after overnight observation & lab work; lump noted in L breast & told to follow/up;
	Social Hx: had baby in 1974; admits 2-3 6 packs beer daily; 1 ppd smoker x's 9 years; prior hx of "the clap".
3/1/84	OV/Dr. [redacted]; unrepaired laceration lower lip; to be seen next week.
10/28/89	OP [redacted] Hosp Radiology; facial lacerations; facial x-rays negative for fx.
1/11/90	OV/Dr. [redacted]; displaced nasal fx; scheduled for surgical repair. (SSF Note: there is no documentation of this surgery having been done.)
5/14/90	ER/[redacted] Hosp; laceration L side of neck w/knife; wound instructions given.
5/18/90	OV/Dr. [redacted]; follow up for neck laceration; referred pt to [redacted] County Primary Care.
10/28/90	OV/[redacted] Ortho Clinic - Dr. [redacted]; fell 2 wks ago on R hip; pain developed; incised/drained clear, yellow fluid;

Through the knee amputation was performed.

7/12/92 Physician's Progress Notes/Orders; (SSF Note: again, there is no time documented as to when this entry was made; however, it was post-op @ x pt was admitted to ICU and was likely prior to availability of Path Report);

Admit ICU; dx: emergency through knee amputation for gas gangrene R lower extremity; post-op orders/routine.

Another 7/12/92 entry (SSF Note: no time documented); Dr. ordered 2 units packed red blood cells (PRBC). (SSF Note: likely to replace surgical blood loss & to boost her hematocrit which was low & to prevent further anemia.)

7/12/92 Pathology Report/specimens R lower leg (came to lab in 2 parts);

Gross Description: ulceration and cellulitis with some soft tissue necrosis;

(SSF Note: this Path Report is somewhat confusing about the term "soft tissue" and specifically what is included in that term; we have checked with a Pathologist who advised soft tissue <u>can</u> include muscle, fascia, fatty tissue, organs, skin or anything that is <u>not</u> bone.

However, please note that the Path Report separately describes the muscle and indicates "acute inflammation and minor fibrosis"; this would indicate there was no necrosis, or irreversible damage to the muscle and that the pathologist who dictated the Report likely did not include the muscle when he used the term "soft tissue" in discussing the necrosis.

Also, the Pathology Report and the Operative Reports do not agree. If the compartments were completely filled with pus, as the surgeon described in the OP Report, the Pathologist would have noted extensive muscle necrosis, and he did not.

In addition, the Pathologist in his report also describes the condition of the skeletal muscle, again contradicting the Operative Report. These discrepancies must be addressed and answered by a qualified medical expert.)

Also noted in Path Report, "no evidence of gangrene".

(SSF Note: this is the key finding in this Path Report. This Pathology Report substantiates earlier lab findings

EXAMPLE 1-17: COVER LETTER FROM ECONOMIST

Economist
West 44th Street
New York, NY 10036-6645
(212)

October 4, 1993

Thomas Moore, Esquire
KRAMER DILLOF LAW FIRM
233 Broadway
New York, NY 10279-0137

SUMMARY ECONOMIC OPINION:

I have studied the relevant economic variables available to date in this case. This Summary Opinion contains the conclusions of my study as of this date. I will support my Opinion by way of expert testimony and detailed analyses at trial. I have no financial interest in any aspect of this case.

was injured at birth.

* Date of Birth: 4/19/83
* Date of Event: at birth or at this time
* Age: 10 presently
* Total Statistical Life Expectancy: 63.6
  [Source: US Department of Health and Human Services]
* Total Worklife Expectancy: 52/HSgrad 48/CollGrad
* Projected Value(s): earnings
* Fringe Benefits: .29
* [Source: US Department of Labor]
* Other Considerations: medically related items

For future value projections, I have used three alternative growth rates. I also generated present value results, should they apply, based on three alternative discount rates. All rates were derived from pertinent historical statistics, produced by US Government Departments.

My conclusions are presented by way of the attached table(s). The attached charts indicate some pertinent statistics.

My Resume is also appended to this Report.

I am prepared to accommodate any queries regarding my Opinion that may arise in this litigation.

, PhD
Economist
LS/wp
Enclosures

EXAMPLE 1-18: LETTER TO OPPOSING PARTY'S ATTORNEY

LAW OFFICES
KRAMER, DILLOF, TESSEL, DUFFY & MOORE
233 BROADWAY
NEW YORK, N.Y. 10279-0137
(212) 267-4177
FAX (212) 233-8525

CHARLES KRAMER (1918-1988)
THOMAS A. MOORE
JAMES R. DUFFY
JUDITH A. LIVINGSTON
THOMAS J. PRINCIPE

JO ANNE KEOGH
OFFICE MANAGER

MATTHEW GAIER
JOHN P. KOESTER
MITCHELL R. DRACH
ANDREW S. TARGUM
WILLIAM T. BURDO
MARY JO BROUSSARD

HENRY H. DILLOF
NORMAN BARD
STANLEY TESSEL
WILLIAM R. DILLOF
OF COUNSEL

June 23, 1995

Smyth & Jonnes
998 Seventh Avenue
New York, New York 10314

Re: Smith v. General Hospital

Gentlemen/Mesdames:

Enclosed please find the bill of particulars for your clients, as well as our combined demand and notice of ebt.

Further, the following information is supplied in response to your other demands. Please update your files accordingly.

In response to your demand for expert witness information, please take notice, that plaintiff is undecided at the present time with regard to the expert witnesses expected to be called to testify at the trial of the above named action.

In response to your demand for statements, please be advised that plaintiff is not in possession of any statements and/or writings made by or given on behalf of your clients.

In response to your demand for witnesses, please be advised that the only witnesses known at this time are the plaintiff, and the defendants, their agents, servants and/or employees.

In response to your demand for photographs please be advised that we have asked the plaintiff if there are any photos of the decedent and will forward same to your office should any exist.

In response to your demand for authorizations, medical reports and collateral source information enclosed please find authorizations for the following:

Smith v. General Hospital, et ano.
June 23, 1995
page 2 of 2

Also enclosed are copies of the bills pertaining to funeral and burial expenses and well as a copy of the Medical Examiner's Autopsy Report.

Kindly advise us what discovery remains outstanding.

If you have any questions regarding the above, kindly contact the undersigned.

Very truly yours,

Thomas A. Moore

enc.

EXAMPLE 1-19: OUTLINE OF PLAINTIFF'S CAUSE OF ACTION

ELEMENTS OF CAUSE OF ACTION	PROBLEM OR COMMENT
1. The defendant's negligence caused the plaintiff's personal injuries.	
A. The tortfeasor is H.H. (driver)	
1. Identified self at scene	
2. Notified insurance company	
3. Witnesses saw driving	
B. The tortfeasor is H.H. (owner of car)	
1. Registration	
a. police report contained license number	
2. Notified insurance company	
C. H.H. drove through the intersection against a red light.	
1. S.S. (plaintiff) and son	Considered biased.
2. K.M. - witness standing on corner	Lives in Hawaii
3. S.M. - driver behind defendant	Intoxicated?
D. H.H. was exceeding the speed limit	55 in 35 zone
1. Witnesses:	
a. plaintiff & son	
b. pedestrian	
c. driver following	
2. Reconstruction by expert, JB.	Extra fee if extra day
a. severity of damage	
E. H.H. hit plaintiff's car.	
1. Witnesses	
2. Positions of cars after the accident	made ethnic remarks
a. policeman	
3. Reconstruction	
a. expert	
F. The collision injured S.S.	
1. Obvious injuries: bleeding, compound fractures, bruises	

2. Expressions: twitching, moaning "I can't move my arms!"	Res gestate
3. Witnesses at scene	
a. pedestrian	
b. driver behind defendant	
c. plaintiff's son	
4. Witnesses called to scene	
a. policeman, (and report)	
b. ambulance attendants. (and report)	Don't remember well.
5. Staff in hospital	
a. doctor in emergency room	
b. nurse in emergency room	
c. X-rays	
d. admission forms	
G. The collision caused the plaintiff's neurological injuries.	
1. No prior problem	
a. family physician	Elderly: may die before trial.
b. army physical	Cursory?
c. medical records	Not really tested.
2. Treating physicians after the accident	
a. emergency room	
b. specialist	
c. consultant	
d. supported by x-rays and other tests	
3. Experts:	
a. Dr. X	Most eminent but soft spoken
b. Dr. Y	Less eminent but forceful
4. Severity and prognosis:	

H. The plaintiff has suffered special damages.
1. Medical expenses
   a. past expenses
      (1) bills

(2) treating physician
b. future damages
(1) treating physician
(2) expert physician
(3) economist
2. Loss of income
a. past income
(1) tax returns and pay records
(a) before accident
(b) after accident
b. future income
(1) economist's projections
(2) employer's and colleagues'
(3) special qualifications

I. The plaintiff has suffered general damages.
1. The pain and fright of the accident
2. Chronic pain
(a) past conscious pain & suffering
(b) future conscious pain & suffering
3. Including loss of the enjoyment of life

J. Proposed Verdict

1. Special Damages
Medical Care
Past $________
Future $________
Loss of Income
Past $________
Future $________

2. General Damages
Past $________
Future $________

3. Deductions, if any $________
4. Interest: $________
5. Total $________

EXAMPLE 1-19A: A.T.L.A.'S DOCUMENTS FROM PARTICULAR CASES

OFFERINGS BY TOPIC: INSURANCE BAD FAITH

DOCUMENTS $95

[ ] CLEVELAND V. FIRE INS. EXCH., 35 ATLA L. Rep. 57 (Mar. 1992) (plaintiff's trial brief in a case alleging fraud and bad faith against an insurer for (1) failing to timely settle a case after an arson investigation failed to link its insured to a fire and (2) denying plaintiff's claim because he had failed to submit to an examination under oath or produce tax documents). No. 1424.

[ ] DEAN V. FIREMAN'S FUND INS. CO., 36 ATLA L. Rep. 293 (Oct. 1993) (plaintiff's complaint and trial brief, the parties' summary judgment motions and consolidated pretrial order, and the jury's verdict in a case alleging bad faith failure to apply the innocent coinsured doctrine in denying benefits to the estate of an insured murdered by his spouse). No. 1855.

[ ] EASTHAM V. NATIONWIDE MUT. INS., 35 ATLA L. Rep. 137 (May 1992) (plaintiffs' motion to determine remaining trial issues, supporting memorandum, proposed jury instructions, and appellate briefs in a case alleging an insurer engaged in a pattern of delay and deceit to avoid paying a claim). No. 1479.

[ ] FIRST NAT'L BANK V. LUSTIG, 37 ATLA L. Rep. 179 (June 1994) (plaintiff's complaint alleging bad faith failure to pay under a fidelity bond). No. 2050.

[ ] FLOWERS V. KEMPER NAT'L INS. COS., 37 ATLA L. Rep. 58 (Mar. 1994) (plaintiff's posttrial memorandum and the court's reasons for judgment in a case alleging an insurer acted in bad faith when it refused to allow its insured to keep his wrecked car and receive the difference between the value of the car before the crash and its salvage value). No. 1961.

[ ] FOX V. HEALTH NET, 37 ATLA L. Rep. 178 (June 1994) (the parties' briefs for and against summary judgment in a case alleging bad faith denial of cancer treatment coverage). No. 2052.

[ ] GLISPY V. SAFEWAY INS. CO., 36 ATLA L. Rep. 292 (Oct. 1993) (plaintiff's motion for partial summary judgment, response to defendants' cross-motion for summary judgment, and statement of facts in a case alleging bad faith refusal to settle a claim within policy limits). No. 1861.

[ ] LITTLES V. BENEFIT TRUST LIFE INS., 35 ATLA L. Rep. 100 (Apr. 1992) (plaintiff's trial and appellate briefs in a suit alleging an administrator of a self-funded employee insurance plan breached a duty of good faith and fair dealing to an insured by denying a benefits claim). No. 1462.

[ ] LUBEZNIK V. HEALTHCHICAGO, INC., 37 ATLA L. Rep. 178 (June 1994) (the parties' appellate briefs and the court's opinion in a case alleging an insurer was obligated to pay for cancer treatment). No. 1890.

[ ] O'MARA V. TIME INS. CO., 36 ATLA L. Rep. 168 (June 1993) (plaintiffs' complaint, the parties' summary judgment memoranda, and the trial court's order in a case alleging bad faith and breach of contract against an insurer that canceled a policy for nonpayment of a premium). No. 1784.

[ ] PATTERSON V. PRUDENTIAL HEALTH CARE PLAN, 37 ATLA L. Rep. 178 (June 1994) (plaintiff's trial memorandum arguing an insurer was obligated to pay for cancer treatment). No. 1894.

[ ] SCALAMANDRE V. OXFORD HEALTH PLANS (N.Y.), INC., 37 ATLA L. Rep. 178 (June 1994) (the trial court's order finding an insurer had violated ERISA by denying coverage for cancer treatment). No. 1896.

[ ] SHIHADEH V. BROWN-MCNELLY INS. FUND, 36 ATLA L. Rep. 248 (Sept. 1993) (plaintiff's arbitration statement, brief on legal issues, and other arbitration documents in a case alleging bad faith refusal to settle a medical negligence claim). No. 1841.

[ ] STEPHENS V. SAFECO INS. CO., 36 ATLA L. Rep. 329 (Nov. 1993) (the parties' and amicus curiae appellate briefs in a case holding that an insured's comparative lack of good faith cannot be used to offset an insurer's bad faith). No. 1898.

[ ] STUMPF V. CONTINENTAL CASUALTY CO., 34 ATLA L. Rep. 19 (Feb. 1991) (the parties' trial and appellate court documents in a case (1) holding an insurer liable for failure to settle within policy limits and for negligent claims investigation and (2) rejecting the insurer's claim it was not liable for its attorney's handling of the case). No. 1150.

[ ] UNITED STATES FIRE INS. CO. V. TRANSPORTATION INS. CO., 36 ATLA L. Rep. 15 (Feb. 1993) (plaintiff's summary judgment motion and memorandum opposing defendant's summary judgment motion on the issue of punitive damages in a case alleging a primary insurer breached a good faith duty to an excess carrier by refusing to offer policy limits to settle the underlying lawsuit). No. 1677.

APRIL 1995 118 38 LAW REPORTER

EXAMPLE 1-19B: A.T.L.A.'S SUMMARIES OF SETS OF CASES

CASE SUMMARY SURVEYS $75

Each survey includes a collection of case summaries appearing in the Law Reporters *from 1988 to the present and a list of relevant articles and legal annotations.*

[ ] ATV Accidents—CS 1
[ ] Premises Owners Liability for Negligent Security—CS 2
[ ] Slip and Fall Accidents—CS 3
[ ] Defective Medical Devices—CS 4
[ ] Abuse of Transference Phenomenon—CS 6
[ ] Airplane Manufacturer Liability—CS 7
[ ] Motorcycle Accidents—CS 8
[ ] Uninsulated Power line Accidents—Utility Liability—CS 9
[ ] Military Hospital Liability—CS 10
[ ] Obstetrics—Liability for Failure to Perform or Timely Perform Cesarean Sections—CS 11
[ ] Swimming and Diving Accidents—CS 14
[ ] Police Torts—CS 15
[ ] Auto Dealer Liability—CS 27
[ ] Construction Site Accidents—CS 28
[ ] Injuries from Asbestos Exposure—CS 29
[ ] Athletic & Recreational Injuries—CS 30
[ ] Premises Liability—Hotels and Motels—CS 32

ULTIMATE OFFERINGS $350

Documents from at least five cases on the subject, a case summary survey, and a bylined article on the topic.

[ ] Blood Bank Liability—UO 1
[ ] Failure to Diagnose Cancer—UO 2
[ ] Manufacturers' & Premises Owners' Liability for Swimming/Diving Accidents—UO 3
[ ] Defective Seat-belt Cases—UO 4
[ ] Tire-rim Assembly Cases—UO 5
[ ] Gas & Fuel Accidents—UO 6
[ ] Motor Vehicle Cases & Preemption—UO 7

ORDER FORM

To order, fill out the form below. For credit card orders, call **1-800-424-2725, ext. 228**, or FAX: **(202) 337-0977**.

Please type or print clearly

Name ____________

Firm ____________

Street ____________

City ____________

State/ZIP ____________

If available, would you like to receive the Document(s) on computer disk? Please indicate your preference below:

Size: ☐ 5¼" ☐ 3½" Format: ☐ WordPerfect ☐ ASCII

☐ **Documents or Disk $95** ☐ **Documents and Disk $150**

Case Title ____________ No. ____________

☐ **Ultimate Offerings $350**

Offering Title ____________ UO No. ____________

☐ **Case Summary Surveys** (not available on disk) **$75 each**

Survey Title ____________ CS ____________

LR Binders $15 each Year ____________

LR Back Issues $10 each Month/Year ____________

LR Annual Indexes $10 each Year ____________

☐ $25 charge for rush orders, regular mail ____________

☐ $50 charge for Fed Ex shipping ____________

Total purchase amount $ ____________

Payment method: (All orders must be prepaid)

Check is enclosed in the amount of $ ____________
(Payable to ATLA/LR)

Charge to: ☐ VISA ☐ MasterCard ☐ American Express

Card Number ____________ Exp. Date ____________

Signature ____________ Date ____________

Mail completed form with payment to:
ATLA/LR, P.O. Box 3717, Washington, DC 20007-4499

EXAMPLE 1-19C: A.T.L.A.'S REQUESTS FOR INFORMATION ON SIMILAR CASES

The Ohio National Life Insurance Co.—Seek info re any fraud cases. Contact W. Daniel Miles III, P.O. Box 4160, Montgomery, AL 36103, (205) 269-2343.

Old Line Life Insurance, U.S. Life Company—Seek information regarding any fraud cases. Contact W. Daniel Miles III, P.O. Box 4160, Montgomery, AL 36103, (205) 269-2343.

Philadelphia Life Insurance Company—Seek info re any fraud cases. Contact W. Daniel Miles III, P.O. Box 4160, Montgomery, AL 36103, (205) 269-2343.

Pioneer Life Insurance Company—Seek information regarding fraud cases. Contact Thomas J. Methvin, P.O. Box 4160, Montgomery, AL 36103-4160, (205) 269-2343.

Provident Life & Accident Insurance Co.—Seek info re any fraud cases. Contact W. Daniel Miles III, P.O. Box 4160, Montgomery, AL 36103, (205) 269-2343.

State Farm Mutual Automobile Insurance Company—Seeking information regarding the practice of State Farm to have chiropractic claims reviewed by an independent evaluation entity known as Professional Evaluation Services. Contact G. Richardson Wieters, P.O. Drawer 6067, Hilton Head Island, SC 29938, (803) 785-8040, fax (803) 785-3506.

Transouth Financial Corp.—Seek information regarding credit insurance or flipping of loans. Contact Thomas J. Methvin, P.O. Box 4160, Montgomery, AL 36103-4160, (205) 269-2343.

Union National Life Insurance Company—Seeking information regarding fraud cases. Contact Julia A. Beasley, P.O. Box 4160, Montgomery, AL 36103-4160, (205) 269-2343.

Westfield Insurance Company, Westfield, Ohio.—Seeking info re any bad-faith failure to pay medical pay provisions of automobile policy issued by this company. Contact Peter C. King, P.O. Box 250, Columbus, IN 47202-0250, (812) 372-8461.

LAWN & GARDEN EQUIPMENT

Homelite Model ST-385 Weed Whacker—Seeking info re similar claims. Plaintiff operating weed whacker with shoulder strap removed injured by unshielded blade when weed whacker was knocked out of his grasp. Machine had no automatic braking mechanism. Call Bill Gunner, (716) 593-1090.

MACHINERY

Cincinnati Horizontal Milling Machine—Seeking information and exchange of discovery in cases or claims against Cincinnati Milacron, Inc. (successor to the Cincinnati Milling Machine Co.), for hand injuries resulting from alleged failure to have a guard and warnings on the milling machine. Contact Dan Mummolo, One Boston Place, Boston, MA 02108, (617) 742-1388.

Mixer—Seek info on cases where plaintiff was scalped by industrial mixer, in particular, "Schold" mixers. Contact Mark Nation, 2251 Lucien Way, Ste. 120, Maitland, FL 32751, (407) 660-9544.

Morbark Woodchipper—Seeking information and exchange of discovery in cases or claims against Morbark Industries, Inc., for hand/arm injuries resulting from alleged inadequate length of the infeed chute on the woodchipper machine. Contact Dan Mummolo, One Boston Place, Boston, MA 02108, (617) 742-1388.

MOTORCYCLES

Helmets—Seeking info re crashworthiness and injuries resulting from helmets manufactured by Florida Safety Products, Fulmer Safety Products, Arthur Fulmer, Inc., or Tennessee Safety Products. Contact Sam N. Gregorio, 1540 Irving Pl., Shreveport, LA 71101, (318) 227-8282.

Sidestand Retraction Defect—One-Vehicle-Accident—Kawasaki, Honda, Suzuki, Yamaha—Failure of sidestand (kickstand) to retract, causing serious injury or death to motorcycle operators. Seven years of litigation information on federal standards, patents, and other relevant discovery against Kawasaki, Suzuki, Honda, and Yamaha available to exchange. Contact Ira H. Leesfield, 2350 South Dixie Hwy., Miami, FL 33133, (305) 854-4900.

MOTOR VEHICLES

—AUTOMOBILES—

1993/1994 Camaro/Firebird—Roof crush/rollover. Contact Clague Van Slyke III, 325 West Franklin, Tucson, AZ 85701, (602) 622-2805.

Corvette—Late Model—Steering, spin-out, battery explosion, fire in driver's footwell, uniframe spot-weld separation, and/or failure; death or serious injury. Contact Edward M. Ricci, P.O. Box 2946, West Palm Beach, FL 33402, (407) 684-6500.

Ford Mustang—Late Model—Seat-belt failure in rear-end collision, fuel-system failure; death or serious injury. Contact Edward M. Ricci, P.O. Box 2946, West Palm Beach, FL 33402, (407) 684-6500.

Fords—Seeking info re door-latch failures. Contact Edward M. Ricci, 1645 Palm Beach Lakes Blvd., Ste. 250, West Palm Beach, FL 33401, (407) 684-6500.

GM—Rear-Seat Lap Belt Only—Death or serious injury. Contact Edward M. Ricci, P.O. Box 2946, West Palm Beach, FL 33402, (407) 684-6500.

GM—Seat Back and Head Restraint—Failure in rear-end collisions; death or serious injury. Contact Edward M. Ricci, P.O. Box 2946, West Palm Beach, FL 33402, (407) 684-6500.

Pontiac/Olds/Chevy—Door-mounted seat-belt system/ejection; death or serious injury. Contact Theodore J. Leopold, 1645 Palm Beach Lakes Blvd., West Palm Beach, FL 33401, (407) 684-6500.

1984 Pontiac T-1000—Rear-end collision gas tank explosion. Seeking any information. Contact David P. Parker, P.O. Box 112, Statesville, NC 28687, (704) 871-0300.

Renault Alliance—Fuel-system failure; death or serious injury. Contact Edward M. Ricci, P.O. Box 2946, West Palm Beach, FL 33402, (407) 684-6500.

Toyota—Motorized Passive Seat Belts—Death or serious injury. Contact Edward M. Ricci, P.O. Box 2946, West Palm Beach, FL 33402, (407) 684-6500.

Vehicle Fires—Absence of inertial fuel cut-off valve; serious burns or death. Contact

EXAMPLE 1-20: DEFENDANT'S NOTICE TO TAKE DEPOSITION UPON ORAL EXAMINATION

SUPREME COURT OF THE STATE OF NEW YORK
COUNTY OF SUFFOLK
--------------------------------------x

Index No.

Plaintiffs

- against -

NOTICE TO TAKE DEPOSITION UPON ORAL EXAMINATION

Defendants
--------------------------------------x

S I R S:

PLEASE TAKE NOTICE, that pursuant to Article 31 of the Civil Practice Law and Rules the testimony, upon oral examination, of plaintiffs will be taken before a Notary Public, who is not an attorney, or employee of an attorney, for any party or prospective party herein and is not a person who would be disqualified to act as a juror because of interest or because of consanguinity or affinity to any party herein, at the Supreme Court, Griffing Avenue, Riverhead, New York, on the 5th day of January, 1996, at 10:00 o'clock in the forenoon of that day with respect to evidence material and necessary in the prosecution or defense of this action:

All the relevant facts and circumstances in connection with the allegations of the pleadings, including negligence, contributory negligence, liability and damages.

That the said person to be examined is required to produce at such examination the following:

A. Plaintiff[s]: All written records regarding the defendants herein, including all correspondence with the defendants; all notes, memoranda, diaries, calendars or outlines prepared in connection with such testimony. In addition, copies of all cancelled checks, receipts or insurance bills or statements regarding special damages must be produced.

B. Defendants [if applicable]: All medical records pertaining to the plaintiff[s] herein.

Dated:

Yours, etc.

TO: Kramer, Dillof, Tessel,
Duffy & Moore, Esqs.
Attorneys for plaintiffs
233 Broadway
New York, NY 10279
[212] 267-4177

EXAMPLE 1-21: PLAINTIFF'S COMBINED DEMAND AND NOTICE OF EBT

SUPREME COURT OF THE STATE OF NEW YORK
COUNTY OF NASSAU
---X
JANE SMITH
Plaintiff,

-against-

COMBINED DEMAND
AND NOTICE OF EBT

GENERAL HOSPITAL and ST. PATRICK'S MEDICAL CENTER,
Defendants.
---X

S I R S :

PLEASE TAKE NOTICE, that pursuant to Article 31 of the Civil Practice Law and Rules, the defendant is hereby required to produce and allow discovery and inspection to be made by the plaintiffs herein, their attorney or others acting on their behalf at the Office of **KRAMER, DILLOF, TESSEL, DUFFY & MOORE, ESQS**. at 233 Broadway, 46th Floor, New York, New York, 10279, thirty days from the date hereof at 10:00 a.m. at which time the plaintiffs will examine, duplicate or copy or photostat the following:

1. Pursuant to CPLR §3101(f), the defendant is to produce and permit plaintiffs to inspect and copy all policies of insurance and excess insurance and policy limitations which policy or policies were in effect during the period of plaintiff's care and any excess, hospital provided insurance, reinsurance, self-insurance, or indemnity agreements which may in whole or in part become available for the payment of any judgment which may be had upon the allegations set forth in the verified complaint and/or bill of particulars of the plaintiffs and to produce a statement of the number of claims and lawsuits

as made against any such policy during the policy period and the amount of claims paid against said policy, excess policy and/or reinsurance policy, and with respect to any hospital defendant. Such defendant is additionally to produce any and all policies of insurance and/or agreements relating to insurance which may provide coverage or excess coverage to any individually named physician defendant or co-defendant in this action.

2. The names and addresses of each person claimed or known, or believed to be a witness to the care and treatment of the plaintiff(s) above named, during the period of plaintiff's care, and/or to any acts or conditions which have been alleged as causing or contributing to the occurrence alleged as causing or contributing to the occurrence alleged in the complaint and bill of particulars, and/or any eye witnesses to any act of culpable conduct by the plaintiff and/or plaintiff's intestate, and/or to any discussion had with the plaintiff(s) with respect to the issue of informed consent. If no such witnesses are known to the defendant, so state in the sworn reply to this item of the demand and this shall be a continuing demand. The plaintiffs will object upon trial as to any testimony of any witnesses not so identified.

3. That pursuant to CPLR §3120 that the defendant produce for discovery and inspection and copying the following:

a) The original medical record of the plaintiff(s) including all billing records, X-rays, scans, pathology slides, gross pathology samples, transfer records, office records, office chart, correspondence with others had with respect to the plaintiff(s) prior to, during, and after the plaintiff(s) care and any prior records, correspondence, and/or medical and laboratory records with respect to the plaintiff(s). In the event that such records and documents and/or items are not under the defendant's custody or control state and identify such item and state the person or entity believed by the defendant to be in possession of such item, document, or record. This is a continuing demand and calls for the production of said items in the event that same shall come into the possession of the defendant or their counsel after reply is made to this initial demand.

b) Any photographs, video tapes, films and/or slides of the plaintiff(s) or any part of the plaintiff's body in the possession or under the control of the defendants, their agents, servants, employees, attorneys or insurance company. This is a continuing demand.

4. That pursuant to CPLR §3101(d), demand is made that the defendant identify by description all persons defendant expects to call as expert witnesses at the time of trial and a detailed written statement as to: a) the subject matter on which each expert is expected to testify; b) the documents, items, objects, and things examined or reviewed by such expert(s) and if microscopic slides or specimens were reviewed state the identifying codes, numbers, or markings upon such items; c) the qualifications of such witness and d) the grounds and basis for each opinion held by said expert witness. In the event of failure to comply with said demand, or to completely

comply therewith, objection will be made at the time of trial to any such expert's testimony which is not in full compliance with this demand. This is a continuing demand.

5. That pursuant to CPLR §3101(e), a copy of each and every statement and other writings or true copy thereof, or transcription of oral statements, taping, photographing, video taping, and/or recording made by or made of the plaintiff(s).

6. A copy of any authorization or consent to deliver to any third person or hospital any pathological specimens, microscopic slides, reports, and/or medical information with respect to the plaintiff(s).

S I R S :

PLEASE TAKE FURTHER NOTICE, that the defendants are to appear at the Office of **KRAMER, DILLOF, TESSEL, DUFFY & MOORE, ESQS.**, 233 Broadway, 46th Floor, New York, New York, 10279 forty days from the date hereof at 9:30 a.m. at which time and place the defendants' testimony as an adverse party will be taken before a Notary Public upon oral questions and that each defendant is to produce at the aforesaid time and place the items set forth in numbered paragraphs 1 through 6 of the Combined Demand to be material relevant and needed as evidence in the within action and request is made that the defendant take such reasonable and prudent steps as they are able to do so to protect, preserve, and maintain said items as potential evidence in this action.

S I R S :

PLEASE TAKE FURTHER NOTICE that pursuant to the CPLR you are required to serve a verified bill of particulars as the defendant(s):

1 - Affirmative defense of culpable conduct on the part of the plaintiff and/or plaintiff's intestate setting forth each and every alleged act or omission constituting the alleged culpable conduct, the date thereof, the place whereof, and the damage or injury alleged to have resulted therefrom. Such bill of particulars must be served within 20 days of the date hereof and upon your failure to do so, an Order will be sought precluding any such testimony and the striking of any such

defense as may be based upon alleged culpable conduct as aforesaid.

2 - Affirmative defense as to the Public Health Law and informed consent set forth each risk, hazard, and alternative which the defendant(s) allege the plaintiff(s) was informed of, the person providing said information, the date(s) and place(s) of each occasion when such information was given to the plaintiff(s), and the persons present on each of said occasion(s).

S I R S :

PLEASE TAKE FURTHER NOTICE, that any authorizations to obtain medical, employment, or other date of or concerning the plaintiff(s) does not authorize the defendant and/or their agents, servants, attorneys, insurance company, or employees to interview the physicians, hospital employees, employers or former employers of the plaintiff(s) without counsel for plaintiff being advised of same in writing and at least twenty days in advance so that plaintiff's counsel can make arrangements to be present for such interview(s). Furthermore, such authorizations are limited to the release of existing medical and employment records only and are valid for no other purpose. Any such medical and/or employment records may not be released to any third persons or anybody else without a further written authorization of the plaintiff(s).

Dated: New York, New York
, 199

KRAMER, DILLOF, TESSEL, DUFFY & MOORE
Attorneys for Plaintiff(s)
233 Broadway
New York, New York 10279-0137
(212) 267-477

TO:

SMYTH & JONNES
Attorneys for Defendants
998 Seventh Avenue
New York, New York 10022

EXAMPLE 1-22: EBT BRIEFING BOOK ON OBSTETRICAL CASES

Summary of Table of Contents

EXAMPLE 1-23: STIPULATIONS FOR EBT

SUPREME COURT OF THE STATE OF NEW YORK
COUNTY OF KINGS
---X

Plaintiff,

-against-

Defendants.

---X

122 Fifth Avenue
New York, New York

December 19, 1995
11:25 a.m.

EXAMINATION BEFORE TRIAL of the Defendant, , by , held at the above-noted time and place, pursuant to Court Order, taken before , a Stenotype Reporter and Notary Public of the State of New York.

- - -

LERNER REPORTING (212) 832-8318

A P P E A R A N C E S: 2

KRAMER, DILLOF, TESSEL, DUFFY
& MOORE, ESQS.
Attorneys for Plaintiff
233 Broadway
New York, New York 10279

BY: , ESQ.
Of Counsel

, ESQ.
Attorney for Defendants
122 Fifth Avenue
New York, New York

BY: , ESQ.
Of Counsel

***

IT IS STIPULATED AND AGREED, by and between the attorneys for the respective parties herein, as follows:

That all rights provided by the C.P.L.R., including the right to object to all questions, except as to form, or to move to strike any testimony at this examination, are reserved for the trial; and, in addition, the failure to object to any questions or to move to strike any testimony at this examination shall not be a bar or waiver of the right to make such objection or motion at, and is reserved for the trial of this action.

That this examination, when transcribed, may be affirmed by the witness before any Notary Public; but the failure to do so or to return the original transcript thereof to counsel for the party on whose behalf it was taken, shall not be deemed a waiver of the rights provided by Rule 3116 of the C.P.L.R., and shall be controlled thereby.

That the filing of the original transcript of this examination is waived.

***

Plaintiff herein, having first been duly sworn by a Notary Public of the State of New York, upon being examined, testifies as follows:

EXAMINATION BY

:

Q State your name for the record.

EXAMPLE 1-24: MEMORANDUM AFTER EBT

AUG-02-1995 22:22 FROM TO 15166248247 P.02

. v. ET AL.
EBT OF DR.

On March 8, 1995 I attended the deposition of Dr. , which was taken at the law offices of This was the first deposition of the defendants in this case, yet to be done is the other target, Dr.

Briefly, this case concerns a failure to diagnose breast cancer by the defendants on March 21, 1991 and again on August 8, 1991 when she made two visits to their offices at the Obstetrics and Gynecology, P.C.

Our theory centers around two diagrams that appear on March 21, 1991 and August 8, 1991. At the March 21st visit, Ms. saw Dr. On the August 8, 1991 visit, she saw Dr. Dr. . described a lump and drew a diagram depicting the lump at the 10:00 position. A look at Dr. ' diagram for March 21, seemingly shows tenderness and pain in the precise area where Dr. found the lump some 5 months later. Dr. testified that the mark he made which appears to be at the 10:00 area, was actually not on the breast but indicates the pain was in the muscle underneath the breast. He descrit.ed the pain, which incidently was the primary reason why Ms. went to see him on March 21, 1991 as being in the pectoralis muscle.

On September 19, 1991 Ms. again, saw Dr. and it was at time that a referral to a surgeon was finally made. He described then a small lump in her right breast. The surgery was performed on November 11, 1991 by Dr at Medical Center.

Since the surgery, Ms. , who did not receive chemo-therapy has not had a reoccurrence of cancer. The surgery was a right lumpectomy, 15 lymph nodes tested and found negative for metastasis.

Our theory is that this breast lump should have been evaluated in March, 1991 when the initial complaint was made. The diagnosis of "prob muscle", in the opinion of Dr. , was a deviation as pain associated with Menses indicated a relationship to breast cancer. Ms. also has a family history of breast cancer, with her mother's sister having been treated for it.

Dr. will make a good physical appearance before a County jury. He is tall, with white hair and gives the appearance of a "Marcus Welby" type of doctor. He resides at

e was licensed to practice medicine in 1959. He served a term in the military from 960-63 in the Army Medical Corp. He is not licensed to practice in any other states and his license has never been suspended or revoked for any reason.

02-1995 22:23 FROM TO 15166248247 P.03

Dr. is a graduate of Medical College in 1959. He attended College where he received his BA in 1955. Right after his graduation from Medical School he did an internship at : Hospital followed by a 4 year residency in OB/GYN at the same institution. This was completed in 1966. The residency program was headed by a Dr. while he was at Hospital. Since then, : has changed its named to Medical Center.

Dr. went into private practice in 1966. He was initially affiliated with Dr. and then in 1979 moved to his present location, in . He became Board Certified in OB/GYN in 1968. He has hospital affiliations with Medical Center and Medical Center. In 1979 he became affiliated with Obstetric and Gynecology, P.C. up until it was devolved in 1994. Dr. was one of the members of the Professional Corporation along with Dr. and a Dr. The nature of the practice of Obstetrics and Gynecology is general OB/GYN. No x-rays or special diagnostic tests like mammograms are done at their office.

Dr. testified he had independent recollection of This independent recollection, however, did not extend to the visit of March 21, 1991, the crucial visit as far as Dr. ' malpractice is concerned.

I had him read into the record each entry in the office chart starting with Ms. first visit of February 9, 1984. She had been treated by him over the years for vaginal infections, including warts on her vagina. None of this, of course, effects our claim of failure to diagnose breast cancer except that the patient never had any complaints regarding her breasts at any of the visits prior to March 21, 1991.

Turning to that visit of March 21, which is mostly in Dr. handwriting, it indicates that the primary reason, and specific complaint which brought to Dr. office was "breast pain". The nature of the breast pain was tenderness which, his records do not indicate how long it had been present. There also in no note whether the pain was constant or intermittent or had changed in severity during her period. Her last menstrual period prior to this visit was February 26, 1991. The note goes on to state that he did "up and down" examination. He did not recall if Ms. winced with pain when he examined her breast, or cried out in any way, something that the plaintiff testified she emphatically did. The note indicates there were "no lumps". There is no mention in the chart at all of her family history for breast cancer. When I asked him if he asked her this, he replied that he could not recall. She had a ~~negative~~ positive family history as her mother's sister had breast cancer in the past.

I then went to the picture that is indicated on his entry for that date on his record for that date. Dr. stated, that the drawing he did was a representation of Ms. breast. There is a mark which indicates the breast pain complaint she sought his advice on. Again, this was the only reason she saw him on that date.

-02-1995 22:23 FROM TO 15166248247 P.04

The mammogram report continued as follows: "...AND A NEGATIVE REPORT SHOULD NOT DELAY BIOPSY IF A DOMINATE MASS OR CLINICALLY SUSPICIOUS MASS IS PRESENT".

Dr. could not tell from the August 8th note of Dr. whether or not Ms. had a clinically suspicious mass never mind a dominate mass. When I asked him why a biopsy on Ms. breast was not performed August 8th, he could not answer.

The office visit for September 19, 1991 where Dr. saw the patient indicates that Ms. still had a lump in her breast. There then is a referral to a surgeon. At this point, on September 19, 1991 it was still unknown whether Ms. had breast cancer. She had complained of breast pain since March 21, but she had not been diagnosed of breast cancer until some 6 months later. Again, no sense of urgency is shown by the fact that an immediate referral to a surgeon was not made.

There is a note on September 3 written by Dr. where it indicates "discussion rebreast". Dr. could not recall any terms of a discussion about the breast of Ms. on September 3rd with Dr.

On the office visit from August 26, 1991 there is no indication that there was a breast lump present. We know it was their based on the September 19th note which indicates "still has lump right breast".

On September 19, she was referred to a surgeon which turned out to be a Dr. Dr. is a general surgeon who does not specialize in breast related diseases. Dr. did not know that Dr. had tried to aspirate Ms. 's breast but had failed to do so successfully. He never found out whether Ms. 's breast lump was ever diagnosed. He never spoke with Dr. at all. He never called Ms. to find out what her diagnosis was after she was referred to a surgeon, nor did anyone from his office according to the chart.

I asked Dr. what the survival rate are for women with Breast Cancer that was two centimeters or more and he replied that he did not know. As I stated earlier surgery was done on November 11, 1991 at Medical Center.

Dr. never had any conversations with Ms. or any members of her family after August 8, 1991. Indeed, for someone who claimed he had an independent recollection of this patient, he could recall discussing nothing with her including his own office visit of March 21, 1991.

It will be interesting to see if Dr. contradicts Dr. recollection of the events in any way. If Dr. will give us the fact that the lump he saw on August

8th and described in the diagram at 10:00 as is in the same area as Dr. ' diagram where he noted the muscle pain on March 21st.

EXAMPLE 1-24A: NOTICE FOR DISCOVERY AND INSPECTION OF OFFICE RECORDS

SUPREME COURT OF THE STATE OF NEW YORK
COUNTY OF

____x

Plaintiffs,

-against-

NOTICE FOR DISCOVERY & INSPECTION

Defendants.

____x

S I R S :

PLEASE TAKE NOTICE, that pursuant to Article 31 of the Civil Practice Law and Rules of the State of New York, all defendants, by their attorneys, are hereby required to produce and allow discovery and inspection to be made by the plaintiffs herein, their attorney or others acting on their behalf at the Office of **KRAMER, DILLOF, TESSEL, DUFFY & MOORE, ESQS**. at 233 Broadway, 46th Floor, New York, New York, 10279, twenty days from the date hereof at 10:00 a.m. at which time the plaintiffs will examine, duplicate or copy or photostat:

1. A copy of the office records, including any and all diagnostic films, maintained __________.

2. A copy of any and all billing records maintained by __________.

3. A copy of any prescription forms maintained by _____________.

4. A copy of any pathology log or pathology records maintained by __________.

5. A copy of the office records, including any and all diagnostic films and the sonograms dated _________, maintained by __________, relevant to ________.

6. A copy of the curriculum vitae of defendant ___________.

PLEASE TAKE FURTHER NOTICE this Notice may otherwise be complied with by service of duplicates of the demanded items upon the office of the undersigned.

Dated: December 8, 1997
New York, New York

KRAMER, DILLOF, TESSEL, DUFFY AND MOORE
Attorneys for the Plaintiff
233 Broadway
New York, New York 10279
Tel: (212) 267 4177

TO:

IVONE, DEVINE & JENSEN
2001 Marcus Avenue
Lake Success, New York 11042

SANTANGELO, BENVENUTO & SLATTERY
111 East Shore Road
Manhasset, New York 11030

EXAMPLE 1-25: MOTION TO STRIKE ANSWER FOR REFUSING TO SCHEDULE EXAMINATION BEFORE TRIAL

SUPREME COURT OF THE STATE OF NEW YORK
COUNTY OF SUFFOLK
---------------------------------------X

JANE SMITH,

Plaintiff,

-against-

GENERAL HOSPITAL and ST. PATRICKS MEDICAL CENTER

Defendants.

---------------------------------------X

NOTICE <u>OF MOTION</u>

Index No.

PLEASE REFER TO HONORABLE

Motion By:	KRAMER, DILLOF, TESSEL, DUFFY & MOORE
Date, Time and Place of Hearing	th, 19 , 9:30 a.m., I.A.S. Part 5, Supreme Court, Suffolk County, Griffing Avenue, Riverhead, New York.
Supporting Papers:	THOMAS A. MOORE
Relief Requested:	Order, pursuant to CPLR §3124, striking the answers of the defendants for their willful failure to submit to and comply with this Court's Order, dated th, 19 for their depositions and pursuant to CPLR §8303 assessing costs and penalties upon said defendants' attorneys for failing to comply with said Order and delaying the prosecution of said action and for such other and further relief as to this Court may seem just and proper.
	Answering affidavits, if any, are required to be served within seven (7) days of the return date of this motion.

DATED: New York, New York
th, 19

Yours, etc.,

KRAMER, DILLOF, TESSEL, DUFFY & MOORE
Attorneys for Plaintiff
233 Broadway
New York, New York 10279
(212) 267-4177

TO: SMYTH & JONNES
Attys for Defts. GENERAL HOSPITAL and ST. PATRICK'S MEDICAL CENTER
998 Seventh Avenue
New York, New York 10019

SUPREME COURT OF THE STATE OF NEW YORK
COUNTY OF SUFFOLK
---------------------------------------X
JANE SMITH,

AFFIRMATION

Plaintiffs,

-against-

GENERAL HOSPITAL and ST. PATRICK'S MEDICAL CENTER

Defendants.

---------------------------------------X

THOMAS A. MOORE, an attorney duly admitted to practice before the Courts of the State of New York and a member of the firm of KRAMER, DILLOF, TESSEL, DUFFY & MOORE, ESQS., attorneys for the plaintiff herein, affirms the following to be true under the penalties of perjury:

I am fully familiar with the facts and circumstances underlying the within application by virtue of a file maintained in our office.

This affirmation is submitted in support of the motion for an Order pursuant to CPLR §3124 striking all defendants' answers for failing to comply with the preliminary conference Order, dated _______________ and pursuant to CPLR §8303 assessing costs and penalties upon said defendants' attorneys for failing to comply with said Order and delaying the prosecution of this action and for such other and further relief as to this Court may seem just and proper.

This is a personal injury action sounding in medical malpractice to the infant plaintiff on or about _______________.

This action has lingered in the discovery stages for several months. The plaintiff's deposition was held on

_________. It was then up to <u>defense counsel</u> to furnish (at least tentative) dates for their respective clients, as provided for by the Preliminary Conference Order (a copy of which is annexed hereto). It is not up to plaintiff's counsel to harass defense counsel for dates. It is incredible that defendants should take such a one-sided view of discovery and ignoring their obligation to the Court and the plaintiff to submit to examinations before trial.

This office has been attempting to schedule the examinations before trial on several occasions but to no avail.

It is respectfully submitted that defendants' refusals constitute attempts to thwart legitimate discovery of relevant, if not crucial, evidence to which plaintiff is clearly entitled.

It is unreasonable and patently unfair in that it deprives plaintiff of the opportunity to prepare a case. Their cavalier ignoring of their obligation and delay of this case should not be tolerated, and sanctions should be imposed. If said defendants' answers are not stricken, it is respectfully submitted that defendants should be made to pay costs for incurring such unnecessary prejudice to the plaintiff and for wasting this Court's time and money.

WHEREFORE, it is respectfully requested that the within motion be granted in its entirety.

DATED: New York, New York
th, 199

THOMAS A. MOORE

SUPREME COURT OF THE STATE OF NEW YORK
COUNTY OF SUFFOLK
--X
JANE SMITH

AFFIRMATION OF GOOD FAITH

Plaintiffs,

-against-

GENERAL HOSPITAL and ST. PATRICK'S MEDICAL CENTER
Defendants.

--X

THOMAS A. MOORE, an attorney duly admitted to practice before the Courts of the State of New York and a member of the firm of KRAMER, DILLOF, TESSEL, DUFFY & MOORE, ESQS., attorneys for the plaintiff herein, affirms the following to be true under the penalties of perjury:

Counsel for movant have attempted to resolve in a good faith effort the issues raised by the attached motion without the need for further judicial intervention. Defendants' continued recalcitrance on these discovery matters has necessitated the instant motion practice.

DATED: New York, New York
th, 19

____
THOMAS A. MOORE

EXAMPLE 1-26: MOTION TO COMPEL DISCOVERY OR TO STRIKE ANSWER

SUPREME COURT OF THE STATE OF NEW YORK
COUNTY OF NASSAU

--------------------------------------X

JANE SMITH, as Administratrix of the Estate of JOHN SMITH, Deceased, and JANE SMITH, Individually,

Plaintiffs,

-against-

DR. JOHN JONES and GENERAL HOSPITAL,

Defendants,

--------------------------------------X

NOTICE OF <u>MOTION</u>

Index No.

Refer to Honorable Justice

Motion By:	KRAMER, DILLOF, TESSEL, DUFFY & MOORE Attorneys for Plaintiffs
Date, Time and Place of Hearing:	,99 , 9:30 a.m.,I.A.S.PART , Supreme Court, County of Nassau, 100 Supreme Court Drive, Mineola, New York.
Supporting Papers:	Affirmation of **THOMAS A. MOORE**
Relief Requested:	Order compelling discovery pursuant to CPLR § 3120 and should the defendants fail to comply, an, Order pursuant to CPLR § 3126(3) striking the answers of both defendants and for such other and further relief as to this Court may seem just and proper. Answering affidavits, if any, are required to be served at least seven days prior to the return date of this motion.

Dated: New York, New York
, 199

Yours, etc.,

KRAMER, DILLOF, TESSEL, DUFFY & MOORE
Attorneys for Plaintiffs
233 Broadway
New York, New York 10279
(212) 267-4177

TO:

SMYTH & JONNES
Attorneys for Defendants
DR. JOHN JONES and GENERAL HOSPITAL
998 Seventh Avenue
New York, New York 10987
(212) 990-3576

SUPREME COURT OF THE STATE OF NEW YORK
COUNTY OF NASSAU
--------------------------------------X
JANE SMITH, as Administratrix of the Estate of JOHN SMITH, Deceased, and JANE SMITH, Individually,

Plaintiffs,

-against-

DR. JOHN JONES and GENERAL HOSPITAL,

Defendants,
--------------------------------------X

AFFIRMATION

Index No.

Refer to Honorable Justice

THOMAS A. MOORE, an attorney duly admitted to practice law in the courts of the State of New York, hereby affirms the following, pursuant to penalties of perjury:

1. Your affirmant is an attorney at law, and a member of Kramer, Dillof, Tessel, Duffy & Moore, the attorneys for the Plaintiffs, **JANE SMITH, as Administratrix of the Estate of JOHN SMITH, DECEASED, and JANE SMITH, Individually.** and as such is fully familiar with the facts and circumstances as hereinafter set forth.

2. This affirmation is executed upon information and belief, the sources of which are in the files and records maintained by the law offices of Kramer, Dillof, Tessel, Duffy & Moore pertaining to this matter.

3. This Affirmation is submitted in support of the present application on behalf of the plaintiff for an order compelling the defendants, Dr. John Jones and General Hospital to produce the outstanding discovery in accordance with CPLR §

3120 and, in the alternative, if the above defendants fail to comply, an order pursuant to CPLR § 3126(3) striking both defendants' answers and for such further relief as this Court deems just and proper.

4. This action sounds in the areas of medical malpractice and the wrongful death of **JOHN SMITH** on or about ______________. The plaintiffs allege that the answering defendants failed to properly treat and diagnosis the deceased complaints and symptoms, which resulted in Mr. Smith suffering a massive myocardial infarction. The suit was instituted by service of the Summons and Complaint on or about __________________ and ________________. (Annexed hereto collectively as Exhibit "A" are copies of the Summons, Complaint and Affidavits of Service).

5. A Bill of Particulars dated _________________ was served. (Annexed hereto as Exhibit "B").

6. Upon the completion of the depositions of defendants Dr. Jones and General Hospital by witness Nurse Clarke on _______________ and ___________________ respectively, the plaintiff requested the production of the following items for discovery:

A. Complete copy of the defendant's office records including the billing record for John Jones.

B. A copy of the intake form if in existence.

C. A copy of the curriculum vitae for Dr. Jones and Dr. Zuckerman, which includes a list of any publications.

D. A copy of the phone logs from ___________ to ____________________, that were kept at the office according to the testimony of Dr. Jones at his deposition.

E. A copy of a properly redacted Emergency Room Log for _______________, with all information included except the names of the patient's other than John Smith.

7. On ______________________ a letter was sent to the defendants formally requesting these discovery items. (Annexed hereto as Exhibit "C"). When there was no response, plaintiff again sent a letter on ______________________ requesting compliance with such discovery. (Annexed hereto as Exhibit "D"). Finally, on __________________, my associate forwarded another letter asking for compliance and informing the defendants that failure to respond would force this office to seek judicial intervention. (Annexed hereto as Exhibit "E').

8. It has been over four months since this outstanding discovery was requested and at the present time we have not received any response regarding when or if same would be provided.

9. The plaintiff has sent several letters in a good faith effort to resolve the issues raised in the attached application. (See Exhibits "C","D", and "E").

10. Plaintiff is baffled as to why defendants have ignored our discovery requests, especially since plaintiff has responded to the defendants requests promptly. The defendants' failure to respond to any of our letters in the last four months indicates a clear message that such discovery will remain outstanding.

11. Since we believe that obtaining the various discovery items requested, including the office records, curriculum vitae, intake forms, phone logs and Emergency Room Log are essential to the prosecution of this case, the defendants have left us no choice but to seek judicial intervention.

12. Further, we ask the Court to set down an Order that should the above named defendants fail to provide the outstanding discovery or fail to respond to the outstanding discovery requests within the time frame that the Court designates, that an Order be issued striking the above named defendants' answer in accordance with CPLR § 3126(3).

WHEREFORE, it is respectfully requested that this Court grant an Order directing the defendants to produce the above mentioned discovery, in accordance with CPLR § 3120 and, in the alternative, if the said discovery is not produced an Order striking the above named defendants' answers in accordance with CPLR § 3126 (3) and for such and other further relief as this Court seems just and proper.

Dated: New York, New York
, 199

____
THOMAS A. MOORE

EXAMPLE 1-26A: PHYSICIAN'S OFFICE RECORD

718-273-1700

Office Hours by Appointment

[redacted], M.D., P.C.
1800 Clove Road
Staten Island, New York 10304

93-310
Case No.

Patient's Name

Referred by ______ or Family Doctor ______

Occupation ______ Date of Birth 5-23-78 Age 14

Compensation ______ Date of Injury 3-3-93 Employer ______

Allergic to —

L-198

3-5-93 jammed Lt. 2nd finger playing basketball

States that while playing basket ball he jammed his left index finger on 3.3.93 It got swollen & a bit painful now feels better wants to get checked.

Px left index finger a bit puffy general alignment normal no gt [illegible] neural [illegible] [illegible] fairly well

X Ray Left Index finger no evident Fx

Dx Contusion & Sprain left Index finger

Buddy taped warm soaks

[illegible] [illegible] [illegible] S/I-146

EXAMPLE 1-26B: PHYSICIAN'S INTAKE FORM

GYNECOLOGY

CASE NO ______ PATIENT'S NAME ______

ADDRESS ████████ (09) INSURANCE Aetna DATE 10/23/90

TEL. NO. ████████ REFERRED BY ______ OCCUPATION ~~clerk~~ Tech. Asst. DOB 25 S M W D

PERSONAL HISTORY ______

PRESENT AILMENT ______

MENSTRUATION: FIRST AT AGE ______ DAYS INTERVENING ______ DAYS DURATION 5-7 AMOUNT ______ PAINS ______

LAST PERIOD 10/1/90 AMENORRHEA ______ MENORRHAGIA ______ DYSMENORRHEA ______ MENOPAUSE ______

VAGINAL DISCHARGE: COLOR ______ CHARACTER ______ AMOUNT ______

URINARY SYMPTOMS: ______

GASTRO-INTESTINAL SYMPTOMS: ______

FAMILY HISTORY ______

OBSTETRICAL RECORD

	DATE	AT TERM	MONTH: MIS-CARRIAGE	MONTH: PRE-MATURE	MONTH: STILL BORN	PREGNANCY COMPLI-CATED	DELIVERY OPERATIVE	MULTIPLE	MONTHS BREAST FED	WEIGHT AT BIRTH	REMARKS
1											
2											
3											
4											

PHYSICAL EXAMINATION: TEMP ______ PULSE ______ RESP ______ BP 106/18 WT 103 HT 5 2"

HEART ______ LUNGS ______ LIVER ______ SPLEEN ______

ABDOMEN ______

BREASTS: SECRETING ______ PAINFUL ______ DISTENDED ______ SKIN REDDENED ______

NIPPLES: CRACKED ______ ERECT ______ FLAT ______ INVERTED ______

LOWER EXTREMITIES ______

PERINEUM: FIRM ______ LACERATED ______ ANUS: HEMORRHOIDS ______ FISSURE ______

VULVA: URETHRAL ORIFICE, INFLAMED ______ RELAXED ______ LEAKAGE ______

VAGINA: SECRETION ______ RELAXED ______ CYSTOCELE ______ RECTOCELE ______

CERVIX: LENGTH ______ THICKNESS ______ LACERATIONS ______ ENDOCERVICITIS ______

UTERUS: POSITION ______ MOBILITY ______ CONSISTENCY ______

______ SIZE ______ TUMORS ______

RIGHT ADNEXA ______ LEFT ADNEXA ______

UTERO-SACRAL LIGAMENTS ______

REMARKS: Pap taken To stay on ______

LABORATORY: ______

DIAGNOSIS: ______

TREATMENT: ______

FORM NO 1261
©1989 HISTACOUNT CORPORATION MELVILLE L.I. N.Y. 11747

SYMBOLS ✓ NORMAL ______ ABNORMAL (UNDERLINE)
DEGREE OF ABNORMALITY X XX XXX

PATIENT'S NAME ______

Staten Island, New York 10310

Health History Summary Date: mo / day / yr EDC 4/16/93

HOLLISTER maternal/newborn RECORD SYSTEM

Patient's name [redacted]
Home address [redacted] STREET
S.I. CITY N.Y. STATE 10309 ZIP

Age 22 Date of birth [illegible] Race or ethnicity [illegible] Religion CATHOLIC Marital status MARRIED Years married 4½ yrs Education 12 yrs
Social Security number 107-58-7127 Occupation Home Work Tel. no. — Home Tel. no. [redacted]
Alternate contact [redacted] Relation to patient MOTHER Work Tel. no. [redacted] Home Tel. no. [redacted]
Referring physician Attending physician LIVORNESE OPTIONAL FOR INSURANCE ETC

Medical History (Patient / Family)

Check and detail positive findings including date and place of treatment. Precede findings by reference number.

1. Congenital anomalies
2. Genetic diseases
3. Multiple births
4. Diabetes mellitus
5. Malignancies
6. Hypertension
7. Heart disease
8. Rheumatic fever
9. Pulmonary disease
10. GI problems
11. Renal disease
12. Genitourinary tract problems
13. Abnormal uterine bleeding
14. Infertility
15. Venereal disease
16. Phlebitis, varicosities
17. Neurologic disorders
18. Metabol./endocrine disorders
19. Anemia/hemoglobinopathy
20. Blood disorders
21. Drug abuse
22. Smoking/alcohol use [checked]
23. Infectious diseases
24. Operations/accidents
25. Allergies/meds sensitivity — S/F Food
26. Blood transfusions
27. Other hospitalizations
28.
29.
30. No known disease/problems

Handwritten notes: Rt ect 9/91 c̄ Laser for endometriosis Dx via laparoscopy
Matewa #100 9/1 lab 4/14
4/9/93 Primary C-Sect ♀ 8 failure to descend

Preexisting Risk Guide

Indicates pregnancy/outcome at risk

31. ☐ Age < 15 or > 35
32. ☐ < 8th grade education
33. ☐ Cardiac disease (class I or II)
34. ☐ Tuberculosis, active
35. ☐ Chronic pulmonary disease
36. ☐ Thrombophlebitis
37. ☐ Endocrinopathy
38. ☐ Epilepsy (on medication)
39. ☐ Infertility (treated)
40. ☐ 2 abortions (spontaneous/induced)
41. ☐ > 7 deliveries
42. ☐ Previous preterm or SGA infants
43. ☐ Infants ≥ 4,000 gms
44. ☐ Isoimmunization (ABO, etc.)
45. ☐ Hemorrhage during previous preg.
46. ☐ Previous preeclampsia
47. ☐ Surgically scarred uterus
48. ☐ Preg. without familial support
49. ☐ Second pregnancy in 12 months
50. ☐ Smoking (> 1 pack per day)
51. ☐
52. ☐
53. ☐

Indicates pregnancy/outcome at high risk

54. ☐ Age ≥ 40
55. ☐ Diabetes mellitus
56. ☐ Hypertension
57. ☐ Cardiac disease (class III or IV)
58. ☐ Chronic renal disease
59. ☐ Congenital/chromosomal anomalie
60. ☐ Hemoglobinopathies
61. ☐ Isoimmunization (Rh)
62. ☐ Alcohol or drug abuse
63. ☐ Habitual abortions
64. ☐ Incompetent cervix
65. ☐ Prior fetal or neonatal death
66. ☐ Prior neurologically damaged infan
67. ☐ Significant social problems
68. ☐
69. ☐
70. ☐

Historical Risk Status

71. ☐ No risk factors noted
72. ☐ At risk
73. ☐ At high risk

Signature

Menstrual History	Onset 13 age	Cycle q 28 days	Length 7 days	Amount	LMP 7 mo/10/yr 92 quality

Pregnancy History Grav Term Pret Abort Live EDC 4 mo/16/yr 93

No	Month/year	Sex	Weight at birth	Wks. gest.	Hrs. in labor	Type of delivery	Details of delivery: Include anesthesia and maternal or newborn complications. Use Risk Guide numbers where applicable.
1							
2							
3							
4							
5							
6							
7							
8							

Hollister HOLLISTER INCORPORATED 2000 HOLLISTER DR. LIBERTYVILLE, IL 60048 TRADEMARK OF HOLLISTER INCORPORATED

HEALTH HISTORY SUMMARY MOTHER'S PHYSICIAN COPY 5870-4

EXAMPLE 1-26C: PHYSICIAN'S CURRICULUM VITAE

CURRICULUM VITAE

DATE: SEPTEMBER 1994

PERSONAL DATA

NAME:

DATE OF BIRTH: DECEMBER 23, 1936

PLACE OF BIRTH: DETROIT, MICHIGAN

MARITAL STATUS: MARRIED

CITIZENSHIP: U.S.A.

SOCIAL SECURITY NUMBER: [redacted]

OFFICE ADDRESS: [redacted] SPRINGFIELD AVENUE
BERKELEY HEIGHTS, NEW JERSEY 07922

TELEPHONE NUMBER: [redacted]

FAX NUMBER: [redacted]

LICENSURE AND EXAMINATION:

STATE LICENCE: NEW JERSEY [redacted]
NEW YORK [redacted]

C.D.S. [redacted]

D.E.A. [redacted]

EDUCATION

	FROM	TO	DEGREE
UNIVERSITY OF MICHIGAN	1954	1958	B.A.
UNIVERSITY OF MICHIGAN	1958	1962	M.D
POST DOCTORAL AND HOSPITAL TRAINING			
KINGS COUNTY HOSPITAL	1962	1963	INTERNSHIP
KINGS COUNTY HOSPITAL	1963	1966	RESIDENCY

ACADEMIC AND PROFESSIONAL APPOINTMENTS

INSTITUTION	POSITION	FROM	TO
COLLEGE OF MEDICINE & DENTISTRY OF N.J.	CLINICAL INSTRUCTOR	1969	1971
COLLEGE OF MEDICINE & DENTISTRY OF N.J.	ASS'T. CLINICAL PROF.	1971	1986

PROFESSIONAL BOARD CERTIFICATIONS

AMERICAN BOARD OF OPHTHALMOLOGY	1968
FELLOW AMERICAN COLLEGE OF SURGEONS	1972
MEMBER UNION COUNTY MEDICAL SOCIETY	1968
FELLOW AMERICAN ACADEMY OF OPHTHALMOLOGY AND OTOLARYNGOLOGY	1969
MEMBER N.J. STATE MEDICAL SOCIETY AND AMA	1968
PRESIDENT N.J. ACADEMY OF OPHTHALMOLOGY AND OTOLARYNGOLOGY	1978
BOARD OF DIRECTORS - MEDICAL EYE SERVICES OF AMERICA	1976
MEMBER INTERNATIONAL EYE SURGEONS	1974
MEMBER OF AMERICAN COLLEGE OF EYE SURGEONS	1986-PRESENT

PUBLIC SERVICE ACTIVITIES

MEMBER STATE BOARD OF MEDICAL EXAMINERS OF NEW JERSEY	1973-1982
SECRETARY OF STATE BOARD OF MEDICAL EXAMINERS OF NEW JERSEY	1979-1982
DEMOCRATIC COUNTY COMMITTEEMAN	1976-1977
BOARD OF DIRECTORS, LIONS, EYEMOBILE FOUNDATION	1976-1977
MEMBER SUMMIT LIONS CLUB	1976-PRESENT

CHAIRMAN OF THE SIGHT COMMITTEE OF THE MEDICAL SOCIETY OF NEW JERSEY — 1978

MEDICAL ADVISORY COMMITTEE VICE PRESIDENT OF THE NATION SOCIETY TO PREVENT BLINDNESS-NEW JERSEY — 1980-PRESENT

HOSPITAL AFFILIATIONS

OVERLOOK, SUMMIT, NEW JERSEY — CHIEF OF OPHTHALMOLOGY

OVERLOOK HOSPITAL STAFF SUMMIT, NEW JERSEY — 1968-PRESENT

SAINT BARNABAS MEDICAL CENTER LIVINGSTON, NEW JERSEY — 1993-PRESENT

PUBLICATIONS

CORNEAL ULCER: A CASE PRESENTATION." , ARTHUR, M.D. AERICAN JOURNAL OF OPHTHALMOLOGY, 1966.

"EXPERIMENTAL SCLERAL SETON IN RABBITS." M.D. AMERICAN COLLEGE OF SURGEONS, SURGICAL FORUM VOL. XXII, 1971.

"GONIOTOMY NEEDLE FOR POSTERIOR CAPSULOTOMIES." ,M.D. D.J. KELMAN RESEARCH FOUNDATION JOURNAL 1976. (IN PRESS) APRIL 1977.

ABSTRACTS AND PRESENTATIONS

"SCLERAL SETON ON THE ALBINO RABBIT FOR FILTERING SURGERY" - PRESENTED AMERICAN COLLEGE OF SURGEONS MEETING, SPRING 1973.

"PHACOEMULSIFICATION AND ITS PLACE WITH THE INTRAOCULAR LENS" - PRESENTED COLLEGE OF MEDICINE AND DENTISTRY OF NEW JERSEY INTRAOCULAR LENS COURSE, DECEMBER 1976.

FACULTY, PHACOEMULISIFICATION COURSE, 1976 - SPONSORED BY CHARLES KELMAN, M.D.

"RESULTS OF 100 PHACOEMULSIFICATION PROCEDURES" - PRESENTED N.J. STATE MEDICAL SOCIETY MEETING, SPRING, 1975.

EXAMPLE 1-26D: EMERGENCY ROOM LOG

Phelps Memorial Hospital Center 441-445 North Broadway North Tarrytown NY 10591

EMERGENCY DEPARTMENT RECORD 016419

DOS/TIME 5/11/94 13:05 REG. BY ADKT DATE OF ONSET/TIME 0/00/00 FAMILY/REFERRING PHYSICIAN KAPLAN, KENNETH-163 ACCOUNT # 204262

AGE 40Y DOB 6/27/53 SEX F RACE W MAR ST M RELIGION NA

NY 10562 0000

.4-762-2290

000000 REL SP 10562

00000 0000

SS# 999999999

WORK RELATED: NO. AUTO ACCIDENT: NO. 722.0

INSURANCE #/CO. 350 EMPIRE BLUE CROSS 07 PLAN 2 NY B/C O/P GROUP # GC-1464 RELATION TO PT. SPOUSE

C/C: pain (L) chest, neck + arm. ONSET TIME: X 2 wks

TIME	T	P	R	BP
184	972	104	20	138/80

ASSESSMENT: A+O NAD Ambulates s̄ difficulty Normal ROM + sensation arms

LMP: 4-3-?? TRIAGE CAT.: II TIME: 1PM B.C. tubal

MED. HX.: ruptured disc C5-C6

ALLERGIES: NKA

PRIMARY NURSE'S HX. TIME 120P

Pt alert ambulatory c/o spasm like pain to (L) neck c̄ radiation to (L) jaw chest + (L) arm. Pt states pain 4/5. c/o gets sweaty from pain. (-) N/V (-) chest tightness. States pain so severe when ambulating unable to walk.

ASSESSMENT: A+Ox3. States has ruptured C-5-C-6 from past head injury. States has pain on & off past few wks. Pain ↑ movement. ... able to move extremities equally c̄ good strength.

IV & MEDICATIONS:

TIME		INIT.
2:50P	cervical soft collar	
2:10P	Toradol 60 mg ... (L) VOGM.	
6:20	Vicodin one tab.	

MRI: C5-C6 central + (L) sided disc herniation; C6-C7 small central + R sided herniation

ORDERS: LAB - XRAY - EKG

TIME		INIT.
	Monitor NSR; O2 sat 98% pulse oximeter	
1:40P	EKG	
2:10P	C-spine complete	
2:10P	HCG (cancel)	
3:30P	MRI neck r/o rupture C5-C6	

TIME OF PHYSICIAN'S EVALUATION:

FINDINGS: [handwritten physician notes, largely illegible] Hx ruptured disc C5-C6 ...

CONSULT #1 NAME: Dr Kaplan. TIME CALLED: 3:05 - EKG discussed. PHONE RESPONSE: not cardiac.

CONSULT #2: Dr. Schulhof 17:30

EKG READING: X-RAY READING:

E.D. PHYSICIAN'S SIGNATURE VERIFICATION OF ORDERS/TREATMENT

ATTENDING PHYSICIAN'S SIGNATURE VERIFICATION OF ORDERS/TREATMENT

NURSE'S SIGNATURE

MEDICAL RECORDS CF002

EXAMPLE 1-27: PLAINTIFF'S ORDER OF PROOF

Client: Sherman, Stewart Index No.________

File No.: ____________

Plaintiff's Order of Proof

A. Liability

1. Sterling Sherman

   a. plaintiff's son; aged 10 then, 14 now
   b. sympathy
   c. passenger: testify to details of accident and father's obvious injuries
   d. problem: teenaged wise guy
   e. solution: serious warning just before trial
   f. objection: father's complaints hearsay
   g. justification: res gestae

2. Kalani Mahi

   a. pedestrian
   b. disinterested
   c. testify to facts of accident including,
      (1) red light
      (2) speed
   d. attractive: tall and handsome, professional volleyball player
   e. problem: lives in Hawaii - really appear?
      Scheduling difficult if case is adjourned

f. Solution: keep in contact, impress with importance

3. Trevor Travis

a. driver behind defendant
b. disinterested
c. best physical position to judge light and speed
d. problem: may have been mildly intoxicated,
(1) denies vehemently,
(2) the policeman believes that this driver was intoxicated, but the policeman didn't take any action because he was coping with the seriously injured plaintiff.
e. solution: none. Allow witness to deny intoxication and rely on the policeman's omission.

B. <u>Liability and Damages</u>

4. Chad McDole

a. policeman called to scene
b. testify to position of autos, to the location and nature of the obvious damage, and to the plaintiff's obvious injuries and complaints.
c. problem: he may have made remarks about WASP's, blondes, and women drivers
d. solution: was trying to defuse the tension and to calm seriously injured plaintiff

e. introduce police report and photographs of scene

5. Sean Travieso

a. ambulance attendant
b. disinterested
c. same testimony as policeman but knowledgeable about nature of injuries
d. vital signs, etc.
e. introduce ambulance record of injuries
f. problem: doesn't seem to have a precise recollection of the facts - seen too many accidents
g. solution: ask only those questions for which the interview shows that he does have answers.
h. objection: not competent to form diagnosis.
i. justification: not giving a diagnosis but testifying to observable medical facts for which he is competent

6. Brian Updegraff

a. expert at reconstructing accidents
b. paid
c. testimony: speed of defendant's car from damage, etc.

C. <u>Damages</u>.

7. Shannon Brewer, R.N.

a. nurse in emergency room
b. disinterested

c. cannot provide diagnosis but may testify regardings symptoms, vital signs, etc.
   (1) expect objection.
d. spent more time with plaintiff than the physician did
e. may introduce hospital records

8. Robert Taterka, M.D.

   a. physician in emergency room
   b. testify to injuries in greater detail
      (1) diagnosis and prognosis though preliminary
      (2) fractures, concussion, etc.
      (3) paralysis
   c. may also introduce hospital records

9. Joseph Spellman, M.D.

   a. treating physician, specialist
   b. thorough diagnosis and prognosis
      (1) especially paralysis
      (2) referred to consultant
   c. introduce office records
   d. future medical treatment and current cost

10. Eric Funk, M.D.

    a. consultant
    b. confirmed treating physician's diagnosis and prognosis
    c. introduce office records
    d. future medical treatment and current cost

11. Michael Thoman, M.D.

    a. specialist who examined medical records and plaintiff
    b. report served on defendant's attorney
    c. confirmed diagnosis and prognosis
    d. future medical treatment and current cost
    e. problem: soft spoken
    f. solution: extensive recital of qualifications, question quietly; let opposing counsel look obnoxious
    g. paid

12. Edwin Fernandez

    a. specialist who examined medical records
    b. report served on defendant's attorney
    c. confirmed diagnosis and prognosis
    d. future medical care and current cost
    e. problem: not so eminent but forceful
    f. solution: if use both experts, call second; don't belabor qualifications: move quickly to review of records and opinion
    g. paid

13. Robert Renck

    a. economist
    b. testify regarding special damages,
        (1) life and work expectancy
        (2) lost income
        (3) cost of future medical care

c. paid
d. problem: extra fee if cross-examination requires his appearance for an extra day
e. solution: none, don't drag out direct examination

14. Todd Schmidt

a. owner of auto repair shop
b. paid
c. testify regarding damage to car (total loss) and value before accident
d. relief from tragedy before the plaintiff testifies

15. Stewart Sherman

a. plaintiff
b. order of witnesses
   (1) last if trial not bifurcated
   (2) after expert on reconstructing accidents if trial is bifurcated
   (3) emotional impact on jury
c. problem: the jurors will become accustomed to his condition if they see him all the time.
d. solution: not present during whole trial – make appearances
e. testify to facts of accident, injuries (especially paralysis), and conscious pain and suffering
f. divorced before accident

D. Rebuttal

16. Jody Brown-Simmons, M.D.

a. family physician for thirty years
b. testify regarding plaintiff's medical history
   (1) especially no neurological problems or fractures
   (2) injuries solely the result of the accident
c. introduce office records
d. problems: very elderly (may die before trial), hard of hearing
e. solutions: use testimony from EBT if necessary; rehearse, be patient, let opposing counsel get frustrated

The Pleadings and Auxiliary Documents 2

In an action for negligence, the attorney must be familiar with eight important documents:

- Notice of claim
- Complaint
- Answer
- Demand for a bill of particulars
- Bill of particulars
- Discovery order
- Report of a medical expert
- Marked pleadings

The parties do, of course, employ other documents, such as the summons, certificate of readiness, and note of issue, but the eight documents listed above are especially relevant to the law of evidence.

2.1 THE NOTICE OF CLAIM

Section 50-e of the General Municipal Law requires the plaintiff to file a notice of claim when the prospective defendant is the City of New York or another public corporation. Other statutes also require a notice of claim, for example:

DEFENDANT	*PROVISION*
1. New York City Transit Auth.	Pub. Auth. Law § 1212, 2980
2. New York City Health & Hosps. Corp.	Unconsol. Laws § 7401(2)
3. Metropolitan Transp. Auth.	Pub. Auth. Law § 1276(2)
4. Port of N.Y. Auth.	Unconsol. Laws § 7107 28 U.S.C. 2401
5. Triboro Bridge & Tunnel Auth.	Pub. Auth. Law § 569-a
6. New York City Hous. Auth.	Pub. Hous. Law § 157 402(a)(13)
7. State of New York	Ct. C1. Act § 10(2) & (3)

Several of these provisions refer back to section 50-e of the General Municipal Law for actions alleging wrongful death.

Fortunately, section 50-e of the General Municipal Law is representative of the form required in all notices of claim. The plaintiff must file the notice within ninety days after the claim arises except that, in a wrongful death action, the personal representative must file the notice within ninety days of his appointment.[1]

> 2. Form of notice; contents. The notice shall be in writing, sworn to by or on behalf of the claimant, and shall set forth: (1) the name and post office address of each claimant, and of his attorney, if any; (2) the nature of the claim; (3) the time when, the place where, and the manner in which the claim arose; and (4) the items of damage or injuries claimed to have been sustained so far as then practicable . . .[2]

However, the notice should not state the amount of the claim unless the prospective defendant is a city with more than a million inhabitants.[3]

---

1. N.Y. GEN. MUN. LAW § 50-e(1)(a) [all statutory citations are to New York law as set out in the latest McKinney and its current supplement].
2. N.Y. GEN. MUN. LAW § 50-e(2).
3. *Id.*

The trial court may correct or disregard a defect in the form of the notice of claim as long as the defect did not affect the time or manner of the service.[4] For example, a demand for money relief is not a jurisdictional defect that makes the notice void. The court would simply order the plaintiff to file a new notice of claim without the monetary demand.[5] If the plaintiff did fail to file the notice of claim in a timely fashion, the plaintiff may make a motion to serve a late notice but only within the applicable statute of limitations.[6] Even then, the court's primary consideration will be whether the defendant or its insurance company received actual notice of the facts underlying the claim within the time for filing the notice or a reasonable time thereafter.[7]

The purpose of the notice of claim is to allow the prospective defendant to investigate the claim promptly and to prepare its defense.[8] Therefore, the plaintiff's attorney must describe how and where the accident occurred as specifically as possible, e.g., giving the number of feet north or south of a well-defined landmark. When possible, the attorney should include photographs or diagrams of the scene on which the exact spot has been marked. Remember, the notice of claim cannot be too specific, but the court may dismiss the claim if the court finds a defect that prejudiced the defendant.[9]

---

4. N.Y. GEN. MUN. LAW § 50-e(6).
5. N.Y. Op. Att'y Gen. (Informal) (Apr. 22, 1986).
6. N.Y. GEN. MUN. LAW § 50-e(5). The statute of limitations is one year and ninety days from the date the claim arises, but it is tolled for infancy.
7. *Id.* Other relevant circumstances include whether the claimant was an infant, incapacitated, or dead, whether he justifiably relied on representations of a settlement, whether he made an excusable error concerning the identity of the public corporation liable, and whether the late filing of the notice would substantially prejudice the corporation in presenting a defense on the merits.
8. Annis v. New York City Transit Auth., 108 A.D.2d 643, 485 N.Y.S.2d 529 (1st Dep't 1985); Caselli v. City of N.Y., 105 A.D.2d 251, 483 N.Y.S.2d 401 (2d Dep't 1984); Eherts v. County of Orange, 215 A.D.2d 524 at 525 (2d Dep't 1995).
9. Caselli v. City of N.Y., 105 A.D.2d 251, 483 N.Y.S.2d 401; Cruz v. City of N.Y., 95 A.D.2d 790, 463 N.Y.S.2d 851 (2d Dep't 1982); Levine v. City of New York, 111 A.D.2d 785 (2d Dep't 1985), and Faubert v. City of N.Y., 90 A.D.2d 509, 455 N.Y.S.2d 24 (2d Dep't 1982).

An additional requirement is a condition precedent to some claims against the City of New York. Section 394a-1.0(d) of the Administrative Code of the City of New York requires that the city have received written notice of a defect in a street or sidewalk fifteen days before the injury occurred so the plaintiff's attorney should obtain a copy of the notice of defect from the Department of Transportation and attach that document to the notice of claim. (See Chapter 6.)

Finally, a complaint and a notice of claim are different documents. Therefore, the plaintiff cannot avoid serving the notice of claim by serving the complaint.[10] In fact, the complaint must recite that more than thirty days have elapsed since the filing of the notice of claim and that the parties have neither settled nor resolved the matter.[11]

Example 2-1 is a completed form for a notice of claim.

2.2 THE COMPLAINT

Section 3017 of the Civil Practice Law and Rules provides that a complaint must include a demand for the relief to which the pleader deems himself entitled. Thus, the plaintiff alleges the elements of the cause of action in his complaint and ordinarily states the amount of the damages he claims. As long as the complaint sets forth the elements of a cause of action in sufficient detail to apprise the defendant of the claim and its material elements, the complaint is sufficient.[12] How-

---

10. Tarquinio v. City of N.Y., 84 A.D.2d 265, 445 N.Y.S.2d 732 (1st Dep't 1982); *aff'd*, 56 N.Y.2d 950.

11. N.Y. GEN. MUN. LAW § 50-i. The three requirements are (a) that the plaintiff served a timely notice of claim, (b) that thirty days have passed since that service without adjustment or payment, and (c) that the plaintiff is commencing his action within one year and ninety days of the event underlying his claim.

12. C.P.L.R. § 3013: "Statements in a pleading shall be sufficiently particular to give the court and parties notice of the transactions, occurrences, or series of transactions or occurrences, intended to be proved and the material elements of each cause of action or defense." Richardson v. King, 36 A.D.2d 781, 319 N.Y.S.2d 218 (3d Dep't 1981).

ever, more specific rules govern the pleading of particular causes of action. We shall examine three examples:

First, C.P.L.R. section 3016 requires specificity in pleading libel or slander, fraud or mistake, and personal injury. Thus, a complaint for libel or slander must state the particular words the plaintiff finds objectionable; a complaint for fraud, mistake, willful default, breach of trust, or undue influence must state in detail the circumstances constituting the wrong, and a complaint for personal injuries arising out of the operation of a motor vehicle in New York must state that the plaintiff has sustained either a serious injury or an economic loss greater than a basic one, as defined by section 5102 of the Insurance Law. The plaintiff's failure to comply with C.P.L.R. section 3016 will cause the court to dismiss the complaint.

Second, in the typical action for negligence, the complaint contains a demand for monetary relief, and that demand sets the upper limit of the plaintiff's recovery.[13] However, in *Loomis v. Civetta Corinno Construction Corp.*,[14] the court of appeals ruled that the trial court should grant a motion to amend the complaint to increase the ad damnum clause in the absence of prejudice to the defendant. According to the court,

> One of the obvious goals of the C.P.L.R. was to liberalize the practice relating to pleadings . . . Thus, in the absence of prejudice to the defendant, a motion to amend the ad damnum clause, whether made before or after the trial, should generally be granted.
>
> Prejudice, of course, is not found in the mere exposure of the defendant to greater liability. Instead, there must be some in-

13. Michalowski v. Ey, 7 N.Y.2d 71, 195 N.Y.S.2d 633 (1959).

14. Loomis v. Civetta Corinno Constr. Corp., 54 N.Y.2d 18, 23; 444 N.Y.S.2d 571, 572-73 (1981). Caveat: the plaintiff must make a formal motion. See Reid v. Weir-Metro Ambulance Service, Inc., 191 A.D.2d 309, 310 (1st Dep't 1993) ("In the absence of a formal motion to amend the ad damnum clause, damages must be limited to the amount sought in the complaint...").

> dication that the defendant has been hindered in the preparation of his case or has been prevented from taking some measure in support of his position . . . .

The court found that the defendant was unable to show that it had been hindered, that the defendant's expert had inspected the items damaged, and that the plaintiff had informed the defendant by letter that she considered her damages to be greater than the amount pleaded.

Assuming that the plaintiff has pleaded his or her damages properly, the plaintiff's attorney may inform the jury of the amount demanded when he or she delivers their summation. In *Tate v. Colabello,*[15] the court of appeals ruled,

> It goes without saying that one of the functions of the jurors in this case was to translate the value of the infant's injuries and her consequent pain and suffering into dollars and cents . . . [I]t was counsel's privilege "to place before the jury his client's contentions in this regard" [and to] . . . state the amount of damages demanded.

Third, according to C.P.L.R. section 3017, a complaint in an action for medical malpractice or against a municipal corporation "shall contain a prayer for general relief but shall not state the amount of damages to which the pleader deems himself entitled." However, if the plaintiff brings this action in the supreme court, he or she must state whether his or her damages exceed the jurisdictional limits of all lower courts, and the defendant may request a supplemental demand that will state the total damages. Mistakenly demanding a particular amount in damages is not a jurisdictional defect, but the court should strike the demand.[16] Moreover, since the dollar amount does not appear in the complaint, the third department has ruled that the plaintiff's attorney should not ask the jury for a specific amount for pain and suffering when deliv-

---

15. Tate v. Colabell, 58 N.Y.2d 84, 87; 459 N.Y.S.2d 422, 424 (1983).
16. Vargas v. Rosal-Archillas, 108 Misc. 2d 881, 438 N.Y.S.2d 986 (Sup. Ct. 1981).

ering his summation in an action for medical malpractice or against a municipal corporation.[17] (This rule is a departure from the general rule in actions for negligence, is controversial, and will require further comment in the chapter on summations.) However, the defendant in such an action "may at any time request a supplemental demand setting forth the total damages . . . ."[18]

Example 2-2 is a complaint, and example 2-2A is a defendant's request for a supplemental demand setting forth the plaintiff's total damages.

2.3 THE ANSWER

2.3.1 In General

The answer is the pleading by which the defendant responds to the allegations contained in the plaintiff's complaint. The defendant must address each allegation individually and will either deny it, admit it, deny it in part while admitting it in part, or assert insufficient information to form a belief. The answer may also allege the defendant's defenses, affirmative defenses, or counterclaims if any.

Naturally, the plaintiff's attorney must read the defendant's answer carefully to ascertain the defendant's position and to determine the contested issues. This determination will help to guide the plaintiff's discovery; for example, if one defendant admits that he owned and controlled the motor vehicle and that he gave the other defendant permission to drive it, then discovery is simplified.

---

17. Bechard v. Eisinger, 105 A.D.2d 939, 481 N.Y.S.2d 906 (3d Dep't 1984); Bagailuk v. Weiss, 110 A.D.2d 284 (3d Dep't 1985). The Court of Appeals declined to resolve this matter in McDougald v. Garber, 73 N.Y.2d 246 (1989).
18. C.P.L.R. § 3017(c).

The plaintiff's attorney also must examine the answer for affirmative defenses, i.e., all defenses that, if not pleaded, will surprise the plaintiff at the trial and including collateral estoppel, the culpable conduct of the plaintiff, payment, release, res judicata, lack of jurisdiction over the person of the defendant, the statute of limitations,[19] or the plaintiff's failure to use a seatbelt.[20] The defendant has the burden of proof on these issues, but the plaintiff must be prepared to contest them.

2.3.2 Defenses

The defendant's attorney must be alert for possible defenses to eliminate or to reduce his or her client's liability while the plaintiff's attorney must prepare to defeat such defenses. We shall examine four examples: workers' compensation, contract, assumption of risk, and failure to mitigate damages.

2.3.2.1 Workers' Compensation

After the defendant serves his or her answer, the plaintiff's attorney must read the defendant's answer carefully to identify all the defenses raised. The attorney must deal immediately with the defenses of lack of jurisdiction or workers' compensation for, if true, such a defense will bar the plaintiff's suit and cause the attorney to waste time and effort.

---

19. C.P.L.R. § 3018(b).
20. Cappadona v. State, N.Y.L.J., May 7, 1987 (Ct. Cl. 1987). The defendant has an obligation at the trial to present expert testimony on how wearing a seatbelt would have reduced the plaintiff's injuries.

As a general rule, if the plaintiff was covered by workers' compensation, then that statute bars a common-law tort action against the plaintiff's employer for injuries sustained in the course of the employment. Workers' compensation is the plaintiff's sole remedy unless the plaintiff can find a third party whose negligence contributed to the injuries.[21] However, an exception to this rule arises when the employee sustains an injury due to an intentional tort perpetrated by the employer or at the employer's direction.[22] The complaint must allege that the employer acted deliberately to harm the plaintiff,[23] or the court will dismiss the complaint.[24] Unfortunately, if the plaintiff's attorney fails to resolve the issue of the applicability of workers' compensation, the court may dismiss the complaint on the eve of the trial.[25]

2.3.2.2 Contract

Sometimes a defendant will allege that a contract protects him or her from a claim based on the defendant's own negligence. Such a defense is possible but only within reasonable limits. Thus, a company that had installed a burglar alarm that failed to sound tried to avoid liability by pleading a contract that purported to relieve the company from all liability for negligence including gross negligence. The court ruled, however, that the relief provided by the contract was so broad that it was against public policy.[26] The court wrote, "Agreements which purport to exempt a party from liability

---

21. Section 10 of the Workers' Compensation Law imposes on the employer the obligation of providing compensation regardless of fault but with some exceptions; section 11 makes this remedy exclusive unless the employer has failed in his obligation, and section 29 preserves the worker's cause of action against any third party.
22. Finch v. Swingly, 42 A.D.2d 1035, 348 N.Y.S.2d 266 (2d Dep't 1973).
23. Mylroie v. GAF Corp., 55 N.Y.2d 893, 449 N.Y.S.2d 21 (1982).
24. Briggs v. Pymm Thermometer, 147 A.D.2d 433, 537 N.Y.S.2d 553 (2d Dep't 1989).
25. Garsten v. MacMurray, 133 A.D.2d 442, 519 N.Y.S.2d 563 (2d Dep't 1987).
26. Arell's Fine Jewellers, Inc. v. Honeywell, Inc., 147 A.D.2d 922, 537 N.Y.S.2d 365, 366 (4th Dep't 1989).

for willful or grossly negligent acts are contrary to public policy and are void . . ., and there is no significant distinction between an agreement which completely relieves a party from liability and one which limits liability to a nominal sum . . . ."

By contrast, in *Howell v. Dundee Fair Association*,[27] the court found the release of liability to be reasonable and valid. This release had been signed by a worker at a race track, not a customer. Hence, section 5-236 of the General Obligations Law[28] was not a bar to the validity of the release. (This section makes such an agreement between the owner or operator of a place of amusement and the fee-paying patron void as against public policy.)

Consequently, the attorneys for the parties must evaluate any pertinent contract to determine whether it purports to bar the claim and whether it is enforceable.

At the end of the chapter are two examples of waivers, i.e., contracts by which one party purports to waive his prospective cause of action for negligence. Note that the plain language of the first form (example 2-3) has resulted in a longer form[29] and that the second form (example 2-4) requires a witness. This second waiver accompanied a lengthy questionnaire, provisions for stress test and a blood test, and a waiver form for the testing.[30]

---

27. Howell v. Dundee Fair Ass'n, 73 N.Y.2d 804, 537 N.Y.S.2d 27 (1988).

28. GEN. OBLIG. LAW § 5-326, as quoted by the court, states: "Every . . . agreement . . . in or in connection with . . . any contract, membership application, ticket of admission or similar writing, entered into between the owner or operator of any . . . place of amusement or recreation, or similar establishment and the user of such facilities, pursuant to which such owner or operator receives a fee or other compensation for the use of such facilities, which exempts the said owner or operator from liability . . . shall be deemed to be void as against public policy and wholly unenforceable."

29. Form provided courtesy of John Pekarik, the president of the Long Island Orienteering Club.

30. These forms are used by the federal fitness center at ARPERCEN, the national headquarters of the army reserve.

2.3.2.3 Assumption of Risk

Assumption of risk is a notion closely related to a contract, and the defense has received considerable attention since the legislature adopted C.P.L.R. section 1411 because the plaintiff's conduct is no longer a complete bar to the suit. (The plaintiff's culpable conduct merely reduces his or her recovery by the percentage by which the plaintiff's conduct was a proximate cause of his or her own injuries.)

However, assumption of risk, properly speaking, is not a matter of culpable conduct; that is, if the plaintiff assumed the risks of his or her conduct, then the defendant did not owe the plaintiff any duty to protect him or her.[31] By assuming the risk of an unintended injury, the plaintiff relieved the defendant of the latter's duty to avoid such an injury, and, therefore, the plaintiff cannot charge the defendant with negligence at all.[32]

We may divide assumption of risk into primary and constructive assumption, the difference being that a primary assumption of risk consists of a party's actual consent to the risk, e.g., by participating in a sporting event, while a construction assumption of risk is imposed by law and is not necessarily complete.

In a case of primary assumption of risk, "Plaintiff's 'consent' is not constructive consent; it is actual consent implied from the act of the electing to participate in the activity . . . ."[33]

---

31. Turcotte v. Fell, 68 N.Y.2d 432, 510 N.Y.S.2d 49 (1986). The cases following Turcotte are legion, e.g., Schiffman v. Spring, 202 A.D.2d 1007, 609 N.Y.S.2d 483 (4th Dep't 1994), and Warech v. Trustees of Columbia University, 203 A.D.2d 54, 610 N.Y.S.2d 480 (1st Dep't 1994); Morgan v. State, 90 N.Y.2d 471 (1997), and Shelmerdine v. Town of Guilderland, 223 A.D.2d 875 (3d Dep't 1996) (soccer player knew of sprinkler head drain covers, so he assumed the risk of injury from stepping on one, losing his balance, and colliding with another player).
32. *Id.*
33. *Id.*, 68 N.Y.2d at 439, 510 N.Y.S.2d at 53.

When the assumption of risk is constructive, the law implies the plaintiff's consent from the plaintiff's voluntarily taking part in an activity in which the danger is inherent but not manifest; hence, the assumption does not necessarily relieve the defendant of all liability.

Two examples will illustrate the difference between primary and constructive assumption of risk. First, in *Turcotte v. Fell*,[34] the court dismissed the injured jockey's complaint because he had assumed the risks inherent in riding horses for money. By contrast, in *Locilento v. John A. Coleman Catholic High School*,[35] the court refused to dismiss the complaint and held that the plaintiff had not assumed the risk of all injuries. The plaintiff, a student, had played in an intramural, not interscholastic, tackle football game and dislocated his shoulder. The court found no actual (i.e., primary) assumption of risk; rather, there was a constructive (i.e., secondary) assumption of risk, which was merely a factor relevant to the jury's assessment of culpable conduct. The question in both examples was whether the danger was manifest so that the plaintiff's assumption of risk was primary, and, as a further result, whether the plaintiff's assumption relieved the defendant of his duty. In the first example, the answer was yes, but, in the second example, the answer was no.

Sometimes, the court must decide whether there was a constructive assumption of risk or none at all, in which case the jury would simply evaluate the culpable conduct of the parties. For example, in *McCabe v. Easter*,[36] the court found that a letter carrier did not assume the risks of walking on icy sidewalks, and in *Tirella v. American Properties Team, Inc.*,[37] the court found that a woman who put her feet into

---

34. Turcotte v. Fell, 68 N.Y.2d 432, 510 N.Y.S.2d 49 (1986).
35. Locilento v. John A. Coleman Catholic High School, 134 A.D.2d 39, 523 N.Y.S.2d 198 (3d Dep't 1987).
36. McCabe v. Easter, 128 A.D.2d 257, 516 N.Y.S.2d 515 (3d Dep't 1987).
37. Tirella v. American Props. Team, Inc., 145 A.D.2d 724, 535 N.Y.S.2d 252 (3d Dep't 1988). But the court noted that the jury could consider the plaintiff's conduct to be culpable.

bath water without noting the temperature of the water did not assume the risk that the water might burn her. However, in *Hernandez v. Hernandez*,[38] the Appellate Division, Second Department, refused to disturb the jury's finding that the plaintiff, who had failed to leave the building upon the first indications of a fire, was culpable and contributed to her own injuries.

In a particular case, the question may be whether either or neither type of assumption of risk is relevant, and the courts do not always make the distinctions clearly.

2.3.2.4 Failure to Mitigate Damages

The plaintiff has a duty to mitigate damages in an action for personal injury, just as in an action for breach of contract. Therefore, in the case of *Bell v. Shopwell, Inc.*,[39] the court granted the plaintiff only part of his lost earnings because he reasonably could have obtained rehabilitation but refused to do so. Moreover, the court found that the plaintiff could have driven a car equipped with special controls and could have held a sedentary job despite his stiff knee.

2.3.3 Payment of Damages in Action for Personal Injury

Either the complaint or the answer may have to comply with the new article 16 of the C.P.L.R. Essentially, that article changes the common-law rule that the successful plaintiff in an action for personal injury can collect his entire judgment from any one of the joint tortfeasors and leave that tortfeasor to seek contribution or indemnity from the others. This traditional rule is still the general rule, but it does not apply to noneconomic losses recoverable from certain tortfeasors.

38. Hernandez v. Hernandez, N.Y.L.J., Jan. 9, 1990 (2d Dep't 1990).
39. Bell v. Shopwell, Inc., 119 A.D.2d 715, 501 N.Y.S.2d 129 (2d Dep't 1986).

Section 1600 defines noneconomic loss as including, but not limited to, pain and suffering, mental anguish, and loss of consortium, i.e., not medical bills or lost earnings. The new rule is that, in an action for personal injury, the plaintiff may not collect from one joint tortfeasor more than that tortfeasor's equitable share of the verdict for noneconomic loss, based on the latter's comparative negligence, if that tortfeasor has been found liable for 50 percent or less of the total liability or if the tortfeasor is the state.[40] However, the percentage is calculated without considering the culpability of any tortfeasor over whom the plaintiff could not obtain jurisdiction.

Naturally, the statute provides exceptions to the new rule. The exceptions to the limitation on the plaintiff's right to recover more than the defendant's share of the plaintiff's noneconomic loss include:

1. Actions based on a written contract of indemnity;
2. A claim for indemnification by a public employee;
3. An action based on a nondelegable duty or respondeat superior;
4. An administrative proceeding;
5. Claims under workers' compensation;
6. Actions requiring proof of intent;
7. Liability for the operation of a motor vehicle;
8. Injuries caused in reckless disregard of the safety of others;
9. An action pursuant to article 10 of the Labor Law (i.e., regarding scaffolding, construction, excavation, demolition, shaftways, and glass doors);
10. Liability for unlawfully discharging hazardous substances into the environment;
11. An action for products liability in which the manufacturer is not a party, and

40. C.P.L.R. § 1601(1).

12. An action against parties who knowingly and intentionally acted in concert to cause the act or failure upon which their liability is based.[41]

In his pleading, each party must address any relevant limitation or exception.

> In any action or claim for damages for personal injury a party asserting that the limitations on liability set forth in this article do not apply [the plaintiff] shall allege and prove by a preponderance of the evidence that one or more of the exemptions set forth in section sixteen hundred two applies. A party asserting limited liability pursuant to this article [the defendant] shall have the burden of proving by a preponderance of the evidence its equitable share of the total liability.[42]

Thus, the plaintiff must allege any applicable exception in the complaint, and, if he does, the defendant must respond to the allegation in the answer. Moreover, if the plaintiff fails to raise a possible exception in his complaint, a shrewd defendant might still include in his answer an allegation denying the exception. In either case, the defendant should be prepared to prove that his share of the total liability does not exceed 50 percent — strictly speaking, the defendant need not allege this separately from his other denials and defenses. The defendant should remember also that the limitation may apply to his claim for contribution or indemnity.[43]

Example 2-5 is a sample answer.

2.4 THE BILL OF PARTICULARS

Either party may have the occasion to supply a bill of particulars in response to the opposing party's demand. The de-

41. C.P.L.R. § 1602(1) (11).
42. C.P.L.R. § 1603.
43. C.P.L.R. § 1602(1).

fendant may require the plaintiff to supply a bill of particulars regarding any claim in the complaint,[44] and the plaintiff may demand a bill of particulars from the defendant regarding any affirmative defense or counterclaim in the answer. In lieu of a demand for a bill of particulars, one party may serve interrogatories on the other, but that practice is rare for a party who has served interrogatories needs the leave of the court to take a deposition from the opposing party in an action for personal injury, wrongful death, or damage to property based solely on a claim of negligence.[45]

2.4.1 The Action for Personal Injury

A bill of particulars may include whatever is necessary to amplify the pleading and respond to the demand, but C.P.L.R. rule 3043(a) provides that the opposing party may require the following details, when relevant, in an action for personal injury:

1. The date and time of the occurrence;
2. The approximate location;
3 The acts or omissions constituting negligence;
4. Whether actual or constructive notice is claimed;
5. If actual notice, when and to whom;
6. The injuries and a description of the permanent ones (if arising from the operation of a motor vehicle, whether the plaintiff suffered a serious injury or an economic loss greater than a basic loss);
7. The time confined to bed and to house;
8. The time incapacitated from employment.
9. The amounts claimed as special damages.

---

44. C.P.L.R. § 3041: "Any party may require any other party to give a bill of particulars of such party's claim, or a copy of the items of the account alleged in a pleading."
45. C.P.L.R. § 3130.

C.P.L.R. rule 3042(g) allows a party to amend the bill of particulars once as of course and prior to the filing of the note of issue. Therefore, the plaintiff's attorney should review the bill of particulars prior to the filing to ensure that all acts of negligence, injuries, and special damages are included.

The plaintiff may also serve a supplemental bill of particulars without the leave of the court, but the law limits this document to "claims of continuing special damages and disabilities . . . [provided that] no new cause of action may be alleged or new injury claimed . . . ."[46] This provision allows the plaintiff to sue for damages that have accumulated since he served the original bill of particulars, but it also allows the defendant to conduct supplemental discovery regarding the supplemental particulars.

At the end of the chapter are examples of a demand for a bill of particulars. Example 2-6 is a lengthy demand from a defendant; example 2-7 is a brief demand from a plaintiff in a notice for an examination before trial.

2.4.2 Failing to Include a Claim in the Bill of Particulars

Failing to include information in a bill of particulars can prevent a party from establishing a claim or an affirmative defense. Naturally, the party demanding the bill of particulars can insist that the opposing party supply the obvious information, such as the approximate location of the occurrence. However, the real danger is that a party's attorney will fail to include information that will be required later to establish his or her client's claim or defense and that the trial court will exclude the evidence or preclude the legal theory. What the court will decide is essentially a function of whether the court believes that the opposing party was prej-

46. C.P.L.R. Rule 3043(b).

udiced in preparing for the trial. As a result, the decision is partly a question of fact, and a shrewd attorney will draft the bill of particulars carefully in order to avoid giving offense.

Be that as it may, the courts seem to be more severe in punishing a failure to specify a theory of recovery than in punishing other omissions. Naturally, the failure to include a claim of negligence in the bill of particulars precludes proving that claim at the trial, and the trial court will not grant a motion to conform the pleading to the proof.[47] For example, in *Forman v. Davidson*,[48] the plaintiff sought to go to the jury on a theory of negligence that he had not included in his bill of particulars. The defendant's attorney had asked the plaintiff's expert a series of questions on the theory, and the plaintiff's attorney then introduced evidence on it. However, the Appellate Division, First Department, ruled that the plaintiff's failure to include the claim in his bill of particulars made his introduction of this claim at the trial an error. The court said,

> This belated injection of a new theory into the case, completely foreign to that disclosed by the bill of particulars, without notice and without opportunity to prepare to meet it and refute it was obviously unfair and prejudicial to defendant . . . . It is not enough to justify injection of a new and surprising theory into a plaintiff's case to point out that defendant's counsel was prepared to cross-examine concerning a possible theory of liability other than that pleaded or particularized. That would be routine preparation for any good trial lawyer readying himself to endeavor to shake a witness' certainty . . . . A trial is manifestly unfair when a party is suddenly called upon to defend on a theory belatedly brought into the case . . . .[49]

---

47. Simino v. St. Mary's Hospital, 107 A.D.2d 800, 484 N.Y.S.2d 634 (2d Dep't 1985); *cf.* Schmeider v. Montefiore Hosp. & Medical Center, 122 A.D.2d 735, 511 N.Y.S.2d 608 (1st Dep't 1986); Princiotto v. Materdomini, 45 A.D.2d 883, 358 N.Y.S.2d 13 (2d Dep't 1974).
48. Forman v. Davidson, 74 A.D.2d 505, 424 N.Y.S.2d 711 (1st Dep't 1980), *but see* Gonfiantini v. Zino, 184 A.D.2d 368 (1st Dep't 1992).
49. *Id.*, 74 A.D.2d at 505-6, 424 N.Y.S.2d at 712.

In *Sharkey v. Locust Valley Marina*,[50] the Appellate Division, Second Department, also ruled that admitting the testimony of the plaintiff's expert on theories not in the bill of particulars was a prejudicial error. The court defined prejudice as "where the matters pleaded are such that an adversary could not have been reasonably expected to have prepared for the variance at trial."

Nevertheless, the courts do expect the party demanding the bill of particulars to act in a timely fashion to correct a deficiency, and the court will examine the bill to determine whether it really gave the opposing party substantial notice of the claim argued at the trial. Consequently, in *McDougald v. Garber*,[51] the Appellate Division, First Department, ruled that the trial court had correctly allowed the plaintiff to prove certain claims that he had not identified specifically in the bill of particulars. The defendant had failed to move for relief either within ten days after receiving the bill (as required by C.P.L.R. rule 3042[d]) or at any time prior to the trial. Moreover, the court found that the specific claims that were in the bill "appear collectively to cover the various theories of liability."

With respect to an injury, the courts hold that the bar to proof applies only if the bill of particulars gave no hint of the newly claimed injury. If the new injury flows from or can be gleaned from the injuries originally claimed, then the court will permit the plaintiff to prove the newly claimed

---

50. Sharkey v. Locust Valley Marina, 96 A.D.2d 1093, 467 N.Y.S.2d 61 (2d Dep't 1983): Tri-State Aluminum Products, Inc. v. Wecher, 128 A.D.2d 697 (2d Dep't 1987). Annot., *Amendment of Pleadings: What Constitutes "Prejudice" to Party Who Objects to Evidence Outside Issues Made by Pleadings so as to Preclude Amendment of Pleadings under Rule 15(b) of Federal Rules of Civil Procedure*, 20 A.L.R. Fed. 448 (1966); Annot., *Answers to Interrogatories as Limiting Parties' Proof at State Trial*, 86 A.L.R.3d 1089 (1978).

51. McDougald v. Garber, 135 A.D.2d 80, 524 N.Y.S.2d 192 (1st Dep't 1988), *rev'd on other grounds*, 73 N.Y.2d 246, 538 N.Y.S.2d 937 (1989).

injury at the trial.[52] The same rule applies to proving special damages.[53] Occasionally, the courts allow notice other than that properly appearing in the pleadings or the bill of particulars if there was clearly no prejudice and if the matter is ancillary. For example, in *Baumis v. General Motors Corp.*,[54] the court of appeals held that the plaintiff's argument that the defendant could not prove arson at the trial because the defendant had not alleged arson as an affirmative defense was without merit since the defendant had informed the plaintiff of its intent to rely on arson as a defense at a pretrial conference some eighteen months before the trial. In fact, the plaintiff's attorney in his opening said that any claim of foul play was nonsense. Hence, the plaintiff was not surprised at the trial.

However, it would be irresponsible and unethical for an attorney to rely upon the court's approving such notice.

In any case, at the end of the chapter are examples of documents which are the defendant's remedy for the plaintiff's failure to serve the bill of particulars which the defendant demanded: a motion to preclude the plaintiff's evidence at the trial and the supporting affirmation (example 2-8).

2.4.3 An Admission Against Interest

Although a party may amend the pleading or bill of particulars, the party's attorney should remember that a statement in the original pleading or bill may constitute an admission against that party's interest and be used as such by the opposing party at the trial. For example, a party may admit that he or she owned and controlled an automobile and then

---

52. Boggi v. Murphy, 105 A.D.2d 768, 481 N.Y.S.2d 423 (2d Dep't 1984); Grey v. United Leasing, Inc., 91 A.D.2d 932, 457 N.Y.S.2d 823 (1st Dep't 1983); Solomon v. Stroler, 82 A.D.2d 756, 440 N.Y.S.2d 200 (1st Dep't 1981).
53. Zapata v. City of N.Y., 96 A.D.2d 779, 465 N.Y.S.2d 729 (1st Dep't 1983).
54. Baumis v. General Motors Corp., 106 A.D.2d 789, 484 N.Y.S.2d 185 (3d Dep't 1984), *aff'd*, 66 N.Y.2d 777, 497 N.Y.S.2d 365 (1985).

amend his or her position, but the amendment does not bar the opposing party from offering the original admission in evidence for "even after amendment, an admission in an original pleading is evidence of the fact admitted."[55] The pleadings are always before the court and need not be offered in evidence,[56] and since they are always in evidence, they need not be marked in evidence.[57] Counsel may refer to them and read them to the jury.

A bill of particulars served by a plaintiff in an action for personal injuries caused by negligence can be found at the end of the chapter as example 2-9.

2.5 THE DISCOVERY ORDER

Certain plaintiffs must or may request a pre-calendar conference at which the judge assigned to the case will issue an order scheduling discovery. As a prerequisite to making this request, the plaintiff may need to file a request for judicial intervention.

2.5.1 The Request for Judicial Intervention

The request for judicial intervention is an outgrowth of New York's individual assignment system for civil actions. The intention is that one judge will make all the rulings in any particular action. Therefore, the system must assign the action to a judge before he can issue any orders. Having purchased an index number[58] and started the action, the

---

55. Coraci v. Yurkin, 12 Misc. 2d 619, 621; 174 N.Y.S.2d 540 (Sup. Ct. 1958); *In re* Richfil Estates, Inc., 197 Misc. 248 (Sup. Ct.), *rev'd on other grounds,* 277 A.D.765 (1st Dep't 1950); Annot., 52 A.L.R.2d 516 (1957).
56. Continental Leather Co. v. Liverpool, Brazil & River Platte Steam Navigation Co., 228 A.D.707, 239 N.Y.S. 229 (2d Dep't 1930).
57. White v. Smith, 45 N.Y. 418 (1871); Field v. Surpless, 83 A.D. 268, 82 N.Y.S. 127 (1st Dep't 1903).
58. C.P.L.R. 306-a.

plaintiff may file a request for judicial intervention in order to have the case assigned to a judge. (The assignment is random.) Of course, either party may file such a request, and Uniform Court Rule 202.6 requires this filing before a party may file a notice of motion, an order to show cause, an application for an ex parte order, a notice of petition, a note of issue, a notice of a medical malpractice action, a statement of net worth pursuant to section 236 of the Domestic Relations Law, or a request for a preliminary conference pursuant to Uniform Court Rule 202.12(a).[59] The form for this request can be found at the end of this chapter (examples 2-10 and 2-10A).

2.5.2 The Pre-Calendar Conference

In an action for medical malpractice, the plaintiff must file a notice of such an action with the clerk of the court within sixty days after issue has been joined,[60] i.e., after the pleadings have been served. With this notice, the plaintiff must file proof of his service of the notice on the other parties and of his service of the authorizations for the defendant to obtain the plaintiff's medical records.[61] Thus, the notice of a medical malpractice action precipitates a pre-calendar conference before the plaintiff files the note of issue.[62] At the conference, the judge should encourage a settlement, simplify or limit the issues, and prescribe a timetable for discovery, offers, and the voluntary examination of expert witnesses pursuant to C.P.L.R. 3101(d). The judge should order the parties to complete discovery within twelve months of the date of the notice and to be ready for trial within eighteen months of the notice. To the extent possible, the judge convening the conference should hear all subsequent mo-

---

59. 22 N.Y.C.R.R. § 202.6. 1007, 1011, and 8018(a).
60. C.P.L.R. Rule 3406(a).
61. *Id.*
62. C.P.L.R. Rule 3406(b).

tions and should preside at the trial. The judge may convene a compliance conference near the end of the prescribed term, and the sanctions for failing to comply with this rule or with the judge's order are attorney's fees, dismissal, and judgment by default.[63]

In some actions for personal injury, the plaintiff may request an expedited preliminary conference that is tantamount to a pre-calendar conference. If a party (the plaintiff or a defendant asserting a counter-claim) is terminally ill allegedly as the result of the culpable conduct of another party, the ill party may file a written request for an expedited preliminary conference.[64] A physician's affidavit must accompany this request, and the affidavit must state that the party is terminally ill, the nature of his or her illness, and his or her life expectancy. The judge must convene the conference within twenty days of receiving the request.[65] Having satisfied himself that the party's illness is genuine and relevant, the judge should prescribe a schedule for discovery, require the parties to complete discovery within ninety days of the conference unless more time is necessary,[66] decide when the plaintiff should file the note of issue and the certificate of readiness, grant the action a trial preference, and order the parties to commence the trial within a year.[67] Subsequent to this order, a motion to dismiss or for summary judgment will not suspend discovery.[68]

The notice of a medical malpractice action and an order pursuant to a pre-calendar conference can be found at the end of the chapter (examples 2-11 and 2-12). In addition, example 2-12A is a physician's affidavit that the plaintiff is terminally ill, and example 2-12B is an order granting the motion to perpetuate the plaintiff's testimony on videotape.

---

63. *Id.*
64. C.P.L.R. Rule 3407(a).
65. *Id.*
66. C.P.L.R. Rule 3407(b)(1).
67. C.P.L.R. Rule 3407(b)(2).
68. C.P.L.R. Rule 3407(b)(3).

2.6 THE REPORTS OF MEDICAL EXPERTS

2.6.1 The General Scheme

Expert testimony is important in most actions for negligence. In order to facilitate the cross-examination of medical experts, rule 202.17 of the Uniform Court Rules requires the exchange of medical reports among the parties in actions for personal injury and wrongful death.

Most of these reports are the result of an expert's examination of the plaintiff, the allegedly injured party, and any party may serve a notice fixing the time and place of such an examination and naming the physician. Before the examination, the party to be examined must serve on the other parties:

1. Copies of the medical reports of the physicians who have already treated or examined him; and
2. Written authorization for the other parties to obtain and copy all hospital records to which those physicians may refer.

After the examination, the party obtaining the physician's report must serve copies on the other parties. If the cause of death is an issue, then the plaintiff must provide authorizations for the other parties to obtain all the hospital records, autopsy, or postmortem reports. The plaintiff's attorney should serve the relevant copies and authorizations with the bill of particulars. No cases may be listed for trial unless the parities have complied with the rules for exchanging medical reports, but a party who intends to rely solely on hospital records may certify that intention in lieu of serving medical reports.

If the plaintiff discovers injuries that did not exist or that were not known to exist when he served the original medical reports, the plaintiff may serve a supplemental medical report on the other parties and specify a time when he may be examined further. Moreover, any party who decides to offer the testimony of additional treating or examining physicians must serve their reports on the other parties at least thirty days before the trial.

> These rules are meant to bind the parties. Hence, rule 202.17(h) provides, . . . the party seeking to recover damages shall be precluded at the trial from offering in evidence any part of the hospital records and all other records, including autopsy or post-mortem records, x-ray reports or reports of other technicians, not made available pursuant to this rule and no party shall be permitted to offer any evidence of injuries or conditions not set forth or put in issue in the respective medical reports previously exchanged, nor will the court hear the testimony of any treating or examining physicians whose medical reports have not been served as provided by this rule.

These rules govern all suits in all judicial departments. Therefore, when preparing a case for trial, the parties' attorneys must comply with the rules for exchanging medical reports. The penalty for failing to comply may include preclusion of testimony and nonsuit.

2.6.2 Judicial Enforcement

The plaintiff's attorney must exchange a medical report if the attorney wants the physician to testify based upon the physician's examination of the plaintiff. If the physician refuses to give the attorney a report to exchange, then the attorney may obtain a court order directing the physician to do so.[69] *Knight v. Long Island College Hospital* provides an example of the unpleasant consequences for the plaintiff of a failure to observe scrupulously the exchange of the reports of medical experts.[70] The Appellate Division, Second De-

69. Lisec v. Abrams, 112 A.D.2d 145, 491 N.Y.S.2d 58 (2d Dep't 1985).
70. Knight v. Long Island College Hospital, 106 A.D.2d 371, 482 N.Y.S.2d 503 (2d Dep't 1984).

partment, reversed and remanded a judgment for the plaintiff in the amount of $1.2 million. The plaintiff had served on the defendants the medical reports of Dr. A and Dr. B, who testified at the trial. The bill of particulars and Dr. A's medical report said that the plaintiff had an organic brain dysfunction. Dr. B's medical report said that he could not tell yet if the plaintiff had such a dysfunction but that time would tell. Dr. B examined the plaintiff again just before testifying and then did testify that the plaintiff was suffering from an organic brain dysfunction. The appellate court held that Dr. B's testimony was improper because his medical report had not said that the plaintiff had an organic brain dysfunction, and, hence, the physician's testimony surprised the defendant.[71]

The plaintiff's attorney in Knight should have served a supplemental medical report on the defendant. This view is confirmed by the decision of the Appellate Division, First Department, in *McDougald v. Garber.*[72] In that case, the appellate court held that the plaintiff's failure to exchange a subsequent medical report until the eve of the trial did not prejudice the defendant. The plaintiff had exchanged the original medical report, and

> the defendants' claim of surprise is considerably weakened by the hospital records, which are replete with nurses' notes as to the patient's responsiveness. While plaintiff may have been technically in violation of the rule, the defendants had almost three weeks after the receipt of the report to prepare for Dr. Kaplan's cross-examination. They are unable to point to any prejudice due to the delay.

The courts also apply an implied rule of reasonableness to the correlation between the report and the physician's testimony. Thus, the courts have held that so long as the medical

---

71. *See also* Manoni v. Giordano, 102 A.D.2d 846, 476 N.Y.S.2d 617 (2d Dep't 1984); Kastner v. Rodriguez, 91 A.D.2d 950, 458 N.Y.S.2d 566 (1st Dep't 1983).

72. McDougald v. Garber, 135 A.D.2d 80, 524 N.Y.S.2d 192 (1st Dep't 1988), *rev'd on other grounds*, 73 N.Y.2d 246, 538 N.Y.S.2d 937 (1989).

report spelled out the injury, the physician may testify regarding the degree of the injury although the report did not do so.[73] Of course, if the physician who is testifying as an expert has neither treated nor examined the plaintiff, then the witness had not produced a report that the rules require the party's attorney to exchange with the other parties. The courts have allowed a physician to testify regarding the plaintiff's condition based solely upon the medical records and without exchanging a report because the physician was not testifying from a personal examination of the plaintiff.[74] In other words, if the physician's testimony is predicated upon expert testimony, medical records, or x-rays that are already in evidence, then the rules for exchanging medical reports do not preclude his testimony.[75]

A more difficult question is presented by the expert testimony of a treating physician who never produced a report. Rule 202.17 seems to say that he must produce a report and that the plaintiff's attorney must serve it on the defendants before the treating physician may testify. However, in *Zimmerman v. Jamaica Hospital*,[76] the Appellate Division, Second Department, held that the defendant was allowed to call one of the doctors who had treated the plaintiff without exchanging his medical report. The court held that the rule applies only to physicians who examine a party in preparation for litigation, and the physician had never prepared a medical report because he attended the plaintiff as a treating physician. The trial attorney should not rely on this deci-

73. Johnson v. School District, 83 A.D.2d 931, 442 N.Y.S.2d 581 (2d Dep't 1981); *cf.*, Holshek v. Stokes, 122 A.D.2d 777, 505 N.Y.S.2d 664 (2d Dep't 1986); Knight v. Long Island College Hospital, 106 A.D.2d 371, 482 N.Y.S.2d 503 (2d Dep't 1984).

74. Markey v. Eiseman, 114 A.D.2d 887, 495 N.Y.S.2d 61 (2d Dep't 1985); Rivera v. City of N.Y., 107 A.D.2d 331, 486 N.Y.S.2d 730 (1st Dep't 1985).

75. Kurth v. Wallkill, 132 A.D.2d 529, 517 N.Y.S.2d 267 (2d Dep't 1987); Kombers v. Lefkowitz, 131 A.D.2d 815, 517 N.Y.S.2d 179 (2d Dep't 1987); Holshek v. Stokes, 122 A.D.2d 777, 505 N.Y.S.2d 664 (2d Dep't 1986); Jorgenson v. Great Atl. & Pac. Tea Co., 119 A.D.2d 730, 501 N.Y.S.2d 396 (2d Dep't 1986).

76. Zimmerman v. Jamaica Hospital, 143 A.D.2d 86, 531 N.Y.S.2d 337 (2d Dep't 1988), *but see* Tiborsky v. Martorella, 188 A.D.2d 795 (3d Dep't 1992).

sion literally. Most likely, *Zimmerman* applies only when the defendant calls the plaintiff's treating physician to the stand. In other words, the plaintiff's attorney may not prevent the defendant from obtaining relevant testimony by failing to obtain a report from a witness under the plaintiff's control.

Finally, if two or more defendants share the services of a physician to examine the plaintiff, then only one of the defendants need serve the resulting medical report on all other parties. If the plaintiff receives a copy of the report, it does not matter from which defendant he received it.[77]

At the end of the chapter is a request for the report of the adverse party's examining physician (example 2-13) and the report of such a physician to the attorney who engaged him (example 2-14).

2.6.3 Motion for Summary Judgment

The attorney must prepare to present a condensed version of his or her client's case when disputing a motion for summary judgment, and this preparation entails reducing prospective testimony to written form in affidavits.

A distinction is in order. A court may grant a defendant's motion to dismiss a cause of action for various reasons,[78] e.g., the complaint's failure to state a cause of action. However, the complaint may contain the correct allegations to state a cause of action, but the evidence may be insufficient on its face to sustain those allegations. In such a situation, the defendant should make a motion for a summary judgment. (A plaintiff may, of course, move for a summary judgment against a counterclaim or an affirmative defense, but the plaintiff rarely can establish his own cause of action this

77. Rhoden v. Montalbo, 127 A.D. 2d 645, 511 N.Y.S.2d 875 (2d Dep't 1987).

78. C.P.L.R. Rule 3211(a)(1)-(11).

way in a case alleging negligence or medical malpractice.[79]) When ruling on such a motion, the court decides whether there is a genuine issue of fact, and, to do so, the court considers evidence in written form. (If there is an issue of fact, the court will deny the motion and leave the evaluation of the competing witnesses to the jury.) Thus, C.P.L.R. Rule 3212(b) reads in part,

> A motion for summary judgment shall be supported by affidavit, by a copy of the pleadings and by other available proof, such as depositions and written admissions. The affidavit shall be by a person having knowledge of the facts; it shall recite all the material facts; and it shall show that there is no defense to the cause of action or that the cause of action or defense has no merit. The motion shall be granted if, upon all the papers and proof submitted, the cause of action or defense shall be established sufficiently to warrant the court as a matter of law in directing judgment in favor of a party. Except as provided in subdivision (c) of this rule [i.e., an immediate trial] the motion shall be denied if any party shall show facts sufficient to require a trial of any issue of fact.

A party shows facts sufficient to create an issue of fact by submitting detailed affidavits from prospective witnesses. The court will consider neither unsworn reports[80] nor hearsay.[81] In many actions for negligence and in every action for medical malpractice, the key affidavit is the one from a medical expert. An affidavit from the party's attorney is insufficient, and so is a pro forma affidavit from an expert.[82]

---

79. Ferraro v. Cinelli, N.Y.L.J., May 10, 1993, p. 27 (A.D. 1st Dep't) and Chahales v. Garber, N.Y.L.J., July 29, 1993, p. 25 (A.D. 2d Dep't), *but see* Cummins v. Rose, N.Y.L.J., Aug. 18, 1992, p. 23 (A.D. 2d Dep't).

80. Gendjoian v. Heaps, N.Y.L.J., Oct. 14, 1992, p. 25 (A.D. 2d Dep't), and Samilenko v. Sosa-Donis, N.Y.L.J., Oct. 16, 1992, p. 27 (A.D. 2d Dep't).

81. Ferraro v. Cinelli, N.Y.L.J., May 10, 1993, p. 27 (A.D. 1st Dep't).

82. Zuckerman v. City of New York, 49 N.Y.2d 557, 562: "mere conclusions, expressions of hope or unsubstantiated allegations or assertions are insufficient." *See also* Bush v. St. Clare's Hospital, 82 N.Y.2d 738 (1993): the finding of a medical malpractice panel that the defendant hospital was not negligent is insufficient to support a motion for summary judgment.

(The defendant doctor could, of course, draft a satisfactory affidavit, and a party to an action for negligence might do so regarding something within that party's competence, e.g., the manner of the car crash.) Once the defendant, for example, has submitted a satisfactory affidavit from his witness to support his or her motion, the plaintiff must submit a similar affidavit from the plaintiff's witness to defeat the motion and to preserve the issue for trial.[83]

As a matter of good office practice, the attorney should ask his or her witness to draft such an affidavit when the witness prepares his or her report — even if the witness does not execute the affidavit at that moment and especially if the witness is an expert who may not be available on short notice. An example of such an affidavit from the plaintiff's medical expert in an action for medical malpractice can be found at the end of this chapter (example 2-15). Note how carefully the expert recites the detailed factual basis for his conclusions.

2.7 THE MARKED PLEADINGS

The attorney must remember that his or her ultimate objective is to persuade the judge and jury and that clarity is a prerequisite to responsible persuasion. Having investigated the case, researched the law, drafted the pleadings, conducted discovery, and disputed motions, the attorney is intimately familiar with the arguments. However, although the judge has supervised the case, he or she is not so familiar

83. Whalen v. Victory Memorial Hospital, N.Y.L.J., Nov. 16, 1992, p. 29 (A.D. 2d Dep't):

> This medical malpractice action arose from the allegedly improper performance of an arteriogram by the defendant, Dr. Allan Keil. On his motion for summary judgment, the defendan Dr. Ramon Cabanas, the plaintiff's attending physician, submitted, *inter alia*, his affidavit detailing the treatment he rendered to the plaintiff as well as hospital records and deposition testimony to support his allegations. Dr. Cabanas established his entitlement to judgment as a matter of law. Thus, the burden shifted to the plaintiff to respond with rebutting medical evidence demonstrating a departure from accepted medical procedures . . . . The attorney's affirmation submitted by the plaintiff simply failed to meet this burden.

with it. Therefore, the court requires marked pleadings for its convenience. A pleading is marked, i.e., annotated, to indicate the opponent's response to each allegation. For example, the defendant has responded to each allegation in the complaint by admitting it, denying it, or professing to lack sufficient knowledge to form a belief.[84]

> The party who has filed the note of issue shall furnish the judge who is to preside at the trial with copies of each pleading, where they have not been superseded by the pre-trial order, plainly marked to indicate which statements are admitted and which controverted by the responsive pleading.[85]

Generally, the plaintiff's attorney files the note of issue, and the pleadings include the complaints, the answers, any reply, the bills of particulars, and any amendments or supplements.[86] At the end of this chapter, you will find a document which consists of the title page for a set of marked pleadings and the marked complaint itself (example 2-16). Please do not begin the trial by alienating the judge: neatness counts!

2.8 ADDITIONAL DOCUMENTS

There are, of course, other documents involved in conducting a lawsuit, and the attorney must be familiar with all of them. Therefore, example 2-17 is a list of the forms which our firm keeps on file in our office. In addition, we have reproduced four more forms: an application for an index number, a summons, a note of issue, and a certificate of readiness. (See examples 2-17A, 2-18, 2-19, and 2-20.)

Since New York now taxes commencing a lawsuit, the plaintiff's attorney's first official act after drafting his pleadings is to purchase an index number. (See example 2-17A for the form.) Only then may the plaintiff commence his suit, and the parties will endorse this index number on every doc-

---

84. C.P.L.R. § 3018(a).
85. C.P.L.R. Rule 4012.
86. C.P.L.R. §§ 3011, 3025, 3041, 3043.

ument they file with the court.[86.1] The attorney should wait to buy the index number until he has drafted the complaint in order to be certain that he has the title of the action correct. Otherwise, he may need to buy a new index number.

As everyone knows, the plaintiff uses the summons to commence his action, and the basic method of service is by personal delivery to the defendant. Any other method requires justification.[87]

The basic difference between the note of issue and the certificate of readiness is that the note of issue puts the case on the calendar, while the certificate of readiness keeps the case on the calendar. Thus, C.P.L.R. 3402(a) provides:

> At any time after issue is first joined, or at least forty days after service of a summons has been completed irrespective of joinder of issue, any party may place a case upon the calendar by filing, within ten days after service, with proof of such service two copies of a note of issue with the clerk and such other data as may be required by the applicable rules of the court....The clerk shall enter the case upon the calendar as of the date of the filing....

In other words, the note of issue tells the court that the defendant has answered the complaint or had an opportunity to do so; that is, there is a real dispute to be tried.[88]

A generation ago, the certificate of readiness was due one year after the note of issue.[89] This document certifies that the pleadings and discovery are complete; that is, that the parties are legally ready for trial. However, pursuant to Uniform Court Rule 202.21(a), the court requires the party to file the certificate of readiness and the note of issue simultaneously (see example 2-19). Naturally, this practice defeats the purpose of the note of issue, but the practice does keep off the calendar those cases which are settled before the conclusion of discovery.

86.1. C.P.L.R. § 8018(c), (d). *See also* C.P.L.R. §§ 306-a and 8018(a), (b).

87. Regarding the summons, see generally C.P.L.R. article 3 and sections 1319, 1345, 6213, 6512, and 1501.

88. BLACK'S LAW DICTIONARY 971 (4th ed. 1968) ("Joinder of issue. The act by which the parties to a cause arrive at that stage of it in their pleadings, that one asserts a fact to be so, and the other denies it.").

89. MARINO, NEW YORK CIVIL PRACTICE LAW AND RULES 279 (1978).

2.9 CONCLUSION

In chapter 1, we explained how an attorney investigates a case. The attorney's understanding grows as he or she learns the facts, and the attorney's arguments improve as he or she outlines those for each side and as he or she revises his or her own to conform to the evidence and to defeat refutation. In chapter 2, we have explained how attorneys express their arguments in a series of responsive documents. This written dialectic should further refine the arguments in the minds of each advocate. Thus, an examination of the pleadings should enable the reader to determine the ultimate issue; for example, did nurse A administer the drug to the patient but fail to record that fact in his chart so that nurse B gave him a second dose, which killed him?

The ultimate issue is not liability: liability is the ultimate conclusion. Instead, the ultimate issue is that specific disagreement whose resolution will led logically and inexorably to a conclusion on liability. The ultimate issue could depend on something as simple as the color of a tissue sample on a slide in the hospital's laboratory: the mis-interpretation of that color led to the erroneous prognosis, which led to the unnecessary amputation, which leads now to a finding of liability and damages. The trial attorney should understand his or her case so well that the attorney can tell the jurors, "Ladies and gentlemen, the science of medicine is complicated, but this case is not. It revolves around the color of a tissue sample on a slide in the hospital's laboratory on the morning of January 17, 1993."

Frankly, by the end of the investigation and pleading, the attorney should be eager to start the trial. Part II explains the use of evidence in the course of that trial.

EXAMPLE 2-1: NOTICE OF CLAIM

Blumbergs Law Products T 1183—Notice of Claim against a Public Authority Pursuant to §50 General Municipal Law: Not for use in the Court of Claims: 6-81

JULIUS BLUMBERG, INC., PUBLISHER, NYC 10013

In the Matter of the Claim of

, An Infant by his Mother and Natural Guardian,

TO: NEW YORK CITY HEALTH AND HOSPITALS CORPORATION
346 Broadway, New York, New York

PLEASE TAKE NOTICE that the undersigned claimant(s) hereby make(s) claim and demand against you as follows:

1. The name and post-office address of each claimant and claimant's attorney is:

, An Infant by his Mother
and Natural Guardian,

Bronx, New York 10458

KRAMER, DILLOF, TESSEL, DUFFY & MOORE
233 Broadway
New York, New York 10279

2. The nature of the claim:

Monetary Damages against New York City Health and Hospitals Corporation for severe and serious personal injuries, conscious pain and suffering, mental anguish and economic losses sustained by claimant herein as a result of the negligence and medical malpracti of New York City Health and Hospitals Corporation by and through Lincoln Medical and Health Center, its clinics, and their agents, servants and/or employees, including the Ruth Baby Clinic, its agents, servants and/or employees.

3. The time when, the place where and the manner in which the claim arose:

From in or about December, 1993 for a continuous course of prenatal course at Ruth Baby Clinic located at 545 East 142nd Street, Bronx, New York through on or about July 3, 19 and during the admission to Lincoln Medical and Health Center, located at 234 East 149t Street, Bronx, New York, from on or about July 3, 1994 through on or about July 7, 1994 including July 4, 1994 when the infant claimant was delivered of his mother at the premises of Lincoln Medical and Health Center and for a continuous course of treatment of the infant plaintiff at Lincoln Medical and Health Center up to the present. By reason of the failure of the Ruth Baby Clinic, and its agents, servants and/or employee to render good and proper prenatal care and treatment and the failure of Lincoln Medica and Health Center and its clinics, and its agents, servants and/or employees, to render good and proper care and treatment during the prenatal, antepartum, intrapartum, postpartum, neonatal and pediatric periods, and its negligent and careless management of the labor and delivery of the infant claimant and his mother, , the infant claimant, was caused to sustain severe and serious injuries.

4. The items of damage or injuries claimed are (do not state dollar amounts)

Infant claimant, , has suffered severe and serious personal injuries, including fetal distress, hypoxia, trauma, brain damage, developmental delays and disabilities, the full extent to which are not yet known, as well as conscious pain and suffering, mental anguish, loss of enjoyment of life and sequelae thereto. Economic losses have been and will be sustained for the cost of medical care, nursing, rehabilitation, therapies and adjunct care.

The undersigned claimant(s) therefore present this claim for adjustment and payment. You are hereby notified that unless it is adjusted and paid within the time provided by law from the date of presentation to you, the claimant(s) intend(s) to commence an action on this claim.

Dated: New York, New York
July 10, 1996

The name signed must be printed beneath

The name signed must be printed beneath

KRAMER, DILLOF, TESSEL, DUFFY & MOORE
Attorney(s) for Claimant(s)
Office and Post Office Address, Telephone Number
233 Broadway
New York, New York 10279
(212) 267-4177

INDIVIDUAL VERIFICATION

State of New York County of New York *ss.:*

being duly sworn, deposes and says that deponent is the claimant in the within action; that she has read the foregoing Notice of Claim and knows the contents thereof; that the same is true to deponent's own knowledge, except as to the matters therein stated to be alleged on information and belief, and that as to those matters deponent believes it to be true.

Sworn to before me, this 10th *day of* July *19* 96

SANDRA DeJESUS
Commissioner of Deeds
City of New York Number 3-6543
Certificate Filed in New York County
Commission Expires Aug. 1, 1997

CORPORATE VERIFICATION

State of New York, County of *ss.:*

being duly sworn, deposes and says that deponent is the of corporate claimant named in the within action; that deponent has read the foregoing Notice of Claim and knows the contents thereof, and that the same is true to deponent's own knowledge, except as to the matters therein stated to be alleged upon information and belief, and as to those matters deponent believes it to be true.

This verification is made by deponent because said claimant is a corporation, and deponent an officer thereof, to wit its

The grounds of deponent's belief as to all matters not stated upon deponent's knowledge are as follows:

Sworn to before me, this day of 19

In the Matter of the Claim of

Notice of Claim Against

Attorney(s) for Claimant(s)
Office and Post Office Address

EXAMPLE 2-2: THE COMPLAINT

SUPREME COURT OF THE STATE OF NEW YORK
COUNTY OF
---x

Plaintiff,

VERIFIED
COMPLAINT

- against -

Defendant.
---x

Plaintiff, above named, complaining of the defendant by his attorneys, respectfully alleges:

AS AND FOR A FIRST CAUSE OF ACTION

1. At all times herein mentioned, the plaintiff, was a resident of the County of , State of New York.

2. At all times herein mentioned, the defendant was a foreign corporation doing business in the State of New York and whose principal place of business was in the Commonwealth of .

3. At all times herein mentioned, the defendant owned, operated, managed and controlled a railroad trestle, located in the village of , County of , State of New York.

4. On or about 19 , plaintiff, while lawfully on the premises of the aforesaid trestle, was caused to fall therefrom.

5. Said occurrence was due to the carelessness and negligence of the defendant, its agents, servants, and/or employees in failing properly to maintain the railroad trestle in a safe condition; in causing, allowing, and/or failing to prevent a trap and a nuisance to exist on said trestle; in failing properly to warn of the existence of said danger, trap, and nuisance; and in failing properly to barricade said site from the public.

6. At all times herein mentioned, the defendant had both actual and constructive notice of said trestle, of the danger, trap, and nuisance aforesaid, and of the public usage of said trestle.

7. By reason of the foregoing, plaintiff sustained severe and serious personal injuries, a severe shock to his nervous system, and certain internal injuries, and was caused to suffer severe physi-

cal pain and mental anguish as a result thereof, and, upon information and belief, some of these injuries are of a permanent and lasting nature; that plaintiff was confined to his bed and home as a result thereof and was incapacitated from attending to his usual activities, all to his damage in the sum of $

WHEREFORE, plaintiff demands judgment against the defendant in such sum as a jury would find fair, adequate, and just.

Dated: New York, New York
July 2, 1996

KRAMER, DILLOF, TESSEL,
DUFFY & MOORE
Attorneys for Plaintiff
233 Broadway
New York, NY 10279
(212) 267-4177

EXAMPLE 2-2A: REQUEST FOR SUPPLEMENTAL DEMAND

SUPREME COURT OF THE STATE OF NEW YORK
COUNTY OF KINGS
-------------------------------------X

Plaintiff

DEMAND FOR TOTAL DAMAGES

-against-

Defendants
-------------------------------------X

K. D. T. D & M

SIRS:

Defendant(s), requests a supplemental demand setting forth the total damages to which the plaintiff(s) deems him or herself to be entitled.

Dated: Manhasset, New York
July 17, 1991

Yours, etc.

Bonomo, Darwin, Geismar and Johnson
Attorneys for Defendant
111 East Shore Road
Manhasset, New York 11030
516 365 6690

TO:

Kramer, Dillof, Tessel, Duffy and Moore
Attorney for Plaintiff
233 Broadway
New York, New York 10279
212 267-4177

EXAMPLE 2-3: WAIVER FOR MINOR

WAIVER OF RIGHT TO SUE

READ CAREFULLY BEFORE SIGNING

Location Of Contest: Caumsett State Park

Date Of Contest: 12/7/96

First, I acknowledge that anyone participating in a sporting event, such as orienteering, consents to those injury causing events which are known, apparent, or reasonably forseeable (Turcotte v. Fell, 68 NY 2d 432, 510 NYS 2d 49 [1986]). During an orienteering contest, the contestant must find flags hidden in the woods with all its hazards; moreover, other people, animals, and vehicles may be using the park simultaneously. Second, I acknowledge that the owner, lessee, or occupant of the premises owes no duty to keep the premises safe for hiking (of which orienteering is a subdivision) or to give warning of hazardous conditions or activities (General Obligations Law # 9-103). Third, I acknowledge that the Long Island Orienteering Club is not an operator of the public park where this contest is being held and that the entry fee for the contest is not a fee for using this public facility (General Obligations Law # 5-326). Fourth, I recognize that a prerequisite for staging an orienteering contest is that the people staging the contest be protected from claims for negligence, including claims by third parties for indemnity or contribution, and from the costs of litigation.

Therefore, in consideration of the Long Island Orienteering Club's allowing me to participate in this contest, I waive any rights or claims for wrongful death, personal injury, or damage to property that I may acquire as a result of this contest, whether from negligence or otherwise. This waiver shall release from liability the Long Island Orienteering Club and its officers, members, and agents, other participants in the contest, the State of New York, the County of Nassau, the County of Suffolk, any governmental subdivision or department, private landowners, lessees, and any other person using or occupying the land where the contest is held. In other words, I shall have no cause of action against anyone for negligence. Moreover, my distributes, heirs, and assigns shall have no such cause of action. Finally, I attest that I am fit, able, and qualified to participate in this contest and that a licensed medical doctor has verified my physical condition.

CONTESTANT'S SIGNATURE: ______________________ DATE: __________

CONTESTANT'S NAME (Print): Liam J. McMullen

CONTESTANT'S ADDRESS (Print): 647 High Street
Port Jefferson, New York 11777

PARENT'S EXECUTION OF WAIVER FOR MINOR

As the parent or guardian of the minor listed above, I hereby execute this waiver of liability on his behalf. I recognize that the Long Island Orienteering Club must rely on the representation of an adult that he is the parent or guardian of a particular child. Therefore, I certify that I am the parent or guardian of the minor named in this waiver and that I possess the legal authority to waive liability on his behalf. In consideration of the Long Island Orienteering Club's accepting my authority and allowing the minor to compete, I agree to indemnify the club and any person listed in the waiver in case my authority should prove insufficient. The indemnity shall include the payment of all damages awarded as a result of this failure of authority and all concomitant attorney's fees including fees in an action against me.

SIGNATURE OF PARENT OR GUARDIAN: Damon McMullen DATE: 12/7/96

NAME OF PARENT OR GUARDIAN (Print): Damon P. McMullen

RELATIONSHIP (Print): Father

ADDRESS OF PARENT OR GUARDIAN (Print): 18 June Ave
Northport, New York 11768

EXAMPLE 2-4: WAIVER FOR ADULT

UNITED STATES PUBLIC HEALTH SERVICE
FEDERAL OCCUPATIONAL HEALTH
REGION VII

CONSENT FOR EXERCISE PROGRAM

Exercise Objectives: The purpose of an exercise program is to develop and maintain cardiorespiratory (aerobic) fitness, muscular strength and endurance, body composition, and flexibility.

Procedures: A structured exercise program based on individual needs (obtained fitness assessment information), interests, and/or physician's recommendations will be given to each participant. Exercises may include aerobic activities (treadmill walking/running, cycling, rowing machine exercise, group aerobic activity, swimming, and other such activities), calisthenics and weight lifting to improve muscular strength and endurance, and flexibility exercises to improve joint range of motion. All aerobic exercise programs involve a warm-up, exercise at target heart rate, and cool down components.

Potential Risks: All exercise programs are designed to place a gradually increasing workload on the cardiorespiratory and musculoskeletal systems in order to effect improvements. The body's reaction to gradually increasing exercise activities cannot be predicted with complete accuracy. Unusual changes during or following an exercise session may occur. These may include muscular or joint injury, abnormal blood pressure, fainting, disorders of heart beat, and/or vary rare instances of heart attack or death.

Potential Benefits: Benefits obtained from a structured and regularly employed exercise program might include a more efficient cardiorespiratory system, an improved musculoskeletal system, a decrease in body fat, a decrease in blood fats, improvement in psychological function, and a decrease in the risk of heart and other diseases.

Confidentially: All participant exercise program information will be treated as privileged and confidential and will not be revealed to any person (other than the fitness staff involved in the participant's exercise program) without expressed written consent. Obtained information, however, may be used for statistical or scientific purposes with right of privacy retained.

Inquiry and Freedom of Consent: I have read the foregoing and I understand the objectives, procedures, potential risks and benefits, and confidentially involved.

Unless otherwise indicated under the "Comments" section below, I certify that I am in good health and have no condition that would limit/prohibit my participation in a structured exercise program.

I understand that if there are any questions about the procedures or methods used during an exercise session I should ask the exercise facility staff.

I realize that injury may result from improper exercise techniques or misuse of exercise facilities or equipment. I agree to be attentive to all instructions given to me and to exercise and use facilities and equipment correctly.

I assume responsibility for monitoring my own condition throughout the exercise program and should any unusual system(s) occur, I will cease my participation and inform the staff.

I shall also notify the staff of any current changes in my medical status. I consent to the administration of any immediate resuscitation measures deemed advisable by the staff.

Comments: ______________________________

____

____

I have read and understand the above information and voluntarily consent to participate in a structured exercise program. I realize that I am free to terminate the exercise program at any time.

PRINTED NAME: McMULLEN, KEVIN LTC

SIGNATURE: Kevin McMullen

AGENCY: MOP-P, ARPERCEN DATE: 24SEP95

WITNESS: Alfred Bromley

EXAMPLE 2.5: THE ANSWER

SUPREME COURT OF THE STATE OF NEW YORK
COUNTY OF
---x

Plaintiff, **ANSWER**

- against -

Defendants.

---x

The defendants, and , by their attorneys **KRAMER, DILLOF, TESSEL, DUFFY & MOORE, ESQS.**, answering the complaint of the plaintiff herein, respectfully allege:

AS AND FOR AN ANSWER TO THE FIRST CAUSE OF ACTION

FIRST: Deny each and every allegation contained in the paragraphs designated "11," "12," "13," "14," "15," "16," and "17" of the plaintiff's complaint.

SECOND: Deny knowledge or information sufficient to form a belief as to all the allegations contained in the paragraphs designated "1," "4," "8," "9," "10," "18," "19," and "20" of the plaintiff's complaint, and leaves all questions of law to the court.

AS AND FOR AN ANSWER TO THE SECOND CAUSE OF ACTION

THIRD: Defendants, and answering paragraph "21" repeats, reiterates and realleges each and every denial and admission concerning paragraphs "1" through "20," inclusive, of the plaintiff's complaint in the answer thereto with the same force and effect as though fully set forth herein at length.

FOURTH: Deny each and every allegation contained in the paragraphs designated "22," "23," "24," and "26" of the plaintiff's complaint.

FIFTH: Deny knowledge or information sufficient to form a belief as to all the allegations contained in the paragraphs designated "25" and "27" of the plaintiff's complaint.

AS AND FOR AN ANSWER TO THE THIRD CAUSE OF ACTION

SIXTH: Defendants, and answering paragraph "28" repeats, reiterates, and realleges each and every denial and admission concerning paragraphs "1" and "27," inclusive, of the plaintiff's complaint in the answer thereto with the same force and effect as though fully set forth herein at length.

SEVENTH: Deny each and every allegation contained in the paragraphs designated "29," "30," "31," and "32" of the plaintiff's complaint.

EIGHTH: Deny knowledge or information sufficient to form a belief as to all the allegations contained in the paragraph designated "33" of the plaintiff's complaint.

AS AND FOR THE ANSWER TO THE FOURTH CAUSE OF ACTION

NINTH: Defendants, and , answering paragraph "34" repeats, reiterates, and realleges each and every denial and admission concerning paragraphs "1" through "33", inclusive, of the plaintiff's complaint in the answer thereto with the same force and effect as though fully set forth herein at length.

TENTH: Deny each and every allegation contained in the paragraphs designated "35," "36," "37," "38," and "39" of the plaintiff's complaint.

ELEVENTH: Deny knowledge or information sufficient to form a belief as to all the allegations contained in the paragraph designated "40" of the plaintiff's complaint.

AS AND FOR AN ANSWER TO THE FIFTH CAUSE OF ACTION

TWELFTH: Defendants, and , answering paragraph "41" repeats, reiterates, and realleges each and every denial and admission concerning paragraphs "1" through "40," inclusive, of the plaintiff's complaint in the answer thereto with the same force and effect as though fully set forth herein at length.

THIRTEENTH: Deny each and every allegation contained in the paragraphs designated "42," "43," and "44" of the plaintiff's complaint.

FOURTEENTH: Deny knowledge or information sufficient to form a belief as to all the allegations contained in the paragraphs designated "45," "46," and "47" of the plaintiff's complaint.

AS AND FOR AN ANSWER TO THE SIXTH CAUSE OF ACTION

FIFTEENTH: Defendants, and , answering paragraph "48" repeats, reiterates, and realleges each and every denial and admission concerning paragraphs "1" through "47," inclusive, of the plaintiff's complaint in the answer thereto with the same force and effect as though fully set forth herein at length.

SIXTEENTH: Deny each and every allegation contained in the paragraphs designated "51," "52," and "53" of the plaintiff's complaint.

SEVENTEENTH: Deny knowledge or information sufficient to form a belief as to all the allegations contained in the paragraphs designated "49," "50," "54," and "55" of the plaintiff's complaint.

EIGHTEENTH: Defendants, and , answering paragraph "56" repeats, reiterates, and realleges each ad every denial and admission concerning paragraphs "1" through "55," inclusive, of the plaintiff's complaint in the answer thereto with the same force and effect as though fully set forth herein at length.

NINETEENTH: Deny each and every allegation contained in the paragraphs designated "57" and "58" of the plaintiff's complaint.

WHEREFORE, the defendants, and demand judgment dismissing the plaintiff's complaint, with the costs and disbursements of this action, together with such other and further relief as to this court may seem just and proper in the premises.

Dated:
New York, New York

KRAMER, DILLOF, TESSEL,
DUFFY & MOORE
Attorneys for Defendants
233 Broadway
New York, NY 10007
(212) 267-4177

EXAMPLE 2-6: DEFENDANT'S DEMAND FOR A BILL OF PARTICULARS

SUPREME COURT OF THE STATE OF NEW YORK
COUNTY OF SUFFOLK
---------------------------------------x

Index No.

Plaintiffs

- against -

DEMAND FOR A VERIFIED BILL OF PARTICULARS

Defendants
---------------------------------------x

S I R S:

PLEASE TAKE NOTICE, that the answering defendant, ., hereby demands that you serve upon the undersigned within twenty [20] days from the date of service hereof, a duly Verified Bill of Particulars with respect to the allegations contained in the Complaint against the answering defendant.

1. State the date and place of birth of each of the plaintiffs and their residence address at the time this action was commenced.

2. Give a statement of each and every act of omission and/or commission which you will claim is the basis of the alleged malpractice or other wrong doing of this answering defendant.

3. State the date, time and place of the alleged occurrence of the alleged malpractice of this answering defendant.

4. State the first and last dates on which it is claimed that this answering defendant treated or advised the plaintiffs herein for the conditions complained of.

5. State the condition or conditions which it is claimed that this answering defendant undertook to treat.

6. Set forth any hospitalizations of the plaintiff indicating the names of the hospitals and the dates of treatment and/or confinements.

7. Set forth a list of the injuries claimed to have been caused by this answering defendant's alleged malpractice or other wrong doing, describing any claimed permanency.

8. Set forth the length of time the plaintiff was confined to:

A. Hospitals

B. Bed

C. Home

9. Set forth, if loss of earnings are to be claimed:

A. The length of time it will be claimed the plaintiff was incapacitated from employment;

B. The last date on which the plaintiff actually worked prior to the alleged medical malpractice;

C. The first date on which the plaintiff actually returned to employment after the alleged medical malpractice;

D. The weekly earnings of the plaintiff as of the the date set forth in "B" above;

E. The names and addresses of the plaintiff's employers as of the dates set forth in "B" and "C" above, together with a description of the nature of plaintiff's occupation.

10. Set forth any and all claimed special damages causally connected to the alleged malpractice or other wrong doing for:

A. Hospitals

B. Physicians

C. Nurses

D. Medical Supplies

E. Loss of Earnings

F. Any other special damages claimed,

identifying each one specifically.

11. Set forth whether or not the plaintiff has made any other claims for the same or similar injuries as are claimed herein,and if so, against whom such claims has been made, the status of such claim, and if litigation was brought or is pending, the Court in which the action was commenced, and the index number and calendar number, if any, assigned thereto.

12. Set forth whether or not the plaintiff has been reimbursed for any claimed economic loss from any collateral source, or if any claim has been made but not yet honored for reimbursement from any collateral source, and if so, set forth the name of that collateral source, and the amount of reimbursement received or claimed. If the collateral source be an insurance company, set forth the policy number under which said claim was made or paid, as well as the name and address of the company.

13. Set forth the Social Security Numbers of the plaintiff[s].

14. Does the plaintiff intend to rely upon the doctrine of informed consent? If so, state in detail the basis for this claim, indicating what risks, hazards, dangers or other information which you claim should have been told to the plaintiff herein by this answering defendant, and which information was not so imparted.

15. State whether or not it is claimed that this answering defendant violated any statutes,rules or regulations, and if so, specify the statute, rule or regulation for which it is claimed this answering defendant violated.

16. Does the plaintiff intend to rely upon the doctrine of res ipsa loquitur? If so, sate the basis for this reliance.

17. State under which exception to Article 16 of the CPLR it is claimed the within action falls under.

Dated:

Yours, etc.

Attorneys for defendant

TO: Kramer, Dillof, Tessel,
Duffy & Moore, Esqs.
Attorneys for plaintiffs
233 Broadway
New York, NY 10279
[212] 267-4177

EXAMPLE 2-7: PLAINTIFF'S DEMAND FOR A BILL OF PARTICULARS

SUPREME COURT OF THE STATE OF NEW YORK
COUNTY OF KINGS

---x

MARY SMITH and JACK SMITH,

Plaintiffs,

COMBINED DEMAND & NOTICE OF EBT

- against -

PETER ROW, ROW BROTHERS GAS & AUTO SERVICE, INC. and BIG CORP., INC.,

Defendants.

---x

SIRS:

* * * * *

PLEASE TAKE FURTHER NOTICE that pursuant to the C.P.L.R. you are required to serve a verified bill of particulars as to the defendants:

1. State the manner in which the complaint fails to set forth a cause of action as set forth in the affirmative defenses contained in the answer.

2. Set forth each and every act or omission alleged to constitute the culpable conduct of the plaintiffs as set forth in the affirmative defenses contained in the answer.

Such bill of particulars must be served within twenty days of the date hereof and upon your failure to do so, an order will be sought precluding any such testimony and the striking of any such defense as may be based upon alleged culpable conduct as aforesaid.

* * * * * *

Dated: February 14, 1996
New York, New York

Yours, etc.

KRAMER, DILLOF, TESSEL, DUFFY & MOORE
Attorneys for Plaintiffs
233 Broadway
New York, NY 10007
(212) 267-4177

TO: **DEFENSE FIRM**

EXAMPLE 2-8: DEFENDANT'S MOTION TO PRECLUDE PLAINTIFF'S EVIDENCE

SUPREME COURT OF THE STATE OF NEW YORK
COUNTY OF SUFFOLK
--X

NOTICE OF MOTION

Index No.

Plaintiff,

-against-

Defendants.

--X

SIRS:

PLEASE TAKE NOTICE, that upon the annexed affirmation of , ESQ., duly affirmed the 30th day of May, 1996, and upon all the pleadings and proceedings heretofore had herein, the undersigned will move this Court, at an IAS Term thereof, to be held at the Supreme Court located at Griffing Avenue, Riverhead, New York, on the 28th day of June, 1996 at 9:30 o'clock in the forenoon of that day, or as soon thereafter as counsel can be heard, for

a. An Order pursuant to C.P.L.R. 3042 precluding the plaintiff from giving evidence at the trial of this action as to the items of which particulars have been demanded, but have not been delivered, and for such other and further relief as to this Court may deem just and proper.

PLEASE TAKE FURTHER NOTICE, that answering affidavits or affirmations, if any, must be served at least seven (7) days prior to the return date of this motion as required by Civil Practice Law and Rules Section 2214(b).

Dated:

Attorneys for Defendant,

TO:

KRAMER, DILLOF, TESSEL,
DUFFY & MOORE
Attorneys for Plaintiff
233 Broadway
New York, NY 10279

SUPREME COURT OF THE STATE OF NEW YORK
COUNTY OF SUFFOLK
---X

AFFIRMATION

Index No.

Plaintiff,

-against-

Defendants.

---X

duly affirms under the penalties of perjury as follows:

1. That I am an attorney duly licensed to practice law in the Courts of the State of New York and I am associated with the law firm of , attorneys for the defendant, and as such I am fully familiar with the facts and circumstances heretofore had herein.

2. This affirmation is submitted in support of the instant motion for an Order precluding the plaintiff from offering any evidence upon the trial of this action in support of the items set forth in said Demands for Verified Bills of Particulars and in accordance with such demands and for such other and further relief as to this Court may seem just and proper.

3. The within action sounds in the alleged malpractice of the defendant and was commenced on or about October 25, 1996. Issue was joined by the service of these moving defendants' Answers on November 13, 1995. Simultaneously therewith, Demands for Verified Bills of Particulars, in accordance with the provisions of the C.P.L.R., were served, copies of which are annexed hereto as Exhibit "A".

4. The plaintiffs have failed to comply with such demands by neglecting to serve the Bills of Particulars, although the time limit for the service of such Bills has expired; no motion to vacate or modify said demands pursuant to C.P.L.R. 3042(a) has been made and these moving defendants did not grant any extension of time to serve the Bills of Particulars, nor did said defendants modify or withdraw the annexed demands.

WHEREFORE, it is respectfully prayed that this Court grant and enter an Order pursuant to C.P.L.R. 3042 precluding the plaintiff from giving evidence at the trial of this action as to the items of which particulars have been demanded, but have not been delivered, and for such other and further relief as to this Court may deem just and proper.

Dated:

EXAMPLE 2-9: BILL OF PARTICULARS

SUPREME COURT OF THE STATE OF NEW YORK
COUNTY OF NEW YORK
--x

Plaintiff,

- against -

VERIFIED BILL OF PARTICULARS

Defendant

--x

(a) The negligence occurred on
at about p.m.

(b) Approximate location.

(c) Bus Number
Direction

(d) Operator of bus -

(e) The acts or omissions constituting the negligence of defendants consisted of: in failing to appropriately train, supervise, and/or control its employee in the proper and safe operation of a passenger bus; including the functioning of the bus doors; in negli gently trapping plaintiff and striking her with said bus door causing her to fall to the pavement and un derneath the wheels of the bus; the defendant was further negligent by failing to stop the bus after the plaintiff had become trapped; in failing to observe whether all passengers had boarded the bus; in im properly maintaining and/or installing bus doors as to create a hazardous condition; in failing to protect the public at large and especially the plaintiff from being injured due to such hazardous conditions. The defendant was also negligent in hiring the de fendant; in failing to investigate the skills, qualifications, and driving record including prior accidents and traffic infractions of the defendant; in allowing and permitting the driver to operate a pas senger bus thereby endangering the public and the plaintiff without the plaintiff is being negligent in any way thereto.

(f) & (g) Both actual and constructive notice are claimed in that the defendants knew or should have known that the plaintiff was trapped by the negligent operation of the bus doors by the agent/employee of the defendant. The failure by the defendant to act upon such notice caused and contributed to plaintiff's injuries and damages. Further the defendant had both actual and constructive notice of the defective condition and/or design of the bus doors, and of the driving record of the defendant, its employee. De spite such notice, the defendant failed to protect against injury and damage to the plaintiff.

(h) Not applicable.

(I) Not applicable.

(j) By reason of the aforesaid accident, the plaintiff sustained the following injuries and complications which were caused, contributed to, and/or aggravated by the defendant's negligence:

Amputation of right arm with local muscle flaps and application of splint thickness skin graft;
Status post mastectomy for breast cancer;
Organic mental syndrome;
Degloved skin extends from right distal clavicle to right forearm with crush of brachial plexus in the axilla, crush of biceps, bronchials, antecubital, fossa, flexor wad of elbow;
Brachial artery divided at antecubital fossa;
No motor function of nerves in right upper extremity prior to amputation;
Emotional distress;

It will be claimed that the above injuries and complications are permanent, protracted, and progressive.

(k) & (l) Plaintiff has been confined to Home for the Aged from the time other discharge from Hospital on , to date and continuing.

(m) Plaintiff claims the following as special damages:
(1) Physicians' services, amounts unknown, to date and continuing;
______ Hospital
New York, NY 10016;

______ Home for the Aged
New York, NY;
(2) Loss of earnings - not applicable.

(3) Hospital expenses, amounts unknown, to date and continuing;
______ Hospital
New York, NY;

______ Home for the Aged
New York, NY;
(4) Nurses' services - unknown

(n) Plaintiff resides at the Home for the Aged, New York, New York.
(o) Not applicable.
(p) Not applicable.
(q) Plaintiff is without knowledge as to this item and respectfully refers all matters of law to the Honorable Court.
(r) Please see item (m) above.
(s) Plaintiff satisfied subdivision four of section six hundred seventy-one of the insurance law due to the loss of plaintiff's right arm.

Dated: New York, New York

EXAMPLE 2-10: REQUEST FOR JUDICIAL INTERVENTION

INTERVENTION

UCS-840 (REV. 1/96)

REQUEST FOR JUDICIAL INTERVENTION

Supreme Court, Kings County
Index No.
Date Purchased

For Clerk Only
IAS entry date
Judge Assigned
RJI Date

In the Matter of the Claim of An Infant
by His Mother and Natural Guardian,

Petitioners,

-against-

Hospital,

Respondents.

Date issue joined:____________ Bill of Particulars served [ ] Yes [X] No

NATURE OF JUDICIAL INTERVENTION (check ONE box only AND enter information)

[ ] Request for preliminary conference
[ ] Note of issue and/or certificate of readiness
[ ] Notice of motion (return date ________)
Relief sought____________)
[ ] Order to show cause
(clerk enter return date__________)
Relief sought____________
[ ] Other ex parte application (specify
________________)

[X] Notice of petition (return date 11/18/96
Relief sought motion for records)
[ ] Notice of medical or dental malpractice action (specify____________)
[ ] Statement of net worth
[ ] Writ of habeas corpus
[ ] Other (Specify____________)
____

NATURE OF ACTION OR PROCEEDING (Check ONE box only)

MATRIMONIAL
[ ] Contested -CM
[ ] Uncontested -UM
COMMERCIAL
[ ] Contract -CONT
[ ] Corporate -CORP
[ ] Insurance (where insurer is a party, except arbitration) - INS
[ ] UCC (including sales, negotiable instruments) -UCC
[ ] *Other commercial__________ -OC [ ]
REAL PROPERTY
[ ] Tax Certiorari -TAX
[ ] Foreclosure -FOR
[ ] Condemnation -COND
[ ] Landlord/Tenant -LT
[ ] *Other Real Property__________ -ORP
OTHER MATTERS
[ ] *____________ -OTH
*If asterisk used, please specify further.

TORTS
Malpractice
[X] Medical/Podiatric -MM
[ ] Dental -DM
[ ] *Other Professional________ -OPM
[ ] Vehicle -MV
[ ] Products Liability________ -PL
[ ] Environmental -EN
[ ] Asbestos -ASB
[ ] Breast implant -BI
*Other Negligence -OTN
[ ] *Other Tort (including intentional)________ -OT
SPECIAL PROCEEDINGS
[ ] ART. 75 (Arbitration) -ART75
[ ] ART. 77 (Trusts) -ART77
[ ] ART. 78 -ART78
[ ] Election Law -ELEC
[ ] Guardianship (MHL Art. 81) -GUARD81
[ ] *Other Special Proceedings -OSP

[] Yes [X] No Municipality: Specify ________ [] YES [X] NO Public Authority: (Specify ______

[] Yes [X] No Does this action/proceeding seek equitable relief?
[X] Yes [] No Does this action/proceeding seek recovery for personal injury?
[] Yes [X] No Does this action/proceeding seek recovery for property damage?

All Cases Except Contested Matrimonial:

Estimate time period for case to be ready for trial from filing of RJI to filing of Note of Issue:

[] 0-12 months [] 12-15 months

Contested Matrimonial Cases Only: (Check and give date)

Has summons been served? [X] No [] Yes. Date__________

Was a Notice of Necessity filed? [X] No [] Yes. Date__________

ATTORNEY(S) FOR PLAINTIFF(S):

NAME	ADDRESS	PHONE
KRAMER, DILLOF, TESSEL, DUFFY & MOORE	233 Broadway New York, NY 10279	(212) 267-4177

ATTORNEY(S) FOR DEFENDANT(S):

NAME	ADDRESS	PHONE
HOSPITAL		

Parties appearing *pro se* (without attorney) should enter information in space provided above for attorneys.

INSURANCE CARRIERS:

RELATED CASES. (if NONE, write "NONE" below)

Title	Index #	Court	Nature of Relationship

"NONE"

I affirm under penalty of perjury that, to my knowledge, other than as noted above, there are and have been no related actions or proceedings, nor has a request for judicial intervention previously been filed in this action or proceeding.

Dated:

(Signature)
Thomas J. Principe
(Print or type name)
Kramer, Dillof, Tessel, Duffy & Moore, Esqs.

Petitioner(s)
(Attorney for Plaintiff)

EXAMPLE 2-10A: REQUEST FOR PRELIMINARY CONFERENCE

B 399—Request for judicial intervention, 22 NYCRR 202.6, 6-88.

JULIUS BLUMBERG, INC., PUBLISHER
62 WHITE STREET, NEW YORK, N.Y. 10013

Supreme Court, Bronx County

Full title of action

Plaintiff(s)
Petitioner(s)

against

Defendant(s)
Respondent(s)

Index No. 21579/91
Date Purchased 9/27/91

For Clerk Only

IAS entry date

Name of assigned judge

Date of assignment

REQUEST FOR JUDICIAL INTERVENTION

☐ Issue joined (date 10/7/91) *(check if applicable)*
XX Bill of particulars served *(check if applicable)*

In the City of New York only:
☐ The City of New York is a party to this action.
☐ The Transit Authority (or MABSTOA) is a party to this action.

NATURE OF JUDICIAL INTERVENTION (check)

☒ Request for preliminary conference
☐ Note of issue and/or certificate of readiness
☐ Notice of motion (return date ....)
Relief sought ....
☐ Order to show cause
(Clerk will enter return date ....)
Relief sought ....
☐ Other ex parte application
☐ Notice of petition (return date ....)
Relief sought ....
☐ Notice of medical malpractice action
☐ Notice of dental malpractice action
☐ Statement of net worth
☐ Writ of habeas corpus
☐ Other (specify): ....

NATURE OF ACTION OR PROCEEDING (check)

Tort
☐ Motor vehicle
XX Medical malpractice
☐ Dental malpractice
☐ Seaman
☐ Airline
☐ ~~Other tort, including but not limited to personal injury,~~ property damage, slander or libel (specify): ....

Special Proceedings
☐ Tax certiorari
☐ Condemnation
☐ Foreclosure
☐ Incompetency or conservatorship
Other special proceeding, including but not limited to:
☐ ~~Article 75 (arbitration)~~
☐ Article 77 (express trusts)
☐ Article 78
☐ Other (specify): ....

OTHER ACTION

☐ Matrimonial (contested)
☐ Matrimonial (uncontested)
☐ Contract
☐ Other (specify): ....

Instructions: Attach rider sheets if necessary to provide required information.
If any party is appearing *pro se* (without an attorney), the required information concerning such party is to be entered in the space provided for attorneys.

SUPREME COURT: COUNTY OF BRONX

Index No. 21579/91
Calendar No.

Plaintiff(s),

—against—

Defendant(s).

Name of assigned judge.

REQUEST FOR PRELIMINARY CONFERENCE

The undersigned requests a preliminary conference.

The nature of the action is MEDICAL MALPRACTICE

The names, addresses and telephone numbers of all attorneys appearing in the action are as follows:

KRAMER, DILLOF, TESSEL,
DUFFY & MOORE, ESQS.
Attorney(s) for Plaintiff
Post Office Address & Tel. No.
233 Broadway
New York, New York 10279
(212) 267-4177

BOWER & GARDNER, ESQS.
Attorney(s) for Defendants
Post Office Address & Tel. No.
110 East 59th Street
New York, New York 10022
(212) 751-2900

Attorney(s) for
Post Office Address & Tel. No.

Attorney(s) for
Post Office Address & Tel. No.

~~Annexed hereto is an Affirmation of Good Faith pursuant to 22 NYCRR 202.12 (a).~~

Dated: March 22, 1993

KRAMER, DILLOF, TESSEL,
DUFFY & MOORE, ESQS.
Attorney(s) for Plaintiff

EXAMPLE 2-11: NOTICE OF A MEDICAL MALPRACTICE ACTION

EXAMPLE 2-11: NOTICE OF A MEDICAL MALPRACTICE ACTION

NOTICE OF MEDICAL OR DENTAL MALPRACTICE ACTION

Malpractice No.: ______________

Calendar ______________

Reserved for Clerk's Use

Index No.: 95-07837

Assigned Judge: Hon. Douglas E. McKeon

SUPREME COURT OF THE STATE OF NEW YORK
COUNTY OF BRONX

---X

An Infant by his Mother and Natural Guardian,

Plaintiff(s),

NOTICE OF MEDICAL MALPRACTICE

-against-

, M.D.,
, M.D., P.C., , C.N.M.
and THE HOSPITAL IN THE CITY OF NEW YORK,

Defendant(s).

Jury Trial Demanded

---X

PLEASE TAKE NOTICE, that the above action for medical malpractice was commenced by service of a Summons, Verified Complaint and Certificate of Merit on February 17, 1995 and that issue was joined therein on March 27, 1995, and the action has not been dismissed, settled or otherwise terminated.

1. **STATE FULL NAME, ADDRESS AND AGE OF EACH PLAINTIFF.**

(Infant) dob 11/27/91 (3 yrs. old)
(Mother) dob 5/4/55 (40 yrs. old)

NY

1

2. **STATE FULL NAME AND ADDRESS OF EACH DEFENDANT.**

(A) M.D. - Avenue, Suite , New York

(B) ., M.D., P.C., Avenue, Suite New York

(C) , C.N.M., Avenue, Suite New York

(D) THE HOSPITAL IN THE CITY OF NEW YORK, Street, New York, New York

3. **STATE ALLEGED MEDICAL SPECIALTY OF EACH INDIVIDUAL DEFENDANTS, IF KNOWN.**

(A) OB/GYN

(B) Medical Facility

(C) Certified Nurse Midwife

(D) Hospital

4. **INDICATE WHETHER CLAIM IS FOR:**

_X_ Medical Malpractice
____ Podiatric Malpractice
____ Dental Malpractice

5. **STATE DATE AND PLACE CLAIM AROSE.**

Claim arose from approximately November 25, 1991 through December 14, 1991 in Bronx County at the defendants facilities and/or offices of the defendants.

6. **STATE SUBSTANCE OF CLAIM.**

The defendants, their agents, servants and employees were careless and negligent in failing to diagnose and respond to the infant's fetal distress; and in failing to diagnose and respond to the cephalopelvic disproportion, tetanic contractions, severe variable decelerations, and chorioamnionitis; in failing to take and record the mother's temperature at frequent intervals; in failing to maintain tocodynamometer recording of uterine contractions; in failing to properly monitor fetal heart rate via external and internal monitor, in failing to obtain fetal

2

scalp or cord PH; in failing to properly and accurately interpret the fetal heart monitor; in failing to properly and accurately record the duration and frequency of contractions; in failing to monitor and record the fetal station; in failing to provide good and proper prenatal and perinatal care; in failing to take and obtain a full, proper and informative history of the mother and to record the same completely and accurately and contemporaneously with the receipt of the information; in failing to consider the significance of the mother's prior obstetrical history; in failing to properly examine the plaintiff's mother; in failing to treat the labor and delivery as part of high risk pregnancy; in failing to arrive at and carry out a proper, appropriate and reasonable plan to manage the labor and delivery; in failing to deliver the infant skillfully and properly; in failing to appropriately and at timely intervals monitor, chart, and be cognizant and aware of the progress and symptoms of the mother and infant; in failing to accurately interpret the fetal heart monitor; in failing to maintain the fetal heart monitor strips; in failing to properly monitor and record the frequency and duration of the contractions; in failing to timely and properly respond to the loss of copious amounts of amniotic fluid and signs of cord compression; in failing to properly and timely respond to premature rupture of the membranes; in failing to timely perform cesarian section; in failing to timely recognize the presence of fetal distress, stress, or compromise; in failing to heed the signs and symptoms of fetal distress or compromise; in failing to properly recognize and record the presence of variable decelerations; in failing to obtain the fetal scalp and cord PH; in failing to obtain and record the fetal station; in failing to prevent an acute hypoxic and/or anoxic insult of the infant; in failing to anticipate and appreciate the possibility of hypoxic and/or anoxic condition of the newborn and to be prepared to treat the same accordingly via qualified physicians in an appropriately equipped facility; in failing to properly suction the infant at birth; in failing to properly and timely treat neonatal depression; in failing to properly and timely resuscitate the infant after birth; in causing severe neonatal intraventricular hemorrhages and neurologic sequelae; in causing asphyxia at birth; in failing to prevent trauma at birth; in failing to monitor the mother's temperature at frequent intervals; in failing to timely and properly respond to the onset of chorioamnionitis, in failing to timely and properly initiate delivery; in improperly administering pitocin; in administering pitocin without tocodynamometer recording; in failing to timely discontinue pitocin; in failing to recognize the presence of and properly treat the complications of delivery; in failing to properly and continuously monitor the fetal heartbeat; in failing to properly place the mother on an external and/or internal fetal monitor; in failing to properly insert an internal fetal monitor; in failing to be cognizant and aware of the mother and infant's vital signs and general overall condition at appropriate times and intervals; in failing to properly chart the course of the mother and infant; in failing to properly and timely administer pitocin; in failing to discontinue the administration of pitocin; and in performing vaginal delivery given the increase in the mother's temperature; the mother's history of a prior cesarian section due to cephalopelvic disproportion; the mother's presentation to the hospital leaking copious amounts of amniotic fluid; the onset of chorioamnionitis; the lack of tocodynamometer recording; the lack of contraction monitoring; the lack of electronic monitoring; the presence of persistent decelerations and decreased variability; and the very rapid active state of labor; in failing to provide good and proper prenatal and perinatal care; in failing to take and obtain a full, proper and informative history of the mother and to record the same completely and accurately and contemporaneously with

3

the receipt of the information; in failing to consider the significance of the mother's prior obstetrical history; in failing to properly examine the plaintiff's mother; in failing to treat the labor and delivery as part of high risk pregnancy; in failing to arrive at and carry out a proper, appropriate and reasonable plan to properly manage the labor and delivery; in failing to deliver the infant skillfully and properly; in failing to appropriately and at timely intervals monitor and chart, and be cognizant and aware of the progress and symptoms of the mother and infant; in failing to accurately interpret the fetal heart monitor; in failing to maintain the fetal heart monitor strips; in failing to properly monitor and record the frequency and duration of the contractions; in failing to timely and properly respond to the loss of significant amounts of amniotic fluid an signs of cord compression; in failing to properly and timely respond to premature rupture of the membranes; in failing to timely perform cesarian section; in failing to timely recognize the presence of fetal distress, stress, or compromise; in failing to heed the signs and symptoms of fetal distress or compromise; in failing to properly recognize and record the presence of variable decelerations; in failing to take and monitor fetal scalp PH; in failing to provide proper and timely intrauterine resuscitation; in failing to timely administer adequate amounts of oxygen in an appropriate manner; in failing to obtain the fetal scalp and cord PH; in failing to monitor and record fetal station; in failing to prevent an acute hypoxic and/or anoxic insult of the infant; in failing to anticipate and appreciate the possibility of hypoxic and/or anoxic condition of the newborn and to be prepared to treat the same accordingly via qualified physicians in an appropriately equipped facility; in failing to properly suction the infant at birth; in failing to properly and timely treat neonatal depression; in failing to properly and timely resuscitate the infant after birth; in causing severe neonatal intraventricular hemorrhages and neurologic sequelae; in causing asphyxia at birth; in failing to prevent trauma at birth; in failing to monitor the mother's temperature at frequent intervals; in failing to timely and properly respond to the onset of chorioamnionitis, in failing to timely and properly initiate delivery; in improperly administering pitocin; in administering pitocin without tocodynamometer recording; in failing to timely discontinue pitocin; in failing to recognize the presence of and properly treat the complications of delivery; in failing to properly and continuously monitor the fetal heartbeat; in failing to properly place the mother on an external and/or internal fetal monitor; in failing to properly insert an internal fetal monitor; in failing to be cognizant and aware of the mother and infant's vital signs and general overall condition at appropriate times and intervals; in failing to properly chart the course of the mother and infant. The defendant's negligence and failures occurred upon the plaintiff's mother's presentation to the hospital on November 25, 1991 and continued to the labor and delivery on November 27, 1991 and through the infant's discharge on December 14, 1991.

7. **(FOLLOWING ITEMS MUST BE CHECKED)**

(a) Proof is attached that authorizations to obtain medical, dental and hospital records have been served upon the defendants in the action ___X___

or

Demand has not been made for such authorizations ______

4

(b) Copies of Summons, Verified Complaint and Certificate of Merit, if required, Answer(s), and the Bill of Particulars, if served are attached _X_

(c) A copy of any demand for arbitration, election of arbitration or concession of liability is attached ___

or

Demand has not been made for arbitration _X_

(d) All information required by CPLR 3101(d)(1)(i) is attached ___

or

A request for such information has not been made ___

or

Such information is not available _X_

8. **STATE NAMES, ADDRESSES AND TELEPHONE NUMBERS OF COUNSEL FOR ALL PARTIES.**

KRAMER, DILLOF, TESSEL, DUFFY & MOORE
Attorney for Plaintiffs
233 Broadway
New York, New York 10279
(212) 267-4177

Attorney for Defendants

New York

Attorney for Defendant
The Hospital

New York, New York

Dated: New York, New York
November 13, 1995

5

Yours, etc.,

KRAMER, DILLOF, TESSEL, DUFFY & MOORE
Attorneys for Plaintiffs
233 Broadway
New York, New York 10279
212-267-4177

6

EXAMPLE 2-12: DISCOVERY ORDER

SUPREME COURT OF THE STATE OF NEW YORK COUNTY OF SUFFOLK
INDIVIDUAL ASSIGNMENT PART 28

INDEX NO. 6735/93

s Administratrix, Individually and of the Estate f , Plaintiff(s) Deceased,

- against -

, M.D., , M.D., lage Internal Medicine roup and Defendant(s) Hosp.

PRELIMINARY CONFERENCE STIPULATION AND ORDER (§§202.8 and 202.12 of the Uniform Rules)

[All items on the form must be completed unless inapplicable.]

It is hereby STIPULATED and ORDERED that disclosure shall proceed as follows:

(1) Insurance Coverage: If not already provided, shall be furnished by Defendants on or before w/in 60 days

(2) Bill of Particulars: Π strikes "including but not limited to" from "3" and "b1" of D physicians' /Vill Int. b.p. + "6" of hospital b.p
(a) Demand for a bill of particulars shall be served by ______ on or before ______.
(b) Bill of particulars shall be served by Defendants ~~on or before~~ within 60 days after EBTs — as to aff. defs.
(c) A supplemental bill of particulars shall be served by Plaintiff as to Items 3, 15, 20b., 20e → D physicians'/ of Vill Int. Med. b.p.s; 13 h.K. → D hospital's b.p. (↓ specific allegations as to each physician) or before w/in 60 days.

(3) Medical Reports and Authorizations: Shall be served as follows: w/in 30 days — Specific A/zs allowing defense counsel to view pathology slides at Memorial Hosp. + Medical Examiner's slides (SUNY Stonybroo[k])

(4) ~~Physical Examination:~~
~~(a) Examination of ______ shall be held ______~~
~~(b) A copy of the physician's report shall be furnished to plaintiff within ______ days of the examination.~~

(5) Depositions: Depositions of
[ ] Plaintiff(s) [ ] Defendant(s) [✓] All Parties
shall be held Plaintiff on or before ~~2/15/94~~ 5/17/94
Respective Attorney's Offices Defendants caption order, ~~on or before 3/...~~ to be completed
10:00 a.m. Non-party witnesses to be completed 6/17/94

(6) Other Disclosure: Defendants to bring original records at EBTs
(a) All parties, on or before w/in 60 days, shall exchange names and addresses of all witnesses, statements of opposing parties and photographs, or, if none, provide an affirmation to that effect.
(b) Authorization for plaintiff(s)' employment records for the period ____________ shall be furnished on or before ____________.
(c) Demand for discovery and inspection shall be served by ____________ on or before ____________. The items sought shall be produced to the extent not objected to, and objections, if any, shall be stated on or before ____________.
(d) Other [interrogatories, etc.] Defendants to respond to Plaintiff's Combined Demand, Notices of D&I within 60 days, with exception of Demand for b.p. addressed on page 1 of order (60 days after EBTS)

(7) End Date for All Disclosure [must be within 12 months]: November 17, 1994.

(8) Impleader: Shall be completed on or before Pursuant to CPLR

(9) Motions: Any dispositive motions(s) shall be made on or before Pursuant to CPLR.

(10) Note of Issue: Plaintiff shall file a note of issue/certificate of readiness on or before November 17, 1994
A copy of this stipulation and order, an affirmation stating that the terms of the stipulation and order have been complied with, and an affidavit of service of the affirmation and note of issue shall be served and filed with the note of issue on or before said date.

(11) If a motion relating to disclosure has raised additional disclosure issues, the parties agree as follows:

Defendant physicians shall withdraw their motion to preclude/compel discovery, currently before court.

(12) Compliance conference shall be held on ____________.

Failure to comply with any of these directives may result in the imposition of costs or sanctions or other action authorized by law.

Dated: 11/17/93

Kramer Dillof Tessel Duffy & Moore
Attorney for Plaintiff(s) by [signature]

____
Attorney for Defendant(s)

____
Attorney for Defendant(s)

Dated: 11/17/93

SO ORDERED:

[signature]
J.S.C.

ADDITIONAL DIRECTIVES

In addition to the directives set forth on the annexed pages, it is further ORDERED as follows:

All defendants to furnish Plaintiff with copies of their clients' records w/in 60 days, to extent not yet provided

Plaintiff shall furnish Defendants with [illegible] IRS 4506 years 1987-1992 within 15 days

Plaintiff shall respond fully to defendant physicians' Combined Demands, to extent not yet provided, within 60 days.

Expert Witness information shall be exchanged pursuant to the CPLR

Dated: 11/17/93

SO ORDERED:

[signature]
J.S.C.

EXAMPLE 2-12A: PHYSICIAN'S AFFADAVIT THAT PLAINTIFF IS TERMINALLY ILL

SUPREME COURT OF THE STATE OF NEW YORK
COUNTY OF NASSAU
-------------------------------------X   Index No.:

Plaintiff,

-against-   **PHYSICIAN'S AFFIDAVIT**

Defendants.
-------------------------------------X

STATE OF NEW YORK)
ss.:
COUNTY OF NEW YORK)

, M.D., deposes and states the following to be true under the penalties of perjury:

1. I am a physician duly licensed in the State of New York and I am certified by the American Board of Pathology in the fields of Anatomic, Clinical and Forensic pathology. As such I am qualified to render opinions in the above captioned matter.

2. I have reviewed all of the pertinent medical records concerning **(plaintiff)** dated February 1984 to the present including the records of her treating oncologist, Dr. Thomas Caputo, and the records concerning her cancer treatment from New York Hospital. The records indicate that March 1992 **(plaintiff)** underwent an exploratory laparotomy, bilateral salpingo-oophorectumy, appendectomy and omentectomy. Her left tube and ovary were noted to be positive for cancer. The omentum was positive for metastic disease. Her right tube and ovary were positive for metastic disease and the washings were also noted to be positive for malignancy. **(Plaintiff)** underwent a regimen of chemotherapy.

3. In July 1995, the records indicate that **(plaintiff)** began complaining of pelvic pain. On July 6, 1995 a fine needle aspiration of a cul-de-sac mass was positive for metastic disease. Further diagnostic tests conformed the presence of recurrent cancer and metastasis into her intra-abdomen. **(Plaintiff)** underwent a regimen of chemotherapy. Her cancer persists despite further chemotherapy and has now spread to her liver.

4. In my medical opinion, stated with a reasonable degree of medical certainty, that **(plaintiff)** is suffering from recurrent metastic ovarian cancer. Her cancer is terminal. She is in imminent danger of death and will not be alive at the time of trial.

Dated: New York, New York
July 9, 1996

____
, M.D.

Sworn to before me this
9th day of July, 1996

____
NOTARY

EXAMPLE 2-12B: ORDER GRANTING MOTION TO PERPETUATE PLAINTIFF'S TESTIMONY ON VIDEOTAPE

At Special Term Part 5 of the Supreme Court of the State of New York, held in and for the County of Nassau, at the Courthouse located at 100 Supreme Court Drive, Mineola, New York 11501, on the ~~2nd~~ 5th day of ~~August~~ September 1996.

P R E S E N T:

HON. GEORGE A. MURPHY, J.S.C.

--X Index No.:

Plaintiff,

-against- **ORDER**

Defendants.

--X

Plaintiff, having moved this Court pursuant to CPLR §3113(b) and 3101(a) and 22 NYCRR 202.15 (1) for an Order granting plaintiff leave to perpetuate her testimony for trial by oral and videotape deposition, and said Order to Show Cause having come on to be heard before me on August 5, 1996,

NOW, upon the reading and filing of the Order to Show Cause dated July 12, 1996, and the Affirmation together with supporting exhibits, dated April 9, 1996 of ESQ., an associate of the law firm **KRAMER, DILLOF, TESSEL, DUFFY & MOORE**, attorneys for plaintiff; an Affirmation in Opposition together with supporting exhibits, dated July 17, 1996 of ESQ., an associate with the law firm of , attorneys for defendants; and the Reply Affirmation together with supporting exhibits, dated July 24, 1996 of ESQ., an associate of the law firm of **KRAMER, DILLOF, TESSEL, DUFFY & MOORE,** attorneys for plaintiff, it is now

ORDERED, that plaintiff's Order to Show Cause for leave to perpetuate plaintiff's testimony is hereby granted in its entirety.

Dated: New York, New York
September 5, 1996

E N T E R:

J.S.C.

ENTERED

SEP 1 3 1996

COUNTY CLERK OF NASSAU COUNTY

EXAMPLE 2-13: LETTER REQUESTING REPORT OF EXAMINING PHYSICIAN

LAW OFFICES

KRAMER, DILLOF, TESSEL, DUFFY & MOORE

233 BROADWAY

NEW YORK, N.Y. 10279-0137

(212) 267-4177

FAX (212) 233-8525

CHARLES KRAMER (1918-1988)
THOMAS A. MOORE
JAMES R. DUFFY
JUDITH A. LIVINGSTON
THOMAS J. PRINCIPE

JO ANNE KEOGH
OFFICE MANAGER

MATTHEW GAIER
JOHN P. KOESTER
MITCHELL R. DRACH
ANDREW S. TARGUM
WILLIAM T. BURDO
MARY JO BROUSSARD

HENRY H. DILLOF
NORMAN BARD
STANLEY TESSEL
WILLIAM R. DILLOF
OF COUNSEL

June 21, 1996

Barrister & Counselors, Esq.
118 East 85th Street
New York, New York 12097

Re: Smith v. Row, et al

Counselors:

On May 12, 1996, a physical examination of the plaintiff, Mary Smith was held by Dr. Bill Ortho at the request of your office. Kindly forward a copy of his report at your earliest convenience.

Thank you.

Very truly yours,

Susan Assist
Paralegal

sa

EXAMPLE 2-14: MEDICAL REPORT

19

Mr.
Kramer, Dillof, Tessel, Duffy & Moore
233 Broadway
New York, N.Y. 10279

RE:

Dear Mr.

was examined on 19 . His records were reviewed. He is noted to be a fifteen year old boy, an only child, the result of a generally uncomplicated full term pregnancy. There is no family history of neurological illness. There is no consanguinity.

was born at Hospital in , weighing six pounds six ounces. The delivery was effected by forceps and the apgar score was said to be nine at one minute. The patient's length was nineteen inches. He was discharged from the hospital with his mother, and his postnatal course was generally unremarkable. The mother describes forceps marks noted after birth, but these are not recorded in the newborn records. The mother surprised me with the photographs of this child at the age of three months and points out what she believes to be forceps marks over his forehead.

walked at thirteen months of age, although he showed poor balance. He didn't talk though until six years of age. He tends to talk to himself, and he laughs to himself. He has been delayed in developing self-help skills, and he has been generally classified as being mentally retarded and "hyperactive and brain injured."

has been placed in the School in the past. Following this he went as a residential student to the School for three years. Then in 19 , he was transferred to the School in where he has been an inpatient for the past eight months. His academic work is still at readiness levels.

takes Thorazine at a dose of 50 mg a day. He takes no other medication. He has never had convulsive seizures.

His interests are somewhat atypical: he likes to line match box cars in a row. He likes to listen to music, and he postures himself to music. He is able to write his name, but his picture of a person is unrecognizable and doesn't achieve a score of more than three and half years. Despite this, he is given an I.Q. score and in some areas as being only mildly retarded. At other times he is described as moderately retarded. The most frequently cited I.Q. is in the range of 50, but that would give him the mental age of seven years. He doesn't appear to be functioning on that level at this time.

On examination this is a well developed and well nourished youngster with a height of sixty-three inches and a weight of one hundred and twenty-six pounds. His head circumference is bigger than average at fifty-seven centimeters. He does show hypertelorism, and he also demonstrates bilateral simian lines. He has been described on previous examinations as being dysmorphic.

walks with a generally symmetrical and secure gait pattern. The Romberg is negative. There is no evidence of any motor, sensory, reflex, or cranial nerve disturbance. Speech is somewhat indistinct but generally fully intelligible. The patient demonstrates some atypical behavior, but his overall performance appears to be that of a moderately retarded child.

This young man demonstrates a syndrome of organic brain dysfunction with mental retardation in the moderately severe range. There are associated behavioral problems as described. Prognosis seems guarded, and it is unlikely that he will ever achieve sufficient independence to function without supervision. He will certainly never be employable. He will require some degree of custodial care for the remainder of his life.

Sincerely yours,

EXAMPLE 2-15: PHYSICIAN'S AFFIDAVIT

SUPREME COURT OF THE STATE OF NEW YORK
COUNTY OF
--------------------------------------X **Index No.:**

and ,

Plaintiffs,

-against- **PHYSICIAN'S AFFIDAVIT**

RADIOLOGY CENTER, and ,

Defendants.
--------------------------------------X

STATE OF NEW YORK)
ss:
COUNTY OF)

Dr. , M.D., being duly sworn, deposes and states the following to be true under the penalties of perjury:

1. I am a physician duly licensed to practice medicine in the State of New York. I am a board certified radiologist, and have practiced in the field of radiology since 19 . As such, I am qualified to render opinions in the above captioned matter.

2. I have reviewed and evaluated the medical records and films pertaining to the decedent including the records of Dr. dated October , 19 through March , 19 ; the mammogram films taken October , 19 at Radiology Center and the corresponding interpretation report signed by Dr. ; the mammogram films taken March , 19 at Mammography & Ultrasonography and the corresponding interpretation report signed by Dr. ; and the subsequent treatment records of Dr. and Medical Center dated from March 19 until the date of death on December , 19 .

3. I have also reviewed the affidavit of , the decedent's husband, wherein he states that he felt a mass in the

medial portion of his wife's right breast in the summer or fall of 19 prior to October 19 and that he continued to feel the same lump after October 19 .

4. Upon my review of Dr. medical records, I specifically noted an undated entry in which indicated the presence of a "2 x 2 1/3 cm mobile cystic mass" in right breast. The entry was accompanied by a diagram which placed the mass in the lower, medial portion of the right breast.

5. On October , 19 , bilateral mammogram x-rays were taken of breast. This routine screening mammography was taken at the Radiology Center and interpreted by Dr.

6. Based upon my review of the above material, it is my opinion to a reasonable degree of medical and radiological certainty that there were deviations from good and accepted medical practice with respect to the mammographies performed and interpreted at the Radiology Center on October , 19 . It is further my opinion to a reasonable degree of medical and radiological certainty that routine screening mammography are falsely negative in 9% to 16% of cancers. It is further my opinion to a reasonable degree of medical and radiological certainty that good and accepted practice requires that when a patient presents with a symptom such as a palpable breast mass, the mammography must be tailored to the patient's specific problem as opposed to routine screening mammography. Specifically, when a patient presents with a breast mass, the mammography study must include the use of markers, compression, magnification and/or specially rotated views

tailored to adequately view the mass. In the face of a palpable breast mass, routine screening mammography is not enough to rule out the presence of cancer and constitutes a deviation from accepted medical practice. Furthermore, when the patient presents with a mass, good and accepted practice requires that the radiologist make recommendations for ultrasound or biopsy in the event the mammography reveals no mass or suspicious findings. Therefore, it is my opinion to a reasonable degree of medical and radiological certainty, that Dr. departed from good and accepted practice on October , 19 when he failed to employ markers and obtain compression, magnification, and/or specially rotated views tailored to adequately view the mass in right breast. It is further my opinion to a reasonable degree of medical and radiological certainty, that Dr. good and accepted practice when he failed to recommend ultrasound or biopsy of the right breast mass in his interpretation of the films. It is further my opinion to a reasonable degree of medical and radiological certainty that in light of breast mass and risk factors, the routine screening mammography conducted on October , 19 by Dr. d/b/a Radiology Center were not sufficient and constituted a deviation from good and accepted practice.

7. It is further my opinion to a reasonable degree of medical certainty, that the above described departures from accepted medical practice were substantially contributing causes to dying from breast cancer. The records reveal that her breast cancer was not diagnosed until March 19 . It is my

opinion to a reasonable degree of medical certainty, that the mass, was present in October 19 , as described by , and would have been revealed and identified through properly performed mammography on October , 19 as described above. Specially tailored mammograms would then have required further medical treatment in the form of a biopsy and/or ultrasound. It is further my opinion to a reasonable degree of medical certainty that this further diagnostic work-up would have revealed breast cancer well before March 19 and would have greatly improved her prognosis and chance of survival.

____
M.D.

Sworn before me this ___
day of , 19 .

____
NOTARY PUBLIC

EXAMPLE 2-16: MARKED PLEADINGS

SUPREME COURT OF THE STATE OF NEW YORK
COUNTY OF KINGS
--x

Plaintiffs,

-against-

MARKED PLEADINGS

DR ______ and
MEDICAL CENTER,

Defendants.
--x

TITLE	PAGE NUMBER
COMPLAINT	1 - 8
VERIFIED ANSWER of	9 - 14
VERIFIED ANSWER of	15 - 20
VERIFIED BILL of PARTICULARS (Defendant DR.	21 - 27
VERIFIED BILL of PARTICULARS (Defendant MEDICAL CENTER)	28 - 34

Respectfully submitted,

KRAMER, DILLOF, TESSEL, DUFFY & MOORE
233 Broadway
New York, New York 10279
(212) 267 -4177

SUPREME COURT OF THE STATE OF NEW YORK
COUNTY OF KINGS
---X

Plaintiffs,

-against-

DR. and
MEDICAL CENTER,

Defendants.

---X

MARKED
COMPLAINT
Index #

Medical Center

DR

Plaintiffs above named, complaining of the defendants by their attorneys, KRAMER, DILLOF, TESSEL, DUFFY & MOORE, ESQS., respectfully allege:

AS AND FOR A FIRST CAUSE OF ACTION ON BEHALF OF

A. | A.

1. At all times herein mentioned, defendant MEDICAL CENTER was a domestic corporation, duly organized and existing under and by virtue of the laws of the State of New York.

D. in form except admits at all times herein A operated a hosp. known as MED. CENTER | D. in form except admits at all times herein A operated a hosp. known as Med. Center

2. At all times herein mentioned, defendant MEDICAL CENTER was the owner of a hospital known as MEDICAL CENTER located at , , New York.

D. in form except admits at all times herein A operated the hosp. | D. in form except admits at all times A owned & operated hosp.

3. At all times herein mentioned, defendant MEDICAL CENTER operated, managed and controlled the aforesaid hospital.

"D" in form alleged. | "D" in form alleged.

4. At all times herein mentioned, each plaintiff was a patient of defendant MEDICAL CENTER.

5. At all times herein mentioned, defendant **DR.** was a physician duly licensed to practice medicine in the State of New York.

6. At all times herein mentioned, each plaintiff was a patient of defendant **DR.**

7. At all times herein mentioned, defendant **DR.** was an agent, servant and/or employee of defendant **MEDICAL CENTER.**

8. During her pregnancy with the infant plaintiff, the mother of the infant plaintiff was a patient of the defendants, their agents, servants and/or employees, and on or about July 13, 1989, the mother of the infant plaintiff was admitted to defendant **MEDICAL CENTER** under the medical diagnosis, care and treatment of the defendants, their agents, servants and/or employees, and the infant plaintiff was delivered of his mother by the defendants, their agents, servants and/or employees on or about July 13, 1989, and thereafter the infant plaintiff remained under the continuing diagnosis, care and treatment of the defendants, and as a result of the foregoing medical diagnosis, care and treatment, including the medical diagnosis, care and treatment rendered during the pregnancy, labor, delivery and pediatric periods, the infant plaintiff sustained severe injuries and complications, including but not limited to brain damage.

9. Said occurrence was due to the carelessness and negligence of the defendants, their agents, servants and/or employees in failing to provide prenatal care and to deliver and

treat the infant plaintiff in the accepted and proper medical manner and all without any fault or lack of care on the part of the plaintiffs herein.

10. By reason of the foregoing, infant plaintiff sustained severe and serious personal injuries, a severe shock to his nervous system and certain internal injuries, and was caused to suffer severe physical pain and mental anguish as a result thereof, and upon information and belief some of these injuries are of a permanent and lasting nature; infant plaintiff was confined to his bed and home as a result thereof, and was incapacitated from attending to what otherwise would have been his regular activities; and there was caused to be expended sums of money for medical and hospital care on his behalf.

11. The amount of damages sought exceeds the jurisdiction of all lower courts which would otherwise have jurisdiction.

12. This action falls within the exceptions to CPLR Section 1602.

AS AND FOR A SECOND CAUSE OF ACTION FOR LOSS OF SERVICES

13. Plaintiffs repeat, reiterate and reallege each and every allegation contained in those paragraphs of the complaint marked and designated 1. through 12. inclusive, with the same force and effect as if hereinafter set forth at length.

14. By reason of the foregoing, plaintiff was deprived of the services of her infant son, and was caused to become obliged to expend sums of money for medical and hospital care on his behalf.

		15. The amount of damages sought exceeds the jurisdiction of all lower courts which would otherwise have jurisdiction.
DKI	3KI	**AS AND FOR A THIRD CAUSE OF ACTION ON BEHALF OF**
admits and denies as above	admits and denies as above	16. Plaintiffs repeat, reiterate and reallege each and every allegation contained in those paragraphs of the complaint marked and designated 1. through 15. inclusive, with the same force and effect as if hereinafter set forth at length.
A	A	17. As a result of the medical diagnosis, care and treatment rendered to plaintiff during the aforesaid labor and delivery and subsequent medical diagnosis, care and treatment by the defendants, their agents, servants and/or employees, plaintiff sustained severe injuries and complications.
A	A	18. Said occurrence was due to the carelessness and negligence of the defendants, their agents, servants and/or employees in failing to treat the plaintiff in the accepted and proper medical manner and all without any fault or lack of care on the part of the plaintiff herein.
A	A	19. By reason of the foregoing, plaintiff sustained severe and serious personal injuries, a severe shock to her nervous system and certain internal injuries, and was caused to suffer severe physical pain and mental anguish as a result thereof, and upon information and belief some of these injuries are of a permanent and lasting nature; the plaintiff was confined to her bed and home as a result thereof, and was incapacitated from attending to her regular activities; and

there was caused to be expended sums of money for medical and hospital care on her behalf.

DKI	DKI	20. The amount of damages sought exceeds the jurisdiction of all lower courts which would otherwise have jurisdiction.

AS AND FOR A FOURTH CAUSE OF ACTION ON BEHALF OF THE INFANT PLAINTIFF FOR LACK OF INFORMED CONSENT

admits and denies as above	admits and denies as above	21. Plaintiffs repeat, reiterate and reallege each and every allegation contained in those paragraphs of the complaint marked and designated 1. through 20. inclusive, with the same force and effect as if hereinafter set forth at length.
D	D	22. Defendants failed to inform the plaintiff of the risks, hazards and alternatives connected with the procedures utilized in connection with the birth of infant plaintiff, so that an informed consent could be given.
D	D	23. Reasonably prudent persons in the plaintiff's position would not have consented to the procedures utilized in connection with the birth of infant plaintiff, if they had been fully informed of the risks, hazards and alternatives connected with said procedures.
D	D	24. The failure to adequately and fully inform the plaintiff of the risks, hazards and alternatives of the procedures utilized in connection with the birth of infant plaintiff, is a proximate cause of the injuries sustained by the infant plaintiff,

D	D	25. As a consequence of the foregoing, there was no informed consent to the procedures utilized in connection with the birth of infant plaintiff.
DKI	DKI	26. The amount of damages sought exceeds the jurisdiction of all lower courts which would otherwise have jurisdiction. **AS AND FOR A FIFTH CAUSE OF ACTION ON BEHALF OF PLAINTIFF FOR LACK OF INFORMED CONSENT**
admits and denies as above	admits and denies as above	27. Plaintiffs repeat, reiterate and reallege each and every allegation contained in those paragraphs of the complaint marked and designated 1. through 26. inclusive, with the same force and effect as if hereinafter set forth at length.
D	D	28. The failure to adequately and fully inform the plaintiff of the risks, hazards and alternatives of the procedures utilized in connection with the birth of infant plaintiff, is a proximate cause of the injuries sustained by plaintiff
DKI	DKI	29. The amount of damages sought exceeds the jurisdiction of all lower courts which would otherwise have jurisdiction. **AS AND FOR A SIXTH CAUSE OF ACTION AGAINST _____ MEDICAL CENTER**
admits and denies as above	admits and denies as above	30. Plaintiffs repeat, reiterate and reallege each and every allegation contained in those paragraphs of the complaint marked and designated 1. through 29. inclusive, with the same force and effect as if hereinafter set forth at length.
D	D	31. Defendant _____ MEDICAL CENTER, prior to the granting or renewing of privileges or employment of defendants,

residents, nurses and others involved in the plaintiffs' care failed to investigate the qualifications, competence, capacity, abilities and capabilities of said defendants, residents, nurses and other employees, including but not limited to obtaining the following information: patient grievances, negative health care outcomes, incidents injurious to patients, medical malpractice actions commenced against said persons, including the outcome thereof, any history of association, privilege and/or practice at other institutions, and discontinuation of said association, employment, privilege and/or practice at said institutions, and any pending professional misconduct proceedings in this State or another State, the substance of the allegations in such proceedings and any additional information concerning such proceedings and the findings of the proceedings; and the **MEDICAL CENTER** failed to make sufficient inquiry of the physician, nurse and/or employees and institutions which should and did have information relevant to the capacity, capability, ability and competence of said persons rendering treatment.

32. Had the defendant **MEDICAL CENTER** made the above-stated inquiry or in the alternative had it reviewed and analyzed the information obtained in a proper manner, privileges and/or employment would not have been granted and/or renewed.

33. By reason of the defendants **MEDICAL CENTER's** failure to meet the aforementioned obligation, plaintiff was treated by physicians, nurses and/or other employees at **MEDICAL CENTER** who were lacking the requisite skills,

abilities, competence and capacity, as a result of which infant plaintiff sustained severe injuries and complications.

DKI DKI

34. The amount of damages sought exceeds the jurisdiction of all lower courts which would otherwise have jurisdiction.

WHEREFORE, plaintiffs demand judgment against defendants in such sum as a jury would find fair, adequate and just.

Dated: New York, New York
December 4, 1991

KRAMER, DILLOF, TESSEL, DUFFY & MOORE
Attorneys for Plaintiffs
233 Broadway
New York, New York 10279
(212) 267-4177

EXAMPLE 2-17: FORMS USED IN THE OFFICE

FORMS USED IN THE OFFICE

1. Greyback
2. Authorizations
3. Authorization letter requesting documents/information
4. Rejection letters
5. Acceptance letters
6. Retainer Statements
7. Fee letters (notice of percentages of what the referring attorney will get)
8. Notice of Claim
9. Summons
10. Attorney/Client verification for Complaints
11. Certificate of Merit for Complaints
12. Default letter (notice to defendants that their time to answer has expired and if they do not respond within a certain amount of time of the date of the letter, a default judgment will be sought)
13. Notice of Medical Malpractice Action
14. Request for Preliminary Conference
15. Request for Judicial Intervention
16. Affidavit of Service
17. Attorney/Client verification for Bill of Particulars
18. Combined Demands and Notice of EBT
19. Demand for Insurance Coverage Information
20. Demand for Surveillance Materials
21. Response to Demand for Total Damages
22. Exchange of Medical Information
23. Letter and Stipulation to defendant to voluntarily withdraw their defense asserting that the Court lacks personal jurisdication over them.
24. Notice of Change of Caption
25. Notice of Entry
26. Notice of Settlement
27. Note of Issue
28. Certificate of Readiness for Trial
29. Attorney's Affidavit for Note of Issue
30. Correction Sheet for Transcripts
31. Letter to Client to execute EBT transcript
32. Letter to defense counsel to execute EBT transcript
33. Stipulations
34. Response to Demand for Expert Witness Information
35. Response to Demanf for Economic Witness Information
36. Affirmation of Good Faith
37. Notice to Take Deposition of Non-Party Witness
38. Notice of Video Taped Deposition
39. Judicial Subpoena
40. Judicial Subpoena Duces Tecum
41. Notice to Produce
42. Notice of Motion
43. Notice of Appeal
44. Bill of Costs

EXAMPLE 2-17A: APPLICATION FOR AN INDEX NUMBER

46-3004R-100M92

COUNTY CLERK, NEW YORK COUNTY

Application for INDEX NUMBER pursuant to Section 8018, C.P.L.R.

FEE $170.00

INDEX NUMBER

Do not write in this space

Spaces below to be TYPED or PRINTED by applicant

TITLE OF ACTION OR PROCEEDING

CHECK ONE

☐	COMMERCIAL ACTION	☐	NOT COMMERCIAL ACTION
☐	CONSUMER CREDIT TRANSACTION	☐	NOT CONSUMER CREDIT TRANSACTION
☐	THIRD PARTY ACTION	☐	NOT THIRD PARTY ACTION

IF THIRD PARTY ACTION MAIN INDEX NO.________________

Name and address of Attorney for Plaintiff or Petitioner. Telephone No.

Name and address of Attorney for Defendant or Respondent. Telephone No.

A. Nature and object of action or Nature of special proceeding ________________

B. Application for Index Number filed by: Plaintiff ☐ Defendant ☐

C. Was a pervious Third Party Action filed? Yes ☐ No ☐

Date Filed________________

COMPLETE THIS STUB

Endorse This INDEX NUMBER On All Papers and advise your adversary of the number assigned. Sec. 202.5, Uniform Rules Of Trial Courts

DO NOT DETACH

Title of Action or Proceeding to be TYPED or PRINTED by applicant

SUPREME COURT, NEW YORK COUNTY

____

v.

____

INDEX NUMBER FEE $170.00

EXAMPLE 2-18: SUMMONS

SUPREME COURT OF THE STATE OF NEW YORK
COUNTY OF NEW YORK
--X

INDEX NO.

Plaintiff designates
NEW YORK
as the place of trial

The basis of the venue:

Defendants place of Business

Plaintiff(s),

- against -

SUMMONS

Defendants Address

New York, N.Y. 10001
COUNTY OF NEW YORK

Defendant(s).
--X

To the above named defendant(s):

YOU ARE HEREBY SUMMONED to answer the complaint in this action and to serve a copy of your answer or, if the complaint is not served with this summons, to serve a notice of appearance, on the Plaintiff's Attorneys within 20 days after the service of this summons, exclusive of the day of service (or within 30 days after the service is complete if this summons is not personally delivered to you within the State of New York): and in case of your failure to appear or answer, judgment will be taken for the relief demanded herein.

A COPY OF THIS SUMMONS WAS FILED WITH THE CLERK OF THE COURT, NEW YORK COUNTY ON ________________________ IN COMPLIANCE WITH CPLR §§305(a) AND 306(a).

Dated: New York, New York
November 29, 1993

KRAMER, DILLOF, TESSEL, DUFFY & MOORE
Attorneys for Plaintiff
233 Broadway
New York, New York 10279
(212) 267-4177

Defendants Address:

Seventh Avenue- New York, N.Y. 10001
Seventh Avenue- New York, N.Y. 10001
Seventh Avenue- New York, N.Y. 10001
Seventh Avenue- New York, N.Y. 10001
Seventh Avenue- New York, N.Y. 10001

EXAMPLE 2-19: NOTE OF ISSUE

NOTE OF ISSUE

(For use of Clerk
(
(
(
(
(
(

Calendar No. (if any) ________
Index No. 100230

Justice Karla Moskowitz
Name of Judge assigned

SUPREME COURT, NEW YORK COUNTY, NY

Plaintiff(s),

- against -

Defendant(s).

Special preference claimed under Special Rules on the ground that plaintiff sustained very serious permanent and protracted personal injuries

NOTICE FOR TRIAL

x Trial by jury demanded
x Of all issues
_ Of issue specified below or attached here to
_ Trial without jury

Filed by attorney for Plaintiff
Date summons served 1/5/95
Date service completed 1/5/95
Date issue joined 1/23/95

NATURE OF ACTION OR SPECIAL PROCEEDING

x Tort
__ Motor vehicle negligence
x Medical malpractice
_ Other tort

__ Contract
__ Contested matrimonial
__ Uncontested matrimonial
__ Tax certiorari
__ Condemnation
__ Other (not itemized above) specify

__ This action brought as a class action

Amount demanded $ Amount demanded exceeds the jurisdiction of all lower Courts
Other relief
Insurance carrier(s), if known:

Attorneys for Plaintiffs Office & P.O. Address Phone No.	KRAMER, DILLOF, TESSEL, DUFFY & MOORE 233 Broadway New York, NY 10279-0137 (212) 267-4177
Attorneys for Defendants Office & P.O. Address Phone No.	FINKELSTEIN, BRUCKMAN, WOHL, MOST & ROTHMAN 575 Lexington Avneue New York, NY 10022 (212) 751-3100

NOTE: Clerk will not accept this note of issue unless accompanied by a certificate of readiness, or, in a medical malpractice action, unless, where applicable, the certificate of readiness previously has been filed and the panel procedures prescribed by court rules pursuant to section 148-a of the Judiciary Law have been completed.

EXAMPLE 2-20: CERTIFICATE OF READINESS

CERTIFICATE OF READINESS FOR TRIAL
Item 1-7 must be checked)

(**For Clerk's Use**)
(**N.I. served**)
(**on**)
( )
( )

	Completed	Waived	Not Required
1. All pleadings served	X		
2. Bill of particulars served	X		
3. Physical examinations completed	X		
4. Medical reports exchanged	X		
5. Appraisal reports exchanged			X
6. Compliance with the Rules in matrimonial actions (22 NYCRR 202.16)			X
7. Discovery proceedings not known to be neccessary completed	X		

8. There are no outstanding requests for discovery.
9. There has been a reasonable opportunity to complete the foregoing proceedings.
10. There has been compliance with any order issued pursuant to the Precalendar Rules (22 NYCRR 202.12).
11. If a medical malpractice action, there as been compliance with any order issued pursuant to 22 NYCRR 202.56.
12. The case is ready for trial.

Dated:____________________

____
Signature - type name below

Attorneys for Plaintiffs KRAMER, DILLOF, TESSEL, DUFFY & MOORE
Office & P.O. Address 233 Broadway
New York, New York 10279-0137

State of New York, County of ss.:

being duly sworn, deposes and says; that depoent is not a party to the action, is over 18 years of age and resides at

That on the day of 19 deponent served the within note of issue and certificate of readiness on

attorney(s) for
herein, at his office at

during his absence from said office
(a) by then and there leaving a true copy of the same with

his clerk; partner; person having charge of said office.
(b) and said office being closed, by depositing a true copy of same, enclosed in a sealed wrapper directed to said attorney(s), in the office letter drop or box.

Sworn to before me on 19

State of New York, County of New York ss.:

ADRIANA PEREZ being duly sworn, deposes and says; that deponent is not a party to the action, is over 18 years of age and resides at NASSAU County

That on the 27th day of February, 1997 deponent served the within note of issue and certificate of readiness on the Attorneys named on front
attorney(s) for the Defendants named on front at their respective addresses

the address designated by said attorney(s) for that purpose by depositing a true copy of same enclosed in a postpaid properly addressed wrapper, in - a post office - official depository under the exclusive care and custody of the United States Postal Service within New York State.

Sworn to before me on February 27, 1997

Admisson of Service Due service of a note of issue and certificate of readiness, of which the within is a copy, admitted
, 19

____
Attorney(s) for Kramer, Dillof, Tessel, Duffy & Moore

THE COURSE OF THE TRIAL II

An advocate generates proof by applying argument to evidence, and, for the legal advocate, that application occurs in a formal proceeding called a trial. Therefore, to understand the law of evidence, the attorney must place the rules of evidence in the context of a trial. For that reason, Part One of this book explains the rules of evidence as they would arise during the course of a trial. We begin Part Two with the court's control of the trial, the formal bifurcation between the issues of liability and damages, and the attorney's opening statement. Logically, the next two topics are the plaintiff's obligation to present a prima facie case and the damages recoverable if he is successful. Finally, we discuss the two events that conclude the advocate's participation in the trial: the court's charge to the jury and the attorney's summations. We discuss the court's charge first because the trial court rules on the attorneys' requests to charge the jury before the attorneys deliver their summations.

The Court's Control of the Trial 3

The principal procedural statute in New York is the Civil Practice Law and Rules,[1] and C.P.L.R. rule 4011 gives the court the power to control the flow of the trial, to determine the sequence in which the issues will be tried, and to control the decorum of the courtroom. However, the court must use its power in an unbiased manner and leave the questions of fact for the jury. This neutrality also implies allowing the parties the proper latitude in introducing evidence. In extreme cases, nevertheless, the court may direct the verdict of the jurors under the supervision of the court, and each attorney may begin his persuasion of the jurors even while selecting them.

3.1 NEUTRALITY

The court should not comment upon the credibility of the witnesses since credibility is an issue of fact for the jury.[2] In fact, the court should not make any comment or statement that lends the court's position to support or bolster a wit-

1. A handy reference for the C.P.L.R. is MARINO and REICH, NEW YORK PRACTICE AND PROCEDURE, 1993 ed., 364 pp.
2. Rivers v. Kumar, 118 A.D.2d 691, 500 N.Y.S.2d 39 (2d Dep't 1986); Madden v. County of Nassau Dep't of Recreation & Parks, 17 A.D.2d 717, 498 N.Y.S.2d 856 (2d Dep't 1986); Rosenberg v. Rixon, 111 A.D.2d 910, 490 N.Y.S.2d 807 (2d Dep't 1985); Heiney v. Pattillo, 76 A.D.2d 855, 428 N.Y.S.2d 513 (2d Dep't 1980).

ness or a party.[3] When the trial court violates these rules and injects itself into the case by asking improper questions or by making comments, the appellate court must reverse the resulting judgment.[4] However, more than one misstep is required. As the Appellate Division, Second Department, held in *Gentile v. Terrace Heights Hospital*:

> Although a trial court is granted wide latitude in controlling the conduct of a trial, here the trial court exercised its discretion improvidently by: (1) interrupting the questioning of witnesses by appellants' counsel both on direct and cross-examination; (2) frequently summarizing the testimony of witnesses while they were still on the stand; (3) responding, on several occasions, to questions asked by counsel of the witness on the stand; and (4) continually admonishing appellants' attorneys that they were repeating material already in the record. This conduct, together with the trial court's sometimes abrupt manner towards appellants' attorneys in the presence of the jury, gave the distinct impression that the court favored the plaintiffs' case. The court's refusal to grant a short continuance to enable appellant Siegel's expert to testify was also unwarranted. The cumulative effect of this conduct was to unfairly and unreasonably restrict the manner in which the appellants' case was presented, and precluded the jury from rendering an impartial verdict.[5]

Naturally, the attorney should not encourage the court to behave this way, thus justifying the opponent's appeal.

---

3. *Id.*; Hotel Utica, Inc. v. Ronald G. Armstrong Eng'g Co., 62 A.D.2d 1147, 404 N.Y.S.2d 455 (4th Dep't 1978).
4. Testa v. Federated Dep't Stores, Inc., 118 A.D.2d 696, 499 N.Y.S.2d 973 (2d Dep't 1986); Lopez v. Linden Gen. Hosp., 80 A.D.2d 1010, 454 N.Y.S.2d 452 (2d Dep't 1982); Gerichten v. Ruiz, 80 A.D.2d 578, 435 N.Y.S.2d 783 (2d Dep't 1981).
5. Gentile v. Terrace Heights Hosp., 57 A.D.2d 585, 393 N.Y.S.2d 592 (2d Dep't 1977).

3.2 THE PRESENTATION OF EVIDENCE

The trial court must give the parties the proper latitude in calling, questioning, and scheduling their witnesses so that the parties have an opportunity to make out a case or defense.[6] Concomitantly, however, the court should force the parties to obey the rules which help the trial to run smoothly.[7]

Ordinarily, the plaintiff's attorney presents the plaintiff's direct case followed by the defendant's attorney presenting the defendant's direct case, but the court has wide discretion to admit evidence out of order and even subject to later connection.[8] It is, nevertheless, incumbent on the plaintiff's attorney to present all of his or her evidence before the plaintiff rests, and the plaintiff may not intentionally hold back evidence for rebuttal.[9] However, the court in its discretion may permit the plaintiff to rest subject to producing medical evidence later and provided that this procedure does not prejudice the defendant.[10] In fact, in *Kennedy v. Peninsula Hospital*,[11] the Appellate Division, Second Department, found reversible error in the trial court's refusal to allow the plaintiff to reopen his case. The plaintiff had failed to present a prima facie case before resting, but the defendants had not begun their direct case when the court granted their motion to dismiss the complaint and denied the plaintiff's request to reopen his case. The appellate court reversed this decision on the grounds that the trial court

---

6. Ellison v. New York City Transit Auth., 63 N.Y.2d 1029, 473 N.E.2d 1171, 484 N.Y.S.2d 797 (1984); Roberts v. St. Francis Hosp., 96 A.D.2d 272, 470 N.Y.S.2d 716 (2d Dep't 1983).
7. Davis-Eckert v. State of New York, 118 A.D.2d 375 (3d Dep't 1986). After the state refused to have its exhibits marked at the pre-trial conference, the court granted the plaintiff's motion to preclude the state from introducing those exhibits.
8. N.Y. C.P.L.R. § 4011. Feldsberg v. Nitschke, 49 N.Y.2d 636, 404 N.E.2d 1293, 427 N.Y.S.2d 751 (1980).
9. Pienewski v. Benbenek, 56 A.D.2d 710, 392 N.Y.S.2d 732 (4th Dep't 1977); Sequin v. Berg, 260 A.D. 284, 21 N.Y.S.2d 291 (3d Dep't 1940).
10. Brzyski v. Schreibe, 314 Pa. 353, 171 A. 614 (1934).
11. Kennedy v. Peninsula Hosp., 135 A.D.2d 788, 522 N.Y.S.2d 671 (2d Dep't 1988).

may allow a party to reopen in order to rectify the defects which have occurred inadvertently and that there was no likelihood of prejudice to the defendants, who knew the substance of the curative proof.[12]

Subsequent to the parties' submission of their direct cases, the trial court has very wide latitude in controlling the nature and scope of the rebuttal testimony,[13] and the court may admit it even after the jury has retired.[14] However, this wide latitude does not mean that there are no rules. For example, rebuttal testimony must rebut. Thus, in *Kapinos v. Alvarado*,[15] the Appellate Division, Second Department, ruled that the trial court had exercised its discretion properly in denying the appellant's request to recall his expert witness in order to rebut the testimony of the defendant's expert. The court wrote:

> The record reveals that the appellant, through this expert, intended to elicit testimony to the effect that the collision occurred in the northbound lane. However, he had ample opportunity to adduce such proof during direct examination . . . . Accordingly, we conclude that the trial court properly refused to permit rebuttal testimony concerning a fact which merely served to bolster the appellant's case after the defendants had rested.[16]

Finally, the court must make a series of rulings during the trial by which the court enforces the rules of evidence and

---

12. *See also* Roberts v. St. Francis Hosp., 96 A.D.2d 272, 470 N.Y.S.2d 716 (2d Dep't 1983); Scimeca v. New York City Transit Auth., 39 A.D.2d 596, 332 N.Y.S.2d 11 (1972), *later appeal*, 42 A.D.2d 745, 346 N.Y.S.2d 308 (2d Dep't 1973), *rev'd*, 34 N.Y.2d 613, 311 N.E.2d 500, 355 N.Y.S.2d 363 (1974); LaTant v. Start, 4 N.Y.2d 890, 150 N.E.2d 711, 174 N.Y.S.2d 469 (1958); Bianchi v. Markese, 276 A.D. 1048, 95 N.Y.S.2d 897 (4th Dep't 1950).
13. Young v. Strong, 118 A.D.2d 974, 499 N.Y.S.2d 988 (3d Dep't 1986); Bailey v. Health Ins. Plan, 116 A.D.2d 546, 497 N.Y.S.2d 400 (2d Dep't 1986); Baumis v. General Motors Corp., 106 A.D.2d 789, 484 N.Y.S.2d 185 (3d Dep't 1984), *aff'd*, 66 N.Y.2d 777, 488 N.E.2d 114, 497 N.Y.S.2d 369 (1985); Yeomans v. Warren, 87 A.D.2d 718, 448 N.Y.S.2d 889 (3d Dep't 1982).
14. People v. Ferrone, 204 N.Y.551, 98 N.E. 8 (1912).

decorum and decides questions of law. For example, the trial court must rule on the admissibility of videotapes,[17] whether a particular witness meets the qualifications of an expert,[18] the admissibility of real or demonstrative evidence,[19] whether a physician will be allowed to testify although the party offering such testimony has not complied with the rules for exchanging medical reports,[20] and whether a party will be allowed to perform experiments that involve the jurors.[21] The trial court should rebuke an attorney who oversteps the bounds of propriety and should instruct the jury to disregard improper remarks and tactics.[22] (It is, however, an error for the trial court to refuse a request to record the summations.[23]) The court must also resolve issues of law, such as whether the plaintiff has suffered a serious injury as defined by the no-fault law.[24]

3.3 QUESTIONS OF FACT FOR THE JURY

The court's role is to conduct the trial, to control the introduction of evidence, and to rule on all related questions,[25] but the jury's role is to resolve all issues of fact. So long as there is evidence from which the jury can decide the dis-

---

15. Kapinos v. Alvarado, 143 A.D.2d 332, 532 N.Y.S.2d 416 (2d Dep't 1988).
16. *Id.* at 332, 532 N.Y.S.2d at 417-18. *See also* Frias v. Fanning, 119 A.D.2d 796, 501 N.Y.S.2d 423 (2d Dep't 1986).
17. Mechanick v. Conradi, 139 A.D.2d 857, 527 N.Y.S.2d 586 (3d Dep't 1988).
18. Locilento v. John A. Coleman Catholic High School, 134 A.D.2d 39, 523 N.Y.S.2d 198 (3d Dep't 1987) (Educator) and Edgewater Apartments, Inc. v. Flynn, 216 A.D.2d 53 (1st Dep't 1995) (Architect).
19. Klombers v. Lefkowitz, 131 A.D.2d 815, 517 N.Y.S.2d 179 (2d Dep't 1987).
20. *Id.*
21. Weinstein v. Daman, 132 A.D.2d 547, 517 N.Y.S.2d 278 (2d Dep't 1987).
22. Hernandez v. Hernandez, 148 A.D.2d 1011, 539 N.Y.S.2d 240 (4th Dep't 1989); Caraballo v. City of N.Y., 86 A.D.2d 580, 446 N.Y.S.2d 318 (1st Dep't 1982).
23. Robinson v. Ferens, 33 A.D.2d 688, 306 N.Y.S.2d 530 (2d Dep't 1969).
24. D'Iorio v. Brancoccio, 115 A.D.2d 634, 496 N.Y.S.2d 293 (2d Dep't 1986).
25. Teitelbaum, Sutto-Barberc & Johnson, *Evaluating the Prejudicial Effect of Evidence: Can Judges Identify the Impact of Improper Evidence on Juries*, 1983 WIS. L. REV. 1147.

pute as an issue of fact, the court should not decide the dispute as a matter of law;[26] for example, the credibility of the witnesses is a question of fact for the jury.[27] The credibility of any expert is also a question for the jury,[28] and the jury must evaluate the failure of a party to call an expert or the significance of one party's calling many more experts than the other.[29]

In an action for medical malpractice, the jury must decide such questions as whether the defendant physician was a member of a partnership, whether there was a physician-patient relationship, whether the treatment was continuous, and whether the defendant's negligence was a proximate cause of the plaintiff's injuries.[30]

Of course, the jury decides questions of ordinary negligence, e.g., whether the plaintiff was reckless in diving into a shallow rock-filled lake,[31] and how the plaintiff fell into the pit where he was found dead.[32] The jury also decides the

---

26. Madden v. County of Nassau Dep't of Recreation & Parks, 117 A.D.2d 717, 498 N.Y.S.2d 856 (2d Dep't 1986); Hermann v. General Tire & Rubber Co., 79 A.D.2d 955, 435 N.Y.S.2d 14 (1st Dep't 1981); Boyle v. Gretch, 57 A.D.2d 910, 395 N.Y.S.2d 797 (4th Dep't 1977); Colozzo v. LoVece, N.Y.L.J., Dec. 2, 1988 (2d Dep't 1988).

27. Rivers v. Kumar, 118 A.D.2d 691, 500 N.Y.S.2d 39 (2d Dep't 1986); Madden v. County of Nassau Dep't of Recreation & Parks, 117 A.D.2d 717, 498 N.Y.S.2d 856 (2d Dep't 1986); Rosenberg v. Rixon, 111 A.D.2d 910, 490 N.Y.S.2d 807 (2d Dep't 1985); Harris v. Armstrong, 97 A.D.2d 947, 468 N.Y.S.2d 740 (4th Dep't 1983), *aff'd,* 64 N.Y.2d 700, 474 N.E.2d 1191, 485 N.Y.S.2d 523 (1984); Birnbaum v. All State Vehicle, Inc., 139 A.D.2d 553 (2d Dep't 1988); O'Brien v. O'Brien, 124 A.D.2d 1029 (4th Dep't 1986).

28. Randolph v. City of N.Y., 69 N.Y.2d 844, 507 N.E.2d 298, 514 N.Y.S.2d 705 (1987); Ledogar v. Giordano, 122 A.D.2d 834, 505 N.Y.S.2d 899 (2d Dep't 1986); O'Connell v. Albany Medical Center Hosp, 101 A.D.2d 637, 475 N.Y.S.2d 543 (3d Dep't 1984); Sternemann v. Langs, 93 A.D.2d 819, 460 N.Y.S.2d 614 (2d Dep't 1983).

29. Mechanick v. Conradi, 139 A.D.2d 857, 527 N.Y.S.2d 586 (3d Dep't 1988).

30. Manning v. Turtel, 135 A.D.2d 511, 496 N.Y.S.2d 775 (2d Dep't 1987); Paladino v. Isasi, 123 A.D.2d 379, 506 N.Y.S.2d 543 (2d Dep't 1986).

31. Ziecker v. Town of Orchard Park, 75 N.Y.2d 761, 551 N.E.2d 99, 551 N.Y.S.2d 898 (1989). *See also* Culkin v. Parks and Recreation Department of the City of Syracuse, 168 A.D.2d 914 (4th Dep't 1990).

32. Horne v. Metropolitan Transp. Auth., 82 A.D.2d 909, 440 N.Y.S.2d 695 (2d Dep't 1981).

issue of damages, e.g., the permanence of the plaintiff's injury when he received no medical care and went to work the day after the accident.[33]

3.4 THE ROLES COLLIDE; THE DIRECTED VERDICT

In the proper circumstance, the trial court has the right to direct a verdict, to set aside a verdict, or to order a new trial.[34] This right is an inherent judicial power, which the legislature has codified in C.P.L.R. section 4404(a):

> After a trial of a cause of action or issue triable of right by a jury, upon the motion of any party or on its own initiative, the court may set aside a verdict or any judgment entered thereon and direct that judgment be entered in favor of a party entitled to judgment as a matter of law or it may order a new trial of a cause of action or separable issue where the verdict is contrary to the weight of the evidence . . . .

This statute actually codifies two different judicial acts: setting aside a verdict as contrary to the weight of the evidence and setting aside a verdict as not supported by sufficient evidence. The first act, setting aside a verdict as contrary to the weight of the evidence, is a factual determination, not a question of law, and results in a new trial. The second act, setting aside a verdict as not supported by sufficient evidence, is a decision of law and leads to a directed verdict terminating the action, i.e., a directed verdict in favor of the party that lost in the jury's verdict. This second judicial act requires the trial court to find that no valid line of reasoning or no permissible inference of fact could possi-

33. Liddy v. Frome, 85 A.D.2d 716, 445 N.Y.S.2d 841 (2d Dep't 1981).
34. N.Y. C.P.L.R. § 4404(a).

bly lead rational individuals to the conclusion that the jury reached.[35]

Despite the differences in terminology and result, the standards to be applied in performing these two judicial acts remain elusive. Hence, the Appellate Division, Second Department, said in *Nicastro v. Park*,[36] one of the leading cases, that the trial court should be wary about setting aside a verdict as against the weight of the evidence when the verdict is in favor of a defendant in a tort action,[37] and the Appellate Division, Fourth Department, has warned that the trial court should not set aside a verdict in favor of the defendant unless "the jury could not have reached the verdict on any fair interpretation of the evidence."[38]

Whatever a fair interpretation is, the courts now apply this standard to verdicts in favor of the plaintiff, too.[39]

> The significance of the fair interpretation standard is that it provides a strong cautionary note by stressing to the court that the overturning of the jury's resolution of a sharply disputed factual issue may be an abuse of discretion if there is any way to conclude that the verdict is a fair reflection of the evidence.
>
> It is significant, however, that the mere fact that some testimony in the record has created a factual issue does not deprive

---

35. Nicastro v. Park, 113 A.D.2d 129, 495 N.Y.S.2d 184 (2d Dep't 1985). Once again, the cases following *Nicastro* are legion, *e.g.*, Kahn v. Queens Surface Transport Corp., 203 A.D.2d 332 (2d Dep't 1994).

36. *Id.*

37. *Id.*, 113 A.D.2d at 134, 495 N.Y.S.2d at 190-91.

38. Tripoli v. Tripoli, 83 A.D.2d 764, 443 N.Y.S.2d 488 (4th Dep't 1981), *aff'd*, 56 N.Y.2d 684, 436 N.E.2d 1319, 451 N.Y.S.2d 717 (1982); Delgado v. Board of Educ., 65 A.D.2d 547, 408 N.Y.S.2d 949 (2d Dep't 1978), *aff'd,* 48 N.Y.2d 643, 396 N.E.2d 481, 421 N.Y.S.2d 198 (1979); Pena v. New York City Transit Authority, 185 A.D.2d 794 (1st Dep't 1992).

39. Moffatt v. Moffatt, 86 A.D.2d 864, 447 N.Y.S.2d 313 (2d Dep't 1982), *aff'd*, 62 N.Y.2d 875, 467 N.E.2d 528, 478 N.Y.S.2d 864 (1984); O'Boyle v. Avis Rent-a-Car, 78 A.D.2d 431, 435 N.Y.S.2d 296 (2d Dep't 1981); Marshall v. Mastodan, Inc., 51 A.D.2d 21, 379 N.Y.S.2d 177 (3d Dep't 1976); Lolik v. Big V Supermarkets, Inc., 86 N.Y.2d 744 (1995).

> the Trial Judge of the power to intervene in an appropriate case. . . .[40]

For the trial attorney, there are two lessons: first, know the difference between setting aside a verdict as contrary to the weight of the evidence and setting aside a verdict as not supported by sufficient evidence, and second, be prepared to argue the relevant motion after the jury's verdict. Of course, the trial court may require the attorneys to submit memoranda before the court makes its decision.

3.5 SELECTING THE JURY: BEGINNING PERSUASION

The trial attorney begins his persuasion of the jurors when he helps to select them: he establishes his *ethos*, he provides his client's general contentions as a framework for the jurors' understanding, and he hints at the evidence by identifying the witnesses. In New York, the new uniform civil rules for selecting juries have restricted the trial attorney to these three devices. These rules came into force on January 1, 1996, and were intended to restrain the conduct of the parties' attorneys during the voir dire because attorneys increasingly were attempting to try the case while selecting the jury. Of course, attorneys inevitably begin the process of persuasion then, but too many were abusing the situation. Nevertheless, the skillful attorney still will be able to begin his persuasion while conforming to the rules. To explain to the reader how to do this, section 3.5 consists of three parts: tactical guidelines for selecting a jury, a summary of the new rules, and an example of an attorney's opening remarks.

---

40. Nicastro v. Park, 113 A.D.2d 129, 135, 495 N.Y.S.2d 184, 189 (2d Dep't 1985) (court held that trial court was right to set aside jury verdict for defendant and to order new trial).

3.5.1 Tactical Guidelines for Selecting a Jury

There is no canonical formulation for cleverly selecting a jury, but the following eleven rules are useful. These rules apply to dealing with the judge, dealing with the jury, the content of the attorney's remarks, and representing the defendant.

The first two rules apply to the attorney's dealings with the judge.

First, avoid demanding that the judge be present for the entire voir dire. The new rules require the trial judge to open the voir dire but leave to his discretion the decision whether to remain.[41] Thus, the rules appear to contradict C.P.L.R. Rule 4107, which still reads, "On application of any party, a judge shall be present at the examination of the jurors." However this question is resolved,[42] the attorney will have better relations with the judge if the attorney refrains from asking the judge to be present. Make such a request only when your opponent's behavior is so egregious that he prevents progress in selecting the jury by feeling free to say anything.

Second, resolve any disagreements with the opposing counsel without bothering the judge for a ruling. The trial judge will appreciate your consideration. If you must seek a ruling, explain your objection briefly and accurately.

The third, fourth, and fifth rules apply to the attorney's dealings with the jurors.

Third, impress the jurors with your conviction and preparation. Their selection is the jurors' first opportunity to evaluate the attorney, and first impressions are important. In this context, it is more important to convince the jurors that you are fair than to provide them with the details of your client's case. Remember that one of the three types of persuasive ap-

---

41. U.C.R. 202.33(e).

42. Baginski v. New York Telephone Co., 130 A.D.2d 362 (lst Dept. 1987) is the old authority.

peal is *ethos*, i.e., the audience's apprehension that the advocate is honest, competent, and helpful. Thus, your demeanor is important. Moreover, being prepared, e.g., having the names of the parties, the lawyers, and the witnesses on your fingertips will tell the jurors that you are competent and helpful. By all means, have this information available in writing, but reduce your notes to a few index cards that you can consult unobtrusively. (See example 3-3.)

Fourth, confront the jurors' prejudices directly. If the written questionnaire or the general oral questions reveal that a particular juror may be biased, e.g., in favor of doctors or against hospitals, explore that bias. Does he believe that doctors are especially believable witnesses or does he have relatives in the profession? If possible, induce the juror to keep an open mind; for example, will he admit that medicine itself is not on trial and that even a good doctor could be negligent on a particular occasion? If you believe that the juror cannot be impartial, then challenge him for cause.[43] The other jurors will respect you for having the courage of your convictions, and your exploration of bias with the excused juror will influence their attitudes. In addition to the general authority to challenge jurors for bias, there is statutory authority for challenges for favor, and a family relationship to a party is a disqualification. Thus, C.P.L.R. 4110(a) provides that a party has grounds to challenge for favor any prospective juror who is an employee or shareholder of a party or an employee, shareholder, officer, or director of any insurance company which issues liability policies (in other words, the insurance company need not be a party to the lawsuit). C.P.L.R 4110(b) provides more stringently that the relatives of a party to the sixth degree are disqualified from serving as jurors. To utilize this statute, the attorney should consult the written questionnaires which the prospective jurors have completed for the court.

---

43. C.P.L.R. 4108.

Fifth, use your peremptory challenges. If you do not like a particular juror, he probably does not like you either. Also consult your client: do he and the prospective juror belong to antipathetic occupations? (Some people claim that electricians and plumbers dislike one another because they are always getting in one another's way at construction sites.)

However, observe the juror's reactions to all the lawyers before you make a decision. C.P.L.R. 4109 provides that each side has three peremptory challenges plus one challenge for every two alternate jurors to be selected. The trial judge may increase and distribute the number of peremptory challenges when there are multiple parties on one side.[44]

Rules six though ten are brief and apply to the content of the attorney's remarks to the jury.

Sixth, provide only a few details about the case. A general statement is sufficient whereas a long recitation will be counterproductive either by boring the prospective jurors (who do not yet know whether they will be chosen) or by eliciting justified objections from the opposing attorneys. Moreover, you will dissipate the emotional impact of your opening statement at the trial.

However, seventh, raise any problems that you anticipate occurring during the trial. For example, after you identify your client, you might ask the jurors whether they can be fair to a party who has a bad driving record.

Eighth, if you represent the plaintiff, mention that your client does not want sympathy. A good time to do this is when you are listing your client's injuries or damages. Expand on this observation in your opening statement, but emphasize the need for human understanding in deciding the case.

Ninth, refer to your client's injuries. However, the worse his physical injuries are, the less you need to say, e.g., if he was rendered a paraplegic. The attorney for the defendant

---

44. C.P.L.R. 4109.

should make clear whether he denies the existence of the injuries or denies that his client caused them.

Tenth, list the plaintiff's damages, i.e., the components of the recovery. You may not mention an amount of money,[45] but you may list the kinds of damages requested, e.g., lost wages or medical bills.

The last tactical guideline applies specifically to the defendant's attorney.

Eleventh, the defendant's attorney must repeatedly press the prospective jurors to keep an open mind, e.g., by asking a prospective juror whether there could have been a reason for the accident other than negligence or whether he will render a verdict out of sympathy. The attorney's essential problem is to keep the jurors from being swept along emotionally with the first telling of the plaintiff's story, the way viewers are swept along by the point of view with which a event is reported on the televised news.

3.5.2 Summary of the New Rules

Section 202.33 of the Unified Civil Rules for the Supreme and County Courts contains the new rules for selecting juries. This section is organized in an ascending order of detail, to wit: the section itself provides the most general rules. Appendix E to 202.33 begins with subdivision A on general principles for attorneys while subdivisions B and C contain the details of the White and Struck methods, respectively. (See example 3-1 for the text of the rules.)

Section 202.33 has four important provisions. First, the trial judge shall hold a settlement conference shortly before the attorneys begin selecting the jury.[46] Second, the trial judge shall preside at the opening of the voir dire, but he has the discretion to decide whether to preside at all or part

45. U.C.R. 202.33, App. E, subd. A(4).
46. U.C.R. 202.33(b).

of the remainder.[47] Third, the trial judge shall limit the time for questioning the prospective jurors. He has the discretion to prescribe either (a) a general period for all the questioning, or (b) a period after which the attorneys must report their progress to him, or even (c) specific periods for questioning panels or individual jurors.[48] Finally, fourth, the trial judge shall determine the mechanical method for striking prospective jurors.[49] The three choices are White's method, the Struck method, or the strike and replace method.[50]

Subdivision A of Appendix E contains the rules governing the conduct of the attorneys. Six of these rules are especially important. First, the attorneys generally shall choose six jurors and two alternates.[51] Second, the jurors shall complete a background questionnaire supplied by the court.[52] (See example 3-2.) The attorneys may examine these questionnaires prior to selecting the jury and may ask the court to supplement the questionnaire with questions appropriate to the specific case.[53] (Do not be afraid to make a reasonable request, but provide the proposed questions.) The purpose of this questionnaire is to eliminate the time devoted to eliciting this information during the voir dire. After the attorneys select the jury, the court will return the questionnaires to the jurors or will destroy them.[54]

We will present the third rule verbatim because this rule allows the attorney to outline his client's case for the first time:

> During the voir dire each attorney may state generally the contentions of his or her client, and identify the parties, attorneys and the witnesses likely to be called. However, counsel may

---

47. U.C.R. 202.33(e).
48. U.C.R. 202.33(d).
49. U.C.R. 202.33(c).
50. U.C.R. 202.33(f).
51. U.C.R. 202.33, App. E, subd. A(2).
52. U.C.R. 202.33, App. E, subd. A(3).
53. *Id.*
54. *Id.*

> not read from any of the pleadings in the action or inform potential jurors of the amount of money at issue.[55]

Thus, the attorney may provide the outline for which the witnesses will provide the evidence, and he may use his inquiries into the suitability of the jurors to embellish the contentions. For example, he may ask, "Has anyone here been hit by a car while walking?"

The fourth rule consists of injunctions. The attorney shall (a) exercise peremptory challenges outside the presence of the prospective jurors,[56] (b) avoid discussing legal concepts such as the burden of proof,[57] and (c) disclose that the trial will be lengthy or subject to an unusual delay.[58] Since one attorney may believe that his opponent is violating these new rules, the fifth important rule in subdivision A provides that the objecting attorney shall unobtrusively ask his opponent to step outside and shall make a determined effort to resolve the dispute. If they cannot resolve it, the attorneys should bring their dispute to the trial judge immediately.[59] Finally, the sixth rule requires the attorneys to inform the judge's clerk when they have finished selecting the jury and whether they will need any special equipment or assistance, e.g., an interpreter, for the trial.

Subdivisions B and C of Appendix E consist primarily of the detailed mechanics of the White and Struck methods, i.e., the seating, questioning, and challenging of the prospective jurors in various rounds. However, the first paragraph of the White method describes how the authors envisaged the questioning, to wit:

> Prior to the identification of the prospective jurors to be seated in the jury box, counsel shall ask questions generally to all of the jurors in the room to determine whether any prospective juror in the room has knowledge of the subject matter, the

---

55. U.C.R. 202.33, App. E, subd. A(4).
56. U.C.R. 202.33, App. E, subd. A(5).
57. U.C.R. 202.33, App. E, subd. A(6). This is the greatest restriction in the new rules.
58. U.C.R. 202.33, App. E, subd. A(7).
59. U.C.R. 202.33, App. E, subd. A(8).

> parties, their attorneys or the prospective witnesses. A response from a juror that requires elaboration may be the subject of further questioning of that juror by counsel on an individual basis. Counsel may exercise challenges for cause at this time.[60]

After the general questioning of the group, the selection continues in rounds consisting of seating prospective jurors, questioning these individuals, and removing any of them for cause.[61] The attorneys question the jurors in the order in which their clients' names appear in the caption.[62] After the questioning and any challenges for cause, the attorneys use their peremptory challenges.[63] The remaining jurors are then sworn.[64]

While the mechanics of the Struck method differ slightly from the White method, the Struck method also allows both general and follow-up questions.[65]

In summary, the trial judge will convene a settlement conference, open the voir dire, prescribe time limits, and choose the method for excusing jurors. The attorneys will select six jurors and two alternates after consulting the jurors' questionnaires. When questioning the prospective jurors, the attorneys may identify the parties, attorneys, and witnesses and may state their clients' contentions briefly. However, the attorneys may not discuss legal concepts, and they should resolve disputes among themselves. Finally, the attorneys use the approved method to excuse prospective jurors.

How then might an attorney begin persuading the jury while conforming to the rules for selecting that jury? Section 3.5.3 contains a proposed example.

---

60. U.C.R. 202.33, App. E, subd. B(10).
61. U.C.R. 202.33, App. E, subd. B(11).
62. U.C.R. 202.33, App. E, subd. B(12).
63. U.C.R. 202.33, App. E, subd. B(13).
64. U.C.R. 202.33, App. E, subd. B(15).
65. U.C.R. 202.33, App. E, subd. C(19).

3.5.3 Opening Remarks to Prospective Jurors

Assume a hypothetical medical malpractice action on behalf of a brain-damaged baby. The attorney for the plaintiff might deliver the following remarks at the beginning of the selection of the jury.

* * * * * *

MR. PRINCIPE: Good morning, ladies and gentlemen. My name is Thomas Principe, and I represent the plaintiff in this lawsuit. The new rules governing the selection of juries limit what the attorneys may say to the prospective jurors. Nevertheless, the law does permit me to tell you the names of the attorneys, the parties, and the prospective witnesses so we can determine whether you have a connection with any of them. The law also permits each attorney to state his client's contentions briefly so we can determine whether you have been involved in a similar situation or would otherwise feel unable to judge the dispute impartially. I believe that the most coherent approach will be for me to begin by giving you the names of the parties and their attorneys; next I will state my client's contentions briefly; then I will identify our witnesses for you. Finally, I will ask questions of the whole group. You should respond if the question applies to you.

Let us begin with the parties and their attorneys. As I said, my name is Thomas Principe, and I am a member of the firm of Kramer, Dillof, Tessel, Duffy, and Moore. Miss Roberta Eng of our firm will assist me. We represent the infant plaintiff, Jessica Reingold, and her mother, Mrs. Diane Reingold. Jessica is suing her mother's obstetrician, Dr. Micah McDole of McDole and Sherman, P.C. Dr. McDole delivered Jessica and is represented by Mr. Randy Dunlop of Murphy and McNiece. Jessica is also suing Maronite Hospital, where she was born, and two of the hospital's former residents, Dr. Sheila Browne and Dr. Jody McCartney. These defendants are represented by Todd Lester of Stowell and Calendar.

My client, the plaintiff Jessica Reingold, has only four contentions. I will state them briefly, but I must warn you not to consider anything I say here to be evidence in this case. First, Jessica suffered catastrophic brain damage at birth because her umbilical cord was squeezed shut and cut off the oxygen to her brain. Second, Dr. McDole's medical malpractice caused this catastrophe because (a) the doctor failed to diagnose that Jessica wasn't positioned properly in her mother's womb, (b) the doctor failed to schedule a caesarian delivery although the baby was large, the mother small, and the delivery overdue, (c) the doctor failed to send Jessica's chart to the hospital, and (d) the doctor delayed reporting to the hospital after the staff informed her that Jessica's mother was in labor. Jessica's third contention is that Maronite Hospital and the resident physicians, Dr. Browne and Dr. McCartney, committed medical malpractice and contributed to Jessica's catastrophic injuries by (a) failing to use the appropriate fetal monitoring machine and (b) not ordering an immediate caesarian delivery when they could not detect a fetal heart beat. In other words, Jessica contends that Dr. McDole created the problem and Maronite Hospital failed to deal with it. The law forbids the attorneys to mention a specific amount of money as damages during the selection of the jury so I will restrict myself to saying that, as her fourth contention, Jessica claims, or rather Mrs. Reingold claims for her brain-damaged child, compensation for her medical bills, custodial care, conscious pain and suffering, and lost income.

Let me finish my introductory remarks, ladies and gentlemen, by identifying the plaintiff's witnesses. These witnesses will include two obstetricians, Dr. Susan Fogarty and Dr. Stacy Mitchell, the toxicologist and pediatrician, Dr. Mark Thomam, and a neurologist, Dr. Matthew Torres. In addition, three nurses on the staff of the hospital will testify:

Nora Rodney, Betty Fitzgerald, and Edith Bellasco. Finally, the plaintiff will call the defendants as witnesses. Mr. Dunlop and Mr. Lester have assured me that they will identify their own witnesses for you so I will end my introductory remarks here.

* * * * * *

This introduction takes only four minutes to deliver, and it conforms to the rules, but it tells the prospective jurors exactly where the plaintiff stands.[66] The contentions are clear (clarity being the greatest virtue at this point in the proceedings), and the list of witnesses assures the jurors that the plaintiff has the evidence to support her contentions. In addition, the trial attorney establishes his *ethos* by delivering this introduction. He is competent because he can state the case fairly and briefly and because he provides all the information without hesitation. This competence is also helpful to the jurors, and the attorney is honest because he refers to the rules and then obeys them. Finally, his use of his client's name makes her a real person, not an abstract party, to the jurors.

We purposely have used an introduction from a hypothetical action for medical malpractice in order to raise two matters: a distinction in the law and a tactical decision. The distinction in the law is between actions for medical malpractice, and all other actions, including actions for personal injury. C.P.L.R. 3101(d)(1)(i) states the general rule, which requires each party to disclose the identities of his expert witnesses including his medical experts. This section also states the exception: in an action for medical malpractice, each party may withhold the identities of his medical ex-

---

66. If the trial attorneys for the various parties agree among themselves to forego introductions and to incorporate all the information into general questions instead, then the attorney can rephrase his statements as interrogatories, e.g., "Has anyone here had a baby in his family suffer brain damage during the delivery?"

perts, but he still must disclose their qualifications and expected testimony. Moreover, each party must identify his nonmedical experts. Thus, in any action other than one for medical malpractice, the adversaries know the identities of one another's medical experts before the attorneys begin selecting the jury so neither attorney has anything to gain by withholding this information from the prospective jurors.

Hence, the tactical decision is whether the attorney should reveal the identities of his medical experts when selecting the jury in an action for medical malpractice. The attorney in the hypothetical introduction above did identify his medical experts. However, the author never does so when representing the plaintiff. He prefers to deny to the defendant's attorney the extra time to prepare for these witnesses. The reader must make his own tactical decisions, however, and he must weigh the advantage of withholding this information against the disadvantage. There may be no advantage if the adversary has deduced the expert's identity from his qualifications. (If the expert's resume says that he is the head of thoracic surgery at the XYZ Hospital, the adversary will determine the expert's identify.) Moreover, the defendant's attorney may ingratiate himself with the prospective jurors by naming his own witnesses after the plaintiff's attorney has declined to reveal his.

Of course, the defendant's attorney may not have deduced the identities of the plaintiff's medical experts, and the plaintiff's attorney may obtain an advantage by withholding this information. For example, the medical expert may be the author of a scientific theory which the defendant's attorney could attack if he had the time to study it. Similarly, the defendant's attorney might obtain an advantage from withholding the identities of his medical experts. The crucial variable may be whether there will be a delay between selecting the jury and beginning the trial. Hence, the reader must make his best estimate of his own situation. The hypothetical introduction illustrates how the attorney should introduce the parties and their attorneys, his client's contentions, and his witnesses. Whether the attorney should identify his medical expert in an action for medical malpractice is problematical; again, the author prefers not to do so.

EXAMPLE 3-1: RULES FOR SELECTING THE JURY (NEW YORK)

UNIFORM CIVIL RULES FOR THE SUPREME AND COUNTY COURTS

202.33 Conduct of the Voir Dire

a. Trial judge. All references to the trial judge in this section shall include any judge designated by the administrative judge in those instances where the case processing system or other logistical considerations do not permit the trial judge to perform the acts set forth in this section.

b. Pre-voir dire settlement conference. Where the court has directed that jury selection begin, the trial judge shall meet prior to the actual commencement of jury selection with counsel who will be conducting the voir dire and shall attempt to bring about a disposition of the action.

c. Method of jury selection. The trial judge shall direct the method of jury selection that shall be used for the voir dire from among the methods specified in subdivision (f) below.

d. Time limitations. The trial judge shall establish time limitations for the questioning of prospective jurors during the voir dire. At the discretion of the judge, the limits established may consist of a general period for the completion of the questioning, a period after which attorneys shall report back to the judge on the progress of the voir dire, and/or specific time periods for the questioning of panels of jurors or individual jurors.

e. Presence of judge at the voir dire. In order to ensure an efficient and dignified selection process, the trial judge shall preside at the commencement of the voir dire and open the voir dire proceeding. The trial judge shall determine whether supervision of the voir dire should continue after the voir dire has commenced and, in his or her discretion, preside over part of or all of the remainder of the voir dire.

f. Methods of jury selection. Counsel shall select prospective jurors in accordance with the general principles applicable to jury selection set forth in Appendix "E" and using the method designated by the judge pursuant to subdivision (c). The methods that may be selected are:

1. "White's method," as set forth in Appendix "E" of this Part;

2. "Struck method," as set forth in Appendix "E" of this Part;

3. "Strike and replace method," in districts where the specifics of that method have been submitted to the Chief Administrator by the Administrative Judge and approved by the Chief Administrator for that district. The strike and replace

method shall be approved only in those districts where the Chief Administrator, in his or her discretion, has determined that experience with the method in the district has resulted in an efficient and orderly selection process; or

4. Other methods that may be submitted to the Chief Administrator for use on an experimental basis by the appropriate Administrative Judge and approved by the Chief Administrator.

APPENDIX "E"

Procedures for questioning, challenging and selecting jurors authorized by section 202.33 of the Rules of the Chief Administrator of the Courts.

A. General principles applicable to jury selection.

Selection of jurors pursuant to any of the methods authorized by section 202.33(e) of the Rules of the Chief Administrator shall be governed by the following:

(1) If for any reason jury selection cannot proceed immediately, counsel shall return promptly to the courtroom of the assigned trial judge or the Trial Assignment Part or any other designated location for further instructions.

(2) Generally, a total of eight jurors, including two alternates, shall be selected. The court may permit a greater number of alternates if a lengthy trial is expected or for any appropriate reason. Counsel may consent to the use of "nondesignated" alternate jurors, in which event no distinction shall be made during jury selection between jurors and alternates, but the number of peremptory challenges in such cases shall consist of the sum of the peremptory challenges that would have been available to challenge both jurors and designated alternates.

(3) All prospective jurors shall complete a background questionnaire supplied by the court in a form approved by the Chief Administrator. Prior to the commencement of jury selection, completed questionnaires shall be made available to counsel. Upon completion of jury selection, or upon removal of a prospective juror, the questionnaires shall be either returned to the respective jurors or collected and discarded by court staff in a manner that ensures juror privacy. With Court approval, which shall take into consideration concern for juror privacy, the parties may supplement the questionnaire to address concerns unique to a specific case.

(4) During the voir dire each attorney may state generally the contentions of his or her client, and identify the parties, attorneys and the witnesses likely to be called. However, counsel may not read from any of the pleadings in the action or inform potential jurors of the amount of money at issue.

(5) Counsel shall exercise peremptory challenges outside the presence of the panel of prospective jurors.

(6) Counsel shall avoid discussing legal concepts such as burden of proof, which are the province of the court.

(7) If an unusual delay or a lengthy trial is anticipated, counsel may so advise prospective jurors.

(8) If counsel objects to anything said or done by any other counsel during the selection process, the objecting counsel shall unobtrusively request that all counsel step outside of the juror's presence, and counsel shall make a determined effort to resolve the problem. Should that effort fail, counsel shall immediately bring the problem to the attention of the assigned trial judge, the Trial Assignment part judge or any other designated judge.

(9) After jury selection is completed, counsel shall advise the clerk of the assigned Trial Part or of the Trial Assignment Part or other designated part. If counsel anticipates the need during trial of special equipment (if available) or special assistance, such as an interpreter, counsel shall so inform the clerk at that time.

B. "White's Method"

(10) Prior to the identification of the prospective jurors to be seated in the jury box, counsel shall ask questions generally to all of the jurors in the room to determine whether any prospective juror in the room has knowledge of the subject matter, the parties, their attorneys or the prospective witnesses. A response from a juror that requires elaboration may be the subject of further questioning of that juror by counsel on an individual basis. Counsel may exercise challenges for cause at this time.

(11) After general questions have been asked to the group of prospective jurors, jury selection shall continue in rounds, with each round to consist of the following: (1) seating prospective jurors in the jury box; (2) questioning of seated prospective jurors; and (3) removal of seated prospective jurors upon exercise of challenges. Jurors removed for cause shall immediately be replaced during each round. The first round shall begin initially with the seating of six prospective jurors (where undesignated alternates are used, additional prospective jurors equal to the number of alternate jurors shall be seated as well).

(12) In each round, the questioning of the seated prospective jurors shall be conducted first by counsel for the plaintiff, followed by counsel for the remaining parties in the order in which their names appear in the caption. Counsel may be permitted to ask follow-up questions. Within each round,

3

challenges for cause shall be exercised by any party prior to the exercise of peremptory challenges and as soon as the reason therefor becomes apparent. Upon replacement of a prospective juror removed for cause, questioning shall revert to the plaintiff.

(13) Following questioning and the exercise of challenges for cause, peremptory challenges shall be exercised one at a time and alternately as follows: In the first found, in caption order, each attorney shall exercise one peremptory challenge by removing a prospective juror's name from a "board" passed back and forth between or among counsel. An attorney alternatively may waive the making of a peremptory challenge. An attorney may exercise a second, single peremptory challenge within the round only after all other attorneys have either exercised or waived their first peremptory challenges. The board shall continue to circulate among the attorneys until no other peremptory challenges are exercised. An attorney who waives a challenge may not thereafter exercise a peremptory challenge within the round, but may exercise remaining peremptory challenges in subsequent rounds. The counsel last able to exercise a peremptory challenge in a round is not confined to the exercise of a single challenge but may then exercise one or more peremptory challenges.

(14) In subsequent rounds, the first exercise of peremptory challenges shall alternative from side to side. Where a side consists of multiple parties, commencement of the exercise of peremptory challenges in subsequent rounds shall rotate among the parties within the side. In each such round, before the board is to be passed to the other side, the board must be passed to all remaining parties within the side, in caption order, starting from the first party in the rotation for that round.

(15) At the end of each round, those seated jurors who remain unchallenged shall be sworn and removed from the room. The challenged jurors shall be replaced, and a new round shall commence.

(16) The selection of designated alternate jurors shall take place after the selection of the six jurors. Designated alternate jurors shall be selected in the manner as described above, with the order of exercise of peremptory challenges continuing as the next round following the last completed round of challenges to regulars jurors. The total number of peremptory challenges to alternates may be exercised against any alternate, regardless of seat.

C. "Struck Method"

(17) Unless otherwise ordered by the Court, selection of jurors shall be made from an initial panel of 25 prospective jurors, who shall be seated randomly and who shall maintain the order of seating throughout the voir dire. If fewer prospective

4

jurors are needed due to the use of designated alternate jurors or for any other reason, the size of the panel may be decreased.

(18) Counsel first shall ask questions generally to the prospective jurors as a group to determine whether any prospective juror has knowledge of the subject matter, the parties, their attorneys or the prospective witnesses. A response from a juror that requires further elaboration may be the subject of further questioning of that juror by counsel on an individual basis. Counsel may exercise challenges for cause at this time.

(19) After the general questioning has been completed, in an action with one plaintiff and one defendant, counsel for the plaintiff initially shall question the prospective jurors, followed by questioning by defendant's counsel. Counsel may be permitted to ask follow-up questions. In cases with multiple parties, questioning shall be undertaken by counsel in the order in which the parties' names appear in the caption. A challenge for cause may be made by counsel to any party as soon as the reason therefor becomes apparent. At the end of the period, all challenges for cause to any prospective juror on the panel must have been exercised by respective counsel.

(20) After challenges for cause are exercised, the number of prospective jurors remaining shall be counted. If that number is less than the total number of jurors to be selected (including alternates, where non-designated alternates are being used) plus the maximum number of peremptory challenges allowed by the court or by statute that may be exercised by the parties (such sum shall be referred to as the "jury panel number"), additional prospective jurors shall be added until the number of prospective jurors not subject to challenge for cause equals or exceeds the jury panel number. Counsel for each party then shall question each replacement juror pursuant to the procedure set forth in paragraph 3.

(21) After all prospective jurors in the panel have been questioned, and all challenges for cause have been made, counsel for each party, one at a time beginning with counsel for the plaintiff, shall then exercise allowable peremptory challenges by alternately striking a single juror's name from a list or ballot passed back and forth between or among counsel until all challenges are exhausted or waived. In cases with multiple plaintiffs and/or defendants, peremptory challenges shall be exercised by counsel in the order in which the parties' names appear in the caption, unless following that order would, in the opinion of the court, unduly favor a side. In that event, the court, after consulting with the parties, shall specify the order in which the peremptory challenges shall be exercised in a manner that shall balance the interests of the parties.

An attorney who waives a challenge may not thereafter exercise a peremptory challenge. Any Batson or other objections

5

shall be resolved by the court before any of the struck jurors are dismissed.

(22) After all peremptory challenges have been made, the trial jurors (including alternates when non-designated alternates are used) then shall be selected in the order in which they have been seated from those prospective jurors remaining on the panel.

(23) The selection of designated alternate jurors shall take place after the selection of the six jurors. Counsel shall select designated alternates in the same manner set forth in these rules, but with an initial panel of not more than 10 prospective alternates unless otherwise directed by the court. The jury panel number for designated alternate jurors shall be equal to the number of alternates plus the maximum number of peremptory challenges allowed by the court or by statute that may be exercised by the parties. The total number of peremptory challenges to alternates may be exercised against any alternate, regardless of seat.

EXAMPLE 3-2: CIVIL VOIR DIRE QUESTIONNAIRE

CIVIL VOIR DIRE QUESTIONNAIRE UCS 137 (12/94)

YOU HAVE BEEN SELECTED TO SERVE AS A PROSPECTIVE JUROR IN A CIVIL CASE. THIS QUESTIONNAIRE IS DESIGNED TO ASSIST COUNSEL AND THE COURT IN SELECTING FAIR AND IMPARTIAL JURORS. PLEASE ANSWER ALL OF THE FOLLOWING QUESTIONS ON THE FORM: HOWEVER, IF THERE IS INFORMATION THAT YOU WOULD PREFER TO KEEP CONFIDENTIAL, INDICATE ON THIS FORM THOSE QUESTIONS AS TO WHICH YOU WOULD LIKE TO SPEAK PRIVATELY TO THE ATTORNEYS OR JUDGE. THE QUESTIONNAIRE IS IN FOUR PARTS. PLEASE PRINT FIRMLY. THANK YOU FOR YOUR COOPERATION.

1. Name____________________

2. Current town/village or geographical area (neighborhood)____________________

3. How long have you lived at your current address?____________________

4. How long have you lived in this country?____________________

5. Years of education or highest degree obtained____________________

6. Occupation (list most recent occupation first)____________________

7. Are you presently employed?__________ And if so, by whom?__________

8. Occupation of other members of your family, including children and their spouses.

   ____

9. Gender and ages of children, ____________________

10. What are your hobbies or recreational activities? ____________________

11. Have you ever served on a state or federal grand jury? ________yes ________no

    Have you ever served on a state or federal trial jury? ________yes ________no

    If yes, state type of case (criminal or civil)____________________

    Did case reach a verdict? ________yes ________no

12. Most recent date of jury service____________________

13. Have you, any relative or close friend ever:

    a. Sued anyone or made a claim for personal injury or property damage? ______yes ______no

    b. Been sued by anyone? ______yes ______no

14. If you were involved in a suit or claim, was it resolved to your satisfaction?__________

AFFIRMATION

I AFFIRM THAT THE STATEMENTS MADE ON THIS QUESTIONNAIRE ARE TRUE AND I UNDERSTAND THAT ANY FALSE STATEMENTS MADE ON THIS QUESTIONNAIRE ARE PUNISHABLE UNDER LAW.

____
Signature of Prospective Juror

Dated:____________________

1. Judge 2. Counsel 3. Counsel 4. Juror's Copy

EXAMPLE 3-3: OUTLINE OF REMARKS IN VOIR DIRE

1

A. PARTIES AND ATTORNEYS

1. PRINCIPE – KDTDM + R. ENG
   rg. JESSICA REINGOLD + MRS. DIANA R.

OBS. 2. MICAH McDOLE – M. + SHERMAN, P.C.
   r. RANDY DUNLOP – MURPHY + McNIECE

3. MARONITE HOSPITAL
   SHEILA BROWNE + JODY McCARTNEY
   r. TODD LESTER – STOWELL + CALENDAR

2

B. CONTENTIONS

1. BRAIN DAMAGE – UMBICAL CORD SQUEEZED

2. McDOLE'S MED. MALP.
   a. DIAGNOSE POSITION
   b. SCHEDULE CAESARIAN
   c. CHART TO HOSPITAL
   d. REPORTING – LABOR

3. HOSPITAL AND RESIDENT'S MED. MALP.
   a. RIGHT FETAL MONITORING MACHINE
   b. IMMED. C. – NO FETAL HEART BEAT

4. DAMAGES: BILLS, CARE, P+S, INCOME

3

C. WITNESSES

1. OBS. - SUSAN FOGARTY + STACY MITCHELL

2. TOX. + PED. - MARK THOMAN

3. NEUR. - MATTHEW TORRES

4. NURSES - NORA RODNEY, BETTY FITZGERALD, EDITH BELLASCO

5. DEFENDANTS

The Bifurcated Trial 4

4.1 THE JUSTIFICATION

The general rule in actions for negligence, other than in those for medical malpractice, is that the issues of liability and damages are tried separately. Only after there has been a finding of liability should the trial proceed to the issue of damages. There are three reasons for this rule: first, it saves time to try liability alone — if there is none; second, the issue of damages is irrelevant unless there is liability; third, it is prejudicial to a defendant to force the defendant to contest liability while the plaintiff parades his or her damages before the jury in order to evoke its sympathy.[1]

4.2 THE SUMMARY OF THE RULES

Rule 202.42 of the court rules of the state of New York contains the provisions for bifurcated trials.[2] The trial court should order a bifurcated trial when that procedure will clarify or simplify the issues or will expedite the trial, and the issue of liability usually should be tried first. During the voir dire, the parties' attorneys may question the prospective jurors on the issue of damages, but the attorneys should

1. Scott v. Pershing Constr. Co., 112 A.D.2d 279, 491 N.Y.S.2d 725 (2d Dep't 1985). If a party objects to a bifurcated trial, the party must make a timely objection, or else waive that right. Sanchez v. Kato, Inc., 115 A.D.2d 646, 496 N.Y.S.2d 482 (2d Dep't 1985); Gee v. New York City Transit Auth., 135 A.D.2d 778, 522 N.Y.S.2d 890 (2d Dep't 1987).
2. 22 N.Y.C.R.R. § 202.42.

not discuss this issue during their opening statements. If the jury subsequently finds the defendant to be liable, then the parties' attorneys may make supplemental opening statements before presenting their evidence regarding damages. Once again, if the jury does find liability, either in favor of the plaintiff on the plainyiff's claim or in favor of the defendant on a counterclaim, then the same judge and jury should try the issue of damages immediately unless the presiding judge finds this procedure impractical.

4.3 WHEN A BIFURCATED TRIAL IS INAPPROPRIATE

A bifurcated trial makes sense as long as the issues of liability and damages are truly distinct. There are actions, however, in which the issues of liability and damages cannot be separated without impairing the rights of a party (i.e., the plaintiff) or in which evidence of the plaintiff's damages is relevant to the issue of liability. In such actions, the trial court would err by precluding the plaintiff from introducing evidence of his or her damages when contesting liability; that is, it would be an error to grant a defendant's request for a bifurcated trial.[3]

The appellate courts have had occasion to rule that granting a request for a bifurcated trial (or ordering one sua sponte) has been an error. Such cases usually involve proving the

3. Scott v. Pershing Constr. Co., 112 A.D.2d 279, 491 N.Y.S.2d 725 (2d Dep't 1985); Schwartz v. Binder, 91 A.D.2d 660, 457 N.Y.S.2d 109 (2d Dep't 1982); DeGregario v. Lutheran Medical Center, 142 A.D.2d 543, 529 N.Y.S.2d 903 (2d Dep't 1988). However, the trial court properly refused to grant the plaintiff a unified trial in Louise B.G. v. New York City Board of Education, 143 A.D.2d 728 (2d Dep't 1988), and the trial court properly refused to allow evidence of the plaintiff's injuries during the liability phase in Fetterman v. Evans, 204 A.D.2d 888 (3d Dep't 1994). *See also* Stanford v. Resler, 206 A.D.2d 468 at 469 (2d Dep't 1994), a case involving an auto accident, in which the court wrote, "It is only where the nature of the inju-

force of an impact or the intent of a touching. Several examples will elucidate the courts' approach.

1. When the speed of the vehicles involved in a two-car collision was in controversy, "the exclusion of evidence of injuries to passengers . . . was reversible error in that such evidence had a direct bearing on the force of the impact and the relative speeds of the vehicles involved."[4]

2. When a pedestrian had been hit by a car, it would have been an error to deny to the plaintiff the right to introduce evidence of her injuries and their extent since the "personal injuries she sustained and the severity of the impact were inextricably intertwined."[5]

3. When the plaintiff claimed that the defendant had pushed him intentionally, but the defendant argued that he only meant to push the plaintiff aside gently, "the severity of plaintiff's injury is relevant to the issue of liability, in that such evidence would aid the jury in determining the force of the blow to plaintiff's mouth and whether defendant's conduct was reasonable under the circumstances."[6]

4. When the plaintiff had been hit by the defendant's motorcycle, and the plaintiff claimed that the defendant had been driving very fast, but the defendant claimed that he had not been driving fast, the "nature of the injuries has an important bearing on the issue of liability."[7]

---

ries has an important bearing on the issue of liability that a joint trial on both issues should be held." The court allowed medical evidence of the plaintiff's resulting amnesia only.

4. Bennetti v. New York City Transit Auth., 22 N.Y.2d 742, 239 N.E.2d 215, 292 N.Y.S.2d 122 (1968).
5. Naumann v. Richardson, 76 A.D.2d 917, 429 N.Y.S.2d 259 (2d Dep't 1980).
6. Jacobs v. Broidy, 88 A.D.2d 904, 450 N.Y.S.2d 586 (2d Dep't 1982).
7. Costa v. Hicks, 98 A.D.2d 137, 470 N.Y.S.2d 627 (2d Dep't 1983).

5. When the defendant argued that the plaintiff's alleged injury was not real or was being exaggerated, then the trial court erred by precluding the plaintiff from offering evidence of the extent of these injuries. The appellate court explained,

> The trial court erred in refusing to permit introduction of evidence of injuries to rebut defendants' claim that plaintiff received no injuries. Although this evidence was offered during the liability phase of the bifurcated trial, such evidence is nonetheless admissible where the nature of the injuries has an important bearing on the issue of liability . . . . At bar, once defendants offered evidence that no accident had occurred, evidence of an injury was a necessary part of plaintiff's case on liability and, thus, plaintiff should have been permitted to offer such evidence . . . .[8] (Citations omitted.)

In other words, although the trial formally might be bifurcated, the plaintiff may have occasion to introduce evidence of his injuries through the back door, i.e., as rebuttal evidence.

6. The plaintiff's right may go beyond offering evidence of his injuries in rebuttal and include a unified rather than a bifurcated trial. For example, in *Lynch v. Nacewicz*,[9] the Appellate Division, Second Department, ruled that the trial court had erred in denying the plaintiff's request for a unified trial. The plaintiff alleged that he had been attacked by the defendant's dog, and the appellate court noted, "proof regarding the nature, extent and gravity of the injuries sustained has an important bearing on the issue of liability insofar as it is relevant to the jury's assessment of the dog's propensities."

---

8. Scott v. Pershing Constr. Co., 112 A.D.2d 279, 280, 491 N.Y.S.2d 725, 726 (2d Dep't 1985).
9. Lynch v. Nacewicz, 126 A.D.2d 708, 511 N.Y.S.2d 121 (2d Dep't 1987), and Hayden v. Sieni, 196 A.D.2d 572 (2d Dep't 1993).

What has been said about the relevance of plaintiff's injuries is equally applicable, of course, to the defendant's injuries on a counterclaim. Moreover, it is conceivable that a defendant would be entitled to show that the plaintiff's injuries were slight in order to dispute liability, e.g., on the issue of the propensity of a dog.[10]

10. *Id.*

The Opening Statement 5

This chapter consists of two parts: advice on composing the opening statement and a sample of an opening statement. Some readers may object that this advice is not germane to a textbook on evidence, but those readers are wrong. The reader can best understand the rules of evidence in the context of their use, and the attorney delivering an opening statement is using those rules because he or she has based the speech on that evidence which he or she knows to be available and admissible. We sometimes speak of imposing an organization on the evidence, but the organization should arise from the evidence. Moreover, the arguments must be justified by the evidence. The attorney should not expect to prove every little thing he or she says in the opening statement. (As Emerson observed, "foolish consistency is the hobgoblin of little minds.") However, the objective is a correspondence between the claim and the proof. The attorney should be able to achieve this correspondence because formulating the opening statement is the final task before the trial.

5.1 APPLYING THE CANONS OF RHETORIC

Delivering an effective opening statement requires skill and preparation. However, nothing about the process is mysterious. Man has known the canons of rhetoric since ancient

Greece. While there is no definitive list of these canons,[1] speakers usually begin their preparation by analyzing six factors: occasion, setting, audience, purpose, subject, and speaker. The four possible purposes are to persuade, inform, entertain, or inspire. Thus, the attorney who will deliver an opening statement can begin his preparation by analyzing the six factors.

1. Occasion: trial of an action for negligence, medical malpractice, etc.
2. Setting: courtroom
3. Audience: jury primarily, judge secondarily
4. Purpose: persuade primarily, inform secondarily
5. Subject: auto accident, brain damaged baby, etc.
6. Speaker: the particular attorney

Naturally, in the course of his preparation, the attorney will make each of these factors more definite. For example, the audience will become the sitting judge or a juror who is exhibiting hostile body language, and the purpose could become to persuade the jury that the amniotic fluid was stained with meconium when the bag of waters ruptured.

Having determined these six factors, the speaker then must determine the mode of discourse and the tone. The four modes of discourse are argumentation, exposition, narration, and description. In the typical action for negligence or medical malpractice, the best mode is narration with frequent interruptions for the exposition of technical terms or concepts as they arise. The attorney also may refer to witnesses or documents as the sources of the facts in the narration. His or her tone, of course, should be conversational but

---

1. For example, Fluharty and Ross list the six initial factors as occasion, audience, speech, response, symbolic medium, and speaker. GEORGE W. FLUHARTY and HAROLD R. ROSS, PUBLIC SPEAKING (New York: Barnes & Noble 1966), p. 8. For a pithy exposition of rhetoric in one volume, see EDWARD P.J. CORBETT, CLASSICAL RHETORIC FOR THE MODERN STUDENT (New York: Oxford Univ. Press, 1965).

serious. In another kind of action, an antitrust action for example, exposition may be a better mode of discourse for the opening statement. Moreover, the facts of the case and the experience and personality of the attorney will influence this choice.

One facet of the law forces the attorney to separate form from intent in his analysis. Traditionally, the attorney is not supposed to make arguments during the opening statement. Instead, he or she should outline for the jurors the evidence which they are about to hear.[2] Of course, the attorney's purpose remains persuasion, and the skilled attorney can work within this restriction. Consequently, the opening statement is a persuasive speech disguised as an informative one; that is, the speech is persuasive in intent but narrative in form, thus conforming to the expectations of the judge but influencing the jury. The attorney composes the narration so that the events suggest the conclusion.

5.2 ORGANIZING THE OPENING STATEMENT

The opening statement for the plaintiff in an action for negligence or medical malpractice usually has four main divisions: the introduction, the principal narration regarding liability, a shorter narration or exposition regarding damages, and a conclusion. The introduction contains certain stock elements including the greeting to the court and the jury, the attorney's identification of him- or herself, his introduction of the plaintiff, and an explanation of the purpose of the opening statement.

The narration of events leading to liability is by far the longest division of the speech; therefore, the attorney must create coherent subdivisions — usually stages in the narration interrupted by explanations. (These stages constitute an example of the organization arising from the evidence.) While the attorney probably will not number these divisions for the jury, he or she should signal the resumption of

2. This rule is, of course, honored as much in the breach as in the observance, and CPLR 4016 does not make this distinction between an opening statement and a summation. However, a lawyer who went beyond telling the jury the facts he intended to elicit would be guilty of relying on matters not yet in evidence.

the narration in some fashion, e.g., by referring to the time of the next event. Besides the narration per se, the attorney will define terms, explain processes, use figurative analogies, point out duties and standards of care, and charge breaches of duty or departures. This narration should carry the plaintiff beyond the accident or the crisis to the result. While anyone with a penchant for purple prose must learn restraint, the attorney should recognize and exploit the fact that he or she is describing a serious human drama with a plot and characters. The plot has development, a crisis, and a resolution, and the characters have personalities, faults, and emotions. Therefore, the attorney's diction and choice of language should be vivid. He or she must lead the jury to visualize the events and to empathize with the client.

The division regarding damages will be considerably shorter than the one regarding liability and may be either narrative or expository. The attorney should begin with a brief description of the plaintiff's injuries and then proceed to an even briefer consideration of monetary damages without mentioning an actual amount. Save the thorough description of the injuries for their emotional impact during the testimony, and save the drier matter of monetary damages for the economic expert. The more catastrophic the injuries, the more the attorney should let them speak for themselves.

The opening statement ends with the conclusion. A conclusion is not a summary, although the conclusion may contain a summary. Instead, a conclusion reaches some resolution or directs some action. In the conclusion to an opening statement, the attorney should urge the jurors to listen to the evidence and to make up their own minds: he or she is confident that a fair hearing will produce a verdict for the client. If the attorney can add some relevant and imaginative remark, he or she should do so. However, do not delay writing the body of your speech while agonizing over your inability to find a clever introduction or conclusion.

The appropriate device will occur to you in time as you work on the speech.

Finally, a few words about composition are in order. It goes without saying that the attorney should speak extemporaneously either from a brief outline or without notes. Do not read the speech from a text (that would require more skill, not less), or deliver the speech verbatim from memory (that would require even more skill). However, this advice does not mean that the attorney should not draft a detailed outline or even a text, nor does it mean that he or she should not practice the speech until the phrasing becomes precise. On the contrary, the attorney should use whichever written or mnemonic devices needed to produce a polished, confident performance. Therefore, in the course of preparation, the attorney may draft several detailed outlines, compose key sentences or even a text, practice the text, revise it as feels comfortable, extract a new outline, and keep reducing the outline. The attorney should not attempt to deliver a text from memory, but should find that he or she could deliver the opening statement in his or her sleep.

5.3 PARTICULAR INJUNCTIONS FOR OPENING STATEMENTS

5.3.1 Content

1. Review only the key events in the drama. At the beginning of the trial, the jury will not be able to absorb the mass of information you have absorbed during months of preparation. Therefore, in the opening statement, you must provide the jury with the outline to which the testimony will add the details.
2. Describe your client's injury accurately. Never overstate it: you would do better to understate it. The jurors

will treat your failure to prove your inflated claim as a failure to prove your client's claim.

3. Mention the names of the witnesses and the parties. Dale Carnegie recommended this simple device to enable the listener to visualize the event and to reassure him that the speaker is telling the truth. If relevant, mention scientific tests and depositions, but do not go into detail.
4. Mention inconvenient facts. Even the worst obstetrical staff does not do everything wrong. In your opening statement, mention those relevant acts which the defendants performed properly but without actually praising the defendants. This ploy will take the sting out of your opponent's allegation of these facts and will convince the jurors of your integrity.
5. Say only a few words about the damages. To expand on your client's injuries during the opening statement is to forfeit their emotional impact later in the trial, i.e., closer to the verdict. Content yourself with giving the jurors the sequence of the events which caused the injuries and a brief indication of their nature.
6. Refrain from asking the jurors for a particular amount of money. Such a figure will not mean anything to the jurors at this stage of the proceedings. In addition, the amount will sound excessive because the jurors will have no idea of the financial burden on the plaintiff. However, tell the jurors that you are not suggesting a figure now but will do so after they have heard the evidence.

5.3.2 Technique and Delivery

1. Walk away from the podium. Move around. Bodily movement will animate your delivery, hold the attention of the jury, and signify your confidence. Leave

your notes, however, in a convenient place where you can refer to them.

2. Use a brief outline of notes as cues to yourself. It would be best if you could speak in an organized and articulate fashion without notes, but such an attempt is unrealistic for most people. Even if you could speak without notes, you should have a brief outline available in case you need it.
3. Make eye contact with every juror. Remember that you are trying to persuade these people and that they are judging you as well as your client. Do not speak directly to only one or two jurors: the others might take offense.
4. Use figurative analogies to explain technical concepts. You cannot teach the jurors medicine or engineering, but the jurors can grasp the gist of the case. For example, compare an aneurysm to a bubble in a tire or a congestive heart failure to a pumping system that has backed up.
5. Explain what you mean without using the demonstrative evidence. Visual aids have a limited place in public speaking.[3] Too often a speaker uses a visual aid as a substitute for forcing himself to formulate his thoughts precisely. How many times have you been bored by a lecture that was really a slide show? When preparing any speech, work until you can explain what you mean without using visual aids, then add visual aids grudgingly. During the opening statement, the jurors are not ready to comprehend the demonstrative evidence, e.g., an anatomical chart, and the attorney rarely should find it necessary to inflict this evidence on them.

3. Professor Seth C. Hawkins of Southern Connecticut State University, the founder of the collegiate circuit in individual events, always prescribed this rule for his tournaments: "Visual aids are permitted but should be neither the organizing principle nor the raison d'etre of the speech." He would also reserve to himself the right to confiscate, pulverize, or eat, as appropriate, any visual aids.

5.4 A SAMPLE OPENING STATEMENT

The following transcript is the opening statement from an actual case, an action for obstetrical malpractice. We have reproduced this speech for two reasons: first, an example will help the reader to grasp the advice we have already given him, and, second, the references to the sources of the facts will demonstrate that admissible evidence must support nearly everything the attorney says. Consequently, we have added three features to the transcript. First, we have made explicit the organization inherent in the speech. Second, we have indicated in parentheses the sources of the evidence which will support each statement. (Note that the general term, expert, means one of several experts, even the defendant.) Third, we have inserted comments about the intent of the speaker.

I. INTRODUCTION

A. The Greeting

MR. MOORE: May it please the Court, Judge Corns, counsel, Kim, ladies and gentlemen of the Jury. This is, as His Honor has just told you, the opportunity that I get representing the Plaintiff in this case to outline for you the proof that we intend to show during the course of this trial. It is really and in its very conception devised to be an aid, as His Honor has already told you, for you, members of the Jury, who are going to follow this case over several weeks. By the nature of human endeavors, that will be piecemeal.

So, this opening statement will give you ahead of time: the picture on the back of the box (as His Honor said) — the roadmap (as I've heard it alluded to at other times) — so you know where we are going and, particularly and most importantly, where each side intends to go during the course of this trial.

COMMENT

This is the introduction to the introduction. It familiarizes the jurors with the purpose of the opening, making them comfortable with the format.

B. Introduce the Plaintiff

Now, you have heard that Chastity Brewer is a severely incapacitated four-year-old child, and I think it is appropriate to begin my opening remarks by first stating something patently obvious to all of you. That is, any time a child is damaged is a tragedy. But that is not the reason that you are here, that this trial is commencing and that this litigation has been going on for several years. The reason is that, as devastating and terrible as these injuries are, we will show you in the course of this trial that they were preventable, that they never should have happened, that Chastity Brewer should be a normal — and I say beautiful (which she still is as you'll see) — young child doing all the things that any four-year-old could do.

COMMENT

This is to let the jury know that we are dealing with very grave injuries that were preventable.

C. The General Purpose of the Opening Statement

It is my purpose now to outline for you not only why I have said what I've just said, but how I intend to show during the course of this trial the truth of what I've said. I expect, and you have the right and duty to expect, that anything that I outline to you right now as my intention to prove, the Plaintiff will be held to. You will make no definitive judgments or decisions on anything at this time. I want you at the end of this trial when you deliberate on this case to consider whether I have lived up to any bargain that I have asked for in this case, and whether indeed proof has been shown consistent with the intentions that I am now setting forth for you. It is only if you find at the end of the case that the proof has been consistent with the positions of the Plaintiff that Chastity would be entitled to a verdict at your hands.

COMMENT

The judge has said that the openings are not evidence, and the defendants are likely to remind the jury that what plaintiff said during the opening is not evidence; therefore, we would like to make the point first: make it clear that the evidence will back up what you are about to say.

D. The Specific Purpose: the Plaintiff's Claim

You know, there is no mystery, medical or otherwise, as to why Chastity Brewer is as she is. Chastity has no genetic defect. Chastity has no congenital abnormalities in her face or any other part of her body. Chastity doesn't suffer from progressive brain damage in which there is no instrumentality that could possibly be involved other than some quirk of nature. Chastity suffers from anoxic encephalopathy. That is a technical phrase. "Encephalopathy": brain damage; "anoxic": caused by a lack of oxygen, and actually, literally, the cessation of oxygen.

We will show you that the most common cause of brain damage in full-term babies, which Chastity was, is a lack of oxygen around the time of birth. We will show you that in Chastity's case, the lack of oxygen around the time of birth was avoidable, that the mechanism of injury should not have been allowed to devastate her brain as it did. Now that, as I am sure you know, brings us to the care given Chastity and her mother prior to her birth.

COMMENT

Since many people believe that a child with brain damage may suffer from some innate defect, at a very early point we will tell the jury that such a cause has no part in this child's injuries.

II. The Narration

A. Mother Became Pregnant and Consulted Obstetrician

1. *First visit and calculation (Kim, office records)*

It was the first pregnancy for Kim and just briefly now, an outline of the prenatal — I am sure you are all familiar with that phrase, literally the prebirth — treatment of the mother and her baby.

January 14, 1983, was the first day that Kim saw obstetricians in this community, who at that time were Keller, Douglas, Cheshire, and Jackson, the professional service corporation herein called Frankfort. They, and particularly Dr. Jackson as you'll hear, during the prenatal course, undertook this case, which, of course, is an everyday, common occurrence in almost all women who are pregnant. By and large, and I believe there will be no disagreement to this, by and large, it was a "normal pregnancy." There was, as you'll hear, some question about the expected date of confinement, as they call it nicely, meaning the expected time that the child will be delivered.

No one in medical circles pretends that there is great exactitude to that concept. However, it is not considered just a guess either. There are parameters, and the most important, as I think you all know, is the last menstrual period, and there is a way of computing the expected date of confinement from the time of the beginning of the last menstrual period. We will show you that when Kim filled out the original form at the doctor's office under the heading "last menstrual period" she put down a question mark. We will show you that Dr. Jackson on the same date wrote in a date, November 25, 1982, and from that came up with an expected date of confinement of September 2, 1983.

COMMENT

As we tell the story of the plaintiff, we weave in the medical terms. This way, when the defendant is the first witness, and uses medical terms, the jury already has some working knowledge of them.

2. *Critical event: sonogram (Kim, office record, technician)*

We will show you, however, that on March 31, 1983, a test was performed on Kim called a sonogram, which is a sonic, or sound-based, system for visualizing the baby in the uterus from which certain determinations can be made, one of which is a notation about the maturity of the baby, how far along the baby is in terms of gestation. By that test, there was roughly a week's difference in terms of the gestational period. In other words, according to the sonogram, and, again, remembering there was not exactitude, but it is a system that has been devised and has been used commonly and is far more accurate in the early part of pregnancy than in the later part — we are talking here about March, not August or September — there was, based on the sonogram, an expected date of confinement about six days earlier than predicted. This will be of some significance, as you'll see in the course of the labor and decision-making in this case. Otherwise, there were the bimonthly visits and the monthly visits and the weekly visits, which I am sure you are all aware of and some of you have experienced yourselves.

3. *Critical event: gained weight (Kim, office record)*

One other important factor, not a complication per se at the time it was happening, but something that was indeed important in terms of obstetrical care, was the weight gain of Kim during this, her first pregnancy. There have been some questions in the examinations before trial — and by the way I think there were some allusions to the fact that obviously a lot has gone on in this case prior to our coming here to try the case. One of the things is that examinations before trial of all the parties have been taken, and testimony of various expert witnesses has been taken. So I probably won't refer to them as such again during the course of my opening statement, but just to make you aware lest you wonder how I could possibly be privy to some of the information that I'll be mentioning, because it would be particularly within the domain of the defendants or their experts. Well, I have obviously had the opportunity to read these depositions, although I only conducted two of them.

COMMENT

The lawyer should tell the jurors how the lawyer knows many of the things he tells them during the opening. It might be through depositions, records, or other discovery. Tell the jury what your sources of information are in a general way.

a. Standard of care in 1983 (expert)

Now it is true, ladies and gentlemen, that obstetrical care and obstetrical knowledge have tended to de-emphasize the concept of weight gain during pregnancy. There was a time some years ago when it was considered to have a greater significance than it has today and, of course, particularly as it did in 1983 and that, of course, is what is going to be at issue. The standards and the appropriate knowledge and care that were available in 1983, that is what will be at issue in terms of medical decisions in this case.

b. Significance of weight gain (office and hospital records, Kim, expert)

Kim, we will show you, gained sixty-one and one-half pounds during her pregnancy. I mentioned that there was some question, by Dr. Keller for one, as to what her nonpregnant weight was. But there is, I believe, no real argument, nor can there be based on the records of the Defendants, that even though there is not a caption, "nonpregnant weight" filled in on the record, there is a number, 130, on the records that was written on January 14, and 130 is what her nonpregnant weight was. When she was admitted to the hospital on September 13, 1983, she weighed, according to the record again, in the hospital, one hundred and ninety-one pounds. The important significance of weight gain and its continuing importance in 1983, and even today, is that weight is a reflection of excessive fluid in the mother's system and can be evidenced by swelling of the ankles, hands, arms, face, neck, and torso of the would-be mother. All pregnant women will have some swelling. The question is the degree, and, therefore, what significance that degree may have. There is no question that this was something that did exist in this case in terms of the weight, and we will prove to you that there was certainly excessive swelling in Kim prior to the time of her labor. She will have the opportunity today to testify concerning her condition. Among other things, putting on shoes became a problem. Rings became out of the question, and, as time went on, her face became distorted because of the bloat, her neck area, her arms.

c. Definition of edema (expert)

So this was swelling, or as the physicians call it, edema, that was out of the ordinary, especially as the pregnancy progressed and as the time of probable or possible delivery came closer. Other than what I mentioned, as I say, it was an uncomplicated pregnancy. The type of pregnancy really that could have resulted, and sometimes does result, in a birth without the need of an obstetrician, without even the need of a medical doctor, general practitioner or otherwise, that could have happened — as some do — at home, because somebody didn't get to the hospital, or on the way to the hospital without complication. We all have heard experiences of backseat babies born without any problem.

COMMENT

Here we stress the normalcy of the pregnancy, other than the swelling. This supports that the baby was healthy prior to labor. Further, we contrast that health to the events during labor.

d. General duty of defendants (expert)

But, ladies and gentlemen, this pregnancy, and particularly this labor, turned out to be one that needed expert obstetrical care, one that would highlight why women go to obstetricians at all, one that would call for the knowledge and the experience of the people to whom she went for such knowledge and experience.

B. Mother's Admission to the Hospital

1. Misleading vaginal discharge (Kim, defendant, hospital records)

Four days before the 13th, on the 9th, which was a Friday evening, Kim had an experience of discharge of fluid, watery fluid, in the vagina, and she had gone to Lamaze classes and had been told that that was a warning sign, and, of course, the warning sign is that possibly the bag of waters, the amniotic sac that encases the baby during the period of gestation, had broken, and, therefore, she should go to the hospital. She went, but it turned out to be a false alarm. Dr. Douglas saw her at the hospital and determined that whatever it was that had come from the vagina was not amniotic fluid, and she was not in labor or apparently about to go into labor. There were some changes in the cervix, and I assume you know, the cervix is the opening of the womb through which the baby passes if it is going to be a vaginal delivery, but otherwise, an indication of imminent labor.

2. *Labor pains begin and mother admitted to the hospital (Kim, hospital records, expert)*

We were seven days past the expected date of confinement and almost two weeks past the date that the sonogram predicted. On the early morning of the 13th, Kim began to have labor pains, and she was in the minority of women that have the labor pains in the back. Some people may not have heard of that, but she had pains in the back, and they were, indeed, labor pains. The contractions were beginning. They were synonymous terms. Contractions would refer to the uterus contracting, which is nature's way of beginning to push the baby from the womb through the birth canal, and, eventually to delivery. The pains are the subjective awareness that a person has. Contractions, as everyone knows, are painful, and, even at the beginning, everyone is aware, and any woman that is having them is aware that she is having them.

That was about around 7:00 A.M. on the 13th. That was a Tuesday in 1983. She had been obviously expecting this day, and you will hear Kim describe the anticipation that she had looking forward to this day. Kim and her husband Mark arrived at the King's Daughters' Hospital here in Frankfort at around 8:00 A.M. According to the records, she was certainly in the hospital and in the examining room by

8:15. She was indeed in labor, and she was seen by Dr. Keller on that occasion.

3. *Identification of the doctors (Kim, office records, hospital records).*

Now just very briefly, there were about sixteen prenatal visits. On four occasions, Kim saw Dr. Douglas. On one occasion, she saw Dr. Keller. On all the other occasions, she saw Dr. Jackson. But she had been told that the fact she was seeing one particular physician almost all the time did not necessarily mean that that physician, namely Dr. Jackson, would be the one who would actually deliver the baby. Kim was aware of that. As it turned out, a physician who was in the hospital and who examined her, and who, as you will hear, was the primary care physician during the whole of this labor was not Dr. Jackson or Dr. Douglas but Dr. Keller.

COMMENT

At this point, we start to lay out the events that form the basis of the malpractice claims.

4. *Critical event: blood pressure (hospital record)*

Vital signs were taken, which are the basic signs of life in a human being, and one of them, as you all know, is blood pressure. The first vital sign taken of Kim, according to the hospital record at 8:15 A.M. on this morning, was blood pressure, and it was a blood pressure of 130/90.

That set Kim apart from the vast majority of women in labor in a hospital because 90 as a diastolic pressure of a woman in labor (the diastolic is the lower number, as you probably know) is considered too high. It is considered a sign of hypertension in the pregnant woman, and to an obstetrician it is a sign that something must be looked for that can be disastrous in the course of a woman's pregnancy, and that is a medical condition called pre-eclampsia. For years, it has bee known that there are three signs of pre-eclampsia. One is hypertension. Two is edema or swelling. And three is protein or albumin in the urine.

5. *Standard of care (expert, hospital records)*

Kim technically was pre-eclampstic at the time of this first vital sign. Now we are not saying that the diagnosis should have been made at that time because certainly another blood pressure would have to be taken. But there was a number in terms of the diastolic, coupled with her swelling, which had existed for several months and had gotten worse. The fact was that in the last week of pregnancy she had gained three and a half pounds. The last visit was a week before. She was one hundred and eighty-eight pounds according to their records, and as I told you, on admission to the hospital she was one hundred and ninety-one and a half pounds. But she was evidently suffering or evidencing an edematous or swollen condition.

6. *Departure re: blood pressure (hospital record, expert)*

At 9:10, fifty-five minutes later and at least forty minutes too long for the taking of another blood pressure, the blood pressure was repeated. I am talking about standards of care that should have been and were well known in obstetrical communities in 1983 to people, to obstetricians, board-certified like Dr. Keller, and to obstetrical nurses, such as were treating this patient at the hospital.

C. Failure of Diagnosis

1. Pre-eclampsia (hospital record, expert)

But in any event, at approximately 9:10 according to the record, another blood pressure was taken. The systolic (the upper number) was the same, 130. The diastolic was 110. By definition — according to the literature and the standards existing in obstetrics, not lawyer's talk or legalese, but in medicine and in obstetrics — by definition, a diastolic of 110 in a pregnant woman is the beginning of severe pre-eclampsia if it is coupled with one or both of the other signs.

COMMENT

Let the jury know that the standards you mention are not standards set by lawyers but are the standards of physicians and the medical profession.

2. Failure of diagnosis (expert)

We will show you that the swelling wasn't disappearing. This woman was diagnosable for surgery at 9:10 and should have been diagnosed as pre-eclamptic at that time, certainly as approaching a serious case or severe case of pre-eclampsia.

Why is pre-eclampsia an important concern in a woman in pregnancy? Because it can be devastating if it goes unchecked, for the mother and for the baby. The hypertension will cause a problem with profusion to all the vital organs of the mother and obviously, therefore, be deleterious to the mother, including the placenta, and, therefore, be deleterious to the baby.

You see, you will hear testimony during the course of this trial that a baby has a circulatory system, and the mother has a circulatory system, and they are separate. The blood that courses through the mother's veins and arteries is separate from the blood coursing through the baby's veins and arteries, and the mother does not transfer, and the reason for the placenta, and the reason the baby is nourished through the placenta, is that from the mother's bloodstream to the baby's bloodstream through the placenta, pass all the nutrients that the baby needs to grow and develop and thrive in the uterus. One of those essential nutrients is oxygen.

If there is a problem with profusion in the mother's circulatory system, as was well known in 1983 and as was well known long before, that can cause a problem with the supply of oxygen to the baby.

COMMENT

Since jurors often think that medicine makes great advances every year, stress that the principles referred to are not new but were basic and well known long before the events in the case.

3. *Further explanation re: oxygen (expert, hospital record)*

Ladies and gentlemen, as in all of us, the oxygen is borne by the bloodstream. But of course, there are no lungs involved in the baby. The whole mechanism of purification and giving of nutrients is given by the mother through her system, passed to the baby, and the blood gets to the vital organs, including the brain, without any use of lungs, without any breathing process.

We will show you that at 9:10 there was a blood pressure of 130, as I said, over 110. We will show you that at 10:25, seventy-five minutes, fifty-five minutes or even sixty minutes longer than any standard of obstetrical practice would have dictated, another blood pressure was taken. That was 140/110. The systolic alone had reached the point of a definition of hypertension.

Even a normal diastolic, 140, according to obstetrical textbooks, is considered the point of hypertension in a pregnant woman, and we will show you that during the course of this trial, and I don't think there is any great argument about it.

4. *Attending physician aware of events and another critical event: urine test (hospital record, nurse)*

Dr. Keller was aware of these events. Nurse Zopff, who was caring for Kim during the labor was aware of these events. At 10:25, nothing was given to the mother for pre-eclampsia, which unquestionably existed at that point. It wasn't really needed. No one needed to know it, but as a matter of act the third element, when only two are necessary for a diagnosis of pre-eclampsia, the third element became evident. They did a little urine test, and they found protein in the urine. She had at that point severe, or certainly the beginning of severe, hypertension. She had excessive edema. And now she had protein in her urine.

COMMENT

We stress how easy it would have been to diagnose the condition because the signs were so obvious.

D. Electronic Fetal Monitor

1. *Standard of care (expert)*

In 1983, it was very, very common to monitor a patient in pregnancy. As they say, to watch so that one could be warned. They had become somewhat sophisticated by that time, because, for about twelve years, there had been available in obstetrical communities, and by 1983, in almost every hospital dealing with obstetrics, something called an electronic fetal monitor, and I am sure you have all heard that phrase. Some of you may be more intimately aware of it and its mechanism than others.

But just very briefly, there was this fetal monitor, which had been a boon to obstetrics. It had been a tremendous breakthrough in obstetrics because all obstetricians knew for a long, long time that the baby had very little means of communicating with the outside world and had very little means of warning the outside world that he or she was in trouble. One of those few ways was the heartbeat of the baby. Before the electronic fetal monitor, the heartbeat was determined by listening to the abdomen of the mother and picking up the baby's heartbeat. Periodic osculation, as they say, listening. But it was an imperfect system at beast. A lot was unfortunately missed. No one could do anything about it. So continuous monitoring was hoped for, and when it was devised it was a tremendous breakthrough. But by 1983, it was not something that was on the periphery of development; it was a central part of everyday obstetrical care. Obstetrics had come a long way in a short time. One of the beauties, as a matter of fact, of human science and medicine is that developments do sometimes come quickly.

2. *EFM Attached (Kim, nurse, hospital records)*

Dr. Keller, or certainly the nurse, whether on Dr. Keller's orders or not, had attached a fetal monitor at around 9:10 A.M. Just very briefly, this was an external fetal monitor. A band is put around the mother's abdomen. It is attached to a machine and through a sound system — there are other ways of external fetal monitoring but this was a doppler or sound system (tachodynometer is the long word) — this machine can give a readout, not just periodically but constantly, of the fetal heart. It also picked up the contractions of the mother, because it was well known even prior to the fetal monitor that the most important time for knowledge concerning the fetal heart was during the contractions of the mother. One of the great problems of periodic listening was that it was almost impossible to listen while the contraction was going on. This was the central development of continuous monitoring, that it gave just as clear a readout during the contraction as it did when the contraction had subsided.

E. Summary of Missed Signs

1. Cervix dilated

a. Standard of care re: progress of labor (hospital record, expert)

At 10:25 — and I use that time because it is a point noted in the record, and I told you the vital signs at that point, I told you the awareness concerning the protein in the urine at that point — let me tell you about the progress of labor. Now the progress of labor is a concept and a phrase well known to obstetricians, and it is self-explanatory, I suppose. It means the progress, not just of the labor per se in terms of pains, but what is happening from the point of the beginning to the point at the end.

One way obviously that is most important in determining progress is the cervix, this opening that the baby is eventually going to have to pass through. What is happening in terms of the cervix? It is thinning out ("effacing"), which it is going to have to do? Is it widening? Is it dilating, which it is going to have to do because the whole baby is going to have to pass through it?

b. Critical event: cervix dilated (hospital record, expert)

Now, according to the record, at 10:25, the cervix was 90 percent effaced, working toward 100, so it was very, very close to full effacement. By the way, that had been the condition on the first examination at 8:15. It had widened the cervix two centimeters. Centimeters is what physicians use. That is what nurses use in obstetrics and have for years and years and still do. There are approximately two and a half centimeters in an inch. Generally, and this is not an exact concept, generally, ten centimeters is full dilation. Obviously, some cervixes are wider than others, but if a cervix is dilated approximately ten centimeters, that is considered full dilation, the widest it is going to be. That is by definition the beginning of what is called the second stage of labor, the first stage being from the onset of regular contractions up to that point, the second phase being from the widest part of the cervix at ten centimeters up to the birth of the baby, and then the third stage, from the birth of the baby to the delivery of the placenta.

COMMENT

In order for the jurors to understand many of the facets of the case, they must learn the medicine involved in labor and delivery. Here we explain the various stages of labor.

2. *Internal fetal monitor*

a. Standard of care (expert)

Available at King's Daughters' Hospital in 1983 and available, again, in almost all obstetrical hospitals or hospitals with obstetrical departments throughout the United States in 1983, was a further development in terms of the electrical fetal monitor called internal monitoring. The tremendous benefit that internal monitoring allowed over external monitoring was it was more accurate. It gave more important information as to what was going on. There is no question that the normal pregnancy with someone going into the hospital in labor leading to a point of delivery in 1983, in all hospitals, there was no need, barring some particular reason, to have more than the external monitor. There were certain reasons well known in 1983 to obstetricians where and when internal monitoring was not just something that was good to have because it gave more accurate information, but where if it was available, it was necessary to use it in accord with certain standards.

Internal monitoring was available at King's Daughters' Hospital. Could it be done? What does that refer to? A lead or an electrode has to be applied to the baby's scalp. We are talking about a baby presenting her head first, as over 90 percent of the babies do. The lead's attached to the baby's scalp leading to the machine and giving a more accurate readout of the heart rate.

The cervix had to be somewhat dilated before the physician could attach the lead to the scalp. There is no question in 1983 that any competent obstetrician should have been able to attach an internal electrode if the cervix was dilated two centimeters. As a matter of fact, it could have been done at one centimeter.

d. Departure (expert)

At 10:25, an internal electrode could have been applied, and, under the circumstances of this case as we will show you by competent medical proof, it should have been done. This woman was now a high-risk pregnancy, high-risk in terms of herself and in terms of the baby she was carrying. The physician was obligated, in accord with everyday accepted standards, not with anything out of the ordinary, but with the applicable mechanism available and the knowledge available to find out as much about the fetal heart as possible so that if, and I say only "if" at this point, any problems were occurring, they would be readily evidenced as early as possible so that means could be taken again to avoid possible injury to the baby. Unfortunately, the internal electrode was not applied at that time.

3. *Meconium*

a. Critical event: meconium (hospital records, defendant, expert)

At 11:00, according to the record, the bag of waters, which was still intact, was deliberately ruptured or broken by Dr. Keller. That was certainly an advisable thing to do at that point because under the circumstances of this case, it was important to find out if the amniotic fluid that would come after the bag of waters was broken was showing any signs of a problem with the baby. Indeed, when the bag of waters was broken, a green-colored substance came out with the amniotic fluid: meconium. Meconium had been passed by the baby. The mechanism of passing meconium by the baby with a vertex or head presentation was generally considered then — and still today — to be as the result of a lack of oxygen to the baby's brain resulting in physiological effects where the little anal sphincter would relax, and what is in the bowel of the baby be passed into the amniotic fluid. What is in the bowel of the baby prior to birth is not stool but meconium, usually dark green in color, a substance that has built up because of some swallowing by the baby. And babies do swallow amniotic fluid in utero, and hair and other substances will pass into the bowel of the baby and remain there and pass into the amniotic fluid if there is this relaxing of the anal sphincter. This is a sign, not a guarantee, that all is not well with the baby, well known in 1983. It was evident at 11:00 a.m., according to the record, because they say not only that the bag of waters had been broken but that meconium staining of the fluid was evident: a further element of risk in this pregnancy aside from the pre-eclampsia that I told you about already.

4. Internal fetal monitor

a. attached (hospital record)

b. enlarged copy of monitoring strip (hospital record, expert, defendant)

Any time that the internal electrode would be applied, to get to the fetal scalp you would have to break the bag of waters. So Dr. Keller did apply the internal monitor at that point. We will show you the monitor strips. Let me very briefly show you what we will be talking about in great detail during the course of the trial — it is really now just for purposes of illustrating, and I'm not going to go into detail — which is part of the fetal monitor strip. The heart rate is on the top, as some of you have probably seen, and the contractions [indicating], when they go up is when the peak of the contraction is reached, and then they recede. You see the great benefit it is. You can tell what is happening with the fetal heart relative to the contractions all along. That is the tremendous benefit of fetal monitor tracing.

COMMENT

We do not usually use exhibits during the opening statement. In this case, we referred to the tapes often during the opening and decided briefly to show the jurors one blow-up of the fetal monitor strip to aid their understanding.

c. explanation of fetal heart rate (expert)

Most importantly, when the internal electrode is applied, there is further and more accurate information given. A baby not doing well in the uterus will, almost invariably, give signs in terms of his or her fetal heart. Just very briefly, the normal fetal heart differs from the rest of our hearts in beats per minute. One hundred twenty to one hundred sixty is approximately the range of normal heartbeats in a baby prior to birth.

These can be monitored, but it is also important whether there are any decelerations or accelerations in the fetal heart that are inappropriate in terms of what is called the baseline, which would be the average fetal heart during a period of time.

d. standard of care (expert)

Now we will show you further that, aside from decelerations or accelerations, the most important concept in terms of fetal well-being, known in 1983, was the variability of the fetal heart and that is, as in all of us, the fact that the constant monitoring of a heart shows that there has to be, under normal circumstance, some variation. There is no constant 140. There is no constant in those of us beyond the stage of being a fetus, whether children, adolescents, or adults, there is no constancy with seventy or eighty. There are fluctuations in the normal fetal heart, and electrical monitoring makes this very, very clear.

e. departure

One of the reasons why at 10:25 the internal monitor should have been applied and why the internal monitor was such a development is that this most important concept of variability cannot be determined on the external monitor. I am not going to get overly technical at this point, but that was a well known concept in 1983. The sound system of picking up the fetal heart exaggerated the existing variability. Therefore, you could not make a proper determination on variability in the fetal heart from the external monitor. What do we see, ladies and gentlemen, however, when the internal monitor was applied at approximately 11:00 A.M.? We see that there was a reduction in the variability in the heart. Now this is evident to anyone trained to read fetal monitors. It would not necessarily be evident to a lay person. It would not necessarily be evident to anyone who had not got proper information and training on how to read a fetal monitor. But it was something that was of vital importance in terms of obstetrical care.

We will show you that when the internal monitor was applied, there was a reduction in variability. There were during the next fifty minutes or fifty-five minutes decelerations in the fetal heart. When you look at them, and if you looked without being educated or without being informed, these decelerations look rather minor: ten beats, maybe fifteen beats, reduction. A couple of times, lower decelerations, which ironically were not the important decelerations. It was the subtle decelerations that were the most common signs in terms of obstetrics and in terms of obstetrical knowledge. Not only was this baby evidencing a problem because of the passage of meconium, but it was evident that this baby was having ongoing hypoxia, ongoing lack of oxygen to her brain, during this period of time. That was evident on the fetal monitor strips, and it was evident by the subtle decelerations in the fetal heart.

f. causality (expert)

These subtle decelerations can be the most ominous sign of distress in a baby as a result of a lack of oxygen. The loss of variability or the reduction of variability is a sign that there is ongoing lack of oxygen. We will show you that there can indeed be lack of oxygen to a baby in labor, but the baby can be born and fortunately recover. The baby can have some signs of depression, be resuscitated by a capable person, maybe have some problems in the nursery or not, but go on to have no obviously discernible damage. The most crucial thing is the constitution of the baby. Some babies can withstand more deprivation of oxygen than others.

Some hearts are more capable of resisting disease than others. Some brains are more resistant to a lack of oxygen than others. The reserve of the baby is the critical thing.

g. departure (expert)

What a reduction of variability shows, and should have shown to the nurses and to Dr. Keller in this pregnancy and this labor, was that this baby was saying not only that she was suffering a lack of oxygen, but that her reserves were becoming dangerously low. That is the sign of lack of variability. That is why it is such an important concept.

Now the baby is saying hypoxia, lack of oxygen, yes, but something must be done very soon; my reserves are running out. The time of irreversible, permanent damage is approaching.

COMMENT

Here we translate the complex medical issues into the very understandable cry for help.

5. *Lack of medication*

a. standard of care (hospital record, expert)

Nothing was ever given to treat the pre-eclampsia, and I am not going to tell you that there is an absolute uniform notion in medicine and obstetrics about the precise treatments of pre-eclampsia, but in 1983, with a blood pressure of 140/110 and previous blood pressures of 130/110 and 130/90, there was one medication that was definitely called for. It was called magnesium sulphate. It doesn't do much for the hypertension. What it was mainly given for was prophylactically, as they say, because what can happen if pre-eclampsia goes unchecked is that it will become eclampsia. The woman will convulse and possibly die, and her baby with her. That never happened in this case.

b. causality (hospital record, defendant, expert)

The magnesium sulphate not being given was not a factor certainly in avoiding something that eventually happened. But ladies and gentlemen, it does indicate a standard of care and appropriate decision-making by Dr. Keller at some time after ll:00 A.M. on this morning. He said in his deposition, and I assume he will say from this witness stand, that it was his plan to probably treat the pre-eclampsia around l2:00, an hour later.

COMMENT

In the opening, we like to show not only the specific acts constituting departures that were the proximate causes of the injury but also a general lack of care in the management of the patient.

F. The Critical Events Accelerate

1. The defendant leaves the hospital (defendant)

Dr. Keller left Kim's side a few minutes after 11:00, according to his testimony. About five minutes later, Nurse Zopff gave Kim a shot of what is called Vistaril, which is a tranquilizer, not a very potent one. That was given what they called intramuscularly in the usual place and a good place to give something intramuscularly is in the buttocks of the patient.

Before Dr. Keller left, although the record is silent, he has testified under oath that he gave the following instructions to Nurse Zopff in words or in substance. He said, in words or in substance, continue to watch the patient, stay with the patient, monitor the blood pressure every ten to fifteen minutes (which by the way should have been happening from the moment the first blood pressure was taken), and watch the fetal monitor.

2. *Departure in leaving (expert, hospital record)*

He left and did not return until the most startling emergency occurred in this case a few minutes until 12:00. He went to his office, I think, at about 11:30. Before that, he was dealing with another of his patients in pregnancy. His office, you will be told, and I'll tell you myself, is a block or a block and a half away. Dr. Keller never should have left the labor area in the case of this woman in her condition — and it was a departure from basic accepted practice for him to do so, to go even to another floor of the hospital let alone to leave the building and go a half block or a block and a half away. The instructions that were given to Nurse Zopff were not complied with, not one of them — staying with the patient, monitoring the blood pressure every ten to fifteen minutes, and watching the fetal monitor. Not one of them was complied with. At 11:25, Nurse Zopff went for lunch.

COMMENT

This sequence, the physician leaving and the nurse going off to lunch, provides a poignant example of neglect.

3. *Departure from good nursing practice (hospital record, expert)*

Now nurses have to go to lunch like the rest of us, and they have their schedule, and it was probably a scheduled lunch approximately in terms of how long Nurse Zopff had been on and how long she expected to work that day, seven something to three something —11:25 is roughly in the middle. But she went to lunch under the circumstances of this case. Another nurse was available in the labor area, as you'll hear, a Nurse Henrietta Millich. Before Nurse Zopff went to lunch, she never gave any of the instructions, which she had not complied with in the first place in terms of the patient. She'd been given them by Dr. Keller, but she never communicated one of them to Nurse Millich.

COMMENT

This conduct compounded the negligence.

Do I have to say that there will be testimony that this does not comply with good, accepted, ordinary obstetrical nursing care? Nurse Millich did not know as much as she should have known because of what should have been but was not communicated to her. She was called into the labor room by Mark. Mark called the nurse because they were concerned that Kim's pains were not reducing. They were concerned that there was an ongoing contraction. Looking at the monitor with their uneducated eye, they saw that the monitor, in terms of the contractions, when it was reducing was not going down to zero. They figured that meant that it was a continuing contraction.

4. *Admission of adverse fact*

As a matter of fact, it doesn't necessarily mean that, as you'll hear. Nurse Millich in coming in made the correct determination that there was not what they call a titanic contraction, which would be a very ominous sign. There is no testimony, and there is no claim in this case that such existed.

5. *Critical event: reduction of variability (hospital record, nurse, expert)*

Nurse Millich came in, and there was a further thing evident on the fetal monitor. As I told you, these subtle decelerations had been evident when the internal electrode was applied. The loss of reduction of variability was evident. Those continued down to and including and beyond the time of Nurse Millich's visit. But furthermore, there was an even more ominous sign in the falling of the baseline of the fetal heart that became evident around the time of Nurse Millich's visit, around twenty or twenty-five minutes to 12:00.

6. *Critical event: mother left supine*

a. standard of care (expert)

The positioning of the mother in labor can be a most important fact and element in terms of profusion to the baby and the passage of blood and oxygen into the baby's blood.

Once you place the mother on her side rather than in the supine position, there can be a tremendous benefit in terms of the supply of oxygen, the profusion from the mother to the baby. This is because of one very, very important, basic fact, well known since the late 1960's, well known for about fourteen or fifteen years prior to Kim's being in labor on that day, a concept that was known as aorta caval compression. Ladies and gentlemen, just very briefly, the main vessel leading back to the heart is the vena cava. The pregnant uterus is heavy, and certainly in this case we were talking about a heavy pregnant uterus. When the mother is lying in the supine position, the uterus will rest on the vena cava and cause a problem with the blood going back to the heart, and it will also lean on the aorta.

Now that will in turn cause problems with the blood being sent out and, therefore, problems with profusion. It was basic in 1983 to be aware that pregnant women should not be allowed to labor indefinitely on their backs, and they should never be allowed to labor on their backs if there is any sign of compromise of the fetal heart.

Now when there is an external monitor, there is a problem. If you turn on the side, the band is not going to pick up the fetal heart that well. But there is no such problem when there is an internal monitor.

This woman should have been turned on her side to labor from the very moment that the signs were seen on the fetal heart monitor when the internal electrode was attached. It should have been ordered by Dr. Keller. Even if it wasn't ordered by Dr. Keller, as the time progressed and the fetal monitor was evidencing what it was evidencing, it was well known, aorta caval compression was well known to obstetrical nurses, and should have been well known to them.

b. departure (hospital record, expert)

This woman was never placed on her side during that period of time between 11:00 and 12:00 P.M. or almost 12:00 P.M., noon. Not placed on her side and not given oxygen. Why do you give oxygen? You give oxygen based on the reason that by oxygenating the mother's bloodstream, she will pass more oxygen to the baby's bloodstream and help the oxygenation of the baby, another basic resuscitative concept. When I say resuscitative, I am not saying that it has to be used only in the most drastic circumstances, but it was a basic tool available at the hospital and should have been available and certainly, based on what was seen on the fetal monitor, for the whole hour in question, it should have been done and absolutely should have been done based on what Nurse Millich saw on the fetal monitor at twenty-five or twenty minutes to 12:00.

Despite the fact that she was never told that this blood pressure needed to be taken every ten to fifteen minutes, that this monitor had to be watched constantly, and that a nurse had to stay with the patient, and by the way, we are not saying for a moment that an obstetrical nurse always has to stay with a patient. No. They come and go, check periodically, but that they should be alerted to problems or possible problems and that is what dictates action. What is appropriate in one instance is only appropriate because of the circumstances of that one instance and therefore not necessarily appropriate in other instances.

COMMENT

Since many of the jurors remembered their own deliveries or those of their spouses, we drew the distinction between what is not necessary if all is going well and what should have been done here because of the problems evident during labor.

G. The Crisis Arrives

1. *Critical event: baby's reserves of oxygen depleted (hospital record, nurse, expert)*

What I said earlier will be clear to you. This was a case that needed obstetrical expert care, nursing and physician.

At about five minutes till 12:00, according to the record, the reserves ended. This baby's reserves ran out, and the problems that had been occurring over these minutes and even hours, and problems that should have been treated and should have alerted the physicians and nurses, eventually came to culmination, and there was what they call a precipitous drop in the fetal heart. The fetal heart went from 140 as it is shown, or 130 on the fetal monitor, down to about 50 in one sharp drop, and you'll see that on the monitor tape. As a matter of fact, for a short moment, and I think you will be able to see this on the monitor tape, it went to zero. Then it came up again and continued at about 50 — an extraordinarily slow and dangerous fetal heart rate. The baby was in desperate straits. The husband ran out and called for a nurse. A resident came in. A call was put in to Dr. Keller. He came. Dr. Jackson, according to the testimony, was also in the office. He came. They performed an emergency caesarean section, and the baby was delivered at 12:17, according to the record, about twenty-two minutes after that precipitous fall.

2. *The crisis (expert)*

Ladies and gentlemen, time now has to be judged in seconds. We will show you from this record — although the experts that have been questioned by the Defendants, and I assume will testify at least through videotape in his case, have doubted the following proposition — I will show you during the course of this testimony that not only was this baby born in a lifeless condition with, of course, a heart not beating, but that that heart was not beating for minutes after and even ten to twenty minutes prior to birth. This baby whose reserves ran out, based on this obvious and precipitous fall at five to 12:00, the heart stopped around ten to twelve minutes after 12:00, and the baby had to stay in the uterus for another ten or nine minutes before delivery. A lack of oxygen brings about damage within five or six minutes. But what does it do to a baby who has been subjected to no oxygen for minutes or even hours prior to that time? What it does is cause permanent, irreversible brain damage — and that is what it caused to Chastity because the obstetrician, Dr. Keller, and the nurses did not see what should have been seen, did not determine what should have been determined, and did not make decisions that should have been made.

We will show you that if this baby could have been delivered even five minutes earlier, and certainly ten or fifteen minutes earlier, the damage could have been greatly reduced or even avoided. That is why minutes were so crucial in this case. That is why the ignoring of the signs and symptoms prior to five to 12:00 were so crucial in this case.

COMMENT

We knew that it was necessary to make the jury keenly aware that every minute that passed was crucial to the baby's well-being.

3. *Re-identify the defendants*

Now the nurses, of course, are the responsibility of the hospital. Dr. Keller is an attending physician and his own responsible party. They are Defendants in this case and those are the claims in general. You will have even more specifics during the testimony, but those are the claims against those Defendants.

4. *The crisis continues (hospital record, nurse, expert)*

This baby was born in this lifeless condition, with no heartbeat, with no breathing, with no muscle tone, with no reflexes, and with no color, the five basic signs used to evaluate newborn babies. This baby had none.

The baby had to get oxygen. Oxygen had been totally cut off for a period of over ten minutes. The oxygen that had been deprived subtly for minutes, even an hour or more, prior to birth had to be gotten to this baby, now into the lungs, because this baby was born and no longer getting oxygen from the mother. Now Chastity had to breathe on her own. Those lungs had to get oxygen so that that oxygen could be passed to the baby's bloodstream and so that the brain among the other vital organs of the baby could get this absolutely necessary nutrition.

5. *The complication of meconium (hospital record, nurse, expert)*

The first total problem to be dealt with was the fact that not only had there been meconium, that passage of the bowel contents evident at 11:00 A.M., but it became evident when they opened this woman's abdomen and opened the uterus to deliver this baby that there was further passage of meconium; that is, the baby had an ongoing reaction to the lack of oxygen and was passing further meconium.

That meconium is not only at this point an absolute sign of the distress that the baby has suffered, but it is a danger to the baby in and of itself, because babies, as I told you, do have breathing movements, and they also have swallowing movements. It is actually the swallowing movements that would explain the presence of the meconium in the bowel. But there are these breathing movements, even though the baby is not breathing and not using her lungs. There are these breathing movements in the uterus and if there is meconium, that meconium can go into the lungs and result in what is called meconium aspiration, which is a critically dangerous thing to a newborn and was existing in this baby.

6. *The crisis continues but the baby survives (hospital record)*

The baby had to be suctioned five different times to get this meconium out and to begin the oxygen. It took valuable seconds, over a minute, to do the suction before the oxygen could even begin, all because this condition was allowed to go on unchecked. At "five minutes of life," this baby had no signs of life. It was absent all of the five parameters of measurement of fetal well-being — tone, reflex, color, heart rate, and respiration.

At ten minutes of life, the only sign of life was a heart rate, and that heart rate was brought about by injecting epinephrine or adrenaline directly into the heart. They tried it in other ways, but it didn't work. At about nine minutes of life, according to the record, they had to inject it directly into the heart — a dangerous procedure, but necessary under the circumstances of this case. That got the heart finally beating. They were doing chest massage, which would circulate the blood, prior to that time, but that was the first time that the baby's heart beat on its own.

III. Subsequent Confirmation of Plaintiff's Version

A. Blood Test: Baby Severely Asphyxiated (laboratory results, expert)

Blood had been drawn after birth. The testing on the blood showed the baby was severely asphyxiated in the minutes prior to birth, severely asphyxiated in the minutes after birth, damaged irreparably around that time. We will prove to you not only that that is more likely than not, which is all the law requires, but is beyond any reasonable question medically or otherwise. This is when the damage to this baby occurred.

B. Diagnosis at Subsequent Treating Hospital (treating physicians)

Now, ladies and gentlemen, this child was transferred to the University of Kentucky Medical Center through its transport team, which uses actual helicopters to transport babies that need intensive neonatal care. There is no question those facilities were not available at King's Daughters'. At about a quarter to 3:00, some few hours after birth, the transport team arrived, and at approximately 3:30, about forty-five minutes later, they left with Baby Chastity. The child remained twenty-four days at the University of Kentucky Medical Center. Even though it apparently is going to be some kind of a very central issue in this case, not only in terms of importance, but in terms of whether it is true or not, the University of Kentucky Medical Center has diagnosed and did diagnose unequivocally that this child was suffering from anoxic encephalopathy, and that this anoxic encephalopathy was caused by asphyxia around the time of birth. That is replete in the University of Kentucky Medical Center record that you will see here in evidence.

C. Examination by Defendants' Expert as Properly Understood under Cross-Examination (witness, plaintiff's expert, test records, etc.)

We will show you that in November of last year, a few short months ago, pursuant to the order of Judge Corns, which was most appropriate, the baby was made available for an examination by physicians of the choice in this particular case of Mr. Rose's firm representing King's Daughters' Hospital.

The baby was flown down with Kim to Alabama, examined by a pediatric neurologist by the name of Dr. Chaleb, who I believe is going to testify in this case, and a test was performed on the baby called an MRI, a rather sophisticated test that tells a lot more about what the brain looks like than a normal x-ray. It is not done with radiation. It tells even more than what was developed after the x-ray, namely a CAT scan, which shows not just one view but several views of the brain. The MRI shows not only several slices of the brain in terms of viewing, but angles of those slices, and can give even more information.

Dr. Chaleb apparently is going to testify in this case that whether oxygen had something to do with this brain damage, infection also had something to do with this brain damage, and he can tell this from the results of this MRI. Ladies and gentlemen, please don't be confused. There was no question that at the University of Kentucky Medical Center, they were concerned about spesis or infection in this baby, but they were concerned about it because of the events just prior to and after birth. They were concerned about it, among other things, because of the meconium aspiration that had occurred — and they were correctly concerned about it, as even Dr. Parker was correctly concerned about it.

COMMENT

Because the defense was going to claim that prenatal infection was a contributing factor to the child's injuries, we directly attacked this defense during the opening. Then, when the defense does mention it, the defense will be challenged to overcome what we asserted against the argument.

But this child was never diagnosed as having an infection. She was given ampicillin and gentimycin for about ten days prophylactially, as she should have been, but she was never seen to have an infection. In any event, if she did have an infection at that time, I don't believe that is what Dr. Chaleb will be talking about, but I'll let him speak for himself. But most importantly, the MRI shows injuries most consistent with anoxic encephalopathy, with anoxia as the mechanism of injury.

IV. The Damages

A. The Baby's Injuries

1. Feeding (treating physician, medical records, Kim)

Just very briefly, Chastity is affected by her injuries in every facet of her existence. She has remained with Kim these years except for short hospitalizations, twice at St. Joseph's in Lexington and once at Humana in Lexington. She has been fed from the first year or so of life through a nasogastric tube, which goes through the nose into the — what they call nasal pharnyx, which would be the part of the throat that goes up behind the nose, then down the esophagus, which is the other tube leading down (other than the trachea) into the stomach. Kim was trained to do this at the University of Kentucky. She has been doing this all these years, except for about a year or a year and a half when the baby was being fed orally. But because the baby wasn't getting proper nutrition, Humana recommended that the nasogastric feeding be reinstituted, and it has been done for about the last year and a half, up to the present.

2. *Operating (treating physician, expert)*

However, it is most likely that the baby, even very soon, will need what they call a gastrostomy, and that is an operation which is an opening in the stomach that allows the feeding to go directly that way rather than via a nasogastric tube, because the baby's nutrition is still not what it should be. There are grave problems in regurgitation, vomiting, gagging. Kim has to constantly be with the baby. The baby can never be left alone for any period of time.

She has to be suctioned. The tube creates mucus and other material in the mouth that needs to be suctioned, and that otherwise can cause grave problems with the baby, Chastity.

3. *Mentally retarded (treating physician, expert)*

We will show you that the child cannot walk and will never be able to walk. She cannot talk, will never be able to talk. She is severely mentally retarded. But we will show you, and you will hear medical testimony — and maybe more importantly, Kim's testimony — of the awareness of this baby, of on the one hand, the way Chastity can suffer and feel all the difficulties and problems that she has, and on the other hand, how at other times, she can be delighted and happy and show it with a beautiful smile, especially in her mother's presence, which she is unquestionably aware of.

B. The Permanent Need for Care (various experts)

We will show you in terms of the damages in this case that, first of all, the child's life expectancy is severely truncated because of her injuries, but we will show you that that life expectancy is greatly dependent upon the constant professional care, and as wonderful as her mother has been and is — and you will hear it testified to — we are talking about professional, round-the-clock care. That care is necessary for this child because this child will always remain at home, will always remain with her mother as she has since her discharge from UK. We will show you that there will be constant need for therapies, which Kim has been trying to do, but obviously in a very nonprofessional way, physical therapy, speech therapy, even though she will never speak, she vitally needs therapies for her vocal system, very necessary to her health and well-being. She needs occupational therapy. She will never be gainfully employed, a very important element of damages that you have to grapple with in this case, and yet occupational therapy is necessary because it has nothing to with an occupation. It is a form of physical therapy, but different from physical therapy per se, very necessary to the baby and her well-being. We will show you there is ongoing medical care that is necessary and will be necessary, of course, over and above what would be necessary for a normal child, and that is what Chastity would be entitled to: what has been brought about as a result of these injuries and what the economic factors are in that regard are the areas of damages.

C. The Monetary Damages (expert in economics)

Primarily, and most importantly, if you decide to make an award in money damages in this case, which is the only award that can possibly be given, you will have to grapple with the devastation of what has occurred, is occurring, and will occur for the rest of the child's life. Chastity's condition is the result of this terrible damage occurring around the time of birth, but not recurring. The damage caused stays, and, therefore, the progress can only be limited, but there is no ongoing, recurring damage, and that is an important concept in terms of causation if — if — damages are appropriate in this case.

COMMENT

During the opening statement, hit only the major aspects of the damages. The details should come during the trial. Never exaggerate the damages.

What then will be appropriate damages for all this loss? That will be another important factor should you award money damages in your verdict. You'll notice I have not mentioned, nor did I in voir dire, specific sums. I want you to hear all the evidence. I want you to hear the medical testimony, the human testimony, and the economic testimony and then be in a position to award the damages that fit this case and only this case in the first place.

COMMENT

Although some lawyers advocate mentioning a dollar amount during the opening, we never have done so. The jury will be more amenable to awarding adequate compensation after hearing the evidence of the plaintiff's needs and their great costs.

V. CONCLUSION

Ladies and gentlemen, I obviously have a point of view, and Kim has a point of view. Do you know what? Our points of view representing this child are irrelevant. What we believe about this case is irrelevant, but what I tell you now is: I believe you should hear the evidence. I am confident that when you have heard all of the evidence in this case — and I urge you to keep an open mind until you receive the instructions of the judge and go out to deliberate in this case — I believe at that time, you will have more than sufficient information to give all sides a just verdict in this case. Thank you.

COMMENT

The jurors know that the lawyer thinks his side should win; therefore, it is not necessary to tell them that. Instead, show your confidence by telling the jurors to decide the case based on the evidence and that justice will be the result.

The Direct Case—Making a Prima Facie Case 6

6.1 THE BURDEN OF PROOF

6.1.1 In General

In an action for negligence, the plaintiff has the burden of pleading and proving, by a fair preponderance of the evidence, that the defendant was negligent[1] as well as the other elements of the cause of action: duty, damage, and proximate cause. The plaintiff need not plead and prove his or her own freedom from contributory negligence since New York adopted the comparative negligence rule on July 1, 1975.[2] On the contrary, if the defendant believes that the plaintiff's negligence was a cause of the accident, the defendant should plead and prove that negligence just as he or she would plead and prove a cause of action or an affirmative defense. Thus, the comparative negligence rule has absorbed what used to be an exception for actions for wrongful death, to wit: that the defendant had the burden of proving the decedent's contributory negligence.[3]

---

1. Schneider v. Kings Highway Hosp., 67 N.Y.2d 743, 490 N.E.2d 1221, 500 N.Y.S.2d 95 (1986). A plaintiff need not prove the exact manner in which the defendant was negligent. A plaintiff need only show the jury that the accident happened as a result of the negligence of the defendant even if the plaintiff cannot show exactly how the defendant was negligent.
2. C.P.L.R. art. 14-A, added by 1975 N.Y. Laws ch. 69, § 1.
3. EST. POWERS & TRUSTS LAW § 5-4.2.

Nevertheless, the mere fact that an accident happened does not mean that someone was at fault.[4] The plaintiff must prove that the defendant was negligent and that the defendant's negligence was the proximate cause of the plaintiff's injuries.[5] In an action arising out of an automobile accident, the plaintiff also must prove that he or she has met the so-called verbal threshold of serious injury as defined by the Insurance Law.[6] Failure to do so will force the trial court to dismiss the suit.[7] Finally, the jury may not speculate when there is no evidence from which to find for the injured plaintiff.[8]

The plaintiff does not satisfy the burden of proof by calling more experts or more witnesses than the defendant does. It is not the number of witnesses that counts but the credibility and relevance of their testimony.[9] Therefore, in *Torem v. 564 Central Avenue Restaurant, Inc.*,[10] the Appellate Division, First Department, overturned the judgment and held that the trial court should have charged the jury more carefully on the plaintiff's burden of proof:

---

4. Rella v. State, 117 A.D.2d 591, 498 N.Y.S.2d 63 (2d Dep't 1986).
5. Boltax v. Joy Day Camp, 67 N.Y.2d 617, 490 N.E.2d 527, 499 N.Y.S.2d 660 (1986) ("To establish a prima facie case of negligence, a plaintiff must show that the defendant's negligence was a substantial cause of events that produced the injury."); Derdiarian v. Felix Contracting Corp., 51 N.Y.2d 308, 414 N.E.2d 666, 434 N.Y.S.2d 166 (1980); Gayle v. Neyman, 91 A.D.2d 75, 457 N.Y.S.2d 499 (1st Dep't 1984).
6. Ins. Law §§ 5104(a) & (c), 5102(d).
7. Thrall v. City of Syracuse, 60 N.Y.2d 950, 459 N.E.2d 160, 471 N.Y.S.2d 51 (1983).
8. Birdsall v. Montgomery Ward & Co., 65 N.Y.2d 913, 483 N.E.2d 131, 493 N.Y.S.2d 456 (1985); LaPlatney v. Whitmor, 111 A.D.2d 1002, 490 N.Y.S.2d 320 (3d Dep't 1985); Friedman v. Sandy Sirulnick Realty Corp., 90 A.D.2d 479, 454 N.Y.S.2d 548 (2d Dep't 1982); Horne v. Metropolitan Transp. Auth., 82 A.D.2d 909, 440 N.Y.S.2d 695 (2d Dep't 1981).
9. Niewieroski v. National Cleaning Contractors, 126 A.D.2d 424, 510 N.Y.S.2d 127 (1st Dep't 1987).
10. Torem v. 564 Cent. Ave. Restaurant, Inc., 133 A.D.2d 25, 518 N.Y.S.2d 620, 622 (1st Dept. 1987), *modified to order new trial on liability*, 134 A.D.2d 158 (1st Dep't 1987).

> We find the instruction inadequate on its face (see PJI 1:23). Among other things, it failed to advise the jury (a) that it was the quality of the evidence, rather than the number of witnesses or the length of their testimony, that would determine what should constitute a preponderance, (b) what plaintiffs were obliged to establish to sustain their burden of proof, and (c) that if the evidence should weigh evenly, it would be the jury's duty to return a verdict for defendants.

6.1.2 The Reduced Burden of Proof

A line of cases in New York talks about the plaintiff's reduced burden of proof when he or she has amnesia or is deceased and, therefore, cannot testify to the events surrounding the incident in question.

6.1.2.1 Amnesia

This supposedly reduced burden of proof is applicable when the plaintiff is an amnesiac as long as the plaintiff proves the amnesia to the satisfaction of the court.[11] For example, in *Sawyer v. Breis & Krump Manufacturing Co.*,[12] the court of appeals reviewed the history of the reduced degree of proof required in a case in which the plaintiff alleged that he had amnesia.[13] The issue before the court was whether the plaintiff must introduce expert testimony to satisfy the burden of proof "by clear and convincing evidence" that the

---

11. Smith v. Stark, 67 N.Y.2d 693, 490 N.E.2d 841, 499 N.Y.S.2d 922 (1986); Rella v. State, 117 A.D.2d 591, 498 N.Y.S.2d 63 (2d Dep't 1986); Iannelli v. Powers, 114 A.D.2d 157, 498 N.Y.S.2d 377 (2d Dep't 1986); Smith v. Sullivan, 99 A.D.2d 776, 472 N.Y.S.2d 28 (2d Dep't 1984); Flynn v. Manhattan & Bronx Surface Transit Operating Auth., 94 A.D.2d 617, 462 N.Y.S.2d 17 (1st Dep't 1983), *aff'd*, 61 N.Y.2d 769, 461 N.Y.2d 291, 473 N.Y.S.2d 154 (1984).
12. Sawyer v. Dreis & Krump Mfg. Co., 67 N.Y.2d 328, 493 N.E.2d 920, 502 N.Y.S.2d 696 (1986).
13. *See* Schechter v. Klanfer, 28 N.Y.2d 228, 269 N.E.2d 812, 321 N.Y.S.2d 99 (1971); Noce v. Kaufman, 2 N.Y.2d 347, 141 N.E.2d 529, 161 N.Y.S.2d 1 (1957); Cole v. Swagler, 308 N.Y. 325, 125 N.E.2d 592 (1957); Jarrett v. Madifari, 67 A.D.2d 396, 415 N.Y.S.2d 644 (1st Dep't 1979).

defendant's acts caused the amnesia.[14] The court held that expert testimony is required to prove that the plaintiff has lost his memory, that the loss is real rather than feigned, and that the defendant's fault caused the amnesia.[15] In other words, the plaintiff must meet a higher burden of proof on the issue of the amnesia in order to obtain a reduced burden of proof for the action.

6.1.2.2 Death

Some cases also posit a reduced burden of proof when the plaintiff is dead and cannot testify regarding what transpired and there are no other witnesses to the occurrence. For example, in *Horne v. Metropolitan Transportation Authority*,[16] the decomposed body of the plaintiff's decedent was found at the bottom of a large pit. He last had been seen a month earlier, and there was evidence that the pit had not been barricaded properly, but there were no bruises on his body. Moreover, the defense presented expert testimony that acute alcoholic ingestion had caused the plaintiff's death and that any fall into the pit had been only a secondary factor. Nevertheless, the jury returned a verdict for the plaintiff. The Appellate Division, Second Department, affirmed the judgment and noted that in an action for wrongful death, when there are no surviving witnesses, the plaintiff has a lower burden of proof, and the jury may place greater weight on circumstantial evidence than in cases in which witnesses testify about how the accident happened.[17]

14. Schechter v. Klanfer, 28 N.Y.2d 228, 269 N.E.2d 812, 321 N.Y.S.2d 99 (1971).

15. Costa v. Hicks, 98 A.D.2d 137, 470 N.Y.S.2d 627 (2d Dep't 1983); Jennings v. State, 55 A.D.2d 745, 389 N.Y.S.2d 442 (3d Dep't 1976).

16. Horne v. Metropolitan Transp. Auth., 82 A.D.2d 909, 440 N.Y.S.2d 695 (2d Dep't 1981).

17. *Id.* at 910, 440 N.Y.S.2d at 696; *cf.* Wingerter v. State, 58 N.Y.2d 848, 446 N.E.2d 776, 460 N.Y.S.2d 20 (1983); Noseworthy v. City of N.Y., 298 N.Y. 76, 80 N.E.2d 744 (1956); Iannelli v. Powers, 114 A.D.2d 157, 498 N.Y.S.2d 377 (2d Dep't 1986); Vitale v. LaCour, 96 A.D.2d 941, 466 N.Y.S.2d 392 (2d Dep't 1983); Rivenburgh v. Viking Boat Co., 83 A.D.2d 625, 441 N.Y.S.2d 534 (2d Dep't

The same court formulated the classic statement of the reduced burden of proof in *Trimble v. City of New York*:

> In a death action the plaintiff is not held to as high a degree of proof of the cause of action as where an injured plaintiff can himself describe the occurrence. While the burden of proving defendant's negligence and the proximate cause of the accident still is on the plaintiff, those essential elements may be established by circumstantial as well as direct evidence. It is enough to show facts and conditions from which the negligence of the defendant and the causation of the accident by that negligence may be reasonably inferred; and in order to establish defendant's negligence plaintiff is not required to exclude or eliminate every other possible cause, or point out the particular act or omission which caused the injury.[18]

Although this case and others, such as *Noseworthy v. City of New York*[19] from the court of appeals in 1956, appear to reduce the plaintiff's burden of proof, several recent cases have held that that is not so. Under *Noseworthy*, the plaintiff's circumstantial evidence regarding the way in which the accident occurred is entitled to greater weight. Therefore, the court should charge the jury that the plaintiff must satisfy the burden of proof, but the charge should refer to the weight that the jury should accord the plaintiff's evidence on the happening of the event.[20] This greater weight applies only to the way in which the accident happened; it does not give the plaintiff a right to ask for such a charge on every issue.[21]

1981), *rev'd,* 55 N.Y.2d 850, 432 N.E.2d 600, 447 N.Y.S.2d 707 (1982); Horne v. Metropolitan Transp. Auth., 82 A.D.2d 909, 440 N.Y.S.2d 909, 440 N.Y.S.2d 695 (2d Dep't 1981); Abbott v. St. Luke's Hosp., 38 A.D.2d 176, 327 N.Y.S.2d 799 (4th Dep't 1972); Cappadona v. State, 156 A.D.2d 505, 548 N.Y.S.2d 778 (Ct. Cl. 1987).

18. Trimble v. City of N.Y., 275 A.D. 169, 171, 88 N.Y.S.2d 325 (2d Dep't 1949).
19. Noseworthy v. City of N.Y., 298 N.Y. 76, 80 N.E.2d 744 (1956).
20. Pederson v. Balzan, 117 A.D.2d 933, 499 N.Y.S.2d 239 (3d Dep't 1986); Oginski v. Rosenberg, 115 A.D.2d 463, 495 N.Y.S.2d 699 (2d Dep't 1985). Moreover, the court errs by refusing to charge the jury regarding the weight of the evidence. Manginaro v. County of Nassau, 172 A.D.2d 593 (2d Dep't 1991).
21. Greer v. Ferrizz, 118 A.D.2d 536, 499 N.Y.S.2d 758 (2d Dep't 1986).

It would probably be most accurate to say that the plaintiff's burden of proof is undiminished but that the trial court will expect the plaintiff to meet this burden in a different manner than if the decedent were alive, i.e., by circumstantial evidence rather than by the direct testimony of the injured party.

However, the Appellate Division, First Department, has made a different distinction, to wit: the plaintiff is entitled to a lesser burden of proof only if he is unable to relate the facts of the accident while the defendant is able. Thus, in *Lynn v. Lynn*,[22] the court held that the plaintiff's amnesia regarding her fall did not entitle her to a lesser burden of proof, and in *Wright v. New York City Housing Authority*,[23] the court held that the death of the plaintiff's decedent also failed to justify reducing the burden. The court wrote,

> Nor is the plaintiff entitled, . . . , to the benefit of a lesser degree of proof because this is a death case. . . . Unlike *Noseworthy*, where "no one except the motorman knew what took place . . . in that deserted subway station" . . ., the identity of the assailant in the instant case and in the manner in which he gained access to the building and confronted the deceased is, . . ., as unknown to defendant Housing Authority as it is to plaintiff.[24]

6.1.3 Duty

The plaintiff in an action for personal injury has the burden of pleading and proving:

1. That the defendant owed a duty of care to the plaintiff;
2. That the defendant breached this duty;
3. That the breach was the proximate cause of the plaintiff's injuries; and
4. That the plaintiff suffered damages.[25]

---

22. Lynn v. Lynn, 216 A.D.2d 194 (1st Dep't 1995).
23. Wright v. New York City Housing Authority, 208 A.D.2d 327 (1st Dep't 1995).
24. *Id.* at 332.
25. Elmlinger v. Board of Educ., 132 A.D.2d 923, 518 N.Y.S.2d 257 (4th Dep't 1987).

In the past several years, no area of the law of evidence has been as active as that of duty. Who owes a duty to whom? What are the boundaries of the duty? The number of cases is mounting, and we offer some insight into the issue with a sampling of appellate cases organized by subject and winning party. Reviewing these cases will give the attorney an appreciation of the concept of duty, which is a recognition by public policy that society believes that the law should impose liability.

6.1.3.1 Landowners

6.1.3.1.1 The Plaintiff

6.1.3.1.1.a Children

(1) *Holtslander v. Whalen & Sons.*[26] Foreseeability is an element of duty. If a defendant should foresee that his actions will invite children to play in the area and if it is foreseeable that they will get hurt if they do play there, then the defendant has a duty to protect these children from harm.

6.1.3.1.1.b Buildings

(2) *Thomassen v. J&K Diner Inc.*[27] The owner of a business and of the land upon which the business is located owes a duty to customers and to other members of the pub-

26. Holtslander v. Whalen & Sons, 70 N.Y.2d 962, 520 N.E.2d 512, 525 N.Y.S.2d 793 (1988), *aff'g* 126 A.D.2d 917, 510 N.Y.S.2d 937 (3d Dep't 1987). *See also* Cruz v. New York City Transit Authority, 136 A.D.2d 196 (2d Dep't 1988).
27. Thomassen v. J&K Diner Inc., N.Y.L.J., Jan. 4, 1990 (2d Dep't 1990). The court cited with approval Restatement of Torts § 422, which states:

> A possessor of land who entrusts to an independent contractor construction, repair, or other work on the land, or on a building or other structure upon it, is subject to the same liability as though he had retained the work in his own hands to others on or outside of the land for physical harm caused to them by the unsafe condition of the structure (a) while the possessor has retained possession of the land during the progress of the work, or (b) after he has resumed possession of the land upon its completion.

lic who are injured due to a defect in the construction of the building caused by an independent contractor — even after the contractor has completed the building and turned it over to the owner.

6.1.3.1.2 The Defendant

(3) *Iannotti v. ConRail.*[28] The recreational use statute (General Obligations Law section 9-103), which grants immunity from liability for ordinary negligence to owners of property who permit members of the public to come on their property to engage in one of several enumerated recreational activities, is applicable to property that — notwithstanding its contemporaneous commercial use — is a type of property not only physically conducive to the particular activity or sport but also appropriate for public use in pursuing the activity as recreation. The application of the statute to such property is an inducement to the owner to make it available to the public and advances the statute's purpose of opening lands to the public for the listed recreational uses. However, the injured party's engaging in one of the enumerated activities does not protect the landowner unless the property is also conducive to the sport and appropriate for public use.[29] Moreover, the landowner loses his protection if he created a hazard which caused the accident.[30] "Whether a parcel of land is suitable and the immunity available is a question of statutory interpretation, and is, therefore, a question of law for the Court . . . ."[31] Hence, in *Albright v. Metz*, the Appellate Division, Third Department, held that a land-

---

28. Iannotti v. Consolidated Rail Corp., 74 N.Y.2d 39, 542 N.E.2d 621, 544 N.Y.S.2d 308 (1989); *see also* Gardner v. Owasco River Ry., 142 A.D.2d 61, 531 N.Y.S.2d 819 (3d Dep't 1988).
29. Ackerman v. Town of Fishkill, 201 A.D.2d 441 (2d Dep't 1994).
30. Hillman v. Penn Central Corp., 204 A.D.2d 902 (3d Dep't 1994).
31. Bragg v. Genesee County Agricultural Society, 84 N.Y.2d 544 at 552 (1994).

fill was a suitable parcel of land for riding a motorized dirt bike.[32]

(4) *Ziecker v. Town of Orchard Park.*[33] An owner of a pool or diving area owes no duty to protect from his own reckless conduct someone who is or should be aware of the dangers of diving. The same principle applies to creeks.[34]

(5) *Nagawiecki v. State of New York.*[35] In an action for negligence against the state as the owner and operator of a ski area, the judgment was in favor of the plaintiff, who had sustained her injuries when she encountered icy conditions, became airborne, and landed on an unpadded pole holding a safety fence. The Appellate Division, Third Department, reversed the judgment and dismissed the complaint since the law imposed no duty upon the state to pad the poles or fences along the access lines to the lift or the facilities located away from the slopes and trails at the base of an outrun and beyond the limits of normal skiable terrain in order to protect such skiers as the plaintiff from the unfortunate consequences of their own actions. The plaintiff, being an experienced skier, knew or should have known that icy conditions would develop late in the day, and, from her own description of the accident, it was clear that she was skiing at an excessive and dangerous rate of speed. To cast the state in liability here would make it an insurer of the safety of the skier upon its premises. While it may be entirely foreseeable that a skier would sustain injuries in a collision with an unpadded pole or fence, that foreseeability alone cannot create a duty when none exists. That materials

32. Albright v. Metz, 217 A.D.2d 123 (3d Dep't 1995), *aff'd*, 88 N.Y.2d 656 (1996).
33. Ziecker v. Town of Orchard Park, 75 N.Y.2d 761, 551 N.E.2d 898, 551 N.Y.S.2d 99 (1989).
34. Culkin v. Culkin, 168 A.D.2d 912 (4th Dep't 1990). The plaintiff was aware of the depth of the water and the presence of rocks.
35. Nagawiecki v. State, 150 A.D.2d 147, 545 N.Y.S.2d 954 (3d Dep't 1989). *See also* Basilone v. Burch Hill Operations, Inc., 199 A.D2d 779 (3d Dep't 1993).

are available to make fences and posts safer or more flexible does not alter this conclusion.

6.1.3.1.2.a Buildings

(6) *Waters v. New York City Housing Authority.*[36] The scope of a landowner's duty to maintain building security should not be extended to embrace the members of the public at large who have no connection to the premises but who might be victimized by predators in the street. Because the defendant-landowner had no relationship at all to the unidentified criminal who attacked the plaintiff and because the plaintiff had no association with the premises, the landlord's duty to maintain security within the building did not extend to her. This conclusion is fatal to her claim regardless of whether her injury was foreseeable. Apparently, this rule also applies to the outdoor areas of a large cooperative apartment development.[37]

(7) In *Appio v. City of Albany,*[38] the Appellate Division, Third Department, outlined the duty which owners of buildings abutting the sidewalk owe to passersby:

> The well-settled general principle of law applicable in cases such as this precludes the imposition of liability on the owner or occupier of property solely by reason of his being an abutter to the public sidewalk where the injury occurred . . . . There is, however, an exception to the general principle where a statute, ordinance or municipal charter imposes liability upon abutting owners or occupiers for injuries caused by their negligent maintenance of the public sidewalk . . . . In order to create such liability, however, the language of the statute, ordinance or charter must not only charge the abutting owner

36. Waters v. New York City Housing Auth., 69 N.Y.2d 225, 505 N.E.2d 922, 513 N.Y.S.2d 356 (1987).

37. Leyva v. Riverbay Corp., 206 A.D.2d 150 (1st Dep't 1994).

38. Appio v. City of Albany, 144 A.D.2d 869, 534 N.Y.S.2d 811, 812 (3d Dep't 1988). *See also* Little v. City of Albany, 169 A.D.2d 1013 (3d Dep't 1991), and Farnsworth v. Village of Postsdam, 288 A.D.2d 79 (3d Dep't 1997).

> or occupier with a duty to maintain the public sidewalk, but it must also specifically state that a breach of that duty will result in liability to those who are injured by defects in the sidewalk . . . . The ordinance herein contains no such language.
>
> An exception to the general principle has also been recognized where the abutting owner or occupier uses the sidewalk for a special purpose; however, before liability can be imposed for negligent maintenance under this exception, it must be established that the sidewalk was constructed in a special manner for the benefit of the abutting owner or occupier . . . .

(7a) *DiPonzio v. Riordan.*[38.1] Even when a customer is on a business's premises, the business is not liable for injuries that are not foreseeable. In *DiPonzio*, a customer at a gas station left his motor running and his car unattended contrary to the rules of the station. The car moved and hit another customer, who sued the station. The Court of Appeals affirmed the appellate division's dismissal of the complaint since the cause of the plaintiff's injuries was outside the foreseeable danger underlying the station's rules, i.e., the danger of fire and explosion.

6.1.3.2 Municipalities

6.1.3.2.1 The Plaintiff

6.1.3.2.1.a Employees

(8) *Haddock v. City of New York.*[39] The city owes to the public a duty not to hire or retain persons who are dangerous or violent. Thus, a nine year old girl, who was raped on a city playground by a parks department employee who had a history of committing violent crimes, had a cause of action against the city for negligent retention.

38.1. DiPonzio v. Riordan, 89 N.Y.2d 578 (1997).

39. Haddock v. City of N.Y., 140 A.D.2d 91, 532 N.Y.S.2d 379 (1st Dep't 1988), *aff'd*, 75 N.Y.2d 478 (1990).

6.1.3.2.1.b Public Roadways

(9) *Kiernan v. Thompson.*[40] A municipality has a continuing duty to maintain its public roadway in a reasonably safe condition, and that duty is independent of the municipality's duty not to create a defective condition.

(10) *Poirier v. City of Schenectady.*[41] A municipality may protect itself by enacting an ordinance that it must receive prior written notice of a defect in the sidewalk or roadway as a condition precedent to the municipality's liability. The court of appeals wrote,

> Practically, prior written notice provisions result in limiting a locality's duty of care over municipal streets and sidewalks by imposing liability only for those defects or hazardous conditions of which its officials have been actually notified exist at a specified location.[42]

Such ordinances typically provide exceptions for defects caused by special uses in favor of the owner of abutting property or by the affirmative act of negligence of the municipality.

6.1.3.2.1.c Public Safety

(11) *Harris v. City of New York.*[43] When the plaintiff requested police protection, and the police department gave him assurances of safety and protection, the department may have created a duty to the plaintiff.

---

40. Kiernan v. Thompson, 73 N.Y.2d 840, 534 N.E.2d 39, 537 N.Y.S.2d 122 (1988).
41. Poirier v. City of Schenectady, 85 N.Y.2d 310 (1995).
42. *Id.* at 314.
43. Harris v. City of N.Y., 147 A.D.2d 186, 542 N.Y.S.2d 550 (1st Dep't 1989); *see also* De Long v. Erie, 60 N.Y.2d 296, 457 N.E.2d 117, 469 N.Y.S.2d 611 (1983); Merced v. City of N.Y., 142 Misc. 2d 442, 534 N.Y.S.2d 60 (Sup. Ct. Bronx 1980), *aff'd*, 75 N.Y.2d 798 (1990).

(12) *Chiplock v. Niagara Mohawk Power Co.*[44] The town owed a duty of care to the homeowner: if the town's employees check a gas leak and tell the homeowner that the homeowner is safe, then the homeowner has a right to rely on that affirmative representation.

(13) *Boland v. State of New York.*[45] The state is liable for relaying the report of child abuse to the wrong local agency thus facilitating further abuse. The legislature intended article 6, title 6 of the Social Services Law to protect the plaintiff's class, not the public at large, and the informant's telephone call substituted for the personal contact required to impose a special relationship on the government.

6.1.3.2.2 The Defendant

6.1.3.2.2.a Employees

(14) *Santangelo v. State of New York.*[46] A municipality owes no duty to a police officer to protect him from harm while he is pursuing or apprehending criminals.

In response to *Santangelo*, the legislature enacted General Municipal Law section 205(g),[47] which extends to policemen the protection granted to firemen by General Municipal Law section 205(a). Thus, the legislature has created a special cause of action in favor of policemen injured or killed as a result of the violation of any federal, state, or municipal law or regulation. Moreover, the statute imposes a standard of strict liability when there is a reasonable connection between the violation and the injury.

---

44. Chiplock v. Niagara Mohawk Power Co., 134 A.D.2d 96, 523 N.Y.S.2d 232 (3d Dep't 1988).
45. Boland v. State of New York, 218 A.D.2d 235 (3d Dep't 1996).
46. Santangelo v. State, 127 A.D.2d 647 (2d Dep't 1987), *aff'd*, 71 N.Y.2d 393 (1988); *see also* Hobbs v. Bowery Sav. Bank, N.Y.L.J., Dec. 29, 1988 (2d Dep't 1988); Campbell v. Lorenzo's Pizza Parlor, Inc., N.Y.L.J., Feb. 1, 1989 (Sup. Ct. Queens 1989); Guadagno v. Baltimore & O. R.R., 142 Misc. 2d 712, 538 N.Y.S.2d 386 (Sup. Ct. Erie 1988), *aff'd*, 155 A.D.2d 981 (4th Dep't 1989).
47. 1989 N.Y. Laws ch. 346 (effective July 12, 1989).

6.1.3.2.2.b Public Roadways

(15) *Bogart v. Town of New Paltz.*[48] *Bogart* was a wrongful death action against a municipal corporation arising out of an automobile accident in which the decedent's car left the roadway, landed in a pond, and sank, asphyxiating the occupants. The plaintiff alleged that the emergency communications center maintained by the municipalities was negligent in responding to a report of the accident given by a third party who happened to pass the scene. The trial court properly dismissed the complaint since the essential elements of a special relationship between the decedents and the municipalities, which is necessary to impose liability, were absent. First, there was no direct contact between the decedents and the municipalities, an element that serves to limit rationally the class of citizens to whom such a special duty exists. Second, the decedents did not rely on any affirmative assurances by the municipalities, and that element is central to the special duty exception. (This element remedies the unfairness resulting when a municipality's undertaking lulled the injured party into inactivity.) In this case, the decedents had no contact with either the third party or the emergency communications center and did not rely on anyone's assurances. Finally, the third party was not the decedents' agent.

6.1.3.2.2.c Public Safety

(16) *Cuffy v. City of New York.*[49] A narrow right to recover from a municipality for its negligent failure to provide police protection arose after the municipality's agent promised protection to a particular citizen and, consequently, created

48. Bogart v. Town of New Paltz, 145 A.D.2d 110, 537 N.Y.S.2d 678 (3d Dep't 1989).
49. Cuffy v. City of New York, 69 N.Y.2d 255, 513 N.Y.S.2d 372 (1978). *See also* Kircher v. City of Jamestown, 74 N.Y.2d 251, 544 N.Y.S.2d 995 (1989) and Merced v. City of New York, 142 Misc. 2d 442, 534 N.Y.S.2d 60 (Sup. Ct. Bronx 1989), *aff'd,* 75 N.Y.2d 798 (1990).

a special duty to that citizen. Essential to the recovery is proof that the plaintiff relied on the promise and that his reliance was causally related to the harm he suffered. In this case, the plaintiff failed to establish such proof.

(17) *Bardavid v. New York City Transit Authority.*[50] The transit authority does not have a duty to protect prospective passengers from assaults by third parties, and the authority does not assume such a duty by installing an electric sign to inform prospective passengers of the arrival of the elevator to take them down to the level of the platform. Thus, the authority did not breach a duty when the sign was out of order.

6.1.3.3 Transportation

6.1.3.3.1 The Plaintiff

6.1.3.3.1.a Common Carriers

(18) *Miller v. Fernon.*[51] A common carrier has a duty to an alighting passenger to stop at a place where the passenger may disembark safely and leave the area.

6.1.3.3.1.b Funeral Processions

(19) *Maida v. Velella.*[52] A funeral home owed a duty to those participating in a funeral procession to avoid creating an unreasonably hazardous situation.

50. Bardavid v. New York City Transit Authority, 61 N.Y.2d 986 (1984).
51. Miller v. Fernon, 73 N.Y.2d 844, 534 N.E.2d 40, 537 N.Y.S.2d 123 (1988). That same duty is owed by every driver who drops off a passenger. Ross v. Ching, 146 A.D.2d 55, 539 N.Y.S.2d 184 (4th Dep't 1989).
52. Maida v. Velella, 69 N.Y.2d 1026, 511 N.E.2d 56, 517 N.Y.S.2d 912 (1987).

6.1.3.3.2 The Defendant

6.1.3.3.2.a Common Carriers

(20) *Marenghi v. New York City Transit Authority.*[53] The transit authority does not owe a duty to potential or future riders to prevent someone who is running to catch a train from knocking down a pedestrian.

6.1.3.4 The Practice of Medicine

6.1.3.4.1 The Plaintiff

6.1.3.4.1.a Pregnancy

(21) *Ferrara v. Bernstein.*[54] The defendant surgeon supposedly performed an abortion on the plaintiff, but the defendant did not inform the plaintiff that a pathology report suggested that she was still pregnant. Three weeks after the abortion, the plaintiff experienced severe cramps and was taken to the emergency room of a hospital. The plaintiff delivered a dead fetus, which she saw, and she subsequently required psychiatric care. The court of appeals affirmed a judgment for the plaintiff and held that there was proximate cause, that the negligent abortion caused the plaintiff's physical pain, and that the abortion caused the miscarriage and, therefore, her emotional distress.

53. Marenghi v. New York City Transit Auth., 74 N.Y.2d 822, 545 N.E.2d 627, 546 N.Y.S.2d 337 (1989).

54. Ferrara v. Bernstein, 81 N.Y.2d 895 (1993).

6.1.3.4.2 The Defendant

6.1.3.4.2.a Pregnancy

(22) *Lancellotti v. Howard.*[55] A mother erroneously diagnosed as pregnant has no cause of action against the physician because the mother suffered no damages. However, the mother does have a cause of action against the physician who erroneously diagnosed a birth defect and thereby caused her to have an unnecessary abortion.[56] Moreover, the mother has a cause of action against the physician who erroneously diagnosed her as not pregnant and then administered to her a drug which did cause a birth defect.[57]

(23) *Prado v. Catholic Medical Center.*[58] No cause of action accrues to either the mother or the baby when the physician's negligence causes the child to be stillborn because a physician is not liable to a person who was never born and because the mother has not been injured. Apparently, what distinguishes *Prado* from *Ferrara* is the physical injury to the mother from the negligent abortion.

(23a) *Ferrara v. Bernstein.*[58.1] The plaintiff experienced a spontaneous miscarriage after an unsuccessful abortion. She experienced emotional distress when she saw the body of the stillborn baby. The plaintiff's distress was compens-

---

55. Lancellotti v. Howard, N.Y.L.J., Nov. 30, 1989 (2d Dep't 1989); *cf.* Lynch v. Bay Ridge Obstetrical & Gynecological Assocs., 72 N.Y.2d 632, 532 N.E.2d 1239, 536 N.Y.S.2d 11 (1988); Martinez v. Long Island Jewish Hillside Medical Center, 70 N.Y.2d 697, 512 N.E.2d 538, 518 N.Y.S.2d 955 (1987).

56. Martinez v. Long Island Jewish Medical Center, 70 N.Y.2d 697, 518 N.Y.S.2d 955 (1987).

57. Lynch v. Bay Ridge Associates, 72 N.Y.2d 632 (1988).

58. Pardo v. Catholic Medical Center, 145 A.D.2d 614, 536 N.Y.S.2d 474 (2d Dep't 1988). But if the mother has suffered distinct physical injuries independent of the stillbirth, her immediate mental distress wrought by the death of her unborn child is a cognizable element of any such independent injury. Buzniak v. County of Westchester, 156 A.D.2d 631, 549 N.Y.S.2d 130 (2d Dep't 1989). In accord with *Pardo, see* Guialdo v. Allen, 171 A.D.2d 535 (1st Dep't 1991).

58.1. Ferrara v. Bernstein, 81 N.Y.2d 895 (1993).

able in a medical malpractice action because the proximate cause of her distress was the physician's failure properly to advise the patient of her condition.

6.1.3.5 Miscellany

6.1.3.5.1 The Plaintiff

6.1.3.5.2 The Defendant

6.1.3.5.2.a Suppliers

(24) *Balsam v. Delma Engineering Corp.*[59] The supplier of gasoline to a gas station owes no duty to the patrons of that gas station if there is an accident while their cars are on line at the station.

(25) *Amatulli v. Delphi Construction Corp.*[60] The manufacturer of an above-ground pool owes no duty to a diver into that pool to protect the diver from the homeowner's having installed the pool below ground so that it looked deeper than it was.

6.1.4 Proximate Cause

6.1.4.1 In General

The plaintiff has the burden of pleading and proving that the defendant's breach of duty was a proximate cause of the plaintiff's injuries. The courts have interpreted this burden to require proof that the defendant's breach was a substantial factor in causing the plaintiff's injuries.[61] However, the plaintiff need not demonstrate the precise manner in which

---

59. Balsam v. Delma Eng'g Corp., 139 A.D.2d 292, 532 N.Y.S.2d 105 (1st Dep't 1988).
60. Amatulli v. Delphi Constr. Corp., N.Y.L.J., Dec. 26, 1989 (2d Dep't 1989).
61. 2 PJI 70; Baker v. Sportservice Corp., 142 A.D.2d 991, 530 N.Y.S.2d 421, 506 N.Y.S.2d 725 (2d Dep't 1986).

the accident occurred or the extent to which his or her injuries were foreseeable.[62]

6.1.4.2 A Superseding or Intervening Cause

A defendant who has breached a duty to the plaintiff may still avoid liability if someone else's superseding or intervening act was the true proximate cause of the plaintiff's injuries.

> [A] defendant is relieved of liability where, after his negligence, an unforeseeable superseding force intervenes which breaks the chain of causal connection and itself causes the injury . . . . Further, a plaintiff's own conduct may be a superseding force absolving a negligent defendant from liability . . . . However, in order to be a superseding cause, a plaintiff's negligence must be more than mere contributory negligence, which would be relevant in apportioning culpable conduct. Rather, such conduct, in addition to being unforeseeable, must rise to such a level of culpability as to replace the defendant's negligence as the legal cause of the accident . . . .[63]

In other words, the superseding cause may be an act of either the plaintiff or a third party, more likely the latter, but this act must exclude the defendant's act as a proximate cause.

In *Mesick v. State of New York,*[64] the Appellate Division, Third Department, cited as an example of a truly superseding cause the case of *Boltax v. Joy Day Camp,*[65] in which the plaintiff dove from a lifeguard chair into a shallow swimming pool. Since the condition of the pool was obvious, it

---

62. McMorrow v. Trimper, 74 N.Y.2d 830, 545 N.E.2d 630, 546 N.Y.S.2d 340 (1989); Derdiarian v. Felix Contracting Corp., 51 N.Y.2d 308, 414 N.E.2d 666, 434 N.Y.S.2d 166 (1980); Schimmenti v. Ply Gem Indus., Inc., N.Y.L.J., Jan. 9, 1990 (2d Dep't 1990).
63. Baker v. Sportservice Corp., 142 A.D.2d 991, 530 N.Y.S.2d 412 (4th Dep't 1988); Mesick v. State, 118 A.D.2d 214, 504 N.Y.S.2d 279, 282 (3d Dep't 1986).
64. Mesick v. State, 118 A.D.2d 214, 504 N.Y.S.2d 279, 282 (3d Dep't 1986).
65. Boltax v. Joy Day Camp, 67 N.Y.2d 617, 620, 490 N.E.2d 527, 499 N.Y.S.2d 660, 661 (1986), *aff'g* 113 A.D.2d 859, 493 N.Y.S.2d 590 (2d Dep't 1985).

was not foreseeable that the plaintiff would engage in such conduct. Further, the conduct of the plaintiff, an experienced swimmer, was found to be so careless that the defendant was absolved of liability. However, if the defendant should have foreseen the intervening act, then the act will not absolve the defendant of liability — although it may justify an apportionment of liability.

In the case before the court in *Mesick*, the plaintiff had been injured in a gym when he tried to climb a rope by taking a running start but slipped and fell. Although the plaintiff's conduct may have been culpable, it was foreseeable and was not so culpable as to break the link between the defendant's negligence and the plaintiff's injury.

6.1.4.3 Applications

We shall illustrate the law of proximate cause by applying the rule to examples of actions for negligence and for medical malpractice.

6.1.4.3.1 Actions for Negligence

Nowhere is the issue of proximate cause more controversial than in swimming pool accidents. The cases involve catastrophic injuries, and yet, in almost every case, the issue of proximate cause is resolved against the injured plaintiff. If the plaintiff's conduct was reckless or the sole proximate cause of his injuries, then the defendant is not liable.[66]

The same approach is evident toward diving accidents at beaches. For example, in *Heard v. City of New York*,[67] the

---

66. Ziecker v. Town of Orchard Park, 75 N.Y.2d 761, 551 N.E.2d 898, 551 N.Y.S.2d 99 (1989); Kritz v. Schum, 75 N.Y.2d 25, 549 N.E.2d 1155, 550 N.Y.S.2d 584 (1989); Campbell v. Muswim Pools, Inc., 147 A.D.2d 977, 537 N.Y.S.2d 412 (4th Dep't 1989); Denkensohn v. Davenport, 144 A.D.2d 58, 536 N.Y.S.2d 587 (3d Dep't 1989) Howard v. Poseidon Pools, Inc., 133 Misc. 2d 50, 506 N.Y.S.2d 523 (Sup. Ct. Allegheny 1986).

67. Heard v. City of New York, 82 N.Y.2d 66 (1993).

lifeguard instructed the plaintiff to leave the jetty but acquiesced in the plaintiff's taking one more dive. He did and was injured. The jury returned a verdict for the plaintiff, but the Appellate Division, Second Department, reversed the judgment. The court of appeals affirmed this decision and held that the lifeguard's acquiescence was not the proximate cause of the plaintiff's injuries because the plaintiff knew the risk from his previous dives and because the plaintiff was no worse off than if the lifeguard had done nothing. However, the court of appeals recognized the possibility of a cause of action in other circumstances and wrote,

> There can be no doubt that a prima facie case is made out when one familiar with a hazard offers direct assurances of safety to one who is unfamiliar with the hazard and who foreseeably relies upon those assurances.[68]

6.1.4.3.2 Actions for Medical Malpractice

In an action for medical malpractice, proximate cause is a very difficult issue. As the Appellate Division, Second Department, observed in *Vialva v. City of New York,* the plaintiff in such an action need not eliminate all other contributing causes in order to make a prima facie case.

> Because causation is always a difficult issue in medicine . . . . , "it bears emphasizing that to establish a prima facie case a plaintiff need not eliminate entirely all possibility that a defendant's conduct was not a cause. It is enough that he offer sufficient evidence from which reasonable men might conclude that it is more probably than not that the injury was caused by the defendant." . . .[69]

In *Ledogar v. Giordano,*[70] the infant plaintiff alleged that the defendants' negligence caused his autism, but the defen-

68. *Id.* at 74.
69. Vialva v. City of N.Y., 118 A.D.2d 701, 703, 499 N.Y.S.2d 977, 979 (2d Dep't 1986); *see also* Hilton v. Jewish Hosp. & Medical Center, N.Y.L.J., Oct. 7, 1986, at 12, col. 4 (Sup. Ct. 1986).
70. Ledogar v. Giordano, 122 A.D.2d 834 (2d Dep't 1986).

dants argued that autism cannot be caused by the physician's negligence. The jury agreed with the plaintiff. Although the trial court set the verdict aside, the Appellate Division, Second Department, reinstated the verdict for three reasons. First, expert testimony is necessary when the causal connection would not be readily apparent to a jury, and the plaintiff presented such expert testimony. Second, the testimony of the plaintiff's experts established a causal connection between the alleged prenatal hypoxia and the plaintiff's autism with a reasonable degree of medical certainty. Third, the plaintiff was not required to eliminate all possibility that his autism resulted from other causes. Therefore, the evidence supported the jury verdict on the issue of liability and the apportionment of fault.

By contrast, the courts sometimes do find that the doctor's conduct was not the proximate cause of the plaintiff's injury. For example, in *Hoffson v. Orentreich*,[71] the plaintiff obtained a verdict against a physician because of the medical treatment the plaintiff had received from the doctor's nurse. The nurse's treatment was not negligent, but the plaintiff argued that the physician was negligent in not examining the plaintiff prior to that treatment. The trial court agreed but set the verdict aside and dismissed the complaint because the physician's failure to examine the plaintiff was not a proximate cause of the plaintiff's injuries. The physician had ordered the nurse to treat the plaintiff for ordinary acne cysts, which she did, but the plaintiff developed an infection and was left with scars. The plaintiff alleged that if the physician had examined the plaintiff, the physician would have discovered a different kind of cyst and would have ordered a different treatment. However, the trial court ruled that there was no evidence to support that allegation and, therefore, that the physician would have ordered the same treatment with the same result. Hence, the physician's failure to examine the plaintiff was not the proximate cause of the plaintiff's injuries.

---

71. Hoffson v. Orentreich, 144 Misc. 2d 411, 543 N.Y.S.2d 242 (Sup. Ct. N.Y. 1989).

6.1.5. Actual or Constructive Notice

6.1.5.1 The Necessity of Proving

The law does not place upon a landowner, a store owner, or a proprietor of property or of a building absolute liability should someone fall on the property or be injured by reason of some defect on the premises. In other words, that a defective condition caused the plaintiff's injuries is not enough to state a cause of action. The plaintiff must also prove either that the defendant caused the defective condition or that the defendant had actual knowledge or constructive notice of the defect.[72] Only then may the defendant be deemed negligent, and, in the absence of this proof, the trial court should dismiss the complaint on a motion for a summary judgment or a directed verdict.[73] For example, the Appellate Division, First Department, wrote in *Blye v. Manhattan and Bronx Surface Transit Operating Authority*:[74]

72. Negri v. Stop & Shop, 65 N.Y.2d 625, 480 N.E.2d 740, 491 N.Y.S.2d 151 (1985); Fink v. Board of Educ., 117 A.D.2d 704, 498 N.Y.S.2d 440 (2d Dep't 1986); Birdsall v. Montgomery Ward & Co., 109 A.D.2d 969, 486 N.Y.S.2d 461 (3d Dep't 1985); *aff'd,* 65 N.Y.2d 913 (1985); Stevens v. Loblaws Mkt., 27 A.D.2d 975, 278 N.Y.S.2d 703 (4th Dep't 1967); Eagan v. Great Atl. & Pac. Tea Co., 252 A.D. 791, 300 N.Y.S. 707 (2d Dep't 1937), *aff'd*, 227 N.Y. 729, 14 N.E.2d 824 (1983). To satisfy the notice requirement, the plaintiff must prove that the defendant actually caused the condition. Proof that the defendant allowed a condition to exist for a short period of time, without proof that the defendant caused the condition, is not sufficient. Fink v. Board of Educ., *supra*; Crandall v. Kocak, 114 A.D.2d 713, 494 N.Y.S.2d 529 (3d Dep't 1985). For two cases dealing with elevators, *see* Burgess v. Otis Elevator Co., 114 A.D.2d 784 (lst Dep't 1985), and Sirigiano v. Otis Elevator Co., 118 A.D.2d 920 (3d Dep't 1986); Kraemer v. K-Mart Corporation, 226 A. D.2d. 590 (2d Dep't 1996).
73. Ivancic v. Olmstead, 66 N.Y.2d 349, 488 N.E.2d 72, 497 N.Y.S.2d 326 (1985); Zino v. City of N.Y., 111 A.D.2d 847, 490 N.Y.S.2d 586 (2d Dep't 1985); Lewis v. Metropolitan Transp. Auth., 99 A.D.2d 246, 472 N.Y.S.2d 368 (1st Dep't), *aff'd,* 64 N.Y.2d 670, 474 N.E.2d 246, 495 N.Y.S.2d 252 (1984); Eddy v. Topps Friendly Mkts., 91 A.D.2d 1203, 459 N.Y.S.2d 196 (4th Dep't), *aff'd,* 59 N.Y.2d 692, 450 N.E.2d 243, 463 N.Y.S.2d 437 (1983).
74. Blye v. Manhattan and Bronx Surface Transit Operating Authority, 124 A.D.2d 106 (1st Dep't 1987). *See also* Francias v. City of New York and MABSTOA, 222 A.D.2d 215 (1st Dep't 1995).

> This court, not long ago, noted that with respect to railroad station entrances and platforms "[t]he law has never exacted of common carriers an absolute duty to maintain approaches and station platforms so as to render it impossible for a passenger to slip or become injured." Rather, the standard is to exercise reasonable care under the circumstances.[75]

Therefore, the plaintiff must establish through competent evidence, such as witnesses or photographs, that the defendant had actual or constructive notice of the dangerous condition for a sufficient time within which to correct it or to warn others of its existence or that the defendant caused the condition.[76]

This rule protects municipalities, lessors, and lessees and typically is applied in such cases as "a slip and fall as the result of a slippery or foreign substance on the floor of a supermarket, grocery or other retail store . . . ."[77] In *Soriano v. State of New York*,[78] the New York Court of Claims listed the elements a plaintiff must establish to hold the state liable for the injuries the plaintiff suffered when his car skidded due to an accumulation of ice and snow on the highway:

> 1. The shoulder was not properly maintained . . . .
> 2. The State was aware and permitted the icy condition to accumulate.
> 3. The State failed to remedy the situation with reasonable diligence . . . .
> 4. The failure to do so was the proximate cause of the injuries sustained herein . . . .

The second element requires the plaintiff to prove that the state had sufficient notice, actual or constructive.

---

75. *Id.* at 111 (quoting Lewis v. MTA, 99 A.D.2d 246, 249).

76. Lewis v. Metropolitan Transp. Auth., 99 A.D.2d 246, 472 N.Y.S.2d 368 (1st Dep't), *aff'd*, 64 N.Y.2d 670, 474 N.E.2d 612, 495 N.Y.S.2d 252 (1984).

77. *Id.* at 250, 472 N.Y.S.2d at 372, *aff'd*, 64 N.Y.2d 670, 474 N.E.2d 612, 495 N.Y.S.2d 252 (1984); *see also* Haddock v. City of N.Y., 140 A.D.2d 91, 532 N.Y.S.2d 379 (1st Dep't 1988).

78. Soriano v. State, N.Y.L.J., Nov. 3, 1986, at 16, col. 1 (Ct. Cl. 1986) (Orlando, J.).

6.1.5.2 The Methods of Proving

As a general rule, there is no particular, required method of proving actual or constructive notice. The plaintiff can satisfy this burden through the testimony of witnesses that the condition existed for a suitable period of time prior to the accident,[79] through the testimony of experts who examined the premises following the accident and can state that the condition was a long-standing one,[80] or through photographs of the scene that show the condition to be long standing.[81] Thus, the Appellate Division, First Department, wrote in *Karten v. City of New York*:[82]

> It has long been settled that photographs may be used to prove constructive notice of the alleged defects shown in the photographs, if they are taken reasonably close to the time of the accident, and there is testimony that the condition at the time of the accident was substantially the same as shown in the photograph . . . .[83]

Sometimes the plaintiff can prove notice through written notification, the defendant's own records, or prior accidents. As the Appellate Division, Second Department, explained in *Iannelli v. Powers*,[84] the courts have consistently held that records of prior similar accidents are admissible and discoverable in a negligence action since they are relevant in establishing both (1) that a particular condition was dangerous and (2) that defendant had notice of the condition.

---

79. Zino v. City of N.Y., 111 A.D.2d 847, 490 N.Y.S.2d 586 (2d Dep't 1985).
80. Ivancic v. Olmstead, 66 N.Y.2d 349, 488 N.E.2d 72, 497 N.Y.S.2d 326 (1985).
81. Batton v. Elghanyan, 43 N.Y.2d 898, 374 N.E.2d 611 (1978); Amorondo v. State, 117 A.D.2d 574, 498 N.Y.S.2d 996 (2d Dep't 1986).
82. Karten v. City of New York, 109 A.D.2d 127 (1st Dep't 1985).
83. *Id.* at 127.

6.1.5.3 Special Requirement of Written Notice of Defect to the City of New York

Section 7-201(c) of the Administrative Code of the City of New York provides that in actions against the city for damage due to a defect in the street, sidewalk, or bridge, the plaintiff has the burden of pleading and proving compliance with the section's requirements for notice. Similar provisions protect other municipalities, and the courts have enforced these provisions.[85]

However, in a particular case, the court may decide that the hazard which caused the accident was not a defect within the meaning of the ordinance. For example, in *Turco v. City of Peekskill*,[86] the court decided that the metal pipe which protruded six inches above the sidewalk adjacent to the highway was not a defect within the meaning of the city's provision for prior written notice, and, in *Montante v. City of Rochester*,[87] the court decided that a sleeve without a signpost inserted was not a defect. Thus, the respective plaintiffs could prove their causes of action without establishing prior written notice. However, in *Poirier v. City of Schenectady*,[88] a case involving the protruding anchor for a missing traffic sign, the court of appeals hinted that it might have decided those two cases differently.[89]

In any case, for New York City to be liable for a personal injury, wrongful death, or damage to property as a result of the dangerous or defective condition of any street, highway, bridge, wharf, culvert, sidewalk, crosswalk, or encumbrance or attachment thereto, someone (not necessarily the plaintiff) must have given the city written notice of the condition or of a previous injury at least fifteen days before the plaintiff's injury, or the city itself must have acknowledged the condition in writing at least fifteen days before the plain-

84. Iannelli v. Powers, 114 A.D.2d 157, 498 N.Y.S.2d 377 (2d Dep't 1986).

85. Poirier v. City of Schenectady, 85 N.Y.2d 310 (1995).

86. Turco v. City of Peekskill, 133 A.D.2d 369, 519 N.Y.S.2d 270 (2d Dep't 1987).

87. Montante v. City of Rochester, 187 A.D.2d 924 (4th Dep't 1992).

88. Poirier v. City of Schenectady, *supra*, n.85.

89. *Id.* at 314.

tiff's injury. Section 7-201(a)(3) & (4) also requires the commissioner of transportation to keep an indexed record of all written notices in a separate book for three years, to make written acknowledgment of all notices the department receives, and to retain the records in the municipal archives for ten years.

Fortunately, the Big Apple Pothole & Sidewalk Protection Corp. will search the records of the department of transportation and produce an extract analogous to the title search performed by an insurance company. Examples 6-1 and 6-2, respectively, which can be found at the end of this chapter, are a cover letter from this corporation to our firm and the corporation's standard form for reporting a defect. Incidentally, the corporation recommends serving the city with a notice to admit that it had received prior written notice of the defect. The attorney would serve the notice to admit pursuant to C.P.L.R. 3123(a) and would append copies of the documents.

6.1.5.4 Illustrative Cases on Notice

Several will cases illustrate the requirement that the plaintiff prove that the defendant had actual or constructive notice of the defective condition which caused the plaintiff's injury. The attorney should be aware, however, that these decisions are essentially findings of fact and that the attorney must be prepared to argue the client's case on that basis. The subjects covered are "slip-and-fall" cases, mechanical devices, robbery, and falling tree limbs.

6.1.5.4.1 "Slip-and-Fall" Cases

6.1.5.4.1.a The Plaintiff

(1) *Newman v. Great Atlantic & Pacific Tea Co.*[90] While shopping at the defendant's supermarket, the plaintiff slipped and fell in a puddle of dirty water near the base of a freezer. The puddle was one and one-half to two feet from the freezer and was six inches wide. The appellate court ruled that the jury could have found either actual or constructive notice.

(2) *Candelier v. City of New York.*[91] The plaintiff alighted from a bus onto an ice-covered sidewalk; he walked ten steps then fell. The appellate court ruled that the jury reasonably could have found that the ice had been on the sidewalk for seven days.

6.1.5.4.1.b The Defendant

(3) *Fischer v. Connor.*[92] The plaintiff, a tenant, fell on an icy walkway leading to his apartment, but he established neither actual nor constructive notice.

(4) *Silver v. Brodsky.*[93] The plaintiff fell on an allegedly slippery floor in a beauty salon, but she testified that there was no visible waxy build-up on the floor, that the lighting

---

90. Newman v. Great Atl. & Pac. Tea Co., 100 A.D.2d 538, 473 N.Y.S.2d 231 (2d Dep't 1984).

91. Candelier v. City of New York, 129 A.D.2d 145 (1st Dep't 1987).

92. Bernstein v. City of N.Y., 69 N.Y.2d 1020, 511 N.E.2d 52, 517 N.Y.S.2d 908 (1987); Fischer v. Connor, 111 A.D.2d 442, 488 N.Y.S.2d 502 (3d Dep't 1985).

93. Silver v. Brodsky, 112 A.D.2d 213, 490 N.Y.S.2d 865 (2d Dep't 1985); *see also* Eddy v. Topps Friendly Mkts., 91 A.D.2d 1203, 459 N.Y.S.2d 196 (4th Dep't), *aff'd,* 59 N.Y.2d 692, 450 N.E.2d 243, 463 N.Y.S.2d 437 (1983). Similarly, in Bauer v. Hirschbedner Associates, 228 A.D.2d 400 (2d Dep't 1996), several employees of a Travelodge slipped and fell on the new marble floors. However, the trial court dismissed the complaint, and the appellate division affirmed this result.

was adequate, and that there did not appear to be a defect in the floor. The court dismissed the complaint because there was no evidence of actual or constructive notice and because the mere happening of the event did not bespeak either notice or negligence.

(5) *Lewis v. Metropolitan Transportation Authority.*[94] The plaintiff slipped on a foreign substance on a train platform belonging to the Long Island Rail Road. She described the substance as "dark . . . oil and sticky and gooky." Following the jury's verdict for the plaintiff, the defendant appealed, and the appellate court reversed the decision and dismissed the complaint. The defendant did not create the condition, and there was no evidence establishing how long the alleged substance was present.

> Thus, in the absence of some evidence that the condition existed for a sufficient period to afford the carrier, in the exercise of reasonable care, an opportunity to discover and correct it, there was no factual issue for the jury. The mere happening of the accident does not establish liability on the part of the defendant.

(6) *Cavaliere v. City University of New York.*[95] The plaintiff fell after losing her balance when she stepped into a hole that was thirteen inches in diameter and four inches deep. The court of claims dismissed her complaint for lack of proof of actual or constructive notice. The court had five reasons. First, the plaintiff and her husband were not credible witnesses. Second, no expert testified regarding the chain of events including the length of time required to create the defective condition. Third, the law does not impose liability for injuries resulting from flaws that are slight or trivial. Fourth, the pho-

---

94. Cruz v. New York City Transit Auth., 136 A.D.2d 196, 526 N.Y.S.2d 827 (2d Dep't 1988); Lewis v. Metropolitan Transp. Auth., 99 A.D.2d 246, 472 N.Y.S.2d 368, 372 (1st Dep't), *aff'd,* 64 N.Y.2d 670, 474 N.E.2d 612, 485 N.Y.S.2d 252 (1984).

95. Cavaliere v. City Univ., N.Y.L.J., Oct. 30, 1986, at 13, col. 1 (Ct. Cl. 1986).

tographs of the hole were inadequate to establish the size of the hole. Fifth, a pedestrian is required to see what the proper use of her senses should reveal. "Claimant's failure to do so constitutes such a culpable act that it completely bars any recovery."

(7)*Torri v. Big V of Kingston, Inc.*[96] The plaintiff slipped and fell over a substance on the floor, but the appellate court affirmed the summary judgment for the defendant. There was no evidence to show how the slippery substance got on the floor; in fact, the evidence that the substance was partially frozen indicated that it had not been there long, and there was no evidence that the defendant either created the condition or had received reports of it. "In the absence of any proof of how long the substance was there prior to the plaintiff's fall, she may not rely on a theory of constructive notice . . . ."

6.1.5.4.2 Mechanical Devices

6.1.5.4.2.a The Plaintiff

(8) *Zino v. City of New York.*[97] The plaintiff, a fireman, was injured when he removed the plug from a defective outlet. The plaintiff produced witnesses who testified that the outlet had been untouched for three years, that it had been installed improperly, and that the city had installed it. Since the defendant had created the faulty condition, there was no need for the plaintiff to prove notice.

---

96. Torri v. Big V of Kingston, Inc., 147 A.D.2d 743, 537 N.Y.S.2d 629 (3d Dep't 1989); *see also* DeVizio v. Hobart Corp., 142 A.D.2d 508, 530 N.Y.S.2d 144 (1st Dep't 1988); Restey v. Victory Mkts., 127 A.D.2d 987, 512 N.Y.S.2d 1022 (4th Dep't 1987); Rabinowitz v. New York Tel. Co., 119 A.D.2d 741, 501 N.Y.S.2d 152 (2d Dep't 1986).

97. Zino v. City of N.Y., 111 A.D.2d 847, 490 N.Y.S.2d 586 (2d Dep't 1985).

(9) *Sirigiano v. Otis Elevator Co.*[98] The plaintiff was injured when alighting from an elevator that did not align properly with the floor. The testimony was that postaccident tests had shown a misalignment and that there had been complaints about the misalignment for six months. The court found, therefore, that there was sufficient evidence of notice.

6.1.5.4.2.b The Defendant

(10) *Ginter v. TWA.*[99] The plaintiff, an airline passenger, was injured when luggage fell out of an overhead storage compartment. The court dismissed the complaint because the airline's personnel had had no notice that the compartment was defective.

6.1.5.4.3 Robbery

6.1.5.4.3.a The Defendant

(11) *Iannelli v. Powers.*[100] The plaintiff's decedent was killed during a robbery in an office building. The plaintiff brought an action for negligence against the landlord and alleged that prior crimes had placed the landlord on notice that crime was likely in the building. The plaintiff also alleged that the defendant had failed to take sufficient precautions to protect the plaintiff's decedent. The appellate court reversed the jury's verdict for the plaintiff, dismissed the complaint, and held that there had not been enough crimes

---

98. Sirigiano v. Otis Elevator Co., 118 A.D.2d 920, 499 N.Y.S.2d 486 (3d Dep't 1986); *see also* Rogers v. Dorcheser Assocs., 32 N.Y.2d 553, 300 N.E.2d 403, 347 N.Y.S.2d 22 (1973); Smith v. Jay Apartments, 33 A.D.2d 624, 304 N.Y.S.2d 304 (2d Dep't 1969). For an endorsement of applying the emergency doctrine to an attempt to escape from a broken elevator, *see* Mas v. Two Bridges Associates, 75 N.Y.2d 680 (1990).

99. Ginter v. Trans World Airlines, Inc., 148 A.D.2d 787, 538 N.Y.S.2d 638 (3d Dep't), *aff'd*, 74 N.Y.2d 754, 543 N.E.2d 741, 545 N.Y.S.2d 98 (1989).

100. Iannelli v. Powers, 114 A.D.2d 157, 498 N.Y.S.2d 377 (2d Dep't 1986).

to put the defendant on notice of the hazard to the decedent. "[T]he possessor of realty is not an insurer of the safety of those who enter upon such realty . . . ."

6.1.5.4.4 Falling Tree Limbs

6.1.5.4.4.a The Defendant

(12) *Ivancic v. Olmstead.*[101] During a windstorm, an overhanging limb fell from a tree and struck the plaintiff causing him serious injuries. Following a verdict for the plaintiff, the defendant moved to dismiss the complaint and then appealed the denial of that motion. The appellate court did dismiss the complaint and observed,

> At least as to adjoining landowners, the concept of constructive notice with respect to liability for falling trees is that there is no duty to consistently and constantly check all trees for nonvisible decay. Rather, the manifestation of said decay must be readily observable in order to require a landowner to take reasonable steps to prevent harm . . . . [In this case] [h]owever, the expert did indicate that the limb hole was about eight-feet high and located in the crotch of the tree which would have made it difficult, if not impossible, to see upon reasonable inspection . . . .

6.2 INDIRECT MEANS OF PROVING THE DIRECT CASE

The evidentiary devices explained in this section are indirect in the sense that the witness testifies to something other than what the party needs to prove, and the party then asks the jury to infer what he needs to prove. For example, the plaintiff may prove that the defendant failed to meet the custom and usage in the industry and then ask the jury to

---

101. Ivancic v. Olmstead, 66 N.Y.2d 349, 351, 488 N.E.2d 72, 497 N.Y.S.2d 326, 327-28 (1985).

infer that the defendant's conduct was negligent. The defendant may present testimony that he acted carefully by habit and then ask the jury to infer that he was careful on the occasion in question. The parties apply essentially the same logic to evidence of modifications or repairs, the violation of public or private rules, and circumstantial evidence. The opposing party, naturally, argues that the inference is unjustified. Remember, proof is the result of the application of reasoning to evidence.

6.2.1 Evidence of Prior Conduct

The relevant prior conduct may be the prior conduct of a party (to raise an inference that the party was or was not negligent on the occasion of the accident) or it may be that of an industry or profession, which conduct a party may claim has ripened into a custom and usage that is evidence of a standard of due care.

6.2.1.1 The Prior Conduct of a Party (Habit)

Prior individual acts of care or carelessness are not admissible to create an inference that the party repeated such conduct in the similar circumstances of the event in question.[102] Moreover, evidence of habit by itself is not admissible. However, the court of appeals held in *Halloran v. Virginia Chemicals, Inc.*:[103] "Proof of a deliberate repetitive practice *by one in complete control of the circumstances* is quite another matter and it should therefore be admissible because it is so highly probative."[104] (Emphasis added.)

---

102. Warner v. New York City Cent. R.R., 44 N.Y. 465, 472 (1874).

103. Halloran v. Virginia Chems, Inc., 41 N.Y.2d 386, 361 N.E.2d 991, 393 N.Y.S.2d 341 (1977).

104. *Id.* at 391, 361 N.E.2d at 994, 393 N.Y.S.2d at 344-45.

The issue in *Halloran* was whether the defendant could submit evidence that the plaintiff had misused the defendant's product in the past in order to show that the plaintiff had misused the product on the date in question. The defendant sought to introduce evidence that it was the plaintiff's custom and usage to use the allegedly defective product in a certain improper manner, but the trial court sustained the plaintiff's objection. The court of appeals ruled, however, that evidence of habit may be admissible to prove negligence. Once the trial court is satisfied that the party performed the conduct a sufficient number of times to rise to the level of a custom or habit, then the evidence of the habit is admissible for the jury's consideration.

Besides using the opposing party's habit against the individual, a party may use his own habit to raise an inference that he acted that way on a particular occasion, e.g., when operating a drill press. In *Rigie v. Goldman*,[105] the defendant, a dental surgeon, sought to introduce evidence of his own custom and practice of informing his patients of the risks and alternatives to surgical procedures. He could not recall what he had told this particular patient, but the doctor testified regarding his custom and practice, and his dental assistant testified to the same custom and practice. The Appellate Division, First Department, held that in a case in which the claim is lack of informed consent, such testimony is proper. The court wrote,

> [T]he testimony to which the plaintiff objects provided an adequate number of prior instances of specific, repetitive conduct by Dr. Levin when confronted with a patient presenting a similar condition to rise to the level of habit. Moreover, Dr. Levin was in complete control of the circumstances in which the operative procedure was performed. Thus, while creating no presumption that the practice was followed in the particular instance at issue, the testimony of Dr. Levin as to his routine practice, corroborated by his dental assistant, was

105. Rigie v. Goldman, 148 A.D.2d 23, 543 N.Y.S.2d 983, 986-87 (1st Dep't 1989).

properly admissible to support an inference by the jury that the practice was followed on the particular occasion in question . . . .

The court of appeals warned the lower courts, however, not to permit evidence of habit to establish a party's propensity to act in accordance with his general character rather than his habitual manner of performing a particular act within his complete control.

Compare *Rigie* with *Glusaskas v. Hutchinson,*[106] in which the Appellate Division, First Department, held that it was reversible error for the trial court to allow a defendant in an action for medical malpractice to introduce a videotape that he had made of himself performing similar surgery. The appellate court held that the circumstances under which the doctor had made the videotape were clearly dissimilar to the plaintiff's surgery.[107] In other words, the videotape was not evidence of the doctor's repetitive performance of an act under his complete control but only of a specific instance performed under the different circumstances created by the taping.

An even more extreme example of an unsuccessful attempt to introduce evidence of habit to allow an inference of careful conduct on the day in question is contained in *Ferrar v. Harris,*[108] in which the plaintiff sought to introduce testimony regarding the prior safe manner in which she had instructed her children to cross the street. The plaintiff did not attempt to show that the instructions had resulted in habitually proper conduct by the infants. Rather, the plaintiff sought to show the "knowledge and experience of the infants in crossing the street." The court of appeals ruled that such evidence is inadmissible because evidence of a plain-

106. Glusaskas v. Hutchinson, N.Y.L.J., July 21, 1989 (1st Dep't 1989).

107. See analysis of *Rigie* and *Glusasakas* in Kramer & Moore, *Medical Malpractice: Habit, Custom and Inferences*, N.Y.L.J., Sept. 5, 1989, at 2, col. 1.

108. Ferrar v. Harris, 55 N.Y.2d 285, 434 N.E.2d 231, 449 N.Y.S.2d 162 (1982), *modified*, 56 N.Y.2d 737 (1982).

tiff's knowledge and experience is inadmissible. In other words, evidence of what a party does on a continuous basis may be admissible, but evidence of what he knows he should do is not.

6.2.1.2 Custom and Usage

A party may prove that he complied with the custom and usage in an industry or profession or that the opposing party failed to comply with such a standard. Thus, the defendant may prove that he or she complied with the recognized custom and usage in the industry in the manner in which he or she performed a certain act as evidence of being careful and prudent.[109] Similarly, evidence that the defendant failed to comply with the recognized and customary practice may indicate negligence.[110]

In *Trimarco v. Klein*,[111] the court of appeals explained the rationale for admitting such evidence. First, a custom and usage in an industry or a profession reflects the judgment and experience of many people. Second, custom bears directly on the feasibility of conduct by focusing on the practicality of a precaution and the readiness with which it can be employed. Third, a custom educates others in the safe way. Such a custom need not be universal, but it must be sufficiently well defined that the relevant party may be charged with knowledge of it.

> However, once its existence is credited, a common practice or usage is still not necessarily a conclusive or even a compelling test of negligence . . . . Before it can be, the jury must be satisfied with its reasonableness, just as the jury must be satisfied with the reasonableness of the behavior which adhered to the custom or the reasonableness of that which did not....After all, customs and usages run the gamut of merit like everything

---

109. Bennett v. Long Island R.R., 163 N.Y. 1, 57 N.E. 79 (1900).

110. Sawyer v. Dreis & Krump Mfg. Co., 67 N.Y.2d 328, 502 N.Y.S.2d 696 (1986); Levine v. Russell Blaine Co., 273 N.Y. 386, 7 N.E.2d 673 (1937).

111. Trimarco v. Klein, 56 N.Y.2d 98, 43 N.E.2d 502, 451 N.Y.S.2d 52 (1982).

else. That is why the question in each instance is whether it meets the test of reasonableness . . . .[112]

The court of appeals explained further that the jury is to judge a deviation from the standard under all the circumstances of the defendant's conduct. The violation of a custom and usage is not negligence, per se, and the jurors must decide whether the standard is reasonable and whether the defendant was wrong to depart from it.

6.2.2 Repairs and Modifications After the Accident

Evidence of the defendant's repairs of the site or his modification to his product is admissible only for limited purposes.

6.2.2.1 Actions for Negligence

It is well settled in New York that evidence of subsequent remedial measures is not admissible on the issue of the defendant's negligence.[113] (A remedial measure may be a physical act, such as a repair, or a letter of warning or instruction.) Nevertheless, such evidence is admissible for other purposes.

---

112. *Id.* at 106-07, 436 N.E.2d at 505, 451 N.Y.S.2d at 56.

113. Weines v. Serps Auto Wreckers, 24 N.Y.2d 845, 248 N.E.2d 601, 300 N.Y.S.2d 852 (1969); DiPaolo v. Somma, 111 A.D.2d 899, 490 N.Y.S.2d 803 (2d Dep't 1985); Heyden v. Gallagher Elevator Co., 94 A.D.2d 936, 464 N.Y.S.2d 887 (4th Dep't 1983); Annot., *Admissibility of Evidence of Repairs, Change of Conditions, or Precautions Taken After Accident*, 64 A.L.R.2D 1296 (1959); *cf.* Robinson v. Reed Prentice Div., 49 N.Y.2d 471, 403 N.E.2d 440, 426 N.Y.S.2d 717 (1980) (held that defendant may show that plaintiff modified or altered product after it left decedent's hands and that manufacturer may not be cast in damages under negligence or strict tort liability for injuries that occurred as a result of strict tort liability for injuries that occurred as a result of that modification); Dudley v. County of Saratoga, 145 A.D.2d 689, 535 N.Y.S.2d 231 (3d Dep't 1988); Ramundo v. Guilderland, 142 A.D.2d 50, 534 N.Y.S.2d 543 (3d Dep't 1988); Hansen v. Honda Motor Co., 104 A.D.2d 850, 480 N.Y.S.2d 244 (2d Dep't 1984).

For example, evidence of the defendant's repairs or alterations to the premises or to a device is admissible if the defendant denies that he owns or controls the property.[114]

6.2.2.2 Actions in Strict Liability

The crucial distinction in cases alleging strict products liability is between defects in manufacturing and defects in design. Thus, in *Caprara v. Chrysler Corp.* [115] and *Rainbow v. Albert Elia Building Co.*,[116] the court of appeals permitted the plaintiff in a strict products liability case based upon a claimed manufacturing defect to introduce evidence of the manufacturer's subsequent modification to the product to establish that the product was defective when made. But such evidence was not admissible in a strict products liability action in which the plaintiff alleged a defect in the design of the product or inadequate instructions for the use of the product or warnings of its danger.[117] Consequently, some plaintiffs have phrased their causes of action as defects in manufacturing in order to introduce the evidence of the manufacturer's modification. In *Perazone v. Sears, Roebuck & Co.*,[118] the Appellate Division, Third Department, held that the trial court must analyze the plaintiff's claims carefully. Only if the claim is really for a defect in manufacturing is evidence of a postmanufacturing change admissible. How the plaintiff characterizes the claim is irrelevant; only the true cause of action matters.

---

114. RICHARDSON, EVIDENCE § 168.

115. Caprara v. Chrysler Corp., 52 N.Y.2d 11, 417 N.E.2d 545, 436 N.Y.S.2d 251 (1981).

116. Rainbow v. Albert Elia Bldg. Co., 79 A.D.2d 287, 436 N.Y.S.2d 480 (4th Dep't 1981), *aff'd*, 56 N.Y.2d 550, 434 N.E.2d 1345, 449 N.Y.S.2d 967 (1982).

117. Haran v. Union Carbide, 68 N.Y.2d 710, 497 N.E.2d 678, 506 N.Y.S.2d 311 (1986).

118. Perazone v. Sears, Roebuck & Co., 128 A.D.2d 15, 515 N.Y.S.2d 908 (3d Dep't 1987).

In *Cover v. Cohen,*[119] the court of appeals added that it was error to admit a federal motor vehicle standard requiring a different type of accelerator spring on 1974 cars than was used on 1973 cars (the car was a Chevrolet) because the defendant had conceded the feasibility of using a different type of spring and because the plaintiff was alleging a defect in design. An internal technical service bulletin that General Motors sent to its dealers after the sale of the car was also inadmissible. However, if the plaintiff has charged the defendant with becoming aware of a defect in the product and failing to warn past purchasers, then a technical service bulletin acknowledging that some 1973 vehicles "may exhibit an erratic idle speed and slow return to idle," if otherwise relevant and together with testimony that an erratic idling speed, slow return to idle, or both may seriously impair the driver's control of the vehicle, is admissible to show that the corporation knew of the defect and failed to warn the purchaser.

6.2.2.3 Feasibility

As an exception to the general rule that evidence of modifications to the design of a product after the accident is inadmissible, such evidence is admissible on the issue of whether modifications in the allegedly defective design were feasible. Thus, in *Cover v. Cohen,*[120] the court of appeals held that evidence that the manufacturer modified the design of a product after the accident is admissible in a defective design case to demonstrate that incorporating the modification was feasible. However, if the defendant concedes that such modifications were feasible, the evidence of the actual modification is not admissible. Such a conces-

---

119. Cover v. Cohen, 61 N.Y.2d 261, 276, 461 N.E.2d 864, 872, 473 N.Y.S.2d 378, 385 (1984) (citing General Motors Corp. v. Dodson, 47 Tenn. App. 438, 338 S.W.2d 655 (1976)); *see* Rozler v. Ford Motor Co., 573 F.2d 1332 (5th Cir. 1978); Bowman v. General Motors Corp., 64 F.R.D. 62 (E.D. Pa. 1974).

120. Cover v. Cohen, 61 N.Y.2d 261, 461 N.E.2d 864, 473 N.Y.S.2d 378 (1984); *see also* Haran v. Union Carbide, 68 N.Y.2d 710, 497 N.E.2d 678, 506 N.Y.S.2d 311 (1986).

sion may be a shrewd trial tactic to prevent the jury from hearing such evidence.

A document may be admissible to prove the feasibility of a modification. For example, in *Barry v. Manglass*,[121] the Appellate Division, First Department, held that a recall letter sent by General Motors to owners and warning that a motor mount might separate was admissible — even though the corporation sent the letter two months after the accident. The trial court, however, must instruct the jury that the recall letter is not an admission that a defect existed or that a defect caused the accident, and that it is admissible only to demonstrate feasibility.

In *Denny v. Ford Motor Co.*,[122] the court of appeals explained the continuing distinction between actions for defective design and those for strict liability.

> In design defect cases, the alleged product flow arises from an intentional decision by the manufacturer to configure the product in a particular way. In contrast, in strict products liability cases involving manufacturing defects, the harm arises from the product's failure to perform in the intended manner due to some flaw in the fabrication process. In the latter class of cases, the flaw alone is a sufficient basis to hold the manufacturer liable without regard to fault . . . .[123]

In cases involving construction of premises, a plaintiff may introduce evidence of other structures. Thus, in *Cruz v. New York City Transit Authority*,[124] the Appellate Division, Second Department, held that proof of the design and construction of similar stairways at other locations was admissible. The plaintiff had sought to show that it was possible to build a similar stairway in a safer fashion in order to show the feasibility as

---

121. Barry v. Manglass, 55 A.D.2d 1, 389 N.Y.S.2d 870 (1st Dep't 1976).

122. Denny v. Ford Motor Co., 87 N.Y.2d 248 (1996).

123. *Id.* at 257 n.3.

124. Cruz v. New York City Transit Auth., 136 A.D.2d 196, 526 N.Y.S.2d 827 (2d Dep't 1988).

well as to define the standard of care in the industry, and the court agreed.

6.2.3 The Violation of a Statute or Private Rule

6.2.3.1 The Violation of a Statute

6.2.3.1.1 The Proof of a Statute

In New York, the courts must take judicial notice of statutes, whether or not the parties have pleaded or proven them.[125] While judicial notice is discussed later in this book, the reader should understand that making a prima facie case or defending an action may involve proving a violation of statute.[126]

6.2.3.1.2 Liability

The defendant's violation of a statute may be mere evidence of negligence, negligence per se, or proof of strict liability. If the defendant is a governmental unit, the violation is very likely, but not necessarily, irrelevant. In addition, the plaintiff's violation of a statute may be a defense or constitute comparative negligence.

6.2.3.1.2.a Negligence

If the defendant did violate a statute and if the plaintiff can prove that the plaintiff is a member of the class the legislature

---

125. C.P.L.R. rule 4511(a).
126. Long v. Murnane Assocs., 68 A.D.2d 166, 416 N.Y.S.2d 413 (3d Dep't 1979). Labor Law § 241(6) imposes absolute liability. *See also* Long v. Forest-Fehlhaber, 74 A.D.2d 167 (3d Dep't 1980).

sought to protect,[127] then the violation is negligence per se.[128] Of course, the plaintiff still must prove that the violation caused the plaintiff's injuries.[129] If the defendant violated a statute meant to protect the plaintiff, and the statute is relevant, the court must charge the jury on the statute even if the defendant has an explanation of why he violated the statute, e.g., circumstances beyond the defendant's control.[130]

6.2.3.1.2.b Governmental Units

When the defendant is a governmental unit, the plaintiff must prove that the defendant was performing a proprietary rather than a governmental function; that is, the injured party must prove that a special relationship between that party and the governmental unit imposed a duty on the government to perform some act for his benefit.[131] If the legislature enacted the statute to protect the general public, and the plaintiff is simply

---

127. Burgbacher v. Lazar, 97 A.D.2d 496, 468 N.Y.S.2d 14 (2d Dep't 1983); Rushnick v. Gerstheimer, 82 A.D.2d 944, 440 N.Y.S.2d 738 (3d Dep't 1981).

128. RESTATEMENT (SECOND) OF TORTS § 286 (1965). In Cordero v. City of N.Y., 112 A.D.2d 914, 492 N.Y.S.2d 430 (2d Dept. 1985), the court noted that the "unexcused violation of a statutory standard of care is negligence and can create liability if found to be a proximate cause of the accident." If there is no proof that the defendant violated a statute, it is reversible error for the court to mention the statute in its charge. Christoforou v. Lown, 120 A.D.2d 387, 502 N.Y.S.2d 184 (1st Dep't 1986).

129. Somersall v. New York Tel. Co., 52 N.Y.2d 157, 418 N.E.2d 373, 436 N.Y.S.2d 858 (1981); Nola v. New York City Transit Auth., 115 A.D.2d 461, 495 N.Y.S.2d 697 (2d Dep't 1985).

130. Hardy v. Sicuranza, 133 A.D.2d 139, 518 N.Y.S.2d 812 (2d Dep't 1987); Gamar v. Gamar, 114 A.D.2d 487, 494 N.Y.S.2d 402 (2d Dep't 1985). In Cincotta v. Johnson, 130 A.D.2d 539, 515 N.Y.S.2d 115, 117 (2d Dep't 1987), the court added:

> The jury should have been instructed that a violation of that rule would represent some evidence of negligence only if it first determined that the rule imposed a standard of care no greater than that which reasonable prudence required (*cf.* Danbois v. New York Cent. R.R. Co., 12 N.Y.2d 234, 237, 238 N.Y.S.2d 921 189 N.E.2d 468) . . . .

131. Miller v. State, 62 N.Y.2d 506, 467 N.E.2d 493, 478 N.Y.S.2d 829 (1984); DeLong v. County of Erie, 60 N.Y.2d 296, 457 N.E.2d 717, 469 N.Y.S.2d 611 (1983); Weiner v. Metropolitan Transp. Auth., 55 N.Y.2d 175, 433 N.E.2d 124, 448 N.Y.S.2d 141 (1982); Pugliese v. City of N.Y., 115 A.D.2d 465, 495 N.Y.S.2d

a member of that class, then the violation of the statute by the municipal defendant will not create a valid claim for negligence.[132]

6.2.3.1.2.c Infants

In *Burgbacher v. Lazar,*[133] the Appellate Division, Second Department, discussed the standard of care imposed upon an infant to comply with a statutory provision. The case dealt with a bicycler's duty to equip his machine with a light as required by Vehicle and Traffic Law section 1236(B). The appellate court approved the following charge to the jury:

> [W]here a statute creates a standard of conduct, a violation of that statute by an adult, constitutes negligence provided such violation was the proximate cause of the accident.

---

700 (2d Dep't 1985). In one recent case, the plaintiff was beaten, raped, and robbed while walking through an isolated subway tunnel that was being renovated. The plaintiff claimed that the transit authority had been negligent in storing construction materials in the tunnel and in declining a recommendation to close the tunnel due to crime there. However, the court of appeals ruled that the defendant's act was governmental, not proprietary, and that causation was speculative. Clinger v. New York City Transit Authority, 85 N.Y.2d 957 (1995). The next day, the Appellate Division, First Department, found that the transit authority was not liable for a token clerk's attack on a passenger. Adams v. New York City Transit Authority, 211 A.D.2d 285 (1st Dep't 1995). For a case involving a rape in a public housing structure, see Jacqueline S. v. City of New York and N.Y.C. Housing Authority, 81 N.Y.2d 288 (1993). The plaintiff, a fourteen-year-old resident of public housing, was abducted from the lobby and raped in the utility room. The housing authority had a common law obligation to provide security against foreseeable attacks on the premises and a statutory duty to comply with M.D.L. 50-a(3), regarding locks and intercoms. There had been crimes including rapes in the project, and although the authority did poll the residents about locks on the outer doors, the authority failed to tabulate the votes for each building individually. Therefore, the appellate division should not have dismissed the complaint.

132. Motkya v. City of Amsterdam, 15 N.Y.2d 134, 204 N.E.2d 635, 256 N.Y.S.2d 595 (1965); Sheu v. High-Forest Corp., 129 A.D.2d 366, 517 N.Y.S.2d 798 (3d Dep't 1987); Stranger v. New York State Elec. & Gas Corp., 25 A.D.2d 169, 268 N.Y.S.2d 214 (3d Dep't 1966). *But see* Smullen v. City of New York, 28 N.Y.2d 66 (1971).

133. Burgbacher v. Lazar, 97 A.D.2d 496, 497, 468 N.Y.S.2d 14, 15 (2d Dep't 1983).

> However, where the violation is by an infant, it is a question of fact for you, the jury, to determine whether or not the infant will be charged with that violation.
>
> If you find that the infant on the basis of his age, his experience, intelligence and development, had the mental capacity to understand the meaning of the statute and to comply therewith, you should charge him with negligence for its violation.
>
> If, on the other hand, you find that the infant lacked the mental capacity to understand its meaning and comply with it, you should not charge him with negligence simply for its violation.

In other words, the violation of a statute is not as strong evidence of negligence against an infant as against an adult.

6.2.3.1.3 Defenses

Proof that the defendant violated a statute is not necessarily dispositive. The violation may be only evidence of negligence or of proximate cause. Some statutes do impose absolute liability upon a defendant,[134] and when a statute does so, neither assumption of risk nor contributory negligence is a valid defense. [135] These defenses are also unavailable when the violation of the statute is negligence per se.[136] However, an important distinction is that a defendant other than the active tortfeasor may or may not be too remote from the conduct to be held liable for the violation of the statute. Thus, the owner of a motor vehicle would be vicariously liable pursuant to the permissive use statute, V.T.L. 388,[136.1] but

134. *E.g.*, LAB. LAW § 240.

135. Koenig v. Patrick Constr. Corp., 298 N.Y. 313, 83 N.E.2d 133 (1948); Long v. Murnane Assocs., 68 A.D.2d 166, 416 N.Y.S.2d 413 (3d Dep't 1979). *See also* Van Gassbeck v. Webatuck Central School District 1, 21 N.Y.2d 239 (1967), re a school bus driver and VTL 1174(b), and Brown v. Christopher St. Owners Corp., 87 N.Y.2d 938 (1996), re: LABOR LAW § 240(1).

136. Martin v. Herzog, 228 N.Y. 164, 126 N.E. 814 (1920). *But see* Tedla v. Ellman, 280 N.Y. 124 (1939), re VTL 85(6).

136.1. Lynch-Fina v. Estate of Wagner, 64 Misc.3d 963 (Sp. Ct. Qns., 1995).

this statute does not impose vicarious liability on the pubic school which contracted for bus service even if V.T.L. 1174(b) does impose liability per se on the driver.[136.2]

In some cases, e.g., General Obligations Law section 9-103 governing certain uses of premises, a statute protects a defendant from liability. When such a statute is relevant, the plaintiff must satisfy the additional burden of proof required by the statute, or the trial court will dismiss the complaint.[137] As an alternative, if the defendant can prove that the plaintiff violated a statute that was designed to protect a class encompassing the plaintiff, then that violation is evidence of the plaintiff's comparative negligence.[138]

6.2.3.2 The Violation of a Private Rule or Regulation

In New York, the plaintiff may introduce evidence of the defendant's work rules when the defendant's business is affected with a public interest and the rules were designed to protect such people as the plaintiff. In most jurisdictions, the private rules that a defendant has adopted for the guidance of its employees in the performance of their duties are admissible on the theory that they are some indication of the care required under the circumstances. New York's rule was formerly to the contrary,[139] and is still narrower, but in *Danbois v. New York Central Railroad*,[140] the court of appeals held that when the defendant's business is "affected with a public interest," the private rules of the company are admissible, and a violation of such a rule may be some evidence of negligence. For example,

---

136.2. Chainani v. Board of Education of the City of New York, 87 N.Y.2d 370 (1995)(V.T.L. requires the bus driver to keep the bus halted and its red lights flashing while discharging passengers who must cross a public street).

137. Hardy v. Gullo, 118 A.D.2d 541, 499 N.Y.S.2d 159 (2d Dep't 1986); Messinger v. Festa, 117 A.D.2d 784, 499 N.Y.S.2d 111 (2d Dept't 1986).

138. Franco v. Zingarelli, 72 A.D.2d 211, 424 N.Y.S.2d 185 (1st Dep't 1980).

139. Longacre v. Yonkers R.R., 236 N.Y. 119, 140 N.E. 215 (1923).

140. Danbois v. New York Cent. R.R., 12 N.Y.2d 234, 189 N.E.2d 468, 238 N.Y.S.2d 921 (1963).

in *Haber v. Cross County Hospital*,[141] the court held that the defendant's failure to abide by its own rule, which required the use of bed rails for all patients over fifty years of age, was some evidence of negligence.

The defendant's private rule is not admissible, however, if it clearly requires a higher standard of care than the reasonable care required by law. Hence, in *Caputo v. New York City Transit Authority*,[142] the Appellate Division, Second Department, held that it would be error to admit a defendant's private rules and regulations into evidence when the standard of care set forth therein is greater than that expected of a reasonable man. The defendant may demand more, but the court may not.

6.2.4 Circumstantial Evidence

6.2.4.1 In General

Circumstantial evidence is direct evidence of the facts presented but indirect evidence of the facts to be proved; that is, it is evidence of facts or circumstances from which the existence or nonexistence of a fact in issue may be inferred.[143]

There are certain instances in which the plaintiff can rely on circumstantial evidence or reasonable inference rather than on direct proof of the defendant's negligence.

Circumstantial evidence is sufficient if it supports the inference of causation or of negligence even though it does not

---

141. Haber v. Cross County Hosp., 37 N.Y.2d 888, 333 N.E.2d 353, 378 N.Y.S.2d 369 (1975); *see also* Schneider v. Kings Highway Hosp., 67 N.Y.2d 743, 490 N.E.2d 1221, 500 N.Y.S.2d 95 (1986); Mertsaris v. 73rd Corp., 105 A.D.2d 67, 482 N.Y.S.2d 792 (2d Dep't 1984); Hughson v. St. Francis Hosp., 96 A.D.2d 829, 465 N.Y.S.2d 578 (2d Dept. 1983).

142. Caputo v. New York City Transit Auth., 86 A.D.2d 883, 447 N.Y.S.2d 535 (2d Dep't 1982), and Lesser v. Manhattan and Bronx Surface Transit Operating Authority, 157 A.D.2d 352 (1st Dep't 1990); judgment for plaintiff reversed because the trial court allowed the defendant's operator's manual into evidence.

143. Black's Law Dictionary 309 (4th ed. 1968).

negate the existence of remote possibilities that the injury was not caused by the defendant or that the defendant was not negligent. "It is enough that he (plaintiff) shows facts and conditions from which the negligence of the defendant and the causation of the accident by that negligence may be reasonably inferred."[144]

In fact, a plaintiff may establish a prima facie case entirely on circumstantial evidence as long as the jury bases its verdict on logical inferences and common experience, not speculation.[145] For example, in *Kaplan v. Central Medical Group of Brooklyn*,[146] the court held that the doctor's having altered his medical records was strong circumstantial evidence of his malpractice.

---

144. Spett v. President Monroe Bldg. & Mfg. Corp., 19 N.Y.2d 203, 205, 225 N.E.2d 521, 523, 278 N.Y.S.2d 818, 829 (1967); *see also* Dryer v. Tishman Realty & Constr. Co., 42 N.Y.2d 883, 366 N.E.2d 873, 397 N.Y.S.2d 785 (1977), *rev'g* 52 A.D.2d 76, 382 N.Y.S.2d 486 (1st Dep't 1976); Barker v. Parnossa, Inc., 39 N.Y.2d 926, 352 N.E.2d 880, 386 N.Y.S.2d 576 (1976). Fed. R. Evid. 401 does not deal specifically with circumstantial evidence but states that "relevant evidence" means evidence (whether demonstrative, circumstantial, or direct) having any tendency to make the existence of any fact more probable. Jackson v. Associated Dry Goods Corp., 13 N.Y.2d 112, 192 N.E.2d 167, 242 N.Y.S.2d 210 (1963); Garippa v. Wisotsky, 305 N.Y. 571, 111 N.E.2d 443 (1953); Dillon v. Rockaway Beach Hosp., 284 N.Y. 176, 179, 30 N.E.2d 373, 375 (1940); Hughes v. Borden's Farm Prods. Co., 252 N.Y. 532, 170 N.E. 132 (1929); *see also* E. Fisch, New York Evidence § 216, at 119 (1977). In Schneider v. Kings Highway Hosp., 67 N.Y.2d 743, 490 N.E.2d 1221, 500 N.Y.S.2d 95 (1986), the court of appeals held that circumstantial evidence of a defendant's negligence can be shown by the fact that the plaintiff was found on the floor next to the hospital bed and that the defendant had violated its own rules and regulations about having the bed rails up. The plaintiff could not testify as to how the accident had happened.
145. Cappadona v. State, N.Y.L.J., May 7, 1987 (Ct. C1. 1987).
146. Kaplan v. Central Medical Group, 71 A.D.2d 912, 419 N.Y.S.2d 750 (2d Dep't 1979).

6.2.4.2 Negative Evidence

Negative evidence is really circumstantial evidence in which the circumstance is the absence of something that should exist. The jury is allowed to draw an inference from the absence of conduct, the loss of papers, or a party's failure to act, which conduct bears only indirectly on the case.[147] For example, in *Zino v. City of New York*,[148] the court charged the jury that it could draw an adverse inference from the defendant city's failure to produce the maintenance records of the situs of the accident.

However, negative evidence is not always admissible. Hence, in *Franco v. Zingarelli*,[149] the court ruled that the jury could not draw an inference from the failure of the police to arrest the defendant. That failure was not relevant to the plaintiff's claim of negligence, and, therefore, that negative evidence was not admissible.

6.2.4.3 Representative Cases

The courts in the following cases decided the motions for the plaintiffs, and discussions of circumstantial evidence tend to focus on the plaintiff's case because he or she has the burden of proof. Either party, however, may employ circumstantial evidence.

---

147. *See* Hoeniy, *Spoliation of Evidence, Preserving the Crown Jewels*, N.Y.L.J., Dec. 23, 1988, at 3, col. 1. Ellinghusen v. Flushing Hosp., 143 A.D.2d 217, 531 N.Y.S.2d 824 (2d Dep't 1988), discussed the plaintiff's right to rely on the absence of notations in hospital records to prove that an event did not take place.

148. Zino v. City of N.Y., 111 A.D.2d 845, 491 N.Y.S.2d 14 (2d Dep't 1985).

149. Franco v. Zingarelli, 72 A.D.2d 211, 424 N.Y.S.2d 185 (1st Dep't 1980).

6.2.4.3.1 "Slip-and-Fall" Cases

6.2.4.3.1.a The Plaintiff

(1) *Spett v. President Monroe Building & Manufacturing Corp.*[150] The plaintiff tripped over a skid (a wooden platform) that was unidentifiable except that it was loaded with a type of cardboard used only by the defendant in its printing business and by no other concern on that floor of the building. "The circumstantial evidence tending to establish Harvey's responsibility for it was sufficient to establish a prima facie case."

(2) *Laidlaw v. Andrew Freedman Home.*[151] The plaintiff, a resident of an old age home, slipped and fell on the wet floor of the bathroom. The evidence established that, on Tuesday of each week, the floor was washed with a wet mop from a wring pail and left to dry as was done on the day of the plaintiff's accident. The appellate court held that the trial court had erred by dismissing the plaintiff's complaint for the inference was reasonable that the defendant had caused the dangerous condition and the plaintiff's injury.

(3) *Hughes v. Borden's Farm.*[152] While walking on the sidewalk in front of the milk company's premises, the plaintiff stepped on a broken milk bottle and injured her foot. The court held that whether the defendant's negligence left the milk bottle on the sidewalk was a question of fact.

(4) *Romano v. City of New York.*[153] The plaintiff was injured when she stepped in a hole in the sidewalk in which was lying part of an automobile spring allegedly from the defendant's junkyard. Whether the junkyard was liable was a question of fact for the jury.

---

150. Spett v. President Monroe Bldg. & Mfg. Corp., 19 N.Y.2d 203, 225 N.E.2d 527, 278 N.Y.S.2d 826 (1967).
151. Laidlaw v. Andrew Freedman Home, 32 A.D.2d 754, 300 N.Y.S.2d 979 (1st Dep't 1969).
152. Hughes v. Borden's Farm Prods. Co., 252 N.Y. 532, 170 N.E. 132 (1929).
153. Romano v. City of N.Y., 254 A.D. 906, 5 N.Y.S.2d 518 (2d Dep't 1938).

(5) *Keegan v. Hohorst.*[154] The plaintiff fell on a grease spot on the sidewalk in front of the defendant's premises. The defendant claimed that he was not responsible for the condition of the sidewalk, but the appellate court affirmed the verdict for the plaintiff.

(6) *Jackson v. Associated Dry Goods Corp.*[155] The plaintiff fell on gravel and stone in a parking lot owned by one defendant. Another defendant, a contractor, had been doing construction work in the vicinity. The inference was reasonable that the contractor was responsible for the condition of the parking lot.

(7) *Cooley v. Trustees, New York & Brooklyn Bridge.*[156] The plaintiff fell on a pile of refuse composed of earth, banana peelings, cigar stumps, etc., situated on the fifth or sixth step from the bottom of a staircase leading to the Brooklyn Bridge. There was no direct evidence of how the pile came to be there except that the defendant's employee would clean the steps every morning about half an hour before the time of the plaintiff's accident and that he swept the steps from top to bottom by accumulating the refuse on each lower step as he proceeded. The appellate court held,

---

154. Keegan v. Hohorst, 235 A.D. 871, 257 N.Y.S.595 (2d Dep't 1932).

155. Jackson v. Associated Dry Goods Corp., 13 N.Y.2d 112, 192 N.E.2d 167, 242 N.Y.S.2d 210 (1963).

156. Cooley v. Trustees, N.Y. & Brooklyn Bridge, 46 A.D.243, 61 N.Y.S. 1 (2d Dep't 1899); *see also* Kelsey v. Port Auth., 52 A.D.2d 801, 383 N.Y.S.2d 801 (1st Dep't 1976) (plaintiff testified that she had seen cigarette butts, paper cups, and wetness on two steps of a stairway some fifteen to twenty minutes before she descended it a second time and then slipped on something that caused her to fall: "Although plaintiff was unable to specify the present condition which caused her to fall, the jury could reasonably infer that the condition present when she first descended the stairway remained unchanged for 15 to 20 minutes and was the proximate cause of the fall."). *But see also* Gordon v. American Museum of Natural History, 67 N.Y.2d 836 (1986): the plaintiff had observed other papers on the steps ten minutes earlier, but the court reversed the judgment for the plaintiff because the time relevant to the papers on which the defendant had slipped was too short to constitute constructive notice.

> From the character of the accumulation, it would seem to be a fair inference that the pile was the result of such sweeping; and, taking its character, the method of procedure of cleaning the stairs, and the time of day when the accident happened, we think there was sufficient [evidence] from which the jury might infer that the defendant was responsible for the condition of the step and the pile of dirt thereon.

6.2.4.3.2 Motor Vehicle

6.2.4.3.2.a The Plaintiff

(8) *Garippa v. Wisotsky.*[157] The plaintiff, a pedestrian, was struck by a truck, which dragged him for two blocks; the truck then left the scene of the accident. The plaintiff testified that, as the truck was dragging him, he smelled fresh baking and noticed that the truck was dark green with lettering on its side. There was evidence that the defendant was a wholesale baker and the owner of a dark green delivery truck that had made a delivery on the same street about the time of the accident. The court affirmed the verdict for the plaintiff.

(9) *Ashton v. J.J. Hafferty, Inc.*[158] The plaintiff's car went off the highway because of rough ground. The evidence was that the defendant had had a contract with the State of New York to level this area, that, at the time of the accident, the surface material was gravel, loam, dirt, and stone, and that the surface was rough. The court held, "[a]n inference could also be drawn that the condition on the highway was created by the respondent."

---

157. Garippa v. Wisotsky, 305 N.Y. 571, 111 N.E.2d 443 (1953); *see also* Demogenes v. Village Carting Co., 44 A.D.2d 155, 354 N.Y.S.2d 7 (1st Dep't 1974) (plaintiff's vehicle struck a large trash receptacle sitting in the roadway and bearing the legend "Village Carting Co."; court held that defendant's name was prima facie evidence of its operation and control, particularly when the defendant offered no evidence in denial).

158. Ashton v. J.J. Haggerty, Inc., 1 A.D.2d 964, 150 N.Y.S.2d 375 (2d Dep't 1956).

(10) *Hunter v. Ford Motor Co.*[159] About four months after the plaintiff had purchased a new Ford truck, he heard a sudden noise while driving, the lower left section of the truck dropped into the road, and the truck went out of control. Consequently, the plaintiff sued the manufacturer and the dealer for negligence and breach of warranty. In affirming the verdict for the plaintiff, the court wrote, "The precise defect need not be named and proved; it is sufficient if the cumulation of circumstances and inferences, which include the pattern of the accident, supports the conclusion that there was a defect which caused the accident."

(11) *Wragee v. Lizza Asphalt Construction Co.*[160] An automobile, heading south and negotiating a left turn, left the road and struck a pole. The driver and his passenger were both killed so their estates sued the owner of property abutting the road. A broken pipe on that property had caused water from the pumps to overflow into the roadway where it turned to ice. The trial court dismissed the complaint, but the appellate court reversed that decision and held that the circumstantial evidence had created a question of fact.

(12) *Pierson v. Dayton.*[161] This case was an action for wrongful death against the supervising driver for the death of the student driver who had only a learner's permit. The student driver lost control of the car on the ice; the car skidded off the road, and the student was killed. The appellate court held that the evidence was sufficient for the jury to draw an inference of negligence against the instructor.

---

159. Hunter v. Ford Motor Co., 37 A.D.2d 335, 337, 325 N.Y.S.2d 469, 471 (3d Dep't 1971); *see also* Depelteau v. Ford Motor Co., 28 A.D.2d 1178, 284 N.Y.S.2d 490 (3d Dep't 1967); Markel v. Spencer & Ford Co., 5 A.D.2d 400, 171 N.Y.S.2d 770 (4th Dep't 1958), *aff'd*, 5 N.Y.2d 958, 157 N.E.2d 713,184 N.Y.S.2d 835 (1959).

160. Wragge v. Lizza Asphalt Constr. Co., 17 N.Y.2d 313, 217 N.E.2d 666, 270 N.Y.S.2d 616 (1966).

161. Pierson v. Dayton, 168 A.D.2d 173 (4th Dep't 1991).

(13) *Coury v. Safe Auto Sales, Inc.*[162] When the plaintiff was a passenger in a car that crossed the center line into the wrong lane and struck another car coming in the opposite direction, the facts raised an inference of negligence.

6.2.4.3.3 Mechanical Devices

6.2.4.3.3.a The Plaintiff

(14) *Rogers v. Dorchester Associates (Otis Elevator).*[163] The door of a self-service elevator malfunctioned, and there was evidence that the door had malfunctioned on previous occasions. Res ipsa loquitur was not applicable, but "circumstantial evidence of sufficient probative force may permit a jury to infer negligence" by the maintenance company, Otis Elevator.

(15) *Sherman v. Concourse Realty Corp.*[164] A tenant entered the lobby of his apartment house and was mugged by someone who entered the lobby after him. The plaintiff presented evidence that the lock, which had been installed on the entrance door for security, had been defective for at least a week. The court ruled that the circumstantial evidence was sufficient for the jury to infer that the assailant was an intruder who had entered the lobby by pushing open the lockless door.

(16) *Johnson v. New York City Transit Authority.*[165] A man was found on the floor with part of a subway shoe lying next to him. The witnesses testified that they did not see what had hit him but that he was walking when his head

---

162. Coury v. Safe Auto Sales, Inc., 32 N.Y.2d 162, 198 N.E.2d 88, 344 N.Y.S. 2d 347 (1973); *see also* Simmons v. Stiles, 43 A.D.2d 417, 353 N.Y.S.2d 257 (3d Dep't 1974).

163. Rogers v. Dorchester Assocs. (Otis Elevator), 32 N.Y.2d 553, 559, 300 N.E.2d 403, 408, 347 N.Y.S.2d 22, 26 (1973).

164. Sherman v. Concourse Realty Corp., 47 A.D.2d 134, 365 N.Y.S.2d 239 (2d Dep't 1975).

165. Johnson v. New York City Transit Auth., N.Y.L.J., Apr. 9, 1987 (1st Dep't 1987).

snapped back and he collapsed. The trial court dismissed the complaint, but the appellate court reinstated it.

6.2.4.3.3.b The Defendant

(17) *Benaquista v. Municipal Housing Authority of the City of Schenectady.*[166] The intercom in a municipal apartment building did not work properly so when a visitor apparently arrived at the main door and buzzed the plaintiff's apartment, she descended the stairs to admit him. She fell on the stairs, injured herself, and sued the housing authority. However, the Appellate Division, Third Department, found that the plaintiff's claim lacked proximate cause since there was no defective condition on the stairs.

166. Benaquista v. Municipal Housing Authority of the City of Schenectady, 212 A.D.2d 860 (3d Dep't 1995).

EXAMPLE 6-1: COVER LETTER REGARDING POTHOLE RECORDS

BIG APPLE POTHOLE & SIDEWALK PROTECTION CORP.

132 Nassau Street New York, NY 10038 (212) 349-5896

RECEIVED
JAN 19
KRAMER, DILLOF, TESSEL
DUFFY & MOORE

ABRAHAM FUCHSBERG
President

January , 19

Kramer, Dillof, Tessel, Duffy & Moore
233 Broadway
New York, New York 10278

Re: BIG APPLE POTHOLE & SIDEWALK SEARCH -

Dear :

Pursuant to your inquiry of January 22, 1992 we have conducted a search of the notices of defective conditions submitted to the Department of Transportation. Enclosed please find the following:

A map of the area specified in your letter: I/F/O Avenue, New York,

A copy of the Proof of Filing for the above map.

A legend explaining the symbols on the map.

A copy of the "Pothole" Law.

A letter from the President which provides some additional information.

There is a charge of $50 if you need an additional map. Please do not hesitate to contact me if you have any questions regarding the search results.

Sincerely yours,

Andrea Glenn

Andrea Glenn
Director

P.S. On the enclosed form, we would greatly appreciate knowing the results of your case. This information is used for statistical purposes only. Thank you.

EXAMPLE 6-2: WRITTEN NOTICE OF DEFECT

BIG APPLE POTHOLE & SIDEWALK PROTECTION CORP.

132 Nassau Street New York, NY 10038 (212) 349-5896

ABRAHAM FUCHSBERG
President

YVETTE DINES
Director

Commissioner Ross Sandler
Department of Transportation
295 Lafayette Street
New York, New York 10012

Dear Commissioner Sandler:

Pursuant to the General Municipal Law Section 50-g and Subdivision d of 394-a-1.0 of Title A of Chapter 16 of the Administrative Code of the City of New York, we hereby notify you of the defects represented on the enclosed maps (19) of this section of Manhattan

VOLUME: PAGES:

Sincerely,

Yvette Dines
Director
Big Apple Pothole & Sidewalk
Protection Corporation

DEPARTMENT OF TRANSPORTATION
DATE AND TIME STAMP

Recoverable Damages and Complicated Judgments 7

The trial attorney must understand which damages are recoverable and to which extent. The substantive question (what may the plaintiff collect?) and the procedural question (which evidence is admissible?) are interwoven to such an extent that understanding one will lead to an understanding of the other. Therefore, in section 7.1 we shall discuss which damages are recoverable under current law, to wit: damages for personal injury, loss of services, wrongful death, and damage to property. In section 7.2, we shall examine specialized verdicts, taxes on lost earnings, payment from a collateral source, payment from a cotortfeasor, and an annuity contract.

7.1 RECOVERABLE DAMAGES FOR CAUSES OF ACTION

7.1.1 Damages for Personal Injury

7.1.1.1 Pain and Suffering

If the plaintiff has suffered a personal injury as a result of the negligence of the defendant, the plaintiff may collect damages for the pain and suffering that he or she has endured and will endure and for the special damages incurred and that will incur.[1] Pain and suffering can be proven by the testimony of the injured party and by expert testimony based upon an examination of the plaintiff and a review of the records. Doctors who treated the plaintiff also may testify to his or her complaint of pain and suffering since the defendant may cross-examine the plaintiff on that issue.

If the plaintiff suffered a physical injury, he or she may sue also for the emotional and psychological injuries associated with it.[2] So long as the plaintiff had some cognition, some awareness of life or of pain, the plaintiff is entitled to recover for his lost enjoyment of life.[3] However, the court must charge the jury that it is to consider the loss of the enjoyment of life as part of the plaintiff's conscious pain and suffering and not as a separate item of damages.[4]

Example 7-1 consists of the ad damnum clauses from three complaints for personal injuries, which complaints demanded damages for conscious pain and suffering.

7.1.1.2 Emotional Injury

The plaintiff's ability to recover for emotional injury, also known as emotional distress, depends upon whether he or

---

1. Buggs v. Veterans Butter & Egg Co., 120 A.D.2d 361, 502 N.Y.S.2d 12 (1st Dep't 1986), re-emphasized the requirement for actual proof of all special damages, both past and future. Speculation will not support a jury verdict. New York's Court of Appeals explained this burden in Cummins v. County of Onondaga, 84 N.Y.2d 322 at 324-5 (1994):

> Plaintiffs have the threshold burden of proving consciousness for at least some period of time following an accident in order to justify an award of damages for pain and suffering . . . . The burden can be satisfied by direct or circumstantial evidence....However, '[m]ere conjecture, surmise, or speculation is not enough to sustain a claim for [pain and suffering] damages' . . . . Without legally sufficient proof of consciousness following an accident, a claim for conscious pain and suffering must be dismissed . . . . (Brackets in original.)

2. Wittrock v. Maimonides Medical Center, 119 A.D.2d 748, 501 N.Y.S.2d 684 (2d Dep't 1986); Hahn v. Taefi, 115 A.D.2d 946, 497 N.Y.S.2d 522 (4th Dep't 1985).
3. McDougald v. Garber, 73 N.Y.2d 246, 536 N.E.2d 372, 538 N.Y.S.2d 937(1989).
4. Nussbaum v. Gibstein, 73 N.Y.2d 912, 536 N.E.2d 618, 539 N.Y.S.2d 289 (1989).

she was in the zone of danger (i.e., whether the defendant owed the plaintiff a duty), whether the plaintiff suffered a physical injury, and whether the plaintiff observed the defendant inflict a physical injury on a member of the plaintiff's immediate family.

Thus, the plaintiff may have a cause of action in three circumstances. First, if the plaintiff did not suffer a physical injury but was within the zone of danger, he or she may recover for emotional injuries flowing from the defendant's negligence.[5] A pregnant woman is ipso facto within the zone of danger when her child is injured. Therefore, she has a cause of action against a physician who negligently and erroneously told her that the baby had a congenital birth defect and, as a result, induced her to have an unnecessary abortion.[6] Similarly, the mother had a cause of action against the physician who negligently failed to diagnose the pregnancy, administered a drug to the mother which harmed the baby and occasioned an abortion.[7] Another mother had a cause of action for emotional distress because the physician's attempt to abort the fetus was unsuccessful, and the mother saw the baby stillborn in a miscarriage.[7.1]

Second, conversely, if the plaintiff was not within the zone of danger but suffered a physical injury anyway, then he may seek damages for emotional injuries and for the emotional injuries inflicted by witnessing the physical injury to someone who was within the zone of danger.[8]

---

5. Battalla v. State, 10 N.Y.2d 237, 176 N.E.2d 729, 219 N.Y.S.2d 34 (1961). A mother may not sue for emotional injuries accompanying the intra-uterine death of a fetus. Tebbutt v. Virostek, 65 N.Y.2d 931, 483 N.E.2d 1142, 493 N.Y.S.2d 1010 (1985); Gastwirth v. Rosenberg, 117 A.D.2d 706, 499 N.Y.S.2d 95 (2d Dep't 1986), and Endresz v. Friedberg, 24 N.Y.2d 478 (1969).
6. Martinez v. Long Island Jewish Medical Center, 70 N.Y.2d 697, 518 N.Y.S.2d 955 (1987).
7. Lynch v. Bay Ridge Associates, 72 N.Y.2d 632 (1988).

7.1. Ferrara v. Bernstein, 81 N.Y.2d 895 (1993).

8. Buzniak v. County of Westchester, 156 A.D.2d 631, 549 N.Y.S.2d 130 (2d Dep't 1989).

Third, if the plaintiff was within the zone of danger and did not suffer a physical injury, but witnessed a serious physical injury to a member of his immediate family, then the plaintiff may sue for the emotional damage suffered by reason of witnessing the injury to the relative.[9] We do not have a definition of immediate family, but the court of appeals has ruled that an aunt is not a sufficiently close relation.[10] In any case, remember that the plaintiff must have been actually within the zone of danger because witnessing an injury to another when you are not within the zone of danger yourself is not compensable.[11] In other words, if the defendant did not owe a duty to the plaintiff, then the emotional injury that the plaintiff suffered as a result of witnessing or participating in the injury of another to whom the defendant did owe a duty is not compensable.[12] For example, the parents did not have a cause of action for emotional distress for watching their son die of meningitis even if the son's death was the result of medical malpractice,[13] and the parents of an infant who was abducted from a hospital did not have a cause of action for their own emotional distress.[14]

---

9. Bovsun v. Sanpieri, 61 N.Y.2d 219, 461 N.E.2d 843, 473 N.Y.S.2d 357 (1984).
10. Trombetta v. Conkling, 82 N.Y.2d 549 (1993).
11. Fargo v. Schulman, 65 N.Y.2d 763, 481 N.E.2d 572, 492 N.Y.S.2d 32 (1985); Schram v. Herkimer Memorial Hosp., 115 A.D.2d 882, 496 N.Y.S.2d 577 (3d Dep't 1985); Maney v. Maloney, 101 A.D.2d 403, 477 N.Y.S.2d 436 (3d Dep't 1984); Osborn v. St. John's Riverside Hosp.,100 A.D.2d 840, 474 N.Y.S.2d 76 (2d Dep't 1984); Birkett v. Kasulke, 97 A.D.2d 630, 469 N.Y.S.2d 32 (3d Dep't 1983); Aquillo v. Nelson, 78 A.D.2d 195, 434 N.Y.S.2d 520 (4th Dep't 1980); McBride v. Brookdale Hosp., 130 Misc. 2d 999, 498 N.Y.S.2d 256 (Sup. Ct. 1986) (court held mother of stillborn fetus cannot sue for her emotional injuries); Collesides v. Westinghouse Elec. Corp., 125 Misc. 2d 413, 479 N.Y.S.2d 475 (Sup. Ct. 1984) (court held mother on escalator can sue for emotional injuries and fright resulting from contemporaneous observation of injury to her daughter when infant's fingers were ripped from her hand after being caught in the comb plate of the escalator.
12. Kennedy v. McKesson Co., 58 N.Y.2d 500, 488 N.E.2d 1332, 462 N.Y.S.2d 421 (1983). *But see* the apparently anomalous decision of the appellate division, fourth department, in Casale v. Unipunch, Inc., 177 A.D.2d 1029 (4th Dep't 1991).
13. Landon v. New York Hospital, 101 A.D.2d 489, 476 N.Y.S.2d 303 (1st Dep't 1984), *aff'd,* 65 N.Y.2d 639 (1985).
14. Johnson v. Jamaica Hospital, 62 N.Y.2d 523 (1984).

7.1.1.3 Surprise Pregnancy

A new and peculiar form of medical malpractice occurs when a woman becomes pregnant despite a purported sterilization or vasectomy.

When a sterilization procedure or a vasectomy fails, and a normal, healthy child is born, the only damages recoverable from the doctor who performed the procedure are the costs of prenatal and delivery care and the emotional injuries associated with the delivery itself.[15] However, if the mother bears a handicapped or injured child, then the parents may recover the special costs of raising and caring for the child.[16] The court may also take into account the mother's shortened life expectancy and award her damages for this loss, i.e., if the surprise pregnancy impairs the mother's health.

7.1.1.4 Loss of Income

7.1.1.4.1 In General

When the plaintiff has suffered an injury that resulted in loss of income, he may seek compensation both for the income he has already lost and for the future loss of income.[17]

---

15. O'Toole v. Greenberg, 64 N.Y.2d 427, 477 N.E.2d 445, 488 N.Y.S.2d 143 (1985); *see* Guilty v. Jewish Hosp., N.Y.L.J., Apr. 8, 1985 (Sup. Ct. 1985) (very critical of *O'Toole*).
16. Alquijay v. St. Luke's Hosp., 63 N.Y.2d 978, 473 N.E.2d 244, 483 N.Y.S.2d 994 (1984); Parks v. Chessin, 46 N.Y.2d 401, 386 N.E.2d 807, 413 N.Y.S.2d 895 (1978). For the analogous claim of wrongful adoption resting on the allegation that the adoption agency had concealed the natural mother's schizophrenia, follow Juman v. Louise Wise Services, 174 Misc.2d 49 (Sp. Ct. N.Y. 1997).
17. Terwilliger v. State, 96 A.D.2d 688, 466 N.Y.S.2d 792 (3d Dep't 1983). In Morales v. City of N.Y., 115 A.D.2d 439, 497 N.Y.S.2d 5 (1st Dep't 1985), the appellate division reduced a verdict for the death of a twenty-five-year-old working father of two infant children from $500,000 to $200,000. On the question of earnings, the majority held:

> The dissent holds that the jury could forecast a dramatic increase in decedent's earnings had he lived. It bases this on the wife's testimony that her husband had "discussed with her his plans to attend an automobile mechanics school and his hopes of opening his own repair shop." Such a forecast would be pure speculation, if not belied by decedent's work record and his never having earned more than $6,000 in any one year since his marriage. The jury award of $500,000 pecuniary damages invested for as little as [5.25 percent] bank interest would pro-

In an appropriate case, damages for lost future income may include lost profits.[18]

Proving the lost earnings of a plaintiff who is an employee is a simple matter. The plaintiff may testify to his or her earnings or produce an employer's records.[19] Even a plaintiff who operates his or her own business or practices a profession and whose income is, at least to some extent, the product of investments and expenditures may prove loss of earnings if personal earnings predominate over a small and purely incidental or supplemental capital investment.[20] When such a plaintiff actually seeks to recover merely lost earnings, rather than profits under the guise of earnings,[21] the plaintiff may prove the nature and extent of the business, his or her particular role in it, and the compensation usually paid to persons conducting such a business for others.[22] That latter item may consist of evidence of the fair and

---

duce an annual return of $26,250. The difference between such an income and that portion of his earnings which the decedent could be expected to use for the benefit of his wife and children (see, EPTL 5-4.3) cannot be supported, as the dissent seemingly does, by such factors as loss of care, love and guidance, even though these factors are proper elements to be considered (see, Richardson v. Lutheran Hosp., 70 A.D.2d 933). Were it otherwise, a jury's determination would be unlimited . . . . *See also* Van Syckle v. Powers, 106 A.D.2d 711 (3d Dep't 1984).

18. Dec v. Brooklyn Heights R.R., 158 A.D. 948, 143 N.Y.S. 1112 (2d Dep't 1913).
19. FED. R. EVID. 803(6); Annot., *Admissibility as Against Objection of Remoteness of Evidence as to Past Earnings, upon Issue as to Amount of Damages in an Action for Personal Injury or Death*, 81 A.L.R.2D 733 (1962).
20. Steitz v. Gifford, 280 N.Y. 15, 19 N.E.2d 661 (1939); Spreen v. Erie R.R., 219 N.Y. 533, 114 N.E. 1049 (1916); Krnold v. City of N.Y., 186 N.Y. 40, 78 N.E. 572 (1906); Annot., *Loss of Profits of a Business in Which Plaintiff Is Interested as a Factor in Determining Damages in Action for Personal Injuries*, 12 A.L.R.2D 288 (1950).
21. Walsh v. New York Cent. & H.R.R., 204 N.Y. 58, 97 N.E. 408 (1912); *See* Annot., *Admissibility of Evidence of Plaintiff's or Decedent's Drawings from Partnership or Other Business as Evidence of Earning Capacity, in Action for Personal Injury or Death*, 82 A.L.R.2D 679 (1962).
22. Weir v. Union R.R., 188 N.Y. 416, 81 N.E. 168 (1907); Masterson v. Village of Mt. Vernon, 58 N.Y. 391 (1874); Annot., *Cost of Hiring Substitute or Assistant During Incapacity of Injured Party as Item of Damages in Action for Personal Injury*, 37 A.L.R.2D 364 (1954).

reasonable wages the plaintiff had paid to others who were employed on prior occasions to perform the same services.

7.1.1.4.2 Expectations

The plaintiff's lost earnings may include not only future earnings but also future earnings that would have been greater than past earnings. For example, that the plaintiff had never earned any money as an opera singer did not prevent the plaintiff from offering evidence of training for an operatic career and the damages resulting from the loss of the quality of the singer's voice.[23] The jury must take into consideration the fact that a plaintiff's "earnings could have been increased if he had not been disabled by the accident,"[24] and that he might have been promoted in his job.[25] (Of course, the jury is not obliged to be convinced.) When the plaintiff has been unemployed, he may show evidence of earnings at the last time of employment and that he was just as capable at the time of the accident.[26]

The only requirement is that the jury must base its award of future lost earnings upon reasonable proof and expectations, not speculation that is unsupported by a suitable work record, training, or experience.[27]

---

23. Grayson v. Irvmar Realty Corp., 7 A.D.2D 346, 184 N.Y.S.2d 33 (1st Dep't 1959) (jury instructed to consider the risks and contingencies of a failure attendant on a particular career).
24. Caliendo v. New York City Transit Auth., 6 A.D.2d 884, 177 N.Y.S.2d 539 (2d Dep't 1958); *cf.* Morales v. City of N.Y., 115 A.D.2d 439, 497 N.Y.S.2d 5 (1st Dep't 1985).
25. Metz v. Great Atl. & Pac. Tea Co., 30 Misc. 2d 258, 215 N.Y.S.2d 175 (Sup. Ct. 1961).
26. Reichman v. Brooklyn Truck Renting Corp., 263 A.D. 1014, 33 N.Y.S.2d 929 (2d Dep't 1942).
27. Lloyd v. Town of Wheatfield, 67 N.Y.2d 809, 492 N.E.2d 396, 501 N.Y.S.2d 323 (1986).

7.1.1.4.3 Income Taxes

May the plaintiff recover the gross loss of income or merely the net loss of income after deducting the income taxes that the plaintiff would have paid? In *Johnson v. MABSTOA*,[28] the court of appeals held, "[T]he damages component of a plaintiff's awards as to lost wages in this action should be based on gross projected earnings and no deduction or consideration of after-tax net should be allowed into evidence or charged to the jury." In order to prevent mistake by the jury, the court of appeals held in *Lanzano v. City of New York*[29] that the trial court should inform the jury that (1) the award is not taxable, (2) the jury should not add or subtract for income taxes, and (3) the jury should follow the ordinary, specific instructions for measuring economic damages.

Nevertheless, a special rule authorizes the deduction of income taxes from the verdict in an action for medical malpractice. C.P.L.R. section 4546, adopted in 1986, sets forth the law. If the plaintiff has claimed lost earnings or an impairment of earning ability, then the court takes evidence outside the presence of the jury to establish the federal, state, and local personal income taxes that the plaintiff would have been obliged to pay. Meanwhile, the court instructs the jury not to deduct income taxes from any award and that the court will make any reduction warranted. After the jury renders its verdict, the court then reduces an award for the plaintiff as may be appropriate. Note that the court does not calculate the reduction on the basis of the entire verdict but only upon that portion awarded for lost earnings or an impairment of earning ability.

28. Johnson v. Manhattan & Bronx Surface Transit Operating Auth., 71 N.Y.2d 198, 519 N.E.2d 326, 524 N.Y.S.2d 415 (1988).

29. *Id.*, Lanzano v. City of N.Y., 71 N.Y.2d 208, 519 N.E.2d 331, 524 N.Y.S.2d 420 (1988).

7.1.2 Loss of Services

When a husband or wife has been injured and one spouse has been deprived of the services of the other, the deprived spouse may recover damages,[30] but that claim derives from the main claim of the injured party. Thus, if the injured plaintiff loses or is found to have been contributorily or comparatively negligent, that finding impairs the right of the deprived spouse to recover damages.

Loss of services includes loss of support, love, companionship, affection, society, sexual relations, solace, and all of the other intangibles that go into making a conjugal relationship.[31] Loss of services may also include the work that the decedent spouse performed for the other spouse in the family's business.[32] In addition, one spouse has a derivative claim for reimbursement of medical expenses if that spouse incurred the expenses by reason of the injury to the other spouse, who is also a plaintiff.[33] However, a spouse may not sue for the loss of services if the spouses celebrated their marriage after the injury occurred.[34]

---

30. Millington v. Southeastern Elevator Co., 22 N.Y.2d 498, 239 N.E.2d 897, 293 N.Y.S.2d 305 (1968); Bessette v. St. Peter's Hospital, 51 A.D.2d 286 (3d Dep't 1976), and Ventura v. Consolidated Edison Co., Inc., 65 A.D.2d 352 (1st Dep't 1978). *Millington* established that a wife, not just a husband, may sue for loss of consortium, and *Bessette* held that the wife's cause of action does not extend to her own emotional distress at the negligent amputation of her husband's leg by a surgeon.
31. *Id.*
32. Wheaton v. Guthrie, 89 A.D.2d 809, 453 N.Y.S.2d 384 (4th Dep't 1982).
33. Lindner v. State, 49 Misc. 2d 908, 268 N.Y.S.2d 760 (Sup. Ct.), *modified*, 30 A.D.2d 615, 290 N.Y.S.2d 698 (3d Dep't 1966), *aff'd*, 27 N.Y.2d 703, 262 N.E.2d 221, 314 N.Y.S.2d 16 (1967); Rush v. Baverle, 49 Misc. 2d 595, 268 N.Y.S.2d 67 (Sup. Ct. 1966).
34. Miller v. Davis, 107 Misc. 2d 343, 433 N.Y.S.2d 974 (Sup. Ct. 1980). In McDougald v. Garber, 73 N.Y.2d 246, 536 N.E.2d 372, 538 N.Y.S.2d 937 (1989), a verdict in the amount of $1.5 million for loss of services was affirmed.

A parent may sue for the loss of the services of an injured child, but the child may not sue for his loss of the services of his injured parent.[35]

7.1.3 Wrongful Death

7.1.3.1 The Elements

The action for wrongful death belongs to the next of kin, but only the personal representative of the decedent's estate may bring it.[36] The personal representative also brings any surviving action for personal injury, conscious pain and suffering, or expenses incurred prior to the decedent's death, but the damages from those actions belong to the estate and, therefore, may pass to different parties pursuant to the decedent's will.[37]

The elements of the cause of action for wrongful death are

1. The death of a human being,
2. Causative negligence,
3. The survival of distributees suffering pecuniary injury, and
4. The appointment of a personal representative for the estate.[38]

The law of New York requires that a child be born alive for its death to constitute the first element of the action so the death of a fetus is not actionable as such,[39] and, therefore, the parents' emotional injury at losing the fetus is not actionable.[40]

---

35. DeAngelis v. Lutheran Medical Center, 58 N.Y.2d 1053, 449 N.E.2d 406, 462 N.Y.S.2d 626 (1983).
36. N.Y. EST. POWERS & TRUSTS LAW § 5-4.1.
37. N.Y. EST. POWERS & TRUSTS LAW § 11-3.2
38. Chong v. New York City Transit Auth., 83 A.D.2d 546, 441 N.Y.S.2d 24 (2d Dep't 1981).
39. Endersz v. Friedberg, 24 N.Y.2d 478, 248 N.E.2d 901, 301 N.Y.S.2d 65 (1969), and LoBello v. Albany Medical Center, 85 N.Y.2d 701 (1995).
40. Tebbutt v. Virostek, 102 A.D.2d 231, 477 N.Y.S.2d 776 (3d Dep't 1976).

7.1.3.2 The Damages

Estates, Powers and Trusts Law section 5-4.3 provides that the damages awarded for wrongful death shall be "fair and just compensation for the pecuniary injuries resulting from the decedent's death to the persons for whose benefit the action is brought," i.e., the distributees. If the distributees also paid or are responsible for the funeral expenses or the medical care incidental to the injury that caused the decedent's death, they may recover those expenses also.[41] Finally, the award includes interest from the date of the decedent's death.[42]

The courts have interpreted pecuniary injuries as including loss of support, services, voluntary assistance, the prospect of inheritance, and medical and funeral expenses. Moreover, "In determining pecuniary loss, it is relevant to consider proof as to age, character and condition of the decedent, his earning capacity, life expectancy, health and intelligence, as well as the circumstances of his distributees."[43]

These definitions may seem straightforward, but they obscure as much as they elucidate so it is necessary to examine different kinds of decedents, distributees, and circumstances. Keep in mind that the measure of damages is actual pecuniary loss.

The most common distributees are surviving spouses and children, but sometimes parents are the survivors.

First, consider the circumstances of an *adult decedent.* When an adult wage earner dies, the major parts of the recovery are loss of income and loss of parental guidance. The jury may consider the decedent's earnings at the time of death, the last known earnings if unemployed, and potential

41. N.Y. EST. POWERS & TRUSTS LAW § 5-4.3.
42. *Id.*
43. Fell v. Presbyterian Hosp., 98 A.D.2d 624, 469 N.Y.S.2d 375 (1st Dep't 1983); *see also* Parilis v. Feinstein, 49 N.Y.2d 984, 406 N.E.2d 1059, 429 N.Y.S.2d 165 (1980).

future earnings.[44] If the decedent earned considerable income and gave it to his family, that sum will be recoverable, but if the money was squandered, that vice will reduce the recovery.[45] Similarly, the courts will reduce a jury's award, sometimes considerably, if the decedent had poor earnings[46] although he was young, had great potential, and supported several children.[47] At the same time, a jury may award lost earnings despite the decedent's having been unemployed — if he had worked and if the plaintiff adduced evidence of the decedent's average earnings when working.[48] When the plaintiff failed to adduce such evidence, however, the court set aside a verdict of $470,000 and ordered a new trial.[49]

Second, consider the circumstances of an *immature decedent.* When a parent dies, a child may seek damages for loss of the parent's care, nurture, and guidance,[50] but when a child dies, the parent's recovery is limited to the pecuniary loss that the parent suffered, which is usually quite small,[51]

---

44. Fell v. Presbyterian Hosp., 98 A.D.2d 624, 469 N.Y.S.2d 375 (1st Dep't 1983); Wingate v. Long Island R.R., 92 A.D.2d 797, 798, 460 N.Y.S.2d 42, 43 (1st Dep't 1983); Gilliard v. New York City Health & Hosps. Corp., 77 A.D.2d 532, 533, 430 N.Y.S.2d 18, 19 (3d Dep't 1980): Ritter v. State, 74 Misc. 2d 80, 344 N.Y.S.2d 257 (Ct. Cl. 1972); *see* Sweeting v. Board of Coop Educ. Servs., 83 A.D.2d 103, 443 N.Y.S.2d 910 (4th Dep't 1981); Lyons v. Devoir, 48 A.D.2d 943, 368 N.Y.S.2d 887 (3d Dep't 1975), *aff'd*, 39 N.Y.2d 1, 346 N.E.2d 243, 382 N.Y.S.2d 475 (1976); Collings v. State, 23 A.D.2d 898, 900, 258 N.Y.S.2d 938, 940 (3d Dep't 1965), *aff'd*, 17 N.Y.2d 542, 215 N.E.2d 500, 268 N.Y.S.2d 314 (1966).
45. Odom v. Byrne, 104 A.D.2d 863, 480 N.Y.S.2d 247 (2d Dep't 1984).
46. Morales v. City of N.Y., 115 A.D.2d 439, 497 N.Y.S.2d 5 (1st Dep't 1985).
47. *Id.*
48. Ritter v. State, 74 Misc. 2d 80, 344 N.Y.S.2d 257 (Ct. Cl. 1972).
49. Richardson v. Lutheran Hosp., 70 A.D.2d 933, 417 N.Y.S.2d 526 (2d Dep't 1979).
50. Tilley v. Hudson River R.R., 29 N.Y. 252 (1864). This is so even if the parent left only adult children. *See also* Weiner v. Lenox Hill Hospital, 193 A.D.2d 380 (1st Dep't 1993), and Gonzalez v. New York City Housing Authority, 77 N.Y.2d 663 (1991).
51. *See, e.g.*, Corrati v. State, 20 A.D.2d 166, 245 N.Y.S.2d 561 (3d Dep't 1963) ($7,500 for death of two-year-old); Gough v. Anson's Dairy, 11 A.D.2d 859, 202 N.Y.S.2d 847 (3d Dep't 1960) ($12,725 for death of twenty-two-month-old).

for New York does not recompense the parent for his emotional suffering.[52] When a child dies, the parents' pecuniary injuries are determined by

1. The age, sex, life expectancy, work expectancy, state of health, and habits of the child;
2. The child's earning potential;
3. The relationship of the decedent to those claiming a pecuniary loss; and
4. The next of kin's health, age, and circumstances.[53]

The jury may consider what the child would have contributed to the distributees, but this must not be guesswork. This rule does not necessarily relegate the parents of a child of tender years to a nominal recovery,[54] but the jury may not speculate, and the appellate courts, therefore, generally affirm small awards for the death of a child. Any other recovery would require too much guesswork.[55]

Example 7-2 is a life expectancy chart. While such a chart is not binding on any party or the jury, the chart is persuasive and a starting point for calculations.

52. Osborn v. Andros Pavilion, 100 A.D.2d 840, 474 N.Y.S.2d 76 (2d Dep't 1984).
53. Franchell v. Sims, 73 A.D.2d 1, 424 N.Y.S.2d 959 (4th Dep't 1980).
54. Parilis v. Feinstein, 49 N.Y.2d 984, 406 N.E.2d 1059, 429 N.Y.S.2d 165 (1980).
55. Bartkowiak v. St. Adalbert's Roman Catholic Church, 40 A.D.2d 306 340 N.Y.S.2d 134 (4th Dep't 1974). In a wrongful death action, a jury may consider increases in future earnings based upon existing facts and circumstances when it is probable that such increases will be forthcoming. Wanamaker v. Pietraszek, 107 A.D.2d 1020, 486 N.Y.S. 2d 523, (4th Dep't 1985); Geary v. Metropolitan St. Ry., 73 A.D. 441, 77 N.Y.S. 54 (1st Dep't 1902). Mere speculation, however, as to how much a young decedent would have earned had he continued to live, or how much he might have contributed to his parent, does not serve as an adequate basis for the determination of damages. Franchell v. Sims, 73 A.D.2d 1, 428 N.Y.S.2d 535 (4t Dep't 1980); Grayson v. Irvmar Realty Corp., 7 A.D.2d 346, 184 N.Y.S.2d 33 (1st Dep't 1959). While there can be no certainty of such proof in a wrongful death action, Zaninovich v. American Airlines, 26 A.D.2d 155, 271 N.Y.S.2d 866 (1st Dep't 1966), the evidence may be received if there is sufficient probability of the decedent's future earnings. Grayson v. Irvmar Realty Corp., *supra*; Geary v. Metropolitan St. Ry., *supra*. This is not to say, however, that the plaintiff may not prove the decedent's prospective earnings, but it is only to emphasize that the jury must be afforded some predicate for its determination of future earnings. *See* Grayson v. Irvmar Realty Corp., *supra*.

7.1.3.3 Expert Testimony

The expert testimony of an economist is admissible to establish the value of the decedent to his family. Until recently, this testimony was not admissible when a housewife died,[56] but that rule changed in 1983 with *DeLong v. County of Erie*,[57] in which the court of appeals observed,

> When the decedent is a housewife who is not employed outside the home the financial impact on the survivors, aside from compensable losses of a personal nature . . . will not involve a loss of income but increased expenditures to continue the services she was providing or would have provided if she had lived.

The court doubted that jurors are knowledgeable regarding the monetary value of a housewife's services and concluded, therefore, that an expert could aid the jury in this evaluation.

7.1.3.4 Surviving Actions

In modern practice, the decedent's cause of action for personal injury survives his or her death, and the decedent's personal representative brings that action together with the wrongful death action but for the benefit of the decedent's estate.

In a surviving action for conscious pain and suffering, the jury may consider the "degree of consciousness, severity of pain and apprehension of impending death along with duration,"[58] Thus, in *DeLong v. County of Erie*,[59] the court af-

56. Zaninovich v. American Airlines, 26 A.D.2d 155, 271 N.Y.S.2d 866 (1st Dep't 1966); *see* Annot., *Admissibility and Sufficiency of Proof of Value of Housewife's Services in Wrongful Death Action*, 77 A.L.R.3D 1175 (1977).

57. DeLong v. County of Erie, 60 N.Y.2d 296, 457 N.E.2d 717, 469 N.Y.S.2d 611 (1983). *See also* Merced v. City of N.Y., N.Y.L.J., Mar. 13, 1987 (Sup. Ct. Bronx 1987).

58. Juidetta v. Bethlehem Steel Corp., 75 A.D.2d 126, 138, 428 N.Y.S.2d 611 (1983).

59. De Long v. County of Erie, 60 N.Y.2d 296, 457 N.E.2d 717, 469 N.Y.S. 2d 611 (1983).

firmed an award of $200,000 for twelve minutes of pain and suffering. Note that punitive damages are recoverable in actions for wrongful death and conscious pain and suffering,[60] but if an adult dies, the spouse's cause of action for loss of services is limited to the time that the adult was alive after the injury occurred.[61]

7.1.4 Damage to Property

The general rule is that a plaintiff whose property has been damaged by the defendant's negligence can recover the difference between its value immediately before and immediately after the accident.[62] However, in an action for damage to an automobile, the plaintiff may recovery only the fair and reasonable cost of the repairs necessary to restore the car to its former condition provided that the cost (1) is less than the diminution in market value due to the damage and (2) does not exceed the value of the automobile before the damage.[63]

In addition, the plaintiff may recover the loss of use of the automobile during the time it was disabled whether it was used for business or for pleasure.[64] However, the total amount recoverable for the damage to the automobile and the loss of its use may not exceed the value of the automobile before the accident.[65] To determine the value of the loss

60. N.Y. EST. POWERS & TRUSTS LAW §§ 5-4.3, 11-3.2(b).

61. Liff v. Schildkrout, 49 N.Y.2d 622, 404 N.Y.2d 1288, 427 N.Y.S.2d 746 (1980).

62. Parilli v. Brooklyn City R.R., 236 A.D. 557, 260 N.Y.S.2d 60 (2d Dep't 1980).

63. Gass v. Agate Ice Cream, Inc., 264 N.Y. 141, 190 N.E. 323 (1934). *See* Wachsman v. Hethering, 31 A.D.2d 552, 294 N.Y.S.2d 760 (1st Dep't 1968) (holding estimate of cost of repairs not admissible without supporting proof of value of car prior to accident); Annot., *Duty of One Suing for Damages to Vehicle as to Minimizing Damages*, 55 A.L.R.3D 936 (1975). In Glazer v. Quittman, 84 Misc. 2d 561, 377 N.Y.S.2d 913 (Justice Ct. 1975), in which the plaintiff was financially unable to have her car repaired or to call an expert witness, her testimony regarding the value of the car before and immediately after the accident presented a prima facie case.

64. Johnson v. Scholz, 276 A.D. 163, 93 N.Y.S.2d 334 (2d Dep't 1949).

65. Gass v. Agate Ice Cream, Inc., 264 N.Y. 141, 190 N.E. 323 (1934).

of use, the plaintiff may use as a criterion the rental value of another automobile used during the repairs[66] even if the plaintiff does not, in fact, rent such a vehicle.[67] Moreover, if the accident wrecked the automobile, the plaintiff may recover both its market value[68] and the value of renting a substitute for a reasonable time until a replacement can be obtained.[69]

A repair bill is not proof per se of the fair and reasonable value of the repairs,[70] but a paid bill is such evidence.[71]

7.2 THE NEW COMPLICATED JUDGMENTS

The successful plaintiff in an action for negligence may receive considerably less than the amount of the jury's verdict — even though the trial court does not reduce the verdict as excessive. The reason is that the trial court must reduce many verdicts in lieu of income taxes on lost earnings, for payments from collateral sources or cotortfeasors, or for the purchase of an annuity contract. Elaborate forms of verdicts make these reductions possible, and the trial attorney must be familiar with both the reductions and the forms so that the attorney will know what to prove and which form to request. We shall begin with the forms.

66. Sellari v. Palermo, 188 Misc. 1057, 70 N.Y.S.2d 554 (County Ct. 1947).
67. Mountain View Coach Lines, Inc. v. Storms, 102 A.D.2d 663 (2d Dep't 1984).
68. Gass v. Agate Ice Cream, Inc., 264 N.Y. 141, 190 N.E. 323 (1934).
69. Allanson v. Cummings, 81 N.Y.2d 16 (4th Dep't 1981), and Cecere v. Harquail, 104 A.D.2d 6 (4th Dep't 1984).
70. Mayo v. Sherwood, 13 N.Y.S.2d 899 (County Ct. 1939); *see* C.P.L.R. rule 5433-a (a paid, certified auto repair bill, not in excess of $1,500 is prima facie evidence of reasonable value).
71. Triangle Waist Co. v. Todd, 223 N.Y. 276, 31, 119 N.E. 85, 86 (1919); Schwartz v. Fletcher, 238 A.D. 554, 558, 265 N.Y.S. 277, 283 (1st Dep't 1933); Model Paper Box Co. v. City of N.Y., 186 Misc. 184, 60 N.Y.S.2d 298 (2d Dep't 1946); Alessi v. Lovell, 152 Misc. 411, 273 N.Y.S. 637 (1st Dep't 1934).

7.2.1 Special Verdicts, General Verdicts with Interrogatories, and Itemized Verdicts

A general verdict is one in which the jury awards a lump sum to one or more parties. C.P.L.R. rule 4111 contains the descriptions of the more elaborate forms of verdicts.

First, a *special verdict*[72] is one in which the jury finds only the facts and leaves the court to determine which party is entitled to the judgment. When the court employs a special verdict, the court submits to the jury either written questions susceptible of brief answers or written forms of the alternative but appropriate findings.

Second, even when the court directs the jury to return a general verdict, the court still may require the jury to answer written *interrogatories*[73] regarding its findings of fact. If the answers are inconsistent with the verdict, the court must direct a verdict in accordance with the answers, but if the answers are inconsistent with the verdict and with one another, then the court must either require the jury to reconsider or order a new trial.

Third, an *itemized verdict*[74] is available (1) in an action for medical, dental, or podiatric malpractice; (2) in an action by a public employee against another public employee or a public employer for personal injury or wrongful death; and (3) in any action for personal injury, injury to property, or wrongful death. In each case, the court instructs the jury that, if it awards damages, it is to render a verdict that specifies the applicable elements of special and general damages and the amount assigned to each element including but not limited to medical expenses, loss of earnings, impairment of earning ability, and pain and suffering. The difference among the three provisions for itemized verdicts is that the first and third, those for medical malpractice and for other

72. C.P.L.R. rule 4111(a), (b).
73. C.P.L.R. rule 4111(c).
74. C.P.L.R. rule 4111(d), (e), (f).

actions, respectively, also require the jury to divide each element of damages between the amounts to compensate the plaintiff for the damages incurred prior to the verdict and the amounts to be incurred after the verdict, i.e., future damages. The second provision, for actions by a public employee, requires no such division.

The information contained in these various verdicts enables the court to perform its calculations in reducing the amount of the verdict.

In an action for negligence, the trial court traditionally asked the jury for a general verdict with interrogatories explaining the reasons for the verdict. The attorney who specializes in negligence must understand the holding of *Davis v. Caldwell*,[75] in which the court of appeals ruled that a general verdict for the plaintiff cannot stand on appeal if the trial court submitted more than one theory of liability to the jury unless there was evidence to support every theory. If the evidence was insufficient to sustain any one of the theories, and there were no written interrogatories explaining which of the theories the jury accepted, then the appellate court must reverse the judgment and order a new trial with written interrogatories. Without such interrogatories, the appellate court cannot tell which theory the jury accepted, and the jury may have found for the plaintiff on a theory of liability not supported by the evidence. Therefore, if the plaintiff's trial attorney plans to submit the client's case to the jury on more than one theory, the attorney has an ethical obligation to propose interrogatories, and the court is obliged to submit appropriate ones to the jury.

However, in a more recent case, *Suria v. Shiffman*,[76] the court of appeals placed the burden of requesting interrogato-

75. Davis v. Caldwell, 54 N.Y.2d 176, 429 N.E.2d 738, 445 N.Y.S.2d 60 (1981); *see also* Russo v. Rifkin, 113 A.D.2d 570, 497 N.Y.S.2d 41 (2d Dep't 1986); Mertsaris v. 73rd Corp., 105 A.D.2d 67, 482 N.Y.S.2d 792 (2d Dep't 1984); Caputo v. Frankel, 89 A.D.2d 595, 452 N.Y.S.2d 649 (2d Dep't 1982). However, a party may waive his right to have a theory submitted to the jury by failing to object to the charge which omits it. Suria v. Shiffman, 67 N.Y.2d 87, 499 N.Y.S.2d 913 (1986).

76. Suria v. Shiffman, 67 N.Y.2d 87, 490 N.E.2d 832, 499 N.Y.S.2d 913 (1986).

ries on the defendants. The jury found that the plaintiff had been contributorily negligent, but there were no interrogatories by which to determine on which of two theories the jury so found. Only one of the two theories predated the comparative negligence rule and, therefore, would have barred any recovery. The court of appeals held that by failing to ask for a special verdict or interrogatories, the defendants had waived their right to appeal the issue. The defendants could have avoided the problem or preserved the issue by a request pursuant to C.P.L.R. section 4111(b) or (c).

When the court is charging the jury on the form of the verdict, the court and the parties should remember that New York accepts the "any five" rule; that is, if any five of the six jurors agree on a verdict or an interrogatory, that settles the matter, and the jury should go to the next question. It is not necessary that the same five jurors agree on every response.[77]

Example 7-3 is the set of interrogatories that constituted the itemized verdict in an action for medical malpractice. Note that the interrogatories lead the jury through the determination of its verdict. Be prepared to propose the interrogatories.

7.2.2 The Reduction in Lieu of Taxes on Lost Earnings in an Action for Medical Malpractice

See the discussion *supra* section 7.1.1.4.3 (Recoverable Damages for Causes of Action/Damages for Personal Injury/ Loss of Income/Income Taxes).

77. Schabe v. Hampton Bays Union Free School Dist., 103 A.D.2d 418, 480 N.Y.S.2d 328 (2d Dep't 1984).

7.2.3 The Reduction for Payment from a Collateral Source

The law provides for reducing a verdict for the plaintiff in proportion to the payments to the plaintiff from collateral sources. However, this reduction is appropriate in only two instances:

1. An action for medical malpractice, and
2. An action by a public employee against his employer or fellow worker for personal injury or wrongful death.

First, C.P.L.R. section 4545(a) applies to actions for medical, dental, or podiatric malpractice in which the plaintiff seeks to recover the cost of medical care, custodial care, rehabilitative services, loss of earnings, or other economic loss. In such a case, the defendant may present evidence that any such past or future expense was or will be, with reasonable certainty, replaced or indemnified, in whole or in part, from any collateral source, such as insurance (except life insurance), Social Security (except those benefits provided under title XVIII of the Social Security Act), workers' compensation, or employee benefit programs (except such collateral sources entitled by law to liens against any recovery by the plaintiff).

If the court finds such a payment from a collateral source, then the court must reduce the award by the amount of the payment minus the amount the plaintiff paid in premiums for such benefits in the two years before the action accrued and minus the projected future cost to the plaintiff of maintaining his or her benefits. (That's right, there may be a reduction of the reduction; buy a calculator and expect a headache!)

Second, C.P.L.R. section 4545(b) is similar but applies in an action by a public employee against either a public employer or a public employee who is subject to indemnification when the action is for a personal injury or wrongful death occurring while the plaintiff was acting within the scope of his employment. The court must reduce the award for payments from collateral sources provided or paid for, in whole or in part, by the public employer and including paid sick leave, medical benefits, death benefits, dependent benefits, a disability retirement allowance, and Social Security (except those benefits provided under title XVIII of the Social Security Act), but not including those collateral sources entitled by law to a lien against the plaintiff's recovery. If the court finds such a payment from a collateral source, then the court must reduce the award by that amount minus the amount the public employee contributed for that benefit.

7.2.4 The Reduction for a Payment by a Cotortfeasor

If the plaintiff settles a claim against one tortfeasor, the plaintiff may reduce thereby his recovery from any other tortfeasor held liable. New York General Obligations Law section 15-108(a) provides:

> When a release or a covenant not to sue or not to enforce a judgment is given to one or two or more persons liable or claimed to be liable in tort for the same injury, or the same wrongful death, it does not discharge any of the other tortfeasors from liability for the injury or wrongful death unless its terms expressly so provide, but it *releases the claim of the releasor against the other tortfeasors to the extent of any amount stipulated by the release or the covenant, or in the amount of the consideration paid for it, or in the amount of the released tortfeasor's equitable share of the damages* under article fourteen of the civil practice law and rules, whichever is the greatest. (Emphasis added.)

Moreover, the plaintiff's release of one tortfeasor frees that tortfeasor from liability to contribute to any other tortfeasor[78] and waives his or her claim to any contribution.[79] (In this context, contribution includes any right of indemnity.)

In other words, the released tortfeasor is out of the action, and a remaining tortfeasor will pay no more than his or her comparative share of the culpable conduct as found by the jury. However, the cotortfeasor may pay less if the release was for an amount large enough.

As a procedural matter, in an action for personal injury, wrongful death, or damage to property, the court takes, out of the hearing of the jury, any evidence of a payment by or a settlement with another joint tortfeasor, or one claimed to be a joint tortfeasor, and offered by a defendant in mitigation of the defendant's own liability for damages. The court then deducts the proper amount, if any, from the jury's award. Thus, the defendant has the burden of pleading and proving that a plaintiff has settled with another tortfeasor, and if the defendant satisfies that burden, then the court must reduce the award by the appropriate amount. The plaintiff has the burden of proving that the release does not justify such a reduction.[80]

In *Hill v. St. Claire's Hospital*,[81] the court of appeals described the hearing that the trial court must conduct when the plaintiff has reached a settlement with a prior or successive tortfeasor and when there is a question regarding the portion of the settlement that was meant to compensate the two plaintiffs for the negligence of a tortfeasor who is still a defendant. The court made clear that "the claim of the releasor is reduced by the greatest of (1) the amount stipulated by the release, (2) the amount of the consideration paid for it, or (3) the released tort-feasor's equitable share of the damages." The trial court must hold a hearing to ascertain that amount and to resolve any question of good faith.

78. N.Y. GEN. OBLIG. LAW § 15-108(b).

79. N.Y. GEN. OBLIG. LAW § 15-108(c).

80. Hill v. St. Clare's Hosp., 67 N.Y.2d 72, 490 N.E.2d 823, 499 N.Y.S.2d 904 (1986).

81. *Id.* at 84, 490 N.E.2d at 829, 499 N.Y.S.2d at 911-12.

> At the contemplated hearing, the trier of fact will *first* determine the amount paid to plaintiffs in settlement by the original tortfeasors, which may or may not be the amount recited in the release. *Next*, he will allocate that amount between the two plaintiffs, based upon the reasonable intent of the parties. *Third*, the fact finder should determine what portion, if any, of the settlement payment should be attributed to each plaintiff's aggravation damages. In so doing he will consider the statement as to allocation, if any, between the original and aggravated injuries contained in the settlement documents and the gravity of the respective injuries and determine whether the amount allocated by the parties was arrived at in good faith. *Finally*, if as to either plaintiff the fact finder allocates any portion of the settlement payment to the aggravation injuries, he should deduct that portion from the damages awarded that plaintiff and direct that judgment be entered for the difference.[82] (Emphasis added.)

This case is complicated rather than representative for not every case with multiple defendants will involve multiple plaintiffs, successive tortfeasors, original and aggravated injuries, and an allocation of the settlement. However, *Hill* is a good example of the process for which the court and the attorneys must be prepared.

7.2.5 The Reduction for an Annuity Contract

C.P.L.R. section 5031 applies to actions for medical, dental, or podiatric malpractice, and section 5041 applies to other actions for personal injury, wrongful death, or damage to property. Otherwise, the two sections are identical and work the innovation, borrowed from civil law countries, of allowing the defendant to pay the plaintiff's future damages through an annuity instead of a lump sum due after judgment.

After applying to the verdict any set-offs, credits, comparative negligence, additurs, or remitturs, the trial court must enter a judgment in a lump sum for all past damages and for

82. *Id.* at 84-86, 490 N.E.2d at 830, 499 N.Y.S.2d at 912.

future damages not exceeding $250,000. Also payable in a lump sum are the expenses of litigation and those attorney's fees related to past damages and to the future damages that are payable in a lump sum. The attorney's fees attributable to the future periodic payments are also payable in a lump sum but are calculated on the present value of the annuity contract. (In other words, all of the attorney's fees are payable in a lump sum, but the fees are based on the present value of the recovery.)

For the future damages in excess of $250,000, the trial court must enter a judgment for the amount of the present value of an annuity contract that will provide for the payment of the remaining amounts of future damages in periodic installments. To calculate the present value of the annuity contract, the court must use the number of years of future damages specified by the jury in the itemized verdict except that the annuity must pay off the award for future pain and suffering within ten years. Moreover, after dividing the amount of future damages by the number of years to determine the first year's payment, the court must calculate a present value sufficient to raise the annual payment 4 percent each year thereafter. Finally, the court's judgment must order the defendant and his or her insurance carrier to guarantee the purchase and payment of the annuity contract.

How will these sections operate? The court's task is complicated but merely arithmetical. The jury, however, must make the estimation and allocation of the plaintiff's future damages. A jury could not possibly speculate on the future values of incomes and medical expenses[83] so the parties must call physicians to testify to the need and cost of future medical expenses[84] and economists to testify as to the plaintiff's future loss of earnings and the cost of future medical expenses.

83. DeLong v. County of Erie, 60 N.Y.2d 296, 457 N.E.2d 717, 469 N.Y.S.2d 611 (1983); Dennis v. Dachs, 89 A.D.2d 511, 488 N.Y.S.2d 1 (1st Dep't 1982); Thornton v. Montefiore Hosp., 120 Misc. 2d 1003, 469 N.Y.S.2d 979 (Sup. Ct. 1983).

84. Friedland v. Meyers, 139 N.Y. 432, 34 N.E. 1055 (1888).

Example 7-4 is the result of all the calculations entailed by the complicated new verdicts — a judgment in an action for medical malpractice, which judgment requires two and one-half pages to state the result. Be prepared to scrutinize such a judgment immediately and carefully to detect errors.

EXAMPLE 7-1: AD DAMNUM CLAUSES FOR CONSCIOUS PAIN AND SUFFERING

For a Death Case

By reason of the foregoing, the plaintiff's decedent sustained severe and serious personal injuries, a severe shock to his or her nervous system, and certain internal injuries, and he or she was caused to suffer severe physical pain and mental anguish as a result.

For an Infant Case

By reason of the foregoing, the plaintiff sustained severe and serious personal injuries, a severe shock to his or her nervous system, and certain internal injuries; the plaintiff was caused to suffer severe physical pain and mental anguish as a result, and, upon information and belief, some of these injuries are of a permanent and lasting nature; the plaintiff was confined to his or her bed and home as a result, and he or she was incapacitated from attending to what otherwise would have been his or her regular activities, and there was caused to be expended sums of money for medical and hospital care on his or her behalf.

For a Slip and Fall Case

By reason of the foregoing, the plaintiff sustained severe and serious personal injuries, a severe shock to his or her nervous system, and certain internal injuries; the plaintiff was caused to suffer severe physical pain and mental anguish as a result, and, upon information and belief, some of these injuries are of a permanent and lasting nature; the plaintiff was obliged to and did expend large sums of money for medical and hospital expenses; the plaintiff may hereafter incur further expenses of a similar nature in an attempt to heal himself or herself of said injuries; the plaintiff was confined to bed and home as a result thereof, and was incapacitated from attending to his or her usual activities, all to his or her damage in the sum of $250,000.

EXAMPLE 7-2: LIFE EXPECTANCY CHART

MALE

The Commissioners 1980 Standard Ordinary

TABLE OF MORTALITY					
Age Last Birthday	Expectation of Life in Years	Number Dying in Each 1000	Age Last Birthday	Expectation of Life in Years	Number Dying in Each 1000
0	70.47	2.63	50	24.93	7.01
1	69.66	1.03	51	24.10	7.63
2	68.73	.99	52	23.28	8.34
3	67.79	.97	53	22.47	9.14
4	66.86	.93	54	21.68	10.02
5	65.92	.88	55	20.89	10.97
6	64.98	.83	56	20.12	11.98
7	64.03	.78	57	19.36	13.04
8	63.08	.75	58	18.60	14.18
9	62.13	.74	59	17.86	15.43
10	61.17	.75	60	17.14	16.81
11	60.22	.81	61	16.42	18.37
12	59.27	.92	62	15.72	20.12
13	58.32	1.07	63	15.03	22.10
14	57.38	1.24	64	14.36	24.28
15	56.45	1.42	65	13.71	26.64
16	55.53	1.59	66	13.07	29.15
17	54.62	1.73	67	12.44	31.82
18	53.72	1.82	68	11.84	34.68
19	52.81	1.88	69	11.24	37.84
20	51.91	1.91	70	10.67	41.41
21	51.01	1.90	71	10.10	45.48
22	50.11	1.88	72	9.58	50.14
23	49.20	1.84	73	9.04	55.42
24	48.29	1.80	74	8.54	61.19
25	47.37	1.75	75	8.07	67.36
26	46.46	1.72	76	7.61	73.83
27	45.54	1.71	77	7.18	80.51
28	44.61	1.71	78	6.76	87.48
29	43.69	1.72	79	6.36	94.85
30	42.76	1.76	80	5.98	103.18
31	41.84	1.81	81	5.61	112.37
32	40.91	1.87	82	5.26	122.75
33	39.99	1.96	83	4.92	134.25
34	39.06	2.06	84	4.61	146.80
35	38.14	2.18	85	4.32	159.52
36	37.23	2.32	86	4.04	172.82
37	36.31	2.49	87	3.78	186.41
38	35.40	2.69	88	3.53	200.28
39	34.49	2.91	89	3.29	214.53
40	33.59	3.16	90	3.05	229.37
41	32.70	3.43	91	2.81	245.21
42	31.81	3.72	92	2.56	262.78
43	30.93	4.03	93	2.29	284.01
44	30.05	4.37	94	2.01	312.83
45	29.18	4.74	95	1.69	357.25
46	28.32	5.12	96	1.35	432.37
47	27.46	5.53	97	1.00	569.08
48	26.61	5.98	98	.67	828.99
49	25.77	6.46	99	.50	1000.00

FEMALE

The Commissioners 1980 Standard Ordinary

TABLE OF MORTALITY					
Age Last Birthday	Expectation of Life in Years	Number Dying in Each 1000	Age Last Birthday	Expectation of Life in Years	Number Dying in Each 1000
0	75.42	1.88	50	29.09	5.14
1	74.58	.84	51	28.23	5.51
2	73.63	.80	52	27.39	5.93
3	72.69	.78	53	26.55	6.38
4	71.74	.77	54	25.71	6.85
5	70.80	.75	55	24.89	7.33
6	69.85	.73	56	24.07	7.80
7	68.90	.71	57	23.25	8.25
8	67.95	.70	58	22.44	8.71
9	66.99	.68	59	21.64	9.21
10	66.04	.69	60	20.83	9.80
11	65.09	.71	61	20.03	10.55
12	64.13	.74	62	19.24	11.49
13	63.18	.78	63	18.46	12.64
14	62.23	.83	64	17.69	13.92
15	61.28	.88	65	16.93	15.30
16	60.33	.93	66	16.19	16.72
17	59.39	.97	67	15.45	18.14
18	58.44	1.00	68	14.73	19.60
19	57.50	1.04	69	14.01	21.24
20	56.56	1.06	70	13.31	23.17
21	55.62	1.08	71	12.61	25.55
22	54.68	1.10	72	11.93	28.49
23	53.74	1.13	73	11.26	32.02
24	52.80	1.15	74	10.62	36.09
25	51.86	1.18	75	10.00	40.61
26	50.92	1.21	76	9.40	45.50
27	49.98	1.24	77	8.83	50.75
28	49.04	1.28	78	8.27	56.40
29	48.10	1.33	79	7.73	62.67
30	47.17	1.38	80	7.22	69.79
31	46.23	1.43	81	6.72	78.00
32	45.30	1.48	82	6.25	87.48
33	44.36	1.54	83	5.80	98.17
34	43.43	1.62	84	5.38	109.96
35	42.50	1.71	85	4.98	122.70
36	41.57	1.83	86	4.61	136.31
37	40.65	1.97	87	4.25	150.75
38	39.73	2.13	88	3.92	166.06
39	38.81	2.32	89	3.60	182.34
40	37.90	2.53	90	3.29	199.81
41	36.99	2.76	91	2.99	218.84
42	36.09	2.98	92	2.69	240.16
43	35.20	3.21	93	2.38	265.41
44	34.31	3.44	94	2.06	298.31
45	33.43	3.68	95	1.72	348.53
46	32.55	3.93	96	1.37	425.35
47	31.68	4.19	97	1.01	565.41
48	30.81	4.48	98	.67	827.93
49	29.94	4.79	99	.50	1000.00

EXAMPLE 7-3: INTERROGATORIES

SUPREME COURT OF THE STATE OF NEW YORK
COUNTY OF ____________

Interrogatories

Question 1A

Was _____ _____ presenting as a footling breach on February _____19____ ?

Yes_____ No_____

At least five jurors must agree on the answer to this question.

1.______ 4.______
2.______ 5.______
3.______ 6.______

I, the undersigned juror, do not concur in the above verdict.

______

If your answer to this question is No, proceed to question 2A.

If your answer to this question is Yes, proceed to question 1B.

Question 1B

Was the failure to diagnose the presentation a departure from good and accepted standards of medical practice?

Yes_____No_____

At least five jurors must agree on the answer to this question.

1._____ 4._____
2._____ 5._____
3._____ 6._____

I, the undersigned juror, do not concur in the above verdict.

____

If your answer to this question was Yes then proceed to question 1C.

If your answer to this question was No then go to question 2A.

Question 1C

Was this departure a substantial contributing factor in causing injury to the infant plaintiff?

Yes_____No_____

At least five jurors must agree on the answer to this question.

1._____ 4._____
2._____ 5._____
3._____ 6._____

I, the undersigned juror, do not concur in the above verdict.

____

Proceed to the next question.

Question 2A

Did the defendant, Dr. ________ depart from good and accepted standards of medical practice in his response to the telephone information concerning ________________________ on __________ ?

Yes_____ No_____

At least five jurors must agree on the answer to this question.

1.______ 4.______
2.______ 5.______
3.______ 6.______

I, the undersigned juror, do not concur in the above verdict.

____

If your answer to this question is Yes, proceed to question 2B.

If your answer to this question is No, proceed to question 3A.

Question 2B

Was this departure a substantial contributing factor in causing injury to the infant plaintiff?

Yes_____ No_____

At least five jurors must agree on the answer to this question.

1.______ 4.______
2.______ 5.______
3.______ 6.______

I, the undersigned juror, do not concur in the above verdict.

____

Proceed to the next question.

Question 3A

Did the defendant_____ Medical Center depart from good and accepted standards of medical practice in the manner of diagnosing and treating prolapsed cord?

Yes_____No_____

At least five jurors must agree on the answer to this question.

1._____ 4._____
2._____ 5._____
3._____ 6._____

I, the undersigned juror, do not concur in the above verdict.

____

If your answer to this question is Yes, proceed to question 3B.

If your answer to this question is No, proceed to the instructions at the top of question 4A.

Question 3B

Was this departure a substantial contributing factor in causing injury to the infant-plaintiff?

Yes_____ No_____

At least five jurors must agree on the answer to this question.

1._____ 4._____ _______
2._____ 5._____
3._____ 6._____

I, the undersigned juror, do not concur in the above verdict.

____

Proceed to the instructions at the top of the next question.

Question 4A

What is the amount of damages, if any, you award to the infant-plaintiff, , for his future loss of earnings?

At least five jurors must agree on the answer to this question.

1._____ 4._____
2._____ 5._____
3._____ 6._____

I, the undersigned juror, do not concur in the above verdict.

____

If you awarded a sum of money to the plaintiff, then proceed to the next question.

If you did not award a sum of money to the plaintiff, then go to question 5.

Question 4B

State the period of years over which the amount awarded for future loss of earnings is intended to provide compensation to the infant-plaintiff, .

_______ years

At least five jurors must agree on the answer to this question.

1.______ 4.______
2.______ 5.______
3.______ 6.______

I, the undersigned juror, do not concur in the above verdict.

____

Proceed to the next question.

Question 5

What is the amount of damages, if any, you award to the infant-plaintiff, ______ for the future cost of an aide, up to the age of 22?

$_____

At least five jurors must agree on the answer to this question.

1._____ 4._____
2._____ 5._____
3._____ 6._____

I, the undersigned juror, do not concur in the above verdict.

____

Proceed to the next question.

Question 6A

What is the amount of damages, if any, you award the infant-plaintiff, ____________ for future residential care expenses from the age of 22 onward?

$_____

At least five jurors must agree on the answer to this question.

1._____ 4._____
2._____ 5._____
3._____ 6._____

I, the undersigned juror, do not concur in the above verdict. _________

____

If you awarded a sum of money to the plaintiff, then proceed to the next question.

If you did not award a sum of money to the plaintiff, then

proceed directly to question 7.

Question 6B

State the period over which the amount awarded for future cost of residential care is intended to provide compensation for the infant-plaintiff, .

_____ years

At least five jurors must agree on the answer to this question.

1._____ 4._____
2._____ 5._____
3._____ 6._____

I, the undersigned juror, do not concur in the above verdict.

____

Proceed to the next question.

Question 7

What is the amount of damages, if any, you award the infant-plaintiff, _________, for his past pain and suffering, including loss of enjoyment of life?

$_______

At least five jurors must agree on the answer to this question.

1._____ 4._____
2._____ 5._____
3._____ 6._____

I, the undersigned juror, do not concur in the above verdict.

____

Proceed to the next question.

Question 8A

What is the amount of damages, if any, you award the infant-plaintiff, ____________, for future pain and suffering including loss of enjoyment of life?

$________

At least five jurors must agree on the answer to this question.

1.______ 4.______
2.______ 5.______
3.______ 6.______

I, the undersigned juror, do not concur in the above verdict.

____

If you awarded a sum of money to the plaintiff, then proceed to the next question.

If you did not award a sum of money to the plaintiff, then report your verdict to the court.

Question 8B

State the period of years over which the amount awarded for future pain and suffering is intended to provide compensation to the infant-plaintiff, .

_______ years

At least five jurors must agree on the answer to this question.

1._____ 4._____
2._____ 5._____
3._____ 6._____

I, the undersigned juror, do not concur in the above verdict.

____

EXAMPLE 7-4: THE JUDGMENT

SUPREME COURT OF THE STATE OF NEW YORK
COUNTY OF
--X

and

JUDGMENT

Plaintiffs,

Index No.

-against-

M.D., P.C.,
DR.
and GENERAL HOSPITAL,
INC.

Defendants.
--X

The above action having come on for trial before the Honorable and a jury on the th day of 19 and the actions against defendants DR. and GENERAL HOSPITAL, INC. having been dismissed and the jury having returned a verdict in favor of the plaintiff on the th day of 19 and against defendant DR. and the jury having awarded the damages as follows:

1)	Past pain and suffering up to the date of verdict in the sum of	$ 1,000,000.00
2)	Future pain and suffering in the future in the sum of	$ 500,000.00
3)	Loss of income up to the date of the verdict in the sum of	$ 500,000.00
	Making a total verdict in favor of the plaintiff in the sum of	$ 2,000,000.00

and the defendants having brought motions to dismiss the complaint, for a new trial on all issues, and for a reduction of damages and the court having denied said motions in their entirety, and the defendants having further moved for an Order pursuant to CPLR 4545, 4546 and 5031 reducing the amount of the damages awarded by the jury and the plaintiff having cross-moved for an Order directing the entry of a judgment nunc pro tunc to . 19 in favor of the plaintiff and against defendants , M.D., P.C. and DR. ., calculating present value at a rate of 6.5%, reducing the $500,000 award for lost income by the sum of $114,568.54 for collateral sources, reducing the remainder of the lost income award after reducing for collateral sources for income taxes at a rate of 48.98% and providing for interest on the present value of the entire judgment, including future damages, and the plaintiff and defendants having agreed to reduce the loss of income award for income taxes at a rate of 48.98% and to reduce future damages to present value utilizing a discount rate of 6.5% and the Court having issued an Order dated 19 · granting plaintiff's cross-motion in its entirety and the Court having reduced the award for loss of income by the sum of $114,568.54 for collateral sources and the Court having further reduced the remainder of the award for lost income for income taxes at a rate of 48.98% in the sum of $188,784, leaving a remaining for past lost income in the sum of $196,647 and the Court further having calculated the present value of future damages after subtracting the first $250,000, utilizing a discount rate of 6.5% (in accordance with the calculations of Legal Economic Evaluations, annexed hereto as Rider "A"), it is

Now, upon the motion of of KRAMER, DILLOF, TESSEL, DUFFY & MOORE, ESQS., it is,

ORDERED, ADJUDGED and DECREED that the plaintiff, DR. , residing at Drive, New York recover judgment against the defendants , M.D., P.C., and DR. residing at , New York in the total present value sum of $1,670,506, and it is further

ORDERED, ADJUDGED and DECREED that the defendants M.D., P.C., and DR. JR., shall pay the following lump sums:

To DR. $ 1,150,650.00, and

To the law firm of KRAMER, DILLOF, TESSEL, DUFFY & MOORE, ESQS. the sum of $ 340,495.00 ($313,872 as and for their attorney's fees and $26,263 as and for litigation expenses) it is further

ORDERED, ADJUDGED and DECREED that defendants M.D. P.C., and DR. be and hereby is directed to purchase and guaranty payment of an annuity contract by an insurance carrier designated as qualified by the Superintendent of Insurance of the State of New York to make the following payments in equal monthly installments to DR. or to his representative, to commence within 30 days of purchase:

a) $ 1,712.52 per month for 10 years or the duration of his life, which ever is less and increasing annually at 4% compounded annually (as and for future pain and suffering)

and it is further

ORDERED, ADJUDGED and DECREED that upon the purchase of said annuity contract, defendants shall within 15 days serve the plaintiffs with a copy of said annuity contract, and it is further

ORDERED, ADJUDGED and DECREED that interest from the date of verdict, September , 19 , on the net present value of $ 1,670,506 shall accrue (at an annual rate of 9%) at the rate of $411.91 per day, of which $82.38 (20% -- the applicable percentage under sliding scale) shall accrue to the law firm of KRAMER, DILLOF, TESSEL, DUFFY & MOORE, ESQS. and $329.52 shall accrue to the plaintiff DR. so that on the date herein, the law firm of KRAMER, DILLOF, TESSEL, DUFFY & MOORE, ESQS. shall recover the additional sum of ____________ and the plaintiff shall recover the additional sum of ____________, together with the costs of this action in the sum of ____________, and that plaintiff have execution on said judgment.

Judgment entered nunc pro tunc as of September 19 on this ____ day of ______________, 19

____
Justice of the Supreme Court

The Court's Charge to the Jury 8

8.1 THE COURT'S RESPONSIBILITY TO CHARGE THE JURY

Even if neither party requests a particular charge, the trial court has the duty to charge the jury and to do so by tailoring the charge to the facts of the case, by stating the facts and the law accurately, by phrasing the charge impartially, and by answering the jury's questions.

8.1.1 In General

The primary purposes of the court's charge to the jury are to define the issues and to specify the processes the jury is to use in deciding those issues so that the jury understands what it must decide and the steps it is to follow.[1] According to the Trial Judge's Guide,[2]

> The instructions of the judge to the jury should outline the issues and explain the law on each issue precisely, accurately

1. In fact, the authors of the *Pattern Jury Instructions* have provided a charge for the judge to give to the jurors at the beginning of the trial (PJI 1:1-14). These sections include explanations of the parties, bifurcated trials, opening statements, objections, motions, summations, the disparate functions of the court and the jury, competent evidence, weighing testimony, conduct during any recess, prohibitions against discussions with others or visiting the scene of the incident, conversations with parties or their attorneys, and the role of alternate jurors.
2. State Trial Judge's Book, appendix 3.

and completely; furnish adequate general information on the law and advisory assistance; develop according to a consistent and logical arrangement; define terms and expressions; be fair and impartial; use ordinary language; be as brief as possible; avoid repetition; and provide appropriate instructions before, during, as well as after the evidence.

The shorter version of the court's duty is that there are two cardinal principles: first, the charge must be clear so that the jury understands it,[3] and second, the charge must be precise and specifically related to the claims of the case.[4] Moreover, the trial court should give the charge orally; that is, the court should not tape record the charge for the jury for jurors are more likely to pay attention to the judge's spoken word than to a tape recording of his or her voice.[5]

8.1.2 Tailoring the Charge

That the court's charge must be clear, unambiguous, and understandable goes without saying and requires no further comment. The court's obligation to tailor the charge to the facts of the case, however, does require additional comment. If a case is lengthy and involved with complex claims of liability and medical issues, the court should marshal the evidence for the jury, include a statement of the parties' contentions, discuss the evidence, and relate the evidence to the principles of law charged.[6] In addition, the charge should contain an explanation of the processes of decision, how damages are computed, and the form of the verdict.[7]

---

3. Cumbo v. Valente, 118 A.D.2d 679, 500 N.Y.S.2d 30 (2d Dep't 1986); People v. Gardner, 59 A.D.2d 913, 399 N.Y.S.2d 146 (2d Dep't 1977).
4. Green v. Downs, 27 N.Y.2d 205, 265 N.E.2d 68, 316 N.Y.S.2d 221 (1970).
5. Fogel v. Lenox Hill Hosp., 127 A.D.2d 548, 512 N.Y.S.2d 109 (2d Dep't 1987).
6. Zimmerman v. Jamaica Hosp., 143 A.D.2d 86, 531 N.Y.S.2d 337 (2d Dep't 1988); Perla v. Daily News, 123 A.D.2d 349, 506 N.Y.S.2d 361 (2d Dep't 1986); Rosenberg v. Rixon, 111 A.D.2d 910, 490 N.Y.S.2d 807 (2d Dep't 1985); Troy v. Long Island Jewish Hosp., 86 A.D.2d 361, 446 N.Y.S.2d 347 (2d Dep't 1982).
7. Regarding the form, see PJI 1:95-7.

As appropriate to the case, the court must adapt the charge to the facts.[8] Thus, in *Pedersen v. Balzan*,[9] the Appellate Division, Third Department, held that the trial court erred by failing to charge "that a driver is charged with observing whatever is within the purview of that driver's unobstructed vision. If the driver does not observe and account for what it [sic] sees, that is negligence." In *Pederson*, the testimony was that the road was straight and level for at least 100 yards before the scene of the accident and that nothing obstructed the defendant's view, but the defendant driver did not see the plaintiff until the car hit the plaintiff. The trial court's charge, however, simply recited the general rule that a person must exercise that degree of care and skill that an ordinarily prudent person would exercise under similar circumstances; that is, the trial court failed to give the jury specific guidance. Another example is that if the facts warrant a charge on the plaintiff's culpable conduct, then the trial court will err if it does not give such a charge.[10]

However, whether the court must marshal the evidence depends upon the complexity of the case. Thus, in *Santalucia v. County of Broome*,[11] the Appellate Division, Third Department, refused to overturn a judgment for the defendant and wrote, "[n]ot withstanding this failure, we find that any contention that the Supreme Court should have marshaled the evidence on its own initiative due to the complexity of the case is without merit . . . ."

---

8. Montanez v. Manhattan & Bronx Surface Transit Operating Auth., 139 A.D.2d 411, 526 N.Y.S.2d 466 (1st Dep't 1988); Rivera v. New York City Health & Hosps. Corp., 72 N.Y.2d 1021, 531 N.E.2d 644, 534 N.Y.S.2d 923 (1988).
9. Pedersen v. Balzan, 117 A.D.2d 933, 499 N.Y.S.2d 239 (3d Dep't 1986).
10. Theodosiou v. CLD Transp. Co., 147 A.D.2d 692, 538 N.Y.S.2d 299 (2d Dep't 1989); Runfola v. Bryant, 127 A.D.2d 972, 513 N.Y.S.2d 55 (4th Dep't 1987); Fitzpatrick v. A.H. Robbins, Inc., 126 A.D.2d 513, 510 N.Y.S.2d 632 (2d Dep't 1987).
11. Santalucia v. County of Broome, 205 A.D.2d 969 (3d Dep't 1994).

8.1.3 Accuracy

The trial court's charge to the jury must be accurate. Hence, when the court marshals the testimony of the various parties and experts, it must do so accurately. An inaccurate restatement of the opinion of an expert on a crucial issue may require an appellate court to reverse the judgment.[12]

Most importantly, the court must give the jury the law that it is to apply to the facts of the case. Clearly, if the court misstates the law or presents the law in a confusing fashion, the appellate court will reverse the judgment. For example, in *Troy v. Long Island Jewish Hospital*,

> The court committed error in its instruction on informed consent. In speaking of that subject, the court stated: "In other words, simply — simple language a doctor must give the patient all the options he has available to him and then allow the patient to make his choice." The appellants excepted to this portion of the charge. A physician's duty is to explain all the facts that "a reasonable medical practitioner under similar circumstances would have disclosed . . . ." Although an earlier portion of the charge contained such language, the court's subsequent attempt to paraphrase the law resulted in a misstatement of the principle and may have caused the jury to misunderstand the appropriate standard.[13]

---

12. Roma v. Blaustein, 44 A.D.2d 576, 353 N.Y.S.2d 44 (2d Dep't 1974).
13. Troy v. Long Island Jewish Hosp., 86 A.D.2d 631, 446 N.Y.S.2d 347 (2d Dep't 1982); *see also* Arbegast v. Board of Educ., 65 N.Y.2d 161, 480 N.E. 2d 365, 490 N.Y.S.2d 751 (1985) (charge on assumption of risk); Flynn v. Manhattan & Bronx Surface Transit Operating Auth., 61 N.Y.2d 769, 461 N.E.2d 291, 473 N.Y.S.2d 154 (1984) (charge on violation of motor vehicle law on obligation of defendant); Coleman v. New York City Transit Auth., 37 N.Y.2d 137, 332 N.E.2d 850, 371 N.Y.S.2d 663 (1975) (charge on jury's obligation vis-á-vis taxability of award); Lee v. City Brewing Corp., 279 N.Y. 380, 18 N.E.2d 628 (1939) (charge to jury on its right to discredit testimony of party whether contradicted or not); Flores v. Flushing Hosp., 109 A.D.2d 198, 490 N.Y.S.2d 770 (1st Dep't 1985) (charge on informed consent in a medical malpractice action); Lium v. Polski, 87 A.D.2d 860, 449 N.Y.S.2d 297 (2d Dep't 1982) (charge on duty of doctor vis-à-vis hospital staff); Gonzalez v. Medina, 69 A.D.2d 14, 417 N.Y.S.2d 953 (1st Dep't 1979) (charge on violation of a statute and charge on standard of care of infant plaintiff);

Two other examples will illustrate how a court may erroneously charge the jury on the law. The first example is *Veal v. New York City Transit Authority,*[14] in which the defendant successfully appealed a verdict for the plaintiff on the grounds of the improper charge to the jury. The trial court had committed two errors. First, it erroneously instructed the jury that the mere occurrence of an accident creates a presumption of negligence and imposes on the defendant a burden of proving that it had properly maintained its train. The trial court's second error was to charge the jury on res ipsa loquitur although the plaintiff had failed to establish that the defendant had had such exclusive control of the instrumentality as to rule out another agency. (The court had avoided using the term res ipsa).

The second example, *Rivera v. MKB Industries, Inc.,*[15] shows how a charge can go awry and result in reversible error. The plaintiff appealed the verdict for the defendant. The plaintiff, an employee of Continental's, had suffered the amputation of his left thumb while working with a machine manufactured and sold to Continental by the defendant's predecessor corporation, Flexitallic. The Appellate Division, Second Department, reversed the decision because of the trial court's numerous mistakes during the charge. Two mistakes were the most prominent. The trial court led the jurors to believe that if they found that the plaintiff's negligence had contributed to the accident, then they were also entitled to find, first, that the machine had not been defectively designed, and second, that the machine did not contain a defect which could have been the proximate cause of the accident.

Taylor v. Dayton Suregrip & Shore Co., 64 A.D.2d 809, 407 N.Y.S.2d 278 (4th Dep't 1978) (charge to jury on its right to discredit testimony of party whether contradicted or not).

14. Veal v. New York City Transit Auth., 148 A.D.2d 443, 538 N.Y.S.2d 594 (2d Dep't 1989).

15. Rivera v. MKB Indus., Inc., 149 A.D.2d 676, 540 N.Y.S.2d 316 (2d Dept. 1989).

8.1.4 Impartiality

The court must charge the jury in an impartial manner, i.e., in a manner not indicating a bias or prejudice for the position of a party.[16] The trial court strayed from this rule in *Theodoropoulos v. New York City Health & Hospitals Corp.*, so the Appellate Division, Second Department, reversed the decision and wrote:

> [N]ot only was the court's marshaling of the facts confusing and inaccurate with regard to certain important details, it also manifested mistrust, skepticism, and bias on the part of the court as to the credibility of decedent's treating-physician, and additionally, with regard to the testimony of defendant's two other medical witnesses.
>
> [T]he cumulative effect of these and other errors "tipped the delicate balance so necessary to the preservation of the requirements of a fair trial" and precluded the jury from reaching an objective and impartial verdict . . . .[17]

8.1.5 Answering the Jury's Questions

The trial court should answer the jurors' questions to ensure that they understand the charge, but if the jurors request a rereading of the entire charge, the court may not require them to specify a particular part of it.[18] However, when the jurors do ask a specific question, the court should not answer it either by rereading the entire charge or by refusing to give further instructions; instead, the court should give a careful and lucid explanation of the problem and of the

16. Theodoropoulos v. New York City Health & Hosps. Corp., 90 A.D.2d 792, 455 N.Y.S.2d 401 (2d Dep't 1982); Blaize v. City of N.Y., 80 A.D.2d 594, 436 N.Y.S.2d 34 (2d Dep't 1981).
17. Theodoropoulos v. New York City Health & Hosps. Corp., 90 A.D.2d 792, 455 N.Y.S.2d 401 (2d Dep't 1982).
18. Kerner v. Surface Transp. Corp., 266 A.D. 356, 42 N.Y.S.2d 296 (1st Dep't 1943).

rules the jurors did not understand.[19] When the wording of a charge has confused the jury, the trial court definitely errs by rereading the confusing part as its response.[20]

There is also the matter of procedure. If the jurors ask a question about the charge, the proper practice is to recall them to the courtroom and to answer the question in open court with the court reporter present.[21] It is absolutely an error for the judge to go to the jury room with the court reporter and to answer the question there without giving the parties' attorneys the opportunity to be present.[22]

8.1.6 Pattern Jury Instructions

The Office of Court Administration has published the *Pattern Jury Instructions*[23] to assist judges in the efficient dispatch of judicial business. These instructions are not prescriptive (the judge must choose among them or adapt them), but the texts and their accompanying commentaries are basic documents for the attorney who is drafting his or her own requests to charge. Volume 1 of the *Pattern Jury Instructions for Civil Trials* contains two hundred eighty-seven charges of general instructions and instructions in actions for negligence. For example, the suggested charge on a claim for nursing by a relative reads,

---

19. *See* People v. Malloy, 55 N.Y.2d 296, 434 N.E.2d 237, 499 N.Y.S.2d 168 (1982); People v. Pena, 50 N.Y.2d 400, 406 N.E.2d 1347, 429 N.Y.S.2d 410 (1980); People v. Duncan, 46 N.Y.2d 74, 385 N.E.2d 572, 412 N.Y.S.2d 833 (1978); People v. Gonzales, 293 N.Y.2d 259, 56 N.E.2d 574 (1944); Snediker v. County of Orange, 89 A.D.2d 560, 452 N.Y.S.2d 111 (2d Dep't), *aff'd*, 58 N.Y.2d 647, 444 N.E.2d 981, 458 N.Y.S.2d 517 (1982); Testa v. Seidler, 81 A.D.2d 715, 439 N.Y.S.2d 469 (3d Dep't 1981); Schwabach v. Beth Israel Medical Center, 72 A.D.2d 308, 424 N.Y.S.2d 208 (1st Dep't 1980); Chanatry v. Williams, 57 A.D.2d 730, 395 N.Y.S.2d 564 (4th Dep't 1977).
20. Bender v. Nassau Hosp., 99 A.D.2d 744, 471 N.Y.S.2d 657 (2d Dep't 1984).
21. Blaha v. Lettmoden, 83 A.D.2d 619, 441 N.Y.S.2d 526 (2d Dep't 1981).
22. *Id.*; Schattner v. Heriman, 247 A.D. 730, 285 N.Y.S. 343 (1936), and Boerum v. Seymour Realty Co., 127 Misc. 577, 217 N.Y.S. 484 (1926).
23. Now in its second edition and substantially supplemented; created by the Committee on Pattern Jury Instructions of the Assoc. of Supreme Court Justices.

PJI 2:318.1

> Such damages also include the reasonable value of the nursing services necessarily performed by the (plaintiff-father, plaintiff-mother) for the infant. If you find that such services were performed, the amount you should award will be measured by the amount customarily paid for such services.

Use the *Pattern Jury Instructions*; cite them, but do not be afraid to adapt them to the evidence in your trial. For your convenience, we have provided example 8-3, which is a list of the pattern jury instructions available in an action for negligence.

8.2 REQUESTS TO CHARGE

The trial attorneys for the parties need not wait to hear how the court charges the jury but may ask the court to deliver particular charges.[24] The court will rule on those requests and will inform the attorneys how it intends to charge the jury before the attorneys deliver their summations. If the attorney for a party disagrees with the court's charge, the attorney must object after the court charges the jury but before the jury retires.

The statute that regulates requests to charge the jury is C.P.L.R. section 4110-b, which reads:

> At the close of the evidence or at such earlier time during the trial as the court reasonably directs, any party may file written requests that the court instruct the jury on the law as set forth in the requests. The court, out of the hearing of the jury, shall

---

24. In preparing requests to charge for the court, which I strongly recommend be done as early in the trial as possible, counsel must own and be acquainted with three texts. The first is the two-volume set entitled *New York Pattern Jury Instructions* (Lawyers Cooperative Publishing Co.). The second is *Jury Instructions on Medical Issues* (Michie Co.). Finally, there is *Jury Instructions on Damages in Tort Actions* (Michie Co.). Not only do these books give counsel a solid foundation in knowing what to request from the court vis-à-vis the charge, but they also summarize vast areas of the law.

> inform counsel of its proposed action upon the requests prior to their arguments to the jury, but the court shall instruct the jury after the arguments are completed. No party may assign as error the giving or the failure to give an instruction unless he objects thereto before the jury retires to consider its verdict stating the matter to which he objects and the grounds of his objection. Opportunity shall be given to make the objection out of the hearing of the jury.

Note that the statute does not require a party to submit requests to charge, but if a party does submit such requests, the court must rule on them and inform the parties' attorneys of its decision before they begin their summations.[25]

For example, the court found the error-in-judgment charge appropriate in *Capolino v. New York City Health and Hospitals Corporation*[26] but inappropriate in *Spadaccini v. Dolan*.[27]

If a party's attorney fails to object to the charge that the court actually gives, the attorney waives the client's right to appeal on the grounds that the charge was improper unless the appellate court rules that the charge contained a fundamental error.[28] Objecting at the precharge conference is not

25. LoFaso v. Jamaica Buses, Inc., 63 A.D.2d 998, 406 N.Y.S.2d 131 (2d Dep't 1978).
26. Capolino v. New York City Health & Hospitals Corp., 199 A.D.2d 173 (1st Dep't 1993).
27. Spadaccini v. Dolan, 63 A.D.2d 110 (1st Dep't 1978).
28. DeLong v. County of Erie, 60 N.Y.2d 296, 457 N.E.2d 717, 469 N.Y.S.2d 611 (1983) (failure to object to court's charge on reliance of "all": not fundamental); Bichler v. Eli Lilly & Co., 55 N.Y.2d 571, 436 N.E.2d 182, 450 N.Y.S.2d 776 (1982); Nallan v. Helmsley-Spear, Inc., 50 N.Y.2d 507, 407 N.E.2d 451, 429 N.Y.S.2d 606 (1980) (failure to object to court's charge on crime rate in vicinity of defendant's building: not fundamental); Saleh v. Sears, Roebuck & Co., 119 A.D.2d 652, 500 N.Y.S.2d 796 (2d Dep't 1986); Rivers v. Kumar, 118 A.D.2d 691, 500 N.Y.S.2d 39 (2d Dep't 1986); Rogers v. Huggins, 106 A.D.2d 621, 483 N.Y.S.2d 110 (2d Dep't 1984) (failure to object to court's failure to charge emergency doctrine: not fundamental); DiGrazia v. Castronova, 487 A.D.2d 249, 368 N.Y.S.2d 898 (4th Dep't 1975); *cf.* McGinn v. Sellitti, 150 A.D.2d 967, 541 N.Y.S.2d 648 (3d Dep't 1989); Scaduto v. Suarez, 150 A.D.2d 545, 541 N.Y.S.2d 826 (2d Dept. 1989); Veal v. New York City Transit Auth., 148 A.D.2d 443, 538 N.Y.S.2d 594 (2d Dep't 1989); Rivenburgh v. Donahue, 147 A.D.2d 689, 538 N.Y.S.2d 464 (2d Dep't 1989).

sufficient,[29] and the attorney must make his or her objection on the record.[30]

Finally, if the court informs the parties' attorneys that it will charge the jury in a given manner but charges the jury differently, the court should give the attorneys an opportunity to make additional closing arguments to the jury on the basis of the charge the court actually gave.[31] Once again, however, the attorney's failure to ask for the additional summation may waive his or her client's objection to the charge.[32]

Reprinted at the end of the chapter are two sets of requests to charge the jury. The first set (example 8-1) was submitted in an action for negligence and includes proposed charges regarding negligence, the breach of an ordinance as evidence of negligence, the duty of a contractor, the duty of the owner or lessor of a building, causality, the burden of proving the plaintiff's negligence, explanations of direct and circumstantial evidence, and drawing inferences. The second set (example 8-2) was submitted in an action for medical malpractice and includes proposed charges regarding the definitions of malpractice and negligence, the duty of a specialist, reliance on expert witnesses, proximate cause, proof of a substantial factor as the proximate cause, the burden of proof in an action for wrongful death, an explanation of direct and circumstantial evidence, economic damages, and damages for conscious pain and suffering. Note that every proposed charge is supported by citations

---

29. McClure v. Bailer's Automotive Serv. Center, 126 A.D.2d 610, 511 N.Y.S.2d 50 (2d Dep't 1987); Zito v. New York State Elec. & Gas, 122 A.D.2d 499, 505 N.Y.S.2d 464 (3d Dep't 1986).
30. Radtke v. Yokose, 87 A.D.2d 220, 453 N.Y.S.2d 43 (3d Dep't 1982).
31. Spadaccini v. Dolan, 63 A.D.2d 110, 407 N.Y.S.2d 840 (1st Dep't 1978). *But see* Getlin v. St. Vincent's Hosp., 117 A.D.2d 707, 498 N.Y.S.2d 849 (2d Dep't 1986), in which the court held that the failure to charge the jury in the manner agreed upon at the precharge conference without notifying counsel does not constitute error when the agreed charge would have been improper. The court noted that the plaintiff's counsel did not ask that the summations be reopened.
32. Getlin v. St. Vincent's Hosp., 117 A.D.2d 707, 498 N.Y.S.2d 849 (2d Dep't 1986).

justifying it. Moreover, these documents are not just boilerplate. Therefore, in another action for medical malpractice, our firm submitted a set of requests to charge the jury regarding negligence and medical malpractice, the duty of a physician, the liability of a hospital for the negligence of its employees, the duty of a hospital to supervise its employees, the duty of a specialist, and the standards of care at the time of the incident.

8.3 REPRESENTATIVE CHARGES

As illustrations, we shall examine three charges to the jury, to wit: the violation of a statute, the doctrine of emergency, and the failure of a party to call a witness under his control.

8.3.1 The Violation of a Statute

If the plaintiff or defendant alleges that the other has violated a statute, and the violation is relevant to a claim or defense, then the court must inform the jury of the statute and of the consequences of failing to adhere to it.[33] The law is not the same, however, regarding the violation of a private rule or regulation. The violation of a rule of a party's employer is only some evidence of negligence so, before delivering a charge, the court must determine that the private rule imposed a standard of care no greater than that which reasonable care required.[34] The violation of a statute, by contrast, can be negligence per se if the legislature designed

33. Montanez v. Manhattan & Bronx Surface Transit Operating Auth., 139 A.D.2d 411, 526 N.Y.S.2d 466 (1st Dep't 1988).
34. Cincotta v. Johnson, 130 A.D.2d 539, 515 N.Y.S.2d 115 (2d Dep't 1987).

the statute to protect a class of which the plaintiff was a member.[35]

8.3.2 The Doctrine of Emergency

An emergency is a sudden, unexpected, and dangerous occurrence that forces a party to act in a manner that would ordinarily be considered negligent; for example, a drunk's driving the wrong way down a one-way street may justify another driver's swerving out of the proper lane to avoid a head-on collision.

The trial court should instruct the jury on the doctrine of emergency, however, only when the evidence suggests that the party faced a true emergency. As the Appellate Division, Second Department, ruled in *Felder v. Carolina Freight Carriers*,

> We find no error in the court's refusal to charge the emergency doctrine (see, PJI 2:141) in this case. The drivers of the vehicles involved in this three vehicle pile-up collision were not presented with any sudden and unforeseen condition. They should reasonably have anticipated and been prepared to deal with the situation with which they were confronted . . . .[36]

By contrast, in *Perez v. Navarro*,[37] the trial court did instruct the jury, and properly so, on the doctrine of emergency because the defendant claimed that he first had noticed the plaintiff's car stopped on the bridge after the car in front of him swerved away. The defendant said that he did not have time to stop, and the appellate court agreed that he may have faced an emergency:

> Similarly unavailing is the defendant's contention that the court erred in charging the emergency doctrine as it related to

35. McCarthy v. Fernandez, N.Y.L.J., Jan. 3, 1990 (2d Dep't 1990).
36. Felder v. Carolina Freight Carriers, 156 A.D.2d 540, 548 N.Y.S.2d 809 (2d Dep't 1989); Perez v. Navarro, 148 A.D.2d 509, 539 N.Y.S.2d 26 (2d Dep't 1989).
37. Perez v. Navarro, 148 A.D.2d 509, 539 N.Y.S.2d 26 (2d Dep't 1989).

> Perez. The unforeseen stalling of the automobile in a traffic lane on the bridge created an emergency, and Perez's actions thereafter must be evaluated in light of this unexpected event . . . . Furthermore, since the actions Perez took on the bridge were in response to an unexpected occurrence, it cannot be said that he intentionally assumed the risk of the defendant's negligence, as Perez's intention was to get off the bridge to avoid an accident. Therefore, the court correctly refused the defendant's request to charge implied assumption of risk . . . .

8.3.3 Failing to Call a Witness Within a Party's Control

The consequences of a party's failure to call a witness within that party's control do not constitute a rule of evidence per se. The rule does not deal with the burden of proof, the admissibility of statements, or the probative value of documents. Rather, the rule results in a charge to the jury: if the trial court finds that a party failed to call a witness within the party's control and that the party has failed to explain the omission satisfactorily, the court should charge the jury that it may draw an inference as a result of those failures.

We shall examine the charge itself, the prerequisite to giving the charge to the jury, some circumstances in which the court should give the charge, and some in which it should decline to do so.

8.3.3.1 The Charge

Pattern Jury Instruction 1:75 (1995 supplement) contains New York's version of the charge to the jury when a party fails to call a witness within the party's control, also known as the missing-witness charge:

> A party is not required to call any particular person as a witness. However, the failure to call a certain person as a witness may be the basis for an inference against the party not calling the witness. For example, in this case the (plaintiff, defendant) did not call AB [identify witness, e.g. treating physician,

> examining physician] to testify on the question of [identify issue, e.g., permanent extent of injury, causation]. (Plaintiff, defendant) (has offered the following explanation for not calling AB [summarize explanation], as a witness or has offered no explanation for not calling AB).
>
> [If explanation is offered] If you find that this explanation is reasonable, then you should not consider the failure to call AB in evaluating the evidence. If, however, you find (the explanation is not a reasonable one, no explanation has been offered) you may, although you are not required to, conclude that the testimony of AB would not support (plaintiff's, defendant's) position on the question of [identify issue] [add if opposing part has offered evidence on the issue]; and would not contradict the evidence offered by (plaintiff, defendant) on this question and you may, although you are not required to, draw the strongest inference against the (plaintiff, defendant) on that question, that opposing evidence permits.[38]

The inference to be drawn from a party's failure to call a witness within that party's control is often confused and misinterpreted. Therefore, the court of appeals wrote in *Matter of Commissioner of Social Services v. Philip DeG*:

> The failure of the respondent to testify does not permit the trier of the fact to speculate about what his testimony might have been nor does it require an adverse inference. It does, however, allow the trier of fact to draw the strongest inference against him that the opposing evidence in the record permits . . . .[39]

Judges will invariably charge the jury that a negative inference is to be drawn against the party who failed to call the witness. Some courts also hold that the inference is a positive one, i.e., that the jury should give the strongest weight to the evidence that is already in the case for the op-

---

38. The charge is based on Noce v. Kaufman, 2 N.Y.2d 347, 141 N.E.2d 529, 161 N.Y.2d 1 (1957). The trial judge may not charge the jury that the failure to call a witness within a party's control is inexcusable because it amounts to a directed verdict. Roma v. Blaustein, 44 A.D.2d 576, 353 N.Y.S.2d 44 (2d Dep't 1974).
39. Commissioner of Social Servs. v. Philip DeG, 59 N.Y.2d 137, 141, 450 N.E.2d 681, 683, 463 N.Y.S.2d 761, 763 (1983).

posing party and that the uncalled witness failed to contradict.[40] This difference is probably only a difference in phrasing since the effect on the weight of the evidence is the same.

8.3.3.2 The Prerequisites in General

Before instructing the jury, the trial court must have substantive and procedural bases for doing so; that is, the court must find that the charge is warranted after the court has given the parties an opportunity to be heard. Procedurally, there are two steps for analysis, as explained by the court of appeals in *People v. Gonzalez.*[41]

> The burden, in the first instance, is upon the party seeking the charge to promptly notify the court that there is an uncalled witness believed to be knowledgeable about a material issue pending in the case, that such witness can be expected to testify favorably to the opposing party and that such party has failed to call him to testify. In some instances, the information may be available prior to trial; at other times, it may not

40. In Felice v. Long Island R.R., 426 F.2d 192 (2d Cir. 1970), the court defined the inference as one allowing a court or jury to "give the strongest weight to the evidence already in the case in favor of the other side and which has not been but might have been effectively contradicted or explained by the absent witness." The *Felice* case and other decisions of the Second Circuit and other courts make it clear that the fulcrum of the adverse inference against the party not calling a witness is the accordance of the "strongest weight" to evidence already in the case in favor of the other party; stated otherwise, the courts will ascribe credibility to the latter evidence. *See* Karavos Compania Naviera S.A. v. Atlantic Export Corp., 588 F.2d 1, 9-10 (2d Cir. 1978); J. Gerbert & Co. v. S.S. Sabine Howaldt, 437 F.2d 580, 593 (2d Cir. 1971); Baldt v. Tabet Mfg. Co., 412 F. Supp. 249, 256 (S.D.N.Y. 1974); Armstrong v. Commerce Tankers Corp., 311 F. Supp. 1236, 1241 (S.D.N.Y. 1969). In Grey v. United Leasing, Inc., 91 A.D.2d 932, 457 N.Y.S.2d 823 (1st Dep't 1983), the court stated that the proper charge should be that "you [the jury] may infer, if you deem it proper to do so, that the testimony of the uncalled person would not . . . support . . . . defendant's . . . version of the case and you may also draw the strongest inferences against . . . defendant . . . that the opposing evidence permits." 1 PJI 75.
41. People v. Gonzalez, 68 N.Y.2d 424, 502 N.E.2d 583, 509 N.Y.S.2d 796 (1986), and People v. Church, 217 A.D.2d 444 (1st Dep't 1995).

> become apparent until there has been testimony of a witness at trial. In all events, the issue must be raised as soon as practicable so that the court can appropriately exercise its discretion and the parties can tailor their trial strategy to avoid "substantial possibilities of surprise" . . . .

Once the party proposing the charge has presented a prima facie case for it, the burden of rebuttal shifts to the other party to account for the absence of the witness. In fact, in *Roma v. Blaustein*,[42] the Appellate Division, Second Department, held that before giving the charge, the trial court must give the adverse party an opportunity to explain why he or she did not call the witness. The court cannot refuse to give a party that opportunity but still give the charge to the jury. According to the court of appeals,

> This burden can be met by demonstrating that the witness is not knowledgeable about the issue, that the issue is not material or relevant, that although the issue is material or relevant, the testimony would be cumulative to other evidence, that the witness is not "available," or that the witness is not under the party's "control" such that he would not be expected to testify in his or her favor.[43]

When deciding the substantive question of whether to give the charge, the trial court must address two issues:

1. Whether the missing witness is available; and
2. Whether the witness is under the control of a party adverse to the one requesting the charge.

As a practical matter, the opposing party may attempt to demonstrate that the witness is unavailable because his or her whereabouts are unknown, he or she is ill or incapacitated, or he is beyond the jurisdiction of the court and cannot be subpoenaed.

---

42. Roma v. Blaustein, 44 A.D.2d 576, 353 N.Y.S.2d 44 (2d Dep't 1974).
43. People v. Gonzalez, 68 N.Y.2d 424, 502 N.E.2d 583, 509 N.Y.S.2d 796 (1986).

Similar to the question of whether the witness is available, the question of whether the witness is within a party's control is a question of law for the court.[44]

> Control, however, has been described as a "relative concept" . . . and . . . does not concern physical availability but rather the relationship between the witness and the parties . . . [I]f a witness, although theoretically "available" to both sides, is favorable to or under the influence of one party and hostile to the other, the witness is said to be in the "control" of the party to whom he is favorably disposed, and an unfavorable inference may be drawn from the failure to call the witness . . . .[45]

A party's relatives, friends, and employees are generally considered to be under the party's control in this sense. Consequently,

> [a] missing witness charge would be appropriate . . . if it is demonstrated that the party had the physical ability to locate and produce the witness, and there was such a relationship, in legal status or on the facts, as to make it natural to expect the party to have called the witness to testify in his favor.[46]

8.3.3.3 Giving the Charge

If the party proposing the charge presents a prima facie case for it and if the opposing party fails to meet its burden of rebuttal, the trial court should give the charge. Besides

---

44. Rehill v. Fraas, 197 N.Y. 64, 90 N.E. 340 (1909). It is generally accepted that you have control of your employees, your relatives, and others who must answer directly to you for their actions, such as the driver of your car. Actually, control simply means that the witness is in a position to give relevant testimony and is related to you by operation of law or by family. Rudnick v. Norwich Pharmaceutical, 34 A.D.2d 912, 311 N.Y.S.2d 363 (1st Dep't 1970), and Gutin v. Frank Mascali & Sons, Inc., 11 N.Y.2d 97 (1962).
45. People v. Gonzalez, 68 N.Y.2d 424, 502 N.E.2d 583, 509 N.Y.S.2d 796 (1986).
46. *See also* People v. Paylor, 70 N.Y.2d 146, 511 N.E.2d 370, 518 N.Y.S. 2d 102 (1987); People v. Prise, N.Y.L.J., June 1, 1987 (Sup. Ct. Kings 1987); Annot., *Relationship Between Party and Witness as Giving Rise to or Affecting Presumption or Inference from Failure to Produce or Examine Witness*, 5 A.L.R.2D 893 (1948).

making this theoretical observation, we can say that some explanations are insufficient to rebut a prima facie case. For example, in *Sternemann v. Langs*,[47] the defendant sought the court's approval to withhold from testifying, for tactical reasons, a witness who was under the defendant's control. The trial court refused to approve the procedure, however, and the appellate court held that the trial court had not abused its discretion. Thus, trial tactics may not explain the failure to call a witness so as to defeat the opposing party's request for the charge.

The trial court even may give the charge in the unusual circumstance in which the controlling party called the witness to the stand but failed to ask the witness material questions on the point in dispute[48] in order to preclude cross-examination on that matter. In fact, this ploy is the ultimate example of failing to call a witness within the party's control.

8.3.3.4 Declining to Charge

Obviously, the court should decline to give the missing witness charge if the witness is either unavailable or not within the control of the opposing party. For example, the court may not give the charge if the witness cannot be subpoenaed because he or she has moved out of the state.[49] There is more to the application of the rule than that, however. Thus, the rule actually requires more than that the witness be within a party's control: the expectation must be that the witness's testimony would be favorable to that party. If the witness is, in fact, adverse to the party, the court

47. Sternemann v. Langs, 93 A.D.2d 819, 460 N.Y.S.2d 614 (2d Dep't 1983).

48. People v. Moore, 17 A.D.2d 57, 230 N.Y.S.2d 880 (3d Dep't 1962).

49. Trainor v. Oasis Roller World, Inc., 151 A.D.2d 323, 543 N.Y.S.2d 61 (1st Dep't 1989); Reehil v. Fraas, 129 A.D. 563, 114 N.Y.S. 17, *rev'd on other grounds*, 197 N.Y. 64, 90 N.E. 340 (1909).

should decline to give the charge even if the witness is technically within his or her control.[50]

Moreover, the witness's testimony should be peculiarly useful to resolve an issue in the trial. Therefore, the trial court should not give the charge if the testimony of the witness would be cumulative or would not be material to a disputed matter. For example, in *Trotta v. Koch*,[51] the Appellate Division, Second Department, ruled that the charge was not applicable to the failure to call the husband of the injured plaintiff to the stand to testify concerning certain alleged conversations since the plaintiff already had conceded that the conversations took place. Since the plaintiff did not dispute the defendant's position on this issue, the missing witness charge was inapplicable.

In *Getlin v. St. Vincent's Hospital*,[52] the same appellate court held that the missing witness charge was inapplicable to the defendants' failure to call to the stand the doctor who had examined the plaintiff for the defense since the defendant's doctor merely would have corroborated the testimony of the plaintiff's doctors. The court wrote, "While the inference may ordinarily arise where a doctor who examined the plaintiff on the defendant's behalf does not testify . . . , where the testimony would be merely cumulative and would not constitute substantial evidence, the inference may not be drawn . . . ."

Distinguish *Getlin* from the holdings in *Griffen v. Nissen*,[53] and *Guzman v. MABSTOA*,[54] which cases held that a plaintiff-patient has the obligation to call to the stand the

---

50. Vollmer v. Automobile Fire Ins. Co., 207 A.D.67, 202 N.Y.S. 374 (3d Dep't 1923).
51. Trotta v. Koch, 110 A.D.2d 631, 494 N.Y.S.2d 664 (2d Dep't 1985).
52. Getlin v. St. Vincent's Hosp., 117 A.D.2d 707, 498 N.Y.S.2d 849 (2d Dep't 1986). *Accord* Weinstein v. Daman, 132 A.D.2d 547, 517 N.Y.S.2d 278 (2d Dep't 1987).
53. Griffen v. Nissen, 89 A.D.2d 808, 453 N.Y.S.2d 277 (4th Dep't 1982).
54. Guzman v. Manhattan & Bronx Surface Transit Operating Auth., 99 A.D. 972, 470 N.Y.S.2d 1006 (2d Dept. 1984); *see also* Siegfried v. Siegfried, N.Y.L.J., Oct. 10, 1986, at 16, col. 2 (2d Dep't 1986).

doctors who treated the plaintiff's injury even if they have not treated the plaintiff for a long time. The presumptions are that a plaintiff has control of the physician who treated him or her and that the treating physician would be favorable to the patient.[55] Since the doctors actually saw and treated the plaintiff's injuries after they occurred, their testimony would not be merely cumulative, unlike the testimony of a doctor who merely examined the plaintiff in preparation for litigation.

Nevertheless, when presenting a case for either a plaintiff or a defendant, the trial attorney must always be aware of the possibility that the attorney's unexplained failure to call a witness within his or her client's control may precipitate a missing witness charge and the drawing of an inference against the client.

---

55. Wilson v. Bodian, 130 A.D.2d 221, 519 N.Y.S.2d 126 (2d Dep't 1987); McClure v. Baier's Automotive Serv. Center, 126 A.D.2d 610, 511 N.Y.S. 2d 50 (2d Dep't 1987).

EXAMPLE 8-1: REQUESTS TO CHARGE IN AN ACTION FOR NEGLIGENCE

SUPREME COURT OF THE STATE OF NEW YORK
COUNTY OF NASSAU

--X

DEBRA and ROBERT

Plaintiffs

-against-

MANAGEMENT INC.,
ENTERPRISES, INC., STEEL
CORP., and INC.,

Defendants.

--X

MANAGEMENT INC.,

Third-Party Plaintiff

-against-

DRUGS,

Third-Party Defendant.

--X

PLAINTIFFS' REQUEST TO CHARGE

Kramer, Dillof, Tessel, Duffy & Moore
Attorneys for Plaintiffs
233 Broadway
New York, NY 10279
(212) 267-4177

SUPREME COURT OF THE STATE OF NEW YORK
COUNTY OF NASSAU
---X
DEBRA and ROBERT

Plaintiffs

-against-

MANAGEMENT INC.,
ENTERPRISES, INC., STEEL
CORP., and INC.,

Defendants.
---X
MANAGEMENT INC.

Third-Party Plaintiff

-against-

DRUGS,

Third-Party Defendant.
---X

As and for their request to charge, plaintiffs request as follows:

1. In order to recover, plaintiff must prove: (1) that there was an unsafe condition; (2) that a defendant was negligent in creating the unsafe condition or in allowing the unsafe condition to exist; and (3) that that defendant's negligence in creating the unsafe condition or in allowing the unsafe condition to exist was a substantial factor in causing plaintiff's injury.

Negligence is the failure to use reasonable care. Reasonable care means that degree of care which a reasonably prudent person would use under the same circumstances. Negligence includes both a foreseeable danger of injury to another and conduct which is unreasonable in proportion to the danger.

Supporting Authorities:

PJI 2:10; 2:90; 2:91.

1

2. The plaintiff claims that the defendants violated the following regulations or ordinances [of which this Court can take judicial notice[1]]:

New York State Industrial Code <16.2(b), which provides as follows:

> Wood Floors. Wood floors shall be kept free from potruding nails, splinters and holes. Boards, planks or other floor surfacing materials shall be properly fastened.

New York State Industrial Code <16.4(b), which provides as follows:

> Stair Treads. The finished surfaces of stair treads shall be of such material and so maintained as to prevent persons from slipping or tripping thereon.

New York State Building Code <764.1(b), which provides as follows:

> Stairways shall be of the fixed type and shall be arranged and constructed for safe ascent and descent. Stairs shall be of sufficient width to serve the occupant.

New York State Building Code <765.4(a)(9), which pertains to stairways and provides as follows:

> Treads shall be set level and true, and top surfaces shall not vary more than one-eighth inch in any run. Risers shall not vary more than one-eighth inch in height on any run. Stair treads and landings shall be provided with nonslip surfaces.

If you find that any of these sections were violated with respect to the condition of the mezzanine platform and top step at issue in this lawsuit, you may regard any such violation as evidence of negligence. The duty imposed by these regulations is absolute and the breach thereof is evidence of negligence without regard to whether or not the defendants had notice of their violations.

---

[1] The Court may take judicial notice of the rules and regulations of the various subdivisions of municipal government. CPLR 4511; **Shepardson by Shepardson v. Town of Schodack**, 83 N.Y.2d 894 (1994).

Supporting Authorities:

> PJI 2:29; PJI 2:151; **Smulczeski v. City Center of Music and Drama, Inc.**, 3 N.Y.2d 498 (1957); **Conte v. Large Scale Development Corp.**, 10 N.Y.2d 20 (1961); **Major v. Waverly and Ogden, Inc.**, 7 N.Y.2d 332 (1960); **McDonald v. NYCH & H Corp.**, 203 A.D.2d 6 (1st Dept. 1994). **See also** Commentary, 1 PJI p.153-54.

3. A contractor, whether he be a general or subcontractor, is required to perform the work for which he was retained, in a reasonably safe manner. If you find that the work performed by either the general and/or the subcontractor, with reference to the mezzanine platform and top step, which are the subject of this action, were not constructed in a reasonably safe condition, then you may find that either the general and/or the subcontractor were negligent.

Supporting Authorities:

> **Rufo v. Orlando**, 309 N.Y. 345 (1955); **Brown v. Welsbach Corp.**, 301 N.Y. 202 (1950); **Gurriel v. Town of Huntington**, 129 A.D.2d 768 (2nd Dept. 1987); **Jasenzak v. Schipp**, 278 App.Div. 660 (2nd Dept. 1951).

4. Defendant, as the owner or lessor of a building, has a duty to use reasonable care to keep the premises in a reasonably safe condition for the protection of all persons whose presence is reasonably foreseeable.

Section 17(a) of the lease required to "make all structural repairs and replacements to the Demised Premises as and when required to keep the same in good condition and repair," including repairs to the "underflooring". That provision required to use reasonable care to keep the premises in safe condition. In order for the plaintiffs to recover, plaintiffs must show that he or she was injured, that the injury occurred in a portion of the premises that was in a defective or unsafe condition; that the defective or unsafe condition of the premises was a substantial factor in causing the injury; and that knew of the defective condition for a sufficient length of time before plaintiff's injury to permit it, in the use of reasonable care, to have corrected it; or that the condition had existed for a sufficient length of time that in the use of reasonable

3

care should have known of its existence and corrected it. Reasonable care means that degree of care that a reasonably prudent lessor would use under the same circumstances.

Supporting Authorities:

PJI 2:90; 2:106.

5. If you find that one or more defendants were negligent, you must next consider whether that negligence was a substantial factor in causing plaintiff's injury. An act or failure to act is a substantial factor in bringing about an injury if a reasonable person would regard it as a cause of the injury. If you find that defendant's negligence was not a substantial factor in causing the injury, then plaintiff may not recover on this claim.

Supporting Authorities:

PJI 2:70; PJI 2:90; PJI 2:91.

6. If you find that the defendant's negligence was a substantial factor in causing plaintiff's injuries, you must next consider whether plaintiff was also negligent and whether plaintiff's conduct was a substantial contributing factor in causing her injuries.

The burden is on the defendants to prove that plaintiff was negligent and that her negligence contributed to causing her injuries. If you find that plaintiff was not negligent, or if negligent that her negligence did not contribute to causing her injuries, you should go no further and report your findings to the court.

Plaintiff claims that she bears no responsibility for negligence in the occurrence of this accident. She maintains that while she was aware of the claimed unsafe condition prior to the accident, she did not have it in mind or memory at the moment of the accident. If you find that in fact she forgot about the condition prior to the accident, then you may find that she bears no culpable responsibility for the happening of the accident. If on the other hand you find that she was aware of the condition and had it in her mind and memory at the time of the accident, then you may find that the plaintiff was negligent.

4

If you find that plaintiff was negligent and that her negligence contributed to her injuries, you must then apportion the fault between plaintiff and defendants.

Weighing all the facts and circumstances, you must consider the total negligence, that is, the negligence of both plaintiff and the defendants which contributed to causing the injuries and determine what percentage of fault is chargeable to each. In your verdict, you will state the percentages you find. The total of those percentages must equal one hundred percent.

Supporting Authorities:

> PJI 2:36; **Gross v. City of New York**, 24 A.D.2d 751 (1st Dept. 1965), affd. 18 N.Y.2d 830 (1966); **Flynn v. City of New York**, 103 A.D.2d 98 (2nd Dept. 1984).

7. Facts must be proved by evidence. Evidence includes the testimony of a witness concerning what the witness saw, heard or did. Evidence also includes writings, photographs, or other physical objects which may be considered as proof of a fact. Evidence can be either direct or circumstantial. Facts may be proved either by direct or circumstantial evidence or by a combination of both. You may give circumstantial evidence less weight, more weight, or the same weight as direct evidence.

Direct evidence is evidence of what a witness saw, heard, or did which, if believed by you, proves a fact. For example, let us suppose that a fact in dispute is whether I knocked over this water glass near the witness chair. If someone testifies that he saw me knock over the glass, that is direct evidence that I knocked over the glass.

Circumstantial evidence is evidence of a fact which does not directly prove a fact in dispute but which permits a reasonable inference or conclusion that the fact exists. For example, a witness testifies that he saw this water glass on the bench. The witness states that, while he was looking the other way, he heard the breaking of glass, looked up, and saw me wiping water from my clothes and from the papers on the bench. This testimony is not direct evidence that I knocked over the glass; it is circumstantial evidence from which you could reasonably infer that I knocked over the glass.

Those facts which form the basis of an inference mut be proved and the inference to be drawn must be one that may be reasonably drawn. In the example, even though the witness did not see me knock over the glass, if you believe his/her testimony, you could conclude that I did. Therefore, the circumstantial evidence, if accepted by you, allows you to conclude that the fact in dispute has been proved.

In reaching your conclusion you may not guess or speculate. Suppose, for example, the witness testifies that the water glass was located equally distant from the court clerk and me. The witness states that he heard the breaking of glass and looked up to see both the court clerk and me brushing water from our clothes. If you believe that testimony, you still could not decide on that evidence alone who knocked over the water glass. Where these are the only proved facts, it would be only a guess as to who did it. But, if the witness also testifies that he heard the court clerk say "I am sorry," this additional evidence would allow you to decide who knocked over the water glass.

Supporting Authorities:

PJI 1:70.

8. Plaintiff has introduced evidence of the condition of the mezzanine platform on the day of the accident. In particular, plaintiff has introduced photographs of the mezzanine platform and top step taken after the accident and has testified as to the condition of the mezzanine platform and top step. If you find that this condition was in fact in existence on the day of the accident and if you find from the nature of the condition that it is reasonable to conclude that this condition had not changed since the time of the construction, you may infer from the evidence submitted by the plaintiff that the mezzanine platform and top step were in fact constructed in this condition.

Supporting Authorities:

Taylor v. NYCTA, 48 N.Y.2d 903 (1979); **Batton v. Elghanayan**, 43 N.Y.2d 898 (1978); **Farrar v. Teicholz**, 173 A.D.2d 674 (2nd Dept. 1991); **Kniffin v. Thruway Food Markets, Inc.**, 177 A.D.2d 920 (3rd Dept. 1991).

6

Respectfully submitted,
KRAMER, DILLOF, TESSEL, DUFFY
& MOORE
Attorneys for Plaintiff
233 Broadway
New York, New York 10279
(212) 267-4177

7

EXAMPLE 8-2: REQUESTS TO CHARGE IN AN ACTION FOR MEDICAL MALPRACTICE

SUPREME COURT OF THE STATE OF NEW YORK
COUNTY OF SUFFOLK

---X

Individually and as
Administrator of the Estate of
, Deceased,

Plaintiff,

-against-

DR. , DR. ,
MEDICAL GROUP,
, M.D., P.C., DR. ,
and HOSPITAL MEDICAL
CENTER,

Defendants.

---X

The plaintiff respectfully requests the Court to charge the jury as follows:

1. Malpractice is professional negligence and medical malpractice is the negligence of a doctor. Negligence is the failure to use reasonable care under the circumstances; doing something which a reasonably prudent doctor would not do under the circumstances or failing to do something which a reasonably prudent doctor would do under the circumstances; it is a deviation or a departure from accepted practice.

A doctor who renders medical service to a patient is obligated to have that reasonable degree of knowledge and ability which is expected of doctors who provide that medical service in the medical community in which the doctor practices.

The law recognizes that there are differences in the abilities of doctors, just as there are differences in the abilities of people engaged in other activities. To practice medicine a doctor is not required to have the extraordinary knowledge and ability that belongs to a few doctors of exceptional ability. However, every doctor is required to keep reasonably informed of new developments in his field and to practice medicine in accordance with approved methods and means of treatment in general use. The standard to which an obstetrician is held is measured by the degree of knowledge and ability of the average obstetrician in good standing in the medical community in which he practices.

In performing a medical service, a doctor is obligated to use reasonable care. By undertaking to perform a medical service, a doctor does not guarantee a good result. The fact that there was a bad result to the plaintiff's decedent, by itself, does not make the doctor liable. The physician is liable only if he was negligent. Whether or not the doctor was negligent is to be decided on the basis of the circumstances existing at the time of the claimed negligence.

If the doctor is negligent, that is, lacks the skill or knowledge required of him in providing a medical service or fails to use reasonable care in providing the service, and such lack of skill or care or knowledge or the failure to use reasonable care is a substantial factor in causing injury or death to the plaintiff's decedent, then the doctor is responsible for the injury or harm caused. This is the standard applicable to defendant physicians.

Supporting Authorities:

> PJI 2:150, 1996 Cum.Supp. p. 340-341. As per Caveat 2 in Comment PJI 2:150 1996 Cum. Supp. p. 341, the error of judgment portion of the charge has been excluded. See also Spadaccini v. Dolan, 63 A.D.2d 110 (1st Dept. 1978).

2. Negligence is a lack of ordinary care. It is a failure to exercise that degree of care which a reasonably prudent person would have exercised under the same circumstances. It may arise from doing an act which a reasonably prudent person would not have done under the same circumstances, or, on the other hand, from failing to do an act which a reasonably prudent person would have done under the same circumstances. This standard is applicable to the hospital and its nurses.

Supporting Authorities:

> PJI 2:10; Commentaries PJI 2:151 1996 Cum. Supp. p. 360-62; Toth v. Community Hospital, 22 N.Y.2d 255, 265 (1968).

3. Dr. law requires him to possess the reasonable skill and knowledge as is possessed by the average specialist in family practice. Thus, as a specialist in family practice, Dr. may be held liable where a general practitioner may not.

Supporting Authorities:

PJI 2:150; Toth v. Community Hospital, 22 N.Y.2d 255, 262-63 (1968).

4. In determining whether the plaintiff has sustained his burden of proving that a defendant was negligent or departed from accepted medical practice, you are not limited to the testimony of the plaintiff's expert witness and the departures from accepted medical practice as testified to by the plaintiff's expert witness. Rather, you may find for the plaintiff on the issue of a defendant's negligence based upon the testimony of the plaintiff's expert witness, a defense expert witness or of a defendant.

Supporting Authorities:

Davis v. Caldwell, 54 N.Y.2d 176 (1981); Behan v. Ivanhoe Co., 263 App.Div. 963 (2nd Dept. 1942); Tumulty v. New York, New Haven & Hartford R.R. Co, 224 App.Div. 131 (2nd Dept. 1928)..

5. To render a defendant liable for malpractice, his malpractice must be a proximate cause of an injury or death. An act or omission is a proximate cause of an injury if it was a substantial factor in bringing about the injury or death, that is, if the act or omission had such an effect in producing the injury or death that reasonable persons would regard it as a contributing cause of the injury or death.

Supporting Authorities:

PJI 2:70

6. There can be several causes of an injury or death. To recover, the plaintiff has to establish only that an act or omission of the defendant was "a" cause, not "the" cause of injury to or the death of   . Any defendant's negligent act or omission need not be the sole cause but need be only "a" cause of an injury to or the death of   in order for the defendant to be held liable.

Supporting Authorities:

PJI 2:71 1995 Cum. Supp. p.167; Dunham v. Canisteo, 303 N.Y. 498, 505-06 (1952); Mortensen v. Memorial Hospital, 105 A.D.2d 151, 158 (1st Dept. 1984); Galioto v. Lakeside Hospital, 123 A.D.2d 421, 422 (2nd Dept. 1986); Ledogar v. Giordano, 122 A.D.2d 834 (2nd Dept.), app. withdrawn, 68 N.Y.2d 911 (1986)

7. Plaintiff does not have to prove with certainty that the negligence of a defendant was a substantial factor in causing injury to or the death of . Rather, plaintiff only had to offer sufficient evidence from which reasonable persons may conclude by reasonable inference that it is more probable than not that a defendant's negligent conduct was a substantial factor in bringing about injury to or the death of . Thus, to recover, plaintiff was not obligated to offer evidence which excludes every other possible cause of injury to or the death of and plaintiff did not have to eliminate entirely each possibility that an act or omission of a defendant was not such a cause.

Moreover, the plaintiff is not required to prove the precise manner in which injury to or the death of occurred or the precise mechanism which caused such injury or death. To this end, in order to find for the plaintiff, you are not required to find that the plaintiff proved the precise nature of a defendant's negligence which caused the injury or death. In determining what was the cause of injury or death, you may rely on an educated medical theory of the expert witness provided that you give credence to that theory.

Supporting Authorities:

PJI 1:70; Schneider v. Kings Highway Hosp. Center, 67 N.Y.2d 743 (1986); Derdiarian v. Felix Contracting Corp., 51 N.Y.2d 308, 315 (1980); Toth v. Community Hosp., 22 N.Y.2d 255, 261 (1968); Pollicina v. Misericordia Hosp. Med. Ctr., 158 A.D.2d 194 (1st Dept. 1990); Jarrett v. Madifari, 67 A.D.2d 396, 405 (1st Dept. 1979); Ledogar v. Giordano, 122 A.D.2d 834 (2nd Dept.), app. withdrawn, 68 N.Y.2d 911 (1986); Vialva v. City of New York, 118 A.D.2d 701, 703 (2nd Dept. 1986); Mertsaris v. 73rd Corp., 105 A.D.2d 67 (2nd Dept. 1984); Hunter v. Ford Motor Co., 37 A.D.2d 335 (3rd Dept. 1971); Monahan v. Weichert, 82 A.D.2d 102, 108 (4th Dept. 1981); Markel v. Spencer, 5 A.D.2d 400, 407-08 (4th Dept. 1958), aff'd, 5 N.Y.2d 958 (1959); Taype v. City of New York, 82 A.D.2d 648 (2nd Dept. 1981); Scott v. Brookdale Hosp., 60 A.D.2d 647 (2nd Dept. 1977); Matter of Blome v. Presti Auto Sales, 43 A.D.2d 1002 (3rd Dept. 1974); Matter of Normile v. Spagnoletti Construction Corp., 27 A.D.2d 169, 171 (3rd Dept. 1957).

8. In a wrongful death action, such as this, the plaintiff has a lesser burden of proof with respect to the principles I have just given you. Thus, in this wrongful death action, the plaintiff, , the administratrix of 's estate is not held to as high a degree of proof as is required of an injured plaintiff who can describe what happened. Thus, you are permitted greater latitude in inferring negligence and/or medical malpractice on the part of a defendant from all of the evidence in the case. If, from all the credible evidence in this case, you conclude that it is more probable than not that a defendant committed medical malpractice and that that malpractice was a substantial factor in causing pain injury to or the death of , you will find for the plaintiff on this issue. However, if that is not your decision, or if you find that the evidence is so evenly balanced that you cannot say that the greater weight of the evidence is on either side of these issues, you will find the defendant was not at fault.

Supporting Authorities:

PJI 1:61; Noseworthy v. New York, 298 N.Y. 76 (1948).

9. Facts must be proved by evidence. Evidence includes the testimony of a witness concerning what the witness saw, heard or did. Evidence also includes writings, photographs, or other physical objects which may be considered as proof of a fact. Evidence can be either direct or circumstantial. Facts may be proved either by direct or circumstantial evidence or by a combination of both. You may give circumstantial evidence less weight, more weight, or the same weight as direct evidence.

Direct evidence is evidence of what a witness saw, heard, or did which, if believed by you, proves a fact. For example, let us suppose that a fact in dispute is whether I knocked over this water glass near the witness chair. If someone testifies that he saw me knock over the glass, that is direct evidence that I knocked over the glass.

Circumstantial evidence is evidence of a fact which does not directly prove a fact in dispute but which permits a reasonable inference or conclusion that the fact exists. For example, a witness testifies that he saw this water glass on the bench. The witness states that, while he was looking the other way, he heard the breaking of glass, looked up, and saw me wiping water from my clothes and from the papers on the bench. This testimony is not direct evidence that I knocked over the glass, it is circumstantial evidence from which you could reasonably infer that I knocked over the glass.

Those facts which form the basis of an inference must be proved and the inference to be drawn must be one that may be reasonably drawn. In the example, even though the witness did not see me knock over the glass, if you believe his/her testimony, you could conclude that I did. Therefore, the circumstantial evidence, if accepted by you, allows you to conclude that the fact in dispute has been proved.

In reaching your conclusion you may not guess or speculate. Suppose, for example, the witness testifies that the water glass was located equally distant from the court clerk and me. The witness states that he heard the breaking of glass and looked up to see both the court clerk and me brushing water from our clothes. If you believe that testimony, you still could not decide on that evidence alone who knocked over the water glass. Where these are the only proved facts, it would be only a guess as to who did it. But, if the witness also testifies that he heard the court clerk say, "I am sorry," this additional evidence would allow you to decide who knocked over the water glass.

Supporting Authorities:

PJI 1:70 1995 Cum. Supp. p.56-57.

10. If you should find that the plaintiff has sustained her burden of proof on the issue of malpractice and thus is entitled to a verdict against the defendants, then you must include in your verdict an award of money for the pecuniary losses sustained by 's husband, and his three children, , and , as a result of her death.

In determining this amount, you should take into consideration the character, habits and ability of the services that she would have performed for her husband and children, the guidance and nurture she would have provided her children and the earnings that she would have spent on the care and support of her husband and children. In this regard, you should consider the care, work and maintenance she would have provided around the family home. You should also consider the intellectual, moral and physical guidance, training, and assistance she would have given to her children, had she lived. In this regard, you should consider that was age 12 at the time of his mother's death, was age 10 at the time of her mother's death and was age 2 at the time of her mother's death. In determining the value of these services, you may exercise your general knowledge and experience regarding the value of each such services in the market place.

You must decide what portion of her earnings would have spent for the care and support of her family. You should also consider the amount, if any, by which if she had lived, would have increased her estate from her earnings and, thus, added to the amount that would have been inherited from her provided you find that her husband and/or children would have been alive to inherit had died when she did.

In considering the damages for pecuniary loss, you should take into account that had a further life expectancy of _____ years and a work life expectancy of ___ years. has a life expectancy of _____ years. Life expectancy and work life expectancy tables are simply statistical averages. A person might live longer or die sooner than the time indicated by those tables. The figures I just mentioned are not controlling but may be considered by you together with the evidence you heard concerning the health, habits, employment and activities of prior to her death and those of in determining what their respective life expectancies were at the time died.

As I stated before, it is the economic value of to her husband and children that you must decide. That value is incapable of exact proof. Taking into account all the factors I have discussed, you must use your own common sense and sound judgment based on the evidence in determining the amount of the economic loss suffered by 's husband and children.

The amount you decide as the amount of economic loss sustained by 's husband and children must represent the full amount of such losses without reduction to present value. You must also decide the period of years for which that amount is intended to provide compensation. You are not to reduce or discount your award to present value. Under the law that is an obligation imposed upon me.

Supporting authorities:

> PJI 2:290; 2:320; DeLong v. County of Erie, 60 N.Y.2d 296, 307 (1983); Gonzalez v. New York City Housing Auth., 77 N.Y.2d 663 (1991); Tilley v. Hudson River R.R. Co., 24 N.Y. 471 (1862).

11. In addition, if you find that the plaintiff has sustained his burden of proof on the issue of malpractice and thus is entitled to a verdict against the defendants, then you must include in your verdict an award of money for the conscious pain and suffering experienced by caused by the defendants. Conscious pain and suffering means pain and suffering of which there was some level of awareness by

Plaintiff is entitled to recover a sum of money which would justly and fairly compensate for the injury and conscious pain and suffering experienced by . In determining this amount, you may take into consideration her physical pain and suffering as well as her mental anguish and emotional distress. You may award damages for any such suffering of which was, at some level, aware from the moment of injury to the moment of death.

Supporting authorities:

PJI 2:280; PJI 2:320; McDougald v. Garber, 73 N.Y.2d 246 (1989).

Respectfully submitted,
KRAMER, DILLOF, TESSEL,
DUFFY & MOORE
Attorneys for Plaintiff
233 Broadway
New York, New York 10279
(212) 267-4177

EXAMPLE 8-3: LIST OF PATTERN JURY INSTRUCTIONS IN AN ACTION FOR NEGLIGENCE

TABLE OF PATTERN JURY INSTRUCTIONS - CIVIL ACTIONS

DIVISION 1. GENERAL CHARGES

A. CHARGE PRIOR TO TRIAL

B. CHARGE AFTER TRIAL

C. GENERAL INSTRUCTIONS NOT APPLICABLE TO ALL CASES

D. CHARGE AFTER VERDICT

DIVISION 2. NEGLIGENCE ACTIONS

A. COMMON LAW STANDARD OF CARE

B. STATUTORY STANDARD OF CARE

C. PLAINTIFF'S NEGLIGENCE

D. ASSUMPTION OF RISK

E. RES IPSA LOQUITUR

F. PROXIMATE CAUSE

G. SPECIFIC NEGLIGENT ACCIDENTS

7

I. LIABILITY OVER

J. DAMAGES

APPENDICES

11

The Summation 9

This chapter explains determining the content of the summation, organizing the summation, and avoiding impermissible remarks during the summation. Finally, this chapter provides a sample summation delivered in a medical malpractice case.

As we have observed in prior chapters, there is nothing mysterious about rhetoric. On the contrary, composing a summation entails the conscious use of well-known techniques. Hence, the summation is a speech whose purpose is frankly persuasive and whose mode is argumentative. In achieving his or her purpose, the attorney should use all three persuasive appeals: *logos*, *pathos*, and *ethos*.[1] *Logos* is the logical appeal, i.e., the proof generated by applying arguments to evidence to establish the client's case. *Logos* should comprise the bulk of the summation. *Pathos* is the emotional appeal, i.e., disposing the jurors to sympathize with the client and inspiring them to decide in the client's favor after the attorney has obtained their intellectual assent through *logos*. Finally, *ethos* is the appeal from the character of the advocate, i.e., the jurors' estimation of him or her as honest and competent. Since the attorney cannot argue directly for his own *ethos*, he must establish it indirectly by his conduct throughout the trial. (Credibility is something different from *ethos*; the former is the judgment that a witness's factual report is worthy of belief.)

1. EDWARD P.J. CORBETT, CLASSICAL RHETORIC FOR THE MODERN STUDENT (New York: Oxford Univ. Press, 1965), p. 38 ff.

9.1 DETERMINING THE CONTENT

We must begin with the assumption that the attorney has prepared thoroughly for the trial. (Refer to chapters 1, 2, and 5.) Remember also that evidence must support nearly everything that the attorney will say during summation. Therefore, during the testimony, the attorney must make brief but accurate notes and must integrate this information with his or her arguments. For the sake of coherence, we will approach this task from the point of view of the plaintiff's attorney.

Taking notes while listening to a witness may be difficult, but taking notes while questioning a witness is impossible. Therefore, the attorney should employ three devices: first, begin the trial with an outline of the witness's expected testimony, which outline the attorney can amend with a few words; second, the attorney should order daily transcripts; and third, during or immediately after the testimony, the attorney should make brief notes which juxtapose the direct, cross, and re-direct examinations. An intelligent assistant (not necessarily a lawyer) who can make neat and accurate notes is a great help.

The notes juxtaposing the successive examinations should look like example 9-1. Turn a yellow pad or a sketch pad sideways; divide the pad into four columns, and then label the columns direct, cross, re-direct, and argument. Do not attempt to take a transcript. In the first column, record the gist of the items of the witness's testimony in the order in which he or she testified to them. In the second column, record the admissions which the defense attorney extracts or attempts to extract from the witness during the cross-examination. However, do not record these items in the order of the cross-examination; instead, record each supposed admission next to the corresponding item from the direct examination. In the third column, record the clarifications, etc. which you extract from the witness during the re-direct examination, and, in the fourth column, note the relevant issue or argument. Check your notes against the daily transcript.

On a daily basis, the attorney should integrate the testimony with a master outline of the case. Example 9-2 is a form with five columns. Before the trial begins, outline your contentions in the first column. During the trial, record the evidence adduced for the plaintiff in the second column, and record the evidence adduced for the defendant in the third column. Do this before you quit for the day. Before preparing your summation, formulate the defendant's expected refutation of your contentions in the fourth column and your rebuttal in the fifth. Thus, this form should relate the attorney's case to the actual evidence and to his or her opponent's arguments.[2]

At this stage of the trial, the attorney will have available the pleadings, the outlines made during pre-trial preparation, the opening statements for each party, the documents introduced, two sets of notes made during the trial, the transcript, and the tentative outline made for the summation but before the trial. The attorney should be ready and eager to reduce this material to a simpler outline concentrating on the questions being contested.

9.2 ORGANIZING THE SUMMATION

9.2.1 In General

A persuasive speech traditionally has five potential divisions: the introduction (*exordium*), the statement of the facts (*narratio*), the logical proof (*confirmatio* or *probatio*),

---

2. Those of you who have been scholastic and collegiate debaters will have noticed the similarity of these two forms to a flow sheet.

the refutation of the opponent's case (*refutatio*), and the conclusion (*peroratio*).[3]

In a summation, the attorney usually combines the proof and the refutation so that he may refute his opponent's arguments on each point immediately after the attorney makes his own argument. The jurors are better able to follow the attorney's reasoning when he uses this approach. The attorney also might combine the statement of the facts with the proof and the refutation if the narration provides a dramatic chronology while retaining argumentative coherence. For example, in a summation in a brain damaged baby case, the plaintiff's attorney might use a dramatic chronology to increase the tension as each act of malpractice builds to the tragic birth. However, the subdivisions of the narration must be directly and rigorously argumentative. Don't hint; accuse, and tell the jury exactly and irrefutably why. Of course, the principle of organization in another case might be the elements of the cause of action, the ultimate issues, the logical contentions, the witnesses, or even the questions in the itemized verdict sheet.

Regardless of the principal scheme of organization, the attorney's presentation of each subcontention must be clear and straightforward. For example, in an action for negligence, the organization might be —

a. first cause of action,
  (1) the duty,
    (a) general,
    (b) specific,
  (2) the act that breached that duty,
  (3) the immediate result, e.g., crash.

or in an action for medical malpractice.

b. second act of malpractice,
    (1) the standard of care,

3. Corbett, *op. cit.*, p. 277.

(2) the act constituting the departure,
(3) the immediate result to the plaintiff.

Since each party's attorney will deliver only one speech in summation, the attorney must integrate refutation of his or her opponent's arguments into the presentation of his or her own contentions. The organization must arise from the material, but there are two principal methods to organize this integration: creating additional subdivisions or creating additional items within each subdivision. For example, an additional subdivision —

a. act of malpractice,
  (1) the standard of care,
  (2) the act constituting the departure,
  (3) the immediate result to the plaintiff,
  (4) the refutation of the defendant's argments.

or additional items within each subdivision —

b. act of malpractice,
  (1) the standard of care,
    (a) plaintiff's argument,
    (b) refutation of the defendant's argument,
  (2) the act constituting the departure,
    (a) plaintiff's argument,
    (b) refutation,
  (3) the immediate result to the plaintiff,
    (a) plaintiff's argument,
    (b) refutation.

The second method is preferable if the opponent has contested a great many points, but such an organization requires frequent internal summaries.

Perhaps the most important aspect of the organization of the summation is that the attorney make conscious choices.

Never attempt to dictate a summation or to deliver one impromptu.[4]

9.2.2 Damages

The attorney will devote more time to the damages in his summation than he devoted to them in his opening statement. Therefore, regardless of the principal divisions into which the attorney organizes his speech, he must further divide the body of his speech between the issue of liability and the issue of damages. If the trial is bifurcated, of course, the attorney will deliver a summation on each question. In either situation, the attorney must argue for his client's economic damages in a precise and straightforward manner. The jurors already will have heard a lucid explanation from the expert witness, so they should be able to follow the attorney's argument if the attorney has the material clear in his own mind and has practiced the explanations. When arguing for a recovery for non-economic damages, e.g., conscious pain and suffering, the attorney must be vivid and courageous. Describe your client's suffering accurately but in such a way as to grip the imagination of the jurors.

In the final appeal to the jury, the peroration, the attorney should return to the drama of the case. Reiterate the facts of the case, but call frankly for the jury to act in favor of your client.

9.2.3 The Defendant

The defendant's attorney will use the same forms and rhetorical approach as the plaintiff's attorney; for example, the defendant's attorney should label the six columns on the

4. In current usage, *extemporaneous* denotes speaking with some brief preparation but without using a text by reading or from memory; *impromptu* denotes speaking with virtually no specific preparation.

flow sheet as the plaintiff's arguments, the plaintiff's evidence, the defendant's arguments, the defendant's evidence, the plaintiff's rebuttal, and the defendant's rebuttal. The defense attorney also must transform his or her notes into one briefer but integrated outline which employs arguments and evidence to address the issues and persuade the jury. Attorneys often see the defense attorney as working at two disadvantages: the attorney speaks first, and the plaintiff has the sympathy of the jury. However, the defendant's attorney may exploit the first disadvantage to counteract the second. Thus, the emotional issue may be defused by addressing it before the plaintiff's attorney has a chance to do so. The defendant's attorney may express sympathy for the plaintiff's tragedy without going so far as to appear insincere. Then the attorney may ask the jurors not to let their sympathy for the plaintiff cloud their judgment and make the defendant another victim. In addition, the defendant's attorney must formulate his or her opponent's specific arguments, raise them in the speech, and refute them decisively. Do not avoid this duty in the hope that your opponent will deliver a weak summation or in the hope that you somehow can distract the jury.

9.2.4 Practice

The attorney must practice the summation aloud. There probably will not be enough time between the last witness and the summations to compose a text, but the attorney should not need a text. Having examined the witnesses, the attorney should be eager to deliver the summation. However, the attorney should reduce his or her thoughts to an outline and then practice speaking from that outline. The attorney should tape-record the speech and then listen to it because listening to the tape will help to eliminate awkward phrases and clichés. In addition, the attorney should ask a colleague to listen to the speech, take notes, and then criticize the composition and arguments. In particular, this colleague should raise those questions which might be in the minds of the jurors. Finally, if possible, the attorney should practice the summation aloud on the day it is to be delivered to the jury. The attorney should be as warmed up intellectually as an athlete is physically.

9.3 AVOIDING IMPERMISSIBLE REMARKS

The C.P.L.R. does not regulate the summation because a summation is not evidence and is controlled by the court.[5] The purpose of the summation is, as its name implies, to summarize the evidence clearly and to persuade the trier of fact that the evidence proves that the position of the attorney's client is correct. To the end of persuasion, the attorney may comment upon the evidence and the witnesses as long as he or she does in a fair, reasonable, and responsible manner.[6] Comments upon the opposition's failure to call a witness are also fair, whether or not the trial court will give a missing-witness charge.[7] The tests of propriety are common sense and logic; thus, while the court will allow legitimate comments upon the evidence, the court will not tolerate personal attacks against a party or a witness.[8]

---

5. Bowen v. Mahoney Coal Corp., 256 A.D. 485, 10 N.Y.S. 454 (1st Dep't 1939).
6. Adams v. Acker, 57 A.D.2d 741, 394 N.Y.S.2d 8 (1st Dep't 1977), *modified* in 58 A.D.2d 574 (1st Dep't 1977): a new trial on common law negligence and violation of G.M.L. 205-a because of the plaintiff's attorney's improper remarks during his summation. Zemliansky v. United Parcel Serv., Inc., 175 Misc. 829, 24 N.Y.S.2d 672 (Sup. Ct. 1940).
7. Seligson, Morris & Neuberger v. Fairbanks Whitney Corp., 22 A.D.2d 625, 257 N.Y.S.2d 706 (1st Dep't 1965).
8. Taormina v. Goodman, 63 A.D.2d 1018, 406 N.Y.S.2d 350 (2d Dep't 1978); Nicholas v. Island Indus. Park, 46 A.D.2d 804, 361 N.Y.S.2d 39 (2d Dep't 1974). In his summation in Taormina, the plaintiff's attorney had accused one of the defendant's experts of selling any testimony for a price and had accused the plaintiff and his attorney of having perjured themselves.

Because the C.P.L.R. does not regulate the summation, it is easier to explain what the trial attorney may not say in the summation than to explain what may be said. The imagination of the unscrupulous attorney can invent many kinds of impropriety, but we shall consider three important kinds: (1) using inflammatory language, (2) suggesting that the jury use a unit of time as the measure of damages for pain and suffering, and (3) – an unsettled area – suggesting a dollar amount for damages in an action for medical malpractice.

9.3.1 Inflammatory Language

A trial attorney must argue forcibly for his or her client, and the attorney may characterize evidence, witnesses, and claims unfavorably. However, the attorney must not use language that is intemperate, unfair, or likely to sway the jury in an irrational manner. Thus, the defendant's attorney may call the plaintiff a liar as a legitimate comment upon the latter's testimony,[9] but the attorney may not call the plaintiff a phony malingerer who was never injured at all and is just suing for the money.[10] Similarly, the defendant's attorney may call the plaintiff's expert a hired gun, but the attorney may not say that the expert is the best that money can buy[11] or that the expert will say anything for a price.[12]

The case of *Vassura v. Taylor*[13] illustrates the cumulative effect of improprieties in a summation in an action for negligence. The Appellate Division, Second Department, reversed the judgment for the defendant and held,

9. Cohen v. Cavelli, 276 A.D. 375, 94 N.Y.S.2d 782 (1st Dep't 1950).
10. Boyd v. Blessey, 96 A.D.2d 816, 465 N.Y.S.2d 563 (2d Dep't 1983).
11. LaRusso v. Pollack, 88 A.D.2d 584, 449 N.Y.S.2d 794 (2d Dep't 1982).
12. Taormina v. Goodman, 63 A.D.2d 1018, 406 N.Y.S.2d 350 (2d Dep't 1978).
13. Vassura v. Taylor, 117 A.D.2d 798, 499 N.Y.S.2d 120 (2d Dep't 1986) (holding that a defendant's verdict had to be reversed due to inflammatory, prejudicial, and erroneous comments that so contaminated the proceedings as to deny plaintiffs a fair trial). The court's analysis is quite deep and thorough. *See also* Roberts v. Stevens Clinic Hospital, Inc., 345 S.E.2d 791 (W. Va. 1986).

> There was evidence to support the jury verdict, but "[t]he record quite palpably reveals that the behavior of defense counsel during the trial created an atmosphere which deprived plaintiffs of a fair trial.". . . "[w]hat was involved [here] was not an isolated remark during questioning or summation, but a seemingly continual and deliberate effort to divert the jurors' and the court's attention from the issues to be determined." . . .

The court's opinion cited several of the defense attorney's more egregious comments during the trial. First, she asked the plaintiff whether he was aware of the medical benefits available under no-fault insurance. Second, she suggested that the measure of damages should be a life's savings or whatever was "in the other fellow's pocket," thereby referring to the financial status of the parties and implying that the defendant had limited financial means. Third, she cast aspersions on the plaintiffs'characters by saying of their claim for diminished sexual activity, "You've got to love a buck; and to just do about anything to open up the bedroom. . . ." Fourth, she made numerous references to other people who had suffered worse injuries, such as "little kids and elderly people" learning to use crutches. Fifth, in her summation, the defense attorney analogized injuries in general to a color spectrum and assigned various injuries to their positions on the spectrum.[14]

The appellate court concluded,

> [T]his was not a case where the attorney was quickly admonished and the jury received immediately curative instructions. . . . Nor was it a situation where an isolated improper remark could be deemed harmless in the face of overwhelming evidence in defendant's favor. . . . Defense counsel's attempt to influence the jurors through these inflammatory, prejudicial and erroneous comments so contaminate the proceedings as to deny the plaintiffs' right to a fair trial. . . .[15]

---

14. Vassura v. Taylor, 117 A.D.2d 798, 499 N.Y.S.2d 120, 121-23 (2d Dep't 1986).
15. *Id.* (Note: since, on retrial, plaintiff was awarded $546,099 by the jury, defense counsel's improper summation clearly had a profound impact upon the jury).

The lesson of *Vassura* is that a trial attorney should not go to the trouble of trying a case and doing a good job (the plaintiffs appealed a verdict of only $113,000) then throw those efforts away by delivering a prejudicial and improper summary.

9.3.2 A Unit of Time as the Measure of Damages for Pain and Suffering

Sometimes a unit of time is a proper measure of damages, e.g., the number of days the plaintiff was out of work as a result of his injuries helps to measure his lost income. However, in an action for negligence, it is improper for one of the parties'attorneys to use a unit of time as the measure of damages to guide the jury in calculating the recovery for such items as pain and suffering[16] or the loss of consortium. In other words, the plaintiff's attorney may not say to the jury: "I want you to place a figure on one day's pain and suffering; multiply that by 365 for a year's pain and suffering, then multiply that by the life expectancy of the plaintiff."

Naturally, this rule leaves the jury without any real guidance.

9.3.3 Suggesting a Dollar Amount in an Action for Medical Malpractice

As a general rule in an action for negligence, the plaintiff's attorney may tell the jury how much money his or her client is requesting and which recovery the attorney wants the jury to return.[17]

---

16. DeCicco v. Methodist Hosp., 74 A.D.2d 593, 424 N.Y.S.2d 524 (2d Dep't 1980). In Lee v. Bank of N.Y., 144 A.D.2d 543 (2d Dep't 1988), the court found counsel's use of the time-unit measure of damages harmless error because the jury did not follow counsel's suggestions.
17. Tate v. Colabello, 58 N.Y.2d 84, 445 N.E.2d 1101 459 N.Y.S.2d 422 (1983).

An unsettled matter is the applicability of this general rule to actions for medical malpractice. The Appellate Division, Third Department, has held in *Bechard v. Eisinger* that the general rule does not apply to such actions and that the plaintiff's attorney may not suggest an amount to the jury or reveal the amount of the claim.[18] The rationale for this exception is that C.P.L.R. section 3017 does not allow the complaint to contain a demand for a specific amount and that this prohibition should be observed throughout the trial. This new view is not unanimous, however, for in *Thornton v. Montefiore Hospital*, the Appellate Division, First Department, modified but let stand a verdict for the plaintiff in an action for medical malpractice in which the plaintiff's attorney had asked the jury to return a verdict of $8 million.[19]

The decision in *Thornton* appears to be more congruent with the legislative intent since the legislature conspicuously failed to adopt a statute that would have forbidden the plaintiff's attorney to suggest an amount to the jury in an action for medical malpractice. Moreover, a summation should assist the jury, guide it, and, in the case of the plaintiff's attorney, let the jury know what the plaintiff wants. Without such guidance, the jury's verdict may be outrageously high or low. The legislature adopted C.P.L.R. section 3017 to prevent the publication by the press of inflated ad damnum clauses; the legislature did not intend to interfere with the ability of a trial attorney to do his or her job.

18. Bechard v. Eisinger, 105 A.D.2d 939, 481 N.Y.S.2d 906 (3d Dep't 1984). In Bagailuk v. Weiss, 110 A.D.2d 284 (1985), the Third Department confirmed its opinion that allowing the plaintiff's attorney to ask for a particular sum for conscious pain and suffering would be to allow him to function as an unsworn witness.

19. Thornton v. Montefiore Hosp., 120 Misc. 2d 1003, 469 N.Y.S.2d 979 Sup. Ct. 1983), *modified*, 99 A.D.2d 1024, 973 N.Y.S.2d 758 (1st Dep't 1984). In the subsequent case of Garcia v. City of New York, 173 A.D.2d 175, 569 N.Y.S.2d 27 (1st Dep't 1991), the court affirmed the judgment although the plaintiff's attorney had suggested a particular amount in his summation: "Plaintiff's counsel is permitted, in summation, to suggest to the jury an amount believed to be appropriate compensation for the injury, . . . " and "We find the jury's total award of damages, . . . , to have been adequately supported in the record." (p. 176).

Nevertheless, the disagreement between the Third and First Departments may be more apparent than real; that is, the First Department may have believed that its modification of the judgment was a sufficient remedy in the case before it for the attorney's use of a specific figure. As another department observed, "[T]he affirmance cannot be viewed as constituting approval of the trial court's ruling on the summation issue, because the issue was not preserved and was not addressed in the briefs on appeal."[20]

The most exhaustive analysis of this issue appears in *Braun v. Ahmed*,[21] in which the Appellate Division, Second Department, ruled that the plaintiff's attorney in an action for medical malpractice may request a specific amount for damages in her summation. The court made six arguments. First, the jurors must ascertain and award damages. Second, it is difficult to translate pain and suffering into dollars and cents. Third, the trial court's only guidance to the jury is an instruction to award the plaintiff reasonable compensation. Fourth, a party's trial attorney has a right to make fair comments on the evidence. Fifth, a party's trial attorney also has a right to place her client's contentions before the jury. Sixth, the legislative history of the 1976 statute prohibiting a claim for a specific amount of damages does not justify extending the prohibition to the summations because the legislature's only purpose was to reduce the publicity accorded exaggerated demands, not to prevent the jury from reacting to the ad damnum clause.[22]

---

20. Braun v. Ahmed, 127 A.D.2d 418, 515 N.Y.S.2d 473 (2d Dep't 1987).

21. *Id.*

22. The Association of the Bar of the City of New York did refer to the jury's reaction when recommending elimination of amounts in ad damnum clauses. However, it did so only because of its belief that the reading of the ad damnum to the jury by plaintiff's counsel in summation may appear to add some official sanction to the sum sued for. That danger is not present when counsel suggests a sum to the jury rather than reading the complaint.

A dissenting opinion accompanied the decision in *Braun*; the issue has not been settled,[23] and the trial attorney should be prepared to argue the matter.

9.4 A SAMPLE SUMMATION

We have reproduced below the summation for the plaintiff from the trial of an action for medical malpractice. However, we have changed the names of the parties and the witnesses.

9.4.1 The Causes of Action

The gist of the case was that the various defendants had failed to foresee, diagnose, or manage a prolapsed umbilical cord. The baby presented himself for birth in the transverse position, i.e., feet first, and the prolapsed position of the umbilical cord cut off the oxygen to the baby, which deficit caused asphyxia and brain damage. Because the baby was large and overdue, he must have been in the transverse position well before the delivery. Hence, the obstetrician should have discovered this position and delivered the baby by a scheduled cesarean section. On the day of the birth, the obstetrician should have reported to the hospital more promptly. Meanwhile, the personnel at the hospital should have used their skill and monitors to detect the fetal heart rate

---

23. In Restey v. Victory Mkts., 127 A.D.2d 987, 512 N.Y.S.2d 938 (4th Dep't 1987), the court held that the trial court had improperly charged the jury to disregard the plaintiff's counsel's estimate of damages for pain and suffering. The amount suggested by counsel can be used by the jury as a guideline. Unfortunately, in McDougald v. Garber, 73 N.Y.2d 246, note at 258, the court of appeals avoided the issue: "We note especially the argument raised by several defendants that plaintiff's attorney was precluded by C.P.L.R. 3017(c) from mentioning, in his summation, specific dollar amounts that could be awarded for nonpecuniary damages. We do not resolve this issue, which has divided the lower courts . . . , inasmuch as the matter was neither presented to nor addressed by the Appellate Division [First Department]."

immediately after the mother's arrival, and they should have discovered the prolapsed umbilical cord sooner than they did so that the baby would have been sooner delivered by an emergency cesarean section. That the emergency cesarean section was not performed in time to prevent the baby's injuries was proven by the fact that the amniotic fluid was discolored with meconium when the bag of waters ruptured. Meconium is the mass of waste that builds up in the baby's intestines during gestation, and a prolapsed cord also causes the baby to excrete meconium. We knew that the amniotic fluid was discolored because the mother testified that it was and because the defendants gave the baby antibiotics as a prophylaxis against infection. Even the incomplete hospital records confirmed the defendants' failure to detect a fetal heart beat, the diagnosis of a prolapsed cord, and the delay in delivering the baby.

9.4.2 Contrast with the Opening Statement

Since the summation is a speech, the attorney should conduct the same analysis he did when preparing his opening statement. The principal difference between these two speeches lies in their modes of discourse. The opening statement is a persuasive speech disguised as an expository one, so the mode of discourse is usually narration. By contrast, the summation is a frankly persuasive speech whose mode is argumentation. (It is, of course, conceivable that the attorney would organize the issues chronologically according to the order of events.)

9.4.3 Principles Illustrated by the Sample

The attorney must compose his summation in an orderly way. First, outline the case for yourself in a pyramid of justification[24] using only the evidence adduced at the trial and the arguments this evidence will support. Avoid wishful thinking and logical leaps. Remember that synthesis should succeed analysis and will make the mass of detail comprehensible to the jury. The jury will be impressed or baffled by the same ideas depending upon how you organize these ideas in relation to one another. The sample summation concluded a trial which entailed weeks of expert testimony.

Second, identify one ultimate issue if possible. Remember that the ultimate issue is not the ultimate conclusion but the specific issue whose resolution will anchor the chain of reasoning which will lead to the ultimate conclusion. Moreover, the ultimate issue should be a simple question of fact. Thus, in the sample summation, the ultimate issue reads, "Was the amniotic fluid stained with meconium when the bag of waters ruptured?" If the fluid was stained, then the plaintiff's claims were correct; if not, the defendants' claims were correct. In other words, if the fluid was stained with meconium, the jury would be led inexorably to conclude that the defendants' negligence caused the plaintiff's injuries by failing to foresee, diagnose, or manage the prolapsed umbilical cord which cut off the oxygen to the baby's brain. The same mechanism would have caused the baby to pass meconium. In its deliberations, the jury was able to make the factual determination that the amniotic fluid was stained by relying on such evidence as the mother's testimony and the defendants' administration of antibiotics to prevent the baby from contracting an infection from the meconium.

Third, consciously select a particular organization for your summation and use this organization explicitly. More than one pattern of organization is possible, but all the alternatives are not equally good. The attorney must make a con-

---

24. See section 1.2.1, The Pleadings.

scious choice among the satisfactory alternatives. The organization for the sample summation was:

I. Introduction
II. Missing Records (*Ethos*)
III. The Defendants' Claim of Polymicrogyria
IV. Transverse Position (First Question on Verdict Sheet)
V. Telephone Call to Obstetrician (Second Question)
VI. Failure to Diagnose and Manage the Prolapsed Cord (Third Question)
VII. Proximate Cause Confirmed
VIII. Damages
IX. Peroration

The obvious alternative would have been to address the first question from the verdict sheet immediately after the introduction. However, we had good reasons to defer the questions. Polymicrogyria was the defendants' alternative explanation for the baby's injuries, and the summation refuted this claim before addressing the first question because the defendants had introduced this explanation at the very end of their direct case. Therefore, the plaintiff needed to dispel this explanation before rebuilding his own case. The summation dealt with the missing and undisclosed records even before the polymicrogyria in order to shape the jury's attitude toward the substantive issues by undermining the defendants' *ethos*. The defendants had given the plaintiff this opportunity by failing to produce records, denying the accuracy of the records they did produce, and withholding the records from their own expert witnesses.

Fourth, use good speech practices. In addition to an explicit outline, these practices include adhering to the outline, using introductions, transitions, conclusions, and internal summaries, repeating key statements, practicing correct pronunciation and articulation, making eye contact with the jurors, making appropriate gestures, speaking at a reasonable rate, and employing a variety in pitch, rate, volume, and pauses to match the meaning of your words. The attorney should keep an outline of one or two pages available on the podium so he may consult it with a glance. Example 9-3 is a reconstruction of such an outline for the sample summation. This is an extreme example in that it is so long, and the outline is so long because delivering the summation consumed two hours. Make your outline as brief as your knowledge of the case will permit. You may find that using contrasting colors of ink for the different levels of organization will help you to find your place more quickly.

Fifth, use some of the limited time available to practice your summation. Preparing to give a speech necessarily implies practicing the speech aloud. There is an irreducibly tentative element in this practice since you must adapt to your opponent's arguments on the day of the summations, but the better practiced you are, the more easily you will adapt. Practice will both clarify your arguments in your own mind and improve your expression of your arguments so that they will be clearer to the jury. (Remember, from the point of view of the jury, there is no difference between a poor argument and an argument poorly expressed.) If possible, tape your practice and listen to the tape. You will discover that the thoughts in your head are not coming out of your mouth. Even your words will not enter the jurors' minds perfectly. Be especially alert for such faults as indefinite pronoun references:[25] in any context, "he" may mean any one of several witnesses to each juror. A juror's blank face or nodding head does not mean that he is following your argument.

Sixth, pursue each contentious issue to its resolution. Do not merely repeat your initial argument and expect the jurors to compare your argument with the opposition's to

25. For effective communication, a personal pronoun requires a noun as its clear antecedent; that is, when the speaker uses the pronoun, the listenter must know to whom the pronoun refers. Hence, if the antecedent is unclear or if the speaker has changed his reference without providing a new antecedent, the speaker will confuse or mislead the listeners. Needless to say, confusing the jurors is not an effective technique for persuading them, but using an indefinite pronoun reference is a very common error.

draw the correct conclusion. Your opponent may have a panoply of evasions and equivocations with which to mislead the jurors. You must be tenacious: do not allow a single fallacy or misrepresentation to escape. In the sample summation, such tenacity destroyed the defendants' arguments regarding the baby's presentation, polymicrogyria, and the general anesthesia. Identify for the jurors the precise disagreement between you and your opponent, then tell the jurors why you are right.

Seventh, devote most of your time during the summation to the issue of liability. In the sample summation, liability absorbed eighty percent of the time while the damages accounted for less than twenty percent, and this division is not unusual. If the defendant wins liability, he need not worry bout the damages, and if the plaintiff wins liability, he probably will receive reasonable damages. Moreover, the jurors have probably heard the expert on damages at length and at the end of the testimony, i.e., immediately before the summations. Therefore, the jurors will not need a repetition of the detail. In fact, a plaintiff's attorney who dwells on the damages risks forfeiting the emotional impact he generated with his discussion of liability. The sample summation does not even spend much time discussing the plaintiff's horrific injuries. By the end of the trial, the jurors understood those injuries and had seen the growing child with the mental age of three. The danger here is that the plaintiff's attorney will overact and alienate the jury.

Eighth, finally, the attorney must trust the jury. The reader may discover that he wants more information about the case than he finds in the sample summation. This is as it should be. The attorney must not compose his summation as if the jurors had not been present for the trial. Say what is relevant at the end of the proceeding: any attempt to review the entire trial will bore the jurors and lose their attention. The jurors, in turn, will lose the thread of the attorney's argument.

9.4.4 The Sample Summation

I. INTRODUCTION

A. THE GREETING

May it please the court, Mr. Justice Lewis, Mr. Adamski, Madam Forelady, and ladies and gentlemen of the jury. You have sacrificed your time beyond what you expected. Nobody could ask you to do more, and we thank you.

You have heard a case of great moment involving a small child, but the issues are far greater than any one person. The issues in this case are the perennial issues that have lived with mankind as long as we have been on this planet: truth and justice.

B. THE VERDICT SHEET

In order to do justice, you will complete a complicated verdict sheet. The first question on the verdict sheet has three parts, five questions have two parts, and two have one part. Fortunately, the verdict sheet is not as involved as it sounds. His honor will read it to you and will explain it in detail. When you retire to the jury room, the complexity of the verdict sheet will be the least of your troubles. The sheet is worded so that you will understand each question. After you have answered each question, you will find instructions for the next question.

By the way, you will determine the probabilities here. His honor will explain the law to you, then you will ask yourselves what's more probable than not. Where does the truth lie in the balance between what the plaintiff says and what the defendant says.

In this case, however, the scales of justice are not tipping slightly one way or another. The probability is overwhelming that this woman, Norma Entemann, has been telling the truth. She told the truth in 1986, she told it in her deposition, and she told it from the witness stand. The ultimate issue in this case is whether there was meconium in the amniotic fluid when the bag of waters ruptured, and Norma Entemann has told you there was.

C. OUTLINE

However, a summation in a medical malpractice case is necessarily long and detailed. I must ask you to concentrate as I address the defendants' suppression of the record, their last-minute claim of polymicrogyria, their negligence in failing to diagnose Andrew's footling breach, in failing to respond quickly to the telephone call from the hospital, and in failing to diagnose and manage Norma Entemann's prolapsed umbilical cord. I will address Andrew's injuries and, finally, the compensation he deserves.

D. TRANSITION IN MOOD

Ladies and gentlemen, as I begin this closing statement on behalf of a terribly damaged child, I ask you to consider that even though no one deliberately injured this child, something has happened which brings to mind what Edmund Burke, an Irish statesman in the British parliament, said two hundred years ago. "Something has happened upon which it is difficult to speak and impossible to be silent."

Ladies and gentlemen, something has happened in this case upon which it is difficult to speak but impossible to be silent. There has been an orchestrated effort by the defense, by the doctors and by the hospital, to deprive this child of justice. They have tried to obfuscate the truth and thereby to trample justice.

COMMENT

The introduction must both outline the summation for the jurors and begin to engage the jurors' emotions. Note that the introduction explicitly introduced the ultimate issue.

II. THE DEFENDANTS SUPPRESSED THE RECORD (*ETHOS*)

The defendants' desperation to suppress the truth is demonstrated by their calling a witness who claimed that his own entries were inaccurate, by their calling the plaintiff's mother a liar although the defendants themselves and their consultants recorded her version of the baby's medical history, by their failing to produce the original record, and by their withholding of the records even from their own expert witnesses.

A. THE DEFENDANTS' WITNESS CLAIMED THAT HIS OWN ENTRIES WERE INACCURATE

A defendant must be desperate to call a witness who denies the accuracy of his own professional records, but from this witness stand, you heard one witness, Dr. Orwin Prentiss, tell you that when he wrote "status post-asphyxia," it wasn't true. Asphyxia never occurred. "I was misled by the information I got from those that observed it. I found out that day, that fateful day that this baby entered the world, that it was false. I never put an addendum here. I never put a question mark here. I never added that I was mistaken, but it's false, and I knew it the day this baby was born."

When this baby was discharged from the hospital six days later, the final diagnosis was left blank. The form does contain the code 768.9, which means asphyxia of the newborn, and the signature was by this same Dr. Prentiss. But he says now that the code was wrong. When I cross-examined him, you heard the doctor say that a clerk picks these code numbers from a book. But how does the clerk pick the code number? By throwing a dart to find a diagnosis at random? Is that the way the defendants were practicing medicine at Maronite Hospital in 1986: putting a random diagnosis in a baby's chart? And those code numbers were on the form when the doctor signed it. "Yeah, but I never checked to see what they were."

The defendants also buried the discharge summary so we must ask: where did the clerk, who knows nothing about newborns, get the exact final diagnosis for this baby: large for gestational age, aspiration pneumonia, or aspiration meconium and asphyxia? Where but from the record? Where could she possibly have gotten the diagnosis but from the record? Nevertheless, the defendant said that the code was wrong. He said, "Oh, these things happen," but he gave you not a word of explanation of how these things happen. It is preposterous that a hospital would list a supposedly false diagnosis about a tiny baby and that the explanation would be, "Oh, a clerk was just meandering along and didn't know what she was doing." I said to the defendant, "You certainly would never sign something you hadn't read." You see, he had read the numbers, but he didn't know what they meant. "No, I'd never sign anything that wasn't true. Yes. I'd never sign anything that wasn't true. And I'd never sign anything I hadn't read." Yet his signature was unmistakable, and the diagnosis was "aspiration pneumonia, asphyxia due to prolapse of cord." But the defendant still maintains that, on April 12, 1986, this diagnosis was false. The witness apparently didn't know what he was signing two months later either. He had forgotten this baby and just signed anything.

Ladies and gentlemen, remember the words, "aspiration pneumonia, aspiration syndrome, and meconium aspiration." You heard me challenge Dr. Prentiss's testimony with the basic textbooks which he recognized as authoritative: Behrman and Avery. Please also remember that international classification of diseases. Do you really believe that amniotic fluid in the lungs is perfectly normal? Does the international classification of diseases assign a code number to something perfectly normal? Where did the hospital's clerk get that diagnosis?

"Aspiration pneumonia, asphyxia due to prolapse of cord." If you summarized this case in eight paragraphs, ladies and gentlemen, you couldn't do it better than those eight words. But it's all false, the defendants say. Isn't this unbelievable? Dr. Mennon is making it up; Dr. Norbert is making it up; and when the diagnosis came out of the defendants' own mouths, the defendants claim that it was false. The defendants summarized the case in essential agreement with the plaintiff, but then they said, "We got carried away. We were mistaken. We didn't know what we were saying." You'll never hear anything like this again.

COMMENT

As well as undermining the defendants' ethos, these arguments establish that the hospital's own records confirm the plaintiff's claim that he was asphyxiated. Note also that we had impeached a witness using learned treatises.

B. THE DEFENDANTS ACCEPTED THE MOTHER'S VERSION OF THE PLAINTIFF'S MEDICAL HISTORY

The defendants confirmed the accuracy of that discharge code, asphyxia of the newborn, when the hospital readmitted the baby. In fact, this baby wasn't out of the hospital for two weeks when he re-entered the hospital for the treatment of a hernia. The defendants then wrote the original diagnosis in the history portion of their own records. Do you remember that the defense attorney asserted in his opening statement, "You will find nowhere in these records meconium aspiration. I defy you." Then I put Dr. Trager on the witness stand, and I asked him, "Did you hear that opening statement? Well, let me show you this record. Aspiration meconium." Yes, aspiration meconium. [Turns to an enlarged copy of this record.] Now, ladies and gentlemen, the previous page of this record shows that this baby is in the hospital on the twenty-sixth for a hernia. This page is the baby's medical history as given by the mother, who said, "aspiration meconium." Where did she get that other than from the medical personnel assisting the delivery?

Now the defendants are accusing the mother of heinous lies. There is no avoiding this issue: the defense has thrown down the gauntlet and accused the baby's mother of having lied about the discolored fluid. "But she has a lawsuit," they say. Of course, she has a lawsuit now, but when she brought her two-week-old baby to the hospital for a hernia operation, what motive did she have to tell anything but the truth in his medical history? Obviously, none. The baby had suffered from meconium aspiration.

The defendants also claim that they accepted the mother's version of the baby's medical history and entered it in their own records because they didn't have access to the baby's chart at that time. The hospital had discharged the baby only nine days earlier, and the defendants didn't have access to the baby's chart when he was re-admitted to the same hospital? They recorded his medical history solely on the mother's word without any verification? Preposterous!

COMMENT

The defendants' acceptance of the mother's version of the baby's medical history so soon after the events demonstrates that they knew that her version was accurate.

C. THE CONSULTANTS ACCEPTED THE PLAINTIFF'S MEDICAL HISTORY

Even the consultants to whom the defendants referred the plaintiff accepted his mother's version of his medical history and acted upon it. For example, look at what was typed into the record as Dr. Trapp was planning to do the CAT scan. This is the CAT scan at Maronite that Dr. Rosen put up on the shadow box. [A visual aid.] "The CAT scan will be done as an outpatient at Maronite and the other blood urine tests, outpatient as well. Follow-up will depend on the results of the tests and also review of the hospital chart to see the extent of asphyxia as pointed out in the discharge diagnosis." Thus, in June of 1986, Dr. Trapp knew that the discharge diagnosis for this baby had been asphyxia.

COMMENT

If the original diagnosis was erroneous, someone would have discovered that.

D. THE DEFENDANTS FAILED TO PRODUCE THE ORIGINAL AND COMPLETE RECORD

The defendants have failed in their duty to produce the plaintiff's original hospital records, and even the copy they did produce is incomplete.

Ladies and gentlemen, where is the note that Dr. Eng should have written at the hospital? The defendants told you that they didn't delay acting during the labor, but where is the note by Dr. Eng that would support this contention? It's not in the record. Vital information should have been recorded on the chart by Dr. Ramdi, but where is it? Not a word.

The missing records are so numerous that I can only list them now. In the copy of the records, there is no pathologist's report on the placenta, no discharge summary, and no third x-ray. There is no notation regarding the baby's prenatal presentation. There is no notation of the time the plaintiff's mother arrived at the hospital, no nurse's notes prior to the delivery, and no record of the fetal heart rate. From the nursery, there is no note explaining the use of the heart monitor or the incubator. We had to obtain the radiologist's report by another route when the defendants failed to produce it, and during their direct testimony the defendants remained silent about their administration of antibiotics.

COMMENTS

This pattern of failing to produce the records should convince the jurors that the defendants were conscious of their own negligence and should induce the jurors to draw conclusions adverse to the defendants on the existing evidence.

E. THE DEFENDANTS EVEN WITHHELD THE RECORDS FROM THEIR OWN WITNESSES

Perhaps the most surprising revelation is that the defendants didn't provide the records to their own expert witnesses. Dr. Bobel didn't read one word in the records. Not one. Then, of course, the parents took their child to Grace-McDole Hospital and Dr. Gollub, and, as great as Dr. Gollub is, he never received the records. Dr. Pekarik never received the records. Dr. Greene never received the records. Dr. O'Connell never received the records. In fact, none of the physicians who testified for the defendants on causation in this case ever received the records from the defendants.

After all this, ladies and gentlemen, Dr. Bobel came to court to testify that events during the birth may have contributed to the baby's injuries but that a genetic abnormality caused most of the injury. Yet the defendants hadn't let this witness see the records either. What kind of excuse is that the defendants didn't want to overtax the expert? What are they talking about? The hospital record is the basic document which anyone should study before testifying as to why the baby was injured, and this basic document demonstrates that there was an extreme emergency around the time of the birth. Why do the defendants consider the fact that the baby was deprived of oxygen to be irrelevant?

Remember Dr. Bobel's testimony. "Doctor, do you think that the records would be helpful in the testimony you're giving to this jury?" "Oh, everything helps." That was his answer. "Exhibit A? The central kernel of the records in this case?" That's the next thing to saying "don't confuse me with the facts." How can a pediatric neurologist get on this witness stand, swear to tell the truth, and tell you why this baby was damaged, but never look at the central records in the case? How? But he did it.

COMMENT

The implication is that the defendants' witnesses would have changed their testimony if they had seen the complete records. In any case, their opinions were uninformed.

* * * * *

Ladies and gentlemen, the defendants' case can't stand scrutiny. The record is a copy, and the copy is incomplete. The defendants and the consultants recorded the mother's version of the baby's medical history shortly after his birth, but now the defendants call her a liar, and their own witness claims that his records are inaccurate. After discussing these attempts to suppress the truth, we must deal with the defendants' last minute defense: the claim that the plaintiff suffers from polymicrogyria.

III. THE DEFENDANTS' ASSERTION OF POLYMICROGYRIA WAS UNPERSUASIVE

The defendants' assertion that the plaintiff suffers from polymicrogyria is unpersuasive. The claim itself demonstrates the defendants' desperation. Moreover, the plaintiff has impeached the expert testimony supposedly supporting the claim, and the CAT scans reveal no evidence of polymicrogyria. Finally, the defendants failed to rebut the refutation of their assertion.

A. THE CLAIM DEMONSTRATES THE DEFENDANTS' DESPERATION

As I said, the defendants' claim of polymicrogyria demonstrates their desperation, and the claim is simply the last in a list of implausible explanations they have offered. For example, the defendants complain that the parents didn't take their baby for a Fragile X test. Their implication is that the parents are hiding something. On the contrary, the parents took the baby for all the relevant tests. Someone suggested that the child had Kannavan's syndrome, but tests ruled it out. Someone else suggested Soto's syndrome, but a bone age test ruled that out. Eventually, the parents realized what had happened to their baby. However, time and again during the trial, the defendants referred to Fragile X so I asked one of them, "Are you saying, Dr. Bobel, that this child had Fragile X?" "I don't know. He never went for the tests." Well, if someone had told you about polymicrogyria, you would know that the baby didn't have Fragile X. I asked, "Dr. Rosen, does Fragile X have anything to do with polymicrogyria?" "No, it doesn't."

I will start my review of these witnesses with the same Dr. Rosen. Isn't it suspicious that the first time you heard the word "polymicrogyria" was from Dr. Rosen, the next-to-the-last witness to take the stand?

Let's examine the defendants' claim that the baby suffers from polymicrogyria. The plaintiff's expert, Dr. Mennon, is a man whose knowledge of brain damage and the infants suffering from it is encyclopedic. On cross-examination, the defense wouldn't give him a chance to say that this child doesn't suffer from polymicrogyria, but you heard what the doctor said on direct examination: the child doesn't have polymicrogyria.

COMMENT

The list of prior explanations undermines the defendants' ethos, and the reference to the plaintiff's expert establishes the plaintiff's position.

B. THE PLAINTIFF IMPEACHED THE DEFENDANTS' EXPERTS.

You also heard my cross-examination of the defendants' witnesses so you know that their claim of polymicrogyria didn't survive cross-examination.

The defense called Dr. Lee Greene, formerly of Maronite Hospital, who came up from Florida for only fifteen hundred dollars. In Florida, he charges three hundred and fifty dollars an hour, but he supposedly came to New York for two days for only fifteen hundred. That figure is either a lie or a favor for the defense. It's probably the latter: he wants to help his old hospital. In any case, remember that I asked him, "You're not denying that the events at birth contributed to the result? It's right in the record." "No, I'm not denying it." His direct testimony had sounded like a denial, but no. He, as opposed to Dr. Prentiss, wasn't going to contradict the hospital record and what he had written.

Remember also their other witness, Dr. Rosen, who was the defendants' expert in pediatric neurology and who was testifying about a child with overwhelming neurological damage. I asked him, "Dr. Rosen, polymicrogyria; is that consistent with what you are saying?" He didn't give you a direct answer. Why? There are two reasons. The first was medical: he said the problem was genetic; then he said that it was probably genetic. I also asked him, "Is there any indication that polymicrogyria is genetic in origin?" "None."

The second reason was personal and far more telling. "Are you trying to help out the defense here, Dr. Rosen?" "What do you mean?" "Well, the fact that the law firm of Adamski and Resnor also represents your hospital. By the way, you're not just an attending physician." In fact, Dr. Rosen is not just an ordinary attending physician. He's part of the administration: he is the director of radiology and has been since the late eighties. This is a man in the administration at Murray Hill Hospital. I don't pretend to quote myself, but I asked him whether Adamski and Resnor's representing Murray Hill Hospital might have affected his objectivity. He replied, "I didn't know that." However, I had asked Dr. Rosen that same question in the Dunphy case tried up in the Bronx two years ago. In two years, could he really have forgotten that Adamski and Resnor represents Murray Hill Hospital?

Ladies and gentlemen, let's examine his testimony. Dr. Rosen consulted the MRI. If you will look at the MRI on the shadow box, you will see that the right side of these pictures is more blurred than the left, and the back of the head is more blurred still. He looked at this MRI and at the CAT scan done at Maronite but at nothing else. So I asked him, "Are you amazed that you're the only one to talk about polymicrogyria?" "Not amazed but surprised." Amazed? If he's correct, he should fall down in a catatonic trance. But at least he has to say he's surprised.

About thirty seconds of Dr. Trapp's testimony was valuable. I said to him, "There's a difference between changes in the brain that are developmental and atrophy, correct?" And he said, "Correct." On the one hand, tissue may fail to develop normally — that's a developmental problem — while on the other hand, tissue may atrophy, i.e., tissue which had already developed wastes away. Dr. Trapp agreed. However, he argued that there is no atrophy in this child's brain according to the medical history. In fact, atrophy would be inconsistent with this developmental anomaly visible from the eighth to the twelfth week of gestation as the gyri, or bumps, were forming in the brain. Don't forget, the defendants claim that there never was a time when the gyri were normal and then became abnormal. These gyri just developed with the polymicro ones as this baby was developing in the womb. It just happened! Nature did it. The condition might have nothing to do with the baby's gestational age, but it has something to do with the developmental process, that's for sure. [Sarcastic.]

Ladies and gentlemen, first of all, Dr. Trapp got the CAT scan and consulted the record, the one we just examined, and added, "left ventriculomegaly non-surgical" — meaning that there is no basis for surgical intervention — "consistent with post hypoxia or IVH," i.e., intraventricular hemorrhage. He came to this conclusion when he had seen only the discharge diagnosis; he did not even have the nursery record. However, this first image of the baby's brain is consistent with an insult around the time of birth. The plaintiff says that this insult was post-hypoxia, but the defendants say absolutely not.

Dr. Gollub did write in the record in 1986, "it is highly probable that the entire clinical picture is secondary to encephalopathy of prenatal origin with ideologic factor of neonatal cerebral hypoxia," and he went on to say that macrocephaly is genetic; yes, part of the family. Big heads are normal in the baby's family. However, what did Dr. Gollub mean by prenatal? Ordinarily, it means before birth and, usually, significantly before birth. But isn't it peculiar that the doctor referred to a *prenatal* ideological factor of *neonatal* cerebral hypoxia? Neonatal means "after birth," so that phrase is a contradiction in terms. What did he mean by prenatal? He knew that there was a prolapsed cord in this case, and as a pediatric neurologist, he would also have known that a prolapsed cord doesn't begin to cause problems when the baby is a neonate, i.e., after he is born. That's impossible! Of course, he never examined the hospital records.

COMMENT

Since jurors are impressed by expert witnesses, especially physicians, the attorney must point out the precise weakness in the testimony of each such witness.

C. THE CAT SCANS DO NOT SHOW EVIDENCE OF POLYMICROGYRIA

Ladies and gentlemen, if you are undecided after hearing the expert witnesses, then you yourselves may consult the CAT scans. These CAT scans should have revealed any polymicrogyria, but they didn't.

Now we go to Grace-McDole Hospital. Although there were MRI's and CAT scans, there was only one contrast study. Remember, the defendants admitted this. Let's look at the beginning of the report. "There is diffuse moderate cerebral atrophy, with proportionate ventricular dilatation. There is no evidence of hydrocephalus. There is a focal component to atrophy in the left frontoparietal area with the degree of porencephalia. This accounts for the noted ventricular assymetry." Remember, despite Dr. Trapp's merely saying "left ventricularomegaly," the report talks about ventricular dilitation, but the left side is much worse than the right. There is bilateral dilitation of the left ventricles. However, no cystic structures are present, and there are no abnormal areas of increased or decreased density, contrast enhancement, or mass effect.

What in the world does all this have to do with polymicrogyria? Back here. [Points to the visual aid.] The frontal parietal area is the focal lesion, and then the atrophy is in the brain. As the brain shrinks, of course, the fluid in the brain increases. The ventricles become enlarged because they occupy the space that was formerly occupied by the normal tissue before it was injured. This phenomenon is incompatible with polymicrogyria.

The defendants' last-ditch evasion was, "Well, the MRI shows the gyri; the CAT scan doesn't." We can't concede that. The defendants used a fourth- or fifth-generation machine for the CAT scan, but it couldn't display the gyri and the cortex of the brain? Or are the defendants claiming that a CAT scan shows atrophy when it isn't there? Do they say that? Atrophy is inconsistent with their claim that the baby had polymicrogyria, a developmental defect, at seven to twelve weeks of gestation.

Dr. Pekarik sent the baby for an MRI in 1989. Dr. Gollub said that the one in 1988 showed the same thing. I will put the report up on the screen. [Uses visual aid.] These are Dr. Gollub's comments on the CAT scan. He writes about the widening, which indicates the atrophy, and he concludes, "static encephalopathy secondary to cerebral hypotonia." This is in 1988 after the third CAT scan. Now we have Dr. Pekarik's comments after he got the report and the MRI from the neurological institute. "Andrew recently had an MRI scan of the brain in axial and sagittal planes. The MRI to my reading shows no change when compared to the CT scan of 1988." That's the one that Dr. Gollub commented on and that I just showed you. Ladies and gentlemen, you can look behind this report, you can look on top of it, you can look underneath it, but it doesn't contain a hint of any problem with this baby's gyri.

But, ladies and gentlemen, developmentally defective gyri are exactly what the defendants finally told you damaged this baby: polymicrogyria. Do you think that we had a right to rely on all these CAT scans and MRI's that were performed? And then the defendants told us that they will bring in a neuro-radiologist, but they didn't give us an inkling of his opinion until he gave it: polymicrogyria. In fact, these CAT scans constitute negative but definitive evidence that the plaintiff does not have polymicrogyria.

COMMENT

We have given the jurors a concrete way to choose among the experts, i.e., the lack of evidence in the CAT scans.

D. THE DEFENDANTS FAILED TO REBUT THE REFUTATION OF THEIR CLAIM.

Finally, despite having saved the assertion of polymicrogyria for the end of their direct case, the defendants have failed to rebut our refutation of their claim. Specifically, they failed to produce the radiologist's report; they called the plaintiff's treating physician, but his testimony failed to support their claim, and the defendants were reduced to feeble attacks against the plaintiff's expert.

You have the CAT scan. We subpoenaed the records from Grace-McDole, but the defendants didn't produce the radiologist's report of the MRI. However, you can see it now: the report is here and in evidence. Fortunately, we knew that there is a radiological institute at the hospital so you will see Dr. Gollub's records. He's in the neurological division of Grace-McDole. It's called a neurological institute, as you will see it imprinted on the MRI, and you will see it listed under Dr. Gollub's name on his reports. Why didn't the defendants want you to see that report?

Now do you want the *coup de grace*? You're going to get it. Consider Dr. Hamilton Grant, the pediatric neurologist who has been treating the child, but who testified for the defendants. He didn't think that the polite and decent thing would be to say, "By the way, I'm testifying against your child even though I'm the treating physician. You're not going to dissuade me, but I'm giving you the courtesy of telling you." I asked him, "Never even occurred to you, doctor, right?" "Never even occurred to me." "Everybody is helped by the truth" was his coy remark.

But here he is in his own words, and you're not going to believe this one. In his report in 1991, he wrote, "An MRI scan of the brain was reviewed. This showed the same left ventricular enlargement without any other abnormalities beyond the extra axial space and sidening" — in other words, as a result of atrophy. To his reading, these gyri are perfect.

Finally, ladies and gentlemen, when the defendants are reduced to calling somebody a liar and a hired gun because he has testified many times, when the defendants don't attempt to show how the witness is wrong on the merits, the defendants are demonstrating that their defense is non-existent. In fact, Dr. Mennon's testimony went uncontradicted, and the defendants' attempt to impeach him was unsuccessful. Dr. Mennon was a pioneer: in 1956, he was the first physician to open a practice in pediatric neurology in the tri-state area. The special certification for this field began only twelve years later in 1968. Unfortunately, you know what a bureaucracy is; consequently, Dr. Mennon didn't take time off from his unbelievably busy practice to do three years of adult neurology. Consequently, the defendants would like you to believe that he isn't qualified to testify. Is that why for years the firm of Dell and Lownes has asked him for his expert opinions?

Ladies and gentlemen, the defendants' assertion that the plaintiff suffers from polymicrogyria was desperate. The weight of their own experts' testimony didn't support it on cross-examination. Meanwhile, the plaintiff's expert and the CAT scans contradict it.

IV. THE DEFENDANT, DR. TRAGER, NEGLIGENTLY FAILED TO DIAGNOSE THE PLAINTIFF'S FOOTLING BREACH

Ladies and gentlemen, both his honor and Mr. Adamski have mentioned the questions which the court will submit to you. The first question is, was the baby in a footling breech presentation on the third? Yes or no. If yes, the failure to recognize it was a departure from good medical practice, and that departure was a substantial factor in the injury to this child.

The plaintiff contends that the defendant, Dr. Trager, did negligently fail to recognize the footling breach based on four subcontentions: the baby could not have changed his position; the baby's size and presentation dictated a scheduled cesarian section; Dr. Trager even failed to send the prenatal sheet to the hospital; and these failures were a negligent cause of the plaintiff's injuries.

A. THE BABY COULD NOT HAVE CHANGED HIS PRESENTATION

Let us start with the baby's presentation: he could not have changed it late in the pregnancy.

Do you remember the testimony of Dr. Trager? He said, "Oh, these babies turn. Oh yeah, they can turn three or four times between the thirty-ninth and the fortieth week. Fortieth and forty-first week." Well, Dr. Norbert and Dr. Manson testified that, on the contrary, it's rare. Then Dr. Rizzo was forced to admit that it's rare, but he still claimed that it could happen. How did he arrive at this opinion? "Oh, like they are in a little tumbler in there." In the thirty-ninth week for a baby who is only a centimeter short of two feet long?

Lets turn to Dr. Mennon. Remember our contention that the baby's head was too big for him to be turning? Remember also that Dr. Bobel rejected that contention but said, "I'm not necessarily meaning anything." I asked him, "What do you mean you're not meaning anything? Do you agree with Dr. Gollub when he said that it's just a normal variant even though it's very large because his parents and everybody in the family have large heads? You don't agree with that?" "No, I don't agree with it."

Dr. Bobel was wrong. Fortunately, the baby's gestational age is undeniable, and nobody can reconcile that age with the defendants' theory that the baby had changed his position. The size of the baby's head also is undeniable, and nobody could reconcile this with the defendants' theory either. Therefore, the defendants claimed that the mother was too old to be pregnant, but no medical expert provided a reasonable medical explanation for the connection with the baby's injury.

Ladies and gentlemen, Dr. Mennon testified that the baby was fifty-eight centimeters long and had a head thirty-nine and a half centimeters in circumference. This baby had a big head; in fact, the doctor'd never seen a head that big. And the baby weighed close to ten pounds. Could he turn around like a tumbler in there with his full length extended? This two foot baby? It's impossible! The extreme rarity is just the beginning. As Dr. Norbert said, it's extremely rare for a baby to turn after the thirty-seventh week. When you add the size of this baby and advance to the fortieth week, it's impossible. It couldn't have happened. Thus, we must ask, why did the defendant miss the baby's position? Or did he miss it? We will never know.

COMMENT

The defendant was charged with discovering the facts during his examination, and, in this case, the facts could not have changed.

B. THE BABY'S SIZE AND PRESENTATION DICTATED A SCHEDULED CESARIAN SECTION

In any case, the baby's position and size dictated that he should have been delivered by elective cesarean section. The defendants admit that they would have done so right away if they had foreseen the baby's presentation a week before the baby suffered asphyxia. A week! At the very latest, they would have done it twelve hours earlier on the morning of the tenth, which was the delivery date. Many hours before the baby suffered asphyxia. The defendants claimed that the mother's obesity obscured the baby's presentation so I asked, "Isn't it true that when a woman is obese in the medical sense it is more difficult to determine the presentation?" "Yes." "And if there's any doubt, you follow the Leopold maneuvers by vaginal exam, and if there is still any doubt, you perform the definitive test, which is a sonogram?" "Yes."

COMMENT

The defendant failed to take the obvious precautions.

C. THE DEFENDANTS FAILED EVEN TO SEND THE PRENATAL SHEET TO THE HOSPITAL

Unfortunately, Dr. Trager and his partner exacerbated his negligence in failing to discover the transverse presentation. Ladies and gentlemen, the defendants should have sent the prenatal sheet to the hospital during the thirty-sixth or thirty-seventh week so that the hospital's personnel would have had available the basic information about the prenatal course. The mother wouldn't be in a position to provide or even to know all that information. The defendants said, "Oh, we didn't start doing that until 1988." Ladies and gentlemen, physicians practicing obstetrics know that babies don't keep a schedule and can come at any time. The mother may have to rush to the hospital, and even the most conscientious attending physician might not arrive for a significant period of time. Was this predicament a revelation in 1988? Was 1988 really the year that obstetricians started sending the prenatal record to the hospital as a precaution in case the attending physician was absent? Is this plausible? No!

By failing to send that prenatal sheet to the hospital, the defendants increased the risk to the plaintiff during the emergency which subsequently arose.

COMMENT

Failing to send the prenatal sheet to the hospital was negligent in itself, but it also exacerbated the other negligence.

D. THE DEFENDANTS' FAILURE TO DETECT THE TRANSVERSE PRESENTATION AND TO SCHEDULE A CESARIAN DELIVERY WAS NEGLIGENCE CAUSING THE PLAINTIFF'S INJURIES.

Unfortunately, Dr. Trager's negligence in failing to discover the transverse position and to schedule a cesarian section was a cause of Andrew's injuries. Ladies and gentlemen, the terrible truth is that this baby was never in a cephalic presentation. The sonogram showed this baby in the transverse presentation. Because of his size, this baby couldn't have turned himself to the cephalic position, and everyone agrees that he made a footling breach on the day of his birth. That's why the surgeon had to deliver him by an emergency cesarean section. The defendants' failure to be aware of the baby's presentation and to plan for it was a basic departure from accepted medical practice, and this departure had catastrophic results.

Outrageously, not only have the defendants failed to produce the original medical record, the copy they have produced contains not one word about the baby's presentation. And where is the original medical record? The defendants haven't given you one iota of explanation for failing to produce it. Does Dr. Legge have it? He bought the practice from Dr. Smith and Dr. Clifford. This fellow is also an attending physician at Maronite. "Did you ever make an effort to get the original record?" I asked him. "No, we never made an effort."

COMMENT

The results are obvious, but the attorney should draw the conclusion for the jury explicitly.

* * * * *

As a result of that departure, this baby was asphyxiated. He could have been born a week earlier in a scheduled cesarean section, spent three days in the nursery, and been sent home to grow up like his brother. You don't think this case is horrendous? Nobody says that medicine is easy, and nobody says that physicians don't practice a great profession. But practitioners of medicine have a tremendous obligation to act responsibly, for failing to perform the correct test or to find what should be found can be disastrous. If a lawyer is incompetent, the client may lose his case. The results may be grave but not disastrous. If a financier miscalculates, people may lose money. Once again, the consequences may be grave but not disastrous. We may say the same thing about a carpenter or a builder. About everyone but the physician, for the physician deals with life, and you can see in this case the repercussions of negligence.

COMMENT

This paragraph counteracts the ethos which doctors naturally possess in the minds of jurors.

V. THE DEFENDANT, DR. TRAGER, DEPARTED FROM GOOD MEDICAL PRACTICE IN FAILING TO RESPOND QUICKLY TO THE TELEPHONE CALL

The essence of the second question is: did Dr. Trager practice good medicine on the information he received during the telephone conversation on the tenth? That's the import of the question, and we must approach the answer directly.

Ladies and gentlemen, the pivotal factual issue in this case is: was there meconium in the amniotic fluid when the bag of waters ruptured? The answer determines whether this baby suffered meconium aspiration, which the defendants deny. The answer also establishes which information Dr. Trager received over the telephone from the hospital and, therefore, whether he responded with sufficient alacrity. The plaintiff contends that there was meconium in the amniotic fluid and that Dr. Trager must have learned this during that telephonic conversation.

A. MECONIUM WAS PRESENT IN THE AMNIOTIC FLUID WHEN THE BAG OF WATERS RUPTURED.

To establish that meconium was present in the bag of wagers when it ruptured, the plaintiff relies on the testimony of his mother, the implausibility of the defendants' alternative explanations, and the remedial measures taken by the hospital.

I. THE MOTHER'S TESTIMONY

First, the mother's testimony established that there was meconium in the amniotic fluid when the bag of waters ruptured.

This mother loves her baby as any mother would, and I think that any mother would love a damaged baby more. That's the essence of motherhood. She's in court to obtain justice for her child, but she's also told you the truth. Ask yourself if she lied under oath during the examination before trial. Ask yourself if she lied during this trial when she told you that brown fluid came from her vagina when the bag of water ruptured on February 10, 1986. When she brought her baby back to Maronite Hospital only two weeks after his birth, she provided the medical history that appears in that record. "Andrew was the ten-pound-and-three-and-a-half-ounce product of a full-term gestation born via emergency cesarean section for prolapsed cord, breech position, and meconium." If you believe that this mother lied to the physicians from whom she was desperately seeking help for her baby, then send her child from this court without a penny.

The baby's mother described the fluid as dark, murky brown. Dr. Norbert testified that meconium is usually green or black. Therefore, he implied that the murky brown fluid couldn't have been meconium. But during my cross-examination of Dr. Trager, I asked him, "Doctor, it can be brown, it can be yellow, it can be green, or it can be a combination of all three. True?" He said, "True." So the mother's testimony that the fluid was brown is plausible. In fact, do you remember, ladies and gentlemen, that on cross-examination the defense asked her not one question on this central issue, not one? Now, if you are going to claim that someone has perjured herself, then you should have the courage to cross-examine her. Otherwise, be silent!

And if you believe that it's just a coincidence that when the surgeons opened her abdomen and uterus they found meconium both times, then you've lost the meaning of the word, coincidence. Ladies and gentlemen, if you believe that one instance of meconium has nothing to do with the other, you believe the impossible.

COMMENT

The mother may be an interested party, but her testimony is credible.

2. THE DEFENDANTS' ALTERNATIVE EXPLANATIONS

Second, the defendants' alternative explanations for the presence of the meconium are implausible. Those explanations were a breech birth and the use of a general anesthesia.

a. Breech Delivery

Listen to what the defendants said about the meconium, i.e., their original version. The defendants claimed that there was no meconium when the bag of water ruptured. No meconium. During the delivery, one of the defendants put his hand into the vagina and diagnosed a prolapsed cord. Eventually, he held the cord off the presenting part. The defendants claim that there was still no meconium. So just as the defendants were finally alleviating the hypoxia and asphyxia in this baby by relieving the constriction on the cord, the baby supposedly passed meconium for the first time. Why? Why, when the baby is getting relief for the first time in hours, does he do what babies do when they're compromised? The defendants' porous explanation is that a baby passes meconium during a breech birth, and this doesn't imply distress. The problem with this explanation is that there was no breech birth. Instead, surgeons delivered the baby by cesarean section. Dr. Mori testified in his examination before trial, as Dr. Norbert has already said, that a breech birth squeezes the meconium from the baby's intestines, but there was no breech birth. The defendants' explanation for the meconium is preposterous. So there you are, ladies and gentlemen, faced with this unbelievable coincidence but with no explanation of why this baby, when finally getting relief from lack of oxygen, decides then to pass meconium. It's impossible.

b. General Anesthesia

The defendants' other alternative explanation was that the surgeons gave the baby a general anesthesia.

Do you believe the defendants' undocumented claim that the general anesthesia depressed the baby's central nervous system although the hospital records say that the baby suffered from asphyxia? Listen to the irony! The surgeons performed the cesarean so quickly because of the prolapsed cord. They didn't give the baby a regional anesthetic because it takes too much time. You heard the expert testimony that in 1986 the preferred mode of anesthesia for a cesarean section was epidural, but the surgeons dispensed with that because it would have been too time-consuming. Therefore, the defendants claim, the general anesthesia and not the prolapsed cord depressed the baby's central nervous system. Unfortunately for the defendants, the last witness, Dr. Rizzo, exposed that defense as a sham. I asked him, "Doctor Rizzo, isn't it true that a properly administered anesthesia (when the subsequent delivery of the baby is timely) does not depress the baby's nervous system?" Do you remember that question? You probably do because I sat down when he said, "Yes." That was the end of that defense, and you never heard of it again.

COMMENT

The defendants' offer of alternative explanations for the presence of the meconium merely strengthened the plaintiff's position because the explanations were implausible.

3. THE REMEDIAL MEASURES

Third, the medical staff at the hospital took remedial measures in the emergency that indicate a prolapsed umbilical cord and the presence of meconium. These measures were an emergency cesarian section and the administration of antibiotics.

a. The Emergency Cesarian Section

Ladies and gentlemen, you were told to decide this case with your intellects, but you should decide this case as total human beings. Your intuition helps. For example, what do you think of the defendants' claim that the baby was doing famously when you know that the medical personnel so rushed the emergency cesarean section that they endangered the mother's life by not waiting to scrub-up and to sterilize the instruments? How does that hit you? The medical staff rushed the cesarian because the prolapsed cord had asphyxiated the baby and, incidentally, had caused him to pass meconium.

b. The Antibiotics

The other remedial measure was the administration of antibiotics to a newborn baby. We will return to this matter when we discuss the hospital's liability, but now it is sufficient to point out that the medical personnel administered the antibiotics to protect the baby from an infection, and he would have contracted that infection from meconium he swallowed in the amniotic fluid before the bag of waters ruptured. Thus, the meconium was already present.

COMMENT

The remedial measures taken by the defendant hospital proved the negligence of the other defendant, the attending physician.

B. DR. TRAGER KNEW FROM THE TELEPHONE CALL HE RECEIVED THAT THERE WAS MECONIUM IN THE AMNIOTIC FLUID

This conclusion brings us to our second conclusion: Dr. Trager must have learned that there was meconium in the amniotic fluid and, therefore, that the baby was suffering from asphyxia.

The argument follows as night the day. If meconium was present in the fluid, does anyone believe for a second that the staff would not have given that information to Dr. Trager when the staff called him back to the hospital? Even if he didn't ask for it, even though he said it's his practice to ask which color the fluid was, can we believe that the other defendants didn't tell him? That would be even more preposterous than the story that the fluid was clear when the bag of waters broke.

The second question is open and shut. Dr. Trager himself said, "I would have told her to go to the hospital right away, and I would have come right away myself." Dr. Norbert added that the attending physician should alert the hospital in case the patient arrives before he does. The defendants did none of that. None of it.

Dr. Norbert said in response to a question that you must change your opinion if your assumptions change; that is, the opinion is wrong if the assumption is wrong. Given a different assumption, you form a different opinion. If there was meconium in the fluid, then certain conclusions are absolutely correct and never change. If you assume that there was no meconium in the fluid, then you reach a different set of conclusions. We saw this with their expert, Dr. Manson.

As I said to him, and as he reluctantly agreed, this case is unusual in that there are so many issues that are not medical ones. The ultimate issues are all factual; they discuss events: meconium or no meconium, what the mother saw when the bags of waters ruptured, the time the doctor took to get to the hospital, the time the mother arrived in the hospital. Moreover, you can decide these issues with little knowledge of medicine, but the answers will tell you whether the defendants practiced good medicine. Ladies and gentlemen, no expert is in a better position than you are to decide whether the assumptions supporting the experts' opinions are correct. These assumptions are factual and are either true or false. For example, was the failure of Dr. Trager to deliver the baby earlier a substantial factor in the injury to this baby? By the doctor's own admission, he would have delivered this baby forty-five minutes earlier if he had done what a doctor should do when learning that the fluid was discolored. So you must decide who is telling the truth. Either way, the consequences are inescapable. Everyone agrees with that. Dr. Norbert agrees, Dr. Manson agrees, and Dr. Trager agrees. There is no doubt that the baby should have been delivered earlier if the meconium was discolored.

When I examined Dr. Rizzo, I said, "Twenty minutes or so is not a long time for most of us in life." And, of course, he knew where I was going. I added, "But not in circumstances like these." And, of course, five minutes is an eternity. Forty-five minutes was a life.

Ladies and gentlemen, you know that there was meconium in the amniotic fluid when bag of waters ruptured. You know this from the mother's testimony, from the implausibility of the defendants' alternative explanations, and from the remedial measures taken at the hospital. Therefore, you also know that Dr. Trager was aware of the meconium. You know this from your own common sense and from his self-alleged practice. Therefore, his delay was a negligent cause of the plaintiff's injuries.

VI. MARONITE HOSPITAL FAILED TO DIAGNOSE AND MANAGE MRS. ENTEMANN'S PROLAPSED UMBILICAL CORD

Ladies and gentlemen, Maronite Hospital was also responsible for the plaintiff's injuries. The hospital's personnel delayed delivering Andrew although they could not detect his fetal heart sounds, and they exacerbated his problems by forcing more meconium into his lungs with positive-pressure oxygen. The hospital confirmed these conclusions by suppressing the record.

A. THE HOSPITAL'S PERSONNEL DELAYED DELIVERING THE BABY ALTHOUGH THEY COULD NOT DISCOVER FETAL HEART SOUNDS

Let us begin with the delay by the hospital's personnel in delivering the baby although they could not detect his fetal heart sounds.

Of course, the time available to the hospital was shorter than it would have been for a scheduled cesarian, but the time was long enough. Seven or eight minutes, the defendants said. The time was twenty-five or twenty minutes to one by the time the defendants had diagnosed the prolapsed cord. They had the mother in the operating room five to seven minutes later, and they delivered the baby in another seven minutes. Record time. But is this our criticism of the hospital? No! The important delay, the negligence, began at two minutes after twelve: the time the mother reported to the hospital as these parents testified and as the hospital record confirms. The defendants claim that the mother didn't arrive in the hospital until 12:15, but the defendants sent her to the lab for a urinalysis, and the lab record shows that she had already given urine by 12:14. In other words, she had arrived at the hospital, saw a member of the staff, was sent to the lab, arrived there, gave urine in her awkward condition, and submitted her sample by one minute before the time that the defendants claim she arrived in the hospital.

Everyone agrees that the mother should have been examined for fetal heart sounds immediately after her arrival at the hospital. Now, whatever you believe about no one apparently detecting the fetal heart sounds, I don't think anyone in this room was reassured by the assertion, "Oh, sometimes you can't find a fetal heart beat, the baby is turning, whatever." Can this be true with an internal fetal heart monitor? I don't mean with a fetoscope. This machine was a monitor which picks up sounds in a much broader area. The defendants used the monitor but couldn't pick up the fetal heart beat; at 12:12, 12:14, 12:15, 12:16, 12:17, 12:18,12:20, there was no fetal heart beat. The defendants needed to find out why, and they needed to find out why immediately. Was the absence of sounds innocuous or very serious? The real reason, of course, was the prolapsed cord. Do you have any doubt? Whatever you believe about the defendants' not finding fetal heart sounds, is there any doubt that it would be an astonishing coincidence if, at the same time that the cord was prolapsed (which can be disastrous for the baby), the nurse just happened not to find the fetal heart beat, but that one occurrence had nothing to do with the other? That defies credulity.

What were the medical personnel doing? This was the crucial time. As I said to Dr. Rizzo, twenty minutes, fifteen minutes are not such a long time ordinarily, but in this situation, they were — and not just twenty or fifteen minutes or ten or five, but even one minute. That twenty minutes was an unconscionable and unexplained delay, but Dr. Eng and Dr. Ramdi have not given you one word of explanation why. Not one word from them appears in the hospital record. Understand me, ladies and gentlemen, I am not asking the defendants for a reason years later when they are fielding easy questions. I am asking for a note in the hospital record on the day of the birth. This is not unreasonable. The nurse who was taking care of the patient, Nurse Atencio, may not have had time to write on the record immediately. However, the defendants now admit that there were at least twenty-five minutes, probably a half hour or even thirty-five minutes, before they diagnosed the prolapsed cord, and yet, the defendants are also claiming that Nurse Atencio didn't have time to write in the hospital record. Both statements can't be true. I admit that when there's an emergency, the care of the patient is paramount to making the record, but everyone admitted that medical personnel must document events after they occur. Moreover, if there was no emergency for those thirty-five minutes, why wasn't there documentation?

What was the fetal heart rate of this baby? The medical personnel took the mother's vital signs, but she wasn't the one in trouble. No one recorded the fetal heart rate from the time this woman got to the hospital to the time her baby was delivered. No one. Isn't it abundantly clear, as Dr. Norbert said, that a pulsating cord does not prevent you from determining the fetal heart rate because you can take the baby's pulse from the pulsating cord itself. That's what the pulsating is, the fetal heart rate. However, the hospital record contains no notation of the fetal heart rate. Was it 120 to 160 beats per minute, i.e., the normal rate? Or was it faint and weak and slow, i.e., the very reason that the cord pulsated? That's the reason the baby was born asphyxiated: the prolapsed cord. This failure to find and record the fetal heart rate is hard evidence of negligence.

COMMENT

The hospital's personnel departed from good and accepted medical practice by failing to appreciate the emergency.

B. THE HOSPITAL'S PERSONNEL EXACERBATED THE BABY'S INJURIES

Ladies and gentlemen, the evidence has borne out everything I said in my opening statement except for one thing. The one thing which I omitted, but which the evidence has shown, was that the defendants exacerbated the child's injuries by forcing positive-pressure oxygen on a baby who had aspirated meconium. Remember, I asked Nurse Callan, "If there is meconium-stained fluid before you give positive-pressure oxygen, you have to visualize the larynx with a laryngoscope, isn't that true?" And Nurse Callan said, "Yes." "Was that done in this case?" And she said, "No." I guess I was delinquent in omitting from my opening statement conduct that was clearly malpractice, for this child's fluid clearly was stained with meconium. There's no doubt about that. The defendants were forced to admit that because no one could erase the entry in the dictation made in the operating room. Dr. Burke, who assisted Dr. Mori during the cesarean section, made that entry.

COMMENT

If the attorney can establish that the negligence was even worse than he claimed, he should do so.

C. THE HOSPITAL HAS CONFIRMED ITS NEGLIGENCE BY SUPPRESSING THE RECORD

Moreover, the hospital has confirmed its negligence by suppressing the record. The pathology report is a basic component of the hospital record. A baby was in the neonatal intensive care unit for six days. When you send a baby there, you also send the placenta for pathological examination. So where is the pathology report? Where is the discharge summary for this baby after he'd been kept in the neonatal intensive care unit for six days? For that matter, where is the follow-up on the x-ray? The report on the first x-ray mentioned the fluid which was, of course, the amniotic fluid with the meconium in it, and recommended a follow-up x-ray. The report on the second x-ray also mentioned the fluid and suggested a follow-up x-ray. Where is that third x-ray? The first two x-rays were taken relatively early on the first day of the baby's life. The physicians took the advice of the radiologist the first time. Did they ignore it the second time? Where is the third x-ray? Why is there no record of the time the plaintiff's mother arrived at the hospital, no nurse's note prior to delivery, and no record of the fetal heart rate? Where are the doctors' notes? Where is the note from the nursery explaining the heart monitor and the incubator? Why did we have to subpoena the radiologist's report from the institute? You know the answer.

* * * * *

Did the defendants depart from good medical practice in diagnosing and managing the prolapsed cord? The answer has to be a resounding yes! They departed from good medical practice both in what they did and in what they failed to do: in not giving the mother oxygen immediately, in not starting an IV immediately, in not turning her to the knee/chest position immediately, in not keeping the hand in the vagina continually on the cord to keep it from being compressed. Ladies and gentlemen, this cord was the baby's lifeline, his *sine qua non* for life and health. That's why a prolapsed cord is an obstetrical emergency!

COMMENT

If the opposing party seems to have confessed his negligence by concealing his actions, help the jury to draw this conclusion.

VII. THE MEDICAL MALPRACTICE WAS THE PROXIMATE CAUSE OF THE BABY'S INJURIES

Ladies and gentlemen, I wish to address directly the issue of the proximate cause of Andrew's injuries. Of course, we addressed this issue when we discussed the negligence of the various defendants because we included the results of that negligence. However, I wish to explain the significance of three events subsequent to Andrew's birth: his Apgar score, the administration of antibiotics to him, and his stormy course in the nursery. These events demonstrate conclusively that the negligence of the various defendants caused his injuries.

A. THE ERRONEOUSLY HIGH APGAR SCORE CONFIRMS THE BABY'S INJURIES

Let us begin with the Apgar score. The hospital's medical personnel gave Andrew an erroneously high score which concealed his injuries.

1. THE BABY'S APGAR SCORE SHOULD HAVE BEEN THREE

First, that score of five was erroneous: it should have been only three. The prolapsed cord harmed the baby, and the proof of this was that the baby was born with two overwhelming signs. The first sign was that the baby's heart rate at birth was only eighty beats per minute. Thus, the baby deserved an Apgar score not of five but, at most, of four and probably three. Remember that I read to Dr. Prentiss from Schaeffer's *Diseases of the Newborn*: a score above four requires a heart rate above one hundred. The other sign was that the baby was limp. A limp baby has no tone. Therefore, that score of one for tone which Dr. Freund admitted he gave this baby was wrong: the score for tone should have been a zero. The combination of a slow heart rate and a limp body would have justified an honest Apgar score of three.

2. THE REASON FOR THE LOW SCORE WAS THE DELAY IN RESUSCITATION

Second, the question then arises: why was this baby born with an Apgar score of three? We know that the general anesthesia was not the reason. By the way, here was a telling admission. Remember that Dr. Manson said, "God's way is the best way." He meant, of course, that it is much better for the baby to breathe on his own just after birth rather than to be resuscitated with oxygen. No one can quarrel with that, but what's God's way prior to birth? God's way prior to birth is that the baby's blood be oxygenated by the mother through the umbilical cord. Unfortunately, what happened here? The medical personnel began resuscitation too late to save this baby from brain damage but not too late to save his life. They held the umbilical cord to end the compression, and God's way operated for seven or ten minutes before the baby was born.

COMMENT

This discussion explains the same process of cause and effect from a different angle.

B. THE DEFENDANTS' ADMINISTRATION OF ANTIBIOTICS TO THE BABY CONFIRMS HIS INJURIES

The next event was that the defendants administered antibiotics to Andrew shortly after his birth.

Thus, even more telling than the Apgar score, is the defendants' false claim that this baby aspirated sterile amniotic fluid. Consider, first, that the defendants thereby admitted that the baby did aspirate fluid. If that fluid did contain meconium, then he aspirated meconium too. Second, there must have been meconium in the fluid unless the defendants are correct that the baby passed the meconium after the bag of waters ruptured and when one of the doctors held the prolapsed cord. That claim, however, is implausible because it posits the strange event of a baby passing meconium when he's finally receiving resuscitation. Third, that the defendants quickly administered antibiotics to the baby demonstrates that they knew that he had aspirated meconium. Didn't it sound strange to you, after you heard Dr. Prentiss explain what happens in the aspiration of meconium, that one of the most important steps is to give the baby antibiotics to prevent pneumonia or pneumonitis? The doctor didn't use the word "prophylactically," but that was the import of his testimony.

The defendants knew that administering antibiotics would be an admission that the baby had aspirated meconium so they never said a word about the antibiotics in their direct testimony. The defendants left you to believe that, if they really were concerned about aspiration of meconium, they would have given the baby antibiotics, and there the supposition lay until my cross-examination. Then you learned that the defendants did give this baby ampicillin and continued it for four days while the baby was in the nursery. In fact, the defendants started the ampicillin in the early hours of the baby's life, and the nurses recorded the administration of these antibiotics in the nurse's notes. You can see those notes in the hospital record.

If these antibiotics weren't a response to the aspiration of meconium, what were they for? Giving antibiotics to a tiny baby is risky: you need a darn good reason. Do you remember the justification that the defendants gave you for giving antibiotics to this baby? You don't because they offered no justification. The answer is in their own records. The defendants gave this baby antibiotics to prevent aspiration pneumonia, and since sterile fluid in the baby's lungs can't cause aspiration pneumonia, then why did they administer antibiotics to combat infection?

Do you want one more indication of the truth? I'll give you the fourth one. You know that the record says that at 4 a.m. the defendants aspirated fluid from the lungs of this baby. What did they aspirate? They aspirated mucus, but they claim it was from the esophagus. You don't need a degree in medicine to know that mucus doesn't come from the esophagus or the stomach. Anyone who has had a cold with congestion in the lungs knows that. The defendants aspirated five c.c.'s of mucus, and you know which mucus they aspirated, brown mucus. There was some talk about meconium being green or black, but Dr. Troper himself testified that it can be brown, green, yellow, or a combination of all three. I will tell you this much: amniotic fluid is not brown.

The reasoning is this. If the defendants gave the baby antibiotics, then he aspirated meconium. If he aspirated meconium, then meconium was present in the amniotic fluid before the bag of waters ruptured. If the baby passed meconium before the rupture, he was asphyxiated by a prolapsed umbilical cord. If his cord was prolapsed, then he was in the transverse position. Finally, if the baby was in the transverse position, Dr. Trager should have detected it; he should have reported to the hospital immediately; and the medical staff should not have delayed the delivery after failing to detect fetal heart sounds. All three of these departures contributed to Andrew's injuries.

C. THE BABY'S STORMY COURSE IN THE NURSERY CONFIRMS HIS INJURIES

The last event was that this baby had a stormy course in the nursery. The record documented the use of a heart monitor and an incubator, the baby's twitching, and abnormal blood gases.

1. THE HEART MONITOR AND THE INCUBATOR

First, Andrew needed a heart monitor and an incubator. This ten-pound-three-ounce bouncing baby supposedly had no reason even to be depressed at birth since we have eliminated the general anesthesia. What was this same baby doing with a heart monitor for six and a half days? What is this same baby doing in an incubator? As Dr. Mennon said, he never heard of such a large baby being in an incubator. What should the defendants be telling us in this record that's so clearly incomplete? What don't we know? For example, we don't know the reason that this baby was taken out of the incubator at three days of life and promptly put back in for a day and a half. Why? In addition, the defendants scoffed at the medical history that the baby had jaundice and was put under lights, but where did they get the information that the baby was put under lights so they could scoff at it? The record that the defendants produced doesn't say that the baby was put under lights although it does say he was jaundiced. This discrepancy has nothing to do with the baby's brain damage, but it is relevant to the credibility of the defendants.

2. THE TWITCHING

Second, Andrew experienced twitching in the nursery. Mothers and fathers don't need to be told that babies in a nursery normally don't experience twitching of the chin and lips. You may not have known the significance of this twitching before the trial, but you knew it wasn't normal. You didn't need the record in which it's documented by the nurse and the doctors to know that. These five, six, or seven notes are not the end of the matter because one of the last notes in the record establishes that the twitching persisted.

This twitching was not only abnormal, it was significant. Remember what Dr. Mennon said about these subtle neonatal seizures. They are not damaging in and of themselves;

they don't require treatment in and of themselves; but they are a sign of what has occurred to the baby's brain. They are a sign that the baby's brain has been irritated by a lack of oxygen. The nurses in the nursery knew this and suggested that a pediatric neurologist examine the baby's chart. Unfortunately, the defendants' expert, Dr. Bobel, didn't take the time to examine this chart to see what it recorded regarding the baby's condition. He just wanted to testify theoretically. In effect, he said, "Don't confuse me with the particulars."

3. THE ABNORMAL BLOOD GASES

Third, Andrew's blood gases were abnormal. Remember how the defense decried Dr. Mennon for referring to the abnormal blood gases? Remember, too, that the defendants' witnesses testified that those blood gases were normal? Were they? Look at the record. [Refers to visual aid.] This sheet alone lists fifteen values. The eighth is low, obviously outside the norm. Seven values are just below the norm. In fact, ten of the fifteen values are low on just this sheet, and that doesn't include the CO_2, the next blood, and the blood pressure which Dr. Mennon said indicated a compensatory acladiosis as a result of acidosis. That's on the next page.

In summary, Andrew's real Apgar score was three because he had been asphyxiated; the defendant gave him antibiotics because the asphyxia had caused him to pass meconium; and his stormy course in the nursery included the use of a heart monitor and an incubator, twitching, and abnormal blood gases, i.e., further indications of the asphyxia from the prolapsed cord and the defendants' negligence.

COMMENT

Explicit reasoning and internal summaries are especially important late in the summation.

D. CONCLUSION

Ladies and gentlemen, the chain of events constituting proximate cause is clear and incontestable. The verdict sheet will ask you whether each departure from good medical practice was a substantial contributing factor in the plaintiff's injuries. You don't have to find that the defendants' departures were the total cause, and his honor will so instruct you. In fact, however, the defendants' departures were the total cause, and you will see that clearly.

This baby experienced an agonal event, like going down for the third time while drowning. Dr. Mennon called it an agonal gasp. It was almost a terminal event, and that event took the discolored fluid down the larynx and into the baby's lungs. The baby had already gasped that fluid before he was born.

This baby took in that fluid, and consider these statistics. One in six babies passes meconium prior to birth, but only one in three hundred of those aspirates that meconium. One in three hundred. Why did this baby agonally take in meconium when two hundred ninety-nine out of three hundred don't? Why?

Ladies and gentlemen, the evidence is inescapable, compelling, and indeed, overwhelming: Andrew's brain was damaged around the time of his birth. The cause documented in this case was not just a lack of oxygen but a lack of oxygen leading to an asphyxia and to an improper exchange of carbon dioxide and oxygen so that his brain tissues were not properly profused with oxygen, and they died. That's how a perfect brain was damaged, and now it has atrophied. The first CAT scan wasn't taken for four months, but the damage was old by then. We don't have the million-in-one chance that Dr. Mennon talked about.

We also don't have the analogy I made earlier to the defendants' position: the analogy of someone being in two plane crashes. What are the chances of being in one? How about being in two? That's what the defendants are claiming here. Supposedly, weeks before the normal amniocentesis, this baby's brain developed improperly and then, coincidentally, at the birth, these extraordinary events occurred followed by foolproof signs that the baby's brain had been damaged. According to the defendants, the first plane crash damaged the baby. All the witnesses up to Dr. Rosen that testified on this subject, and all the documents that refer to the subject say that the second plane crash also damaged him. But then Dr. Rosen stepped into the breach for the defendants and claimed that the second plane crash was just a smoke screen. Just smoke; there was no fire. There was no damage. This baby's injury wasn't an injury. His brain was never damaged because it hadn't developed in the first place. * * * * *

Please remember, ladies and gentlemen, that the ultimate question in this case is: was there meconium in the amniotic fluid when the bag of waters ruptured? If there was meconium in the fluid, then the baby had passed it as a result of asphyxia caused by the prolapsed umbilical cord. Moreover, the defendants' negligence allowed the prolapsed cord to cause this asphyxia. Dr. Trager had failed to detect the baby's transverse position although a baby of that age and size could not have turned, and the doctor should have scheduled a delivery by cesarian section. He also should have reported to the hospital sooner on the day of the delivery because the staff at the hospital must have informed him of the meconium over the telephone. In addition, if there was meconium in the amniotic fluid, then the medical staff at the hospital was negligent because the staff failed to discover the reason for the absence of fetal heart sounds and, therefore, failed to deliver the baby in a timely fashion.

Of course, if there was no meconium in the amniotic fluid, then the defendants' negligence did not cause Andrew's injuries. However, we know that there was meconium in the fluid. First, Norma Entemann saw the discolored fluid. Second, the defendants' alternative explanations for the baby's passing meconium are implausible: there was no breech birth, and the general anesthesia would not have depressed the baby's central nervous system. Finally, third, the hospital took remedial measures: the discovery of the prolapsed cord triggered the emergency cesarian section, and the administration of antibiotics necessarily implies that the baby had aspirated meconium in the amniotic fluid. Thus, meconium was present in the fluid, and the defendants' negligence did cause Andrew's injuries.

COMMENT

It is important to remind the jurors of the ultimate issue and to review the precise reasoning for them.

VIII. THE PLAINTIFF SHOULD RECEIVE MONETARY DAMAGES TO COMPENSATE HIM FOR HIS INJURIES

Since we know that the defendants are liable for Andrew's injuries, we must consider the damages to which he is entitled.

A. INTRODUCTION

1. APPEAL TO PATHOS

However, before I discuss Andrew's damages, I'd like to mention something that you've seen in this courtroom. The law of the State of New York has show you that an injured child is equal to a mighty institution and to the physicians who practice within its walls. Equal. And the right to a trial by jury in a civil case is the right of all. And yet, who but a fool would say that we have arrived at a state of perfection? We have not, and we know it; but, ladies and gentlemen of the jury, disparate as our backgrounds are, ask yourselves this question. If equality does not start with the law and is not emblazoned in the citadel of law which is this courtroom, then doesn't equality end right here? What, then, is just and fair compensation for what has happened to this child?

2. DEFUSING THE EFFECT OF THE ASTRONOMICAL NUMBERS

Questions four, five, six, seven, and eight address this child's damages. You heard some big numbers from the experts, but I think that by now you understand that the size of those figures is misleading if taken literally. After the trial, if you render a verdict for the plaintiff, his honor will hold a hearing and then set the real present value of the verdict. You are not to discount these seemingly enormous sums to their present values. To talk about awarding current dollars for expenses incurred fifty years from now is as meaningless as using dollars from 1930 now without recognizing the decline in their purchasing power.

COMMENT

The attorney must set the emotional tone, and he must counteract the effect of seemingly astronomical demand for damages.

B. THE PLAINTIFF'S DAMAGES FOR HIS LOSS OF HIS EARNING CAPACITY

The individual questions are not really difficult, ladies and gentlemen. For example, question four asks about the plaintiff's loss of earning capacity, i.e., his loss of earnings during his expected working life.

The discounted sum does bear a relationship to reality because, if you reduce that sum, you reduce its real value after discounting. If you reduce the number of years of a working life or reduce the amount the plaintiff would have earned, you thereby reduce his eventual discounted recovery, and that is the worst thing you can do. If you want to reduce the recovery, and there's no reason that you should, you must reduce the dollar amount only in parallel with the years. Otherwise, the ultimate reduction will be even greater than you intend.

More specifically, the plaintiff contends that he would have received annual increases of 5.13 percent in income over his expected working life if he had not been injured and had been a college graduate. This is an extremely conservative projection: the plaintiff could have been anything. His father has a Ph.D. and has dedicated his life to teaching. Remember that dollars of income far in the future multiply in number but lose their value. Therefore, $6,303,903 for the loss of Andrew's earning capacity is a reasonable recovery. The defendants have asked you to reduce this amount because the plaintiff would have spent some of his earnings on himself. Of course, he would. That's the joy of productivity: to do with it as you will, but the defendants took that ability from him.

COMMENT

The defendants apparently had confused an action for personal injuries with an action for wrongful death.

The defense also has claimed that the growth rate of 5.13 percent is too high and that the rate should be 4 percent. The defense has, of course, no obligation to produce witnesses, as his honor has told you, but we can't have a lawyer telling an economist that the rate of growth will be 4 percent and not 5.13 percent. A lawyer may not substitute his opinion for evidence. Our expert stands alone as the expert in economics in this trial. If 4 percent, rather than 5.13 percent, is the reasonable expectation for the years in question, where is the expert testimony to that effect?

Of course, when it's discounted, the recovery will be a mere fraction of the sum you will calculate at 5.13 percent, but you must award the plaintiff the undiscounted sum. Therefore, you will calculate the appropriate sum, neither more nor less, and award that sum to the plaintiff in those future dollars.

We have made only a conservative adjustment in the plaintiff's life expectancy because, as Dr. Mennon testified, the plaintiff's injuries will not affect his life expectancy with reasonable probability up to age seventy, which statistics say is his life expectancy. You can do the arithmetic as well as I can. His working life would be forty-three years, i.e., from the age of twenty-two to sixty-five. His life expectancy when he needs a companion will be forty-eight years. However, you must specify those years in answer to the appropriate questions.

COMMENT

The calculations are only arithmetical, but the jury must grasp its role accurately and must rely on the evidence.

C. THE PLAINTIFF'S DAMAGES FOR THE FUTURE COST OF A HOME HEALTH AIDE

Question five asks for the cost of a home health aide for just one shift per day. The child's grandmother, who has been such a boon, is now elderly and in need of care herself. For now, the plaintiff asks for a home health aide for only one shift a day, seven days a week. Unfortunately, the cost of a home health aide will grow faster than the general rate of inflation over the next ten years so the undiscounted cost will be $361,561.

Meanwhile, the child needs schooling. He needs the stimulation of others and constant care. He can't just be left at home: that would be cataclysmic for his development. Therefore, he needs something like school, and you heard about the cost.

D. THE PLAINTIFF'S DAMAGES FOR THE COST OF HIS RESIDENTIALCARE FROM AGE TWENTY-TWO UNTIL HIS DEATH

Question six asks for the cost of Andrew's residential care from the age of twenty-two until his death. Beginning at age twenty-two, when his mother will be in her late sixties and his father well into his seventies, the plaintiff will need companionship and care so that he doesn't become a vegetable lying at home. As I have explained, Andrew's life expectancy from the age of twenty-two until his death will be forty-eight years since his injuries will not significantly shorten his life.

COMMENT

The jury may reject the mortality tables and the plaintiff's experts, but the jury may not merely speculate. Therefore, its verdict should be in a reasonable range of the evidence.

E. THE PLAINTIFF'S DAMAGES FOR CONSCIOUS PAIN AND SUFFERING

Question seven asks you which sum of money you award to Andrew for his pain and suffering to date, and question eight asks which amount you award to Andrew for his future pain and suffering. In both cases, pain and suffering includes the plaintiff's loss of the enjoyment of life. This child now has the mental age of a three-year-old, and he will probably reach the mental age of a six-year-old. You certainly know the awareness of a six-year-old. It's not that of a sixteen-, twenty-, or forty-year-old, but it will be the mental age of this child forever. Will $2,000,000 fairly and justly compensation Andrew for never having had a moment of normalcy in his first ten years? You must decide.

COMMENT

The damages for pain and suffering are the most elusive ones, and the law of evidence prevents the attorneys and the court from giving the jurors any real guidance.

IX. PERORATION

Ladies and gentlemen, the total of $40,910,774 in damages is alien to the value of a dollar today, but real dollars have a value far greater than those future dollars I've been discussing. In any case, this total compensates the plaintiff, but it doesn't begin to compensate Andrew. If I climbed to the top of the Williamsburg Savings Bank, the tallest building in Brooklyn, and shouted to the throng below, "Would all the money in the world compensate this boy for this tragic enfoldment of his life?" would there be anyone who would suggest an amount that would compensate him? No!

Don't you think that even if Andrew received nothing from this trial but could walk from this courtroom with his life restored, he would rejoice? Without a penny, he would rejoice! Ladies and gentlemen, think of the words of the woman in the Bible who said, "All you who pass by the way, look and see if there be any sorrow likened to my sorrow." Would that fairly depict the enormity of the loss to a not-so-tiny human being?

Before you deliver your verdict deciding what is fair and just compensation to Andrew for his remaining years in this world, think of the following. You will leave this courthouse today or tomorrow believing that you have done justice, but think of a year from now, when this case comes to mind in a moment of solitude. Will you think then that what you awarded today was fair and just compensation for this child? And ten years from now, when this case has almost faded from your memory, when part 15 or room 109A comes fondly to mind and Andrew with it, will you think then that what you awarded now was just compensation as he enters the last refuge of his life, an institution such as the Devereau Home? Twenty and thirty and forty years from now, and he will far outlive us all, will the recovery you give him now still be fair compensation for his devastation?

Ladies and gentlemen of the jury, only you can say, and I leave you with this thought. You, in doing the right thing in this case, can forever look at yourselves with pride because this act of yours in dispensing justice is the essential element of our democracy. The essential one!

Thank you.

COMMENT

At the end of a long summation closing a long trial, the attorney must re-awaken the sympathies of the jurors.

EXAMPLE 9-1: NOTES JUXTAPOSING THE EXAMINATIONS

WITNESS:

DIRECT	CROSS	RE-DIRECT	ARGUMENT
1.			1.
2.	2.	2.	2.
3.	3.	3.	3.
4.	4.	4.	4.
5.			5.
6.	6.	6.	6.
7.			7.

EXAMPLE 9-2: FLOW SHEET OF CONTENTIONS, EVIDENCE, AND REFUTATION

PLAINTIFF'S CONTENTIONS	PLAINTIFF'S EVIDENCE	DEFENDANT'S EVIDENCE	DEFENDANT'S REFUTATION	PLAINTIFF'S REBUTTAL
I.				
A.				
B. 1.				
2.				
II. A. 1.				
2.				
3.				
B. 1.				
2.				
C. 1. a.				
b.				
2.				
3.				

EXAMPLE 9-3: OUTLINE FOR SUMMATION

1

I. INTRODUCTION
   A. GREETING
   B. VERDICT SHEET
      1. NOT AS COMPLICATED: 3, 2, 1
      2. PROBABILITIES – JURY
      3. a. NORMA ENTEMANN,
         b. ULTIMATE ISSUE: MECONIUM
   C. OUTLINE
   D. ORCHESTRATED EFFORT

II. DEFENDANTS SUPPRESSED RECORD
   A. CLAIMED OWN ENTRIES INACCURATE
      1. DR. PRENTISS
      2. CLERK: 768.9
      3. WOULDN'T SIGN
      4. "ASPIRATION PNUEMONIA, ASPIRATION SYNDROME, AND MECONIUM ASPIRATION,"
      5. "ASPIRATION PNUEMONIA, ASPHYXIA DUE TO PROLAPSE OF CORD,"
   B. ACCEPTED MOTHER'S VERSION
      1. RE-ADMITTED,
      2. OPENING STATEMENT,
      3. RECORD (VA),
      4. WHERE HEAR? MOTIVE?
      5. ACCESS TO CHART
   C. CONSULTANTS ACCEPTED
      1. DR. TRAPP – PLANNED CAT SCAN
   D. FAILED TO PRODUCE ORIGINAL AND COMPLETE RECORD
      1. DRS. ENG AND RAMDI – DELAY?
      2. MISSING: PATHOLOGIST — NURSE'S NOTES
         DISCHARGE SUMMARY — FETAL HEART RAT
         THIRD X-RAY — HEART MONITO
         PRENATAL PRESENTATION — INCUBATOR
         TIME ARRIVED

2

3. RADIOLOGIST'S REPORT AND ANTIBIOTICS,

E. WITHHELD FROM OWN WITNESSES

1. BOBEL, GOLLUB, PEKARIK, GREENE, O'CONNELL,
2. BOBEL - OVERTAX? BASIC DOC'T, "EVERYTHING HELPS"

III. POLYMICROGYRIA UNPERSUASIVE

A. DESPERATION

1. IMPLAUSIBLE: KANNAVAN'S, SOTO'S, FRAGILE X
2. DIDN'T ASK P'S EXPERT

B. IMPEACHED Ds' EXPERTS

1. DR. GREENE: $1,500, DIDN'T DENY BIRTH CONTRIBUTED
2. DR. ROSEN:
   a. NOT GENETIC, ADAMSKI + RESNOR, DIR. OF RADIOLOGY,
   b. SURPRISED!
3. DR. TRAPP: DEV. V. ATROPHY, CONSISTENT W. INSULT
4. DR. GOLLUB: PRE NATAL V. NEO NATAL

C. CAT SCANS DON'T SHOW POLYMICROGYRIA

1. CONTRAST STUDY: BRAIN SHRANK
2. ADVANCED CAT SCANS DON'T SHOW: PEKARIK + GOLLUB

D. FAILED TO REBUT REFUTATION

1. RADIOLOGIST'S REPORT
2. DR. GRANT - TREATING PHYSICIAN
   a. DIDN'T WARN b. BUT SHOWS ATROPHY,
3. DR. MENNON: UNCONTRADICTED, PIONEER, FIRM

IV. DR. TRAGER - FOOTLING BREACH (Q. 1)

A. COULD NOT HAVE CHANGED

1. DR. TRAGER - BABIES TURN
2. DR. RIZZO - RARE BUT
3. DR. BOBEL - NOT MEAN ANYTHING
4. → WRONG: GESTATIONAL AGE, HEAD, LENGTH
5. DR. MENNON: 58 LONG, 39 1/2 CIRC., 10 LBS.
6. DR. NORBERT: EXTREMELY RARE AFTER 39TH

3

B. DICTATED SCHEDULED CAESARIAN
1. WEEK, 12 HOURS
2. LEOPOLD, SONOGRAM
C. PRENATAL SHEET
1. BASIC INFO. 2. 1988 IMPLAUSIBLE
D. CAUSED P's INJURIES
1. SONOGRAM SHOWS TRANSVERSE
2. COULDN'T CHANGE
3. EMERGENCY CAESARIAN
4. RECORD ?
∴ 5. ASPHYXIATION

V. RESPOND TO TELEPHONE CALL (Q. 2)
PIVOTAL ISSUE: MECONIUM
A. PRESENT WHEN RUPTURED
1. MOTHER
a. EBT, TRIAL, TWO WEEKS, RECORD
b. BROWN
c. D DIDN'T CROSS-EXAMINE
d. SURGEONS
2. Ds' ALTERNATIVE EXPLANATIONS
a. BREACH DELIVERY: RELIEF ? NONE !
b. GENERAL ANESTHESIA: DR. RIZZO - DOESN'T
3. REMEDIAL MEASURES
a. EMERGENCY CAESARIAN
b. ANTIBIOTICS
B. KNEW MECONIUM
1. STAFF MUST HAVE TOLD
2. DR. NORBERT - ASSUMPTIONS
3. QUESTIONS OF FACT FOR JURY
4. DR. TRAGER: ADMITTED EARLIER

4

VI. MARONITE FAILED TO DIAGNOSE AND MANAGE

A. DELAYED DESPITE FETAL HEART SOUNDS

1. NEGLIGENCE BEGAN 12:02
2. CLAIMS 12:15 BUT URINALYSIS BY 12:14
3. EXAMINE IMMEDIATELY
4. DELAY UNEXPLAINED: 25, 30, 35; RECORD
5. PULSATING CORD

B. EXACERBATED

1. FORCING POSITIVE PRESSURE OXYGEN
2. NURSE CALLAN: DIDN'T VISUALIZE

C. SUPPRESSING RECORD

1. PATHOLOGY—PLACENTA
2. DISCHARGE SUMMARY
3. FOLLOW-UP X-RAY
4. MOTHER'S ARRIVAL
5. NURSE'S NOTE PRIOR
6. DOCTOR'S NOTES
7. FETAL HEART + INCUBATOR
8. RADIOLOGIST'S REPORT

VII. PROXIMATE CAUSE

A. ERRONEOUSLY HIGH APGAR SCORE

1. THREE: HEART RATE, LIMP
2. DELAY IN RESUSCITATION: GOD'S; TOO LATE

B. ANTIBIOTICS

1. ADMIT ASPIRATED FLUID
2. MECONIUM – WHEN RELIEVED?
3. ANTIBIOTICS – Ds KNEW!
   a. SILENT b. RISKY
4. ASPIRATED MUCOUS
   a. ESOPHAGUS !? b. BROWN

C. STORMY COURSE IN NURSERY

1. HEART MONITOR AND INCUBATOR
   a. DR. MENNON b. RECORD? JAUNDICE – LIGHTS?
2. TWITCHING
   a. ABNORMAL b. BRAIN IRRITATED
3. ABNORMAL BLOOD GASES
   a. VA

5

D. CONCLUSION
1. AGONAL EVENT
2. STATISTICS: 1-6, 1-300
3. LACK OF OXYGEN
4. TWO PLANE CRASHES
5. ULTIMATE QUESTION: MECONIUM

VIII. MONETARY DAMAGES
A. INTRODUCTION
1. MIGHTY INSTITUTION
2. NUMBERS MISLEADING
B. LOSS OF EARNING CAPACITY
1. PARALLEL WITH YEARS
2. 5.13% CONSERVATIVE: PH.D.
3. $6,303,903
4. SPEND ON SELF
5. 4%: LAWYER CAN'T SUBSTITUTE
6. 70 YEARS - DR. MENNON
7. WORK: 43 LIFE: 48
C. FUTURE HOME HEALTH AIDE
1. ONE SHIFT, GRANDMOTHER
2. FASTER THAN INFLATION: $361,561
3. SCHOOLING
D. RESIDENTIAL CARE - 22
1. COMPANIONSHIP + CARE: 48
E. CONSCIOUS PAIN AND SUFFERING
1. MENTAL AGE: 3, 6
2. $2,000,000

IX. PERORATION
A. $40,910,774 ALIEN
B. DOESN'T COMPENSATE: BANK, WOMAN
C. THINK: TOMORROW, 1 YEAR, 10; 20, 30, 40

THE TESTIMONY OF WITNESSES AND DEMONSTRATIVE EVIDENCE

III

Part One dealt with the investigation of the case, the preparation for trial, and the pleadings. Part Two dealt with the course of the trial in the order of events. Part Three deals with the presentation of evidence in a logical and temporal order. Thus, Chapter 10 explains the presentation of witnesses, e.g., swearing them, and Chapter 11 explains the competence of witnesses including privileges and the dead man's statute. The next two chapters discuss using lay and expert witnesses, respectively, to establish the party's direct case. Most of Chapter 12 is devoted to the exceptions to the general rules governing the testimony of lay witnesses, and Chapter 13 explains the limited relevance of the testimony of expert witnesses. Besides presenting witnesses, the attorney impeaches witnesses. Chapter 14 deals with impeaching one's own witnesses and with rehabilitating one's own witness after the opposing party has charged the witness with a recent fabrication. Chapter 15 explains the general rules for cross-examination and then examines the six principal methods of impeaching the credibility of the opposing party's witnesses. Finally, all evidence does not consist of testimony so Chapter 16 explains the common forms of demonstrative evidence, such as photographs and x-rays.

Presenting Witnesses 10

10.1. EXCLUDING THE WITNESSES FROM THE COURTROOM

10.1.1 A Witness Who Is Not a Party

A witness who is not a party does not have a right to be present in the courtroom when he or she is not testifying. An attorney for a party may wish to exclude such a witness in order to prevent him or her from hearing another witness's testimony or the questions propounded and adjusting his or her testimony accordingly. Therefore, at the beginning of the trial, either party may move to exclude all prospective nonparty witnesses from the courtroom. While the trial court has the discretion to grant or deny that motion, the appellate courts have found that it is difficult to understand what reason there is, or could be, for denying such a motion.[1]

1. People v. Cooke, 292 N.Y. 185, 190-191, 54 N.E.2d 357, 359-60 (1944); *see also* FED. R. EVID. 615; Philpot v. Fifth Ave. Coach Co., 142 A.D. 811, 128 N.Y.S. 35 (1st Dep't 1911). In cases involving brain-injured children and in which one parent has been named as the parent and natural guardian, the courts have allowed the exclusion of the other parent because he or she was to testify. The trial attorney might want to amend the caption to name both parents as plaintiffs to avoid this problem.

10.1.2 A Witness Who Is a Party

The rule permitting a witness to be excluded from the courtroom does not apply where the witness is a party. The general rule is that the trial court may not exclude either a party or his attorney from the courtoom during the trial.[2] There are, however, exceptions. For example, in *Monteleone v. Gestetner Corp.*,[3] the trial court held that "a seriously and irrevocably deformed infant plaintiff may be excluded from the liability portion of his own trial,"[4] and that the issue of liability would be tried first in a bifurcated trial pursuant to 22 N.Y.C.R.R. section 202.42. The court in *Monteleone* found that a trial court should apply a two-part test when the defendant moves to exclude the plaintiff from the courtroom during the liability phase of the trial by asking, sequentially:

1. Would the plaintiff's appearance or conduct unfairly prejudice the proceedings in his favor by substantially impairing the jury's performance of its fact-finding task?
2. Can the plaintiff comprehend the proceedings or aid his or her counsel? ("If the trial court concludes that the plaintiff can understand the proceedings and assist his attorney in any meaningful way, he cannot be involuntarily excluded regardless of prejudicial impact."[5])

---

2. Carlisle v. County of Nassau, 64 A.D.2d 15, 408 N.Y.S.2d 114 (2d Dep't 1978); Annot., *Nonparty: Propriety and Prejudicial Effect of Permitting Nonparty to Be Seated at Counsel's Table*, 87 A.L.R.3D 238 (1978).
3. Monteleone v. Gestetner Corp., 140 Misc. 2d 841, 531 N.Y.S.2d 857 Sup. Ct. 1988).
4. *Id.* at 843, 531 N.Y.S.2d at 859.
5. Monteleone v. Gestetner Corp., 140 Misc. 2d 841, 845, 531 N.Y.S.2d 857, 860 (Sup. Ct. 1988).

Note four caveats:

1. The exclusion is exceptional;
2. The exclusion is from the liability phase of the bifurcated trial only;
3. The plaintiff's appearance or conduct must be so extreme that it would prejudice the jury; and
4. The plaintiff must also be incapable of understanding the proceedings or aiding his or her counsel; that is, the plaintiff must be a young infant or be mentally impaired.

Consequently, in *Caputo v. Joseph J. Sarcona Trucking Co.*,[6] the Appellate Division, Second Department, upheld the trial court's exclusion of the plaintiff from the liability phase, stating as follows:

> Although the physical condition of a plaintiff, in and of itself, is not enough to justify his involuntary exclusion from any phase of the trial . . . when a plaintiff is both physically and mentally incapable and his mental incapacity prevents him from assisting counsel in any meaningful way, then the decision to exclude the plaintiff from the liability phase of a trial lies within the sound discretion of the trial court . . . . Here, Caputo's presence in the courtroom would have impaired the jury's ability to objectively perform its task because he physically appeared to be in a state of unawareness . . . . Moreover, he had been judicially declared to be mentally incompetent prior to trial.[7]

However, in *Mason v. Moore*,[8] the Appellate Division, Third Department, ruled that the trial court should not have excluded the five-year-old plaintiff because the issues of lia-

---

6. Caputo v. Joseph J. Sarcona Trucking Co., 204 A.D.2d 507, 611 N.Y.S.2d 655 (2d Dep't 1994).
7. *Id.* at 507-8.
8. Mason v. Moore, ___ A.D.2d ___, 641 N.Y.S.2d 195 (3d Dep't 1996).

bility and damages were so closely intertwined. While the courts continue to analyze this issue,[9] the attorney for a deformed plaintiff should not bc surprised if the attorney for the defendant moves to exclude the plaintiff from the courtroom during the liability phase of a bifurcated trial. Even where the plaintiff is not excluded from the courtroom, the author suggests that plaintiff's attorney bring a seriously injured client to the courtroom only intermittently, so as to avoid the jury becoming desensitized to the injuries.

10.2 SWEARING THE WITNESSES

Every witness in a civil proceeding must be sworn in in order to testify. Moreover, C.P.L.R. section 2309(b) provides: "an oath or affirmation shall be administered in a form calculated to awaken the conscience and impress the mind of the person taking it in accordance with his religious or ethical beliefs." Accordingly, a witness need not swear on a bible if he or she objects to doing so. Where such a situation arises, the witness may declare and affirm that he or she will tell the truth.

An infant's testimony in a civil case may not be unsworn.[10] The trial court must, therefore, determine whether an infant of tender years understands the oath.[11] For example, in *Tuohy v. Gaudio*,[12] the Appellate Division, Second Department, held that a brain-damaged child is not automatically excluded from testifying, but rather the trial court should conduct a preliminary conference to determine whether the infant has sufficient mental capacity to testify.

---

9. *See also In re* Richardson-Merrill, Inc. Benedectin Prod. Liab. Litig., 624 F. Supp. 212 (S.D. Ohio 1985); Gage v. Bogarth, 505 N.E.2d 64 (Ind. App. 1987).
10. Stoppick v. Goldstein, 174 A.D. 306, 160 N.Y.S. 947 (2d Dep't 1916).
11. C.P.L.R. § 2309(b). However, if the infant is unable to testify because of age or inability to appreciate the oath, then the jury may rely upon circumstantial evidence, Stein v. Palisi, 308 N.Y. 293, 125 N.E.2d 575 (1955). *See* Annot, *Competency of Young Child as Witness in Civil Case*, 81 A.L.R.2D 386 (1962).
12. Tuohy v. Gaudio, 87 A.D.2d 610, 448 N.Y.S.2d 41 (2d Dep't 1982).

Clearly, if the infant cannot understand the oath, he or she is incompetent and may not testify.

A witness who cannot speak English or who cannot speak or hear may use an interpreter. If no official interpreter is available, the trial court should appoint, as an official interpreter, someone who can speak both English and the language to be interpreted and this person must swear that he or she will interpret the testimony accurately.[13]

Finally, in limited circumstances, the courts have permitted witnesses to testify through electronic media. Thus, when the plaintiff's attorney delayed completing the cross-examination until the defendant's witness had left for vacation, the court allowed the witness to complete his or her testimony by speakerphone.[14] In another case, the court permitted an elderly plaintiff who was confined to a nursing home in Florida to testify via telephone while being videotaped.[15] An administrative tribunal has likewise allowed a nonparty witness who was outside New York to testify by telephone.[16]

10.3 PRELIMINARY REQUIREMENTS GOVERNING TESTIMONY AND DOCUMENTS

A witness may not testify on every subject within his or her personal knowledge. The witness's testimony must meet the preliminary requirement of being relevant and material. An offer to prove the contents of a writing must further meet the requirements of the best-evidence rule.

---

13. W. RICHARDSON, EVIDENCE § 476 (J. Prince 10th ed. 1973) [hereafter cited as RICHARDSON, EVIDENCE].
14. Superior Sales & Salvage, Inc. v. Time Release Sciences, Inc., ___ A.D.2d ___, 643 N.Y.S.2d 291 (4th Dep't 1966).
15. Ferrante v. Ferrante, 127 Misc. 2d 352, 485 N.Y.S.2d 960 (Sup. Ct. 1985).
16. Matter of Hoffman, 138 A.D.2d 785, 525 N.Y.S.2d 423 (3d Dep't 1988).

10.3.1 Relevant and Material

In order to be admissible, evidence must be both relevant and material. Evidence is relevant if it logically tends to prove that which is at issue. Evidence is material if it has an effective influence on the issues. For the most part, attorneys use these terms interchangeably; however, evidence could be logically relevant but trivial and, therefore, immaterial.

The following thirteen items are examples of evidence that the courts have found to be irrelevant and immaterial.

1. The plaintiff has changed his or her name to "Americanize" it.[17]
2. A police officer or the defendant in an action for negligence has received citations for bravery.[18]
3. The defendant, an employee, was fired after the accident.[19]
4. In an action for negligence, the plaintiff is wealthy, the defendant is poor, or vice versa.[20]
5. The plaintiff in a wrongful death action has remarried or has adopted a child.[21]
6. The defendant is insured.[22]
7. The plaintiff is a person of good character.[23]

---

17. Sandy v. Wicks, 260 A.D. 1046, 24 N.Y.S.2d 424 (2d Dep't 1948).
18. Kesten v. Forbes, 273 A.D. 646, 78 N.Y.S.2d 769 (1st Dep't 1948).
19. Engel v. United Traction Co., 203 N.Y. 321, 96 N.E. 731 (1911).
20. Annot., *Prejudicial Effect of Admission, in Personal Injury Action of Evidence as to Financial or Domestic Circumstances of Plaintiff,* 59 A.L.R.2D 371 (1958).
21. Alberino v. Long Island Jewish-Hillside Medical Center, 87 A.D.2d 217, 450 N.Y.S.2d 857 (2d Dep't 1982).
22. Costa v. Hicks, 98 A.D.2d 137, 470 N.Y.S.2d 627 (2d Dep't 1983); Ward v. Kovacs, 55 A.D.2d 391, 390 N.Y.S.2d 931 (2d Dep't 1977). Note that the court has the discretion either to grant a motion for a mistrial, should such evidence get in accidentally, or to give a curative instruction. Galuska v. Arbaiza, 106 A.D.2d 543, 48 N.Y.S.2d 846 (2d Dep't 1984); Rush v. Sears, Roebuck & Co., 92 A.D.2d 1072, 461 N.Y.S.2d 559 (3d Dep't 1983).
23. Kravitz v. Long Island Jewish Hosp., 113 A.D.2d 577, 497 N.Y.S.2d 51 (2d Dep't

8. The defendant offered to settle the case.[24]
9. The defendant, a doctor, rendered services without a fee.[25]
10. The parties are of particular races.[26]
11. In a case in which the defendant has conceded liability, that the defendant, a driver, was intoxicated when he or she struck the plaintiff.[27]
12. The defendant, a driver, was or was not arrested.[28]
13. At an inquest on damages, what the character of the plaintiff is for truthfulness. (The plaintiff's credibility is relevant, but his or her character is not.)[29]

10.3.2 The Best Evidence Rule

A party who seeks to prove the contents of a writing must produce the original or account for its absence.[30] If the original writing has been destroyed, lost, or similarly accounted for, then the party may prove its contents by secondary evidence.[31] However, even if the court rules that secondary evi-

---

1985) (the court went on to state that in an inquest the plaintiff's credibility as a witness is in issue, but his or her character for truthfulness is not relevant); Lium v. Polski, 87 A.D.2d 860, 449 N.Y.S.2d 297 (2d Dep't 1982); Liberto v. Worcester Mut. Ins. Co., 87 A.D.2d 477, 452 N.Y.S.2d 74 (2d Dep't 1982).

24. Universal Carloading & Distrib. Co. v. Penn Cent. Transp. Co., 101 A.D.2d 61, 474 N.Y.S.2d 502 (1st Dep't 1984).
25. Lium v. Polski, 87 A.D.2d 860, 449 N.Y.S.2d 297 (2d Dep't 1982).
26. Serpe v. Rappaport, 103 A.D.2d 771, 477 N.Y.S.2d 403 (1st Dep't 1984); Abbate v. Solan, 257 A.D. 776, 15 N.Y.S.2d 332 (1st Dep't 1939); Bowen v. Mahoney Coal Corp., 256 A.D.485, 10 N.Y.S.2d 454 (1st Dep't 1939).
27. Obercon v. Glebatis, 89 A.D.2d 762, 454 N.Y.S.2d 46 (3d Dep't 1982).
28. RICHARDSON, EVIDENCE § 506.
29. Kravitz v. Long Island Jewish Hosp., 113 A.D.2d 577, 497 N.Y.S.2d 51 (2d Dep't 1985).
30. RICHARDSON, EVIDENCE § 568; FED. R. EVID. 901-903, 1001-0002; Annot., *Best Evidence: Admissibility in Evidence of Sound Recordings as Affected by Hearsay and Best Evidence Rule*, 58 A.L.R.3D 598 (1974).
31. Dependable Lists, Inc. v. Malek, 98 A.D.2d 679, 469 N.Y.S.2d 754 (1st Dep't 1983); Hoffman v. Lehman, 204 Misc. 1053, 126 N.Y.S.2d 608 (Sup. Ct. 1952), *modified*, 286 A.D. 487, 145 N.Y.S.2d 105 (1st Dep't 1955), *aff'd*, 2 N.Y.2d 824, 140 N.E.2d 749, 159 N.Y.S.2d 839 (1957).

dence is admissible, the court still may refuse to admit the secondary evidence proferred. For example, one court rejected a document which purported to be a photostat of a fax of a lease because the document exhibited "none of the standard indicia of facsimile transmission."[31.1]

It must be remembered that the best-evidence rule excludes secondary evidence, such as oral testimony or an unexecuted carbon, of the contents of a writing. The rule does not, by itself, exclude an original writing in place of oral testimony. For example, in *Flynn v. MABSTOA*,[32] the defendant objected to the plaintiff introducing a policeman's memo book, which contained the entry, "unidentified passenger reported he had hit the bike rider," on the ground that it was not the best evidence. The court of appeals rejected that argument because the plaintiff had not introduced the memo book to "prove the contents of another original written document."[33] Although the memo book may have been inadmissible as hearsay, the defendant made no such objection.

The legislature has gradually adapted the C.P.L.R. to advances in technology, i.e., to methods of recording entries other than on a page of paper. Thus, rule 4539 reads in part:

> If any business, . . ., in the regular course of business . . . has made, kept or recorded any writing . . . and in the regular course of business has recorded, copied or reproduced it by any process which accurately reproduces or forms a durable medium for reproducing the original, such reproduction, . . . , is as admissible in evidence as the original, whether the original is in existence or not . . . .

This version of the rule leaves open the question of the precise scientific process, but the new rule 4539(b), effective No-

---

31.1.Glatter v. Borten, 233 A.D.2d 166 (1st Dep't 1996).

32. Flynn v. Manhattan & Bronx Surface Transit Operating Auth., 61 N.Y.2d 769, 461 N.E.2d 291, 473 N.Y.S.2d 154 (1984).

33. *Id.* at 771, 461 N.E.2d at 293-94, 473 N.Y.S.2d at 156.

vember 1, 1996, endorses the use of optical disks without actually mentioning them.

> (b) A reproduction created by any process which stores an image of any writing, entry, print or representation and which does not permit additions, deletions, or changes without leaving a record of such additions, deletions, or changes, when authenticated by competent testimony or affidavit which shall include the manner or method by which tampering or degradation of the reproduction is prevented, shall be as admissible in evidence as the original.

This amendment permits a reproduction from an optical disk to satisfy the best-evidence rule and the amendment does not require the record to have been created in the ordinary course of business. However, there may still be a hearsay objection to the contents of the reproduction which is not a business record.[34]

10.3.3 Self-Serving Declarations

Sometimes a party seeks to introduce the original of a document he created after the incident that gave rise to the lawsuit. Such bogus best evidence is called a self-serving declaration and is inadmissible to bolster the testimony of the party's witnesses. A self-serving declaration is inadmissible, because "it would be manifestly unsafe to permit a party to litigation to create evidence for himself."[35] Thus, the written report of a defendant's motorman,[36] a party's favorable motor vehicle acci-

---

34. Alexander and Shea, "Evidence Update: State and Federal," lecture, New York County Lawyers' Assoc., Dec. 3, 1996.
35. FED. R. EVID. 801(d)(1); RICHARDSON, EVIDENCE § 357.
36. FED. R. EVID. 801(d)(1); Werber v. City of N.Y., 87 A.D.2d 768, 449 N.Y.S.2d 225 (1st Dep't 1982). In Galanek v. New York City Transit Auth., 53 A.D.2d 586, 385 N.Y.S.2d 62 (1st Dep't 1976), the court held that the introduction of the accident report of the motorman was an error, but it was a harmless error.

dent report,[37] or the plaintiff's workers' compensation report regarding how the accident happened[38] may not be offered as evidence of their contents because they are self-serving. Nevertheless, if the report was prepared in the ordinary course of business and is admissible pursuant to that exception to the hearsay rule,[39] the document is admissible even if it contains self-serving material.[40] Another significant exception may allow a party to introduce a self-serving statement where the opposing party has accused the witness of a recent fabrication.[41] Finally, the report may be admissible solely as a prior inconsistent statement to impeach the witness.[42]

10.3.4 Objections

If the attorney for one party believes that the opposing party is offering evidence that (1) is irrelevant or immaterial, (2) violates the best-evidence rule, or (3) is merely a self-serving declaration, the attorney should object. C.P.L.R. section 4017 provides:

> Formal exceptions to rulings of the court are unnecessary. At the time a ruling or order of the court is requested or made a party

---

37. Newcomb v. Frink, 278 A.D. 998, 105 N.Y.S.2d 704 (3d Dep't 1951); Trampush v. Kastner, 242 A.D. 803, 274 N.Y.S. 771 (2d Dep't 1934); *see also* Morini v. Murphy, 285 A.D. 1154, 140 N.Y.S.2d 294 (2d Dep't 1955) (the court held that the motor vehicle accident report of one defendant may not be used to prove the negligence of a codefendant; that report would be a self-serving statement by the defendant, which the plaintiff may not use to his or her advantage).
38. Anderson v. Permanent Land No. 7 Corp., 18 Misc. 2d 240, 192 N.Y.S.2d 548 (2d Dep't 1959).
39. C.P.L.R. § 4518.
40. Toll v. State, 32 A.D.2d 47, 299 N.Y.S.2d 589 (3d Dep't 1969); Bromberg v. City of N.Y., 25 A.D.2d 885, 270 N.Y.S.2d 425 (2d Dep't 1965); Bishin v. New York Cent. R.R., 20 A.D.2d 921, 249 N.Y.S.2d 778 (3d Dep't 1964). For a case in which a police officer's report of a motor vehicle accident was inadmissible as a business record because the source of the information was unclear, see Murray v. Donlan, 77 A.D.2d 337 (2d Dep't 1980).
41. *See* section 14.3 (recent fabrication) *infra*.
42. Donohue v. Losito, 141 A.D.2d 691 (2d Dep't 1988).

> shall make known the action which he requests the court to take or, if he has not already indicated it, his objection to the action of the court.

The trial court has the discretion to exclude the jury from the courtroom during an argument concerning a question of the admissibility of evidence,[43] as it may during the argument of a motion to dismiss.

43. C.P.L.R. rule 4011: "The court may determine the sequence in which the issues shall be tried and otherwise regulate the conduct of the trial in order to achieve a speedy and unprejudiced disposition of the matters at issue in a setting of proper decorum."

The Competence of Witnesses to Testify 11

11.1 THE DEFINITION OF COMPETENCE

The term "competent" does not refer primarily to the evidence but to the ability of the witness to testify to certain matters. Either the witness is competent to testify to the matter in issue, or he is not.

The general rule is that an adult witness is presumed to be competent to testify regarding all matters that are relevant and material until a party shows the contrary to the court's satisfaction.[1] By statute, a person shall not be excluded from being a witness by reason of the person's interest in the event or because he or she is a party or the spouse of a party.[2] Also by statute, a person who has been convicted of a crime is competent to testify although the opposing party may prove the conviction in order to undermine the weight of the witness's testimony.[3] Even a person who has suffered a serious brain injury is competent so long as he or she can understand the oath and can give a coherent account of the facts.[4] (This rule applies to a brain-damaged

1. Calandara v. Norwood, 81 A.D.2d 650, 438 N.Y.S.2d 381 (2d Dep't 1981); Aguilar v. State, 279 A.D. 103, 108 N.Y.S.2d 456 (3d Dep't 1951). A witness is not incompetent to testify simply because he or she is interested in the outcome of the case, but the court should charge the jury that the witness is interested.
2. C.P.L.R. § 4512. *See also* C.P.L.R. § 4502 (one spouse is not competent to testify against the other in action founded upon adultery except to prove the marriage, disprove the adultery, or disprove a defense).
3. C.P.L.R. § 4513.
4. Barker v. Washburn, 200 N.Y. 280, 93 N.E. 958 (1911).

child as well.)[5] In fact, a child is not ipso facto incompetent.[5.1] However, the trial court must inquire into the competence of any small child to testify.[5.2]

In any case the trial court must make its own determination regarding competence. That a witness was ruled incompetent to testify at a deposition, for example, does not automatically render the witness incompetent to testify at the trial.[6]

Although an adult generally is competent to testify, he or she may fail by defect or excess. By defect we mean that the witness may lack the ability to perceive the event, and this lack of ability need not be obvious. For example, in *People v. Bazalar,*[7] a witness testified to an admission allegedly made by the defendant. Since the defendant spoke in Spanish, however, the defense was entitled to impeach the witness's ability to understand Spanish.

Conversely, a witness may be incompetent by excess if hypnosis has enhanced his or her recollection. The court of appeals has identified three ways in which hypnosis may taint a witness's testimony. The court explained that:

> [A] witness may be affected in three primary respects as a result of having been hypnotized: (1) he may become susceptible to suggestions given intentionally or unintentionally by the hypnotist or others present during the session; (2) the subject may confabulate or intentionally fabricate incidents in order to fill memory gaps or to please those conducting the hypnotic session; (3) a witness who recalls an event under hypnosis which he had previously recollected may experi-

---

5. Tuohy v. Gaudio, 87 A.D.2d 610, 448 N.Y.S.2d 42 (2d Dep't 1982).

5.1. Jensen v. Shady Pines, Inc., 32 A.D.2d 648 (2d Dep't 1989) (plaintiff was six years old).

5.2. For a case in which the court failed to do so, *see* People v. Rose, 223 A.D.2d 607 (2d Dep't 1996), and for a case in which the trial court did make the proper inquiry, *see* People v. Scott, 86 N.Y.2d 864 (1995). *See also* Kapuscinski v. Kapuscinski, 75 A.D.2d 576 (2d Dep't 1980); Rittenhouse v. Town of North Hempstead, 11 A.D.2d 957 (2d Dep't 1960).

6. Sessa v. City of N.Y., 114 A.D.2d 444, 494 N.Y.S.2d 360 (2d Dep't 1985).

7. People v. Bazalar, 211A.D.2d 839, 621 N.Y.S.2d 224 (3d Dep't 1995).

ence an artificially enhanced confidence in his subsequent recollection of that incident, thereby unfairly impairing defendant's ability to cross-examine that witness.[8]

Consequently, a witness may not testify while under hypnosis,[9] and the statements the witness made while hypnotized outside the courtroom are admissible neither as evidence in chief nor to impeach the witness.[10] This complete exclusion applies to civil cases as well as criminal ones. For example, in *Bennett v. Saeger Hotels, Inc.*,[11] the infant plaintiff sought to introduce her hypnotically enhanced recollection on the issue of whether she jumped, fell, or was pushed from a seventh floor window of the defendants' hotel. The trial court correctly granted the defendant's motion in limine to restrict the plaintiff's testimony to her pre-hypnotic recollection. However, even after hypnosis, a witness may repeat the testimony which he or she gave before the hypnosis if the party offering the testimony can establish that post-hypnotic suggestion has not tainted the testimony.[12]

Finally, several rules of evidence prevent a competent witness from testifying. Since they are particularly important in actions for negligence, we will examine three of these rules, to wit, the attorney-client privilege, the physician-patient privilege, and the dead man's statute.

---

8. People v. Tunstall, 63 N.Y.2d 1 (1985).
9. *See generally* Alderman & Barrette, *Hypnosis on Trial: A Practical Perspective on the Application of Forensic Hypnosis in Criminal Cases*, 18 CRIM. L. BULL. 5 (1982); Falk, *Post-Hypnotic Testimony — Witness Competency and the Fulcrum of Procedural Safeguard*, 57 ST. JOHN'S L. REV. 30 (1982); Mickenberg, *Mesmerizing Justice: The Use of Hypnotically Induced Testimony in Criminal Trials*, 34 SYRACUSE L. REV. 927 (1983); Note, *Hypnosis in Our Legal System: the Status of Its Acceptance in the Trial Setting*, 16 AKRON L. REV. 517 (1983); Note, *Probative Value of Testimony from the Hypnotically Refreshed Recollection*, 14 AKRON L. REV. 609 (1981); Note, *Awakening from the Exclusionary Trance: A Balancing Approach to the Admissibility of Hypnotically Refreshed Testimony*, 61 TEX. L. REV. 719 (1982); Note, *Hypnosis in Court: A New Twist on the Old Memory Game*, 13 U. BALT. L. REV. 112 (1983).
10. People v. Hults, 76 N.Y.2d 190 (1991).
11. Bennett v. Saeger Hotels, Inc., 209 A.D.2d 946 (4th Dep't 1994).
12. People v. Hughes, 59 N.Y.2d 523, 453 N.E.2d 484, 466 N.Y.S.2d 255 (1983); People v. DeSantis, N.Y.L.J., Jan. 16, 1986 (Nassau County Ct. 1986).

11.2 PRIVILEGED COMMUNICATIONS

New York recognizes seven evidentiary privileges:

1. The attorney-client privilege.[13]
2. The physician-patient privilege.[14]
3. The clergyman-penitent privilege.[15]
4. The psychologist-client privilege.[16]
5. The social worker-client privilege.[17]
6. The husband-wife privilege.[18]
7. The rape crisis counselor-client privilege.[19]

In a civil action, a witness may invoke the fifth amendment's privilege against self-incrimination, but the attorney for the opposing party may comment upon that invocation in the attorney's summation to the jury — even if the witness invoking the privilege is a party.[20] In addition, New York does not recognize nonstatutory privileges;[21] that is, the statute has absorbed the common law.

---

13. C.P.L.R. § 4503.
14. C.P.L.R. § 4504.
15. C.P.L.R. § 4505.
16. C.P.L.R. § 4507; People v. Wilkins, 65 N.Y.2d 172, 480 N.E.2d 373, 490 N.Y.S.2d 759 (1985); Martin, *Psychologist-Client Privilege*, N.Y.L.J., Aug. 9, 1985, at 1, col. 1.
17. C.P.L.R. § 4508.
18. C.P.L.R. § 4502.
19. C.P.L.R. § 4510.
20. Marine Midland Bank v. John E. Russo Produce Co., 50 N.Y.2d 31, 405 N.E.2d 205, 427 N.Y.S.2d 961 (1980); Martin, *Use of Privilege Against Self-Incrimination in Civil Cases*, N.Y.L.J., Nov. 10, 1983, at 1, col. 1; Litchford, *Privilege Against Self-Incrimination in Civil Litigation*, 57 FLA. B.J. 139 (1983). *See* C.P.L.R. § 4501 (a witness not excused from answering relevant question solely on the ground that the answer may tend to establish that the witness owes a debt or is subject to a civil suit).
21. A nonstatutory privilege is described in Annot., *Disgrace: Privilege of Witness to Refuse to Answer Question Tending to Disgrace or Degrade Him or His Family*, 88 A.L.R.3D 209 (1978); FED. R. EVID. 501 (privileges are governed by the state's law). *See The Federal Law of Privileges*, 16 LITIG. No 1, at 32 (Fall 1989).

11.2.1 The Attorney-Client Privilege

C.P.L.R. section 4502(c) contains New York's version of the attorney-client privilege and provides that confidential communications between an attorney and client are privileged. Thus, the attorney may not disclose the contents of that communication unless the client has waived the privilege, and the client cannot be compelled to disclose the contents. The privilege is applicable in actions, hearings, and administrative proceedings.

The need to interpret this privilege arises in an action for negligence when the defendant argues that his or her incident and accident reports are neither discoverable nor admissible because they were prepared solely for his or her attorney and not for the operation of his business. C.P.L.R. section 3101(g) provides that the parties shall disclose any written report of an accident if the report was prepared in the regular course of business "except as is otherwise provided by law." Thus, the incident or accident report that the party prepared solely for his or her attorney or insurance carrier and with no business purpose is not discoverable or admissible.[22] However, few reports are prepared solely for that purpose: most are prepared with future business operations in mind.[23] Thus, if there was any business rationale for preparing the report, the report is not privileged. Consequently, the Appellate Division, Second Department, has held that incident reports prepared by a hospital following unusual or iatrogenic events are not privileged because the

22. Ellis v. County of Broome, 112 Misc. 2d 19, 445 N.Y.S.2d 957 (Broome County Ct. 1981); Masters v. Hassenpflug, 110 Misc. 2d 998, 443 N.Y.S.2d 210 (Sup. Ct. 1981); *cf.* Pataki v. Kiseda, 80 A.D.2d 100, 437 N.Y.S.2d 692 (2d Dep't 1981); Montag v. YMCA of Oneida County, 122 Misc. 2d 382, 471 N.Y.S.2d 437 (Sup. Ct. 1982).
23. Viruet v. City of N.Y., 97 A.D.2d 435, 467 N.Y.S.2d 285 (2d Dep't 1983); Chaplin v. Pathmark Supermarkets, 107 Misc. 2d 541, 435 N.Y.S.2d 497 (Sup. Ct. 1980).

hospital was motivated by the desire to prevent such events in the future.[24]

Consequently, shrewd administrators have learned to have separate forms for accident reports, per se, and for reports to insurers. This strategy has permitted the courts to hold that simultaneously, "written accident reports prepared in the regular course of business are subject to disclosure,"[25] and that the legislature did not intend to abolish the distinction between those reports and reports to insurance carriers.[26]

> There is, however, a sharp distinction between accident reports which result from the regular internal operations of any enterprise, . . . , and those which are made . . . in connection with the report of an accident to a liability insurer. The latter constitute, at the minimum, materials prepared for litigation which are conditionally exempt from disclosure under C.P.L.R. 3101 (subd [d]) . . . .[27]

The plaintiff's attorney should be alert for an accident report that is so sketchy that it is a subterfuge. The attorney may then subpoena the report to the insurance carrier as the real accident report. In any case, the court should reject a party's merely conclusory assertion that it prepared a particular report solely for litigation.[27.1]

Finally, some recent cases have favored the corporate body. For example, the communication between the corporation's attorney and a former employee may be privileged if

---

24. Pataki v. Kiseda, 80 A.D.2d 100, 437 N.Y.S.2d 692 (2d Dep't 1981). A lay witness cannot testify to the speed of a passing motorcycle based solely upon hearing the sound of the engine. Grant v. New York Tel. Co., 114 A.D.2d 350, 493 N.Y.S.2d 871 (2d Dep't 1985).
25. Vavallo v. Consolidated Edison Co. of New York, Inc., 83 A.D.2d 904 (2d Dep't 1981).
26. Schneider v. Schneider, 94 A.D.2d 700 (2d Dep't 1983).
27. Williams v. Metropolitan Transportation Authority, 99 A.D.2d 530, 531 (2d Dep't 1984).

27.1. Agovino v. Taco Bell 5083, 225 A.D. 569 (2d Dep't 1996); Commerce & Industry Insurance Co. v. S.H. Laufer Vision World, Inc., 225 A.D.2d 313 (1st Dep't 1996); Martino v. Kalbacher, 225 A.D.2d 862 (3d Dep't 1996).

the attorney had communicated with the same employee on the same subject while the latter still was an employee,[28] and, after a corporate merger, the new management retains any privilege which arose in favor of its predecessors.[29]

---

28. Radovic v. City of New York, 168 Misc. 2d 58, 642 N.Y.S.2d 1015 (Sup. Ct. N.Y. 1996).
29. Tekni-Plex, Inc. v. Meyner and Landis, 89 N.Y.2d 123, 651 N.Y.S.2d 954 (1996).

11.2.2 The Physician-Patient Privilege

The need to interpret the physician-patient privilege arises even more frequently than the need to interpret the attorney-client privilege.

11.2.2.1 The General Statement of the Rule

The legislature has broadened the category of practitioners who must preserve the patient's confidences. Thus, the current version of C.P.L.R. section 4504(a) reads, "unless the patient waives the privilege, a person authorized to practice medicine, registered professional nursing, licensed practical nursing, dentistry, podiatry or chiropractic shall not be allowed to disclose any information which he acquired in attending a patient in a professional capacity, and which was necessary to enable him to act in that capacity."

Although the statute is phrased as forbidding the physician to disclose certain information, the statute "also serves to protect the patient from being compelled to disclose the substance of a communication made to the medical profession in an attempt to obtain treatment."[30] The plaintiff in an action for medical malpractice puts his or her physical condition in issue and may not claim the privilege. To the extent, however, that the plaintiff's condition is not in issue, the privilege still stands. Even where the privilege applies, however, a witness may not refuse to reveal relevant medical incidents or facts, even while he or she need not reveal confidential communications with his or her physician.[31]

---

30. Williams v. Roosevelt Hosp., 66 N.Y.2d 391, 396, 488 N.E.2d 94, 97, 497 N.Y.S.2d 348, 351 (1985).
31. Bolos v. Staten Island Hospital, 217 A.D.2d 643 (2d Dep't 1995).

11.2.2.2 The Necessary Relationship

For the privilege to apply, there must be a physician-patient relationship.[32] This relationship usually does not exist when the physician examines the plaintiff for the defendant or the defendant's insurance carrier.[33] For example, in *Kusterman v. Glick*,[34] the trial court permitted the examining physician to testify concerning a comment the plaintiff's husband had made to the physician during the examination. The comment was an admission against interest, relevant to the husband's action for loss of services. Since there was no physician-patient relationship between the examining physician and the plaintiff or her husband, there was no privilege.

Nevertheless, the physician-patient relationship may arise in an emergency, such as in an ambulance[35] or even as the result of an attempted suicide.[36]

11.2.2.3 The Communication Was Necessary for Treatment

In order to be privileged, the information that the patient disclosed to the physician must have been necessary for treatment[37] and the patient must have disclosed the infor-

---

32. Maggio v. State, 88 A.D.2d 1087, 452 N.Y.S.2d 719 (3d Dep't 1982).
33. Griffiths v. Metropolitan St. Ry., 171 N.Y. 106, 63 N.E. 808 (1902); Annot., *Construction and Effect of Statute Removing or Modifying in Personal Injury Actions Patient's Privilege Against Disclosure by Physician*, 25 A.L.R.2D 1429 (1982).
34. Kusterman v. Glick, 107 A.D.2d 664, 484 N.Y.S.2d 31 (2d Dep't 1985).
35. Duggan v. Phelps, 82 A.D. 509 (2d Dep't 1903).
36. Meyer v. Knights of Pythias, 178 N.Y. 63 (1904).
37. Henry v. Lewis, 102 A.D.2d 430, 478 N.Y.S.2d 263 (1st Dep't 1984); Holiday v. Harrows, Inc., 91 A.D.2d 1062, 458 N.Y.S.2d 669 (2d Dep't 1983) (information in the emergency room's records specifying times patients were treated is not privileged); Moore v. St. John's Episcopal Hosp., 89 A.D.2d 618, 452 N.Y.S.2d 669 (2d Dep't 1982) (information in the hospital's records listing the prior assaults by the patient who assaulted the plaintiff is not privileged); Polsky v. Union Mut. Stock Life Ins. Co., 80 A.D.2d 777, 436 N.Y.S.2d 744 (1st Dep't 1981).

mation with the intent that it be confidential.[38] Thus in *Williams v. Roosevelt Hospital*,[39] a case involving the examination before trial of the mother of a brain-damaged infant, the court of appeals held that the defendant's attorney could question the mother regarding the facts of her own prior and subsequent medical care but not regarding the communications enveloping that care. The court explained that the privilege seeks to protect "confidential communications, not the mere facts and incidents of a person's medical history. . . . "

> A witness may not refuse to answer questions regarding matters of fact, such as those posed in this case, as to whether her children had any physical or congenital problems, whether she was in the care of a physician or was taking medication during a certain period of time, or concerning the facts surrounding an abortion merely because those topics relate to events that required medical care or advice from a physician.

Moreover, the burden of proof rests on the person asserting the privilege to demonstrate that the circumstances justify its application.[40]

11.2.2.4 A Waiver of the Privilege

The physician-patient privilege protects communications to, and the medical records of, doctors and hospitals.[41] The plaintiff, however, waives his or her privilege regarding all medical treatment related to an action[42] when the plaintiff

---

38. People v. Christopher, 101 A.D.2d 504, 476 N.Y.S.2d 640 (4th Dep't 1984), *rev'd in part*, 65 N.Y.2d 417, 482 N.E.2d 45, 492 N.Y.S.2d 566 (1985); Bernstein v. Lore, 59 A.D.2d 650, 398 N.Y.S.2d 388 (4th Dep't 1977).
39. Williams v. Roosevelt Hosp., 66 N.Y.2d 391, 488 N.E.2d 94, 497 N.Y.S.2d 348 (1985).
40. *Id.*, 66 N.Y.2d at 396-97, 488 N.E.2d at 97, 497 N.Y.S.2d at 351-52.
41. Cynthia B. v. New Rochelle Hosp. Medical Center, 60 N.Y.2d 452, 458 N.E.2d 363, 470 N.Y.S.2d 122 (1983); New York City Council v. Goldwater, 284 N.Y. 296, 31 N.E.2d 31 (1940).
42. Iseman v. Delman Medical-Dental Bldg., 113 A.D.2d 276, 495 N.Y.S.2d 747 (3d Dep't 1985).

commences an action for negligence or personal injury.[43] The decision in *Williams, supra*, resolved the confusion concerning the specifics of the waiver and the scope of the defendant's ensuing discovery.[44]

In addition to waiving the privilege by commencing the action, a party may waive the privilege at the examination before trial by answering objectionable questions on unrelated medical treatment[45] or by answering interrogatories.[46]

Of course, for the waiving of the physician-patient privilege to be relevant, someone's physical condition or medical treatment must be in issue. Normally, the plaintiff may not put the defendant's medical condition in issue by alleging that the defendant's medical condition caused the accident.[47] In an appropriate case, however, a defendant may waive his or her privilege by affirmatively placing his or her medical condition in issue. In *Swartz v. Koster*,[48] for example, the trial court granted the plaintiff's motion to compel the defendant to provide authorizations for his medical records after the plaintiff alleged that the defendant had been driving the car but was too ill to do so because he had had serious heart surgery. In his original answer to the

43. Koump v. Smith, 25 N.Y.2d 287, 250 N.E.2d 857, 303 N.Y.S.2d 858 (1969). *See also* Dillenbeck v. Hess, 73 N.Y.2d 278 (1989), which held that a plaintiff cannot put the defendant's physical condition in issue so as to defeat the latter's privilege by alleging that the defendant's intoxication caused the automobile accident; Schenk v. Devall, 20 A.D.2d 900 (3d Dep't 1994), which held that even the plaintiff's claim that the defendant infected her with herpes will not defeat his privilege; and Schnobrich v. Schnobrich, 198 A.D.2d 850 (4th Dep't 1993), another accident case.

44. Herbst v. Bruhn, 106 A.D.2d 546, 483 N.Y.S.2d 363 (2d Dep't 1984); Scharlack v. Richmond Memorial Hosp., 102 A.D.2d 886, 477 N.Y.S.2d 184 (2d Dep't 1984); Hughson v. St. Francis Hosp., 93 A.D.2d 491, 463 N.Y.S.2d 224 (2d Dep't 1983). *See also* Dalley v. LaGuardia Hospital, 130 A.D.2d 543 (2d Dep't 1987), and Sibley v. Physicians' Hospital, 126 A.D.2d 629 (2d Dep't 1987), for obstetrical cases.

45. Herbst v. Bruhn, 106 A.D.2d 546, 483 N.Y.S.2d 363 (2d Dep't 1984).

46. Waldman v. A.H. Robbins Co., 129 Misc. 2d 331, 493 N.Y.S.2d 274 (Sup. Ct. 1985).

47. Dillenbeck v. Hess, 73 N.Y.2d 278, 536 N.E.2d 1126, 539 N.Y.S.2d 707 (1989), and Williams v. McGinty, 205 A.D.2d 617 (2d Dep't 1994).

48. Swartz v. Koster, 129 Misc. 2d 342, 493 N.Y.S.2d 82 (Sup. Ct. 1985).

plaintiff's interrogatories, the defendant had admitted that he was the driver, but he denied this in his amended answers. The trial court found that the defendant's physical condition was not itself in issue but was in controversy. In order to be discoverable, "the alleged impairment — mental or physical — . . . [must] relate to, contribute to, or in some way attempt to mitigate the claims for damages or other relief sought by the plaintiff."[49]

11.2.2.5 A Deceased Party

That a party to the action is deceased neither dissolves the privilege nor makes it absolute. Thus, if the plaintiff brought an action which waived the privilege by operation of law, then the privilege remains waived, and the physician must disclose the information required except information that would tend to disgrace the memory of the decedent.[50] Moreover, C.P.L.R. section 4504(c) provides that the decedent's personal representative, surviving spouse, or next of kin may waive the privilege for the decedent.[51] This section does not require that a personal representative be appointed in order to obtain the decedent's medical records because the surviving spouse or next of kin could sign the authorization. At least one trial court has held that such an authorization is sufficient,[52] but the principle is still disputed by physicians and hospitals who do not want to give copies of their records to attorneys. Public Health Law section 17 requires the disclosure of medical records only to doctors and hospitals; the provision says nothing about at-

---

49. *Id.*
50. C.P.L.R. rule 4504(c).
51. There are two other cases: if the personal representative's interest is adverse to the decedent's and if the validity of the decedent's will is in question. *Cf.* Annot., *Death: Who May Waive Privilege of Confidential Communication to Physician by Person Since Deceased*, 97 A.L.R.2D 393 (1964).
52. *In re* Gerkin, 106 Misc. 2d 643, 434 N.Y.S.2d 607 (Sup. Ct. 1980).

torneys. However, in *Matter of Striegel v. Tofano,*[53] the trial court held that, despite this omission, the patient and his attorney have an absolute right to obtain copies of the patient's own medical records. This right is not so clear outside the context of litigation.[54] Apparently, however, contemplating litigation is sufficient to make the patient's right absolute.[55]

The question of waiving the privilege protecting a decedent's medical records often arises in an action for wrongful death. Thus, in *Prink v. Rockefeller Center, Inc.,*[56] the court of appeals held that an action for wrongful death had waived both the decedent's physician-patient privilege and his husband-wife privilege concerning the defendant's mental condition because his unwitnessed death had occurred under circumstances consistent with either negligence or suicide. Prior to his death, the plaintiff's intestate had been under the care of a psychiatrist, but the decedent's wife refused to disclose what her husband had told her about his reasons for seeing the psychiatrist. The court found that maintaining the action had waived both privileges.[57]

Finally, it should be noted that the patient's privilege for confidential communications to his or her psychologist is not identical to the physician-patient privilege. Instead, the statute creating the privilege for psychologists (C.P.L.R. section 4507) makes this privilege analogous to the attorney-

---

53. Striegel v. Tofano, 92 Misc. 2d 113, 399 N.Y.S.2d 584 (Sup. Ct. 1977).

54. Cynthia B. v. New Rochelle Hospital Medical Center, 60 N.Y.2d 452 (1983) at 460, n.3: ". . . , in New York, although patients may exercise a considerable degree of control over their records, there is no statute that expressly allows them to obtain direct and complete access to their medical records regardless of whether litigation is pending. . . . This court has not had occasion to decide whether there is an absolute common-law right to unconditional disclosure of a patient's medical or psychiatric records. Nor have other courts found such a right. . . . " (citations omitted.)

55. Hill v. Springer, 132 Misc. 2d 1013 (Sup. Ct. N.Y. 1986).

56. Prink v. Rockefeller Center, Inc., 48 N.Y.2d 309, 398 N.E.2d 517, 422 N.Y.S.2d 911 (1979).

57. Koump v. Smith, 25 N.Y.2d 287, 250 N.E.2d 857, 303 N.Y.S.2d 858 (1969) (plaintiff's death does not alter waiver of privilege).

client privilege. Nevertheless, the plaintiff in an action for defamation who claims damages for mental distress and psychological counseling puts his or her mental health in issue so as to waive the privilege for the psychological counseling received before the tort.[58]

11.3 THE DEAD MAN'S STATUTE

11.3.1 The Rule

C.P.L.R. section 4519, entitled "Personal Transaction or Communication Between Witness and Decedent or Mentally Ill Person," is commonly known as the dead man's statute. This statute provides that a person interested in the outcome of an action, or his or her predecessor in interest, will not be examined on behalf of himself or herself or of his or her successor against the personal representative or survivor of a decedent, the committee of an incompetent, or the successor in interest of such a person concerning "a personal transaction or communication between the witness and the deceased or mentally ill person." By exception, the interested person may testify if the personal representative, survivor, or committee has testified to the transaction or if the testimony of the decedent or the incompetent has been introduced in some form, such as by being read from the transcript of a prior proceeding. Moreover, the statute does not prevent any person from testifying to the facts or results of an accident arising from the operation of a motor vehicle in New York, an aircraft over the state, or a vessel on the waters of the state, "but this provision shall not be con-

58. LeVien v. LaCorte, 649 N.Y.S.2d 728 (Sup. Ct. Suffolk 1996).

strued as permitting testimony as to conversations with the deceased."[59]

For a witness to be incompetent to testify pursuant to the dead man's statute, he must be both interested in the event and testifying against the interest of the estate. Thus, in *Bechard v. Eisinger,*[60] the Appellate Division, Third Department, held that a wife who had discontinued her derivative action was no longer a person interested in the event and, thus, she could testify to her husband's conversations with the defendant, a doctor. Similarly, in *Cotter v. Mercedes Benz,*[61] the Appellate Division, First Department, held that an employee of the defendant was not a person interested in the event and, consequently, the employee could testify to his conversations with the plaintiff's intestate prior to the accident. Finally, in *Friedman v. Sills,*[62] the Appellate Division, Second Department, noted that the dead man's statute applies only when a party offers the testimony against the estate. The statute does not bar testimony in favor of a decedent against a surviving party.

11.3.2 Circumventing the Rule

The bar of the dead man's statute is waived when any party reads into evidence the decedent's prior testimony regarding the transaction. The party opposing the estate is then free to testify about all matters concerning the transaction or com-

59. Northrop v. Kay, 5 A.D.2d 957, 171 N.Y.S.2d 660 (4th Dep't 1958) (the court held that the defendant could testify regarding the facts surrounding the automobile accident but not about the conversation with the decedent to the effect that the decedent had instigated the race that caused the accident); Annot., *Automobile Accident: Testimony as to Facts of Automobile Accident as Testimony to a "Transaction" or "Communication" with a Deceased Person Within Dead Man's Statute,* 80 A.L.R.2D 1296 (1961); Radigan, *The Dead Man's Statute — Alive and Well in Surrogate's Court*, 50 N.Y. ST. B.J. 470 (1980).
60. Bechard v. Eisinger, 105 A.D.2d 939, 481 N.Y.S.2d 906 (3d Dep't 1984).
61. Cotter v. Mercedes Benz, 108 A.D.2d 173, 488 N.Y.S.2d 390 (1st Dep't 1985).
62. Friedman v. Sills, 112 A.D.2d 343, 491 N.Y.S.2d 793 (2d Dep't 1985).

munication with the decedent. Such a waiver by prior testimony is effective whether the decedent's personal representative or the opposing party reads the decedent's deposition into evidence.[63] The waiver is also effective if A takes B's deposition and then B dies. A may read B's deposition into evidence and effect a waiver of the statute.[64] For example, in *Ward v. Kovacs*,[65] the plaintiff alleged that she had had a conversation with the defendant, a doctor. The defendant died after the examination before trial, in which he denied the conversation had taken place. The plaintiff sought to introduce the defendant's deposition because it constituted prior testimony during which the defendant's attorney could have examined him in full. Accordingly, the plaintiff had effectuated a waiver for the defendant and the plaintiff could then testify fully regarding her conversation with the decedent. The court observed that the language of the statute, if read literally, permitted any party to introduce the decedent's deposition. The court then confronted the question of whether it should read into the statute the qualification that the decedent's personal representative must have introduced the deposition. The court decided not to do so and stated five reasons, explaining as follows:

- First, the rationale of the dead man's statute was only marginally applicable because the decedent had stated his version of the incident for the record under oath and subject to examination by the adversary.
- Second, the decedent's personal representative could have offered the deposition for the truth of its contents.
- Third, the surviving party is subject to cross-examination on her version.

63. Tepper v. Tannenbaum, 65 A.D.2d 359, 411 N.Y.S.2d 588 (1st Dep't 1978); Ward v. Kovacs, 55 A.D.2d 391, 390 N.Y.S.2d 931 (2d Dep't 1977).
64. Siegel v. Waldbaum, 59 A.D.2d 555, 397 N.Y.S.2d 144 (2d Dep't 1977).
65. Ward v. Kovacs, 55 A.D.2d 391, 390 N.Y.S.2d 931 (2d Dep't 1977).

> - Fourth, the decedent's inability to rebut the plaintiff's testimony with his own live testimony is a proper subject for discussion during the summations and the charge.
> - Finally, fifth and most important, a trial is a search for the truth.
>
> Where a party has died after his deposition has been taken, we should not encourage a situation where counsel for the decedent is placed in the position of being able to determine whether it is better for his client that the deposition be admitted into evidence, thus "opening the door" to "survivor" testimony, or whether it is perhaps wiser to withhold it and thus to leave the door closed.

Therefore, the argumentative balance was against reading into the statute a qualification that only the decedent's personal representative could introduce the decedent's deposition and thereby waive the dead man's statute.

Even a violation of the statute is not always reversible error. For example, in *Peters v. Morse,*[66] the Appellate Division, Third Department, held that a violation of the dead man's statute was harmless error because independent evidence supported the plaintiff's claim.[67]

Nevertheless, the courts' flexibility is not limitless. Although A, the survivor, may defeat the dead man's statute by introducing the deposition of B, the decedent, A may not defeat the statute by introducing his own deposition taken when B was still alive but unable to be present. Thus, in *Matter of Mead,*[68] the Appellate Division, Fourth Department, wrote:

> The deposition is not admissible under C.P.L.R. 3117 (use of depositions) because that section does not authorize the use of deposition where the witness later becomes unavailable to testify because of the operation of the Dead Man's Statute. The

66. Peters v. Morse, 112 A.D.2d 559, 491 N.Y.S.2d 495 (3d Dep't 1985).
67. *Id. See also* Young v. Strong, 118 A.D.2d 974, 499 N.Y.S.2d 988 (3d Dep't 1986) (the court held that where the introduction of incompetent evidence was a harmless error, the incompetent evidence merely corroborated the competent testimony).
68. In the Matter of the Estate of Arthur W. Mead, 129 A.D.2d 1008 (4th Dep't 1987).

> statute speaks of unavailability only in terms of the distance of the witness from the place of trial, the death of the witness, or his physical or mental inability to attend or testify. . . .
>
> [A] deposition may be admissible under the common-law rule concerning former testimony. . . . [However] [i]n the instant case, Arthur Mead, unlike the decedent in *Siegel*, was unable to be present and confront their witness. . . . [H]e was in a nursing home and, . . . was incapable of handling his affairs.[69]

69. *Id.* at 1009.

Using Lay Witnesses to Establish the Direct Case 12

12.1 INTRODUCTION

The plaintiff ordinarily presents his or her direct case before the defendant does, but no rule requires the plaintiff to call the plaintiff's witnesses in any particular order. In an action for negligence, the plaintiff's attorney will often call the attorney's client, the injured party, first in order to explain how the accident happened. Sometimes the witness best able to provide that explanation is the policeman who investigated the accident. In actions for medical malpractice, the plaintiff almost always calls the defendant doctor as his or her first witness. Similarly, no rule requires the defendant to call his or her witnesses in any particular order.

The ordinary or lay witness is one who observed some act and testifies to what he saw or heard on that occasion, e.g., what was said or how the automobiles entered the intersection. Thus, a witness is "one who testifies to what he has seen, heard, or otherwise observed."[1] The witness must testify without leading questions from the attorney for the party who called him, without giving opinions or drawing conclusions, and from his own recollection.

The remainder of this chapter discusses the exceptions to these rules, to wit, examining the witness by using leading questions, allowing the lay witness to express an opinion,

1. BLACK'S LAW DICTIONARY 1778 (4th ed. 1968).

and allowing the witness to refresh his recollection or to introduce his past recollection recorded.

12.2 EXAMINING THE WITNESS BY USING LEADING QUESTIONS

12.2.1 The General Rule

The general rule is that it is improper for the attorney to ask the witness leading questions on his or her direct case.[2] A leading question is a question which:

1. Calls for only a "yes" or "no" answer, e.g., "Didn't you slow down as you approached the corner?"
2. Suggests an answer to the witness, e.g., "Which part of the crosswalk did you use when you crossed the street?"
3. Assumes facts that are in controversy, e.g., "Where were you standing when the defendant's car ran the red light?"

Exceptions to the rule against leading questions allow such questions in certain circumstances. For instance, the plaintiff's attorney may pose leading questions to the defendant when the plaintiff calls the defendant as a witness for the plaintiff on the plaintiff's direct case.[3] The court has the discretion to permit leading questions,[4] particularly when the questions relate to matters not in dispute[5] or when the witness appears to have exhausted his or her memory. In the latter situation, the attorney may direct the witness's atten-

2. FED. R. EVID. 611(c), 614(a), 614(b).
3. *See* section 12.2.2 *infra*.
4. Walls v. Randall, 81 N.Y. 164 (1880).
5. W. RICHARDSON, EVIDENCE § 482 (J. Prince 10th ed. 1973) [hereinafter cited as RICHARDSON, EVIDENCE].

tion to a particular fact.[6] The court may also permit the attorney to ask leading questions of children, the illiterate, or the aged.[7]

In addition, the judge may ask the witness leading questions provided the judge does so in such a manner as to appear impartial and not to indicate a preference for an answer or a party.[8] (The attorneys for the parties may, of course, ask leading questions on cross-examination.)

Beware of the occasion where the trial judge goes too far in questioning the witnesses. Such conduct can, albeit rarely, result in a reversal on appeal. The Appellate Division, First Department, did so in *Campbell v. Rogers & Wells,*[9] observing as follows:

> Upon review of the trial court's conduct in this matter it appears that . . ., the trial court questioned numerous witnesses, dictated the length of answers, at times suggested answers, and generally interjected itself into the proceedings. . . . While we find that no bias or prejudice was displayed, we conclude that the court's conduct could not have allowed the jury to review the case in the "calm untrammeled spirit necessary to effect justice" . . . .[10]

---

6. O'Hagan v. Dillon, 76 N.Y. 170 (1879); Hunter v. Szabo, 117 A.D.2d 778, 499 N.Y.S.2d 426 (2d Dep't 1986); Rodriguez v. Manhattan & Bronx Surface Transit Operating Auth., 117 A.D.2d 541, 498 N.Y.S.2d 826 (1st Dep't 1986); Griffen v. Griswold, 114 A.D.2d 596, 494 N.Y.S.2d 441 (3d Dep't 1985).
7. RICHARDSON, EVIDENCE § 482.
8. Gunderson v. All Am. Commerce Corp., 275 A.D. 572, 575, 90 N.Y.S.2d 3, 6 (1st Dep't 1949). The trial justice, undoubtedly feeling that he was tactful, frequently interfered with direct examination by counsel of defendant's witnesses and followed that by undue cross-examination. As the record did not require clarification by the court's questions and counsel were experienced, the intervention was not warranted. Kamen Soap Prods. Co. v. Prusansky & Prusansky, Inc., 11 A.D.2d 676, 201 N.Y.S.2d 875 (1st Dep't 1960) ("However, we have concluded that plaintiffs were deprived of a fair trial and an unprejudiced consideration of the case by the jury because of the trial judge's repeated lengthy cross-examination and unnecessary criticism of plaintiff's counsel; and because the judge so far injected himself into the proceedings that the jury could not review the case in the calm and untravailed spirit necessary to effect justice.").
9. Campbell v. Rogers & Wells, 218 A.D.2d 576 (1st Dep't 1995).
10. *Id.* at 579.

12.2.2 Leading Questions to a Defendant Called by the Plaintiff

If the plaintiff calls the defendant to the stand or if the witness is deemed hostile or adverse to the plaintiff, then the plaintiff's attorney may ask the witness leading questions and conduct a full cross-examination.[11] As the Appellate Division, Second Department, held in *Segreti v. Putnam Community Hospital*:

> The trial court also erred in improperly curtailing plaintiff's examination of defendant Chang as a hostile and expert witness. As an adverse party, Dr. Chang was a hostile witness subject to cross-examination when called to the stand by the plaintiff. . . . The trial court improperly ruled that Dr. Chang should not be required to testify concerning whether the procedures he followed constituted proper medical practice or not. *It was prejudicial error for the trial court to so prevent plaintiff's counsel from leading and cross-examining Dr. Chang as a hostile witness as to hold him bound by the latter's answers.*[12] (Emphasis added.)

It is proper for the plaintiff to call the defendant doctor to establish the plaintiff's direct case, and this ploy may be shrewd trial strategy because the testimony will fix the defendant's position on the issues early in the trial. In such a situation, the plaintiff's attorney should prepare what amounts to a counter-hypothetical question.[12.1]

---

11. Becker v. Koch, 104 N.Y. 394, 401, 10 N.E. 701, 703 (1887).

12. Segreti v. Putnam Community Hosp., 88 A.D.2d 590, 449 N.Y.S.2d 785 (2d Dep't 1982).

12.1. *See* § 15.7.2.

12.3 ALLOWING THE LAY WITNESS TO EXPRESS AN OPINION

12.3.1 The General Rule

The general rule is that a lay witness may testify only to the facts and not to opinions or conclusions because it is the jury's role to draw the conclusions from the facts.[13] Thus, the trial court will not permit a witness to state his opinions regarding whose negligence caused the accident,[14] that the plaintiff was acting in a careful or a careless manner,[15] or that more than one attendant was needed to supervise a playground properly.[16]

As we have noted, since it is for the jury to draw the conclusions from the evidence, a question that asks the witness to draw a conclusion is objectionable.[17] Nevertheless, the courts have determined that a witness cannot separate some sense impressions from the event. Consequently, it is proper for a witness to testify that the defendant was driving "fast" or "too fast."[18] Sometimes such testimony is the only way the witness can describe what he or she observed, and the courts are loath to prevent a witness from stating such a conclusion. Thus, an opinion is permissible where it relates to an incident or fact that the witness cannot describe un-

---

13. Grey v. United Leasing, Inc., 91 A.D.2d 932, 457 N.Y.S.2d 823 (1st Dep't 1983); Annot., *Admissibility of Opinion Evidence as to the Cause of an Accident or Occurrence*, 38 A.L.R.2D 13 (1934); Annot., *Admissibility of Opinions as to Point of Impact or Collision in Motor Vehicle Case*, 66 A.L.R.2D 1048 (1959).
14. Crofut v. Brooklyn Ferry Co., 36 Barb. 201 (N.Y. Sup. Ct. 1862).
15. McCarragher v. Rogers, 120 N.Y. 526, 24 N.E. 812 (1890).
16. Storms v. City of Fulton, 263 A.D. 927, 32 N.Y.S.2d 395 (4th Dep't 1942).
17. *See* FED. R. EVID. 704.
18. Costa v. Hicks, 98 A.D.2d 137, 470 N.Y.S.2d 627 (2d Dep't 1983) (the ages of the lay witnesses negated their ability to render an accurate estimate of speed: the witnesses were nine, eleven, and twelve at the time of the trial); LoFaso v. Jamaica Buses, Inc., 63 A.D.2d 998, 406 N.Y.S.2d 131 (2d Dep't 1978). A lay witness cannot testify to the speed of a passing car based upon the sound of the engine. Grant v. New York Tel. Co., 114 A.D.2d 350, 493 N.Y.S.2d 871 (2d Dep't 1985).

less the witness expresses it in the form of an opinion.[19] Such opinions, however, must not rely on subjects that require special knowledge or skills as a basis for forming a conclusion; that is, the lay witness may not testify as an expert.

12.3.2 The Allowable Testimony

In *Hardy v. Merrill*, the court of appeals listed some of the subjects upon which a lay witness may give an opinion:

> [A]ll concede the admissibility of the opinion of nonprofessional men upon a great variety of unscientific questions arising every day, and in every judicial inquiry. These are questions of identity, handwriting, quantity, value, weight, measure, time, distance, velocity, form, size, age, strength, heat, cold, sickness, and health; questions, also, concerning various mental and moral aspects of humanity, such as disposition and temper, anger, fear, excitement, intoxication, veracity, general character and particular phases of character, and other conditions and things, both moral and physical, too numerous to mention. . . .[20]

Hardy was decided in 1974, but the courts of New York have since accumulated a more specific list of matters upon which a lay witness may give an opinion:

1. A train was operated with a terrific jerk.[21]
2. A trolley car stop was unusual.[22]
3. An automobile was going fast.[23]
4. An automobile was traveling at a certain speed.[24]

---

19. Collins v. New York Cent. & H.R. R.R., 109 N.Y. 243 (1888); FED. R. EVID. 701; Annot., *Requisite Foundation or Predicate to Permit Non-Expert Witness to Give Opinion, in a Civil Action, as to Sanity, Mental Competency or Mental Condition*, 40 A.L.R.2D 15 (1955); Annot., *Admissibility of Non-Expert Opinion Testimony as to Weather Conditions*, 56 A.L.R.3D 575 (1974).
20. Howell v. Mills, 56 N.Y. 226 (1874).
21. Fellows v. I.R.T. Co., 117 Misc. 64, 190 N.Y.S. 547 (1st Dep't 1921).
22. Lombardi v. New York State Rye, 224 A.D. 438, 231 N.Y.S. 306 (4th Dep't 1928).
23. *See* note 18 *supra*.
24. Larsen v. Vigliarolo Bros., 77 A.D.2d 562, 429 N.Y.S.2d 273 (2d Dep't 1980); Marcucci v. Bird, 275 A.D. 127, 88 N.Y.S.2d 333 (3d Dep't 1949) (rule does not apply to estimating speed of motorcycle).

5. A person appeared to be intoxicated.[25]
6. The apparent physical condition of a person that can be seen by ordinary observation, e.g., his general strength, vigor, feebleness, illness, state of unconsciousness, and comparative condition from day to day.[26]
7. An estimate of the depth of a hole or a depression.[27]
8. Color, weight, size, quantity, light, and darkness.
9. The inferences of identity, race, language, persons, visibility, sounds, and the like.[28]

Finally, that the witness answers a question by stating that the witness *believes* or *thinks* that something was so does not make the answer objectionable.[29] Thus, the witness may properly say, "I believe that the car was going about forty miles per hour," or "I think that the hole in the sidewalk was about two inches deep." However, when the question calls for a specific answer on a matter central to the issues in the case, the witness may not so qualify the answer. For example, a witness may not testify that he or she thought that the traffic light was red for the plaintiff. In other words, a witness may testify to a belief regarding mediate contraries but not immediate contraries.

---

25. Ellison v. New York City Transit Auth., 63 N.Y.2d 1029, 473 N.E.2d 1171, 484 N.Y.S.2d 797 (1984); Ross v. Robert Bar & Grill, 83 A.D.2d 550, 441 N.Y.S.2d 987 (2d Dep't 1981); Allan v. Keystone Nineties, Inc., 74 A.D.2d 992, 427 N.Y.S.2d 107 (4th Dep't 1980).
26. RICHARDSON, EVIDENCE § 364.
27. Buckhout v. City of Niagara Falls, 199 A.D. 263, 193 N.Y.S. 38 (4th Dep't 1921).
28. RICHARDSON, EVIDENCE § 364; Annot., *Admissibility of Opinion Based on Experiment to Show Visibility or Line of Vision*, 78 A.L.R.2D 153 (1961); Annot., *Identification of Accused by His Voice as Opinion Evidence*, 70 A.L.R.2D 978 (1919).
29. FED. R. EVID. 701; Annot., *Effect of Witness Qualifying His Testimony with "I Think," "I Believe" or the Like When Expressing Thereby Indistinct Observation or Recollection*, 4 A.L.R. 978 (1919).

12.3.3 The Opinion of a Party

The appellate courts appear more reluctant to permit a party to testify to an opinion than they are to permit a disinterested witness to do so.

Trial attorneys should be familiar with the decision by the Appellate Division, First Department, in *Christoforou v. Lown*.[30] In that case, the plaintiff testified that inadequate lighting had caused her to trip and fall down a short staircase. The appellate court reversed the jury's verdict in the plaintiff's favor and dismissed the complaint, finding that there was no "objective proof . . . from which the jury could conclude that there was an absence of due care."[31] The dissent interpreted that holding to mean that a plaintiff may not testify, as a lay witness, to inadequate lighting and to who knows what else, and that expert testimony will now be required. The dissent may have overstated the ramification of the holding a bit. The relevant distinction is not between a lay person and an expert but between an interested witness and a disinterested one.

The issue was broached by the Appellate Division, Second Department, the following year in *Swoboda v. We Try Harder, Inc.*,[32] in which the court reversed the judgment for the defendant. The court found reversible error in the trial court's admission of the defendant's testimony that the plaintiff had been traveling sixty to sixty-five miles per hour on his motorcycle at the moment of the collision. The defendant had been driving automobiles for thirty-one years and concomitantly estimating the speed of other vehicles. However, the appellate court wrote, "at no time did he ever state that he had any experience in estimating the speed of motorcycles. In the absence of such a foundation, the opinion testimony as to the motorcycle's specific speed should not have been admitted . . . ." That rationale seems somewhat disingenuous and probably dis-

30. Christoforou v. Lown, 120 A.D.2d 387, 502 N.Y.S.2d 184 (1st Dep't 1986).
31. *Id.* at 391, 502 N.Y.S.2d at 87.
32. Swoboda v. We Try Harder, Inc., 128 A.D.2d 862, 513 N.Y.S.2d 781 (2d Dep't 1987).

guised the court's reluctance to take one party's word for the other's speed aside from the competence of lay witnesses to judge such matters.

The Appellate Division, Second Department, did approve the trial court's admission of the testimony of a disinterested lay witness in *Kapinos v. Alvarado*.[33] The appellate court held that it was proper to admit the nonexpert testimony of a police officer, a disinterested witness, regarding the point of impact of the colliding vehicles. The officer had predicated his opinion upon the location and position of the vehicles when he had arrived at the scene. The court held:

> Contrary to the plaintiff's contention, we find that the trial court properly permitted the officer to testify as to his conclusions, without having qualified him as an expert, since his testimony constituted observations not requiring any particular expertise. . . .

It would thus appear that the operative distinction is not the relevant expertise of the witness, but whether or not the witness is interested in the outcome.

12.4 REFRESHING THE WITNESS'S RECOLLECTION

A witness who has no present recollection of a fact or conversation may refresh his or her recollection by consulting any paper or memorandum, whether written by the witness or not.[34] However, the witness must testify first that he or she cannot re-

33. Kapinos v. Alvarado, 143 A.D.2d 332, 532 N.Y.S.2d 416 (2d Dep't 1988).

34. See Annot., *Refreshment of Recollection by Use of Memoranda or Other Writings,* 83 A.L.R.2D 473 (1962). When the writing does not refresh the recollection of the witness, see Brown v. Western Union Tel. Co., 26 A.D.2d 316, 274 N.Y.S.2d 52 (4th Dep't 1966); FED. R. EVID. 612. *See* FED. R. EVID. 803(5) for the rule on past recollection recorded. If the witness does not indicate inability to remember, then the document may not be shown to refresh witness's recollection. Nappi v. Gerdts, 103 A.D.2d 737, 477 N.Y.S.2d 202 (2d Dep't 1984).

call sufficient facts to testify from memory.[35] In the leading case of *Howard v. McDonough*, the court of appeals phrased the rule as follows:

> A witness may, for the purpose of refreshing his memory, use any memorandum, whether made by himself or another, written or printed, and when his memory has thus been refreshed, he must testify to facts of his own knowledge, the memorandum itself not being evidence.[36]

The Appellate Division, Second Department, applied this rule in *Newman v. Great Atlantic & Pacific Tea Co.*[37] and held, "the trial court erred in preventing plaintiff from refreshing the recollection of the assistant manager of defendant [store] at the time of the accident with an accident report supplied to plaintiff by the defendant."

After the witness has used the writing to refresh his or her recollection, the opposing party has a right to inspect the writing. This includes the right to inspect any paper the witness consulted, not merely the one the witness used to refresh his recollection on the witness stand.[38]

In *Matter of Slotnick v. State of New York,*[39] the New York Court of Claims held that by using a certain writing to refresh the witness's recollection, the party had waived the privilege afforded by Education Law section 6527(3). (Section 6527[3] protects from disclosure the proceedings or records of a medical quality assurance review or a malpractice prevention program.)

Clearly, the courts are enforcing two rules and, by analogical equivocation, referring to both as refreshing the recollec-

35. Nappi v. Gerdts, 103 A.D.2d 737, 477 N.Y.S.2d 202 (2d Dep't 1984).

36. Howard v. McDonough, 77 N.Y. 592, 593 (1879). *See also* People v. Raja, 77 A.D.2d 322 (2d Dep't 1980).

37. Newman v. Great Atl. & Pac. Tea Co., 100 A.D.2d 538, 473 N.Y.S.2d 231 (2d Dep't 1984).

38. State v. Mucci, 25 N.J. 423, 136 A.2d 761 (1957). The witness's recollection may be refreshed by a tape recording. Herrmann v. General Tire & Rubber Co., 79 A.D.2d 955, 435 N.Y.S.2d 14 (1st Dep't 1981).

39. Slotnik v. State, 129 Misc. 2d 553, 493 N.Y.S.2d 731 (Ct. Cl. 1985).

tion of the witness. The first rule is that a witness who cannot remember the event may use a writing to stimulate his or her memory while on the stand, but the opposing counsel may examine this writing. Then, during cross-examination, the opposing counsel may impeach the witness for merely repeating the contents of the writing, rather than really remembering the event. The second rule is that a witness may prepare for his or her testimony by consulting a writing before the witness reports to court and even if the witness remembers the event, but the opposing counsel may examine this writing also. The witness waives any privilege once he or she relies on this document to testify at the trial or even at the examination before trial. Thus, if the witness gave a deposition, the opposing counsel may obtain the documents on which the witness relied by serving a notice of discovery and inspection. For example, in *Merrill Lynch Realty Commercial Services, Inc. v. Rudin Management Co., Inc.,*[40] an action for a commission, the Appellate Division, First Department, held that the chronology drawn up by one of the plaintiff's officers and relied on by the plaintiff for his deposition was discoverable. "We find that the chronology is relevant and that any privilege adhering to it has been waived . . . ."[41]

12.5 INTRODUCING A WITNESS'S PAST RECOLLECTION RECORDED

Theoretically, introducing a witness's past recollection recorded is quite different from using a writing to refresh the witness's recollection.[42] When employing past recollection

40. Merrill Lynch Realty Commercial Services, Inc. v. Rudin Management Co., Inc., 94 A.D.2d 617 (1st Dep't 1983).
41. *Id. See also* Herrmann v. General Tire & Rubber Co., 79 A.D.2d 955, 435 N.Y.S.2d 14 (1st Dep't 1981).
42. Muth v. J&T Metal Prods. Co., 74 A.D.2d 898, 425 N.Y.S.2d 858 (2d Dep't 1980); Fine, *Past Recollection Recorded in New York*, N.Y.L.J., Aug. 27, 1980, at 1, col. 2.

recorded, the party offers the document in evidence as a substitute for the witness's oral testimony rather than having the witness testify after consulting the document. Moreover, the witness must have created the document embodying the witness's past recollection recorded, whereas a witness may refresh his or her recollection from a writing created by anyone.

Admitting the document into evidence is an exception to the hearsay rule and the courts have accepted the exception because the document may be the best and only record of what occurred. In addition, the person who created the document is on the stand and subject to cross-examination, and the trial court will usually conduct a voir dire on the admissibility of the document.

In *Calandara v. Norwood,*[43] the Appellate Division, Second Department, outlined the formal requirements for introducing a document as past recollection recorded:

> There are three criteria for admission of a written memorandum, made by a witness, under the rule of past recollection recorded: (1) that it was made at or about the time of the matters to which it relates, (2) that its accuracy at the time of its making is presently certified to by the witness and (3) that there is a necessity for its introduction due to the witnesses' present inability to recall the facts of the matter.[44] At the foundation of this rule, like most hearsay exceptions, is an apparent trustworthiness.[45] In the instant case, that apparent trustworthi-

---

43. Calanda v. Norwood, 81 A.D.2d 650, 438 N.Y.S.2d 381, 382-83 (2d Dep't 1981). *See also* Howard v. McDonough, 77 N.Y. 592, 593 (1879):

> 2. When a witness has so far forgotten the facts that he cannot recall them, even after looking at a memorandum of them, and he testified that he once knew them and made a memorandum of them at the time or soon after they transpired, which he intended to make correctly, and which he believes to be correct, such memorandum, in his own handwriting, may be received as evidence of the facts therein contained, although the witness has no present recollection of them.

44. *See* RICHARDSON, EVIDENCE § 469.

45. *See* People v. Raja, 77 A.D.2d 322, 433 N.Y.S.2d 200 (2d Dep't 1980); Ianelli v. Consolidated Edison Co., 75 A.D.2d 223, 428 N.Y.S.2d 473 (2d Dep't 1980).

> ness was diminished by the 4-1/2 month gap between the accident and the statement. While there is no rigid rule as to how soon after the event the statement must have been made,[46] under the circumstances at bar the delay was too great. . . .

In *Ianelli v. Consolidated Edison Co.*,[47] the same court went further and observed that "if a witness does not remember having seen the memorandum before, he may testify that, from his handwriting, habits, or usual course of business in reference to matters of that nature, he has a present conviction or belief that the statements are correct."[48] The court noted that the doctrine is grounded upon a guarantee of correctness. If the trial court believes that the witness made the record honestly and without a motive to falsify, the court will allow the party to introduce the document as a past recollection recorded. However, if the witness prepared the record solely for litigation, then the court will exclude it.[49] If the record was not a business record and was always under the control of one party, the trial court will examine the integrity of the document thoroughly before admitting it.[50]

Consequently, in *Ianelli*, the court ruled that the memorandum by the defendant's insurance investigator was inadmissible for four reasons. First, the memorandum was an account of the accident given by the plaintiff's intestate while in the hospital just a few days after the accident and, therefore, was taken in violation of Judiciary Law section 480. Second, the intestate had not signed the memorandum. Third, the investigator was unable to state under oath that

---

46. *See, e.g.*, Toll v. State, 32 A.D.2d 47, 299 N.Y.S.2d 589 (3d Dep't 1969) (fifteen days); People v. Caprio, 25 A.D.2d 145, 268 N.Y.S.2d 70 (2d Dep't) (twenty-eight hours), *aff'd*, 18 N.Y.2d 617, 219 N.E.2d 204, 272 N.Y.S.2d 385 (1966).
47. Ianelli v. Consolidated Edison Co., 75 A.D.2d 223, 428 N.Y.S.2d 473 (2d Dep't 1980).
48. *Id.* at 228-31, 428 N.Y.S.2d at 476-78.
49. *Id.* at 231, 428 N.Y.S.2d at 478.
50. *Id.* at 230, 428 N.Y.S.2d at 477.

the intestate was coherent and not drugged. Fourth, since the investigator worked for the defendant's insurance company, the memorandum was subject to challenge as biased.

Remember, however, that a memorandum which is not admissible as evidence in chief as a past recollection recorded may be admissible for another purpose or in another way. Thus, the memorandum may be admissible to prove that a party made the statement,[51] or it may qualify as a business record if the declarant had a duty to report the information.[52]

12.6 COMBINING A REFRESHED RECOLLECTION WITH A PAST RECOLLECTION RECORDED

A new attorney may be forgiven for believing that refreshing a witness's recollection and introducing a witness's past recollection recorded are mutually exclusive alternatives. Fortunately, they are not. The witness from whom the trial attorney is attempting to extract testimony is often recalcitrant. In fact, the witness is often the opposing party. This witness typically will admit to as little refreshed recollection as possible, but the witness will probably feel constrained to admit to some. Moreover, if the witness made the memorandum, the witness will be reluctant to claim that the record was inaccurate when he or she made it.[52.1] Therefore, the opposing party's attorney may combine such refreshed recollection as the attorney can extract from the witness with the witness's past recollection recorded for the remaining facts in the memorandum. The appellate courts have endorsed this approach. For example, in *People v. Briggs,*[53] the Appellate Division, Fourth Department, held:

---

51. Donohue v. Losito, 141 A.D.2d 691 (2d Dep't 1988).

52. Murray v. Donlan, 77 A.D.2d 337 (2d Dep't 1980).

52.1. But see the interesting and contrary example explained in the sample summation reprinted in chapter 9.

53. People v. Briggs, 190 A.D.2d 995 (4th Dep't 1993).

> Defendant contends that the memorandum was inadmissible because the witness recalled some of the events set forth in the memorandum. Although the witness had some general memory of the events, he was unable to remember a number of facts recited in the memorandum and, therefore, the memorandum was properly admitted to augment his memory as past recollection recorded . . . .[54]

The court of appeals reached the same conclusion on similar reasoning in *People v. Taylor*.[55]

> . . . [A] memorandum made of a fact known or an event observed in the past of which the witness lacks sufficient present recollection may be received in evidence as a supplement to the witness's oral testimony . . . .
>
> When such a memorandum is admitted, it is not independent evidence of the facts contained therein, but is supplementary to the testimony of the witness. The witness' testimony and the writing's contents are to be taken together and treated in combination as if the witness had testified to the contents of the writing based on present knowledge . . . . Admission of the memorandum is a matter for the exercise of the court's discretion in determining whether the proponent has made a sufficient showing of the accuracy of the recording and its reliability . . . .
>
> The above requirements are most easily met where the witness testified about a memorandum in which the witness personally recorded information based on his . . . observations.[56]

Example 12-1, found at the end of the chapter, is a transcript of the plaintiff's attorney cross-examining the defendant-doctor. Also included are the two pages of the hospital record to which the attorney referred the witness. Notice how the attorney maneuvers from attempting to refresh the witness's recollection to using the hospital record as past recollection recorded and back again without any explicit

54. *Id.* at 996.
55. People v. Taylor, 80 N.Y.2d 1 (1993).
56. *Id.* at 8, 9.

mention of this change in justification. As professors in law school would ask, should the defendant's attorney have objected to these switches?

EXAMPLE 12-1: REFRESHING RECOLLECTION AND PAST RECOLLECTION RECORDED

75

date?

Q The date was July 18th; is that correct?

A Yes.

MR. : I think it was the 17th.

THE WITNESS: Oh, yes.

MR. : The stress test, I think, was the 17th.

MR. : Here it is. (Handing.)

A The 18th.

Q It would be on the 18th?

A Yes.

Q Do you know what time of day you wrote that note?

A I can't recollect.

Q The note preceding it is dated July 18th, and it's marked 3:00 A.M. or P.M.?

A 3:00 A.M.

Q Would that refresh your recollection as to when you noted your conversation with Mr. ?

A I can't say.

Q Would it be fair to say it was sometime after 3:00 A.M. on--

A Oh, yes.

Q --the 18th?

A Yes.

PLEASE SIGN ALL NOTES

SUBJECTIVE FINDINGS: e.g. patient's complaints
OBJECTIVE FINDINGS: e.g. rash, B.P., dyspnea, lab findings
ASSESSMENT OF PROBLEMS PLAN: a. Diagnostic b. Therapeutic c. Patient's Education

DATE/TIME	
7/17/ 30 4Pm	DDG: F.S. 4pm 321mg/dl, Dr. ____ called Regular Insulin 5u ordered & given. No s/s of hypo/hyperglycemia. Will continue to monitor.
7/17/ pm 7	Ddg: Pt. c/o chills & being shaky. No c/o dizziness, skin ↓warm-↑good turgor. BP 160/78 T.99.5, P.84. B.S. 222mg/dl No S/S of hypo/hyperglycemia. Dr notified & aware. Continue to monitor. No new orders - Will continue to closely monitor.
7/18/ 3AM	Nsg Pt alert & oriented when observed on rounds. Pt c/o of being weak & shaky, & extremely nervous. Dr ____ notified Valium 5 mg ordered & given. c̄ good results. Observed pt sleeping quietly through the night. In no acute distress. Pt for discharge in the A.M.
7/18/	medicine Pt pulled out back. probably 2° to stress test will postpone discharge

(CONTINUE ON REVERSE SIDE IF NECESSARY)

BSH 6-8 86) MADISON BUSINESS FORMS

HOSPITAL
PROGRESS RECORD

76

Q When was the stress test performed on Mr. ?

A I believe it was the 17th. July 19th--oh, no. I am sorry. That is--that's an error. July 17th.

Q You are referring to the cardiology special testing report?

A Yes.

Q Does that indicate what time of day the stress test took place on the 17th?

A No.

Q Did you at any time review the records from the cardiology department regarding the stress test?

MR. : At what time?

Q At any time before testifying today.

A The records available here?

Q I think they are in a separate chart, but they have the cardiac exercise report and they also have adjoining EKG strips.

A No.

Q You didn't review that?

A No.

Q At some time after the stress test was performed on the 17th did you visit the patient?

A Yes.

77

Q This was before the 18th. You can refer to the progress notes.

A The first one I see is the 18th.

Q Referring to a medical attending note, July 17, 1991--

A Yes.

Q --is that your handwriting?

A Yes.

Q Does that refresh your recollection as to when you saw the patient on the 17th?

A As a rule, I make rounds early in the morning.

Q Do you know approximately what time?

A 8:00 to 10:00 in the morning.

Q Can you read that note on the 17th into the record?

A Sure.

(Reading) Patient found to have large bulbar ulcer. Patient with no complaints today, no epigastric distress. Physical exam, alert and oriented times three; vital signs stable, afebrile. HEENT exam, normal; chest, clear; heart, S1 and S2 with no murmur; abdomen, benign; extremity, no cyanosis, clubbing or edema.

DATE/TIME | PLEASE SIGN ALL NOTES

7/17/ medical attending note

Pt fd to have large bulbar ulcer. Pt c̄ no complaints today no epigastric distress.

PE) alert oriented X3
VS stable afebrile
HEENT: wnl
Chest: clear to A+P
heart: $S_1 + S_2$ ∅ M
abd: benign
EXT: no cce.

Imp/ Duodenal ulcer
d2.
Zantac 150 PO BID
consider D/C tomorrow

Pt told that sugars are running high & that he may require insulin therapy. He states that @ home sugars are well controlled & will not go on insulin. Tolinase is at maximum recommended dose.

Using Expert Witnesses to Establish the Direct Case 13

Expert testimony is not universally admissible, but such testimony is necessary in nearly all actions for medical malpractice and in most actions for negligence. This chapter begins with the qualifications of an expert witness, then discusses those cases in which expert testimony is required or permitted, the issues to which expert testimony is relevant, and the necessary basis for the expert's opinion. The discussion will then focus on the testimony of medical experts and, finally, on identifying and using the opposing party's expert.

13.1 THE QUALIFICATIONS OF AN EXPERT WITNESS

The trial court determines as a matter of law whether a witness is qualified to testify as an expert.[1] No rule prescribes the exact manner in which the witness must have acquired the witness's expertise. In general, either study alone or observation and experience without formal study may qualify

1. Meiselman v. Crown Heights Hosp., 285 N.Y. 389, 398, 34 N.E.2d 367, 372 (1941); Annot., *Testing Qualifications of Expert Witness Other Than Handwriting Expert, by Objective Tests or Experiments*, 78 A.L.R.2d 1281 (1961). FED. R. EVID. 706 deals with court-appointed experts.

a witness to be an expert.[2] For example, in *People v. Greene*, the witness's qualification included a short course, but consisted principally of experience conducting wood fracture analysis. He was thus qualified to testify that the broken chair leg found outside the bar came from a broken chair inside the bar.[3]

If a party has asked the court to allow expert testimony, and the court has determined that expert testimony is appropriate, the court must give the party's attorney an opportunity to establish that the witness is an expert in the field.[4] In other words, the court may not rule that the witness is not qualified to testify as an expert on the issue involved simply because the witness is not an expert in the broader field of learning. For example, in *Werner v. Sun Oil Co.*, the Court of Appeals held that just because the witness was not an expert in the larger field of industrial plastics did not mean that he could not have testified about a particular plastic pump with which he was very familiar.[5] Conversely, a witness may testify if his field of expertise is broader than necessary. Thus, in *Edgewater Apartments v. Flynn*, a registered architect testified regarding the source of the water damaging the building.[6] In addition, the term "expert" is not synonymous with author or lecturer; so a physician may testify as an expert even if she has neither published nor lectured.[6.1] In fact, a physician may testify as an expert in a field outside her own specialty.[6.2]

---

2. Meiselman v. Crown Heights Hosp., 285 N.Y. 389, 398, 34 N.E.2d 367, 372 (1941); see Annot., *Chiropractor's Competency as Expert in Personal Injury Action as to Injured Person's Condition, Medical Requirements, Nature and Extent of Injury, and the Like*, 52 A.L.R.2d 1384 (1957); Annot., *Qualification of Nonmedical Psychologist to Testify as to Mental Condition or Competency*, 78 A.L.R.2d 919 (1961).
3. People v. Greene, 153 A.D.2d 439 (2d Dep't 1990). The court affirmed the defendant's convictions for murder and rape.
4. Cruz v. Madison Detective Bureau, Inc., 137 A.D.2d 86, 528 N.Y.S.2d 372 (1st Dep't 1988); Lucilento v. Coleman Catholic High School, 134 A.D.2d 39 (3d Dep't 1987); DeLuca v. Kameros, 130 A.D.2d 705 (2d Dep't 1987).
5. Werner v. Sun Oil Co., 65 N.Y.2d 839, 482 N.E.2d 921, 493 N.Y.S.2d 125 (1985).
6. Edgewater Apartments v. Flynn, 216 A.D.2d 53 (1st Dep't 1995).

6.1. Khatri v. Lazarus, 225 A.D.2d 302 (1st Dep't 1996).

6.2. Julien v. Physician's Hospital, 231 A.D.2d 678 (2d Dep't 1996).

13.2 THE CASES IN WHICH EXPERT TESTIMONY IS REQUIRED OR ALLOWED

Certain causes of action require the testimony of an expert in order to present a prima facie case, such as most actions for medical malpractice.[7] However, an expert's opinion is not always required or even admissible. In fact, expert testimony is admissible in an action for negligence only when the trial court decides that the issue is beyond the ordinary knowledge of the jury.[8] Since the jury is the final arbiter of the facts, expert testimony is admissible only when the jury will need help in analyzing the facts or in reaching a decision based upon the facts.

In *Dougherty v. Milliken,*[9] the Court of Appeals explained the two classes of cases in which expert testimony is admissible. First are those cases in which the jury's conclusions depend upon facts that are not common knowledge but are peculiarly within the knowledge of the individuals who are experts by study or experience. Second are those cases in

---

7. Meiselman v. Crown Heights Hosp., 285 N.Y. 389, 34 N.E.2d 367 (1941); Hunter v. Szabo, 117 A.D.2d 778, 499 N.Y.S.2d 426 (2d Dep't 1986).
8. FED. R. EVID. 702; Chafoulias v. 240 E. 55th St. Tenants Corp., 141 A.D.2d 207, 533 N.Y.S.2d 440 (1st Dep't 1988). In an action to recover damages for the personal injuries the plaintiff sustained when she fell down two stairs in the vestibule of an apartment building, the plaintiff presented evidence sufficient to establish the existence of material issues of act by means of her verified complaint, bill of particulars, depositions, attorney's affidavit, photographs, and supporting documents, and thus, the trial court improvidently granted a summary judgment dismissing her complaint. The plaintiff's theory of optical confusion, i.e., that the defendant was negligent in failing to distinguish the steps in any meaningful fashion and that the failure to warn the plaintiff was exacerbated by the proximity of the steps to the entrance door of the building, is both legally sufficient and adequately supported by the record to preclude a summary judgment. In particular, the issues involving the safety of the vestibule are not so complex as to require the plaintiff to present expert testimony in order to establish her prima facie case, and a reasonable interpretation of her statement that she "never saw the stairs" is consistent with her theory that the steps were so indistinguishable from the platform above and below them and so close to the door that they could not be seen. In any event, the significance of plaintiff's actions is a question for the jury.
9. Dougherty v. Milliken, 163 N.Y. 527, 57 N.E. 757 (1900).

which both knowledge of the facts and the conclusions to be drawn from them depend upon professional or scientific knowledge and skill. In the first class of cases, the expert witness may testify only to those facts, but in the second class, the expert also may state his or her conclusions.[10] In the more recent case of *Selkowitz v. County of Nassau*, the Court of Appeals observed that whether to admit expert testimony is primarily a question in the discretion of the trial court. However, the Court added that such testimony has been found appropriate "to clarify a wide range of issues calling for the application accepted professional standards. This includes the standard of care for contractors . . . , fire fighters . . . , window washers, and mariners . . . to name but a few."[11] Thus, a physician may testify that an injury is permanent,[12] an economist may present his calculations regarding the market value of the services performed by the average housewife,[13] and a retired policeman may describe the proper police procedure when stopping to investigate a stranded automobile on the Long Island Expressway.[14]

Sometimes, however, expert testimony is neither necessary nor admissible. Thus, in *Corelli v. City of New York,*[15] the Appellate Division, First Department, ruled that expert testimony would not be admissible on the issue of the appearance and condition of the flagstones at the site of the accident because a jury is capable of resolving such an issue

10. *Id.*, 163 N.Y. at 533, 57 N.E. at 760.

11. Selkowitz v. County of Nassau, 45 N.Y.2d 97, 101-02, 379 N.E.2d 1140, 1142, 408 N.Y.S.2d 10, 12 (1978). Interestingly, the court held that expert testimony is not admissible concerning the everyday rules of the road and driving but is admissible concerning high-speed chases by the police. On the trial court's direction, *see* Rosen v. Salem Truck Leasing, Inc., 108 A.D.2d 907, 485 N.Y.S.2d 793 (2d Dep't 1985); Rodriguez v. Board of Educ., 104 A.D.2d 978, 480 N.Y.S.2d 901 (2d Dep't 1984).

12. Dufel v. Green, 84 N.Y.2d 795 (1995).

13. DeLong v. County of Erie, 60 N.Y.2d 296 (1983).

14. Anderson v. Miniz, 125 A.D.2d 281 (2d Dep't 1986).

15. Corelli v. City of N.Y., 88 A.D.2d 810, 450 N.Y.S.2d 823 (1st Dep't 1982); *see also* Rosen v. Salem Truck Leasing, Inc., 108 A.D.2d 907, 485 N.Y.S.2d 793 (2d Dep't 1985).

without an expert's help. In another case, it was held that expert testimony may not be necessary to establish that the person who suffers a broken bone experiences pain.[16] The standard of care in an action for legal malpractice. has been held to be an improper subject for expert testimony.[17]

It should be noted that in most of these cases the trial court allowed some testimony by the expert but refused to let him address certain other questions. For example, in *Crawford v. Gallagher,* the court permitted the expert in reconstructing accidents to testify regarding the accident, but refused to let him testify regarding the standard procedures of the state police.[18]

There is, of course, a division of labor between the trial court and the jury. The court decides (1) whether expert testimony is required, (2) which qualifications a witness must possess to testify as an expert, and (3) whether the witness possesses those qualifications. The jury decides the weight to be accorded to the conflicting testimony of the various experts. In fact, the jury may accept or reject the testimony of any expert and is not required to accept either party's expert as authoritative.[19]

---

16. Carver v. Medical Soc'y, 334 S.E.2d 125 (S.C. 1985).
17. Entelisano Agency v. Felt, 135 A.D.2d 1096 (4th Dep't 1987).
18. Crawford v. Gallagher, 199 A.D.2d 235 (2d Dep't 1993).
19. Randolph v. City of N.Y., 69 N.Y.2d 844, 507 N.E.2d 298, 514 N.Y.S.2d 705 (1987); Mechanick v. Conradi, 139 A.D.2d 857, 527 N.Y.S.2d 586 (3d Dep't 1988); Halvorsen v. Ford Motor Co., 132 A.D.2d 57, 522 N.Y.S.2d 272 (3d Dep't 1987); Ledogar v. Giordano, 122 A.D.2d 834, 505 N.Y.S.2d 899 (3d Dep't 1986); Starobin v. Hudson Transit Lines, 112 A.D.2d 987, 493 N.Y.S.2d 12 (2d Dep't 1985); Hill v. Bresnick, 112 A.D.2d 919, 492 N.Y.S.2d 435 (2d Dep't 1985); Baumfield v. State, 107 A.D.2d 27, 84 N.Y.S.2d 348 (3d Dep't 1985); O'Connell v. Albany Medical Center Hosp., 101 A.D.2d 637, 475 N.Y.S.2d 543 (3d Dep't 1984); Desnoes v. State, 100 A.D.2d 712, 474 N.Y.S.2d 602 (3d Dep't 1984) (the jury may reject one party's expert testimony even if the other party has not rebutted it with expert testimony); Sternemann v. Langs, 93 A.D.2d 819, 460 N.Y.S.2d 614 (2d Dep't 1983). In Hall v. Yonkers Professional Hosp., 115 A.D.2d 637, 496 N.Y.S.2d 297 (2d Dep't 1985), the appellate court held that an out-of-state doctor is not precluded from being an expert. The fact that the doctor was licensed in a different state affected only the weight of his testimony.

13.3 THE ISSUES ON WHICH EXPERT TESTIMONY IS RELEVANT

The trial court sometimes allows an expert to testify to an ultimate question of fact, e.g., the negligence of the defendant. Nevertheless, the trial court decides in each case whether it will restrict the expert to explaining the facts that are beyond the jury's knowledge or if it will permit the expert to analyze the facts and deliver an opinion on an ultimate issue of fact.[20]

13.3.1 Representative Issues

The courts have found expert testimony to be relevant and admissible on the following issues of fact, which are arranged by subject.

13.3.1.1 Motor Vehicles

- Whether the police handled a high speed chase properly.[21]

---

20. *Compare* Dougherty v. Milliken, 163 N.Y. 527, 57 N.E. 757 (1900) (the court would only allow the expert to explain the intricacies of construction) *with* Jenks v. Thompson, 179 N.Y. 20, 71 N.E. 266 (1994) (the court ruled that the expert should have been allowed to give his opinion on the negligence of the defendant); *see* FED. R. EVID. 704; Annot., *Necessity of Expert Testimony to Show Causal Connection Between Medical Treatment Necessitated by Injury for Which Defendant is Liable and Allegedly Harmful Effects of Such Treatment*, 27 A.L.R.2d 1263 (1952); *see also* Stauch v. Hirschman, 40 A.D.2d 711, 336 N.Y.S.2d 678 (2d Dep't 1972)(it was improper for an expert to testify that engaging in basketball practice was dangerous because that was the ultimate issue for the jury). In Weiss v. Alexander's Rent-a-Car, Inc., 40 A.D.2d 879, 337 N.Y.S.2d 930 (2d Dep't 1972), the plaintiff, a lessor of a car, testified that the wheel had pulled to the left, that the brakes had failed, and that the car had hit a tree. Although the car was destroyed and the expert never examined it, it was held error not to permit the expert to testify when he stated that he was familiar with the car model, etc., because there was a reasonable degree of scientific certainty about what had caused the car to behave as the plaintiff described.
21. Selkowitz v. County of Nassau, 45 N.Y.2d 97, 379 N.E.2d 1140, 408 N.Y.S.2d 10 (1978).

- Whether automobile tires could have made a sixty-foot-long skid mark unless the automobile had been exceeding the speed limit.[22]
- Whether experiments conducted after the accident could establish what someone could have seen in the roadway at the distance of 466 feet from the spot of the accident.[23] (The appellate courts have ruled that the trial court errs when it excludes testimony about an experiment designed to show the range of vision of a passenger on a bus in order to show that the passenger could not have seen the condition of the roadway from his seat.[24])
- A state trooper who saw the defendant speeding shortly before the accident, but who lost sight of the car before it hit the plaintiff, may testify to the speed of the car before it hit the plaintiff.[25]

13.3.1.2 "Slip and Fall" Cases

- Whether the existence of a change in the level between a sidewalk and an automobile parking area was unsafe unless the difference between the levels was made conspicuous.[26]
- Whether a step had been constructed in a manner that conformed to safe, standard, and proper practice.[27] (The expert had not inspected the step until two and one-half years after

22. Saladow v. Keystone Transp. Co., 241 A.D. 161, 271 N.Y.S.293 (1st Dep't 1934); Annot., *Expert and Opinion Evidence as to Tire Marks or Marks on or Near Highway*, 23 A.L.R. 2d 131-41, 153 (1952); Annot., *Opinion Evidence as to Speed of Motor Vehicle Based on Skid Marks and Other Facts*, 29 A.L.R.3d 248 (1970).
23. Havecker v. Weiss, 237 A.D. 856, 261 N.Y.S. 494 (2d Dep't 1932).
24. Thomas v. Central Greyhound Lines, Inc., 6 A.D.2d 649, 180 N.Y.S.2d 461 (1st Dep't 1958), *new trial ordered*, 8 A.D.2d 606 (1959); *see also* Washington v. Long Island R.R., 13 A.D.2d 170, 214 N.Y.S.2d 115 (2d Dep't 1961); Annot., 78 A.L.R. 2d 152 (1961).
25. Mechanick v. Conradi, 139 A.D.2d 857, 527 N.Y.S.2d 586 (3d Dep't 1988).
26. Decker v. R.H. Macy & Co., 3 A.D.2d 756, 160 N.Y.S.2d 826 (2d Dep't 1957); Annot., *Safety of Condition, Place, or Appliance as Proper Subject of Expert or Opinion Evidence in Tort Actions*, 62 A.L.R.2d 1246 (1958).
27. Pine v. Moawood, 1 A.D.2d 903, 149 N.Y.S.2d 612 (2d Dep't 1956).

the accident, but the condition of the step had not changed substantially in the meantime.)

- Whether the manner of laying a throw rug in the hallway was contrary to the good and established practice known to landlords.[28]
- That a terrazzo floor becomes slippery when wet, and whether rubber mats are usually used to overcome that condition.[29]

13.3.1.3 Other Construction

- Whether a furnace pit had been constructed properly.[30]
- Whether there were defects in the construction of a waterslide that made it dangerous to use.[31]

13.3.1.4 Medical Malpractice

- Generally, whether a defendant departed from or complied with the standards of good and accepted medical practice.
- Whether the custom and usage in hospitals was to avoid placing a patient near an open window after surgery if the patient had been extremely nervous when admitted and was to receive drugs during his postoperative recovery.[32]
- If the plaintiff sustained an injury after the administration of a needle to draw blood, then expert testimony is admissible to establish that the defendant's employees drew the blood negligently.[33]

---

28. Ordway v. Hillirad, 266 A.D. 1056, 44 N.Y.S.2d 819 (4th Dep't 1943).
29. Pignatelli v. Gimbel Bros., 285 A.D. 625, 140 N.Y.S.2d 23 (1st Dep't), *aff'd*, 309 N.Y. 901, 131 N.E.2d 578 (1955).
30. Behsmann v. Waldo, 36 Misc. 863, 74 N.Y.S.929 (City Ct. 1901), *aff'd*, 38 Misc. 820, 78 N.Y.S. 1108 (County Ct. 1902).
31. Kenny v. Douglas Manor Ass'n, 252 A.D. 780, 299 N.Y.S. 384 (2d Dep't 1937); Annot., *Admissibility of Evidence of Absence of Other Accidents or Injuries from Customary Practice or Method Asserted to be Negligent*, 42 A.L.R.2d 1055 (1955).
32. Liebrecht v. Gotham Sanitarium, Inc., 284 A.D. 781, 134 N.Y.S.2d 762 (1st Dep't 1954).
33. Muniz v. American Red Cross, 141 A.D.2d 386, 529 N.Y.S.2d 486 (1st Dep't 1988).

13.3.1.5 Other Personal Injuries

- The trial court should permit an expert familiar with cartwheeling to testify if the plaintiff has alleged that the defendant failed to supervise the students' cartwheeling thereby allowing the plaintiff to be injured.[34]
- If the plaintiff alleged that he was injured by the chemicals used by the defendant, only a physician may testify as an expert to the causal connection between the defendant's chemicals and the plaintiff's injuries.[35]
- Based upon his examination of the plaintiff and his review of the medical records, a physician may testify that the plaintiff sustained a concussion, a brain injury, and a blackout as a result of the accident.[36]
- Expert testimony is permitted regarding the costs and value of a homemaker's services in a case involving her injury or death.[37]

13.3.1.6 Miscellany

- Whether the method used to move a heavy safe was good practice.[38]
- In a case against an insurance company for bad faith in refusing to settle a case against its assured, an experienced trial attorney may testify regarding the probability of success, the award, trial strategy, and the potential for settlement.[39] (However, the witness may do so only in a general way and he may not answer hypothetical questions about the particular case in dispute.[40])

---

34. Franck v. Minisink Valley School Dist., 136 A.D.2d 588, 523 N.Y.S.2d 573 (2d Dep't 1988).
35. Kracker v. Spartan Chem. Co., N.Y.L.J., Oct. 10, 1989 (Sup. Ct. Nassau 1989).
36. Daliendo v. Johnson, 147 A.D.2d 312, 543 N.Y.S.2d 987 (2d Dep't 1989).
37. Merced v. City of N.Y., 142 Misc. 2d 442, 534 N.Y.S.2d 60 (Sup. Ct. Bronx 1987), *rev'd on other grounds*, 75 N.Y.2d 798 (1990).
38. Wolfe v. Mosler Safe Co., 139 A.D. 848, 124 N.Y.S. 541 (4th Dep't 1910).
39. Kulak v. Nationwide Ins. Co., 47 A.D.2d 418, 366 N.Y.S.2d 927 (4th Dep't 1975).
40. *Id.*, rev'd for admitting hypothetical questions about the particular case, 40 N.Y.2d 140 (1976).

13.3.2 Custom and Usage

An expert may testify to the custom and usage within a given field when the custom and usage are relevant.[41] The expert also may testify regarding the proper standard of care as defined by standard practice. For example, in a case in which an automobile had run into the wall dividing the roadway, the Court of Appeals held that the trial court properly admitted evidence that the defendant had not maintained the wall in accordance with the standard practice applicable to warning signs and reflectors.[42] Similarly, the Appellate Division, First Department, found that the trial court had erred in not permitting the plaintiff's expert to testify to the custom and usage applicable to wet terrazzo floors.[43] Of course, the attorney presenting the expert must lay a foundation. Thus, before the expert testifies that the ramp violated custom and usage,[44] there must be a relevant custom or usage, the expert must know it, and the expert must be able to state it.

The relevant custom and usage may be the custom and usage of one of the parties. For example, in *Cappel v. Board of Education, Union Free School District No. 4,*[45] the plaintiff,

41. Duffy v. Owen A. Mandeville, Inc., 5 N.Y.2d 730, 152 N.E.2d 669, 177 N.Y.S.2d 713 (1958), *rev'd on other grounds*, 5 N.Y.2d 730 (1958); *see also* Clark v. Iceland S.S. Co., 6 A.D.2d 544, 179 N.Y.S.2d 708 (1st Dep't 1958) for an excellent review of this subject.

42. Kovalsky v. City of Watervliet, 5 A.D.2d 324, 171 N.Y.S.2d 887 (3d Dep't 1958). In Isserles v. Gil-Ed Corp., 14 A.D.2d 857, 221 N.Y.S.2d 129 (1st Dep't 1961), involving a ski towrope accident, the appellate court held that it had been an error to exclude the testimony of the plaintiff's expert witness "concerning the custom and practice of other ski-tow operators in guarding against accidents of this kind." In Meyer v. West End Equities, Inc., 12 N.Y.2d 698, 185 N.E.2d 915, 233 N.Y.S.2d 479 (1962), the Court of Appeals held that it had been an error to exclude an expert witness's testimony that a thirty-degree ramp was an improper pitch according to custom and usage.

43. Berman v. H.J. Enters, 13 A.D.2d 199, 214 N.Y.S.2d 945 (1st Dep't 1961).

44. Meyer v. West End Equities, Inc., 13 A.D.2d 938 (1st Dep't 1961).

45. Capppel v. Board of Educ., Union Free School Dist. No. 4, 70 A.D.2d 848, 337 N.Y.S.2d 836 (2d Dep't 1972).

age five, was injured on the school's playing field by the goal cage for field hockey. The cage had not been anchored, although children could reasonably be expected to climb it and play about it. Consequently, the Appellate Division, Second Department, held that the trial court had erred in dismissing the complaint: "It was error to bar proof of defendant's prior self-imposed custom and practice with respect to precautions taken in securing the field hockey goal cage when not in use."

13.3.3 Limitations

The attorney should remember that experts may not testify on all issues. For example, a trial court has held that a handwriting expert may not testify to the state of mind of the writer.[46] The Court of Appeals has made it clear that one expert may not testify that another expert is not credible.[47] Likewise an expert may not testify that identifications by eyewitnesses are unreliable.[48]

The expert should address the relevant issue then let the attorneys argue and the jury decide. Thus, when the defendant has presented an expert on auto safety to testify that if the plaintiff had used his seat belt, he would not have sustained the injuries he suffered, the plaintiff's attorney properly cross-examined the expert to show that if the plaintiff had worn his seat belt, then he might have sustained other injuries. It was also proper for the plaintiff's attorney to make the same argument on summation.[49]

---

46. Cameron v. Knapp, N.Y.L.J., Oct. 29, 1987 (Sup. Ct. N.Y. 1987).
47. People v. Williams, 6 N.Y.2d 18, 159 N.E.2d 549, 187 N.Y.S.2d 750 (1959).
48. People v. Greene, 223 A.D.2d 474, 637 N.Y.S.2d 79 (1st Dep't 1996), and People v. Kelley, 220 A.D.2d 456, 631 N.Y.S.2d 926 (2d Dep't 1995).
49. Baker v. Hlavachek, 51 A.D.2d 739, 379 N.Y.S.2d 481 (2d Dep't 1976).

13.4 THE BASIS OF THE EXPERT'S OPINION

13.4.1 The General Rule

Once the trial court has decided to allow a witness to testify as an expert, upon what can the expert base this opinion? Clearly, the expert may use all of the facts that are in evidence and within the expert's knowledge and expertise, such as the testimony of other witnesses, documents, photographs, medical records, and x-rays. In *Hambsch v. New York City Transit Authority*, the Court of Appeals held that the trial court had erred by allowing a physician to testify as an expert on the basis of x-rays that had not been admitted into evidence.[50] In another case, the Court of Appeals ruled that the trial court had erred by allowing a physician to testify based upon a conversation that the witness had had with a radiologist several days before the trial.[51] The Appellate Division, First Department, followed that precedent in *Cornier v. Spagna*, in which the court ruled that unless the radiologist's testimony was in evidence, it was improper to allow the expert to base his testimony partially on the radiologist's opinion[52]; and the Appellate Division, Second Department, ruled in *Cleary v. City of New York* that it was improper to allow an expert to base his testimony on the ambulance report unless that report was in evidence.[52.1] An

---

50. Hambsch v. New York City Transit Auth., 63 N.Y.2d 723, 725, 469 N.E.2d 516, 518, 480 N.Y.S.2d 195, 197 (1985); Hugelmaier v. Sweden, 144 A.D.2d 934, 534 N.Y.S.2d 253 (4th Dep't 1988); Perla v. Daily News, 123 A.D.2d 349, 506 N.Y.S.2d 361 (2d Dep't 1986). However, a physician's affidavit based upon his reading of the medical records would be sufficient to defeat a motion for summary judgment. Nandy v. Albany Medical Center Hospital, 155 A.D.2d 833 (3d Dep't 1989).

51. *See also* Cassano v. Hagstrom, 5 N.Y.2d 643, 159 N.E.2d 348, 187 N.Y.S.2d 1 (1959); O'Shea v. Sarro, 106 A.D.2d 435, 482 N.Y.S.2d 529 (2d Dep't 1984); Borden v. Brady, 92 A.D.2d 983, 461 N.Y.S.2d 497 (3d Dep't 1983); Chang Chiu v. Garcia, 75 A.D.2d 594, 426 N.Y.S.23 803 (2d Dep't 1980); People v. Flynn, 129 Misc. 2d 176, 492 N.Y.S.2d 882 (Sup. Ct. 1985), and Aetna Casualty & Surety Co. v. Barile, 86 A.D.2d 362 (1st Dep't 1982).

52. *See* Cornier v. Spagna, 101 A.D.2d 140, 475 N.Y.S.2d 7 (1st Dep't 1984).

52.1. Cleary v. City of New York, 234 A.D.2d 411 (2d Dep't 1996).

expert witness who has examined the plaintiff's injuries may testify, of course, to those facts and base his or her opinion on that examination.

Nevertheless, in *Hambsch*, the Court of Appeals had recognized that it is proper, in limited circumstances, for an expert witness to base his opinion on matters that are not in evidence:

> "It is settled and unquestioned law that opinion evidence must be based on facts in the record or personally known to the witness." . . . In *People v. Sugden*, 35 N.Y.2d 453, 363 N.Y.S.2d 923, 323 N.E.2d 169, we recognized two limited exceptions to this rule and held that an expert may rely on out-of-court material if "it is of a kind accepted in the profession as reliable in forming a professional opinion" or if it "comes from a witness subject to full cross-examination on the trial" (*id.*, at pp. 460, 461, 363 N.Y.S.2d 923, 323 N.E.2d 169).
>
> In order to qualify for the "professional reliability" exception, there must be evidence establishing the reliability of the out-of-court material . . . .[53]

In other words, the Court of Appeals seemed to say that the facts that are not in evidence must come from the expert's own observation or from a witness who will testify.

The Appellate Division, Second Department, applied its understanding of these exceptions in three subsequent cases that allowed an expert to base the expert's opinion on matters not yet in evidence. In the first case, *Holshek v. Stokes*, in 1986,[54] the Court wrote,

> Additionally, the doctor's testimony, that the plaintiff had suffered a torn meniscus was properly admitted, although based in part on an x-ray and report not in evidence. An expert may rely upon material not in evidence, if it is of a kind accepted in the profession as reliable in forming a professional opinion. Here, the material relied upon met this test. Additionally, while not in evidence, the defendant had a copy of both the x-

53. Hambsch v. New York City Transit Auth., 63 N.Y.2d at 723, 725-26, 469 N.E.2d at 516, 518; 480 N.Y.S.2d 195, 197 (1984).

54. Holshek v. Stokes, 122 A.D.2d 777, 505 N.Y.S.2d 664 (2d Dep't 1986).

ray and the report; accordingly, he was not foreclosed from effective cross-examination.

The second case was *Flamio v. State of New York,*[55] where the appellate court ruled, in 1987, that an expert witness may base his or her opinion on the out-of-court but written statement of a witness who does testify at the trial. Finally, in 1988, in *Karayianakis v. L&E Grommery, Inc.*,[56] the court found that a medical expert's reliance on x-rays that were not in evidence was an error but not a prejudicial or reversible one.

Since so many of the important cases involve reliance on x-rays, we should explain that New York treats an x-ray as a writing. Therefore, the best evidence rule requires the production of the x-ray. However, if a party can explain why the x-ray is unavailable, the party may introduce secondary evidence of its contents, such as a contemporaneously written report by the treating physician or the testimony of someone else who examined the x-ray.[57]

13.4.2 Speculation and Certainty

The opinion of an expert is admissible even if it relates to an ultimate question of fact,[58] but the expert may not base his or her opinion on speculation.[59] Unfortunately, the courts struggle to explain this rule beyond saying that the facts must support the expert's opinion. Thus, the Appellate Divi-

55. Flamio v. State, 132 A.D.2d 594, 517 N.Y.S.2d 756 (2d Dep't 1987).
56. Karayianakis v. L&E Grommery, Inc., 141 A.D.2d 610, 529 N.Y.S.2d 358 (2d Dep't 1988).
57. Schozer v. William Penn Life Insurance Co. of New York, 84 N.Y.2d 639 (1994).
58. People v. Cronin, 60 N.Y.2d 430, 458 N.E.2d 351, 470 N.Y.S.2d 110 (1983); cf. Colon v. Bridge Plaza Rental Corp., 46 A.D.2d 13, 360 N.Y.S.2d 896 (1st Dep't 1974); Lopez v. Yannotti, 24 A.D.2d 758, 263 N.Y.S.2d 532 (2d Dep't 1965).
59. DeFrancisci v. Baron, 97 A.D.2d 453, 467 N.Y.S.2d 419 (2d Dep't 1983); Natasi v. State, 55 A.D.2d 724, 389 N.Y.S.2d 175 (3d Dep't 1976); Kinch v. Adams, 46 A.D.2d 467, 363 N.Y.S.2d 119 (3d Dep't), *aff'd*, 38 N.Y.2d 792, 345 N.E.2d 341, 381 N.Y.S.2d 869 (1975).

sion, First Department, wrote in *Matter of Aetna Casualty & Surety Co. v. Barile*:

> It is settled and unquestioned law that opinion evidence must be based on facts in the record or personally known to the witness . . . . While it is true that in many cases the cause or effect of a physical injury can be proved in no other way than by the opinions of experts specially qualified by experience and study, it is equally true that such opinions, to be of any value, must be based upon facts in evidence, and either known to the witness or assumed to be true (*Marx v. Ontario Beach Hotel & Amusement Company,* 211 N.Y. 33, 39; . . .). that is not to say that an expert may not offer an opinion unless he has personally viewed the items on which he bases that opinion. It is only to say that he may not speculate, he may not guess. His opinion must be supported either by acts disclosed by the evidence or by facts known to him personally . . . . Indeed, his testimony may be based on photographs taken immediately after the event . . . . What is essential is that the facts upon which the opinion is based be established or "fairly inferable" from the evidence. . . .[60]

In addition to the rule that the expert may not speculate, there is the rule that the expert must predicate his or her opinion upon a reasonable degree of certainty, another ambiguity. The expert must be certain within the confines of the expert's knowledge and the limitations of the question.[61] In other words, when the expert is asked for an opinion, the expert may not *guess* or *think* that the defendant did something improperly. However, the expert may testify on the basis of probability; for example, an expert in reconstructing accidents may testify to the probable point of impact on the street,[62] and a physician need not use the formula "a reasonable degree of medical certainty."[62.1]

---

60. Aetna Casualty & Sur. Co. v. Barile, 86 A.D.2d 362, 364-65, 450 N.Y.S.2d 10, 12 (1st Dep't 1982). *See also* Sawyer v. Dreis & Krump Manufacturing, 67 N.Y.2d 328 (1986).

61. O'Neill v. Cross County Hosp., 61 A.D.2d 1008, 402 N.Y.S.2d 633 (2d Dep't 1978); Schrantz v. Luancing, 527 A.2d 967 (N.J. 1986).

62. People v. Spurling, 199 A.D.2d 624 (3d Dep't 1993). *See also* Leahy v. Allen, 221 A.D.2d 88 (3d Dep't 1996).

62.1. Rodriguez v. New York City Housing Authority, 238 A.D.2d 125 (1st Dep't 1997).

13.4.3 Hypothetical Questions

The party offering the testimony of an expert witness need not employ hypothetical questions to elicit that testimony.[63] C.P.L.R. rule 4515 now provides:

> Unless the court orders otherwise, questions calling for the opinion of an expert witness need not be hypothetical in form, and the witness may state his opinion and reasons without first specifying the data upon which it is based. Upon cross-examination, he may be required to specify the data and other criteria supporting the opinion.[64]

The hypothetical question is still permissible and the legislature did not intend C.P.L.R. rule 4515 to suggest otherwise.[65] If, however, the attorney does ask the expert a hypothetical question, then the question should include all the pertinent facts and should not omit any that, if included, would alter the witness's opinion. Thus, the Court of Appeals has held that it was improper for the plaintiff's attorney to ask a medical expert to assume that the decedent had been in good health at the time of the accident when the plaintiff's own evidence had shown that the decedent had been suffering from several ailments.[66] At the same time, a hypothetical question is not improper merely because it as-

---

63. Annot., *Hypothetical Questions: Modern Status of the Rule Regarding Use of Hypothetical Questions in Eliciting Opinion of Expert Witness*, 56 A.L.R.3d 300 (1974).

64. C.P.L.R. rule 4515, FED. R. EVID. 705, 703; *see* Tarlowe v. Metropolitan Ski Slopes, 28 N.Y.2d 410, 414, 271 N.E.2d 515, 518, 322 N.Y.S.2d 665, 668 (1971), in which the court of appeals said:

    > An expert need not give technical reasons or bases for his opinion on direct examination. The matter may be left for development in cross-examination. If the facts in the hypothetical question are fairly inferable from the evidence, the expert may state his opinion without further foundation. The extent to which he elaborates or fails to elaborate on the technical basis supporting the opinion affects only the weight of the expert testimony.

65. Buck Constr. Corp. v. 200 Genessee St., 109 A.D.2d 1056, 487 N.Y.S.2d 198 (4th Dep't 1985).

66. Middleton v. Whitridge, 213 N.Y. 499, 515, 108 N.E.2d 192, 198 (1915).

sumes only part of the evidence: the question may assume any state of facts for which there is sustaining evidence.[67] If there is other evidence, then the attorney for the opposing party may develop the significance of that evidence during the attorney's cross-examination of the expert.[68] In fact, the trial court has the discretion to permit a party to supply a defect in the evidence in order to enable the expert to answer the hypothetical question,[69] but the question may not assume facts that are not in evidence at all and that cannot be supplied to remedy the defect.[70] Finally, that some of the evidence on which the question relies is permissible hearsay may affect the weight to be given the expert's answer, but not the admissibility of the answer.[71]

13.5 THE USE OF MEDICAL EXPERTS AS WITNESSES

The discussion of the use of the medical expert is divided into two parts. The first is the medical expert who testifies regarding liability in an action for medical malpractice. The second part is the medical expert who testifies regarding the plaintiff's injuries in an action for negligence.

---

67. Cole v. Fall Brook Coal Co., 159 N.Y. 59, 53 N.E. 670 (1899). The courts have held that the expert testimony of a psychiatrist is admissible even when based in part on testimony that is not in evidence. People v. DiPiazza, 24 N.Y.2d 342, 248 N.E.2d 412, 300 N.Y.S.2d 545 (1969). *See also* People v. Sugden, 35 N.Y.2d 453, 323 N.E.2d 169, 363 N.Y.S.2d 923 (1974); People v. Stone, 35 N.Y.2d 69, 315 N.E.2d 787, 358 N.Y.S.2d 727 (1974).
68. Stearns v. Field, 90 N.Y. 640 (1882).
69. Jarvis v. Metropolitan St. Ry., 65 A.D. 490, 72 N.Y.S. 829 (2d Dep't 1901).
70. O'Shea v. Sarro, 106 A.D.2d 435, 482 N.Y.S.2d 529 (2d Dep't 1984).
71. People v. Rudd, 196 A.D.2d 666 (2d Dep't 1993).

13.5.1 Liability in an Action for Medical Malpractice[72]

In most actions for medical malpractice, the plaintiff must present the testimony of a medical expert to establish that the defendant doctor departed from the accepted standards of medical practice and that the doctor's malpractice was the proximate cause of the plaintiff's injuries.[73] Moreover, by statute, the plaintiff must present expert testimony on the issue of the plaintiff's lack of informed consent.[74]

The attorney should be aware, however, that not all actions for medical malpractice require expert testimony to establish a prima facie case. In the case of *Lawrence v. Bluestone,*[75] the plaintiff hemorrhaged and had to be hospitalized after his dentist extracted two teeth. At the trial, the plaintiff failed to present expert testimony that the defendant had departed from the applicable standard of care so the defendant moved for a judgment in his favor. The trial court disagreed.

> [W]hen common sense and ordinary experience suggest that the condition is incompatible with skillful or successful treatment opinion evidence is not necessary until defendant has presented opinion evidence to rebut the common sense interference which the jury may draw.
>
> Common sense and ordinary experience do indeed suggest that a dentist performing extractions properly would examine both the extracted teeth and the sockets for chips or fragments.

---

72. For a complete discussion of the expert witness in the medical malpractice action, *see* C. KRAMER & D. KRAMER, MEDICAL MALPRACTICE (4th ed. 1983).
73. Fiore v. Galang, 64 N.Y.2d 999, 478 N.E.2d 188, 489 N.Y.S.2d 47 (1985); Meiselman v. Crown Heights Hosp., 285 N.Y. 389, 34 N.E.2d 367 (1941). The appellate court affirmed a summary judgment for the defendant because the affidavit from the plaintiff's expert did not even assert that the defendant's departure was the proximate cause of the plaintiff's injury. Amsler v. Verrilli, 119 A.D.2d 786 (2d Dep't 1986).
74. C.P.L.R. § 4401-a.
75. Lawrence v. Bluestone, N.Y.L.J., Feb. 15, 1978 (Sup. Ct. 1978).

> If the examination is carefully done, it should lead to discoveries which would have enabled defendant in the present case to forestall plaintiff's hemorrhaging. So much, at least, the jury could properly infer absent any opinion evidence which defendant might have presented to rebut the inference . . . .

The court's opinion collected examples of cases in which the appellate courts have allowed a plaintiff to rely on common sense without expert testimony, to wit: a psychiatrist who beat his patient in the course of treatment,[76] a doctor who failed to disclose that he had lost a broken surgical needle in the plaintiff's rectal tissue,[77] a hospital that left a suicidal patient near an open window,[78] a dentist who extracted the wrong tooth,[79] and a psychiatrist who had sexual intercourse with a patient.[80] The court in *Lawrence* also observed, "the rule of res ipsa loquitur may be applied to the same effect," and gave three more examples: a nerve condition apparently resulting from trauma from an anesthetic applied during an operation on an area unrelated to the injury,[81] a twenty-three-month-old child with an infection who was anesthetized for surgery but died before the opera-

---

76. Hammer v. Rosen, 7 N.Y.2d 376, 165 N.E.2d 750, 198 N.Y.S.2d 65 (1960).
77. Benson v. Dean, 232 N.Y. 52, 133 N.E. 125 (1921). However, the plaintiff needed to present expert testimony when he claimed that the defendant's negligent use of a needle to draw blood injured the plaintiff's arm. Pipers v. Rosenow, 39 A.D.2d 240 (2d Dep't 1972).
78. Meiselman v. Crown Heights Hosp., 285 N.Y. 389, 34 N.E.2d 367 (1941); Wright v. State, 31 A.D.2d 421, 300 N.Y.S.2d 153 (4th Dep't 1969).
79. Griffin v. Norman, 192 N.Y.S. 322 (App. Term, 1st Dep't 1922).
80. Roy v. Hartogs, 85 Misc. 2d 891, 381 N.Y.S.2d 587 (App. Term, 1st Dep't 1976). An attorney does not commit an ethical violation, ipso facto, by having sexual intercourse with a client, and the bald accusation of sexual intercourse by the opposing party is insufficient to raise the question. Edwards v. Edwards, 165 A.D.2d 362 (1st Dep't 1991). Of course, there are now rules forbidding an attorney to have intercourse with a client whom he is representing in a matrimonial matter, but there is no cause of action, i.e., no violation of the rules, if the intercourse did not occur until after the representation was concluded. Sanders v. Rosen, 159 Misc. 2d 563 (Sup. Ct. N.Y. 1993).
81. Mattlick v. Long Island Jewish Hosp., 25 A.D.2d 538, 267 N.Y.S.2d 631 (2d Dep't 1966).

tion,[82] and a dentist who broke the patient's jaw while extracting a tooth.[83]

13.5.1.2 Who Is an Expert

For a witness to testify as an expert, the only real requirement is that the witness be an expert in the view of the court. Hence, courts have allowed nurses[84] and pharmacologists[85] to testify as experts because those witnesses' training had made them experts in the fields of medicine involved. There is certainly no requirement that the witness be a physician in the same field of medicine as the defendant.[86] Moreover, the expert's testimony is admissible even if the expert's views are neither popular nor in accord with the medical community's, since the jury may find that the standard of care in the medical community is wrong.[87] The medical expert need not be licensed in New York for New York does not recognize a local standard of care; rather,

82. Sawyer v. Jewish Chronic Disease Hosp., 234 N.Y.S.2d 372 (Sup. Ct. Kings 1962).
83. Zettler v. Reich, 256 A.D. 631, 11 N.Y.S.2d 85 (1st Dep't 1939), *aff'd* 281 N.Y. 729 (1939).
84. Johnson v. Hermann Hosp., 659 S.W.2d 124 (Tex. App. 1983). In Keane v. Sloan Kettering Hosp., 96 A.D.2d 505, 464 N.Y.S.2d 548 (2d Dep't 1983), the appellate court held that a doctor can testify as an expert even if the doctor was in medical school when the malpractice occurred. What counts is his or her knowledge of medical care when the doctor testifies.
85. Karasik v. Bird, 98 A.D.2d 359, 470 N.Y.S.2d 605 (1st Dep't 1984); *cf.* McDonnell v. County of Nassau, 129 Misc. 2d 228, 492 N.Y.S.2d 699 (Sup. Ct. 1985) (the court ruled that a psychologist who had never worked in a general hospital could not testify as an expert against a hospital and a psychiatrist); Cummnings v. Fondak, 122 Misc. 2d 913, 474 N.Y.S.2d 356 (1st Dep't 1983).
86. However, no statutory basis exists for allowing a certified psychologist to render a medical diagnosis sufficient to establish a serious injury under the no fault auto insurance law. Hohlakes v. Rizzo Associates, 164 Misc. 2d 374 (Sup. Ct. Kings 1995). *See* Annot., *Competency of Physician or Surgeon of School of Practice Other Than That to Which Defendant Belongs to Testify in Malpractice Case*, 85 A.L.R.2d 1022 (1962).
87. Douglas v. Lombardino, 693 P.2d 1138 (Kan. 1985). In Riley v. Wieman, 137 A.D.2d 309, 528 N.Y.S.2d 925 (3d Dep't 1988), the appellate court ruled that there is no need to apply the locality rule to the expert's testimony because the defendant was board-certified and the locality for board certification is national.

New York recognizes only a uniform, nationwide standard of medical care.[88]

Finally, when testifying in an action for personal injury, the expert need not use the words, "with a reasonable degree of medical certainty."[89] As a matter of fact, there are no magical words that the expert must use. Instead, the trial court simply must be satisfied that the witness's testimony is not speculative or guesswork and the expert must state his or her opinion with conviction and belief.

13.5.1.3 The Defendant as the Plaintiff's Expert

In an action for medical malpractice, the plaintiff may call the defendant doctor to the stand and examine the defendant doctor to establish the plaintiff's direct case, thereby forcing the defendant doctor to become one of the plaintiff's experts. The court of appeals provided the classic rationale for this rule in the seminal case of *McDermott v. Manhattan Eye, Ear & Throat Hospital*:

> It is quite clear that no such burden or unfairness is occasioned by the practice of compelling a doctor, who is actually a defendant in the malpractice action, to testify as an expert. It is, therefore, not inconsistent to permit the plaintiff to question the defendant as an expert even though we would not accord him the same right with respect to an unwilling witness who is in no way connected with the action. The very inability of a plaintiff in a malpractice action to compel the attendance and testimony of a "disinterested" medical witness underscores the need and importance of allowing such a plaintiff the opportunity of questioning his adversary as an expert.

---

88. Hirschberg v. State, 91 Misc. 2d 590, 398 N.Y.S.2d 470 (Ct. Cl. 1977). *But see* Prooth v. Wallsh, 105 Misc. 2d 653 (Sup. Ct. N.Y. 1980).
89. Miller v. National Cabinet, 8 N.Y.2d 277, 168 N.E.2d 811, 204 N.Y.S.2d 129 (1960); Ward v. Kovacs, 55 A.D.2d 391, 390 N.Y.S.2d 931 (2d Dep't 1977), and Mattot v. Ward, 48 N.Y.2d 455 (1979).

In short, a plaintiff in a malpractice action is entitled to call the defendant doctor to the stand and question the defendant doctor both as to his or her factual knowledge of the case (i.e., as to the defendant's examination, diagnosis, treatment, and the like) and as an expert for the purpose of establishing the generally accepted medical practice in the community. While it may be the height of optimism to expect that such a plaintiff will gain anything by being able to call and question (as an expert) the very doctor the plaintiff is suing, the decision whether or not to do so is one which rests with the plaintiff alone.[90] Remember, however, that the plaintiff may not generally call another physician, such as a subsequent treating physician, and then cross-examine that physician.[91]

13.5.2 The Plaintiff's Injuries in an Action for Negligence

13.5.2.1 The Presentation of Expert Medical Testimony

A party's offer of an expert's testimony begins with a review of the expert's qualifications and the direct examination of a medical expert may include a statement of his or her qualifications even though the opposing party's attorney offers to concede them.[92] After the attorney for the party offering the witness's testimony establishes that the attorney served the witness's medical report on the other parties, that attorney may ask the witness to testify about the witness's examination of the plaintiff and his or her review of the

90. McDermott v. Manhattan Eye, Ear & Throat Hosp., 15 N.Y.2d 20, 203 N.E.2d 469, 255 N.Y.S.2d 65 (1964). *See also* Segreti v. Putnam Community Hosp., 88 A.D.2d 590, 449 N.Y.S.2d 785 (2d Dep't 1982).
91. Cuccia v. Brooklyn Medical Group, 171 A.D.2d 836 (2d Dep't 1991).
92. Counihan v. Werbelovsky's Sons, 5 A.D.2d 80, 168 N.Y.S.2d 829 (1st Dep't 1957).

medical records in order to establish the nature and scope of the plaintiff's injury.

Expert medical testimony is unnecessary unless the court finds that the plaintiff's injuries are not obviously the consequence of the claimed negligence. If the hospital records and the plaintiff's condition demonstrate clearly that the injuries are the result of the accident, then expert medical testimony is not necessary to establish the plaintiff's prima facie case.[93]

If a party does present the testimony of a medical expert, the expert is competent to answer a hypothetical question even though the expert did not examine the plaintiff until years after the accident.[94] For example, a physician is competent to testify that the decedent had diabetes before the accident, that the diabetes had been under control, and that the injury affected the diabetic condition.[95] A medical witness who examined the plaintiff merely to testify at the trial is not competent to testify regarding the plaintiff's complaints of pain.[96] However, in a hypothetical question, the plaintiff's attorney may ask the witness to assume that the pains existed.

---

93. Shaw v. Tague, 57 N.Y. 193, 177 N.E. 417 (1931); Mitchell v. Coca Cola Bottling Co., 11 A.D.2d 579, 200 N.Y.S.2d 478 (3d Dep't 1969). In Lieberman v. Colen, N.Y.L.J., Dec. 3, 1964, at 17, col. 2 (1st Dep't 1964), the court said:

    > [T]he trial judge erred in instructing the jury to disregard all testimony of the plaintiff as to pain and suffering, disability and loss of earnings after the day of the accident because of his failure to produce medical testimony. Where the results of an alleged act of negligence are such that they are within the experience and observation of a layman, the jury or court sitting as a trier of the facts can draw a conclusion as to causal relationship without the necessity of expert medical testimony. The ruling was prejudicial to plaintiff's case and in the interests of justice there should be a new trial.

    See also Capelouto v. Kaiser Found. Hosp., 7 Cal. 3d 889, 500 P.2d 880, 103 Cal. Rptr. 856 (1972) (court held no expert testimony was necessary to establish infant plaintiff's pain and suffering because of gravity of injury or ailment and because infants can feel pain and communicate distress through sound and gesture).
94. Grunfelder v. Brooklyn Heights R.R., 143 A.D.89, 127 N.Y.S. 1085 (2d Dep't 1911), *aff'd*, 206 N.Y. 720, 100 N.E. 1128 (1912).
95. Eisenberg v. City of N.Y., 285 A.D. 831, 137 N.Y.S.2d 103 (2d Dep't 1955).
96. Slacke v. Yellow Taxi Corp., 260 A.D. 1046, 24 N.Y.S.2d 490 (2d Dep't 1940).

13.5.2.2 Proximate Cause and the Phrasing of the Expert's Testimony

A medical expert may give his or her opinion of the cause or nature of the plaintiff's injuries without phrasing that opinion as a certainty. Terms such as "apparently" and "I think" are not speculative.[97] More specifically, competent medical experts may express opinions upon ascertained physical conditions of suffering or bad health, e.g., whether a previous injury might have caused the plaintiff's condition. Thus, a medical expert's testimony that the plaintiff's injury resulted in a "possible backward herniation of the disc" was admissible.[98] Similarly, a physician's opinion of when during a hospital stay the plaintiff's injury occurred, which opinion was couched in terms of the "possibles," was admissible because the physician's "opinion was accompanied by detailed explanation based on the evidence."[99]

When the plaintiff's doctor was asked the hypothetical question of whether the accident was a competent producing cause of the plaintiff's injuries, and the doctor answered "My opinion is that the accident described could constitute a competent and producing cause of findings which I made on the examination of this man," the Appellate Division, Third Department, held that the word "could" was not spec-

---

97. Reich v. Evans, 7 A.D.2d 765 180 N.Y.S.2d 159 (3d Dep't 1958).
98. Zipprich v. Smith Trucking Co., 2 N.Y.2d 177, 139 N.E.2d 146, 157 N.Y.S.2d 966 (1956); *see also* Ernest v. Boggs, 12 N.Y.2d 414, 416, 190 N.E.2d 528, 529, 240 N.Y.S.2d 153, 155 (1963), and Mitchell v. Nason's Delivery, Inc., 75 A.D.2d 965 (3d Dep't 1980).
99. O'Neill v. Cross County Hosp., 61 A.D.2d 1008, 402 N.Y.S.2d 633 (2d Dep't 1978). *See* Matott v. Ward, 48 N.Y.2d 455, 399 N.E.2d 532, 423 N.Y.S.2d 645 (1979) (plaintiff's expert originally testified that an accident was not the sole cause of the injury, but later he corrected himself and said he was reasonably certain the cause was the accident); Gurecki v. Gurecki, 92 A.D.2d 606, 459 N.Y.S.2d 1017 (2d Dep't 1983) and Matter of Cyr v. Bero Construction Corp., 75 A.D.2d 914 (3d Dep't 1980); Annot., *Expert Opinion: Admissibility of Expert Medical Testimony as to Future Consequences of Injury as Affected by Expression in Terms of Probability or Possibility*, 75 A.L.R.3d 9 (1977).

ulative and that the doctor's answer was sufficient to establish the causal relationship.[100]

Nevertheless, the testimony of a medical expert is inadmissible if it is speculative. For example, the testimony of the defendants' expert that a subsequent accident could have caused the plaintiff's condition was inadmissible in the absence of evidence establishing either the physical effect of the subsequent accident or that the plaintiff had suffered an injury.[101]

13.5.2.3 The Future Consequences of the Injury

A physician may, of course, testify regarding his or her prognosis, i.e., the probable course of the injury, and regarding the permanence of the injury. However, the physician may not testify regarding damages that are merely possible or wholly speculative.[102] Nevertheless, the plaintiff may establish the degree of future pain and suffering either by inference from the injury or by expert medical testimony.[103] If there is already evidence that the plaintiff's injuries are permanent, then evidence of the plaintiff's life expectancy is admissible.[104]

---

100. Cunningham v. Maxwell, 6 A.D.2d 366, 176 N.Y.S.2d 720 (3d Dep't 1958). A disagreement among a party's expert witnesses will not destroy party's case. Mudano v. Philadelphia Rapid Transit Co., 289 Pa. 51, 137 A. 104 (1927); *see* Annot., 66 A.L.R.2d 1118, 1125 (1959).

101. Drollette v. Kelly, 286 A.D. 641, 146 N.Y.S.2d 55 (3d Dep't 1955); *see also* Buris v. Lewis, 2 N.Y.2d 323, 327, 141 N.E.2d 424, 427, 160 N.Y.S.2d 853, 857 (1957) ("medical opinion lacks probative force where the conclusions are 'contingent, speculative or merely possible' and does not rise to the level of substantial evidence").

102. Gurecki v. Gurecki, 92 A.D.2d 606, 459 N.Y.S.2d 1017 (2d Dep't 1983).

103. *See* Ayres v. Delaware L.&W.R.R., 158 N.Y. 253, 263, 53 N.E.22, 31, 40 N.Y.S. 11, 20 (1899); Annot., *Requisite Proof to Permit Recovery for Future Medical Expenses as to Items of Damages in Personal Injury Action*, 69 A.L.R.2d 1261 (1960).

104. Barone v. Forgette, 286 A.D. 588, 146 N.Y.S.2d 63 (3d Dep't 1952); Annot., *Admissibility of Mortality Tables in Personal Injury Actions as Dependent Upon Showing of Permanency of Injury*, 50 A.L.R.2d 419 (1956).

A medical expert may testify that the accident activated, precipitated, or aggravated a particular condition, and "one who has negligently forwarded a diseased condition and thereby hastened and prematurely caused death cannot escape responsibility even though the disease probably would have resulted in death at a later time without his intervention."[105] Finally, a plaintiff may present evidence that, as a consequence of the injury sustained in the second accident, that second accident aggravated a prior injury.[106]

13.6 DISCOVERING THE IDENTITY OF THE OPPOSING PARTY'S EXPERT

C.P.L.R. section 3101(d), effective July 1, 1985, provides for discovering the opposing party's expert and other information. Although it does not deal with evidentiary issues, per se, this section has had a tremendous impact upon evidentiary issues in trials. The section provides in part:

> Upon request, each party shall identify each person whom the party expects to call as an expert witness at trial and shall disclose in reasonable detail the subject matter on which each expert is expected to testify, the substance of the facts and opinions on which each expert is expected to testify, the qualifications of each expert witness and a summary of the grounds for each expert's opinion.[107]

If, for some good cause, a party retains an expert too late before the trial to give the appropriate notice, the trial court

105. Dunham v. Village of Canisteo, 303 N.Y. 498, 104 N.E.2d 872 (1952); McCahill v. New York Transp. Co., 201 N.Y. 221, 224, 94 N.E. 616, 617 (1911). When adjudicating a claim for workmen's compensation, the courts have wrestled with the question of whether the stress of the job (i.e., no particular accident) caused the worker's death or whether his deathwas just the result of the wear and tear of life. Matter of Goldman v. White & Case, 9 A.D.2d 160 (3d Dep't 1959), and DiCicco v. Liebmann Breweries, Inc., 11 A.D.,2d 613 (3d Dep't 1960).

106. Wagner v. Mittendorf, 232 N.Y. 481, 134 N.E. 539 (1922).

107. C.P.L.R. § 3101(d)(1)(i).

should not preclude the expert's testimony but may make whatever order is just.

Significantly, in an action for medical, podiatric, or dental malpractice, the party complying with the demand may omit the names of his or her expert witnesses while disclosing the other information. In any action, further disclosure of the expert's expected testimony requires a court order upon a showing of special circumstances. However, one party may take the testimony of another party's treating or retained medical expert without a court order but in accordance with C.P.L.R. section 3101(a)(3), i.e., in an action for negligence or an intentional tort but not in an action for medical malpractice.

Finally, any party in an action for medical malpractice may make a written offer to all the other parties that each disclose the names of the expert witnesses each expects to call and make them available for oral examination. If all the other parties accept the offer, each must present his or her own expert witnesses for the oral examination. Moreover, if a party accepts the offer but fails to comply, the court will preclude that party from offering expert testimony at the trial.

In order to discover the identity, background, and prospective testimony of an opponent's experts, the attorney should serve a formal demand for that information. Example 13-1 is a sample of such a demand from an action for medical malpractice. For the information regarding any other expert or for the identity of a medical expert in an action for personal injuries, the attorney would add such an item to the demand. See example 13-2 for such a paragraph in a comprehensive notice demanding various items. Example 13-3 is a sample of a response to such a demand before he or she has selected her expert witnesses, and example 13-4 is a further response to the demand after he or she has selected his or her experts. All examples can be found at the end of this chapter

13.7 USING THE OPPOSING PARTY'S EXPERT

Using the opposing party's expert encompasses two situations:

1. Retaining an expert consulted by the opposing party, and
2. Using the substance of the report prepared by the opposing party's expert.

13.7.1 Retaining an Expert Consulted by the Opposing Party

Sometimes a party will consult an expert whom the opposing party already has consulted and the first party may learn that the expert informed the opposing party that the latter had the poorer argument. May the second party to consult an expert retain the expert? Since the opposing party did not retain the expert, the answer is yes. The trial court in *Napolitano v. H.G. Grable Co.,*[108] faced such a situation and held,

> The court does not feel, in this case, that the fact that the expert was retained after being contacted by the plaintiff is material. To hold otherwise would be disastrous, for a litigant could conceivably call leading experts in anticipation of their retention by his adversary and thereafter claim their disqualification thus leaving the adversary without a desirable expert.

The court quoted the Appellate Division, Second Department, in *Gugliano v. Levi*:

> The refusal of a retainer by an expert should not serve as a ground for his disqualification were he retained by an adversary. An expert is free to choose for whom he wishes to work. That is

108. Napolitano v. H.G. Grable Co., 116 Misc. 2d 58, 455 N.Y.S.2d 79 (Sup. Ct. 1982).
109. *Id.* at 60, 455 N.Y.S.2d at 81, *cf.* Gugliano v. Levi, 24 A.D.2d 591, 262 N.Y.S.2d 372 (2d Dep't 1965).

> not to say that this is not a proper subject for inquiry upon a trial.[109]

This inquiry could result in a charge that one party had actually hired away the other's expert. Mere contact between the expert and the opposing party, however, does not create an inference of impropriety. Therefore, the Appellate Division, Fourth Department, held in *Matter of County of Onondaga v. Hiawatha Plaza Associates*:

> Generally, an expert may be retained by only one side and an adversary should not seek his opponent's expert. The rationale for the rule is to avoid placing the expert in the unethical position of accepting retainers from both sides . . . . [However] We conclude that the brief contact in 1984 between the County of Onondaga and the appraiser for Niagara Frontier Services, Inc., was insufficient to invoke the general rule . . . .[110]

Sometimes the parties to litigation hired one expert jointly before starting the litigation. For example, partners may hire an accountant or an appraiser to help them to liquidate their partnership. In such a case, either party may call the expert as a witness.[111] Moreover, the plaintiff may call as a witness a medical doctor who examined the plaintiff on the defendant's behalf.[112]

13.7.2 Using the Substance of an Expert's Report

In 1987, in *Gilly v. City of New York,*[113] the Court of Appeals finally ruled that the plaintiff may elicit as part of plaintiff's direct case the substance of a report prepared by a physician

110. Matter of County of Onondaga v. Hiawatha Plaza Associates, 195 A.D.2d 1009 (4th Dep't 1993).
111. Rosen Trust v. Rosen, 53 A.D.2d 342 (4th Dep't 1976).
112. Liddy v. Frome, 85 A.D.2d 716 (2d Dep't 1981).
113. Gilly v. City of N.Y., 69 N.Y.2d 509, 508 N.E.2d 901, 516 N.Y.S.2d 166 (1987), and Ingleston v. Francis, 206 A.D.2d 745 (3d Dep't 1994).

who examined the plaintiff on behalf of the defendant. (The defendant's attorney would have served this report on the plaintiff's attorney, of course.) The court noted that the physician was not being compelled to express an opinion against his will but only to relate to the jury conclusions which he had already formulated and disclosed. In addition, there is no danger that by giving this limited evidence the physician would be thrust into an ethical dilemma or pulled apart by competent loyalties. Once a physician has served the report on an adversary, the report ceases to be for the defendant's exclusive use. However, a party may not subpoena the other's medical expert and force that expert to testify.[114]

---

114. Gugliano v. Levi, 24 A.D.2d 591, 262 N.Y.S.2d 372 (2d Dep't 1965).

EXAMPLE 13-1: DEMAND FOR EXPERT WITNESS INFORMATION

SUPREME COURT OF THE STATE OF NEW YORK
COUNTY OF WESTCHESTER
---X
JANE DOE and JOHN DOE,

Plaintiffs,

-against-

BRONX DOCTOR'S GROUP, DR. ROSE SMITH,
EAST END GENERAL HOSPITAL,

Defendants.
---X

DEMAND FOR EXPERT WITNESS INFORMATION

Index No.

S I R S:

PLEASE TAKE NOTICE, that pursuant to C.P.L.R § 3101 (d) (1) and Jasopersaud v. Rho, 169 A.D.2d 184, 572 N.Y.S.2d 700 (2nd Dep't 1991), plaintiff demands that you serve upon the undersigned the following:

1. The qualifications of each medical expert witness including:

   (a) The medical school attended by each expert;

   (b) Any and all board certifications of each expert;

   (c) Areas of special expertise of each expert;

   (d) All States in which each expert is licensed; and

   (e) The location and nature of any and all internships, residencies and/or fellowships performed by each expert.

2. The subject matter, in reasonable detail, on which each expert is expected to testify and the substance of the facts and opinion on which each expert is expected to testify.

3. A summary of the grounds and basis of each expert's opinion.

4. The above Demand is a continuing one from the date of this notice through trial.

PLEASE TAKE NOTICE, that in the event of your failure to comply with this Demand, the undersigned will object to the defendant introducing into evidence any testimony relating to the items and information dated herein.

Dated: **New York, New York**
May 17, 1996

KRAMER, DILLOF, TESSEL, DUFFY & MOORE
Attorneys for Plaintiffs
233 Broadway
New York, New York 10279-0137
(212) 267-4177

TO: **DEFENSE FIRM**

EXAMPLE 13-2: PARAGRAPH DEMANDING INFORMATION REGARDING EXPERTS

3. Pursuant to Section 3101(d) of the C.P.L.R. and Rule 202.17 of the Uniform Rules for New York State trial courts, demand is hereby made that you set forth the name and address of each person whom the defendant(s) expect(s) to call as an expert witness at trial, such expert's qualifications, the subject matter upon which such expert is expected to testify, the substance of the facts and opinions on which such expert is expected to testify, and the grounds for each opinion.

EXAMPLE 13-3: RESPONSE TO DEMAND FOR EXPERT WITNESS INFORMATION

SUPREME COURT OF THE STATE OF NEW YORK
COUNTY OF NEW YORK
---------------------------------------X
JANE SMITH

Plaintiff,

-against-

GENERAL HOSPITAL and ST. PATRICK'S MEDICAL CENTER,

Defendants.
---------------------------------------X

RESPONSE TO DEMAND FOR EXPERT WITNESS INFORMATION

INDEX NO.

Plaintiffs will call one or more physicians with specialties which include orthopedics, and/or orthopedic surgery who will testify that defendants were careless and negligent in failing to provide good and proper post operative care to the infant plaintiff; in failing properly to examine and observe the right arm; in failing to obtain proper post operative x-rays; in improperly and prematurely removing fixation pins from the arm; in improperly and prematurely removing the cast; in failing properly to immobilize the arm; in failing to maintain sufficient and proper immobilization; in failing to treat the infant plaintiff in accordance with good and accepted medical care; the infant plaintiff sustained the following injuries and complications all of which caused, contributed to and/or aggravated by the defendant's negligence; severe increase in and aggravation of cubitus varus deformity of right arm, requiring right humeral osteotomy; deformity of right arm and wrist; limitation of function and motion of right arm and wrist; emotional distress; all of which injuries and complications are permanent protracted and progressive.

Dated: New York, New York
November 2, 1993

KRAMER, DILLOF, TESSEL, DUFFY & MOORE
Attorneys for Plaintiffs
233 Broadway
New York, New York 10279
(212) 267-4177

To: Attorneys for Defendants

EXAMPLE 13-4: FURTHER RESPONSE TO DEMAND FOR EXPERT WITNESS INFORMATION

SUPREME COURT OF THE STATE OF NEW YORK
COUNTY OF SUFFOLK

---X

ALEXANDER , an Infant under the age of 14 years, by his Mother and Natural Guardian, and , Individually,

Plaintiffs,

-against-

MICHAEL , M.D., HOWARD M.D., MOLIN , M.D., FELD, M.D., NETH , M.D., ALFRED M.D., , P.C., & , P.C. and HOSPITAL MEDICAL CENTER,

Defendants.

FURTHER RESPONSE TO DEMAND FOR EXPERT WITNESS INFORMATION

---X

SIRS:

PLEASE TAKE NOTICE that plaintiffs, as and for their response, pursuant to §3101(d) of the New York State's Civil Practice Law and Rules ("C.P.L.R."), to defendants demand for expert information, states as follows:

The plaintiffs will call as a witness at trial one or more physicians duly licensed to practice medicine in the State of New York. Each of these physicians is Board Certified in Obstetrics and Gynecology.

These physicians have each graduated from one of the following medical schools: University School of Medicine; Medical School; University School of Medicine, and; University of School of Medicine.

These physicians have each completed an approved internship at one of the following facilities: Hospital; General Hospital; Hospital, and; Hospital.

These physicians have each completed an approved residency in Obstetrics and Gynecology at one of the following facilities: Hospital Center; Hospital; Hospital, and; Hospital,

These physicians, to the extent that they are called, shall testify based upon their experience and training, the records, films, tapes, documentary evidence, depositions and trial testimony and any other material offered into evidence that may form the subject matter for such testimony.

These physicians shall testify that, to a reasonable degree of medical certainty, the defendants

departed from good and accepted medical practice in that they were careless and negligent in failing to render proper prenatal care to the mother. The grounds for this opinion are that: (1) the defendants failed to arrive at an accurate estimate of the gestational age of the fetus; (2) the defendants allowed pregnancy with the infant plaintiff to proceed approximately three weeks beyond the due date, and; (3) the defendants failed to anticipate the possibility of and manage the existence of cephalopelvic disproportion.

The defendants further departed from good and accepted medical practice in that they were careless and negligent in failing to render proper medical care during the labor and delivery of the infant plaintiff. The grounds for this opinion are that: (1) the defendants failed to appreciate the significance of and/or properly act upon the meconium stained amniotic fluid which became apparent upon the artificial rupture of membranes; (2) the defendants failed to appreciate the significance of and/or properly act upon signs of fetal distress such as decelerations in the fetal heart rate and decreased variability of the fetal heart during the labor and delivery; (3) the defendants failed to appreciate the significance of and/or properly act upon failure to progress during labor i.e the failure of her cervix to become engaged; (4) the defendants failed to deliver the infant plaintiff in a timely fashion; (5) the defendant's failed to perform a timely caesarean section delivery of the infant plaintiff; (6) the defendants failed to anticipate the possibility of and properly manage the existence of cephalopelvic disproportion; (7) the defendants failed to appreciate the significance of and properly act upon failure to properly progress in labor; (8) the defendants allowed the fetus to suffer prolonged distress; (9) the defendants failed to properly resuscitate the fetus in utero by giving oxygen to the mother and failed to alleviate the fetal distress suffered by the fetus; (9) the defendants did nothing to ascertain the degree of hypoxia that the infant plaintiff had suffered, including failing to utilize fetal scalp sampling; (10) the defendants delivered the infant plaintiff in a traumatic fashion, and; (11) the defendants caused or permitted to occur a skull fracture and intracranial hemorrhage to the fetus.

The above-named defendants further departed from good and accepted medical practice in that they were careless and negligent in failing to render proper post natal care to the mother and infant plaintiff in that; (1) the defendants caused and or allowed the infant plaintiff to suffer a skull fracture and an intracranial hemorrhage; (2) the defendants failed to properly and adequately resuscitate the newborn; (3) the defendants failed to properly examine the newborn and assess his condition, and; (4) the defendants failed to recognize and treat the infant plaintiff's skull fracture.

Moreover, these physicians will further testify, to a reasonable degree of medical certainty, that as a result of the above referenced departures from accepted medical practice and procedures, the defendants caused, aggravated, contributed to, and/or were significant factors in the injuries and damages to the infant plaintiff including: brain damage; perinatal hypoxia; perinatal asphyxia; intracranial hemorrhage; subdural and cerebral hemorrhage; skull fracture; static encephalopathy; developmental delay; seizure disorder; generalized convulsive epilepsy; spastic diplegia; spastic quadriplegia; hypsarrhythmia; lethargy; intractable seizures; hypotonia; hyperreflexia; visual impairment; hyporeflexia, and; microcephaly.

Dated: New York, New York
December 19

KRAMER, DILLOF, TESSEL, DUFFY & MOORE
Attorneys for Plaintiffs
233 Broadway
New York, N.Y. 10279
(212) 267-4177

TO:

Attorneys for Dr.
, Dr. ,
Dr. Dr.
and
P.C.
s/h/a &
P.C.
Bypass
New York

Impeaching and Rehabilitating a Witness with Prior Statements 14

A party is necessarily concerned with the effect of his or her witnesses' testimony. Unfortunately, a witness's testimony sometimes surprises the party who called the witness to the stand so that party may seek to undermine the witness's testimony by showing that he or she made a prior inconsistent statement in writing or under oath. At other times, the opposing party may attack the witness's testimony as the product of a recent fabrication so the party who called the witness may wish to rehabilitate the witness by showing that he or she made a prior consistent statement at a time when the witness had no motive to falsify his or her testimony.

14.1 Contradicting Your Own Witness

The general rule is that a party may not attack the credibility of the party's own witness, i.e., a witness the party called to the stand.

> When a party offers a witness in proof of his cause, he thereby, in general, represents him as worthy of belief. He is presumed to know the character of the witnesses he adduces; and having thus presented them to the Court, the law will not permit the party afterwards to impeach their general reputation for truth, or to impugn their credibility by general evidence, tending to show them to be unworthy of belief; for this would enable him to destroy the witness if he spoke against him, and to make

> him a good witness if he spoke for him, with the means in his hand of destroying his credit if he spoke against him.[1]

Despite this general rule, the witness's answers do not bind the party who called him or her and that party may contradict the witness with other evidence on the issue in dispute.[2] Thus, "a party may prove any material fact in the case by other witnesses, even though the effect is to contradict his own witness."[3] Thus,

> although a party, to a certain extent, vouches for the credibility of a witness he . . . puts on the stand, in civil cases, at least, it has been held that such party has the right to claim a witness mistaken and to contradict his . . . witness, not for the purpose of impeachment, but to prove a material fact.[4]

14.2 Impeaching Your Own Witness

14.2.1 Impeaching a Witness Who Is Not a Party

Two exceptions, one statutory and the other common-law, permit the party who called the witness to impeach him or her. The statutory exception is the narrower one and applies to a witness who is not the opposing party. C.P.L.R. section 4514 provides: "In addition to impeachment in the manner permitted by common law, any party may introduce proof that any witness has made a prior statement inconsistent with his testimony if the statement was made in a writing subscribed by him or was made under oath."

---

1. GREENLEAF ON EVIDENCE § 442 (16th ed.).
2. Quick v. American Can Co., 205 N.Y. 330, 98 N.E. 480 (1912). FED. R. EVID. 607 states that any party, even the one who called him, may attack the credibility of a witness.
3. W. RICHARDSON, EVIDENCE 508 (J. Prince, 10th ed. 1973) [hereinafter cited as RICHARDSON, EVIDENCE].
4. People v. Reed, 40 N.Y.2d 204 at 207 (1976).

Thus, to impeach the credibility of his or her own witness, a party may use only a prior inconsistent statement contained in a writing subscribed by the witness or made by the witness under oath. The trial court will not admit the prior inconsistent statement for its truth but merely to undermine the credibility of the witness.[5] However, the impeaching party may confront his or her own witness with the witness's accident report,[6] deposition,[7] or prior testimony.[8]

Assume, for example, that the plaintiff must prove that the defendant had notice of a defective condition and that to do so the plaintiff calls the defendant's janitor as a witness. On direct examination, the attorney for the plaintiff asks the janitor whether, prior to the accident, he knew that the step was broken, and the witness denies such knowledge. If the attorney then shows the janitor a statement he signed stating that he had known of the defective condition for several weeks before the accident and the janitor persists in his denial, the statement would be admissible but only to undermine the witness's credibility and not as evidence in chief. Therefore, if the plaintiff has no other evidence of notice, the plaintiff will fail to present a prima facie case,[9] and the trial court will dismiss his or her complaint.

Moreover, the witness's credibility is a collateral matter so the plaintiff may not attempt to prove the truth of the facts contained in the prior statement in order to impeach the witness.[10]

5. Roge v. Valentine, 280 N.Y. 268, 20 N.E.2d 751 (1939); Annot., *Binding Effect upon Party Litigant of Testimony of His Witness at a Former Trial*, 74 A.L.R.2d 521 (1960).
6. Robinson v. New York City Transit Authority, 105 A.D.2d 614, 481 N.Y.S.2d 85 (1st Dep't 1984).
7. Rodford v. Sample, 30 A.D.2d 588, 290 N.Y.S.2d 30 (3d Dep't 1968).
8. Millington v. New York City Transit Authority, 54 A.D.2d 649, 387 N.Y.S.2d 865 (1st Dep't 1976).
9. Scarbrough v. Schenck, 76 Misc. 2d 1074, 352 N.Y.S.2d 825 (Sup. Ct. 1974), *aff'd* 47 A.D.2d 718 (2d Dep't 1975).

14.2.2 Impeaching a Witness Who Is an Adverse Party

By exception, the common law permits one party to impeach his or her own witness when that witness is an adverse party and to use the witness's prior inconsistent statement as evidence in chief.[11] This exception is actually a corollary to the rule allowing a party's admission into evidence as an exception to the hearsay rule. The adverse party finds him- or herself impeached by his or her own admission because the law allows one party to call an adverse party as a witness and then to cross-examine the latter on the direct examination.

For example, in *McDermott v. Manhattan Eye, Ear & Throat Hospital*,[12] the Court of Appeals held that the plaintiff in an action for medical malpractice may call the defendant to the stand for interrogation as if under cross-examination. Thus, the plaintiff who calls the defendant in such an action has the right to cross-examine the defendant as an adverse and hostile witness and to impeach the defendant's credibility in all the ways we discussed in the chapter on cross-examination.[13] Consequently, the Appellate Division, Second Department, held in *Segreti v. Putnam Community Hospital*, that "[t]he trial court also erred in improperly curtailing plaintiff's examination of defendant Chang as a hostile and an expert witness. As an adverse par-

10. *Id.*; People v. McCormick, 303 N.Y. 403, 103 N.E.2d 529 (1952).
11. Koester v. Rochester Candy Works, 194 N.Y. 92, 87 N.E. 77 (1909).
12. McDermott v. Manhattan Eye, Ear, and Throat Hospital, 15 N.Y.2d 20, 203 N.E.2d 469, 255 N.Y.S.2d 65 (1964).
13. *See* Spampinato v. ABC Consolidated Corp., 35 N.Y.2d 283, 319 N.E.2d 196, 360 N.Y.S.2d 878 (1974); Becker v. Koch, 104 N.Y. 394, 10 N.E. 701 (1887); Annot., *Impeachment of Adverse Party Called under Rule Relating to Calling and Interrogation of Adverse Party as Witness at Trial*, 35 A.L.R.2d 759 (1953). In a matrimonial case, Cross v. Cross, the court of appeals held, ". . . by calling him [her husband] as a witness the plaintiff did not become forced to admit as true every fact to which he testified." 108 N.Y.628 at 629 (1883).

ty, Dr. Chang was a hostile witness subject to cross-examination when called to the stand by plaintiff." [14]

However, to be subjected to cross-examination during the direct examination by the party who called him or her, the witness really must be an adverse party. The plaintiff in *Cuccia v. Brooklyn Medical Group*,[15] an action for a wrongful death due to medical malpractice, discovered that the witness's mere association with the defendants is insufficient.

> At trial, the plaintiff's counsel attempted to cross-examine Dr. Solomon, a treating physician of the deceased, as an expert witness. The trial court properly prohibited the witness from being cross-examined in this manner . . . . Doctor Solomon, who was a member of the defendant partnership, the Empire Medical Group, at the time the alleged malpractice occurred, but not at the time of trial, had not been named as a defendant. In addition, as trial counsel stressed to the jury in his summation argument, no allegations of medical malpractice were being made as against Dr. Solomon.[16]

14.3. REHABILITATING YOUR OWN WITNESS AFTER THE CHARGE OF A RECENT FABRICATION

14.3.1 In General

The term recent fabrication means "the defense is charging the witness not with mistake or confusion, but with making

14. Segreti v. Putnam Community Hospital, 88 A.D.2d 590, 449 N.Y.S.2d 785 (2d Dep't 1982).
15. Cuccia v. Brooklyn Medical Group, 171 A.D.2d 836 (2d Dep't 1991).
16. *Id.* at 836-7. However, a party may show by cross-examination the bias of a witness who has settled with an adverse party or whose employer (read: partner) has. Hill v. Arnold, 640 N.Y.S.2d 892 (1st Dep't 1996).

up a false story well after the event."[17] Ordinarily, a party may not corroborate the testimony of the party's own witness by presenting the previous statements in which the witness told the same story.[18] However, if an adverse party attacks the witness's testimony as a recent fabrication, then the party who called the witness may properly show, for the purpose of rehabilitation, that the witness made a statement consistent with his or her testimony on direct examination and at a time when the witness had no motive to falsify his or her report. Such a prior consistent statement normally would be inadmissible as self-serving and even the exception will not ordinarily permit the introduction of a prior statement from an interested witness or a party because the witness must have had no motive to lie.[19] In other words, the witness must have had "no motive to color his explanations of the accident when he made them."[20] Nevertheless, if the defendant charges the plaintiff with a recent fabrication, i.e., with making up a story or having no injury at all, then the recent fabrication rule allows the plaintiff's attorney to introduce a prior consistent statement that the client made when his need for treatment overbore any motive to falsify the client's report.

The witness's recent fabrication need not be recent in the sense of occurring just before the trial. Instead, it must be recent in the sense of occurring after his motive to lie arose.

---

17. People v. Singer, 300 N.Y. 120, 89 N.E.2d 710 (1949), and People v. Seit, 86 N.Y.2d 92 (1996).
18. RICHARDSON, EVIDENCE § 519, and People v. McDaniels, 81 N.Y.2d 10 (1994).
19. That is, the party should not testify to his own prior statement. Someone else should to it for him.
20. Alexander v. Kramer Bros. Freight Lines, Inc., 273 F.2d 373 (2d Cir. 1959); *see also* FED. R. EVID. 801(d)(1); Giordano v. Eastern Utils., Inc., 9 A.D.2d 947, 195 N.Y.S.2d 753 (2d Dep't 1959); Annot., *Admissibility for Purpose of Supporting Witness Impeached by Charge of Recent Fabrication of Prior Statements by Him Consistent with His Testimony*, 75 A.L.R.2d 939 (1961). In Mandzych v. Karl, 33 A.D.2d 786, 307 N.Y.S.2d 139 (2d Dep't 1969), the court held that it was error to admit as a prior consistent statement the defendant's motor vehicle report, which he filed fourteen months after the accident.

The Court of Appeals explained this distinction in *People v. Singer*:[21]

> Of course, if the word "recent" in this court's formulation of the exception, ... means that the witness' statements at the trial must have been assailed as having been fabricated at some point just before the trial, this was no case for applying the exception. But we think that "recent" as so used, has a relative, not an absolute meaning: It means, . . . that the defense is charging the witness not with mistake or confusion, but with making up a false story well after the event . . . . "Recently fabricated" means the same thing as fabricated to meet the exigencies of the case . . . .[22]

14.3.2 Rehabilitating the Witness Who Is Not a Party

One party may accuse an adverse party's witness of a recent fabrication whether the witness is a party or not. For example, in *Flynn v. MABSTOA*,[23] the Appellate Division, First Department, considered the admissibility of an index card written by a passenger on the bus at the time of the accident. The card bore her name and address and the statement, "People on the bus said 'stop, you hit the boy on the bike.'" The passenger gave the index card to another passenger but testified for the plaintiff.

At the trial, the defendant argued that the bus driver had not hit the boy on the bike and that the witness had not heard such a remark from another, unidentified passenger. The trial court allowed the plaintiff to introduce the index card to buttress the witness's testimony pursuant to the recent fabrication rule. The appellate court held this to be proper. "The court appropriately permitted the plaintiff to demonstrate — through a memorandum made at the acci-

---

21. People v. Singer, 300 N.Y. 120 (1949).
22. *Id.* at 124.
23. Flynn v. Manhattan and Bronx Surface Transit Operating Authority, 94 A.D.2d 617, 462 N.Y.S.2d 17 (1st Dep't 1983), *aff'd* 61 N.Y.2d 769 (1984).

dent scene many years before the trial — that her version of what had transpired at the time of the incident was not a recent fabrication."

In another case, a witness identified a burglar at the latter's trial, but the defendant's counsel claimed that the witness had contrived the identification after the defendant was arrested. Therefore, the trial court admitted a police artist's sketch of the defendant because the artist drew the sketch from particulars given by the witness two months before the arrest.[24]

14.3.3 Rehabilitating the Witness Who Is a Party

The court is more likely to exclude a prior consistent statement by a party because a party more often has a motive to misstate the facts. For example, in *Melendez v. Lang*,[25] an action arising from an automobile accident, the court refused to admit a letter from a defendant driver's insurance broker. The letter, which the broker composed at the same time he completed the accident report, provided more details than those provided by the driver and it exculpated him. "The letter was prepared more than 24 hours after the accident, during which time appellant had the opportunity to reflect upon the possible benefits he could derive from a favorable letter."[26]

However, in the correct circumstances, a party may convince the trial court to admit the party's own prior consistent statement to rebut a charge of recent fabrication. An important civil case illustrating this possibility is *Lichtrule v. City Savings Bank*,[27] in which the plaintiff claimed that she had been injured because of the excessive speed of the revolving door at the entrance to the defendant's building. The defendant called a police officer who testified that he

24. People v. Coffey, 11 N.Y.2d 142 (1962).
25. Melendez v. Lang, 54 A.D.2d 864 (1st Dep't 1976).

had spoken to the plaintiff after the accident and that she told him that she had been struck by a man coming out of the building. In rebuttal, the plaintiff offered to prove that at the time she was admitted to the hospital, she told her doctor she had been struck by a revolving door. The trial court excluded the evidence, but the Appellate Division, Second Department, held that the exclusion was an error:

> As the question with respect to the manner in which the accident occurred was a vital issue and the jury inquired of the court as to any statement made by plaintiff at the time of her admission to the hospital, it was vital to the proper presentation of plaintiff's case that the evidence of her statement should have been before the jury.

14.3.4 Caveats

As always, when employing a rule of law, the attorney must beware of the pitfalls. We will mention a few.

First, the recent fabrication rule will not be applicable if the opposing counsel has not accused the witness of a recent fabrication. For example, in *Cherico v. City of New York,*[28] the Appellate Division, First Department, held that the history portion of a hospital record is admissible when the defendant has argued that the plaintiff fabricated his or her version of the accident.[29] However, if the defendant is not alleging a recent fabrication regarding how the accident happened but merely that the defendant was not negligent, the plaintiff may not introduce the history portion of the hospital record. In *Cherico*,

> [d]efendant Somma did not attempt at trial to introduce any evidence suggesting that Mr. DiPaolo had changed his account of the manner in which he was injured at any time after the

---

26. *Id.* at 865.
27. Lichtrule v. City Savings Bank, 29 A.D.2d 565, 286 N.Y.S.2d 307 (2d Dep't 1967).
28. Cherico v. City of New York, 88 A.D.2d 889, 452 N.Y.S.2d 606 (1st Dep't 1982).

> accident. In the absence of such a claim of recent fabrication, the prior consistent statements are clearly inadmissible hearsay which would only serve to improperly bolster Mr. DiPaolo's trial testimony . . . .[30]

Second, the cross-examiner's position may not be clear, and the attorney for the party who presented the witness should be prepared to introduce any prior consistent statement and to argue that the statement is admissible. The cross-examiner, meanwhile, should decide whether charging the witness with a recent fabrication would enhance his or her client's case or backfire.

Third, the attorney must beware of reading something into the prior statement that is not there; that is, the statement may be too imprecise to be admitted as consistent.[31]

---

29. *See also* Romanchuck v. County of Westchester, 40 A.D.2d 877, 337 N.Y.S.2d 926 (2d Dep't 1972), *aff'd* 34 N.Y.2d 906 (1974) (the plaintiff, five years of age, claimed to have been struck by county truck while he was on a sled; the defendant denied the accident, and the defendant's attorney attacked the father's testimony on cross-examination; the court held it was error under the recent-fabrication rule to exclude the history portion of the hospital record, which indicated that the child had been struck by a moving vehicle); Abrams v. Gerold, 37 A.D.2d 391, 326 N.Y.S.2d 1 (2d Dep't 1971); Theban v. Lowerre, N.Y.L.J., Apr. 21, 1964, at 16, col. 5 (2d Dep't 1964).
30. DiPaolo v. Somma, 111 A.D.2d 899, 491 N.Y.S.2d 27 (2d Dep't 1985).
31. Pomer v. Chen, 187 A.D.2d 497 (2d Dep't 1992).

Cross-Examination 15

Chapter 15 discusses the purposes and rules of cross-examination, not the techniques of drawing out witnesses.[1]

15.1 THE GENERAL RULES

15.1.1 The Purposes of Cross-Examination

Cross-examination is "the examination of a witness upon a trial or hearing, or upon taking a deposition, by the party opposed to the one who produced him, upon his evidence given in chief, to test its truth, to further develop it, or for other purposes."[2] In other words, the purpose of cross-examination is to test the mental capacity, veracity, and accuracy of the witness.[3] For example, the attorney for the opposing party may show that the witness has an erroneous understanding of the traffic regulations or the rules of the road.[4] Generally, a witness may be cross-examined about all matters that tend to discredit the witness, but the range and extent of the cross-examination that will be permitted, especially regarding the credibility of a witness, is within the

1. For the classic introductory text on technique, *see* FRANCIS L. WELLMAN, THE ART OF CROSS-EXAMINATION, 4th ed. (New York: Collier Books, 1932), 476 pp.
2. BLACK'S LAW DICTIONARY 450 (4th ed. 1968).
3. People v. Lustig, 206 N.Y. 162, 170, 99 N.E. 183, 186 (1912).
4. Dauch v. Theed, 209 A.D. 682, 686, 205 N.Y.S. 306, 308 (2d Dep't 1924).

trial court's discretion. The Court of Appeals stated the rule in *Langley v. Wadsworth:*

> So far as the cross-examination of a witness relates either to facts in issue or relevant facts, it may be pursued by counsel as a matter of right, but when its object is to ascertain the accuracy or credibility of a witness, its method and duration are subject to the discretion of the trial judge and unless abused its exercise is not the subject of review.[5]

The trial court should limit the cross-examination of the witness to the matters to which he or she testified on direct examination. A cross-examiner who persists in inquiring about matters that were not brought out on direct examination makes the witness the cross-examiner's own concerning those matters. As a consequence, the cross-examiner would be limited to the means available for a party to impeach his or her own witness.[6]

15.1.2 Collateral Matters

When addressing either the facts or the witness's credibility, the cross-examiner is bound by the witness's answers on collateral matters and may not produce evidence to establish that the witness's answers are untruthful.[7] Thus, if the

---

5. Langley v. Wadsworth, 99 N.Y. 61, 1 N.E. 106 (1895).
6. Bennett v. Crescent Athletic-Hamilton Club, 270 N.Y. 456, 1 N.E.2d 963 (1936).
7. W. Richardson, Evidence § 491 (J. Prince 10th ed. 1973) [hereinafter cited as Richardson, Evidence]. However, although the cross-examiner is bound by the answer, the witness is not bound. For example, in People v. Catalanotte, 41 A.D.2d 968, 244 N.Y.S.2d 72 (2d Dep't 1973), *aff'd*, 36 N.Y.2d 192, 325 N.E.2d 866, 366 N.Y.S.2d 403 (1975), in which the defendant's testimony was attacked on a collateral issue involving bank accounts, although the cross-examiner was held bound by defendant's answers, the appellate courts held that the trial court had erred by rejecting the defendant's offer of rebuttal testimony to explain the bank accounts, because the witness is not limited by his answer. Getlin v. St. Vincent's Hosp., 117 A.D.2d 707, 498 N.Y.S.2d 849 (2d Dep't 1986); Serpe v. Rappaport, 103 A.D.2d 771, 477 N.Y.S.2d 403 (1st Dep't 1984).

witness denies being a prostitute, the cross-examiner is bound by her answer, and may not present independent evidence of that fact, unless the witness has been convicted of being a prostitute. The rationale for this rule is that collateral matters are irrelevant to the claims in the case and tend to confuse the jury.[8] Hence, the trial court must be alert to the issues in order to separate the germane from the irrelevant or prejudicial. The court's duty is to prevent the latter from entering the trial.

Unfortunately, it is not always easy to determine whether a particular matter is collateral. A witness's bias, interest, or hostility is not a collateral matter, and the cross-examiner may prove such bias, etc., despite the witness's denial.[9] However, the cross-examiner may not present evidence to impeach the character of a witness in a civil action.[10] For example, in *Davis v. Blum*,[11] an action for medical malpractice, the Appellate Division, Second Department, reversed a verdict for the defendant and ordered a new trial because the trial court had allowed the defendant to introduce evidence that the plaintiff was an alcoholic in order to show that the plaintiff tended to exercise poor judgment. The appellate court held that such evidence was "akin to evidence of character and habit which is generally inadmissible in civil cases to raise the inference that a party acted in a particular way on the occasion in issue."[12]

Another example of evidence that is inadmissible because it is directed to a collateral matter is the testimony of

8. DiPaolo v. Somma, 111 A.D.2d 899, 490 N.Y.S.2d 803 (2d Dep't 1985); Ellison v. New York City Transit Auth., 61 N.Y.2d 853, 473 N.Y.S.2d 976 (1984), *aff'd,* 98 A.D.2d 659, 470 N.Y.S.2d 144 (1st Dep't 1983).
9. Bennett v. Crescent Athletic-Hamilton Club, 270 N.Y. 456 (1936).
10. Kravitz v. Long Island Jewish Hosp., 113 A.D.2d 577, 497 N.Y.S.2d 51 (2d Dep't 1985).
11. Davis v. Blum, 70 A.D.2d 583, 416 N.Y.S.2d 57 (2d Dep't 1979).
12. *Id.,* 70 A.D.2d at 584, 416 N.Y.S.2d at 59; *cf.* Halloran v. Virginia Chems., Inc., 41 N.Y.2d 386, 393 N.Y.S.2d 341 (1977). However, New York does permit proof of a business, professional, or other institutional practice or custom as probative evidence that the practice or custom was followed on a specific occasion.

an expert on the credibility of the eyewitnesses. Such testimony would confuse the jury and would require a trial within a trial to determine whether the eyewitnesses had testified accurately. Therefore, expert testimony on this issue is inadmissible.[13] Instead, the cross-examiner should probe the witnesses' powers of observation and memory and, if possible, present demonstrative evidence and witnesses who can contradict the opposing party's witnesses on the facts.

15.1.3 Calling and Cross-Examining the Adverse Party in an Action for Medical Malpractice

When the plaintiff in an action for medical malpractice calls the defendant as a witness on the plaintiff's direct case, the plaintiff's attorney may ask the defendant leading questions. In effect, the plaintiff's attorney may cross-examine the defendant during the direct examination, and the plaintiff may even force the defendant to become the plaintiff's expert witness. Thus, in *Segreti v. Putnam Community Hospital*, the Appellate Division, Second Department, held,

> It was prejudicial error for the trial court to so prevent plaintiff's counsel from leading and cross-examining Dr. Chang as a hostile witness as to hold him bound by the latter's answers . . . [Moreover], it is well settled that a plaintiff in a medical malpractice action may call as a witness the doctor against whom she brought the action and question him as a medical expert . . . .[14]

---

13. People v. Kelley, 631 N.Y.S.2d 926 (2d Dep't 1995); People v. Greene, 637 N.Y.S.2d 79 (1st Dep't 1996); United States v. Fosher, 590 F.2d 381 (1st Cir. 1979); *but cf.* People v. Cronin, 60 N.Y.2d 430, 470 N.Y.S.2d 110 (1983); *see also* Martin, *Expert Opinion on Eyewitness Testimony*, N.Y.L.J., Feb. 14, 1986 at 1, col. 1.
14. Segreti v. Putnam Community Hosp., 88 A.D.2d 590, 592, 449 N.Y.S.2d 785, 786 (2d Dep't 1982); *see also* Arlene W. v. Robert D., 36 A.D.2d 455, 324 N.Y.S.2d 333 (4th Dep't 1971).

15.1.4 The Methods of Impeaching the Credibility of the Opposing Party's Witnesses

In addition to using cross-examination to test the memory, knowledge, and understanding of the opposing party's witness, the attorney may attempt to destroy the witness's credibility, i.e., "that quality in a witness which renders his evidence worthy of belief."[15] More specifically, the witness's credibility consists of the jurors' belief that the witness is telling the truth as he or she knows it. Several methods are available to the attorney for impeaching the credibility of the opposing party's witnesses, but the rules governing each method limit the attorney's questions.

The principal methods of attacking the credibility of a witness are by showing that:

1. The witness made a prior inconsistent statement.
2. The witness has been convicted of a crime.
3. The witness has committed an immoral, vicious, or criminal act which may reflect unfavorably on the witness's character and thus prove that he or she is unworthy of belief.
4. The witness is biased in favor of the party calling him or her, hostile toward the opposing party, or interested in the outcome of the case.
5. The witness's opinion, if he or she is an expert, is contrary to recognized authority.
6. The witness has a bad reputation for truth and veracity.

---

15. BLACK'S LAW DICTIONARY 440 (4th ed. 1968).

15.2 THE WITNESS HAS MADE A PRIOR INCONSISTENT STATEMENT

The attorney may impeach the opposing party's witness most directly by showing that the witness has made a prior and inconsistent statement about the same facts. The statement may have been an unsworn oral one, a signed writing, or testimony. In addition, the attorney must understand the distinction between a prior inconsistent statement made by a witness who is not a party and a statement by a witness who is a party. The party's prior inconsistent statement is also an admission against interest and, thus, constitutes evidence-in-chief. The prior inconsistent statement of a witness who is not a party, however, merely impairs the witness's credibility and the cross-examiner may not offer the statement as evidence supporting his or her client's case.[16]

15.2.1 An Unsworn Oral Statement

Before the trial court will admit a prior inconsistent statement, the attorney must confront the witness with it by specifying the time and place the witness supposedly made it, the person to whom the witness made it, and the substance of the language the witness used.[17] If the attorney fails to lay this foundation, he or she may not use the statement to impeach the credibility of the witness. If the witness denies having made the statement or declares that the witness does not remember it, the attorney still has laid the foundation and may offer the evidence of the statement dur-

---

16. FED. R. EVID. 801(d)(a)(a), 607, 613, 801(c); Roge v. Valentine, 280 N.Y. 268 (1939); Robinson v. New York City Transit Auth., 105 A.D.2d 614, 481 N.Y.S.2d 85 (1st Dep't 1984).

17. Ahmed v. Board of Educ., 98 A.D.2d 736, 469 N.Y.S.2d 435 (2d Dep't 1983); Morris v. Palmer Oil Co., 94 A.D.2d 911, 463 N.Y.S.2d 631 (3d Dep't 1983); Bombard v. County of Albany, 94 A.D.2d 910, 463 N.Y.S.2d 633 (3d Dep't 1983).

ing the defendant's case (if the attorney represents the defendant) or during the rebuttal (if the attorney represents the plaintiff).[18] Note that the attorney does not introduce the prior inconsistent statement while the witness is testifying if the witness denies having made it.

The following example will illustrate the rule. During the direct examination, an eyewitness to the accident testified for the plaintiff that the traffic light had been green for the plaintiff. When cross-examined by the defendant's' attorney, the witness denied that during a conversation with a police officer at the scene of the accident, he said he had not noticed the color of the light. Having laid the foundation, the defendant's attorney could call the police officer during the defendant's direct case to establish the conversation as a prior inconsistent statement.

Since a party's prior inconsistent oral statement is also an admission against interest, the attorney need not lay a foundation before offering that statement in evidence.

15.2.2 A Signed Writing

Before the attorney conducting the cross-examination may introduce a signed writing as a prior inconsistent statement to impeach the witness, "the paper must be shown or read to the witness and marked for identification and, if subscribed, the signature and in case he so demands, the paper must be

18. Loughlin v. Brassil, 187 N.Y. 128, 79 N.E. 854 (1907). For electronically recorded prior statements, *see* Sloan v. New York Cent. R.R., 45 N.Y. 125 (1871); Annot., *Evidence Secured by Mechanical or Electronic Eavesdropping Device as Admissible Against Witness for Purpose of Impeachment or Showing of Prior Inconsistent Statement*, 94 A.L.R.2D 1295 (1964); Annot., *Admissibility of Sound Recordings in Evidence for Impeachment Purpose*, 58 A.L.R.2D 1048 (1957); for the proper method, *see also* Ahmed v. Board of Educ., 98 A.D.2d 736, 469 N.Y.S.2d 435 (2d Dep't 1983); Ryan v. Dwyer, 33 A.D.2d 878, 307 N.Y.S.2d 565 (4th Dep't 1969); Wolfe v. Madison Ave. Coach Co., 171 Misc. 707, 13 N.Y.S.2d 741 (1st Dep't 1939).

shown to him."[19] In *Larkin v. Nassau Electric Railroad Co.*,[20] the Court of Appeals outlined the procedure. First, if the witness admits to signing the written statement, his or her admission is sufficient to prove the statement, but the impeaching party is entitled to a clear and direct admission – otherwise, other witnesses may be presented on the issue. Second, if the witness denies signing the statement, then the impeaching party may prove that the witness's signature is genuine. Third, after obtaining the admission or proving the signature, the impeaching party may offer the writing in evidence immediately during the case or during rebuttal. Fourth, the witness's signature is merely some evidence that he or she made or authorized the statement contained in the writing, unless the writing is a contract. The witness may claim that he or she did not read the statement, in which case the jury will evaluate that claim. Finally, the attorney for the impeaching party may not read the witness's prior statement to the jury or use the statement as the basis for cross-examination until the trial court has admitted the statement into evidence.

15.2.3 Testimony

When the prior inconsistent statement consists of testimony that the witness gave before another court or at a hearing at the motor vehicle bureau, the usual procedure is for the attorney for the impeaching party to request that the adversary concede that the cross-examiner has correctly read the series of questions and answers from the stenographer's minutes. Such a concession proves the prior inconsistent statement. Without it, the cross-examiner is theoretically obliged to call the stenographer or some other person who heard the witness testify. However, and as a practical matter, this procedure is unnecessary if the stenographer certified the transcript as a complete and accurate record of what was said.[21]

---

19. Larkin v. Nassau Elec. R.R., 205 N.Y. 267 (1912).

20. *Id.* at 270, 98 N.E. at 468.

21. *E.g.*, C.P.L.R. § 3116(b).

15.3 THE WITNESS HAS BEEN CONVICTED OF A CRIME

15.3.1 The Rule

In New York, C.P.L.R. section 4513 provides that the cross-examiner may prove that the opposing party's witness has been convicted of a crime "for the purpose of affecting the weight of his testimony, either by cross-examination, upon which he shall be required to answer any relevant question, or by the record. The party cross-examining is not concluded by such person's answer."[22] Since the statute requires that the witness have been convicted, evidence that the witness was arrested or indicted is inadmissible.[23]

15.3.2 The Crime

Within the meaning of the statute, a crime is either a misdemeanor or a felony. A traffic infraction is neither, and, therefore, evidence that the witness committed such an infraction is not admissible.[24] Note, however, that a traffic

22. C.P.L.R. § 4513. FED. R. EVID. 609 sets forth specific rules governing the admissibility and exclusion of testimony and convictions.
23. People v. Morrison, 195 N.Y. 116 (1909); Annot., *Impeachment of Witness by Evidence or Inquiry as to Arrest, Accusation, or Prosecution*, 20 A.L.R.2D 1421 (1951); Annot., *Prior Convictions: Propriety, in Impeaching Credibility of Witness in Civil Case by Showing Former Conviction or Questions Relating to Nature and Extent of Punishment*, 67 A.L.R.3D 761 (1975). In People v. Sandoval, 34 N.Y.2d 371, 357 N.Y.S.2d 849 (1974), the Court of Appeals held that if evidence may be offered at the trial on cross-examination, such as conviction of a crime, etc., that the opposing party deems prejudicial, that party may, prior to the offer, request a hearing in limine to have the court exclude the evidence. However, Guarisco v. E.J. Milk Farms, 90 Misc. 2d 81, 393 N.Y.S.2d 883 (Civ. Ct. 1977), held that the *Sandoval* principle does not apply to a civil case because C.P.L.R. § 4513 contains no exceptions and, therefore, the judge has no discretion.
24. C.P.L.R. § 4501; DeStasio v. Janssen Dairy Corp., 279 N.Y. 501 (1939); McQuage v. City of N.Y., 285 A.D.249, 136 N.Y.S.2d 111 (1st Dep't 1954); *see also* Annot., *Cross-Examination of Automobile Driver in Civil Action with Respect to Arrest or Conviction for Previous Traffic Offenses*, 20 A.L.R.2D 1217 (1951); Annot., *Traffic Offenses: Use of Unrelated Traffic Offense Conviction to Impeach Credibility of Witness in a State Civil Court*, 88 A.L.R.3D 74 (1978).

violation, such as reckless driving or driving while intoxicated, is a misdemeanor and, therefore, evidence of the witness's conviction is admissible.[25] Similarly, the statute does not permit the impeaching party to introduce evidence of:

1. The witness's conviction of a police offense;
2. Adjudication of the witness as a youthful offender, juvenile delinquent, or wayward minor;[26]
3. The imposition on the witness by an administrative officer of a fine for a dereliction of duty or an infraction of rules;
4. The witness's expulsion from a city department, or
5. The suspension or revocation of the witness's license to operate a motor vehicle.[27]

15.3.3 The Procedure

If the witness admits to having been convicted of a crime, the attorney may proceed to show the nature of the crime.[28] If the witness denies being convicted of a crime, the cross-examiner is not bound by the witness's answer but may prove that the witness was convicted,[29] typically by producing the record of the conviction.[30] Even if the witness con-

25. Woodward v. Phipps, 261 A.D. 865, 26 N.Y.S.2d 393 (3d Dep't 1941); Geiger v. Weiss, 245 A.D. 817, 281 N.Y.S. 154 (2d Dep't 1935).
26. People v. Sarra, 283 A.D. 876, 129 N.Y.S.2d 201 (2d Dep't 1954); See v. Wormser, 129 A.D. 596, 113 N.Y.S. 1093 (2d Dep't 1908). In People v. Vidal, 26 N.Y.2d 249, 306 N.Y.S.2d 336 (1970), the Court of Appeals held that although the cross-examiner could not prove the witness had been adjudicated a juvenile delinquent, the cross-examiner was not precluded from asking the witness about specific criminal acts, because the opposing party may show that the witness has committed criminal, vicious, or immoral acts.
27. Tryon v. Willbank, 234 A.D. 335, 255 N.Y.S.2d 27 (4th Dep't 1932).
28. Moore v. Leventhal, 303 N.Y. 534, 538, 104 N.E.2d 892, 894-95 (1952); People v. Sorge, 301 N.Y. 198, 201 (1950).
29. People v. McCormick, 278 A.D. 410, 105 N.Y.S.2d 571 (1st Dep't 1951), *aff'd*, 303 N.Y. 403 (1952).
30. C.P.L.R. § 4513.

cedes the conviction, the cross-examiner still may produce the record of conviction for the jury.[31]

A witness who has been impeached by a conviction for a crime may, if he wishes, proclaim his innocence in the face of the conviction[32] or explain the circumstances surrounding the conviction.[33]

15.3.4 When the Witness Is a Party

That a party was arrested has no probative value and is inadmissible in a civil action involving the same facts.[34] Similarly, that the witness was not arrested cannot be shown as circumstantial evidence of anything, such as credibility or due care.[35]

However, evidence of a party's conviction of a crime is admissible in a civil action involving the same facts.[36] Thus, in an action for wrongful death, the plaintiff may introduce evidence that the defendant has been convicted of the manslaughter of the plaintiff's intestate. However, the defendant in the civil action may not introduce evidence that he or she

---

31. McQuage v. City of N.Y., 285 A.D. 249, 136 N.Y.S.2d 111 (1st Dep't 1954).
32. Schindler v. Royal Ins. Co., 258 N.Y. 310, 179 N.E. 711 (1932); Sims v. Sims, 75 N.Y. 466 (1870).
33. People v. Tait, 234 A.D. 433, 255 N.Y.S.2d 455 (1st Dep't), *aff'd*, 259 N.Y. 599 (1932). *See* Annot., *Pardon as Affecting Impeachment by Proof of Conviction of Crime*, 30 A.L.R.2D 893 (1953).
34. Dance v. Town of Southampton, 95 A.D.2d 442, 467 N.Y.S.2d 203 (2d Dep't 1983); Franco v. Zingarelli, 72 A.D.2d 211, 424 N.Y.S.2d 185 (1st Dep't 1980); 2 BENDER'S NEW YORK EVIDENCE § 73.02[2] (1962).
35. RICHARDSON, EVIDENCE § 506.
36. *In re* Rechtschaffen, 278 N.Y. 336, 340, 16 N.E.2d 357, 359 (1938); Schindler v. Royal Ins. Co., 258 N.Y. 310, 179 N.E. 711 (1932); Annot., *Conviction or Acquittal as Evidence of the Facts on Which It Was Based in Civil Action,* 18 A.L.R.2D 1287 (1951). In S.T. Grand, Inc. v. City of N.Y., 38 A.D.2d 467, 330 N.Y.S.2d 594 (1st Dep't 1972), *aff'd*, 32 N.Y.2d 300, 344 N.Y.S.2d 938 (1973), the appellate courts held that a prior conviction on the same issue as the civil case is not merely evidence of negligence but complete estoppel or res judicata as to that issue.

was acquitted in the criminal action stemming from the same facts.[37]

15.4 THE WITNESS HAS COMMITTED AN IMMORAL, VICIOUS, OR CRIMINAL ACT

The courts of New York take the position that witnesses "whose lives indicate an abandonment or lack of moral principles, and show them to be lewd and debased characters, void of shame or decency, have not usually a great respect for the truth, or the sanctity of an oath."[38] Therefore, the courts permit a cross-examiner to interrogate the opposing party's witness about the immoral, vicious, or criminal acts the witness has committed. However, if the witness denies the accusation, the cross-examiner is bound by the answer and may not introduce evidence of this collateral matter.[39] (Note the distinction between this ground of impeachment and impeachment for the conviction of a crime.)

The interrogation must relate to matters of moral turpitude, e.g., whether the witness had sold or used narcotics,[40] operated

37. Massey v. Meurer, 25 A.D.2d 729, 268 N.Y.S.2d 735 (1st Dep't 1966); Etheridge v. City of N.Y., 121 N.Y.S.2d 103 (Sup. Ct. 1953), *aff'd,* 283 A.D. 867, 129 N.Y.S.2d 915 (1st Dep't 1954).

38. Osborne v. Seligman, 39 Misc. 811, 812, 81 N.Y.S. 346, 347 (1st Dep't 1903). *See* FED. R. EVID. 608(b). In People v. Duffy, 36 N.Y.2d 258, 367 N.Y.S.2d 236 (1975), the Court of Appeals held that it was proper to cross-examine the witness about his use of narcotics during a trial in which the defendant was charged with the crimes of robbery and grand larceny. However, in the very next year, the Court of Appeals held that the prosecution may not cross-examine the defendant about his prior bad acts in order to show his propensity to commit the crime charged. People v. Wright, 41 N.Y.2d 172 (1976). Annot., *Use of Drugs as Affecting Credibility of Witness*, 65 A.L.R.3d 705 (1975); Annot., *Impeachment of Witness with Respect to Intoxication*, 8 A.L.R.3D 749 (1966).

39. People v. Sorge, 301 N.Y. 198 (1950); Serpe v. Rappaport, 103 A.D.2d 771, 477 N.Y.S.2d 403 (1st Dep't 1984); RICHARDSON, EVIDENCE § 491. Remember, however, that extrinsic evidence is admissible to show that the witness is biased, interested, or hostile. Badr v. Hogan, 75 N.Y.2d 629 (1990), and People v. Knight, 80 N.Y.2d 845 (1992).

40. People v. Webster, 139 N.Y. 73 (1893); Annot., *Use of Drugs as Affecting Competency or Credibility of Witness*, 52 A.L.R.2D 848 (1957).

a brothel, or had illicit sexual relations.[41] The interrogation is not proper if it inquires about the witness's failure to pay rent, expulsion from a church, society, labor union, or fire department,[42] religious beliefs or lack thereof,[43] a dishonorable discharge from the armed forces,[44] or having been visited by the police while a resident on a certain street.[45] Questions of this type are attacks on the witness's private life. They do not test credibility but merely degrade the individual and bring him or her into disrepute with the jury and are, therefore, improper.[46] Even when asking a question which may be proper, the attorney must act in good faith – there must be a reasonable factual basis for the question.[47]

---

41. RICHARDSON, EVIDENCE § 498; People v. Giblin, 115 N.Y. 196 (1889). The opposing party may show that the witness, a lawyer, had been disbarred, Hyman v. Dworsky, 239 A.D. 413, 417, 267 N.Y.S. 539 (3d Dep't 1933), or suspended from the practice of law, Batease v. Dion, 275 A.D. 451, 90 N.Y.S. 851 (3d Dep't 1949).
42. RICHARDSON, EVIDENCE § 499; *see also* McQuage v. City of N.Y., 285 A.D. 249, 136 N.Y.S.2d 111 (1st Dep't 1954).
43. Brink v. Stratton, 176 N.Y. 150 (1903), and People v. Wood, 107 A.D.2d 830 (2d Dep't 1985).
44. Annot., *Admissibility and Effect of Evidence or Comment on Party's Military Service or Lack Thereof,* 9 A.L.R.2D 606 (1950).
45. George v. Owners Trucking Corp., 264 A.D. 831, 35 N.Y.S.2d 475 (4th Dep't 1942).
46. *Id. See also* Cortis v. Grenor Co., 20 A.D.2d 704, 247 N.Y.S.2d 205 (1st Dep't 1964), in which the appellate court held that the trial court had erred by permitting the defendant's attorney to read many pages of an affidavit from a previous matrimonial action and containing unsavory details, because "extrinsic evidence may not be introduced on this collateral issue." In People v. Alamo, 23 N.Y.2d 630, 633, 298 N.Y.S.2d 681, 682-83 (1969), the Court of Appeals held that a witness may be cross-examined about his criminal and immoral acts (even when he has not been convicted) if there is a reasonable basis for the attack. *Accord*, People v. Schwartzman, 24 N.Y.2d 241, 299 N.Y.S.2d 817, *cert. denied*, 396 U.S. 846 (1969); People v. Sorge, 301 N.Y. 198, 200 (1959), and People v. Knight, 80 N.Y.2d 845 (1992).
47. People v. Simpson, 109 A.D.2d 461 (1st Dep't 1985). The court quoted People v. Alamo: "The rule that evolves from the cases is that questions such as these . . . to the defendant . . . as a witness are not error if the prosecutor asked them in good faith, that is to say, if he had some reasonable basis for believing the truth of things he was asking about." 23 N.Y.2d 630, 633 (1969).

In *Gedrin v. Long Island Jewish Hospital,*[48] the Appellate Division, Second Department, explained the rule, applied it, and approved two attempts to impeach the witness. The appellate court explained that the trial court, in its discretion, controls the admission of evidence for impeaching witnesses. However, a witness in a civil action may be cross-examined regarding any immoral, vicious, or criminal act that would show the individual to be unworthy of belief. The court then approved the defense attorney's cross-examination of the plaintiff's mother about two specific acts of misconduct – assaulting a policeman and petty larceny. Although the first charge was adjourned and the second reduced, the attorney had a basis on which to question the witness regarding the incidents.

15.5 THE WITNESS IS BIASED, HOSTILE, OR INTERESTED IN THE OUTCOME

"The witness's bias in favor of the party calling him, or his hostility to the party against whom he testifies, may be shown to affect his credibility. . . . For the same purpose, it is competent to show the interest of the witness in the case."[49] There is no particular ground for or method of showing bias or hostility except the application of common sense to the facts of the case, e.g., that the witness is related to the party who called him or was fired by the opposing party. Moreover, New York does not require the cross-examiner to lay a foundation in order to show bias or hostility by first asking the witness about the factual basis.[50] As the Court of Appeals explained in *People v. Brooks,*[51]

48. Gedrin v. Long Island Jewish Hosp., 119 A.D.2d 799, 501 N.Y.S.2d 426 (2d Dep't 1986).

49. RICHARDSON, EVIDENCE § 503.

50. People v. Brooks, 131 N.Y. 321 (1892); Luce v. St. Peter's Hosp., 85 A.D.2d 194, 448 N.Y.S.2d 855 (3d Dep't 1982); Thompson v. Korn, 48 A.D.2d 1007, 368 N.Y.S.2d 923 (4th Dep't 1975); Annot., *Necessity and Sufficiency of Foundation for Discrediting Evidence Showing Bias or Prejudice of Adverse Witness,* 87 A.L.R.2D 407 (1963). *See also* FED. R. EVID. 611(b).

51. People v. Brooks, 131 N.Y. 321 (1892).

> The hostility of a witness towards a party against whom he is called may be proved by any competent evidence. It may be shown by cross-examination of the witness, or witnesses may be called who can swear to facts showing it. There can be no reason for holding that the witness must first be examined as to his hostility, and that then, and not till then, witnesses may be called to contradict him, because it is not a case where the party against whom the witness is called is seeking to discredit him by contradicting him. He is simply seeking to discredit him by showing his hostility and malice; and as that may be proved by any competent evidence we see no reason for holding that he must first be examined as to his hostility.[52]

The foregoing rule also applies to the case of a witness who is interested in the outcome of the litigation.[53] For example, the Appellate Division, Second Department, has held that the trial court erred by not allowing the opposing party to show that the witness had settled his claim with the party who called him.[54]

When attempting to impeach a witness for bias in favor of a party, the cross-examiner may show that the witness and the party are friends.[55] Similarly, when impeaching a medical expert for hostility against a party, the cross-examiner may ask the witness about the number of physical examinations he or she has performed on behalf of the defendants, the witness's fee as a medical witness, membership in the society on whose behalf the testimony is given, and threats to get even with the plaintiffs.[56] Finally, an adverse party may show that the witness is hostile to a party other than the one examining him or her, i.e., to another plaintiff or defendant.[57]

---

52. *Id.* at 325.
53. G. Mottla, New York Evidence — Proof of Cases § 370 (2d ed. 1966).
54. Pretto v. Leiwant, 80 A.D.2d 579, 435 N.Y.S.2d 778 (2d Dep't 1980).
55. Bombard v. County of Albany, 94 A.D.2d 910, 463 N.Y.S.2d 633 (3d Dep't 1983).
56. People v. Milks, 70 A.D. 438, 74 N.Y.S. 1042 (4th Dep't 1902); Annot., *Cross-Examination of Expert Witness as to Fees, Compensation and the Like*, 33 A.L.R.2d 1170 (1954).
57. Garnsey v. Rhodes, 138 N.Y. 461 (1893).

15.6 THE OPINION OF THE EXPERT WITNESS IS CONTRARY TO RECOGNIZED AUTHORITY

The cross-examiner may impeach the credibility of medical and other expert witnesses by showing that the expert's opinion is contrary to recognized authority in his field. However, as a prerequisite, the witness must first acknowledge as authoritative the author or treatise to which the cross-examiner refers.[58] Thus, in an action for personal injuries resulting from the explosion of a battery in the plaintiff's automobile, the Appellate Division, First Department, held that the trial court should have permitted the plaintiff's attorney to lay a foundation for cross-examining an expert witness about the statements and opinions in treatises by recognized authorities, which opinions varied from the expert's.[59] Although the statement in the treatise is not evidence-in-chief, the Appellate Division, Second Department, drew an important distinction in the important case of *Vialva v. City of New York.*[60] *Vialva* suggests that if the expert agrees with the statement in the treatise and if the witness adopts the statement, it thereby becomes evidence-in-chief. (The treatise itself, of course, is not evidence, whether the witness agrees with it or not.) However, *Vialva* is merely an instance of a witness testifying in a particular way when prompted to do so by the opposing attorney via a textbook.

58. FED. R. EVID. 803(18) goes well beyond New York's rule. The federal rule allows the attorney to use texts for direct examination. In addition, any witness may establish that the text is authoritative. *See* Annot., *Use of Medical or Other Scientific Treatises in Cross-Examination of Expert Witnesses,* 60 A.L.R.2D 77 (1958).

59. Hastings v. Chrysler Corp., 273 A.D. 292, 77 N.Y.S.2d 524 (1st Dep't 1948); *see also* People v. Feldman, 299 N.Y. 153, 168 (1949) (the witness knew of the books and that they were standard works on the subject); Egan v. Dry Dock, E.B.B.R.R., 12 A.D. 556, 42 N.Y.S. 188 (1st Dep't 1896); Ruth v. Fenchel, 21 N.J. 171, 121 A.2d 373 (1956).

60. Vialva v. City of N.Y., 118 A.D.2d 701, 499 N.Y.S.2d 977 (2d Dep't 1986).

The troublesome question of the extent to which the witness must recognize the treatise as authoritative was addressed by the highest court of New Jersey in *Ruth v. Fenchel.*[61] At the trial, the plaintiff's attorney asked the defendant's medical expert, "Do you recognize Key and Conwell?" The witness answered, "Yes, they are very, very capable." He said that he had read those authors, but not that particular volume.[62] On cross-examination, another of the defendant's medical experts "characterized the Key and Conwell treatise as 'an excellent text book, one of the text books I have in my library.'"[63] The court held that when

> the cross-examiner directs the attention of the expert witness to the contents of treatises expressing an opinion at variance with the opinion of the witness, and does so not to prove the contrary opinion but merely to call into question the weight to be attached by the fact finder to the opinion of the witness, the law of this State allows such use of the treatise *even if not relied upon by the witness in arriving at his opinion, provided the witness admits that the treatise is a recognized and standard authority on the subject.*[64] This was decided in *New Jersey Zinc & Iron Company v. Lehigh Zinc & Iron Company* . . . .[65]

The court in *Ruth v. Fenchel* approved the following cross-examination from *New Jersey Zinc:*

Q Do you remember Whitney's *Metallic Wealth of the United States?*

A Yes sir. I know that quite well.

Q Is it considered a standard book and referred to as such generally?

A Yes sir. It is a standard book.

61. Ruth v. Fenchel, 21 N.J. 171, 121 A.2d 373 (1956).
62. *Id.* at 173-74, 121 A.2d at 374.
63. *Id.* at 174, 121 A.2d at 374.
64. Emphasis added.
65. *See* New Jersey Zinc & Iron Co. v. Lehigh Iron & Zinc Co., 59 N.J.L. 189, 35 A. 915 (1896).

Q And referred to as such by scientific men?

A Yes sir.[66]

Twenty years after *Ruth*, the Appellate Division, Second Department, reached the same conclusion in *Mark v. Colgate University.*[67] The court held that the cross-examiner is not limited to using books and articles read by the expert witness as long as the witness recognizes as authoritative the treatise the cross-examiner does use. In a nutshell, the cross-examiner may use for cross-examination any treatise on which the witness relied during the direct examination[68] and if the witness has not relied on the treatise, it may be used if the witness recognizes it as authoritative.

15.7 THE WITNESS HAS A BAD REPUTATION FOR TRUTH AND VERACITY

To impeach the opposing party's witness, the attorney may demonstrate that the witness has a bad reputation for truth and veracity in the community in which he or she lives.[69] In *Spira v. Holoschutz,*[70] the trial court outlined the procedure for this method of impeachment:

> All that is necessary for a party to an action to do in order to impeach the testimony of an adverse witness is to show by an impeaching witness that he, the impeaching witness, knows the general reputation for truth and veracity of the witness whose testimony it is sought to impeach, in the community in which the witness resides. If the witness says that he does know such reputation he may then be asked what that reputa-

66. Ruth v. Fenchel, 21 N.J. 171, 176-77, 121 A.2d 373, 376 (1956).
67. Mark v. Colgate Univ., 53 A.D.2d 884, 385 N.Y.S.2d 621 (2d Dep't 1976).
68. RICHARDSON, EVIDENCE § 373.
69. FED. R. EVID. 608(a); Richardson, Evidence §§ 494-97.
70. Spira v. Holoschutz, 38 Misc. 754 (N.Y. Mun. Ct. 1902). *See also* Carlson v. Winterton, 147 N.Y. 652 (1895); Elmendorf v. Ross, 221 A.D.376, 222 N.Y.S.737 (3d Dep't 1927); Sturmwald v. Schreiber, 69 A.D. 476, 74 N.Y.S. 995 (2d Dep't 1902).

> tion is, and if he says that it is not good, he may be asked whether from such knowledge he would believe such witness on his oath.

Note that the impeaching witness may not testify about any specific instance of the original witness's lack of veracity but merely about his or her reputation for veracity. However, when cross-examining the impeaching witness, the attorney for the party who called the original witness may question the impeaching witness about his or her knowledge of specific instances.[71] Finally, the attorney should bear in mind that the testimony impeaching a witness's reputation is limited to the individual's reputation for truth and veracity and may not show that reputation as bad in other respects, such as for chastity.

---

71. Annot., *Admissibility of Testimony as to Reputation of Party or Witness at Place of Employment or Occupation*, 82 A.L.R.3D 525 (1978).

Demonstrative Evidence 16

Demonstrative evidence is "evidence addressed directly to the senses without intervention of testimony."[1] In other words, the jury can see the evidence for what it is, e.g., a photograph of the scene of the accident, although a witness's testimony may be necessary to identify, explain, or introduce the evidence. The trial court has the authority to compel the production of demonstrative evidence, such as photographs, records, or papers that are present in the courtroom.[2] This chapter will discuss the demonstrative evidence used most often in actions for negligence: photographs, movies and recordings, diagrams and models, x-rays and blood samples, premises, and hospital and repair bills.

16.1 PHOTOGRAPHS

16.1.1 The General Rule

The general rule is that admitting photographs into evidence rests in the sound discretion of the trial court.[3] So long as the photograph is relevant to the issue of liability or damages and accurately reflects the condition of the scene

1. BLACK'S LAW DICTIONARY 419 (4th ed. 1968).
2. Bloodgood v. Lynch, 293 N.Y. 308, 56 N.E. 718 (1944).
3. Markey v. Eiseman, 114 A.D.2d 887, 495 N.Y.S.2d 61 (2d Dep't 1985); Wesler v. Kassl, 109 A.D.2d 740, 485 N.Y.S.2d 844 (2d Dep't 1985); People v. Winchell, 98 A.D.2d 838, 470 N.Y.S.2d 835 (3d Dep't 1983).

at the time of the incident or accurately reflects the plaintiff's injuries, then the court should admit the photograph for the jury's consideration.[4] Anyone who is familiar with the scene at the time of the incident may testify that the photograph is an accurate depiction;[5] this witness need not be the photographer. However, if no one testifies that the photograph accurately reflects the scene or product at the relevant time, the photograph is not admissible.[6] For example, if the photograph purports to show the positions of the automobiles after the collision, there must be preliminary testimony that the automobiles were not moved before the photograph was taken.[7] Of course, the photograph is inadmissible if the witnesses testify that it is not a fair representation.[8]

Once admitted into evidence, the photograph may be the basis for expert testimony like any other evidence.[9] There are situations in which the setting or occurrence cannot be duplicated, and, in those situations, a photograph may be the best evidence of the condition at the crucial time.[10]

16.1.2 Posed Photographs of the Scene

Although posed photographs are generally not admissible, some such photographs are.[11] Thus, one foreign court admitted a photograph of the scene of a highway accident, which

4. FED. R. EVID. 901, 403 (the general exclusionary rule); see Busch, *Photographic Evidence*, 4 DEPAUL L. REV. 195 (1955).
5. Archer v. New York, N.Y. & H. R.R., 106 N.Y. 589 (1887); Annot., *Authentication or Verification of Photograph as Basis for Introduction in Evidence*, 9 A.L.R.2D 899 (1950).
6. Keefner v. City of Albany, 77 A.D.2d 747, 430 N.Y.S.2d 877 (3d Dep't 1980).
7. Roberson v. Keogh, 66 A.D.2d 816, 411 N.Y.S.2d 370 (2d Dep't 1978).
8. People v. Tortorice, 142 A.D.2d 916 (3d Dep't 1988).
9. Markey v. Eiseman, 114 A.D.2d 887, 495 N.Y.S.2d 61 (2d Dep't 1985); Bolm v. Triumph Corp., 71 A.D.2d 429, 422 N.Y.S.2d 969 (4th Dep't), *aff'd*, 33 N.Y.2d 151 (1974).
10. Bolm v. Triumph Corp., 71 A.D.2d 429, 422 N.Y.S.2d 969 (4th Dep't 1979).
11. Annot., *Admissibility of Posed Photograph Based on Recollection of Position of Persons or Moveable Objects*, 19 A.L.R.2D (1951).

photograph showed a witness standing on the road and pointing to certain marks on the roadway, because the only purpose of the witness's presence in the picture was to draw attention to fixed marks that were present immediately after the accident.[12] Sometimes a map marked by a witness during the witness's testimony is a more lucid alternative.[13]

16.1.3 Photographs of Injuries

The trial court has the discretion to admit photographs of the plaintiff's injuries, even if the injuries are unsightly, when the plaintiff offers the photographs on the issue of damages and the photographs are relevant to the jury's understanding of the plaintiff's injuries.[14] In other words, gruesome photographs are not necessarily inadmissible.[15] Hence, the court properly admitted color photographs of the plaintiff lying on a Stryker frame with Crutchfield tongs attached to his scalp.[16] Even though the plaintiff's scars are obvious to the jury, the plaintiff may introduce the photographs of the injuries so that the appellate court can better understand their nature[17] or so that the jury can assess the

---

12. Square Deal Cartage Co. v. Smith's Adm'r, 307 Ky. 135, 210 S.W.2d 340 (1948).
13. *See* section 16.3 *infra*.
14. Gallo v. Supermarkets Gen. Corp., 112 A.D.2d 345, 491 N.Y.S.2d 796 (2d Dep't 1985); Caprara v. Chrysler Corp., 71 A.D.2d 515, 423 N.Y.S.2d 694 (3d Dep't 1979), *aff'd*, 52 N.Y.2d 114, 417 N.E.2d 545, 436 N.Y.S.2d 251 (1981); Note, *Admission of Gruesome Photograph in Homicide Prosecution*, 16 CREIGHTON L. REV. 73 (1982).
15. Knox v. City of Granite Falls, 245 Minn. 11, 19, 72 N.W.2d 67, 73 (1955). In fact, photographs of the plaintiff showing his lacerations and sutures and taken while the plaintiff was still in the hospital were held admissible in New v. Cortright, 32 A.D.2d 576, 299 N.Y.S.2d 43 (3d Dep't 1969). *See* Gomaco Corp. v. Faith, 550 So. 2d 482 (Fla. App. 1989).
16. Caprara v. Chrysler Corp., 71 A.D.2d 515, 423 N.Y.S.2d 694 (3d Dep't 1979), *aff'd*, 52 N.Y.2d 114, 417 N.E.2d 545, 436 N.Y.S.2d 251 (1981).
17. Carlisle v. County of Nassau, 64 A.D.2d 15, 408 N.Y.S.2d 114 (2d Dep't 1978).

plaintiff's pain and suffering.[18] Courts have admitted color slides of a plaintiff's injuries as well as black-and-white photographs.[19]

The court of appeals has ruled, however, that it was prejudicial to admit a photograph of the decedent in an action for wrongful death.[20]

16.1.4 Photographs to Prove Notice

As we discussed in chapter 6, photographs are admissible to prove that the defendant had constructive notice of a defective or dangerous condition.[21] If a witness at the deposition marked a photograph to indicate the place at which the accident occurred, that photograph is admissible at the trial, assuming the party's attorney laid a proper foundation for the photograph at the deposition.[22]

If, between the time of the accident and the taking of the photograph, there have been minor changes in the condition of the premises that do not affect any important issue, the

---

18. Krueger v. Frisenda, 218 A.D.2d 685 (2d Dep't 1995).
19. Annot., *Admissibility in Evidence of Colored Photographs*, 53 A.L.R.2D 1102 (1978).
20. Smith v. Lehigh Valley R.R., 177 N.Y. 379, 384, 69 N.E. 729, 730 (1904), and Allen v. Stokes, 260 N.Y. 600 (1940); Annot., *Admissibility in Wrongful Death Action, of Photograph of Decedent Made in Her Lifetime*, 74 A.L.R. 928 (1960). *See also* Annot., *Admissibility of Photograph of Corpse in Prosecution for Homicide or Civil Action for Causing Death*, 73 A.L.R.2D 769 (1960). However, in Mayes v. County of Nassau, 31 A.D.2d 638, 295 N.Y.S.2d 989 (2d Dep't 1968), the appellate court held that although the trial court should not have admitted the photograph of the deceased plaintiff, the error was not prejudicial as to require an unconditional reversal.
21. *See also* Taylor v. New York City Transit Auth., 48 N.Y.2d 903, 400 N.E.2d 1340, 424 N.Y.S.2d 888 (1976); Batton v. Agradgon, 43 N.Y.2d 898, 374 N.E.2d 611, 403 N.Y.S.2d 717 (1973), and Karten v. City of New York, 109 A.D.2d 126 (1st Dep't 1985). Although these cases pre-date written notice ordinances, the means of proving constructive notice are still appropriate against private defendants and for other kinds of accidents.
22. Roach v. City of Albany, 282 A.D. 807, 122 N.Y.S.2d 437 (3d Dep't 1955).

trial court should admit the photograph into evidence.[23] However, if the change was substantial[24] or if repairs have been made, the court should not admit the photograph. The reason in the latter case is that an opposing party may prove subsequent repairs only if control of the premises is an issue.[25] For example, if the exterior staircase had no handrail at the time of the accident, and that fact underlines the plaintiff's claim of negligence, it would be prejudicial to the defendant to admit a photograph that was taken months later and that shows a handrail.

Of course, the parties may dispute whether a particular photograph accurately represents the condition of the scene

---

23. FED. R. EVID. 407; Amsler v. City of N.Y., 172 A.D. 63, 58 N.Y.S. 219 (1st Dep't 1916). *See also* Robertson v. Giangrasso, 7 A.D.2d 733, 735, 180 N.Y.S.2d 627, 628 (2d Dep't 1958), which held that "it was error to exclude the testimony proffered by appellant as to the condition of respondents' vehicle and the photograph taken *one-half hour after the accident* away from the scene thereof." (Emphasis added.) The court cited Simon v. Ora Realty Corp., 1 N.Y.2d 388, 393, 135 N.E.2d 580, 582, 153 N.Y.S.2d 39, 42 (1956) ("the trial court should have permitted the introduction of evidence of the condition of the ash can *on the day following the accident* since, without proof to the contrary it was reasonable to assume that its then condition was substantially the same as at the time in question." (Emphasis added.) *See also* Peil v. Reinhart, 127 N.Y. 381, 385, 27 N.E. 1077, 1078 (1891) ("[T]here was no error in the reception of the evidence of the condition of the stair carpet the morning following the injury."); Coffin v. Cunningham, 11 A.D.2d 1082, 206 N.Y.S.2d 353 (4th Dep't 1960) (a witness who had arrived at the scene of an accident shortly after it had occurred could properly testify to the fire marks that appeared in newly fallen snow and led to a vehicle involved in the accident).
24. In Dugan v. Dieber, 32 A.D.2d 815, 302 N.Y.S.2d 423 (2d Dep't 1969), the appellate court held that it was prejudicial to the plaintiff to admit photographs taken of a street where apartment houses had replaced private houses and that showed different parking conditions with cars not parked close together. *But see* Saporito v. City of N.Y., 14 N.Y.2d 474, 202 N.E.2d 369, 253 N.Y.S.2d 985 (1964), in which the court of appeals held that it was error to exclude the defendants' offer of photographs of the condition of the roadway when the plaintiff claimed that there had been a hole in the roadway, for "[i]t did not impair the admissibility of these photographs that they showed the building abutting the street, or the presence of rubbish or other debris on the sidewalk, if, as was testified by several witnesses, they correctly showed the condition of the pavement 15 feet out into the street."
25. Scudero v. Campbell, 288 N.Y. 328, 43 N.E.2d 66 (1942); Feinstein v. New York City Transit Auth., 17 Misc. 2d 45, 190 N.Y.S.2d 304 (2d Dep't 1958) (evidence that a subway platform had been sanded after the accident was not admissible).

at the time of the incident, and both may introduce photographs. Thus, in an action against a county for the death of a passenger in an automobile that had gone over a precipitous embankment into a river, the court of appeals held that the trial court had properly permitted the plaintiff to show that the guardrails had not been installed at the time of the accident because the defendant had introduced, as a fair representation of the conditions at the time of the accident, a photograph of the roadway showing that there had been guardrails.[26]

Example 16-1, at the end of the chapter, is the paragraph demanding that the opposing party produce any relevant photograph.

16.2 MOVIES, VIDEOTAPES, AND TAPE RECORDINGS

16.2.1 Admissibility

Motion pictures or videotapes are admissible only if they are relevant and only if they are not cumulative, sensational, or prejudicial.[27] Thus, a motion picture of an allegedly injured plaintiff working around the house or a "day-in-the-life" film of an injured party might be relevant, but the film must be accurate, and the person who made the film must

26. Huston v. City of Chenango, 253 A.D. 56, 1 N.Y.S.2d 252 (3d Dep't 1934), *aff'd*, 278 N.Y. 646, 16 N.E.2d 301 (1938).

27. Boyarsky v. G.A. Zinnerman Corp., 240 A.D. 361, 270 N.Y.S. 134 (1st Dep't 1934); Gibson v. Gunn, 206 A.D. 464, 202 N.Y.S. 19 (1st Dep't 1923); Annot., *Use of Motion Pictures as Evidence*, 62 A.L.R.2D 686 (1958). On authentication, see People v. Turnstall, 97 A.D.2d 523, 468 N.Y.S.2d 32 (2d Dep't 1983); Peters v. Wiles, *Videotaping of Surgery for Use as Demonstrative Evidence in Medical Malpractice Litigation*, 16 DUQUESNE L. REV. 360 (1978); Wells, *Motion Pictures in Evidence*, 8 BROOKLYN L. REV. 290 (1939); *see also* Repple v. Barnes Hosp., 778 S.W.2d 819 (Mo. App. 1989); Annot., *Authentication or Verification of Moving Pictures as Basis for Introduction in Evidence*, 9 A.L.R.2D 921 (1950).

testify to the facts surrounding the film. In other words, the rule for introducing films differs from the rule for introducing still photographs since any person with knowledge of the scene may testify that the photograph is an accurate representation. He need not be the photographer, but the witness who introduces moving pictures must have participated in the filming.

A good example of how a court evaluates the admissibility of a movie or videotape is *Mechanick v. Conradi,*[28] in which the Appellate Division, Third Department, upheld the trial court's refusal to admit a videotape by which the plaintiff intended to show the sighting distances at the scene of the accident between his motorcycle and the defendant's vehicle. The appellate court observed that admitting such a videotape lies in the discretion of the trial court, depends on the circumstances of the case, and requires that the videotape not exaggerate any feature the party seeks to prove. The court then pointed out the videotape's deficiencies, to wit:

> [T]he videotape depicted a full-size van heading south on Route 147 instead of a motorcycle. It presented a north-bound view of what defendant would have seen but never shows what plaintiff would have seen while traveling south. Moreover, the videotape could have unfairly misled the jury since the van was clearly more visible than the motorcycle. Additionally, large red cones were placed on the side of the road as visual reference markers which were obviously not there at the time of the accident. The use of a telephoto lens also enhanced defendant's alleged sight distance. Finally, the van was operated at speeds no greater than 55 miles per hour, which, while consistent with plaintiff's claim that he was not speeding, contradicted the trooper's testimony that plaintiff was speeding.

Therefore, the trial court had properly refused to admit the videotape.

28. Mechanick v. Conradi, 139 A.D.2d 857, 527 N.Y.S.2d 586 (3d Dep't 1988).

Audiotapes are also admissible, but they are admitted less often than movies or videotapes because it would be a rare instance in which an audiotape could depict the accident, the scene, or an injury. However, if authenticated as accurate, a tape recording of a person speaking may be admissible to establish an admission against interest.[29] In addition, tapes of 911 calls may be admissible as excited utterances[30] or present-sense impressions. (See chapter 17.)

16.2.2 Discovery

The rule in New York is that the plaintiff is entitled to discovery of all surveillance films or videotapes made of the plaintiff for the defendant and of redacted copies of the defense attorney's memoranda about the tapes. However, the defendant need not produce the tapes and the memoranda until after he or she has taken the plaintiff's deposition, and, if the defendant does not introduce the surveillance tapes at the trial, the plaintiff's attorney may not even comment on this choice.

According to one commentator in 1993, "the use of videotape evidence has grown dramatically over the last 10 years as the cost associated with its production has dropped and as more companies have become willing and able to perform surveillance."[31] One result of the popularity of this form of investigation was that every appellate division was required to rule on the discovery of these tapes, but the four departments formulated three different rules.[32] Fortunately, the court of appeals heard two companion cases from the

29. Tepper v. Tannenbaum, 65 A.D.2d 359, 411 N.Y.S.2d 588 (1st Dep't 1978).
30. People v. Lewis, 635 N.Y.S.2d 872 (4th Dep't 1995).
31. James P. Connors, *Assault on an Effective Way to Expose Fraud,* N.Y.L.J., Dec. 1, 1993, at 2.
32. Marte v. W. O. Hickok Manufacturing Co., 154 A.D.2d 173 (1st Dep't 1990); Careccia v. Enstrom, 174 A.D.2d 48 (3d Dep't 1992); Kane v. Her-Pet Refrigeration, 181 A.D.2d 257 (2d Dep't 1992); and DiMichel v. South Buffalo Railway Co., 178 A.D.2d 914 (4th Dep't 1991).

Fourth Department. Thus, in *DiMichel v. South Buffalo Railway Co.* and *Poole v. Consolidated Rail Corporation*,[33] the court held,

> [W]e agree . . . that surveillance films should be treated as material prepared in anticipation of litigation, and as such, are subject to a qualified privilege that can be overcome only by a factual showing of substantial need and undue hardship.
>
> That the plaintiffs in both these cases have a substantial need to view surveillance films before trial is manifest.[34]

In other words, any plaintiff's need for the films overcomes the defendant's privilege almost ipso facto.

The legislature codified the central holding of *DiMichel* in C.P.L.R. section 3101(i): " . . . , there shall be full disclosure of any films, photographs, video tapes or audio tapes, including transcripts or memoranda thereof, involving a person referred to in paragraph one of subdivision (a) of this section. There shall be disclosure of all portions of such material, including out-takes, rather than only those portions a party intends to use." C.P.L.R. section 3101(a)(1) enumerated a party or the officer, director, member, agent, or employee of a party.

However, the attorney still must refer to the court's opinion in *DiMichel* for other elements of the court's decision, and the attorney should remember that the court was concerned to protect each party from dishonesty by the other. Thus, although the court decided that the possibility of the defendant's manipulating the tape required that the plaintiff receive a copy before the trial, the possibility of the plaintiff's altering his testimony required that the defendant be allowed to withhold that copy until after he had taken the plaintiff's deposition.[35] Moreover, if the defendant produces

---

33. DiMichel v. South Buffalo Railway Co., 80 N.Y.2d 184, 590 N.Y.S.2d 1 (1992).
34. *Id.* at 196.
35. *Id.* at 197. This was the position of the Appellate Division, First Department, in Marte v. W.O. Hickok Manufacturing, 154 A.D.2d 173 (___) and in Rodgers v. City of New York, N.Y.L.J., June 11, 1992, at 24.

the surveillance film but decides not to use it at the trial, then the plaintiff's attorney may not even comment on this choice.[36] Most commentators have interpreted this prohibition as implying a fortiori that the plaintiff may not introduce the surveillance film as part of his or her direct case,[37] but one court has allowed the plaintiff to introduce the defendant's surveillance films during the damage phase.[38]

16.3 DIAGRAMS, MODELS, ANATOMICAL EXHIBITS, AND DEMONSTRATIONS

The trial court has considerable latitude to admit diagrams, models, etc.,[39] and a map, diagram, or model that has been properly authenticated is clearly admissible.[40] A diagram or survey need not have been made by a surveyor or have been drawn to scale. Anyone, e.g., an investigator, may have drawn the diagram, and it becomes admissible when the witness testifies regarding how the area was measured and certifies the diagram's accuracy.[41] For example, in an action for wrongful death due to the collapse of a temporary bridge, the plaintiff produced what he claimed was a model of the bridge. The plaintiff called a witness who testified that he had constructed the model and who detailed the

36. *DiMichel, supra* at 199.
37. For example, Susan C. Roney and Laurie Styka Bloom, letter to ed., N.Y.L.J., Oct. 28, 1993, at 2.
38. Baird v. Campbell, N.Y.L.J., Oct. 30, 1992, at 34 (Sup. Ct. Queens).
39. *See* Ladd, *Demonstrative Evidence and Expert Opinion*, 1956 WASH. U. L.Q. 1; Article, *Charts, Graphs and Mini Summations*, 16 LITIG. 1, at 21 (Fall 1989).
40. Clegg v. Metropolitan St. Ry., 1 A.D. 207, 37 N.Y.S. 130 (2d Dep't 1896), *aff'd*, 159 N.Y. 550, 54 N.E.2d 1089 (1899).
41. Annot., *Evidence: Use and Admissibility of Maps, Plats, and Other Drawings to Illustrate or Express Testimony*, 9 A.L.R.2D 1044 (1950); Annot., *Admissibility in Evidence, in Automobile Negligence Action, of Charts Showing Braking Distance, Reaction Times, Etc.*, 9 A.L.R.3D 976 (1966).

construction. Another witness testified that the model correctly represented the bridge at the time of the accident. The trial court then admitted the model into evidence although the defendant disputed the model's accuracy.[42]

The trial court has the discretion to permit a party's attorney to use anatomical charts or models of parts of the body.[43] It is proper for the attorney to use a skull to explain to the jury the nature of the injuries to the plaintiff's eye.[44] In such a case, *McNaier v. Manhattan Railway Co.*, the appellate court wrote:

> The objection of defendant to the use of a skull to explain to the jury the nature of plaintiff's injuries is not well taken, nor was the objection to the exhibition of the surgical instruments, by which the operation was performed, valid . . . . To suppose that the sight of a skull and the instruments, used, as they were, to explain the injury and the operation necessary to relieve it, should have "inflamed the passion of the jury" is quite unreasonable.[45]

The party's attorney or witness may draw the chart or diagram, and the trial court has the discretion to permit the use of a blackboard.[46]

---

42. Coolidge v. City of N.Y., 99 A.D. 175, 90 N.Y.S. 1078 (1st Dep't 1904), *aff'd*, 185 N.Y. 529, 77 N.E. 1192 (1906). *See* Annot., *Propriety, in Trial of Civil Action, of Use of Model of Object or Instrumentality or of Site or Premises, Involved in the Accident or Incident*, 69 A.L.R.2D 424 (1960).
43. Dietz v. Aronson, 244 A.D. 746, 299 N.Y.S.2d 66 (2d Dep't 1935).
44. McNair v. Manhattan Ry., 51 Hun. 644, 4 N.Y.S. 310 (Gen. Term 2d Dep't 1889), *aff'd*, 123 N.Y. 664, 26 N.E. 750 (1890).
45. *Id.* at 645, 4 N.Y.S. at 311; *see* Annot., *Propriety in Trial of Civil Action, Use of Skeleton or Model of Human Body or Part*, 58 A.L.R.2D 689 (1958).
46. McKay v. Lasher, 121 N.Y. 477, 483, 24 N.E. 711, 712 (1890); *see also* Haley v. Hockey, 199 Misc. 512, 103 N.Y.S.2d 717 (Sup. Ct. 1950) (it was proper to place figures on a blackboard during the plaintiff's summation). *See* Annot., *Counsel's Use in Trial of Personal Injury or Wrongful Death Case of Blackboard, Chart, Diagram or Placard, Not Introduced in Evidence Relating to Damages*, 86 A.L.R.2D 239 (1962).

A party's attorney may even arrange a demonstration. Hence, in *Uss v. Town of Oyster Bay,*[47] the court of appeals held that the trial court should have permitted a demonstration, although the circumstances were not identical to those of the accident, because the opposing party had an unrestricted right to cross-examine the person performing the demonstration. However, in *DiSanto v. County of Westchester,*[48] a slip and fall case, the trial court properly refused to let the plaintiffs demonstrate that fuel and water do not mix and that fuel floats thereby creating a slippery condition. The plaintiff could not prove that this demonstration would replicate the conditions at the scene of the accident.

Example 16-2 is a map of a county park.[49] Assume that an equestrian organization held a point-to-point contest on the same Sunday that an orienteering club held an orienteering contest and that a rider trampled an orienteer. A witness, such as an employee of the park, could testify to the accuracy of the map and then mark on this copy the sign saying "No Horses Beyond This Point" and the spot of the accident.

16.4 X-RAYS AND BLOOD SAMPLES

16.4.1 X-Rays

A medical test can result in demonstrative evidence when the test produces an object, such as an x-ray negative.

C.P.L.R. rule 4532-a establishes three requirements for admitting x-rays into evidence in an action for personal injury. First, the name of the injured party, the date, an identifying number, and the name and address of the supervising physi-

---

47. Uss v. Town of Oyster Bay, 37 N.Y.2d 639, 399 N.E.2d 147, 376 N.Y.S.2d 449 (1975).

48. DiSanto v. County of Westchester, 210 A.D.2d 628 (3d Dep't 1994).

49. The map is provided by the courtesy of John Pekarik, the president of the Long Island Orienteering Club.

cian must be inscribed photographically on the x-ray. Second, at least ten days before the trial, the attorney for the party offering the x-ray must serve on the opposing party's attorney a notice of intention to offer the x-ray into evidence and the availability of the x-ray for inspection. Third, an affidavit from the supervising physician must accompany the notice and attest both to the inscribed information and that the physician would so testify.

Note that the attorney's compliance with this section must be strict and literal, or the trial court will not admit the x-ray unless it qualifies for admission under C.P.L.R. rule 4518, the business record exception.[50] Judge Joseph McLaughlin, in his commentary to C.P.L.R. rule 4532-a,[51] states that the section has a flaw in it that allows a party to introduce x-rays without calling a physician to interpret them. While that technically may be true, the trial court has the discretion to rule that the jury cannot interpret the x-ray and that the plaintiff's failure to call a physician to do so will result in nonsuiting the complaint.

16.4.2 Blood Samples

When relevant, e.g., when the blood alcohol level of a party is in issue, the results of a blood test are admissible. Generally, the person who performed the test must testify regarding the test performed, the results it produced, and what they mean. However, the technician's supervisor may testify instead.[52] Another problem with such evidence has always been that the party offering it had to establish the chain of

50. Galuska v. Arbaiza, 106 A.D.2d 543, 482 N.Y.S.2d 846 (2d Dep't 1984).
51. 7B McKinney's C.P.L.R. §§ 3401-5100 Supp. Pamphlet 420 (1987).
52. Amaro v. City of N.Y., 40 N.Y.2d 30, 351 N.E.2d 665, 386 N.Y.S.2d 19 (1976). Note that the chain of custody of a photograph or a tape recording is not so important because such an item has its own identifiable characteristics whereas one sample of blood or drugs looks much like another. People v. Arena, 65 A.D.2d 182 (4th Dep't 1978).

custody of the blood sample to the smallest detail: any lapse or mistake usually meant that the test's results were not admissible.[53] In *Timmons v. Hecker*,[54] however, the Appellate Division, Second Department, held, "any purported deficiencies in the chain of custody relating to blood samples taken from the deceased . . . went to the weight and not the admissibility of the resulting report." Then the pendulum swung back. In *North v. Travelers' Insurance Co.*, the Appellate Division, Fourth Department, denied the defendant's motion for summary judgment because there was no evidence regarding how the plaintiff's blood sample was obtained, handled, or analyzed.[55]

The results of a test for blood alcohol are admissible in an action for personal injuries even if the person tested was not convicted of drunken driving and even if he did not consent to the test, as long as the test was performed legally and properly.[56]

Example 16-3 consists of the results of common blood tests. Note that, in accordance with a recent trend, the form includes the normal range next to the result of each test.

16.5 INSPECTION OF THE PREMISES

C.P.L.R. section 4110-c provides for the jury's inspection of premises. If the trial court decides that viewing the place where the accident or its cause occurred, the place where the injuries were sustained, or other relevant premises will help the jury to determine a material factual issue, then the court has the discretion to order the jury conducted to that place before the summations. The court may be present dur-

---

53. For a DNA test, see Pepole v. Vega, ____A.D.2d____, 639 N.Y.S.2d 511 (3d Dep't 1996); for a test on suspected narcotics, see People v. Torres, 213 A.D.2d 797, 632 N.Y.S.2d 645 (3d Dep't 1995), *appeal denied*, 86 N.Y.2d 784 (1995).
54. Timmons v. Hecker, 110 A.D.2d 762, 488 N.Y.S.2d 49 (2d Dep't 1985).
55. North v. Travelers' Insurance Co., 218 A.D.2d 901 (3d Dep't 1995).
56. Fafinski v. Reliance Ins. Co., 106 A.D.2d 88, 484 N.Y.S.2d 729 (4th Dep't 1985).

ing the inspection, and the parties and their attorneys have a right to be present, but an official appointed by the court must keep the jurors together. The sole purpose of the inspection is to permit the jury to observe the place or premises, and neither the court, the parties, their attorneys, nor the jurors themselves may discuss the case.

The attorney should remember that whether to permit an inspection of the premises is discretionary with the court.[57] That a juror visited the scene of the accident is not inherently prejudicial,[58] but the court must assure itself that this improper act will not affect the jury's deliberation. If the juror's visit will affect the deliberations, then the trial court must grant a mistrial.

16.6 HOSPITAL AND REPAIR BILLS

Two statutory provisions govern using bills as evidence. One provision applies to hospital bills; the other applies to all repairs and services, including medical care, but only up to the amount of $1,500.

The provision governing hospital bills is C.P.L.R. rule 4518(b), which states that a hospital bill is admissible and is prima facie evidence of the facts contained therein provided that the bill bears a certification that it is correct, that each of the items was supplied necessarily, and that the amount charged was reasonable. There is no monetary limit.

The provision governing bills for repairs and services is C.P.L.R. rule 4533-a. This rule provides that a party may introduce an itemized bill, receipted or marked paid, for repairs or services not exceeding $1,500. Such a bill is prima facie evidence of the reasonable value and necessity for the repairs provided that the business that made the repairs certifies the bill and includes a verified statement that no part

57. Cole v. Lawas, 97 A.D.2d 912, 470 N.Y.S.2d 747 (3d Dep't 1983).
58. Alford v. Sventek, 53 N.Y.2d 743, 421 N.E.2d 831, 439 N.Y.S.2d 339 (1981).

of the payment will be refunded to the debtor and that the charges are the customary ones. In addition, the party offering the bill in evidence must, at least ten days before the trial, serve on the other parties a notice of intention accompanied by a true copy of the bill. Finally, only one such bill from the same provider to the same customer may be introduced in one action.

Since C.P.L.R. rule 4533-a applies to services as well as repairs, the court of appeals has construed the rule to govern medical bills as well as bills for repairs to property.[59] The bill constitutes prima facie evidence of the facts it contains, creates a true presumption, and must be rebutted by evidence to the contrary, or the trial court must find that the amount of the bill is binding on the opposing party. However, a medical bill cannot establish that the defendant's negligence was the proximate cause of the plaintiff's injury.[60]

Example 16-4 is a sample of a certified hospital bill.

59. River v. State, 115 Misc. 2d 523, 454 N.Y.S.2d 408 (Ct. Cl. 1982).
60. *Id.*

EXAMPLE 16-1: DEMAND FOR PHOTOGRAPH

2. Demand is hereby made that you produce for inspection and photocopying any and all photographs in your possession or in the custody or control of any party that you represent, depicting the location which is the subject of this occurrence, the location where the accident occurred, or depicting the plaintiff or the plaintiff's physical condition, injuries, disability, or any lack thereof, for inspection and photocopying. Please take notice that an application will be made at trial to preclude any photographs not produced in response to this demand.

EXAMPLE 16-2: MAP

Orienteering

involves the mind and the body. With the aid of a map and compass, you find your way on foot across the countryside from check point to check point. Your imagination and skills choose the best route. The course has orange and white markers (check points or controls) at the locations designated on your map. You visit each control in sequence and punch a score card. Each punch perforates your card with a different design verifying your visit.

Orienteering courses are usually set in a pleasant forest environment and you set your own pace. You can treat orienteering as a highly competitive race of navigational skill and physical speed or as a hike through the woods with the added fun of finding the orange and white controls. Orienteering can be enjoyed by everyone. Meet organizers generally set short courses for new orienteers and longer, more complicated courses for experienced orienteers. At large meets there are over 35 categories based upon age, sex and skill level. These categories for males and females are broken down into age groups from under 12 to over 55 years of age spread over 6 different courses of various lengths and levels of difficulty. You orienteer on a course comparable to your experience and fitness. Course lengths range from under 3 to over 12 KM in length.

Orienteering is usually an individual effort but it is also common to see groups or families hiking around an orienteering course together. Orienteering lends itself to many variations and can be done from a canoe, on skis, on horseback, or on a bicycle. the skills learned can be used by hunters, hikers, and backpackers. Fitness and experiencing the outdoors come naturally with this sport.

Long Island Orienteering Club

62 KNOLLWOOD DRIVE, CARLE PLACE, N.Y. 11514
Affiliate Member of United States Orienteering Federation ©

road, paved
road dirt
trails
uncrossable fence
fence
building , ruin
wall
concrete trough
pit boulder
junkpile
ditch
marsh or pond
dense vegetation
woods
open
bank
depresion

Rev 8/95

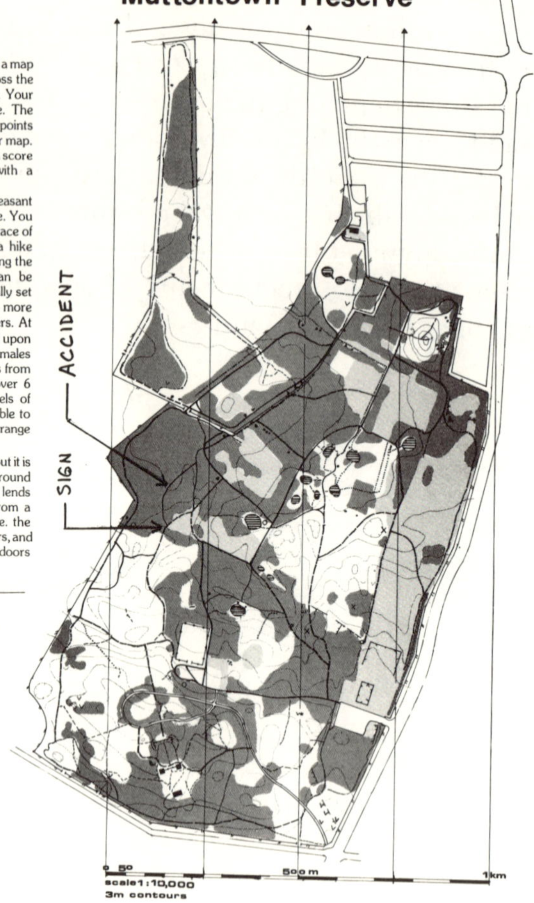

EXAMPLE 16-3: RESULTS OF BLOOD TESTS

MEDICAL DIRECTOR
708 993-1500
800 597-8026

National Health Laboratories Incorporated
LABORATORY REPORT
"Quality Results Through Exceptional People"

ELMHURST, IL 60126
CLIA #14D0703742
CAP #44212-01

DATE REPORTED	DATE RECEIVED	PATIENT NAME – I.D.	PHONE	AGE	SEX
15-SEP-95	15-SEP-95	MCMULLEN, KEVIN		48	M

DATE COLLECTED	TIME COLLECTED	HOSPITAL I.D.	REQUISITION NO.	ACCESSION NO.
14-SEP-95	6:00 AM		A07340751	4383450-5

CLIENT NAME/ADDRESS		TEST REQUESTED
P.H.S.	87014-4	PROFILE 2292-4.
HEALTH UNIT RM 2010	[SL]	
9700 PAGE BLVD	[90]	
SAINT LOUIS, MO 63121	9031-56505.002	

PHYSICIAN	VOLUME	FASTING	PATIENT SS#	COMMENTS
		YES		

TEST NAME	RESULT	UNITS	REFERENCE RANGE
GLUCOSE, PLASMA OR SERUM:			
GLUCOSE	82	MG/DL	65 - 115
CORONARY RISK PROFILE I:			
CHOLESTEROL	173	MG/DL	DESIRABLE: <200
TRIGLYCERIDES	57	MG/DL	30 - 150
HDL-CHOLESTEROL	43	MG/DL	30 - 75
CHOL/HDL RATIO	4.0		AV:4.2-7.3
LDL (CALCULATED)	119	MG/DL	< 130
LDL/HDL RATIO	2.8		< 3.1
VLDL (CALCULATED)	11	MG/DL	< 39
RISK FACTOR	< 1		=< 1

EXAMPLE 16-4: CERTIFIED HOSPITAL BILL

MED CTR
BLVD
, NY 11421

215

:EN 21 F / / / /

1 30 B23

DRIVE
NY 11

RY OF CHARGES				
C U	9DAYS@	1300.00	11700.00	11700.00
E.R. VISIT	236		65.00	65.00
LAB/MICRO	421		5989.00	5989.00
CYTO PATHOLOGY	423		88.00	88.00
VASCULAR LAB	119		170.00	170.00
BLOOD PROCESS	426		625.00	625.00
RADIOLOGY	432		3960.00	3960.00
CAT SCAN	434		290.00	290.00
ULTRA DIAG	127		373.00	373.00
EKG	429		280.00	280.00
EEG	446		70.00	70.00
PHARMACY	415		2502.55	2502.55
RESP/PULMONARY	442		2145.00	2145.00

SUB-TOTAL OF CHARGES 28257.55 28257.55

9/22

DRG

Covered by Blue Cross at B/C rates
$3641.85

Bal. — 0 —

I DO HEREBY CERTIFY THAT THE SAID BILL IS TRUE AND CORRECT. THAT EACH OF THE ITEMS SHOWN THEREON WAS NECESSARILY FURNISHED OR SUPPLIED AND THAT THE AMOUNT OF THE CHARGES THEREFOR IS THE FAIR AND REASONABLE VALUE THEREOF.

****BENEFITS ARE ASSIGNED TO THE HOSPITAL****

T O T A L S 28257.55 28257.55

Medical Records Dept.

PAY THIS AMOUNT 0

MED CTR
, NY

Cross-Examination 15

Chapter 15 discusses the purposes and rules of cross-examination, not the techniques of drawing out witnesses.[1]

15.1 THE GENERAL RULES

15.1.1 The Purposes of Cross-Examination

Cross-examination is "the examination of a witness upon a trial or hearing, or upon taking a deposition, by the party opposed to the one who produced him, upon his evidence given in chief, to test its truth, to further develop it, or for other purposes."[2] In other words, the purpose of cross-examination is to test the mental capacity, veracity, and accuracy of the witness.[3] For example, the attorney for the opposing party may show that the witness has an erroneous understanding of the traffic regulations or the rules of the road.[4] Generally, a witness may be cross-examined about all matters that tend to discredit the witness, but the range and extent of the cross-examination that will be permitted, especially regarding the credibility of a witness, is within the tri-

---

1. For the classic introductory text on technique, *see* FRANCIS L. WELLMAN, THE ART OF CROSS-EXAMINATION, 4th ed. (New York: Collier Books, 1932), 476 pp.
2. BLACK'S LAW DICTIONARY 450 (4th ed. 1968).
3. People v. Lustig, 206 N.Y. 162, 170, 99 N.E. 183, 186 (1912).
4. Dauch v. Theed, 209 A.D. 682, 686, 205 N.Y.S. 306, 308 (2d Dep't 1924).

al court's discretion. The Court of Appeals stated the rule in *Langley v. Wadsworth:*

> So far as the cross-examination of a witness relates either to facts in issue or relevant facts, it may be pursued by counsel as a matter of right, but when its object is to ascertain the accuracy or credibility of a witness, its method and duration are subject to the discretion of the trial judge and unless abused its exercise is not the subject of review.[5]

The trial court should limit the cross-examination of the witness to the matters to which he or she testified on direct examination. A cross-examiner who persists in inquiring about matters that were not brought out on direct examination makes the witness the cross-examiner's own concerning those matters. As a consequence, the cross-examiner would be limited to the means available for a party to impeach his or her own witness.[6]

15.1.2 Collateral Matters

When addressing either the facts or the witness's credibility, the cross-examiner is bound by the witness's answers on collateral matters and may not produce evidence to establish that the witness's answers are untruthful.[7] Thus, if the

---

5. Langley v. Wadsworth, 99 N.Y. 61, 1 N.E. 106 (1895).
6. Bennett v. Crescent Athletic-Hamilton Club, 270 N.Y. 456, 1 N.E.2d 963 (1936).
7. W. RICHARDSON, EVIDENCE § 491 (J. Prince 10th ed. 1973) [hereinafter cited as Richardson, Evidence]. However, although the cross-examiner is bound by the answer, the witness is not bound. For example, in People v. Catalanotte, 41 A.D.2d 968, 244 N.Y.S.2d 72 (2d Dep't 1973), *aff'd*, 36 N.Y.2d 192, 325 N.E.2d 866, 366 N.Y.S.2d 403 (1975), in which the defendant's testimony was attacked on a collateral issue involving bank accounts, although the cross-examiner was held bound by defendant's answers, the appellate courts held that the trial court had erred by rejecting the defendant's offer of rebuttal testimony to explain the bank accounts, because the witness is not limited by his answer. Getlin v. St. Vincent's Hosp., 117 A.D.2d 707, 498 N.Y.S.2d 849 (2d Dep't 1986); Serpe v. Rappaport, 103 A.D.2d 771, 477 N.Y.S.2d 403 (1st Dep't 1984).

witness denies being a prostitute, the cross-examiner is bound by her answer, and may not present independent evidence of that fact, unless the witness has been convicted of being a prostitute. The rationale for this rule is that collateral matters are irrelevant to the claims in the case and tend to confuse the jury.[8] Hence, the trial court must be alert to the issues in order to separate the germane from the irrelevant or prejudicial. The court's duty is to prevent the latter from entering the trial.

Unfortunately, it is not always easy to determine whether a particular matter is collateral. A witness's bias, interest, or hostility is not a collateral matter, and the cross-examiner may prove such bias, etc., despite the witness's denial.[9] However, the cross-examiner may not present evidence to impeach the character of a witness in a civil action.[10] For example, in *Davis v. Blum*,[11] an action for medical malpractice, the Appellate Division, Second Department, reversed a verdict for the defendant and ordered a new trial because the trial court had allowed the defendant to introduce evidence that the plaintiff was an alcoholic in order to show that the plaintiff tended to exercise poor judgment. The appellate court held that such evidence was "akin to evidence of character and habit which is generally inadmissible in civil cases to raise the inference that a party acted in a particular way on the occasion in issue."[12]

Another example of evidence that is inadmissible because it is directed to a collateral matter is the testimony of an ex-

---

8. DiPaolo v. Somma, 111 A.D.2d 899, 490 N.Y.S.2d 803 (2d Dep't 1985); Ellison v. New York City Transit Auth., 61 N.Y.2d 853, 473 N.Y.S.2d 976 (1984), *aff'd,* 98 A.D.2d 659, 470 N.Y.S.2d 144 (1st Dep't 1983).
9. Bennett v. Crescent Athletic-Hamilton Club, 270 N.Y. 456 (1936).
10. Kravitz v. Long Island Jewish Hosp., 113 A.D.2d 577, 497 N.Y.S.2d 51 (2d Dep't 1985).
11. Davis v. Blum, 70 A.D.2d 583, 416 N.Y.S.2d 57 (2d Dep't 1979).
12. *Id.,* 70 A.D.2d at 584, 416 N.Y.S.2d at 59; *cf.* Halloran v. Virginia Chems., Inc., 41 N.Y.2d 386, 393 N.Y.S.2d 341 (1977). However, New York does permit proof of a business, professional, or other institutional practice or custom as probative evidence that the practice or custom was followed on a specific occasion.

pert on the credibility of the eyewitnesses. Such testimony would confuse the jury and would require a trial within a trial to determine whether the eyewitnesses had testified accurately. Therefore, expert testimony on this issue is inadmissible.[13] Instead, the cross-examiner should probe the witnesses' powers of observation and memory and, if possible, present demonstrative evidence and witnesses who can contradict the opposing party's witnesses on the facts.

15.1.3 Calling and Cross-Examining the Adverse Party in an Action for Medical Malpractice

When the plaintiff in an action for medical malpractice calls the defendant as a witness on the plaintiff's direct case, the plaintiff's attorney may ask the defendant leading questions. In effect, the plaintiff's attorney may cross-examine the defendant during the direct examination, and the plaintiff may even force the defendant to become the plaintiff's expert witness. Thus, in *Segreti v. Putnam Community Hospital*, the Appellate Division, Second Department, held,

> It was prejudicial error for the trial court to so prevent plaintiff's counsel from leading and cross-examining Dr. Chang as a hostile witness as to hold him bound by the latter's answers . . . [Moreover], it is well settled that a plaintiff in a medical malpractice action may call as a witness the doctor against whom she brought the action and question him as a medical expert . . . .[14]

---

13. People v. Kelley, 631 N.Y.S.2d 926 (2d Dep't 1995); People v. Greene, 637 N.Y.S.2d 79 (1st Dep't 1996); United States v. Fosher, 590 F.2d 381 (1st Cir. 1979); *but cf.* People v. Cronin, 60 N.Y.2d 430, 470 N.Y.S.2d 110 (1983); *see also* Martin, *Expert Opinion on Eyewitness Testimony*, N.Y.L.J., Feb. 14, 1986 at 1, col. 1.
14. Segreti v. Putnam Community Hosp., 88 A.D.2d 590, 592, 449 N.Y.S.2d 785, 786 (2d Dep't 1982); *see also* Arlene W. v. Robert D., 36 A.D.2d 455, 324 N.Y.S.2d 333 (4th Dep't 1971).

15.1.4 The Methods of Impeaching the Credibility of the Opposing Party's Witnesses

In addition to using cross-examination to test the memory, knowledge, and understanding of the opposing party's witness, the attorney may attempt to destroy the witness's credibility, i.e., "that quality in a witness which renders his evidence worthy of belief."[15] More specifically, the witness's credibility consists of the jurors' belief that the witness is telling the truth as he or she knows it. Several methods are available to the attorney for impeaching the credibility of the opposing party's witnesses, but the rules governing each method limit the attorney's questions.

The principal methods of attacking the credibility of a witness are by showing that:

1. The witness made a prior inconsistent statement.
2. The witness has been convicted of a crime.
3. The witness has committed an immoral, vicious, or criminal act which may reflect unfavorably on the witness's character and thus prove that he or she is unworthy of belief.
4. The witness is biased in favor of the party calling him or her, hostile toward the opposing party, or interested in the outcome of the case.
5. The witness has a bad reputation for truth and veracity.
6. Extrinsic documents contradict the witness's testimony.

15. BLACK'S LAW DICTIONARY 440 (4th ed. 1968).

15.2 THE WITNESS HAS MADE A PRIOR INCONSISTENT STATEMENT

The attorney may impeach the opposing party's witness most directly by showing that the witness has made a prior and inconsistent statement about the same facts. The statement may have been an unsworn oral one, a signed writing, or testimony. In addition, the attorney must understand the distinction between a prior inconsistent statement made by a witness who is not a party and a statement by a witness who is a party. The party's prior inconsistent statement is also an admission against interest and, thus, constitutes evidence-in-chief. The prior inconsistent statement of a witness who is not a party, however, merely impairs the witness's credibility and the cross-examiner may not offer the statement as evidence supporting his or her client's case.[16]

15.2.1 An Unsworn Oral Statement

Before the trial court will admit a prior inconsistent statement, the attorney must confront the witness with it by specifying the time and place the witness supposedly made it, the person to whom the witness made it, and the substance of the language the witness used.[17] If the attorney fails to lay this foundation, he or she may not use the statement to impeach the credibility of the witness. If the witness denies having made the statement or declares that the witness does not remember it, the attorney still has laid the foundation and may offer the evidence of the statement during the defendant's case (if the attorney represents the de-

16. FED. R. EVID. 801(d)(a)(a), 607, 613, 801(c); Roge v. Valentine, 280 N.Y. 268 (1939); Robinson v. New York City Transit Auth., 105 A.D.2d 614, 481 N.Y.S.2d 85 (1st Dep't 1984).

17. Ahmed v. Board of Educ., 98 A.D.2d 736, 469 N.Y.S.2d 435 (2d Dep't 1983); Morris v. Palmer Oil Co., 94 A.D.2d 911, 463 N.Y.S.2d 631 (3d Dep't 1983); Bombard v. County of Albany, 94 A.D.2d 910, 463 N.Y.S.2d 633 (3d Dep't 1983).

fendant) or during the rebuttal (if the attorney represents the plaintiff).[18] Note that the attorney does not introduce the prior inconsistent statement while the witness is testifying if the witness denies having made it.

The following example will illustrate the rule. During the direct examination, an eyewitness to the accident testified for the plaintiff that the traffic light had been green for the plaintiff. When cross-examined by the defendant's' attorney, the witness denied that during a conversation with a police officer at the scene of the accident, he said he had not noticed the color of the light. Having laid the foundation, the defendant's attorney could call the police officer during the defendant's direct case to establish the conversation as a prior inconsistent statement.

Since a party's prior inconsistent oral statement is also an admission against interest, the attorney need not lay a foundation before offering that statement in evidence.

15.2.2 A Signed Writing

Before the attorney conducting the cross-examination may introduce a signed writing as a prior inconsistent statement to impeach the witness, "the paper must be shown or read to the witness and marked for identification and, if subscribed, the signature and in case he so demands, the paper must be shown to him."[19] In *Larkin v. Nassau Electric Railroad Co.*,[20] the

18. Loughlin v. Brassil, 187 N.Y. 128, 79 N.E. 854 (1907). For electronically recorded prior statements, *see* Sloan v. New York Cent. R.R., 45 N.Y. 125 (1871); Annot., *Evidence Secured by Mechanical or Electronic Eavesdropping Device as Admissible Against Witness for Purpose of Impeachment or Showing of Prior Inconsistent Statement*, 94 A.L.R.2D 1295 (1964); Annot., *Admissibility of Sound Recordings in Evidence for Impeachment Purpose*, 58 A.L.R.2D 1048 (1957); for the proper method, *see also* Ahmed v. Board of Educ., 98 A.D.2d 736, 469 N.Y.S.2d 435 (2d Dep't 1983); Ryan v. Dwyer, 33 A.D.2d 878, 307 N.Y.S.2d 565 (4th Dep't 1969); Wolfe v. Madison Ave. Coach Co., 171 Misc. 707, 13 N.Y.S.2d 741 (1st Dep't 1939).
19. Larkin v. Nassau Elec. R.R., 205 N.Y. 267 (1912).
20. *Id.* at 270, 98 N.E. at 468.

Court of Appeals outlined the procedure. First, if the witness admits to signing the written statement, his or her admission is sufficient to prove the statement, but the impeaching party is entitled to a clear and direct admission – otherwise, other witnesses may be presented on the issue. Second, if the witness denies signing the statement, then the impeaching party may prove that the witness's signature is genuine. Third, after obtaining the admission or proving the signature, the impeaching party may offer the writing in evidence immediately during the case or during rebuttal. Fourth, the witness's signature is merely some evidence that he or she made or authorized the statement contained in the writing, unless the writing is a contract. The witness may claim that he or she did not read the statement, in which case the jury will evaluate that claim. Finally, the attorney for the impeaching party may not read the witness's prior statement to the jury or use the statement as the basis for cross-examination until the trial court has admitted the statement into evidence.

15.2.3 Testimony

When the prior inconsistent statement consists of testimony that the witness gave before another court or at a hearing at the motor vehicle bureau, the usual procedure is for the attorney for the impeaching party to request that the adversary concede that the cross-examiner has correctly read the series of questions and answers from the stenographer's minutes. Such a concession proves the prior inconsistent statement. Without it, the cross-examiner is theoretically obliged to call the stenographer or some other person who heard the witness testify. However, and as a practical matter, this procedure is unnecessary if the stenographer certified the transcript as a complete and accurate record of what was said.[21]

---

21. *E.g.*, C.P.L.R. § 3116(b).

15.3 THE WITNESS HAS BEEN CONVICTED OF A CRIME

15.3.1 The Rule

In New York, C.P.L.R. section 4513 provides that the cross-examiner may prove that the opposing party's witness has been convicted of a crime "for the purpose of affecting the weight of his testimony, either by cross-examination, upon which he shall be required to answer any relevant question, or by the record. The party cross-examining is not concluded by such person's answer."[22] Since the statute requires that the witness have been convicted, evidence that the witness was arrested or indicted is inadmissible.[23]

15.3.2 The Crime

Within the meaning of the statute, a crime is either a misdemeanor or a felony. A traffic infraction is neither, and, therefore, evidence that the witness committed such an infraction is not admissible.[24] Note, however, that a traffic

---

22. C.P.L.R. § 4513. FED. R. EVID. 609 sets forth specific rules governing the admissibility and exclusion of testimony and convictions.
23. People v. Morrison, 195 N.Y. 116 (1909); Annot., *Impeachment of Witness by Evidence or Inquiry as to Arrest, Accusation, or Prosecution*, 20 A.L.R.2D 1421 (1951); Annot., *Prior Convictions: Propriety, in Impeaching Credibility of Witness in Civil Case by Showing Former Conviction or Questions Relating to Nature and Extent of Punishment,* 67 A.L.R.3D 761 (1975). In People v. Sandoval, 34 N.Y.2d 371, 357 N.Y.S.2d 849 (1974), the Court of Appeals held that if evidence may be offered at the trial on cross-examination, such as conviction of a crime, etc., that the opposing party deems prejudicial, that party may, prior to the offer, request a hearing in limine to have the court exclude the evidence. However, Guarisco v. E.J. Milk Farms, 90 Misc. 2d 81, 393 N.Y.S.2d 883 (Civ. Ct. 1977), held that the *Sandoval* principle does not apply to a civil case because C.P.L.R. § 4513 contains no exceptions and, therefore, the judge has no discretion.
24. C.P.L.R. § 4501; DeStasio v. Janssen Dairy Corp., 279 N.Y. 501 (1939); McQuage v. City of N.Y., 285 A.D.249, 136 N.Y.S.2d 111 (1st Dep't 1954); *see also* Annot., *Cross-Examination of Automobile Driver in Civil Action with Respect to Arrest or Conviction for Previous Traffic Offenses*, 20 A.L.R.2D 1217 (1951); Annot., *Traffic Offenses: Use of Unrelated Traffic Offense Conviction to Impeach Credibility of Witness in a State Civil Court*, 88 A.L.R.3D 74 (1978).

violation, such as reckless driving or driving while intoxicated, is a misdemeanor and, therefore, evidence of the witness's conviction is admissible.[25] Similarly, the statute does not permit the impeaching party to introduce evidence of:

1. The witness's conviction of a police offense;
2. Adjudication of the witness as a youthful offender, juvenile delinquent, or wayward minor;[26]
3. The imposition on the witness by an administrative officer of a fine for a dereliction of duty or an infraction of rules;
4. The witness's expulsion from a city department, or
5. The suspension or revocation of the witness's license to operate a motor vehicle.[27]

15.3.3 The Procedure

If the witness admits to having been convicted of a crime, the attorney may proceed to show the nature of the crime.[28] If the witness denies being convicted of a crime, the cross-examiner is not bound by the witness's answer but may prove that the witness was convicted,[29] typically by produc-

---

25. Woodward v. Phipps, 261 A.D. 865, 26 N.Y.S.2d 393 (3d Dep't 1941); Geiger v. Weiss, 245 A.D. 817, 281 N.Y.S. 154 (2d Dep't 1935) . A fortiori, a conviction of a felony for driving under the influence is admissible to impeach the witness — even if the witness is the plaintiff whose intoxication is an issue in his action for personal injuries. Scotto v. Daddario, 235 A.D.2d 470 (2d Dep't 1997).
26. People v. Sarra, 283 A.D. 876, 129 N.Y.S.2d 201 (2d Dep't 1954); See v. Wormser, 129 A.D. 596, 113 N.Y.S. 1093 (2d Dep't 1908). In People v. Vidal, 26 N.Y.2d 249, 306 N.Y.S.2d 336 (1970), the Court of Appeals held that although the cross-examiner could not prove the witness had been adjudicated a juvenile delinquent, the cross-examiner was not precluded from asking the witness about specific criminal acts, because the opposing party may show that the witness has committed criminal, vicious, or immoral acts.
27. Tryon v. Willbank, 234 A.D. 335, 255 N.Y.S.2d 27 (4th Dep't 1932).
28. Moore v. Leventhal, 303 N.Y. 534, 538, 104 N.E.2d 892, 894-95 (1952); People v. Sorge, 301 N.Y. 198, 201 (1950).
29. People v. McCormick, 278 A.D. 410, 105 N.Y.S.2d 571 (1st Dep't 1951), *aff'd*, 303 N.Y. 403 (1952).

ing the record of the conviction.[30] Even if the witness concedes the conviction, the cross-examiner still may produce the record of conviction for the jury.[31]

A witness who has been impeached by a conviction for a crime may, if he wishes, proclaim his innocence in the face of the conviction[32] or explain the circumstances surrounding the conviction.[33]

15.3.4 When the Witness Is a Party

That a party was arrested has no probative value and is inadmissible in a civil action involving the same facts.[34] Similarly, that the witness was not arrested cannot be shown as circumstantial evidence of anything, such as credibility or due care.[35]

However, evidence of a party's conviction of a crime is admissible in a civil action involving the same facts.[36] Thus, in an action for wrongful death, the plaintiff may introduce evidence that the defendant has been convicted of the man-

---

30. C.P.L.R. § 4513.
31. McQuage v. City of N.Y., 285 A.D. 249, 136 N.Y.S.2d 111 (1st Dep't 1954).
32. Schindler v. Royal Ins. Co., 258 N.Y. 310, 179 N.E. 711 (1932); Sims v. Sims, 75 N.Y. 466 (1870).
33. People v. Tait, 234 A.D. 433, 255 N.Y.S.2d 455 (1st Dep't), *aff'd*, 259 N.Y. 599 (1932). *See* Annot., *Pardon as Affecting Impeachment by Proof of Conviction of Crime*, 30 A.L.R.2D 893 (1953).
34. Dance v. Town of Southampton, 95 A.D.2d 442, 467 N.Y.S.2d 203 (2d Dep't 1983); Franco v. Zingarelli, 72 A.D.2d 211, 424 N.Y.S.2d 185 (1st Dep't 1980); 2 BENDER'S NEW YORK EVIDENCE § 73.02[2] (1962).
35. RICHARDSON, EVIDENCE § 506.
36. *In re* Rechtschaffen, 278 N.Y. 336, 340, 16 N.E.2d 357, 359 (1938); Schindler v. Royal Ins. Co., 258 N.Y. 310, 179 N.E. 711 (1932); Annot., *Conviction or Acquittal as Evidence of the Facts on Which It Was Based in Civil Action,* 18 A.L.R.2D 1287 (1951). In S.T. Grand, Inc. v. City of N.Y., 38 A.D.2d 467, 330 N.Y.S.2d 594 (1st Dep't 1972), *aff'd*, 32 N.Y.2d 300, 344 N.Y.S.2d 938 (1973), the appellate courts held that a prior conviction on the same issue as the civil case is not merely evidence of negligence but complete estoppel or res judicata as to that issue.

slaughter of the plaintiff's intestate. However, the defendant in the civil action may not introduce evidence that he or she was acquitted in the criminal action stemming from the same facts.[37]

15.4 THE WITNESS HAS COMMITTED AN IMMORAL, VICIOUS, OR CRIMINAL ACT

The courts of New York take the position that witnesses "whose lives indicate an abandonment or lack of moral principles, and show them to be lewd and debased characters, void of shame or decency, have not usually a great respect for the truth, or the sanctity of an oath."[38] Therefore, the courts permit a cross-examiner to interrogate the opposing party's witness about the immoral, vicious, or criminal acts the witness has committed. However, if the witness denies the accusation, the cross-examiner is bound by the answer and may not introduce evidence of this collateral matter.[39] (Note the distinction between this ground of impeachment and impeachment for the conviction of a crime.)

---

37. Massey v. Meurer, 25 A.D.2d 729, 268 N.Y.S.2d 735 (1st Dep't 1966); Etheridge v. City of N.Y., 121 N.Y.S.2d 103 (Sup. Ct. 1953), *aff'd,* 283 A.D. 867, 129 N.Y.S.2d 915 (1st Dep't 1954).

38. Osborne v. Seligman, 39 Misc. 811, 812, 81 N.Y.S. 346, 347 (1st Dep't 1903). *See* FED. R. EVID. 608(b). In People v. Duffy, 36 N.Y.2d 258, 367 N.Y.S.2d 236 (1975), the Court of Appeals held that it was proper to cross-examine the witness about his use of narcotics during a trial in which the defendant was charged with the crimes of robbery and grand larceny. However, in the very next year, the Court of Appeals held that the prosecution may not cross-examine the defendant about his prior bad acts in order to show his propensity to commit the crime charged. People v. Wright, 41 N.Y.2d 172 (1976). Annot., *Use of Drugs as Affecting Credibility of Witness*, 65 A.L.R.3d 705 (1975); Annot., *Impeachment of Witness with Respect to Intoxication*, 8 A.L.R.3D 749 (1966).

39. People v. Sorge, 301 N.Y. 198 (1950); Serpe v. Rappaport, 103 A.D.2d 771, 477 N.Y.S.2d 403 (1st Dep't 1984); RICHARDSON, EVIDENCE § 491. Remember, however, that extrinsic evidence is admissible to show that the witness is biased, interested, or hostile. Badr v. Hogan, 75 N.Y.2d 629 (1990), and People v. Knight, 80 N.Y.2d 845 (1992).

The interrogation must relate to matters of moral turpitude, e.g., whether the witness had sold or used narcotics,[40] operated a brothel, or had illicit sexual relations.[41] The interrogation is not proper if it inquires about the witness's failure to pay rent, expulsion from a church, society, labor union, or fire department,[42] religious beliefs or lack thereof,[43] a dishonorable discharge from the armed forces,[44] or having been visited by the police while a resident on a certain street.[45] Questions of this type are attacks on the witness's private life. They do not test credibility but merely degrade the individual and bring him or her into disrepute with the jury and are, therefore, improper.[46] Even when asking a question which may be proper, the attorney must act in good faith — there must be a reasonable factual basis for the question.[47]

---

40. People v. Webster, 139 N.Y. 73 (1893); Annot., *Use of Drugs as Affecting Competency or Credibility of Witness*, 52 A.L.R.2D 848 (1957).
41. RICHARDSON, EVIDENCE § 498; People v. Giblin, 115 N.Y. 196 (1889). The opposing party may show that the witness, a lawyer, had been disbarred, Hyman v. Dworsky, 239 A.D. 413, 417, 267 N.Y.S. 539 (3d Dep't 1933), or suspended from the practice of law, Batease v. Dion, 275 A.D. 451, 90 N.Y.S. 851 (3d Dep't 1949).
42. RICHARDSON, EVIDENCE § 499; *see also* McQuage v. City of N.Y., 285 A.D. 249, 136 N.Y.S.2d 111 (1st Dep't 1954).
43. Brink v. Stratton, 176 N.Y. 150 (1903), and People v. Wood, 107 A.D.2d 830 (2d Dep't 1985).
44. Annot., *Admissibility and Effect of Evidence or Comment on Party's Military Service or Lack Thereof*, 9 A.L.R.2D 606 (1950).
45. George v. Owners Trucking Corp., 264 A.D. 831, 35 N.Y.S.2d 475 (4th Dep't 1942).
46. *Id. See also* Cortis v. Grenor Co., 20 A.D.2d 704, 247 N.Y.S.2d 205 (1st Dep't 1964), in which the appellate court held that the trial court had erred by permitting the defendant's attorney to read many pages of an affidavit from a previous matrimonial action and containing unsavory details, because "extrinsic evidence may not be introduced on this collateral issue." In People v. Alamo, 23 N.Y.2d 630, 633, 298 N.Y.S.2d 681, 682-83 (1969), the Court of Appeals held that a witness may be cross-examined about his criminal and immoral acts (even when he has not been convicted) if there is a reasonable basis for the attack. *Accord*, People v. Schwartzman, 24 N.Y.2d 241, 299 N.Y.S.2d 817, *cert. denied*, 396 U.S. 846 (1969); People v. Sorge, 301 N.Y. 198, 200 (1959), and People v. Knight, 80 N.Y.2d 845 (1992).
47. People v. Simpson, 109 A.D.2d 461 (1st Dep't 1985). The court quoted People v. Alamo: "The rule that evolves from the cases is that questions such as these . . . to the defendant . . . as a witness are not error if the prosecutor asked them in good faith, that is to say, if he had some reasonable basis for believing the truth of things he was asking about." 23 N.Y.2d 630, 633 (1969).

In *Gedrin v. Long Island Jewish Hospital,*[48] the Appellate Division, Second Department, explained the rule, applied it, and approved two attempts to impeach the witness. The appellate court explained that the trial court, in its discretion, controls the admission of evidence for impeaching witnesses. However, a witness in a civil action may be cross-examined regarding any immoral, vicious, or criminal act that would show the individual to be unworthy of belief. The court then approved the defense attorney's cross-examination of the plaintiff's mother about two specific acts of misconduct — assaulting a policeman and petty larceny. Although the first charge was adjourned and the second reduced, the attorney had a basis on which to question the witness regarding the incidents.

15.5 THE WITNESS IS BIASED, HOSTILE, OR INTERESTED IN THE OUTCOME

"The witness's bias in favor of the party calling him, or his hostility to the party against whom he testifies, may be shown to affect his credibility. . . . For the same purpose, it is competent to show the interest of the witness in the case."[49] There is no particular ground for or method of showing bias or hostility except the application of common sense to the facts of the case, e.g., that the witness is related to the party who called him or was fired by the opposing party. Moreover, New York does not require the cross-examiner to lay a foundation in order to show bias or hostility by first asking the witness about the factual basis.[50] As the Court of Appeals explained in *People v. Brooks,*[51]

---

48. Gedrin v. Long Island Jewish Hosp., 119 A.D.2d 799, 501 N.Y.S.2d 426 (2d Dep't 1986).

49. Richardson, Evidence § 503.

50. People v. Brooks, 131 N.Y. 321 (1892); Luce v. St. Peter's Hosp., 85 A.D.2d 194, 448 N.Y.S.2d 855 (3d Dep't 1982); Thompson v. Korn, 48 A.D.2d 1007, 368 N.Y.S.2d 923 (4th Dep't 1975); Annot., *Necessity and Sufficiency of Foundation for Discrediting Evidence Showing Bias or Prejudice of Adverse Witness*, 87 A.L.R.2d 407 (1963). *See also* Fed. R. Evid. 611(b).

51. People v. Brooks, 131 N.Y. 321 (1892).

> The hostility of a witness towards a party against whom he is called may be proved by any competent evidence. It may be shown by cross-examination of the witness, or witnesses may be called who can swear to facts showing it. There can be no reason for holding that the witness must first be examined as to his hostility, and that then, and not till then, witnesses may be called to contradict him, because it is not a case where the party against whom the witness is called is seeking to discredit him by contradicting him. He is simply seeking to discredit him by showing his hostility and malice; and as that may be proved by any competent evidence we see no reason for holding that he must first be examined as to his hostility.[52]

The foregoing rule also applies to the case of a witness who is interested in the outcome of the litigation.[53] For example, the Appellate Division, Second Department, has held that the trial court erred by not allowing the opposing party to show that the witness had settled his claim with the party who called him.[54] A recent case from the first department is *Hill v. Arnold*, 226 A.D.2d 232 (1st Dep't 1996).

When attempting to impeach a witness for bias in favor of a party, the cross-examiner may show that the witness and the party are friends.[55] Similarly, when impeaching a medical expert for hostility against a party, the cross-examiner may ask the witness about the number of physical examinations he or she has performed on behalf of the defendants, the witness's fee as a medical witness, membership in the society on whose behalf the testimony is given, and threats to get even with the plaintiffs.[56] Finally, an adverse party may show that the witness is hostile to a party other than the one examining him or her, i.e., to another plaintiff or defendant.[57]

---

52. *Id.* at 325.
53. G. MOTTLA, NEW YORK EVIDENCE — PROOF OF CASES § 370 (2d ed. 1966).
54. Pretto v. Leiwant, 80 A.D.2d 579, 435 N.Y.S.2d 778 (2d Dep't 1980).
55. Bombard v. County of Albany, 94 A.D.2d 910, 463 N.Y.S.2d 633 (3d Dep't 1983).
56. People v. Milks, 70 A.D. 438, 74 N.Y.S. 1042 (4th Dep't 1902); Annot., *Cross-Examination of Expert Witness as to Fees, Compensation and the Like*, 33 A.L.R.2D 1170 (1954).
57. Garnsey v. Rhodes, 138 N.Y. 461 (1893).

15.6 THE WITNESS HAS A BAD REPUTATION FOR TRUTH AND VERACITY

To impeach the opposing party's witness, the attorney may demonstrate that the witness has a bad reputation for truth and veracity in the community in which he or she lives.[58] In *Spira v. Holoschutz*,[59] the trial court outlined the procedure for this method of impeachment:

> All that is necessary for a party to an action to do in order to impeach the testimony of an adverse witness is to show by an impeaching witness that he, the impeaching witness, knows the general reputation for truth and veracity of the witness whose testimony it is sought to impeach, in the community in which the witness resides. If the witness says that he does know such reputation he may then be asked what that reputation is, and if he says that it is not good, he may be asked whether from such knowledge he would believe such witness on his oath.

Note that the impeaching witness may not testify about any specific instance of the original witness's lack of veracity but merely about his or her reputation for veracity. However, when cross-examining the impeaching witness, the attorney for the party who called the original witness may question the impeaching witness about his or her knowledge of specific instances.[60] Finally, the attorney should bear in mind that the testimony impeaching a witness's reputation is limited to the individual's reputation for truth and veracity and may not show that reputation as bad in other respects, such as for chastity.

---

58. FED. R. EVID. 608(a); Richardson, Evidence §§ 494-97.
59. Spira v. Holoschutz, 38 Misc. 754 (N.Y. Mun. Ct. 1902). *See also* Carlson v. Winterton, 147 N.Y. 652 (1895); Elmendorf v. Ross, 221 A.D.376, 222 N.Y.S.737 (3d Dep't 1927); Sturmwald v. Schreiber, 69 A.D. 476, 74 N.Y.S. 995 (2d Dep't 1902).
60. Annot., *Admissibility of Testimony as to Reputation of Party or Witness at Place of Employment or Occupation*, 82 A.L.R.3D 525 (1978).

15.7 EXTRINSIC DOCUMENTS CONTRADICT THE WITNESS

The attorney may cross-examine witnesses using extrinsic documents or materials outside their testimony, in other words, using learned treatises, counter-hypothetical questions, public documents, or published documents. The attorney's intent in using each of these four methods is to weaken the witness's testimony by impeaching his credibility or his *ethos*. The attorney properly uses learned treatises and counter-hypothetical questions to attack an expert witness, but the attorney may use public documents and published documents to attack any witness to whose testimony the documents are relevant.

15.7.1 Learned Treatises

We may divide cross-examining an expert witness using a learned treatise into definitions, specific purposes, preparation, use during cross-examination, the direct and indirect results, and use in the summation.

15.7.1.1 Definitions

The direct examination of a witness consists of questions from the party who called him in order to elicit his knowledge in admissible form.[61] By contrast, cross-examination consists of questions by the adverse party to test the truth of the witness's evidence.[62] An expert witness is a witness

---

61. BLACK'S LAW DICTIONARY 664 (4th ed. 1968): "The examination of a witness consists of the series of questions put to him by a party to the action, or his counsel, for the purpose of bringing before the court and the jury in legal form, the knowledge which the witness has of the facts and matters in dispute, or of probing and sifting his evidence previously given."

62. *Id.* 450: "The examination of a witness upon a trial or hearing, or upon taking a deposition, by the party opposed to the one who produced him, upon his evidence given in chief, to test its truth, to further develop it, or for other purposes."

who possesses specialized knowledge which the jury requires in order to decide a question of fact.[63] For our purposes, the most important qualification is that the expert's opinion must be based on principles generally accepted in the relevant scientific community.[64] Finally, a learned treatise is a scholarly publication which embodies the knowledge of an expert in written form.

We must also distinguish credibility from *ethos*. Credibility is the jury's perception that the witness's factual report is accurate because he is honest and was able to observe the events.[65] In contrast, *ethos* is the persuasive appeal from the jury's perception that the advocate is honest, competent, and trying to assist the jury.[66] Every witness needs credibility, but an expert witness also needs *ethos* because he offers an opinion; that is, he becomes a disguised advocate for the party who called him.

15.7.1.2 Specific Purposes

The attorney who cross-examines such an expert using a learned treatise is pursuing one of four specific purposes: adoption, contradiction, rejection, or consultation. When pursuing the specific purpose of adoption, the attorney is attempting to induce the witness to adopt the statement in the

63. *Id.* 688. Frye v. United States, 293 F. 1013 (D.C. Cir. 1923); Kulak v. Nationwide Mutual Insurance Co., 40 N.Y.2d 140 (1976); Selkowitz v. County of Nassau, 45 N.Y.2d 97 (1978); and De Long v. County of Erie, 60 N.Y.2d 296 (1983).

64. Frye v. United States, 293 F. 1013 (D.C. Cir. 1923) (the basic rule); People v. Wesley, 83 N.Y.2d 417 (1994) (the rule's continued validity in New York); and People v. Middleton, 54 N.Y.2d 42 (1981) (the court may consult judicial decisions or the scientific literature to decide this issue).

65. BLACK'S LAW DICTIONARY 440 (4th ed. 1968): "... one who is entitled to have his oath ... accepted as reliable, not only on account of his good reputation for veracity, but also on account of his intelligence, knowledge of the circumstances, and disinterested relation to the matter in question."

66. CORBETT,CLASSICALRHETORICFORTHEMODERNSTUDENT80(1965):"Theethical appeal is exerted, according to Aristotle, when the speech itself impresses the audience that the speaker is a man of sound sense (phronesis), high moral character (arete), and benevolence (eunoia)."

treatise thereby converting that statement into evidence in chief.[67] Example 15-1 provides a successful example of such an attempt. The attorney induced the defendant's medical expert to agree with statements in various treatises, to wit: that a fetus who has suffered an hypoxic insult may still have normal blood gases at delivery, that he may show no signs of respiratory depression, that an overdue pregnancy risks such an hypoxic event, that such a baby is more susceptible to stress during labor, that a marked decrease in amniotic fluid is an ominous sign possibly related to hypoxia, that a finding of oligohydramnios indicates fetal asphyxia absent other explanations, and that length of gestation is one obstetrical factor related to autism.

When pursuing the specific purpose of contradiction, the attorney impeaches the expert's *ethos* by demonstrating that the expert's testimony contradicts the accepted knowledge in the field. Specifically, the attorney asks the witness if he agrees with the statement in the learned treatise. For example, each side in a lawsuit might present expert testimony regarding the monitoring of the flow of oxygen during anesthesia and regarding the causality between this flow and the plaintiff's coma. The respective opponents would then challenge each other's experts using learned treatises.

The third specific purpose is to impeach the expert's *ethos* by inducing him to reject every one of several proffered treatises as not being authoritative. If you cannot induce your opponent's expert to adopt your position, and if you cannot demonstrate that the accepted scientific knowledge in his field contradicts him, the reason probably will be that the expert has refused to acknowledge anyone else's work as authoritative. This is his right, but the attorney can make such a witness appear closed-minded, egotistical, uncooperative, and generally foolish. Take your time when confronting such a witness. In particular, name each author

---

67. Vialva v. City of New York, 118 A.D.2d 701 (2d Dep't 1986).

of a textbook and list each author's qualifications on the pretext of carefully identifying the learned treatise before asking the witness whether it is authoritative. Example 15-2 is the transcript an attorney's cross-examination of such a witness. The author will allow the reader to decide whether the witness looked foolish.

Finally, the attorney's fourth specific purpose may be to impeach both the credibility and the *ethos* of the witness by demonstrating that his testimony contradicts his own writings or a treatise which he consulted in order to testify. It is virtually impossible for the witness to deny that either of these works is authoritative, but the attorney should lay the foundation by asking the expert which works he consulted or wrote before the attorney challenges the expert.

15.7.1.3 Preparation

The basis of effective cross-examination is preparation, not genius. Remember that the allies expended months of preparation to produce four days of blitzkrieg in Desert Storm. This preparation will entail preparation in the expert's field (e.g., medicine), for the witness, and of the questions; and we may further divide the preparation in the medicine between learning the medicine and discerning the opponent's position.

Learning the medicine entails summarizing the medical records, consulting your experts, collecting your own library of treatises, making bibliographic searches, studying the treatises, and marking the crucial passages. A highly specialized firm, such as Kramer Dillof, can perform all these functions in house, but other firms may not be so equipped or may desire an outside check on their work. Therefore, the Medical Records Review Service has kindly provided examples 15-3 and 15-4. Such a service will subpoena the medical records, organize, summarize, and review them, conduct a bibliographic search, and obtain an expert witness. Example 15-3 is a letter explaining the firm's services, and example 15-4 is the result of a bibliographic search of the periodical literature on anesthesia with hypoxia.[68] When we requested this search, the Medical Records Review Service told us that the starting point would be the *Guidelines for Patient Care in Anesthesiology* issued by the American Society of Anesthesiologists for the relevant year and then several standard textbooks. However, we wanted an example of the computer printout for periodical literature. Although the Medical Records Review Service does not advertise this function, the partners told me that attorneys often hire them to mark passages in a treatise, which passages contradict the expected testimony of the opponent's expert.

The subject of passages brings us to preparing for the medicine by discerning the opponent's position. You must construct your opponent's arguments carefully, but you should not find this task intellectually difficult. Your starting point is the pleadings, i.e., the complaint, the answer, and the respective bills of particulars. The plaintiff's medical records are the second stop, and your own expert should help you to deduce your opponent's position from these documents. Third, Uniform Court Rule 202.17 requires the parties to exchange the reports of their examining physicians, and C.P.L.R. 3101(d)(1)(i) provides that each party shall disclose in reasonable detail the subject matter of its expert's testimony, his qualifications, and a summary of the grounds for his opinion. These reports and disclosures should make your opponent's position clear enough for you to determine which statements in a learned treatise will contradict the opponent's expert.

Having prepared for the opponent's position on the medicine, the attorney should, if possible, prepare for his oppo-

---

68. For other forms and reports from the Medical Records Review Service, Inc., see examples 1-2, 1-14, 1-15, and 1-16 or contact MRRS directly at 1420 Woodland Avenue, Suite #1, Des Moines, Iowa 50309, telephone (800) 984-6777.

nent's expert as an individual, and this preparation entails identifying the witness and investigating the witness's opinions. C.P.L.R. 3101(d)(1)(i) states the general rule that each party shall identify the experts he expects to call and their qualifications; but the same section provides that a party may withhold the name of its medical, dental, or podiatric expert in an action for medical, dental, or podiatric malpractice. The parties may agree, of course, to share this information,[69] but assume they do not. The attorney still may be able to deduce the physician's identity. Any physician who examined the plaintiff may testify, but a party may call an expert who will testify on the basis of the medical records alone. (This ploy may or may not be a clever tactic because the expert will not have examined the patient.) However, the attorney may uncover the witness's identity even then. For example, there may be few experts in his field, or the opposing firm may frequently use the same expert in similar cases. Finally, the expert's qualifications, supplied pursuant to C.P.L.R. 3101, may enable the attorney to identify him. In fact, the more prominent the expert is, the easier it is to identify him. Even if you are unable to identify a particular expert, you may be able to narrow the field to such a small number that you can investigate each. One caveat: do not be surprised if the defendant calls the plaintiff's treating physician without warning the plaintiff.

Having identified the expert, you will investigate his opinions. Medline or the Medical Records Review Service will conduct a bibliographic search of the expert's publications for you. You can also investigate the expert's testimony in previous trials by obtaining a list of these trials from a

69. C.P.L.R. 3101(d)(1)(ii): "In an action for medical, dental or podiatric malpractice, any party may, by written offer made to and served upon all other parties and filed with the court, offer to disclose the name of, and to make available for examination upon oral deposition, any person the party making the offer expects to call as an expert witness at trial . . . .If all parties accept the offer, each party shall be required to produce his or her expert witness for examination upon oral deposition . . . ."

service provided by the *Jury Verdict Review and Analysis.*[70] (See example 15-5.) However, examine the summaries in the printed editions of the reporter before ordering the transcripts to ensure that the issues were similar to the ones in your case. Finally, using these treatises and transcripts does not require bringing steamer trunks into the courtroom. Compile one loose-leaf binder with photostats from the relevant treatises, the list of cases in which the expert has testified (especially for the same firm), and the relevant pages from any transcript. (Have the transcript of the expert's entire testimony available.) The Medical Records Review Service warns me that when the parties do identify their experts in advance of the trial, the expert often makes small but intentional mistakes in the citations to his publications in order to make them difficult to find.

Having prepared for the medicine and the witness, the attorney must prepare his questions using the learned treatises. Work backwards. Specifically, find the exact statement which will contradict the opponent's expert, then formulate the questions leading up to the challenge once the expert acknowledges the treatise as authoritative. Finally, formulate the questions which will lead up to asking whether the treatise is authoritative. Practice your questions in their proper sequence so you do not have to read them.

15.7.1.4 Use During Cross-Examination

The critical prerequisite to using the learned treatise during cross-examination is that the witness must accept the proposed treatise as authoritative. There is, of course, some dispute over whether the witness must agree to the term "authoritative" rather than to its substance. Examples 15-6 and 15-7 are appellate briefs dealing with attorneys reading from medical textbooks. In example 15-6, our firm objected

---

70. Published monthly by Jury Verdict Review, 24 Commerce Street, Suite 1722, Newark, N.J. 07102, telephone (201) 624-1665 & 1666.

to the court's allowing the defendant's attorney to read from a textbook despite our expert's refusal to recognize it as authoritative; and in example 15-7, our firm objected to the court's refusing to allow us to cross-examine the defendant's expert using a treatise which he had recognized as standard but would not call authoritative. Our firm's position on judicial policy has three parts: first, the court should not allow the witness to evade cross-examination through a subterfuge; however, second, some treatises really are not authoritative; and third, having made a ruling, the court must enforce it against both parties.

In any case, the attorney must approach the witness in careful steps. Ensure that you are using the edition of the textbook that was current when the events occurred. (The treatise must represent the consensus of scientific knowledge at the time, and the witness may accept that the statement was authoritative when made.) Ask the witness whether physicians must use learned treatises, whether he uses any, and only then whether a particular treatise is authoritative. If he balks, you may ask him whether he will recognize the treatise as authoritative while reserving the right to disagree with it. Finally, you may ask the witness whether he agrees with a particular statement in the text.

The witness, of course, may adopt any one of different attitudes. He may reject all treatises as authoritative, reject some but accept others, or accept all for what they are worth. Once he has heard the quotation from the treatise, the witness may claim that the treatise is wrong or not the scientific consensus, or he may deny the contradiction and claim that the attorney has misconstrued the quotation or taken it out of context.

15.7.1.5 The Results

What will be the direct result of all this effort? Be certain of one thing: the witness will not break down on the stand like the murderer on *Perry Mason*. Of course, the witness may discredit himself if he refuses to accept any text as authoritative. More likely, he will deny any contradiction or will agree to some qualification of his opinion. This qualification may be important but undramatic so the attorney must explore the qualification for the jury. The witness also may reveal that his opinion rests on a certain view of the facts, e.g., that there was no meconium staining the amniotic fluid when the bag of waters broke during the delivery. He should admit that if the facts were different, his opinion would change. This admission will allow the attorney to out-maneuver his opponent on the facts, and it will open the way for a counter-hypothetical question. Finally, if the witness does adopt the statements in the treatise as his own, then those statements become evidence indirectly through his testimony; but this evidence is not equivalent to an opinion on the plaintiff's injuries.

The indirect results of cross-examining an expert using a learned treatise consist of further cross-examination. Read example 15-1 carefully. The attorney confronted the defendant's expert with a series of learned treatises. In each case, the attorney induced the witness to agree to a statement in the text, and then she used that agreement to extract further admissions. Moreover, she repeated the process until the defendant's expert had virtually become the plaintiff's expert. After using the learned treatise, the attorney may turn to an examination of the medical records or a counter-hypothetical question, and the attorney may use the admissions from one expert to frame questions for subsequent experts.

15.7.1.6 The Summation

Unfortunately, new attorneys often overlook using the results of the cross-examination during the summation. The attorney must not expect the jurors to formulate his arguments for him . . . ever! Even if the jurors laughed at the witness, they may lose the significance of his testimony during the subsequent weeks of the trial. Thus, the attorney must integrate each witness's testimony into the attorney's arguments. For example, if the witness abandoned an opinion, the attorney must remind the jurors of this and explain its significance to them.

15.7.2 Counter-Hypothetical Questions

The second method of impeaching the testimony of an expert witness is by asking him a counter-hypothetical question. We will divide the discussion of this method into definition, preparation, introduction, the answer, and using the answer.

15.7.2.1 The Definitions

The definitions are easy. *Black's Law Dictionary* defines a hypothetical question as

> A combination of assumed or proved facts and circumstances, stated in such a form as to constitute a coherent and specific situation or state of facts, upon which the opinion of an expert is asked, by way of evidence at a trial. (Citations omitted.)

* * *

> . . . the witness should be asked whether he is able to form an opinion therefrom and if so to state his opinion (citation omitted.)[71]

A counter-hypothetical question is simply a hypothetical question which contains at least one change in the facts assumed. The attorney asks the counter-hypothetical to demonstrate that the expert's answer to the original hypothetical was not dispositive — everything depends on the facts. In order to ask the counter-hypothetical, the cross-examiner may need to assume facts which are not yet in evidence but which he reasonably expects to place into evidence; that is, he asks the question subject to connection later.

15.7.2.2 Preparation

The preparation for asking a counter-hypothetical question is similar to that for using a learned treatise. Assuming that the attorney has learned the medicine or other specialty, he must phrase the question carefully including only the pertinent facts, numbering the elements if necessary, and supporting each item with evidence. However, this evidence may be disputed and need not have been introduced before the cross-examiner asks the counter hypothetical.[72]

---

71. BLACK'S LAW DICTIONARY 877 (4th ed. 1968). *See also* WELLMAN, THE ART OF CROSS-EXAMINATION 119-20 (4th ed. 1936): "A hypothetical question is supposed to be an accurate synopsis of the testimony that has already been sworn to by the various witnesses who have preceded the appearance of the medical expert in the case. The doctor is then asked to assume the truth of every fact which counsel has included in this question, and to give the jury his opinion and conclusions as an expert from these supposed facts."

72. PRINCE, RICHARDSON ON EVIDENCE §390 (9th ed. 1964): "It is not necessary that the facts be established beyond all controversy: each side may shape its question according to its own theory. Cowley v. People, 83 N.Y. 464, 470. But a question which assumes a material fact which has no support in the evidence is im proper and must be excluded. People v. Patrick, 182 N.Y. 131, 172–3."

As part of this preparation, the attorney should draft the hypothetical question which his opponent is likely to ask, then the attorney should compare the two questions to isolate the factual difference. If he is lucky, this fact will be one easily grasped by the jurors, e.g., the color of a slide in the lab, which color was misinterpreted and led to an unnecessary amputation. When you compose the final version of your own question, compile a chart to justify it. Draw three columns. In the first column, list the elements of the question; in the second, note the form in which the supporting evidence has already appeared, e.g., a particular witness at the E.B.T.; and, in the third note the form in which the supporting evidence will be admitted at the trial.

15.7.2.3 Using the Question

Having formulated his counter-hypothetical question, the attorney must ask it, of course; I will say introduce it although that term is not technically accurate. The attorney must lead up to his counter-hypothetical slowly. I still find useful the advice we received from Wellman's book when we were in law school.[73]

First, ask the witness to repeat the substance of your opponent's hypothetical question. When the witness cannot, his standing with the jury will decline. Second,

ask the witness whether your opponent showed him the hypothetical question in advance. This practice is not unethical, but the jury may find that it undermines the witness's *ethos* as a neutral expert. Third, ask the witness which facts in the hypothetical question are important and which he could discard without changing his opinion. Grad-

---

73. The list in the next paragraph has been compiled from WELLMAN, THE ART OF CROSS-EXAMINATION (4th ed. 1936), chapters 5 & 6.

ually narrow the real factual issues for the jury. Fourth, determine whether a single sentence or a twist in the question served as the foundation for the answer, e.g., that the precise level of oxygen would *always* or *never* lead to a coma. Ask if the witness suggested this phrasing to the opposing counsel. Fifth, probe the phrasing of the question to determine whether the phrasing begs the question by including the ultimate conclusion in different words. Sixth, inquire whether the expert would change his opinion if the assumed facts changed. He will discredit himself if he says no, and he will open himself to the counter-hypothetical if he says yes. Finally, seventh, if there is some dispute about the credibility of other witnesses, ask the witness whom he would have consulted if he had been called in as the attending physician. (This assumes, of course, that the witness would have questioned the personnel, e.g., the nurses, on whose testimony the attorney is relying.)

When you have finished these preliminaries, alert the witness that you are going to ask him a hypothetical question, and make every effort to appear reasonable. (This means reasonable to the judge and jury, not to the opposing counsel.) While you should not announce the basis of each fact assumed, have ready your chart showing the evidentiary basis of each fact. (This chart is not evidence, of course, but you will be able to satisfy the judge at the sidebar that your question is proper.) Ask your counter-hypothetical question carefully. List the elements in a logical order: number them if necessary; review the list with the witness; point out the difference from the original hypothetical, ask him if he can form an opinion; then ask him for his opinion.

15.7.2.4 The Answer

Once the witness has answered, have him repeat his answer for the jury, and insist that he give you a definite response. You must use your own judgment about letting the witness expand on his answer, but beware of allowing an expert to explain away his answer. However, you may ask further hypothetical questions; for example, if lack of oxygen did cause the coma, what is the prognosis?

Besides inducing the expert to qualify his opinion, the attorney may have revealed to the jury that a slight change in the disputed facts will change the conclusion, or that the critical factual element of the opponent's hypothetical is supported by very slight evidence, or that the expert's answer to the original question depended on the phrasing of the question.

15.7.2.5 Using the Answer

Finally, the attorney must use the answers he has extracted. The answers may lead to other questions, but they must lead to argument in the summation. For example, assume that the expert has admitted that if the amniotic fluid was stained with meconium, then a prolapsed umbilical cord must have asphyxiated the baby. In his summation, the attorney for the plaintiff would argue, based on other evidence, that the amniotic fluid was stained with meconium; then he would return to the expert's testimony and use the answer to his counter-hypothetical to draw the conclusion.[74]

15.7.3 Public Documents

We now leave expert witnesses and turn to ordinary ones, i.e., to cross-examination using public documents or published documents. The distinction is that a public document is a governmental document while a published document is a private but circulated document.

---

74. For an example of this procedure, see the sample summation in §9.4.5.

Although public documents are now generally admitted pursuant to statute, they have a long history in the common law.[75] In any case, we may divide our discussion of public documents into definitions, preparation, admission, content and effect, and use during cross-examination.

15.7.3.1 The Definitions

We may define documentary evidence as evidence in the form of a written record and a public document as a record evincing or connected with the public business or the administration of public affairs, preserved or issued by a department of the government,[76] i.e., not necessarily created by the government. Some examples of public documents are birth, death, and marriage certificates, weather reports, agricultural inspection certificates, autopsy reports, and sewer surveys.

15.7.3.2 Preparation

The preparation for using a public document begins, of course, with determining the issues and relevant facts. For example, where did the autos collide? Could a large puddle have accumulated at that spot? Could the witness have identified the cyclist who ran down the pedestrian? Having determined the issues and possible facts, the attorney should consider whether any public documents contain relevant evidence and whether he can use any such document in his direct case or to contradict a witness for the opposition. Preparation also includes obtaining the correct certificate or witness to introduce the document.

---

75. HOGUE, ORIGINS OF THE COMMON LAW 218-27 (1966). Royal records were conclusive evidence of their contents, not just prima facie evidence.

76. BLACK'S LAW DICTIONARY 568 (4th ed. 1968) for both definitions.

15.7.3.3 Admission

Assuming that the attorney has obtained a relevant public document, he must convince the court to admit the document into evidence. There are four bases for admitting a public document. To supplement this discussion, we have provided the following table of statutes. The entries are intended to be illustrative, not exhaustive or definitive.

TABLE OF STATUTES

The sections listed below are the principal ones governing the admission of documents.

C.P.L.R.	
4518.	Business records.
4520.	Certificate or affidavit of public officer.
4521.	Lack of record.
4522	Ancient filed maps, surveys and records affecting real property.
4523.	Search by title insurance or abstract company.
4524.	Conveyance of real property without the state.
4525.	Copies of statements under article nine of the uniform commercial code.
4526.	Marriage certificate.
4527.	Death or other status of missing person.
4528.	Weather conditions.
4529.	Inspection certificate issued by United States department of agriculture.
4530.	Certificate of population.
4531.	Affidavit of service or posting notice by person unavailable at trial.
4532.	Self-authentication of newspapers and periodicals of general circulation.
4532-a.	X-rays, magnetic resonance images, computed axial tomographs, positron emission

	tomographs, electromyograms, sonograms and fetal heart rate monitor strips in personal injury actions.
4533.	Market reports.
4533-a.	Prima facie proof of damages.
4534.	Standard of measurement used by surveyor.
4538.	Acknowledged, proved or certified writing, conveyance of real property without the state.
4539.	Reproductions of original.
4540.	Authentication of official records of court or government office in the United States.
4541.	Proof of proceedings before justice of the peace.
4542.	Proof of foreign records and documents.
4543.	Proof of facts in writing by methods other than those authorized in this article.
D.R.L. Art. 3.	Solemnization, Proof and Effect of Marriage.
E.P.T.L. 2-1.7	Presumption of death from absence; effect of exposure to specific peril.
Ins. L. 311	Filing of report on examination [superintendent].
P.H.L. 10	Legal presumptions; evidence [reports of public health officers].
Art. 41.	Vital Statistics.
4103.	Vital statistics, evidence.

Meanwhile, the four bases for admitting a public document into evidence are: the general statute for public documents created by public officials, the various statutes for specific public documents, the statute for business records, and the residual common law exception.

Remember that these documents are hearsay and therefore must be admitted pursuant to some exception to the hearsay rule. The first basis, the general statute for public documents created by public officials, is embodied in C.P.L.R. 4520, Certificate or affidavit of public officer.

> Where a public officer is required or authorized, by special provision of law, to make a certificate or an affidavit to a fact ascertained, or an act performed, by him in the course of his official duty, and to file or deposit it in a public office of the state, [then] the certificate or affidavit so filed or deposited is prima facie evidence of the facts stated.

In other words, such a document is admissible when certified, i.e., without a witness laying a foundation, but the official must have performed the act himself or have ascertained the fact himself, and he must have created the document in the form of an affidavit or certificate.[77]

Since the statutory basis is so narrow, the legislature also created the second basis: the various statutes admitting specific public documents. Many of these statutes apply to what we would call vital statistics, e.g., births, deaths, marriages, population, and the weather. Note also that some of these documents are created by private parties, such as physicians and title insurance companies, and that certified copies are admissible as such.

The third basis for admitting a public document is the exception to the hearsay rule for business records. Obviously, the government keeps business records, and C.P.L.R. 4518(c) makes certified copies of such records admissible pursuant to the same tests as other business records but without a witness;[78] that is, the certificate must recite that the records were made in a timely fashion, etc.[79] However, despite the

---

77. For example, Mace v. Cardone, 35 Misc.2d 163 (App. Term 1962) (Certificate of notary public admissible pursuant to C.P.L.R. 4520), and People v. Brown, 221 A.D.2d 270 (1st Dep't 1995) (Certificate of medical examiner admissible pursuant to C.P.L.R. 4520).

78. C.P.L.R. 4818(c) refers to C.P.L.R. 2306. Hospital records; medical records of department or bureau of a municipal corporation or of the state and to C.P.L.R. 2307. Books, papers and other things of a library department or bureau of a municipal corporation or of the state.

79. People v. Mertz, 68 N.Y.2d 136, 147-8 (1986).

language of the statute, such records are admissible without a judicial subpoena.[80]

Finally, the fourth basis for admitting a public document is the residual common law exception for public documents.[81] It is hard to specify the scope of the residue, however. We can only approach it in a negative way. Obviously, the residue would not include a business record, a document covered by a specific statute, or an affidavit or certificate created by a public official pursuant to his duty and embodying his own act or a fact he ascertained. (The common law rule might encompass such a document, but we are discussing the residue of the rule after factoring out the statutory exceptions.) The primary use of the residual common law rule is to admit the reports of official and detailed investigations, e.g., the report of the Medical Review Commission of the State Commission on Corrections on whether a particular prisoner committed suicide.[82] Probably a sewer survey or another official map would be admissible pursuant to the common law exception if the document did not qualify as an ancient map.

---

80. Joyce v. Kowalcewski, 80 A.D.2d 27 (4th Dep't 1981).

81. Consolidated Midland Corp. v. Columbia Pharmaceutical Corp., 42 A.D.2d 601 (2d Dep't 1973) (common law exception for public documents broader than statutory exception); Greenberg v. Manlon Realty, Inc., 43 A.D.2d 968 (2d Dep't 1974) (if statutory exception inapplicable, admission of document requires testimony for foundation); People v. Garneau, 120 A.D.2d 112 (4th Dep't 1986) (results of breathalyzer test not admissible pursuant to common law exception); People v. Gower, 42 N.Y.2d 117 (1977) (foundation for breathalyzer); People v. Hoats, 102 Misc.2d 1004 (Monroe 1980) (admitted breathalyzer test) and People v. Kollore, 151 Misc.2d 384 (City Ct. of Mt. Vernon 1991) (admitted report of Dept. of Motor Vehicles).

82. Kozlowski v. City of Amsterdam, 111 A.D.2d 476 (3d Dep't 1985); *see also* Cramer v. Kuhns, 213 A.D.2d 131 (3d Dep't 1995) (federal report on kickstands inadmissible as too cursory); Kelly v. Diesel Construction Division of Carl A. Morse, 35 N.Y.2d 1 (1974) (accident report by elevator inspector admissible); and Steven v. Kirby, 86 A.D.2d 391 (4th Dep't 1982) (report for State Liquor Authority inadmissible). For statutory authority to admit reports, see Insurance Law 311(d) and Public Health Law 10(2).

15.7.3.4 Content and Effect

We must consider the content and effect of public documents once they are in evidence. Remember that admitting a document does not necessarily constitute admitting every statement in the document. For example, a police report of an auto accident may be admissible as a business record, and the officer's record of what he observed, e.g., the positions of the autos, would be admissible. However, a bystander's report of how the accident happened would not be admissible because the bystander would not be acting pursuant to a duty or making an admission against interest.[83] (The bystander could, of course, testify in person.) In general, the admissible content of a public document depends on the document's purpose. However, the courts are slowly expanding the matters they will admit in these documents. Thus, a death certificate originally was admissible only to prove the fact of death;[84] then it became admissible to prove the cause of death.[85] Most recently, the court of appeals has

---

83. Kelly v. Diesel Construction Division of Carl A. Morse, 35 N.Y.2d 1 (1974) (statement to elevator inspector inadmissible); Greenberg v. Prudential Insurance Co. of America, 266 A.D. 685 (2d Dep't 1943) (statement in death certificate that victim had jumped in front of the train was inadmissible); and Welz v. Commercial Travelers Mutual Accident Association of America, 266 A.D. 688 (2d Dep't 1943) (statement in medical examiner's report that the victim fell on the subway platform was inadmissible).
84. PRINCE, RICHARDSON ON EVIDENCE §366 (9th ed. 1964).
85. *Id.*: Principally by admitting the certificate as a business record pursuant to statute. *See* Anderson v. Commercial Travelers Mutual Accident Association, 73 A.D.2d 769 (3d Dep't 1979) (vital statistics admissible as public records); Brownrigg v. Boston & Albany Rail Road Co., 8 A.D.2d 149 (1st Dep't 1959) (death certificate admissible as prima facie evidence of facts contained); Duffy v. 42nd Street, M.&S. Avenue Railway, 266 A.D. 865 (2d Dep't 1943) (death certificate admissible regarding cause of death); Gioia v. State, 22 A.D.2d 181 (4th Dep't 1964) (death certificate and hospital report admissible regarding cause of death); *In re* Estate of Whittaker, 120 Misc.2d 1021 (Sur. Rensselaer 1983) (death certificate admissible for facts in addition to death); and Stein v. Lebowitz-Pine View Hotel, Inc., 111 A.D.2d 572 (3d Dep't), *appeal. denied*, 65 N.Y.2d 611 (1985) (coroner's report admissible on cause of death).

ruled that the death certificate is admissible on the issue of suicide in a civil action for the proceeds of an insurance policy.[86] However, if my opponent tried to introduce a death certificate or an autopsy report, not for the proposition that the decedent was run over by a subway train, but for the proposition that the decedent jumped in front of the train, I would rely on the traditional rule and object. In sum, the attorney must evaluate each document individually on the basis of the relevant statute and the cases.

The evidentiary effect of a public document is a much simpler matter. A public document admitted pursuant to one of the statutes is prima facie evidence of its proper contents; that is, the trier of fact must accept the evidence unless the adverse party adduces contradictory evidence. In other words, the document creates a rebuttable presumption. However, a public document admitted pursuant to the common law exception is merely some evidence of its contents.[87]

15.7.3.5 Use During Cross-Examination

Finally, let us consider the use of these public documents in cross-examination. Attorneys do not use public documents solely or even primarily to impeach witnesses. However, the attorney may use such a document to demonstrate that the witness is lying or at least wrong. Example 15-8 is a monthly weather report from the National Oceanic and Atmospheric Administration. One of the author's partners[88] used such a report to win a conviction when he was an assistant D.A. in Queens. The defendant took the stand to testify that, on the day in question, he was in Columbia, South Carolina. Fortunately, the prosecutor had read Wellman's

86. Brown v. Equitable Life Assurance Society of the United States, 69 N.Y.2d 675 1986). The result in this case depended on the plaintiff's having introduced expert testimony to rebut the presumption against suicide.

87. Bogdan v. Peekskill Community Hospital, 168 Misc.2d 856 (Sp. Ct. West. 1996).

88. Thomas J. Principe.

advice "not to disclose your 'trump card' . . . until you have so completely committed the witness to the details of his story as to make it impossible to offer any plausible explanation of the damaging document with which you intend to destroy him."[89] During his cross-examination, the prosecutor challenged the defendant to prove that he was in South Carolina by describing the weather. The defendant responded by describing a warm day with the sun shining. The prosecutor thereupon produced a certified copy of the weather report showing that Columbia, South Carolina had received several inches of rain that day. The jury convicted the defendant.

15.7.4 Published Documents

The final method of cross-examination using extrinsic documents consists of using published documents to impeach the witness, and we may divide this discussion into definition, admission, content and effect, and use in cross-examination.

15.7.4.1 Definition

Black's Law Dictionary defines "publish" as to circulate or to make known to people in general.[90] Thus, a public document is a non-governmental but circulated record that was reproduced in some written form, e.g., the farmer's almanac or the *New York Times.*

For our purposes, we are interested in two kinds of published documents: scientific calculations and quantitative reports. By scientific calculations, we mean the time of the tides, the phases of the moon, the rising and setting of the moon and of the sun, and even the time of an eclipse. These events were predictions when the almanac was printed, but

89. WELLMAN, THE ART OF CROSS-EXAMINATION 138 (4th ed. 1936).
90. BLACK'S LAW DICTIONARY 1397 (4th ed. 1968).

these events are simply matters of calculation so the attorney may use the almanac after the event as evidence of its occurrence. By a quantitative report, we mean the closing prices on the stock exchange or on the commodity exchanges. These records are mere ministerial acts, but each precise event is uncertain and must be ascertained as it occurs. Calendars and road maps are further examples of these two kinds of documents, and the sources of published documents are obvious.

15.7.4.2 Admission

The method of obtaining the admission of a published document is judicial notice. There is no general statute for the judicial notice of facts as opposed to judicial notice of law; however, the principle is well established.[91] Moreover, the procedure is simple and usually informal. The attorney makes a motion to have the court take judicial notice of the fact and provides the court with the documents necessary to its decision,[92] e.g., a copy of the almanac. (Strictly speaking, the court does not take judicial notice of the almanac but of the fact, i.e., that a full moon rose at a particular time on the date in question.) The adverse party, of course, has the right to be heard in opposition to the motion,[93] and the motion it-

91. One hundred years of cases will confirm this. Hunter v. New York, Ontario, and Western R.R. Co., 116 N.Y. 615 (1889); Ecco High Frequency Corp. v. Amtorg Trading Corp., 81 N.Y.S.2d 610 (Sp. Ct. N.Y. 1947), *aff'd,* 274 App. Div. 982 (1st Dep't 1948); People v. Alicea, 25 N.Y.2d 685 (1969); American Broadcasting Companies, Inc. v. Wolf, 76 A.D.2d 162 (1st Dep't1980), *aff'd*, 52 N.Y.2d 394 (1981); Crater Club, Inc. v. Adirondack Park Agency, 86 A.D.2d 714 (3d Dep't 80), *aff'd,* 57 N.Y.2d 990 (1982); St. Lawrence County Dept. of Social Services v. Steve CC, 92 A.D.2d 1038 (3d Dep't 1983); and People v. Jones, 73 N.Y.2d 427 (1989).

92. Walton v. Stafford, 14 App. Div. 310 (1st Dep't 1897), *aff'd*, 162 N.Y. 558 (1900).

93. *In re* Justin EE, 153 A.D.2d 772 (3d Dep't 1989), *appeal. denied*, 75 N.Y.2d 704 (1990).

self lies in the sound discretion of the court.[94] The standard for that discretion is that the court should take judicial notice of facts which people cannot reasonably dispute.[95]

15.7.4.3 Content and Effect

Once the court has taken judicial notice of the fact, the content of the evidence is straightforward: the data in the tide table or on the face of the calendar. However, the court's judicial notice of the evidence is conclusive, for the court should take judicial notice only of facts which are indisputable. Nevertheless, and this is very important, judicial notice may not decide the real issue. In other words, if the issue is whether the witness could have seen the defendant well enough to identify him, judicial notice of the rising of the moon is conclusive as to that fact, but other facts may bear on the issue.

15.7.4.4 Use During Cross-Examination

This may become clearer as we discuss the actual use of the published document in cross-examination. The reader will remember the famous case in which Abraham Lincoln defended a man accused of murder, and the key witness for the prosecution claimed that he was able to identify the defendant in the woods at night because the witness saw the defendant in the moonlight.[96] Lincoln won the case by using

94. *See* notes 91 and 92. In addition, *see* Cole Fischer Rogow, Inc. v. Carl Ally, Inc., 29 A.D.2d 423 (1st Dep't 1968), *aff'd,* 25 N.Y.2d 943 (1969), and for an abuse of discretion, see Hoya Saxa, Inc. v. Gowan, 149 Misc.2d 191 (App. T., 1st Dep't 1991), and People v. Kennedy, 68 N.Y.2d 569 (1986).

95. Some examples are Elkaim v. Elkaim, 176 A.D.2d 116 (1st Dep't), *appeal dismissed*, 78 N.Y.2d 1072 (1991) (bank records); Montenes v. Metropolitan Street Railway Co., 77 A.D. 493 (2d Dep't 1902) (almanacs); Schenectady Discount Corp. v. Dziedzic, 31 N.Y.S.2d 636 (Schen. Co. Ct. 1941) (calendars); and Vadney v. United Traction Co., 193 A.D. 329 (3d Dep't 1920), *aff'd*, 233 N.Y. 643 (1922) (dictionaries).

96. WELLMAN, THE ART OF CROSS-EXAMINATION 73-5 (4th ed. 1936).

an almanac which showed that the moon had not risen until three hours after the shooting. Lincoln used this evidence in his summation to argue that the witness's probable reason for lying was that he had committed the murder.

A hypothetical example will illustrate how the judicial notice of the published document is conclusive on that fact but not necessarily on the issue. Suppose the witness had been out in the woods at Caumsett State Park competing in an orienteering contest, i.e., trying to find all the flags in the woods quicker than anyone else did. However, this orienteering contest was being held at night. Near the fourteenth flag, someone shot another competitor to death about forty feet away from the witness. At the trial, the witness testified that he saw the defendant commit the murder, and the prosecutor obtained judicial notice that there was a full moon that night. However, when cross-examining the witness, the defense attorney introduced a certified copy of the weather report showing that there was thick cloud cover at the time of the murder. Could the witness really have identified the murderer? Maybe.

15.7.5 Summary

The reader should grasp the differences among our four methods of cross-examination using extrinsic documents, i.e., using a learned treatise, a counter-hypothetical question, a public document, or a published document. The attorney uses a learned treatise or a counter-hypothetical question to impeach an expert witness, but the attorney may use a public or published document to impeach any witness. As a kind of evidence in itself, the learned treatise is none at all; the answer to the counter-hypothetical question is an expert opinion of a tentative kind; the public document is prima facie, i.e., presumptive, evidence of its contents; and the published document is conclusive evidence but of a narrow fact. During cross-examination, each of these devices is more important for impeaching the witness than for establishing a fact. The four methods of cross-examination also differ in the way the attorney introduces them. The attorney essentially asks the permission of the adverse witness to use the learned treatise, but the attorney constructs the counter-hypothetical out of other and disputed evidence. The attorney introduces a public document on the basis of an official certificate or, occasionally, a witness, but the attorney introduces a published document by moving for judicial notice. Finally, the attorney must exploit the results of the cross-examination in his summation.

EXAMPLE 15-1: ADOPTION OF LEARNED TREATISE (APPELLATE BRIEF)

To be argued by
Judith A. Livingston or
Matthew Gaier
New York County Clerk's Index No. 19506/87

Supreme Court

State of New York
Appellate Division – First Department

LOUIS ACEVEDO, an Infant by His Mother and Natural Guardian, NORMA RODRIGUEZ,

Plaintiffs-Respondents,

against

NEW YORK CITY HEALTH AND HOSPITALS CORPORATION, and DR. MALCOLM ROTHBARD,

Defendants-Appellants,

and

DR. JAMES RORIE, and DR. JOEL NOVENSTERN,

Defendants.

BRIEF OF PLAINTIFFS-RESPONDENTS

KRAMER, DILLOF, TESSEL, DUFFY & MOORE
Attorneys for Plaintiffs-Respondents
233 Broadway
New York, NY 10279
(212) 267-4177

JUDITH A. LIVINGSTON
NORMAN BARD
MATTHEW GAIER
Of Counsel and on the Brief

THE REPORTER COMPANY, *Printers and Publishers, Inc.*
30 Vesey Street, New York, NY 10007—212-732-6978
(5650 - 1998)
Reproduced on Recycled Paper

compression and trauma, as was the lay testimony regarding the appearance of the newborn's head. The trauma and compression caused ischemia, which caused brain damage as evidenced by the mental retardation, seizures, and motor difficulties. There was thus substantial basis for the plaintiffs' theory of causation and the jury's finding in that regard was clearly based upon a fair interpretation of the evidence. If there is any doubt in this regard, it is easily dispelled by reference to the testimony of the defendants' own expert in pediatric neurology.

(4)

The Testimony Of The Defendants' Pediatric Neurologist Undermines Their Arguments Attacking Causation And Confirms The Viability Of Plaintiffs' Theory Of Causation

When called by the defense, Dr. Regina DeCarlo testified that hypoxia is a lack of oxygen to any tissue, hypoxemia is when the oxygen carrying capacity of the blood is less than it should be and ischemia is when the blood supply that carries the oxygen to the tissues is interrupted (1248). It was her position, on direct examination, that with damage from any of these mechanisms, you would see immediate damage at birth (1251). She further testified on direct that "it would be unusual to see a child who has severe neurological or developmental issues now who never had any type of motor development [problem]... at some point in time" (1259).

On cross examination, Dr. DeCarlo agreed that Louis' condition is organic and that he has central nervous system dysfunction (1274). She could not state what she believes caused this injury and could only say that the cause is unknown (1274-77, 1280-81). She identified rubella and genetics as possible causes, but acknowledged that there is no indication of either here (1320-21), and she eventually agreed that she could rule them out (1329-30).

When asked whether the events surrounding Louis' birth caused his injuries, Dr. DeCarlo responded that "it's possible, but it's unlikely" (1282-83). The reason she found it unlikely was remoteness -- the 2 1/2 year gap from birth to diagnosis (1284-85). While her opinion was based in part on there being no motor development problems "at some point in time" (1259), she acknowledged that cerebral palsy, which was noted at Metropolitan Hospital when Louis was 2 to 2 1/2 years old, deals with motor development and indicates that there were very likely developmental lags (1302). She further admitted that she had never looked at a single record on this issue (1303). Dr. DeCarlo admitted that "these problems very likely started before 2" and "could have started before 1, certainly" (1305, 1309).

Dr. DeCarlo then completely undermined the significance of the normal Apgar scores in ruling out a birth related injury. She admitted that babies who suffer various conditions and insults while in the uterus prior to delivery can definitely and have good Apgar scores (1311). She further admitted that babies can have significant insults that will cause brain injury and still have normal Apgar scores (1311-12). She testified that Apgar scores have a limited purpose, that a child can have hypoxic damage ***hours or days*** before and have a normal Apgar and can even be born without a cortex in his brain and still have normal Apgar scores (1312-14). A child can suffer hypoxia hours or days before delivery, sustain neurological damage from it, have a complete recovery and the child will then have good Apgar scores without any apparent problems (1317-18). Recognizing the Textbook of Neonatology by N.R.C. Robertson as one of main textbooks used as a reference in neonatology, Dr. DeCarlo agreed with the statement from that book that hours or days before delivery, the fetus may suffer a hypoxic insult severe enough to cause neurologic damage, but by the time the mother goes into labor, he may have made a complete biochemical recovery and have normal blood gases -- her agreement was with the portion about a biochemical recovery (1368-69). She further agreed with the statement that since

35

the child suffers no intrapartum asphyxia, he may show no signs of respiratory depression at birth, have good Apgar scores and good breathing (1369).

This testimony is extremely significant in view of the fact that the abnormal FAD/OCT test was the day before delivery and the oligohydramnios, late decelerations, CPD and Pitocin stimulation had all gone on several hours before the delivery, the Pitocin was stopped an hour and a half before the delivery and the meconium stained placenta indicated continued hypoxia hours earlier. The jury could have viewed Dr. Wilson's and Dr. DeCarlo's testimony as establishing causation based upon hypoxia hours before the delivery.

Dr. DeCarlo agreed that a post dates pregnancy is known to be a risk factor to the baby and a risk factor for the occurrence of hypoxic events (1340). She acknowledged that a post dates pregnancy puts the baby at risk for hypoxic events and that a post term baby is particularly susceptible to hypoxic damage, under the right set of circumstances (1340-41).

When confronted with the text "Neonatal-Perinatal Medicine, Diseases Of The Fetus And Infant", 5th Ed., by Avery Fanaroff, she testified that she "absolutely" agrees with the statement that the fetus of a post term pregnancy is more susceptible to stress during labor than the fetus of a normal pregnancy (1343-44). Her agreement with this statement made it her own such that it became evidence in chief. See PJI 1:90.2.

It was her understanding that Louis was not symptomatic of post maturity in that he was not hypoglycemic or "wasted" (1347). However, she later acknowledged that a post mature baby looks wasted, thinner than usual, long fingernails, could have meconium staining, and has cracked leathery skin (1418-19). A post term baby could appear the same way (1419). Significantly, she admitted that the only description of this baby's skin in the record was "leathery, cracked, wrinkled" (1417). It is also significant that Norma testified that Louis had long fingernails and

36

wrinkled skin (493), his aunt described his skin as reddish and peeling (803), and the record indicated that the placenta was meconium stained (2553).

When read a portion of the chapter on post-term pregnancies from the above referenced text, Dr. DeCarlo agreed that in general a marked decrease in the amount of amniotic fluid "could be an ominous sign, yes" (1349-50). She agreed that oligohydramnios could be a result of the hypoxia induced change in the distribution of factors (1350). She agreed that oligohydramnios is, without any other symptomology in a post-mature infant, "certainly a risk factor, it is a dangerous sign" (1347).

Dr. DeCarlo agreed with a statement from the text "Neonatology Pathophysiology And Management Of The Newborn", by Dr. Gordon B. Avery, that a finding of oligohydramnios always must be considered indicative of fetal asphyxia unless absent renal function, parenthesis or rupture of the membranes can be demonstrated (1351-53).

Dr. DeCarlo agreed that the mortality in babies delivered after 42 weeks doubles and this happens because the placental unit is not functioning properly anymore (1356-57). She admitted that the mortality after 42 weeks is the extreme and that short of mortality, oligohydramnios could be one of the parameters to indicate that the placenta is no longer functioning properly (1357-58).

Dr. DeCarlo then made various admissions which tied the post term condition with the existence of CPD and Pitocin to essentially confirm the underpinnings of Dr. Charash's theory. She agreed that labor can be very traumatic to a baby and that stimulated labor in the face of CPD can be even more traumatic (1360). She admitted that if you have oligohydramnios and CPD and a Pitocin stimulated labor in the face of secondary arrest, the baby will be more

37

vulnerable to the effects of Pitocin induced trauma if you have persistent late decelerations and she then admitted that late decelerations are by definition persistent (1361-63).

Dr. DeCarlo agreed that children with pervasive developmental disorders, with which she diagnosed Louis (1241), and autistic features or autism have a higher correlation of obstetrical complications (1364). She testified that autistic children could have obstetric events in their history and there would be a causal relation if it leads to perinatal encephalopathy (1365-66). She agreed that in this post mature pregnancy, there was oligohydramnios, late decelerations, an abnormal or suspicious stress test, secondary arrest of labor, Pitocin and CPD and that all those are risk factors for causing neurologic injury that should be considered (1366).

After recognizing as authoritative and widely used and read by people who study autism, the Journal of Autism and Developmental Disorders in High-functioning Females and Males With Autism, by Catherine Lord, Dr. DeCarlo agreed in part with the statement that obstetrical complications must be considered along with other potential factors and only one obstetrical factor, gestation estimated greater than 42 weeks, was specifically associated with autism (1372).

While Dr. DeCarlo recognized that Perinatal Factors in Infantile Autism by Joanne Finegan published in the Journal of Psychology and Psychiatry is one of the journals in the field, she disagreed with the statement made in that article that autistic children have a high rate of obstetrical events that may have caused brain damage (1373). She then admitted that you could have a correlation, but not necessarily a correlation of cause and effect (1375-76). The correlation known to the medical community is that a child subject to postmaturity, oligohydramnios, trauma around delivery, is known to develop pervasive developmental disorder (1376-77). She then admitted that since medicine is not an exact science, one of the basic ways medicine is understood is that you do not know for certain, but you look for a correlation between a certain given set of facts and an outcome (1378).

From the article Childhood Autism: An Investigation of Etiological Factors in 25 Cases, from the British Journal of Psychiatry, Dr. DeCarlo agreed with the following statement (1381):

> This investigation shows autistic children can be differentiated from controls by their longer gestation period and history of more complications during labor delivery and the neonatal period. There is ample evidence to substantiate the increased risk to babies born after the 287th day of gestation.
>
> Walker has commented on the definite fall in the mean oxygen saturation of the blood in the umbilical vein after the 41st week in mothers and the age range 25 to 30, the baby being considered to have been at serious risk from intrauterine anoxia

She acknowledged that Louis was born after the 287th day of gestation (1380).

Dr. DeCarlo's testimony thus confirmed that post datism poses risk to the fetus and makes it more vulnerable to injury, that CPD and Pitocin can increase the risk of trauma in a post term baby, that an injury could happen hours before delivery and the child will be born in seemingly good condition, and that autistic-like injuries can result from perinatal insults. In short, Dr. DeCarlo confirmed the validity of the plaintiffs' causation theory and undermined the defendants' two points of criticism -- good Apgars and autism. There is no doubt that the jury's findings of causation should be sustained.

39

EXAMPLE 15-2: REFUSAL TO RECOGNIZE TEXT AS AUTHORITATIVE (TRANSCRIPT)

926

As "expert" OBST

SUPREME COURT OF THE STATE OF NEW YORK
COUNTY OF NEW YORK: TRIAL TERM PART 26
- X
LOUIS ACEVEDO, an Infant by his Mother and
Natural Guardian, NORMA RODRIGUEZ,

Plaintiff,

- against -

NEW YORK CITY HEALTH AND HOSPITALS
CORPORATION, DR. JOEL NOVENSTERN
and DR. MALCOLM ROTHBARD,

Defendants.

- X
Index Number: 19506/87
80 Centre Street
New York, New York
October 9, 1996

BEFORE:

HONORABLE KARLA MOSKOWITZ, Justice.
And a Jury

APPEARANCES:

KRAMER, DILLOF, TESSEL & MOORE
Attorneys for the Plaintiff
233 Broadway
New York, New York, 10279

BY: JUDITH LIVINGSTON ESQ.

MCALOON, FRIEDMAN & MANDEL
Attorneys for the Defendants
116 John Street
New York, New York, 10038

BY: GUNTHER H. KILSCH, ESQ.
JOHN BONACCOLTA, CSR
DEBRA SALZMAN, CSR
OFFICIAL COURT REPORTERS

John A. Bonaccolta, C.S.R., Official Court Reporter

[redacted] - By Defendants - Cross

Q Did you attempt to find in any regard what this note of January 13 means?

A No.

Q The standard -- going back to my question before, the standard of care in 1978 was to effectuate delivery by the end of the 42nd week if that delivery had not occurred; isn't that true?

MR. KILSCH: Objection, your Honor. It was asked and answered.

THE COURT: Sustained.

Members of the jury, disregard the question.

Q Doctor, did you review, sir, to find out what the standard of care was in 1978 regarding effectuating delivery for a postdate pregnancy?

A I did not review any materials, no.

Q You told us you teach, sir?

A Yes.

Q Is that in a classroom setting or clinically?

A Both.

Q One of the textbooks, I take it, you utilize and have utilized regularly over the years is the book entitled "Williams on Obstetrics," in

John A. Bonaccolta, C.S.R., Official Court Reporter

[redacted] - By Defendants - Cross

the 15th Edition then and now up to the 20th or 21st, right, sir?

A I don't recall.

Q You don't recall which edition?

A There's so many editions, yes.

Q One of the books you would regard as generally authoritative, reserving the right to disagree with any portion of it, is "Williams Obstetrics, 15th Edition," which would be the applicable edition in this case, right?

A No.

Q No what?

A I don't regard it as authoritative. It's a good reference book; it's not authoritative.

Q When you say "it's a good reference book," is that the -- do you mean it's something you refer to to find out what should be done under given circumstances?

MR. KILSCH: Objection.

THE COURT: Overruled.

You may answer.

A I refer to it for general information, not so much what should be done. I know what should be done. That's my job.

[redacted] - By Defendants - Cross

Q What should be done, according to the standards?

MR. KILSCH: Objection.

MS. LIVINGSTON: Allow me.

Q This "Williams Obstetrics, 15th Edition," is the 1976 -- published in 1976. Therefore, sir, the applicable "Williams" for the year in question 1978, you know that, right, sir?

A I don't recall. I'd have to see when the next one came out. I don't remember.

Q You know it was after 1980, I believe it was, right, sir?

MR. KILSCH: Objection.

THE COURT: Reframe the question.

Q The next one came out in 1980?

A Okay.

Q You refer to "Williams" --

MR. KILSCH: Objection.

Q -- "on Obstetrics"?

THE COURT: Overruled.

A Yes, I have read "Williams" text of obstetrics.

Q Do you refer medical students to "Williams on Obstetrics," sir?

[redacted] - By Defendants - Cross

A Yes, I do.

Q You refer medical students to "Williams on Obstetrics" because you want them to understand the applicable principals involved?

A Yes.

Q Because you want them to understand what should or should not be done under given circumstances?

A That's a little bit too specific. I can't answer that yes or no.

Q Do you refer medical students to "Williams on Obstetrics" because you find it a source of valuable information in the obstetrics field?

MR. KILSCH: Objection.

THE COURT: Overruled.

A Yes.

Q You consider it generally authoritative, reserving the right to disagree with any particular sentence or paragraph in it; don't you, sir?

A No.

Q Did Mr. Kilsch tell you before you got on the witness stand, if you don't recognize a book as authoritative, I can't read from it? Did he tell you that?

[redacted] - By Defendants - Cross

MR. KILSCH: Objection.

THE COURT: Overruled.

A No.

Q Did you know that, sir?

A I've learned it from some people, yes.

Q Did you check, sir, for 1978 the fact the standard of care was to effectuate delivery once the 42nd week was completed?

MR. KILSCH: Objection.

THE COURT: Sustained.

Members of the jury, disregard that question.

Q Doctor, when you were preparing this case and reviewing this case to know what the standards of care were in 1978, did you go to "Williams" as a source?

A No.

Q One of the reasons, sir, to suspect there might be cephalopelvic disproportion in a given patient is their height, correct?

A No.

Q Doctor, it is well known in 1978 and since then a patient with a short stature is more likely to have cephalopelvic disproportion?

[redacted] - By Defendants - Cross

A No.

Q It's published in the literature; wasn't it?

MR. KILSCH: Objection, your Honor.

THE COURT: Sustained.

Members the jury, disregard that question.

Q You surely recognize the book of "Obstetrics and the Newborn, 1977"? The book entitled "Obstetrics and the Newborn," by Norman Abeischer and Evan V. MacKay, do you recognize that as generally authoritative, reserving the right to disagree with any portion of it, regarding the fact that a patient with a short stature is suspicious for cephalopelvic disproportion?

MR. KILSCH: Objection, your Honor.

THE COURT: Sustained.

Members of the jury, disregard that question.

Q Doctor, do you recognize a generally authoritative volume entitled "Obstetrics and the Newborn," by Abeischer and MacKay, published in 1977?

A No.

[redacted] - By Defendants - Cross

Q Not only was it well known in 1978 that a woman with a short stature was more likely to have CPD, it was common sense; wasn't it, sir?

MR. KILSCH: Objection.

THE COURT: Overruled.

A No.

Q Surely, Doctor, you recognize the writing of Emanuel A. Friedman who you have told us about and who you have referred to; don't you?

A Yes, I know Emanuel Friedman.

Q You would recognize, sir, as generally authoritative what Dr. Emanuel A. Friedman has to say about the warnings of cephalopelvic disproportion; wouldn't you, sir?

A No.

Q You have been quoting us throughout the morning from Dr. Emanuel A. Friedman; haven't you?

A We talked about the -- about the Friedman curve, yes.

Q You even said to us, sir -- you were talking about the guidelines from Dr. Friedman and his guidelines and his studies and his reports; weren't you, sir?

A I believe I said general guide -- general

John A. Bonaccolta, C.S.R., Official Court Reporter

[redacted] - By Defendants - Cross

guidelines.

Q I take it, sir, you were referring to Dr. Emanuel A. Friedman because you found his work to be generally authoritative, reserving the right to disagree with any portion of it; is that true, sir?

A No.

Q Doctor, would you recognize the article by Dr. Emanuel A. Friedman entitled --

MR. KILSCH: Objection.

Q "Pathophysiology of Labor" as generally authoritative, reserving the right to disagree with any portion?

A No.

THE COURT: Overruled.

Q You knew in 1978 that when a woman was 5 feet tall or less, that should be a warning to the doctors of the likelihood of cephalopelvic disproportion, true, sir?

A No.

Q You ever find out how tall this mother was?

A I believe she was 4-11. I think she's under 5 feet.

Q 4-10?

John A. Bonaccolta, C.S.R., Official Court Reporter

[redacted] - By Defendants - Cross

A Thank you.

Q When you were quoting us statistics this morning, sir, in response to Mr. Kilsch's questions and statistics from Dr. Friedman, I take it you got those statistics by reading Dr. Friedman, correct?

MR. KILSCH: Objection to the form.

THE COURT: Overruled.

A It's hard to remember because it's just part of the general knowledge. It's in textbooks. That's a pretty much standard-like percentage that's in the books.

Q When you were quoting us statistics from Dr. Friedman, were you quoting them because you read Dr. Friedman?

MR. KILSCH: May we approach the -- I have an objection. It's based on --

THE COURT: I don't want speeches. I'm going to overrule the objection.

Q When you were quoting us statistics this morning from Dr. Friedman, is it because you read Dr. Friedman?

A I have read Dr. Friedman in the past. Specifically to this case no, I did not reread it. That is general knowledge. The 85 percent-15

John A. Bonaccolta, C.S.R., Official Court Reporter

[redacted] - By Defendants - Cross

percent breakdown is general knowledge in obstetrics.

Q This general knowledge is codified somewhere, isn't it, sir? It's written down somewhere; isn't it?

A Yes.

MR. KILSCH: Objection.

Q It's written down in Dr. Friedman's book?

A I'd have to go back and look again.

Q You surely want to know what his book says about what you're telling us is written in his book; wouldn't you?

MR. KILSCH: Objection.

THE COURT: Sustained.

Disregard that question, members the jury.

Q It is not 85 percent, sir, it is 95 percent of nulliparous patients who are engaged at the time of labor beginning; isn't that true?

MR. KILSCH: Objection, your Honor.

THE COURT: It's a problem with the form. I'll sustain it.

Q You kept quoting us 85 percent this morning, Doctor; remember that?

[redacted] - By Defendants - Cross

A Yes.

Q You told us 85 percent of nulliparous patients are engaged at the time labor starts?

A Yes.

Q You got that quote from Dr. Friedman's book, sir?

A I just answered that question. It's general knowledge. I cannot remember specifically where the number came from.

Q You were sure; were you not?

MR. KILSCH: Objection.

THE COURT: Sustained.

Q Emanuel A. Friedman wrote the definitive textbooks on labor and arrest of labor called "Labor" --

MR. KILSCH: Objection, your Honor.

Q It's the definitive textbook?

MR. KILSCH: Who says? Who's testifying?

THE COURT: Reframe the question, counsel. Sustained.

Q The book that you were telling us -- quoting from this morning and the statistics you were quoting from this morning came from the volume

[redacted] - By Defendants - Cross

entitled "Labor, Clinical Evaluation and Management, Second Edition, by Emanuel A. Friedman, Professor of Obstetrics and Gynecology, Harvard Medical School, Obstetrician- Gynecologist in Chief Beth Israel Hospital, Boston, Massachusetts, Second Edition, 1978," right?

MR. KILSCH: Objection, your Honor.

THE COURT: Overruled.

A No.

Q Regarding the exact statistics, since you kept saying 85 percent, would you be interested in knowing what the correct statistic was, sir?

MR. KILSCH: Objection.

THE COURT: Sustained.

Members of the jury, disregard the question.

Q Doctor, regarding the statistics that you have been testifying, would you recognize Dr. Emanuel A. Friedman, the Harvard Medical School book entitled "Labor Clinical Evaluation and Management, Second Edition," as generally authoritative, reserving the right to disagree with any portion of it?

MR. KILSCH: Objection.

THE COURT: Overruled.

A No.

Q Most engagement takes place three weeks before labor, approximately, in nulliparous patients; doesn't it, sir?

A No.

Q Would you recognize what Dr. Friedman has to say in that regard?

MR. KILSCH: Objection, your Honor.

THE COURT: Sustained.

Members of the jury, disregard that question.

Q By the way, Doctor, when you teach these residents, you tell us you teach, you use books to teach them, right?

A Yes.

Q When you want them to learn what's proper and what's not, you teach them from books in part; do you not, sir?

MR. KILSCH: Objection. Asked and answered.

THE COURT: Overruled.

Q Do you not?

A It is one of the methods I use.

[redacted] - By Defendants - Cross

Q One of the methods so they can know what to do and what not to do, right, sir?

A In the most general terms, yes.

Q Tell me this, Doctor: This test done on January 27th on this postterm mother in her 43rd week or 44th week by dates, was at best suspicious, correct?

MR. KILSCH: Objection to the form.

THE COURT: Sustained.

Members of the jury, disregard the question.

Q The test, oxytocin challenge test that is called, the nonstress test, as it was begun, was suspicious, correct?

A Yes.

Q And there is no doubt it was suspicious by what you have told us; isn't that true, sir?

A Yes.

Q Anybody who knew what they were doing should know for a mother such as this in her 43rd week, perhaps, of pregnancy, you shouldn't have decelerations on a nonstress test or OCT under these circumstances, correct?

MR. KILSCH: Objection to the form.

John A. Bonaccolta, C.S.R., Official Court Reporter

S/I -506

EXAMPLE 15-3: LETTER OF INTRODUCTION (MEDICAL RECORDS REVIEW SERVICE)

MEDICAL RECORDS REVIEW SERVICE INC.

Date

Mr./Ms. I. M. Lawyer
ABC Law Offices
123 Fourth Street
Anytown, USA 12345

Re: Medical Records Review Service, Inc. (MRRS, Inc.)

Dear Mr./Ms. Lawyer:

By means of introduction, Medical Records Review Service, Inc. (MRRS, Inc.) is a litigation support business located in Des Moines, Iowa. In July 1998, we will celebrate our seventh anniversary in business and have clients in 18 states. We are retained by attorneys and law firms to assist in litigation revolving around medical records. Provided with the appropriate information, we are able to assist our clients in identifying and determining which sets of providers' records to retrieve.

Upon receipt, we visually review those documents for comprehensiveness. Once comprehensive records have been retrieved, we perform in-depth visual reviews and produce either Quick Look Reports or more detailed chronological summaries. Our staff includes several registered nurse reviewers, as well as physical, occupational and speech therapist reviewers, a registered pharmacist reviewer and an accredited records technician. Our registered nurse reviewers have clinical backgrounds and experience in orthopaedics, neurology, neurosurgery, general medical/surgical, trauma, infectious disease, pediatrics and geriatrics.

In working with our clients, both plaintiff and defense attorneys, we have developed questionnaires and forms which allow the attorneys to obtain a comprehensive medical history from or about the injured party, as well as a detailed medical history of the event in question and the patient's care from that point forward. We have been told this system and the forms we have created works well for our clients who deal in personal injury litigation. It also assists us in working with our attorney-clients.

In addition to producing reports and summaries, we are often retained to perform library and electronic key word medical research. We maintain our own medical library with over 1,800 medical textbooks, as well as several medical journals and periodicals. Additionally, we subscribe to 5 medical databases, including MedLine and have computer access to nearly every medical school library in the country.

We have spent years developing a network of credentialed physicians in virtually every major medical speciality who are available for telephone consultation or to personally review records. These doctors are board certified and treat patients at least 50% of their time. If retained to perform an in-depth review, these experts will render an objective medical opinion. Should their review reveal negligence occurred, they are willing to testify as to their findings and opinions.

We have been told by our clients the services we provide are invaluable saving time, money and to avoid surprises at depositions and/or trial. We would like the

SUZANNE S. FOGARTY
THERESA T. THOMAN
1420 Woodland Avenue
Suite #1
Des Moines, Iowa
50309-3204

phone 515•244•MRRS
(6777)
1•800•984•MRRS

fax 515•244•1131

mrrsth3@aol.com

piecing together medical records

Mr./Ms. I. M. Lawyer
Date
Page 2
opportunity to talk with you about your legal practice. Perhaps, we can identify specific areas in which MRRS, Inc. could be of assistance. We are enclosing copies of our business cards, brochures and testimonials written by several of our clients. We publish a quarterly newsletter and enclose a copy of our most recent edition, as well as some past editions which include additional information about our company, our services and our reviewers.

If you are interested, we would be happy to provide you with a list of references and would encourage you to talk with some of our clients about our organization and our work. In the meantime, we look forward to hearing from you in the very near future.

Cordially,

Suzanne S. Fogarty
President
MRRS, Inc.

enclosures
c:\genmktg.lt1

EXAMPLE 15-4: COMPUTER PRINTOUT OF BIBLIOGRAPHICAL SEARCH (MEDICAL RECORDS REVIEW SERVICE)

Medical Records Review Service, Inc
1420 Woodland Ave #1/Des Moines,IA 50309-3204/1-800-984-6777

PaperChase provides 10,085,491 references -- all references found in the following databases of the National Library of Medicine and the National Cancer Institute*. You are searching all four databases simultaneously.

Database	Indexing Began	Updated	Current through
MEDLINE	1966	weekly	June 1998 Update, Part 3
HealthSTAR	1975	monthly	May 1998 Update
AIDSLINE	1980	monthly	May 1998 Update
*CANCERLIT	1980	monthly	April 1998 Update

LIST	REFERENCES	LIST	REFERENCES
A) ANESTHESIA, GENERAL	19817	I) *ON E&G	1
B) INTRAOPERATIVE COMP...	10172	J) ANOXIA	23908
C) SURGERY, OPERATIVE	15261	K) CEREBRAL ANOXIA	4209
D) *SUM BC	25286	L) *SUM JK	27083
E) HYPOXIA	11016	M) *ON F&L	6
F) *ON A&B	701	N) *ON G&L	14
G) *ON A&D	1253	O) ACIDOSIS	11927
H) *ON E&F	1		

MEDICAL RECORDS REVIEW SERVICE INC.

*****AMERICAN JOURNAL OF EMERGENCY MEDICINE*****

(REFERENCE 1 OF 6)
85097294

Foex P
Cardiac arrest during anesthesia.

In: Am J Emerg Med (1984 May) 2(3):241-5

ISSN: 0735-6757

<Anesthesia, General/AE> <Heart Arrest/ET>
<Intraoperative Complications/ET>

<Anesthetics/AE> <Anoxia/CO> <Coronary Circulation/DE>
<Coronary Disease/CO/ET> <Emergencies> <Human> <Risk>
<Medline File>

[No Abstract Available]

*****SURGICAL CLINICS OF NORTH AMERICA*****

(REFERENCE 2 OF 6)
69138026

Schweizer O Howland WS

1420 Woodland Avenue
Suite #1
Des Moines, Iowa
50309-3204

phone 515•244•MRRS
(6777)
1•800•984•MRRS

fax 515•244•1131

mrrsth3@aol.com

Medical Records Review Service, Inc
1420 Woodland Ave #1/Des Moines,IA 50309-3204/1-800-984-6777

Some metabolic changes associated with anesthesia and operation.

In: Surg Clin North Am (1969 Apr) 49(2):223-31

ISSN: 0039-6109

<Acid-Base Equilibrium> <Acidosis/ET> <Anesthesia, General>
<Carbohydrates/ME> <Surgery, Operative>

<Adenosine Triphosphate/BL> <Adult> <Aged> <Anoxia/CO>
<Blood Glucose/BL> <Ethyl Ethers/PD> <Female> <Glycolysis/DE>
<Halothane/PD> <Human> <Lactates/BL> <Male> <Metabolism/DE>
<Middle Age> <Pyruvates/ME> <Shock, Hemorrhagic/CO> <Thiopental/PD>
<Medline File>

[No Abstract Available]

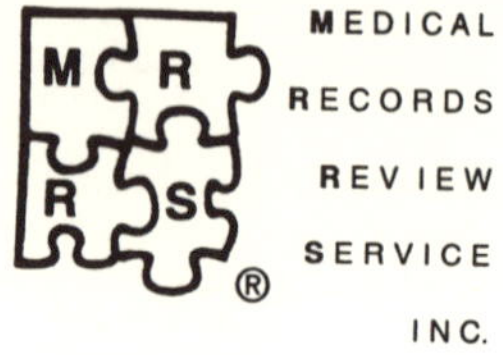

1420 Woodland Avenue
Suite #1
Des Moines, Iowa
50309-3204

phone 515•244•MRRS
(6777)
1•800•984•MRRS

fax 515•244•1131

mrrsth3@aol.com

Medical Records Review Service, Inc
1420 Woodland Ave #1/Des Moines,IA 50309-3204/1-800-984-6777

*****ACTA ANAESTHESIOLOGICA SCANDINAVICA. SUPPLEMENTUM*****

(REFERENCE 3 OF 6)
97057608

Kochs E
Monitoring of the central nervous system.

In: Acta Anaesthesiol Scand Suppl (1996) 109:60-1

ISSN: 0515-2720

<Central Nervous System/PH> <Monitoring, Physiologic>

<Anesthesia, General> <Cerebral Anoxia/DI> <Cerebral Ischemia/DI>
<Electroencephalography> <Evoked Potentials/PH>
<Evoked Potentials, Somatosensory/PH> <Human> <Intensive Care>
<Intraoperative Complications/DI> <Ischemia/DI>
<Monitoring, Intraoperative> <Spinal Cord/BS/PH>
<Intraoperative Monitoring> <Medline File>
<Health Planning & Administration File>

[No Abstract Available]

Institutional address:
Institut fur Anaesthesiologie
Technische Universitat
Munchen.

*****ANAESTHESIA*****

(REFERENCE 4 OF 6)
98038177

Aarhus D Soreide E Holst-Larsen H
Mechanical obstruction in the anaesthesia delivery-system mimicking severe bronchospasm.

In: Anaesthesia (1997 Oct) 52(10):992-4

ISSN: 0003-2409

<Anesthesia, General/IS> <Anesthesia, Obstetrical/IS> <Anoxia/ET>
<Bronchial Spasm/DI> <Intraoperative Complications>

<Adult> <Case Report> <Diagnosis, Differential>
<Equipment Failure> <Female> <Filtration/IS> <Human>
<Medline File>

We present a case where mechanical obstruction in the anaesthesia delivery system caused by plastic wrapping from a filter was misinterpreted as severe bronchospasm. The patient suffered severe hypoxia before the problem was solved by using a free-standing self-expanding ventilation bag. This near-fatal incident emphasises the importance of thorough equipment checking routines, rapid troubleshooting and how equipment failure may be misinterpreted as a medical complication. It also shows how transparent container material can become a medical hazard.

Institutional address:
Department of Anaesthesiology
Rogaland Central Hospital
Stavanger
Norway.

*****CANADIAN ANAESTHETISTS SOCIETY JOURNAL*****

(REFERENCE 5 OF 6)
67013579

Dickson RC
Some physiological factors affecting operative risk.

In: Can Anaesth Soc J (1966 Jan) 13(1):1-13

ISSN: 0008-2856 (Published in English and French)

<Adrenal Glands/PH> <Anesthesia, General/AE> <Anoxia>
<Blood Volume/PH> <Surgery, Operative>

<Human> <Kidney/PH> <Pituitary-Adrenal System/PH> <Vasopressins/PH>
<Medline File>

[No Abstract Available]

*****CANADIAN JOURNAL OF ANAESTHESIA*****

(REFERENCE 6 OF 6)
97376141

Glaisyer HR Parry M Bailey PM
The LMA for the application of postoperative CPAP [letter]

In: Can J Anaesth (1997 Jul) 44(7):784-5

ISSN: 0832-610X

<Anesthesia, General/AE> <Anoxia/ET/TH> <Laryngeal Masks>

<Case Report> <Human> <Oxygen/BL> <Postoperative Period>
<Surgical Procedures, Operative> <Surgery, Operative> <Letter>
<Medline File> <Health Planning & Administration File>

[No Abstract Available]

Registry Numbers: 7782-44-7 (Oxygen)

EXAMPLE 15-5: NEW YORK STATE JURY VERDICT REVIEW AND ANALYSIS

New York State Jury Verdict Review and Analysis®

A MONTHLY STATEWIDE REVIEW OF NEW YORK SUPREME AND FEDERAL DISTRICT COURT CIVIL JURY VERDICTS WITH COMMENTARY BY IRA J. ZARIN, ESQ.

Providing

— A BASIS FOR EVALUATION AND SETTLEMENT OF COMPARABLE CASES.
— AN OVERVIEW OF STATEWIDE COURT EXPERIENCE WITH TRIAL ANALYSIS NOT REFLECTED IN APPELLATE REVIEW.
— NAMES OF EXPERT WITNESSES TESTIFYING FOR PLAINTIFFS AND DEFENDANTS.
— THEORIES OF LIABILITY AND DEFENSE AS ACCEPTED OR REJECTED BY JURIES.
— PERTINENT TRIAL DATA FOR FURTHER REFERENCE.

Published Monthly
Subscription Price $150 Per Year

The cases summarized herein are obtained and selected from a current and ongoing survey of the Supreme and the Federal District Courts in the State of New York. However members of the bar are encouraged to advise this publication of any current plaintiff or defendant jury verdict they believe to be of sufficient interest to warrant publication.

Volume IV, Issue 2 — January, 1987

Table of Contents Page

$954,000 Verdict - Med Mal - Fail. of hospital to perform blood study during admin. of Heparin - Hematoma in thigh........ 1
$502,000 Verdict - Med Mal - Negligent performance of barium enema - Perforated rectum - Wrongful death................ 4
Defendant's Verdict - Med Mal - Alleged negligent handling of nerve root during disc surgery - Dropped foot................. 5
$250,000 Verdict - Med Mal - Unnecessary removal of prosthetic eye implant causes permanent facial deformity............ 8
$370,000 Gross Verdict - Auto/Pedestrian - Severe soft tissue trauma causes significant cosmetic deformity to thigh......... 9
$297,500 Verdict - Labor Law case - Failure to maintain scaffold in encumbrance free manner - Fall - Trimalleolar fracture. 10
$270,000 Gross Verdict - Jones Act case - Failure of ship captain to obtain medical treatment for crewmember exhibiting severe abdominal complaints - Ruptured appendix and peritonitis.. 11
$250,000 Verdict - Premises Liab. - Doorman negligently provides pass key to acquaintance of tenant's - Tenant assualted. 13
VERDICTS—AT—A—GLANCE... 15

$954,000 VERDICT - MEDICAL MALPRACTICE - FAILURE OF HOSPITAL TO PERFORM SECOND ORDERED BLOOD STUDY DURING ADMINISTRATION OF HEPARIN - HEMATOMA IN AREA OF THIGH - SIGNIFICANTLY DIMINISHED USE OF LEG AND HYPERSENSITIVITY TO TOUCH. **Albany**

This was a medical malpractice action in which the plaintiff, aged 53 at the time of the incident, contended that as a result of the negligence of the staff at the defendant hospital, who failed to perform a second ordered blood work-up during the administration of Heparin following a diagnosis of deep veined thrombophlebitis, internal bleeding remained undetected, resulting in the formation of a hematoma in the area of the thigh which greatly compromised the femoral nerve, resulting in hypersensitivity to touch and severely diminished use of the leg. The plaintiff further contended that the co- defendant private attending vascular surgeon negligently failed to ascertain that the required tests were not performed, resulting in the continuation of the Heparin and

(cont'd on next page)

$502,000 VERDICT - MEDICAL MALPRACTICE - NEGLIGENT PERFORMANCE OF BARIUM ENEMA - PERFORATED RECTUM - FAILURE TO IMMEDIATELY HOSPITALIZE PATIENT FOLLOWING PERFORATION - DEATH ACTION. **Broome** **This was a medical malpractice, death action in which the plaintiff contended that as a result of the negligence of the defendant radiologist, who, during the performance of a barium enema, overinflated a balloon utilized in the procedure and who improperly placed the balloon in the upper area of the rectum, the decedent suffered the perforation of the rectum. The plaintiff further contended that the defendant radiologist and the co-defendant family physician, who had referred the plaintiff to the radiologist, negligently failed to immediately hospitalize the plaintiff, substantially diminishing her chances of surviving. The decedent was hospitalized that evening and died approximately one month later.**

The evidence revealed that the decedent had visited the defendant family physician with a history of rectal bleeding of short duration and that the family physician performed a sigmoidoscopy. The evidence additionally established that although the family physician suspected benign polyps, he properly advised the performance of a barium enema to utilize the contrast material to rule out cancer. The family physician referred the decedent to the defendant radiologist, whose offices were situated several doors away, and the barium enema was performed that morning. The plaintiff's expert radiologist maintained that based upon a review of the x-rays taken during the barium enema, it was obvious that the defendant radiologist had overinflated the balloon utilized in the procedure and had improperly placed it in an excessively high area of the rectum in which the rectal walls are less pliable. The expert contended that as a result, the rectum perforated. The plaintiff's expert further contended that use of the balloon in this case was improper in and of itself because the balloon carries certain risks and that it is only necessary in the case of an incontinent patient, of which there was no indication in the instant case.

The defendant's expert radiologist denied that the balloon was overinflated or improperly positioned and contended that the perforation is a normal risk of the procedure which can occur in the absence of negligence. The plaintiff countered that the opinion of its expert, who is a world renowned radiologist, should be given more weight than the conclusions of the defendant's expert. The evidence further revealed that after the perforation occurred, the defendant radiologist walked the plaintiff back to the family physician and the radiologist contended that he advised the family physician of the perforation and that in the absence of hospitalization, the plaintiff faced a significantly greater risk of death. The family physician denied that the radiologist advised him that the injury posed such a grave hazard in the absence of hospitalization. The family physician prescribed an oral antibiotic, specific for one type of bacterium found in the rectum, and advised the plaintiff to return home and rest and consult him upon a change of symptoms. The evidence revealed that over the ensuing several hour period, the plaintiff suffered severe symptoms of septicemia and was hospitalized that evening.

The plaintiff's expert contended that the family physician should have realized that a perforation of the rectum dictated immediate hospitalization and that as a result of the delay in such hospitalization, the rectal contents and barium continued to invade the retroperitoneal area, significantly depriving the decedent of a substantial chance of recovery. The expert further contended that the defendant radiologist should have hospitalized the decedent when it became apparent that the defendant family physician failed to do so. The defendant radiologist contended that he could not so hospitalize the patient because he did not have admitting privileges. The plaintiff countered that the defendant radiologist should have contacted any number of other physicians who had such admitting privileges once the family physician failed to immediately hospitalize the decedent. The plaintiff contended that as a result of the delay, the decedent suffered severe symptoms which were much greater than would have been the case if she had been immediately hospitalized and provided proper treatment, including the use of I.V. broad spectrum antibiotics.

The evidence revealed that the decedent was in and out of intensive care during the one month period between the incident and her death. The plaintiff further presented several relatives who maintained that the decedent appeared to be in great pain, had become extremely gaunt, and that she expressed the belief that she would not survive. The decedent did not work outside the home and the plaintiff presented an expert economist who maintained that replacement value of her

(cont'd on next page)

(Cont'd)

homemaker services would approximate $28,000 per year. The jury found the defendant radiologist 70% negligent, the defendant family physician 30% negligent, and awarded $502,000. Plaintiff's radiologist: Alexander R. Margulis from Chicago. Plaintiff's economist: Frank Corcione from Bethlehem, Pa. Index no. 133237; Judge Robert Kuhnen, 12-16-86. Attorneys for plaintiff: Alan J. Friedlander and Lee D. Daniel of Friedlander, Friedlander, Reizes & Joch in Waverly, N.Y.; Attorney for defendant radiologist: John O'Mara of Davidson & O'Mara in Elmira, N.Y.; Attorney for defendant family physician: Carlton Thompson of Levene, Goulden & Thompson in Binghamton, N.Y.

COMMENTARY: The plaintiff presented a world renowned radiologist who utilized the x-rays taken during the performance of the barium enema to clearly explain to the jury the manner in which the balloon was overinflated and improperly positioned, resulting in the perforation of the rupture. This testimony probably resulted in the finding of 70% liability against the defendant radiologist whom, the expert contended, negligently caused the injury, notwithstanding the failure of the family physician to immediately hospitalize the decedent even though he had the primary responsibility to do so. The plaintiff further strenuously argued that the defendants had acted egregiously in failing to immediately hospitalize the patient and stressed that as a result of this failure, the rectal contents and barium continued to invade the retroperitoneal cavity for an unnecessary length of time, significantly depriving the decedent of a reasonable chance for survival. Regarding damages, the plaintiff presented several relatives who offered vivid descriptions of the pain and suffering entailed and who related that the decedent knew that she would not survive. Additionally, although the decedent did not work outside the home, the plaintiff presented an expert economist who maintained that the replacement value of her household services would amount to some $28,000 per year. Finally, the size of the award probably also reflected an acceptance by the jury that the defendants had acted in an extremely egregious manner in failing to immediately hospitalize the decedent upon such a life threatening perforation of the rectum.

EXAMPLE 15-6: OBJECTION TO ALLOWING CROSS-EXAMINER TO READ FROM TEXTBOOK (APPELLATE BRIEF)

To be argued by
Matthew Gaier

Time requested: 15 minutes

New York State Supreme Court

Appellate Division—Second Department

MARGARET DORN and THOMAS DORN,

Plaintiffs-Appellants,

against **93-09653**

DR. HENRY Z. BAREKET, DR. LOUIS H. LEFKOWITZ,

Defendants-Respondents,

and

DR. VINCENT J. FREDA,

Defendant.

BRIEF OF PLAINTIFFS-APPELLANTS

KRAMER, DILLOF, TESSEL, DUFFY & MOORE
Attorneys for Plaintiffs-Appellants
233 Broadway
New York, NY 10279
(212) 267-4177

MATTHEW GAIER
Of Counsel and On the Brief

Rockland County Clerk's Index No. 3538/89

THE REPORTER COMPANY, INC.—Walton, NY 13856—800-252-7181
Syracuse Office, University Building, Syracuse, NY 13202—315-426-1235
NYC Office—30 Vesey St., New York, NY 10007—212-732-6978—800-800-4264
(5929—1994)
Reproduced on Recycled Paper

Dr. Bareket's use of the procedure under the circumstances present during Margaret Dorn's delivery was an appropriate exercise of obstetrical judgment (395).

Thus, the stage was set for a battle of the experts. Whichever party's expert was believed by the jury would, in all likelihood, prevail on the issue of liability.

(E)
The Use of Medical Textbooks

Early in the trial, defense counsel sought to lend credibility to his defense that an episioproctotomy is a recognized and accepted procedure to be employed by an obstetrician to facilitate a delivery by referring to a medical textbook. While eliciting testimony from his own client, Dr. Bareket, defense counsel inquired about medical texts (122-123):

> Q. Doctor, are there texts, to your knowledge, which discuss the use of an episioproctotomy in situations where it is warranted, such as shoulder dystocia and other situations?
>
> A. I'm sure I'm not aware of all the texts, but in the last eight years of private practice, I have come across articles and other reference books whereby the need, the indication, for episioproctotomy is called for.
>
> In fact I can't quote exactly the page, but one of the principal authors in this country of obstetrics, his name is Manual Freedman from Harvard, has said --
>
> MR. TURKEWITZ: Objection.
>
> THE COURT: Sustained.
>
> Q. Without telling us what the -- is he the author of the text?
>
> A. Yes.

6

Q. You can't tell us what he said.

A. He's the author of a text.

Q. Is that called "Management of Labor"?

A. It's called "Management of Labor", yes.

Q. Does that discuss, without telling us what it said, the technique of episioproctotomy and so forth?

MR. TURKEWITZ: Objection.

THE COURT: He can say yes or no to that.

MR. BALL: Yes. We won't quote the text.

THE COURT: Does he do that, yes or no?

A. Yes.

This contrived testimony clearly had the effect of informing the jury that the text recognized an episioproctotomy as an acceptable obstetrical procedure during a delivery. However, defense counsel's use of the same medical text did not stop there.

While cross examining plaintiffs' expert, Dr. Siegel, defense counsel deliberately read from the Freedman text despite Dr. Siegel's refusal to recognize it as authoritative. Defense counsel asked Dr. Siegel whether he considered the text to be authoritative and Dr. Siegel responded that he had never even read it (326-327). Defense counsel, nevertheless, over plaintiffs' objection, proceeded to read a passage from the book (327). The exchange was as follows (327):

Q. Do you recognize his book "Management of Labor," second edition, as an authority in the field of obstetrics and gynecology?

A. I never read it, so I cannot say whether it is or not.

7

Q. Well, would you agree with the following statement, Doctor --

MR. TURKEWITZ: Objection.

THE COURT: Let him finish.

MR. TURKEWITZ: I'd like a side bar. I think it's quite clear what he's going to do.

THE COURT: I know the basis of your objection, but I can't make a ruling on a question until I hear the question. I'll listen carefully.

Q. I am just going to finish the question, Doctor, okay? Doctor, would you agree with the following statement with regard to shoulder dystocia: several approaches are acceptable, but one should never hesitate to perform an episioproctotomy to provide maximal space in this situation.

Do you agree with that statement, Doctor?

A. No.

The judge did not sustain the objection. With the court's de facto approval of the text, defense counsel made sure to refer to it again before completing his cross examination of Dr. Siegel (353).

Having found a weapon with which to undermine the all important testimony of plaintiffs' expert on the critical issue in the case, defense counsel later compounded the prejudicial effect of his improper use of the text by again referring to it on summation and, over the objection of plaintiff's counsel, paraphrasing the same passage (603-604):

> Dr. Siegel had not even read "The Management of Labor" by Dr. Manual Freedman, a professor of obstetrics and gynecology at Harvard University, and he did not agree with the statement which I read to him, that one should not hesitate --

8

MR. TURKEWITZ: Objection.

MR. BALL: -- to use episioproctotomy.

THE COURT: Just a minute. There's been an objection. If you are objecting to Mr. Ball commenting on the testimony in the case, that's the jury's memory that controls there.

MR. TURKEWITZ: About something not in evidence, your Honor.

THE COURT: Again that's their recollection that controls.

MR. BALL: He was asked this question, Judge.

THE COURT: That's your argument, and that's why I'm saying this, and I'm saying it's the jury's recollection that controls.

Please proceed, if you would.

MR. BALL: That one should not hesitate to use an episioproctotomy to gain the maximum amount of room for delivery in a situation of shoulder dystocia.

Undoubtedly, these repeated improper references to the Freedman text on the central issue in the case irreparably damaged the credibility of plaintiffs' expert in what amounted to a pure battle of the experts and furnished inappropriate, invalid and misleading support for the defendants' theory of the case.

It is notable that in stark contrast to defense counsel's unabashed contempt for the rules of evidence with respect to the use of textbooks, plaintiffs' counsel displayed great restraint with respect to using a medical text which supports plaintiffs' claim that an episioproctotomy is not a proper obstetrical procedure to be employed during a delivery (66-69, 419-421). While questioning defendant Dr. Bareket, plaintiffs' counsel inquired about the text "Williams on Obstetrics" (66-69). Dr. Bareket testified that he keeps a copy of the text in his office (66) and that it is "one of the texts we may refer to on various issues" (68), but he nevertheless maintained that it is not "an authoritative text" (66, 67, 68). Because of Dr. Bareket's refusal to find that the text was authoritative, plaintiffs' counsel did not read from the sections of the text dealing with episiotomies (68). Again, during cross examination of the defendants' expert, Dr. Howard, plaintiffs' counsel refrained from reading from "Williams on Obstetrics," after the witness refused to concede its authoritativeness (419-421).

(F)
The Jury's Verdict

The jury returned a verdict in favor of the defendant, finding that Dr. Bareket did not depart from accepted medical practice.

10

POINT I

THE JUDGMENT FOR THE DEFENDANT SHOULD BE REVERSED AND A NEW TRIAL ORDERED BASED UPON DEFENSE COUNSEL'S IMPROPER AND PREJUDICIAL USE OF A MEDICAL TEXTBOOK

This Court has repeatedly and consistently held that before an attorney may read from a medical treatise or textbook during the cross-examination of an expert witness, the expert must first accept or recognize the book as authoritative. Labate v. Plotkin, 195 A.D.2d 444 (2nd Dept. 1993); Serota v. Kaplan, 127 A.D.2d 648, 650 (2nd Dept. 1987); Ithier v. Solomon, 59 A.D.2d 935 (2nd Dept. 1977); Mark v. Colgate University, 53 A.D.2d 884, 886 (2nd Dept. 1976); Roveda v. Weiss, 11 A.D.2d 745, 746 (2nd Dept. 1960).

As this Court explained in Ithier v. Solomon, 59 A.D.2d at 935:

> It is well settled that an expert may be questioned through the use of a scientific work or treatise. However, in order to lay a foundation for the use of such material, he must first admit to its authoritativeness (*People v Feldman*, 299 NY 153; *Mark v Colgate Univ.*, 53 AD2d 884; *Hastings v Chrysler Corp.*, 273 App Div 292; Richardson, Evidence [Prince, 10th ed], § 373).

As each of the above cited cases makes clear, a violation of this rule constitutes reversible error.

This Court's recent decision in Labate v. Plotkin, 195 A.D.2d 444, is virtually indistinguishable from the present case. The plaintiff in that case sued her obstetrician, alleging that her daughter sustained injuries as a result of the defendant obstetrician's medical malpractice during the labor and delivery. The jury determined that the obstetrician had not departed from accepted medical standards in his care of the plaintiff. In reversing the judgment entered in favor of the defendant, this Court held:

11

> [D]uring cross-examination the defense counsel improperly utilized hearsay statements from medical textbooks and articles which the plaintiff's experts had not accepted as authoritative. It is well settled that on cross-examination an expert witness may be confronted with a passage from a treatise or book which contradicts the opinion the expert witness previously expressed on the stand, only after the expert witness has excepted the treatise or book as authoritative (*see, Mark v. Colgate Univ.*, 53 A.D.2d 884, 886, 385 N.Y.S.2d 621). In light of the numerous instances in which the defense counsel utilized passages of books not accepted as authoritative, we find that the plaintiff was unduly prejudiced and is entitled to a new trial (*see, Mark v. Colgate Univ., supra*, 53 A.D.2d, at 886, 385 N.Y.S.2d 621).

Id.

Notably, the Court reached the conclusion that the defense counsel's conduct was reversible error even though he did not read directly from the books, but from his notepad. The Court stated:

> [A]lthough the defense counsel did not read directly from the books, his questions clearly indicated to the jury that the statements which he read off his notepad were taken from those texts.

Id. It is thus clear that this Court recognizes the significant effect that readings excerpted from textbooks can have upon a jury's view of an expert's credibility, where the material read is inconsistent with his or her testimony.

This Court's holding in Roveda v. Weiss, 11 A.D.2d at 746, is similarly instructive. That case stemmed from an automobile accident for which the defendant conceded liability. During the trial on damages, there was conflicting testimony from medical experts as to whether the plaintiff had sustained injuries to her back and neck. The jury's verdict reflected their finding that no such injuries were sustained as a result of the accident. The plaintiff appealed, contending that the verdict was inadequate, that remarks by the trial judge precluded a fair trial

12

and that the court committed reversible error in rejecting and admitting certain evidence. After rejecting the plaintiff's first two arguments, this Court found that the trial court's rulings with respect to the use of medical texts on cross examination constituted "errors of law serious enough to necessitate reversal." Id. The Court observed as follows:

> Dr. Sherman, one of plaintiffs' medical experts, stated on cross-examination that he had never heard of a Dr. Armstrong, the author of a certain medical book, nor heard of the book itself. Nevertheless, over objection, the court permitted counsel to elicit the witness' opinion as to the correctness or incorrectness of a statement which counsel read from the book. The witness disagreed with the statement, which conflicted with his testimony. Similar rulings were made on the cross-examination of another of plaintiffs' medical experts, Dr. Braaf, and on the cross-examination of one of defendant's medical experts. The court's rulings in permitting the use of textbooks, which had not been accepted as authoritative by the witness in each instance, were erroneous. Such rulings permitted violation of the hearsay evidence rule (*People v. Feldman*, 229 N.Y. 153, 167-168; *Hastings v. Chrysler Corp.*, 273 App. Div. 292).

Id.

The holdings of this Court, as discussed above, have not only evinced an unwavering policy of precluding readings from a medical text on cross examination where the expert does not accept the text as authoritative, but have clearly recognized that significant damage can be done to an expert's credibility and, consequently, to a party's case, by virtue of an improper reading from such a text.

Nowhere is the prejudice that flows from an improper use of a medical textbook greater than in a case, such as the present one, where the determination of the issue of liability turns on which expert the jury believes. In this classic battle of the experts, the damage done by defense counsel's repeated references to the medical text, "The Management of Labor," undoubtedly affected the jury's verdict.

The deleterious effects of this impropriety were even more damaging since the passage read from the text went to the core of the dispute between the two experts and the pivotal issue in the case -- whether an episioproctotomy is a recognized and accepted obstetrical procedure to be employed during a delivery.

It is indisputable that defense counsel's use of the text was improper.[1] After being asked whether he considered the book an authority in the field of obstetrics, Dr. Siegel responded, "I never read it, so I cannot say whether it is or not." (327). Despite the expert's refusal to recognize the text, defense counsel brazenly, over plaintiffs' objection, read from the book and asked Dr. Siegel whether he agreed with the statement (327). Dr. Siegel responded that he did not (327). The situation was virtually identical to that in Roveda, where, after plaintiff's medical expert stated that he had not heard of a book, defense counsel "elicit[ed] the witness' opinion as to the correctness or incorrectness of a statement which counsel read from the book." 11 A.D.2d at 746. This Court found that the trial judge committed reversible error in permitting that use of the text. Id.

---

[1] While the error asserted by the plaintiffs-appellants on this appeal stems from defense counsel's use of the book "The Management of Labor" on cross examination of the plaintiffs' expert, his use of the same text while examining defendant Dr. Bareket was highly questionable under existing case law which holds that an expert may not testify that his opinions were based upon authoritative text. See Foggett v. Fischer, 23 App. Div. 207 (2nd Dept. 1897); McEvoy v. Lommel, 78 App. Div. 324 (1st Dept. 1903); DeFalco v. Long Island College Hosp., 90 Misc.2d 164 (Sup. Kings 1977), aff'd., 62 A.D.2d 1180 (2nd Dept. 1978).

14

Moreover, as in Labate, there were "numerous instances" in which defense counsel made references to the book. While we do not know from the opinion in Labate the degree of importance of the subject matter read from the text vis-a-vis the issue of liability, it could not have been more important than was the subject matter of the reading to the issue of liability in the present case.

The ultimate issue to be decided by the jury in the case at bar was whether Dr. Bareket departed from accepted obstetrical practice by performing an episiotomy that extended down into the plaintiff's rectum. The defense claimed, and their expert testified, that this procedure was an acceptable method of facilitating a delivery of a child and that it was completely within the judgment of the physician as to when to employ the procedure. Plaintiffs' argument, as propounded to the jury through their expert, was that an obstetrician should never deliberately extend an episiotomy into a woman's rectum during a delivery. By reading a passage from a text, not recognized as authoritative, which stated that such a procedure is acceptable, defense counsel improperly undermined the most important aspect of the testimony of the plaintiffs' expert witness. As a result, the plaintiffs clearly and indisputably suffered extreme prejudice.

This prejudice was only compounded by defense counsel's other references to the text and by his recitation of the same passage during summation. Defense counsel's improper use of the book on summation clearly "reinforced the prejudicial impact" of the original impropriety (O'Shea v. Sarro, 106 A.D.2d 435, 438 (2nd Dept. 1984)) and left the jury with the indelible impression that the defendants' expert rather than the plaintiffs' expert was telling the truth.

As a result of these improprieties, the plaintiffs were deprived of their right to a fair trial.

15

CONCLUSION

THE JUDGMENT IN FAVOR OF THE DEFENDANTS SHOULD BE REVERSED AND A NEW TRIAL ORDERED

Respectfully submitted

Kramer, Dillof, Tessel, Duffy & Moore
Attorneys for Plaintiffs
233 Broadway
New York, NY 10279
(212) 267-4177

Matthew Gaier, Esq.
Of Counsel and on the Brief

16

EXAMPLE 15-7: OBJECTION TO REFUSING TO ALLOW CROSS-EXAMINER TO READ FROM TEXTBOOK (APPELLATE BRIEF)

To be argued by
Judith A. Livingston
or Matthew Gaier
New York County Clerk's Index No. 21705/85

New York State Supreme Court

Appellate Division – First Department

JOCELYN PALESTRANT, An Infant by her Father and Natural Guardian, ABRAHAM PALESTRANT and ABRAHAM PALESTRANT,

Plaintiffs-Appellants,

against

DR. EMILIO A. GARCIA, DR. IRWIN GRIBETZ and IRWIN GRIBETZ, M.D., P.C.,

Defendants-Respondents.

BRIEF OF PLAINTIFFS-APPELLANTS

KRAMER, DILLOF, TESSEL, DUFFY
& MOORE
Attorneys for Plaintiffs-Appellants
233 Broadway
New York, NY 10279
(212) 267-4177

Of Counsel:
JUDITH A. LIVINGSTON
NORMAN BARD
MATTHEW GAIER

THE REPORTER COMPANY AND THE WALTON REPORTER, INC.
30 Vesey St., New York, NY 10007—212-732-6978
(9528 – 1997)
Reproduced on Recycled Paper

POINT II

THE COURT COMMITTED PREJUDICIAL ERROR IN NOT PERMITTING CROSS-EXAMINATION OF DR. BROWN WITH RESPECT TO A MEDICAL TEXT WHICH HE RECOGNIZED AS A STANDARD TEXT, COMMONLY USED BY PEDIATRICIANS INCLUDING HIMSELF

Dr. Brown testified, in essence, that what was felt by Mrs. Palestrant in May and June was different from the Wilms' tumor that was found at the hospital during the August 1984 operation (2285). Dr. Brown was of the view that the mass could not be palpated in May or June of 1984 (2276). In an attempt to affect his credibility on this point, he was asked whether or not he recognized the textbook **Principles of Pediatrics**, by Dr. Frank Oski, Director and Chairman of the Department of Pediatrics of the John Hopkins School of Medicine (2304). Dr. Brown responded that it is a standard text which is commonly used by pediatricians and that he uses it, but he maintained that he does not view it as being authoritative and that no textbooks are truly authoritative (2304-05). In view of Dr. Brown's determination that no books are authoritative, the trial court prevented any questioning with reference to the text. The testimony and colloquy were as follows:

> Q Do you recognize reserving the right to disagree with any portion of the volume Principle of Pediatrics by Dr. Frank Oski, Director and Chairman of the Department of Pediatrics of the John Hopkins School of Medicine, 1990 Edition, do you recognize that?
>
> MS. MORELLI: Objection.

- 48 -

MS. LIVINGSTON: Reserving the right to agree or disagree with any portion.

MS. MORELLI: Objection.

THE COURT: You may answer.

A It's a standard text.

Q Would you agree, sir, or disagree--

MS. MORELLI: Objection.

THE COURT: We did not get the answer to the question.

A I don't view it as being authoritative. I agree it's a standard text that encompasses-- it's a commonly used text by pediatricians.

Q One you use, sir?

A On occasion.

Q You say you use it on occasion, and use it to refer to on occasions for the benefit of what is written therein; is that right, sir?

MS. MORELLI: Objection.

THE COURT: Do you recognize it as authoritative?

THE WITNESS: None of the textbooks are truly authoritative. They're used as a guideline for reviewing illnesses hand complaints includes Wilms' tumor.

Q This is on you will utilize has a guideline; correct, sir?

MS. MORELLI: Objection.

THE COURT: Form. Sustained.

MS. LIVINGSTON: May I read from it?

THE COURT: That is what we're trying to determine.

The question is, do you recognize it as an authority because if you do then there is something else that will follow. If you don't, we won't follow.

THE WITNESS: ***I don't accept any text as being truly authoritative.***

Q What about being authoritative, since you refer to it, what about-- withdrawn.

Let me ask you, when you say you refer to it when you're treating children, this is a point of reference you might go to treat the people to get the information to treat the people--

MS. MORELLI: Objection.

THE COURT: Miss Livingston, for our purposes he does not recognize it as an authority. So, any continued probing in this regard would be inappropriate. We can move on to the next question.

Dr. Brown was then confronted with two other texts which he testified are not authoritative (2307-08; 2311-12). The trial court's ruling with respect to the use of medical texts was erroneous and, since the issue under cross-examination with reference to the texts was a critical issue in the case, the plaintiffs were severely prejudiced and a reversal is required.

- 50 -

Dr. Brown testified that the textbook **Principles of Pediatrics**, by Dr. Frank Oski, is a standard text which is commonly used and which he himself uses. The trial court's limitation of the use of that text and its preclusion from further inquiry into other texts was improper and unduly restrictive. **Hastings v. Chrysler Corp.**, 273 App.Div. 292 (1st Dept. 1948). In fact, the trial court's tolerance of Dr. Brown's semantic gamesmanship with the word "authoritative" is contrary to this Court's holding in **Spiegel v. Levy**, 201 A.D.2d 378, 379 (1st Dept. 1994), where the Court observed that a "the physician could not foreclose full cross-examination by the semantic trick of announcing that he did not find the work authoritative."

This Court made clear in **Spiegel** that semantic gamesmanship with the word "authoritative" may not be employed to prevent a proper cross-examination with the use of medical texts. Thus, when an expert witness testifies that a text is "a standard text," that it is commonly used and that he himself uses it, he has in fact recognized that the text is "authoritative" within the meaning of the rule.

This was the specific holding of the New Jersey Supreme Court in **Jacober v. St. Peter's Med. Ctr.**, 128 N.J. 475, 608 A.2d 304 (1992). In that medical malpractice action, one of the defendant's expert's conceded, as did Dr. Brown here, that one of the textbooks raised on cross-examination was a standard text, but he said, as did Dr. Brown, "...I don't think it's authoritative, if that's what you're getting at" **Id**. at 308. Interestingly, it should be observed that the doctor

- 51 -

refused to accept as authoritative his own work, acknowledging that it was authoritative only for himself. The trial court ruled that unless the witness accepted the text as "authoritative", he cannot be cross-examined with it.

With respect to a medical text in which the defense neonatology and pediatrics expert had written a chapter, the Supreme Court's opinion notes as follows:

> "Q. Do you accept this book as one of the standard and authoritative textbooks in the field?
>
> A. No.
>
> Q. Even though you, yourself, are an author in the first edition of this book?
>
> A. That's correct."
>
> The court prevented plaintiffs' counsel from cross-examining Dr. Auld on the medical literature because Dr. Auld did not concede that those texts were authoritative.

Id. at 309.

The plaintiff further sought to cross-examine another defense neonatologist and pediatrician with a text which he recognized as standard, but not authoritative. The Court quoted the testimony as follows:

> "Q. Do you know the book Neonatal/Perinatal Medicine edited by Dr. Behrman?
>
> A. I recognize it.

> Q. Do you recognize this as one of the standard treatises in the field?
>
> A. It's a standard textbook, yeah.
>
> * * * * * *
>
> Q. By standard, Doctor, do you mean standard in that it is recognized in the field by other practitioners as an authoritative source for reference?
>
> A. Well, I don't think any textbook is really authoritative, it has a set of opinions that some * * * clinicians would agree with and others would be very controversial.
>
> * * * * * *
>
> A. * * * Authoritative sort of sounds to me as though it implies that one opinion is the correct opinion that's expressed in a particular book, and that's simply not the way that any textbook is written."

Id. at 309.

The trial court and Appellate Division determined that the Supreme Court's earlier decision in **Ruth v. Fenchell**, 21 N.J. 171, 121 A.2d 373 (1956), precluded any further inquiry once the experts refused to state that the texts were authoritative. The Supreme Court addressed this specific issue and reversed the verdict in favor of the defendants on the ground that the limitation on the use of the medical texts was improper. In so holding, the Supreme Court stated as follows:

> In the present case, both the trial court and Appellate Division held that *Ruth* prevented plaintiffs' counsel from cross-examining defense experts about the medical literature. Although Auld and Skolnick

- 53 -

> refused to declare the proffered texts "authoritative," they implicitly conceded as much. Auld admitted that the Klaus and Fanaroff book was "a standard text," and Skolnick acknowledged Dr. Stanley James as an "eminent neonatologist" who authored a "standard textbook."
>
> Under *Ruth, supra*, those statements constituted sufficient acknowledgement that the texts are "recognized and standard authority on the subject." 21 N.J. at 176, 121 A.2d 373. Indeed, *Ruth* allowed the cross-examination of an expert witness who had stated merely that a treatise was "very, very capable." *Id.* at 173, 121 A.2d 373. *Ruth* requires an expert only to recognize a text as standard authority, not expressly to declare the text "authoritative." *See Ecleberry v. Kaiser Found. N. Hosps.* 226 Or. 616, 359 P.2d 1090, 1093-94 (1961)(expert's admission that textbook was "commonly used" deemed sufficient to render the work authoritative).
>
> Here, the trial court's exclusion of the statements from learned treatises precluded the jury from adequately assessing the defense expert's credibility.

Id. at 311.

It should further be noted that the Supreme Court observed that the federal rule, FRE 803(18), which had been adopted by the majority of the States, "expands the use of learned treatises on cross-examination...." **Id**. at 312. The Court ultimately adopted the federal rule as New Jersey's common law.

The holding in **Jacober**, seems to be the standard prevailing rule in the United States -- if an expert acknowledges that a text is a standard text, the text is deemed to be authoritative. See **Pound v. Medney**, 337 S.E.2d 772 (Ct.App.

1985)("a standard treatise on the subject" is authoritative); **State Hwy. Dept. v. Willis**, 128 S.E.2d 351 (Ct.App. 1962)(same); **Mize v. State**, 240 S.E.2d 11 (1977)(authoritativeness is established where the witness has testified that he is familiar with the work, that he studied under the authors of the book, that he used it during his studies and that it was accepted as one of many books in the field). Thus, in **Brannen v. Prince**, 421 S.E.2d 76 (Ct. App. 1992), where a neurosurgeon testified that he was familiar with a journal called "Neurological Surgeries" and acknowledged that the periodical was commonly read and used as a reference by members of the neurosurgical and other medical professions with interest in this area, this was sufficient to permit cross-examination of the witness. So too in **Crain v. Wakeman, M.D., Inc.**, 800 S.W.2d 105 (Mo.App. 1990) and **Grippe v. Momtazee**, 705 S.W.2d 551 (Mo.App. 1986), the Court held that the general acceptance of the text within the profession is sufficient to warrant cross-examination.

The plaintiffs in the present case have met each and every one of the tests set down by the above cases. Dr. Brown recognized that the book is a standard textbook, is commonly used and that he himself uses it. This is sufficient to warrant cross-examination on that textbook. Dr. Brown's statement that no book is authoritative highlights the semantical absurdity of his position. All medical schools throughout the world teach medicine through the use of medical textbooks and articles. It is simply ludicrous for a doctor to state that no medical text is

- 55 -

authoritative when his entire profession, including himself, is taught through books and articles.

The semantical interpretation of the word "authoritative" by the witness cannot be the sole requirement of the law. Just as a witness is not required to use the magic words "reasonable degree of medical certainty" (**Mattot v. Ward**, 48 N.Y.2d 455 (1979)), or "proximate cause" (**Lipsius v. White**, 91 A.D.2d 271 (2nd Dept. 1983)), so long as the opinion indicates that the doctor intended to signify a probability supported by a rational basis (**Ward v. Kovacs**, 55 A.D.2d 391 (2nd Dept. 1977)), the word "authoritative" cannot be regarded as an absolute requirement. As long as the testimony conveys that the text is an authority, that is all that is required and an expert may not be permitted to thwart a proper cross-examination by disavowing the substantive authoritativeness by relying on a semantical distinction. Any other rule would elevate form over substance, a principle which this Court recognized in **Spiegel v. Levy**, is inappropriate.

EXAMPLE 15-8: LOCAL CLIMATOLOGICAL DATA (NOAA)

LCD-30-94728-PD-9806

13817
KRAMER DILLOF, TESSEL DUFFY & MOORE
233 BROADWAY
NEW YORK NY 10279

For address correction, please return a photocopy of this page to Subscription Services indicating changes

NATIONAL CLIMATIC DATA CENTER
151 PATTON AVE RM 120
ASHEVILLE, NC 28801–5001

OFFICIAL BUSINESS, PENALTY FOR PRIVATE USE $300

FIRST CLASS
POSTAGE AND FEES PAID
NOAA
PERMIT G–19

FEBRUARY 1998
NEW YORK C.PARK, NY

LOCAL CLIMATOLOGICAL DATA

NOAA, National Climatic Data Center

I certify that this is an official publication of the National Oceanic and Atmospheric Administration (NOAA). It is compiled using information from weather observing sites operated by NOAA–National Weather Service / Department Of Transportation–Federal Aviation Administration and received at the National Climatic Data Center (NCDC), Asheville, North Carolina 28801.

ACTING DIRECTOR

NOTICE

Effective July 1, 1996, the National Weather Service & Federal Aviation Administration began using the METAR format for Hourly Observations.

We welcome your questions or comments, please contact us at 704–271–4800 (voice), 704–271–4876 (fax), 704–271–4010(TDD) or orders@ncdc.noaa.gov

United States Department of Commerce | National Oceanic and Atmospheric Administration | National Environmental Satellite Data, and Information Service

FEBRUARY 1998
NEW YORK C.PARK, NY

FEBRUARY 1998
LOCAL CLIMATOLOGICAL DATA
NOAA, National Climatic Data Center

NEW YORK C.PARK, NY
CENTRAL PARK OBSERVATORY (NYC)
Lat: 40°47' N Long: 73°58' W Elev (Ground): 132 Feet
Time Zone: EASTERN WBAN: 94728 ISSN #:0198–3601

	TEMPERATURE °F						DEG DAYS BASE 65°			SNOW/ICE ON GND(IN)		PRECIPITATION (INCHES)		PRESSURE (INCHES OF HG)		WIND SPEED = MPH DIR = TENS OF DEGREES			MAXIMUM				
										0700 LST	1300 LST	2400 LST	2400 LST						5-SEC		2-MIN		
DATE	MAXIMUM	MINIMUM	AVERAGE	DEP FROM NORMAL	AVERAGE DEW PT	AVERAGE WET BULB	HEATING	COOLING	WEATHER	DEPTH	WATER EQUIV	SNOW-FALL	WATER EQUIV	AVERAGE STATION	AVERAGE SEA LEVEL	RESULTANT SPEED	RES DIR	AVERAGE SPEED	SPEED	DIR	SPEED	DIR	DATE
1	2	3	4	5	6	7	8	9	10	11	12	13	14	15	16	17	18	19	20	21	22	23	24
01	46	31	39	8	22	32	26	0				0.0	0.00	30.13	30.20	0.0	05	3.6	15	03	11	01	01
02	49	35	42	11	28	37	23	0				0.0	0.00	30.15	30.22	1.4	24	4.1	17	20	13	19	02
03	49	39	44	12	30	39	21	0	RA			0.0	T	30.06	30.13	2.7	04	5.9	23	06	15	07	03
04	42	35	39	7	28	35	26	0	RA BR			0.0	0.29	29.84	29.91	16.4	08	16.7	43	06	31	06	04
05	36	34	35	3	29	33	30	0	RA BR			0.0	1.07	29.53	29.60	15.8	06	16.2	41	07	30	07	05
06	44	31	38	6	12	29	27	0	UP			0.0	0.00	29.78	29.85	5.8	04	7.5	25	04	16	06	06
07	42	31	37	5	20	31	28	0				0.0	0.00	29.93	30.00	9.3	08	10.0	29	06	22	07	07
08	41	29	35	3	22	30	30	0				0.0	0.00	29.93	30.00	9.9	08	10.9	28	06	23	07	08
09	48	30	39	7	23	33	26	0				0.0	0.00	30.04	30.11	1.7	05	4.3	18	09	14	09	09
10	50	35	43	11	28	36	22	0	HZ			0.0	0.00	30.14	30.21	2.9	11	5.4	14	07	10	18	10
11	50	37	44	11	35	40	21	0	RA BR HZ			0.0	0.64	30.00	30.07	2.3	14	5.1	16	18	13	15	11
12	54	44	49	16	28	41	16	0	RA HZ			0.0	0.36	29.44	29.51	7.0	28	10.1	33	20	23	30	12
13	45	32	39	6	22	33	26	0				0.0	0.00	29.82	29.89	9.0	32	10.4	29	31	21	30	13
14	37	24	31	-2	5	23	34	0				0.0	0.00	30.04	30.12	4.5	36	8.2	21	07	15	32	14
15	33	17*	25*	-8	0	20	40	0				0.0	0.00	30.38	30.45	2.8	04	5.5	17	30	13	07	15
16	41	27	34	0	16	28	31	0				0.0	0.00	30.43	30.50	1.5	10	5.6	15	14	11	19	16
17	41	36	39	5	34	36	26	0	RA BR			0.0	1.27	30.08	30.14	13.0	09	13.7	37	06	26	08	17
18	46	40	43	9	26	36	22	0	RA BR HZ			0.0	0.65	29.56	29.63	12.6	09	13.0	39	09	30	09	18
19	51	39	45	11			20	0	RA HZ			0.0	0.15	29.61		4.5	31	6.5	21	30	17	30	19
20	50	43	47	12	38	43	18	0	RA BR			0.0	0.10	29.61	29.67	3.1	30	5.0	15	30	10	30	20
21	47	41	44	9	29	37	21	0				0.0	0.00	29.67	29.73	9.8	32	10.8	31	35	22	33	21
22	51	40	46	11	28	38	19	0				0.0	0.00	29.97	30.04	4.5	32	6.1	22	32	16	32	22
23	43	39	41	6	33	37	24	0	RA BR			0.0	0.41	29.80	29.87	15.1	08	15.4	52*	07	34*	08	23
24	41	35	38	2	36	37	27	0	RA BR UP			0.0	0.78	29.24	29.31	9.1	04	11.7	40	07	29	07	24
25	48	37	43	7	30	38	22	0	RA UP			0.0	T	29.47	29.54	15.5	32	15.6	39	34	28	32	25
26	58	42	50*	14	26	39	15	0				0.0	0.00	29.76	29.83	6.4	32	8.1	25	32	17	32	26
27	58*	36	47	10	26	38	18	0				0.0	0.00	29.76	29.82	1.0	29	5.3	21	33	14	32	27
28	53	42	48	11	36	42	17	0	RA BR			0.0	0.09	29.76	29.83	4.5	10	6.4	22	07	16	08	28
	46.2	35.0	40.6	■■			24.1	0.0	< MONTHLY AVERAGES	TOTALS->		0.0	5.81	29.85		3.6	04	8.8	<- MONTHLY AVERAGES				
	5.9	8.1	7.0	■■	<------------- DEPARTURE FROM NORMAL ------------->								2.54	SUNSHINE, CLOUD, & VISIBILITY TABLES ON PAGE 3									

DEGREE DAYS

	MONTHLY TOTAL	MONTHLY DEPARTURE	SEASON TO DATE TOTAL	SEASON TO DATE DEPARTURE
HEATING:	676	-203	3211	-393
COOLING:	0	0	0	0

GREATEST 24-HR PRECIPITATION: 1.92 DATE: 17-18
GREATEST 24-HR SNOWFALL: 0.0 DATE:
GREATEST SNOW DEPTH: DATE:

SEA LEVEL PRESSURE		DATE	TIME
MAXIMUM	30.58	15	0934
MINIMUM	29.23	24	1615

NUMBER OF DAYS WITH →

MAXIMUM TEMP ≥ 90:	0	MINIMUM TEMP ≤ 32:	9	PRECIPITATION ≥ 0.01 INCH:	11
MAXIMUM TEMP ≤ 32:	0	MINIMUM TEMP ≤ 0:	0	PRECIPITATION ≥ 0.10 INCH:	10
THUNDERSTORMS:	0	HEAVY FOG:	0	SNOWFALL ≥ 1.0 INCH:	0

HOURLY PRECIPITATION

(WATER EQUIVALENT IN INCHES)

NEW YORK C.PARK, NY

FEBRUARY 1998 NYC WBAN # 94728

DATE	FOR HOUR (LST) ENDING AT 1	2	3	4	5	6	7	8	9	10	11	12
01												
02												
03												
04												
05	0.10	0.09	0.09	0.07	0.03	0.04	0.05	0.04	0.06	0.11	0.04	0.08
06	T	T										
07												
08												
09												
10												
11												
12	0.14	0.10	0.03	T			0.01	0.09				T
13												
14												
15												
16												
17												
18	0.19	0.30	0.11	0.03	0.01	0.01	T					
19	T	0.04										
20												
21	0.01											
22												
23												
24	0.13	0.13	0.04	0.03	0.01	0.09	0.01	0.01	0.07	0.01	0.02	0.01
25	T	T							T			
26												
27												
28												T

DATE	FOR HOUR (LST) ENDING AT 13	14	15	16	17	18	19	20	21	22	23	24	DATE	Sum if Different (See Note 2)	2400 LST Water Equiv.
01													01		0.00
02													02		0.00
03		T											03		T
04					T	0.01	0.03	0.04	0.05	0.06	0.03	0.06	04	0.28	0.29
05	0.05	0.06	0.06	0.04	0.03	0.01	0.02	0.01	T				05	1.08	1.07
06													06	T	0.00
07													07		0.00
08													08		0.00
09													09		0.00
10													10		0.00
11								T	0.01	0.09	0.23	0.29	11	0.62	0.64
12	T		0.01										12	0.38	0.36
13													13		0.00
14													14		0.00
15													15		0.00
16													16		0.00
17			0.01	0.05	0.04	0.04	0.15	0.14	0.18	0.24	0.19	0.22	17	1.26	1.27
18												0.01	18	0.66	0.65
19													19	0.04	0.15
20		0.01	0.01	0.01	0.01	0.01	0.02	0.01	0.01	0.01	T	T	20		0.10
21													21	0.01	0.00
22													22		0.00
23				T	0.02	0.04	0.06	0.03	0.10	0.05	0.03	0.05	23	0.38	0.41
24	0.01	0.03	0.02	0.02	0.03	0.05	0.03	0.02	0.02	0.01	T	0.01	24	0.81	0.78
25													25		T
26													26		0.00
27													27		0.00
28							0.05	T	T	T	0.04		28		0.09

MAXIMUM SHORT DURATION PRECIPITATION (See Note 1)

Time Period (Minutes)	5	10	15	20	30	45	60	80	100	120	150	180
Precipitation (Inches)												
Ending Date												
Ending Time (Hour/Min)												

Date and time are not entered for TRACE amounts.

Note 1: NCDC derives these data from one-minute ASOS values. The table is not printed when inconsistent with ASOS hourly totals.

Note 2: The sum of the hourly totals is given when it differs from the daily total. NWS does not edit ASOS hourly values but may edit daily and monthly totals. Hourly, daily, and monthly totals are printed as reported by the ASOS site.

NOAA, National Climatic Data Center

PAGE 2

REFERENCE NOTES & SUPPLEMENTAL SUMMARIES

* = Extreme for the month (last occurence if more than one)
T = Trace precipitation amount
+ = also occurs on earlier date
FG+ = Heavy fog, visibility .25 miles or less
BLANK entries denote missing or unreported data

Resultant wind is the vector sum of the wind speeds and directions divided by the number of observations.

Wind direction is recorded in tens of degrees (2 digits) clockwise from true north. '00' = calm, 'VR' = variable.

Precipitation is for the 24-hour period ending at the time indicated in the column heading.

Water Equivalent of snow on the ground is reported only when the depth is 2 or more inches.

NORMALS ARE FOR THE YEARS 1961-1990

WEATHER NOTATIONS

QUALIFIER	WEATHER PHENOMENA		
DESCRIPTOR	PRECIPITATION	OBSCURATION	OTHER
BC Patches	DZ Drizzle	BR Mist	DS Duststorm
BL Blowing	GR Hail	DU Widespread Dust	FC Funnel Cloud
DR Low Drifting	GS Small Hail and/or Snow Pellets	FG Fog	+FC Tornado Waterspout
FZ Freezing	IC Ice Crystals	FU Smoke	PO Well-Developed Dust/Sand Whirls
MI Shallow	PE Ice Pellets	HZ Haze	SQ Squalls
PR Partial	RA Rain	PY Spray	SS Sandstorm
SH Shower(s)	SG Snow Grains	SA Sand	GL Glaze
TS Thunderstorm	SN Snow	VA Volcanic Ash	
VC In the Vicinity	UP Unknown Precipitation		

Intensity (as indicated on pages 4 to 6):
'+' = Heavy ' ' = Moderate '-' = Light

NEW YORK C.PARK, NY
FEBRUARY 1998

Ceilometer (30-second) data are used to derive cloudiness at or below 12,000 feet. This cloudiness is the mean cloud cover detected during sunrise to sunset (SR-SS), or midnight to midnight (MN-MN).

Satellite data are used to derive cloudiness above 12,000 feet. Effective Cloud Amount is based on the cloud cover and the transparency of the clouds within the satellite field of view (approx. 31x31 miles).

Sky Condition is based on the sum (not to exceed 8) of the sunrise to sunset cloud cover below and above 12,000 feet. Both ceilometer and satellite data must be present to compute Sky Condition. Clear = 0-2 oktas, Partly Cloudy = 3-6 oktas, Cloudy = 7-8 oktas.

A Heating (Cooling) Degree Day is the difference between the average daily temperature and 65 degrees F. The HDD season begins July 1, the CDD season begins January 1.

Dew Point is the temperature to which the air must be cooled to achieve 100% relative humidity. Wet Bulb is the temperature the air would have if cooled at constant pressure by evaporation of moisture into it, to 100% relative humidity.

Snow Depth, Snowfall, and Sunshine data may come from nearby sites that the National Weather Service deems Climatologically representative of this site.

ADDITIONAL NOTES:

DATE	SUNSHINE TOTAL MINUTES	SUNSHINE PERCENT POSSIBLE	CLOUDINESS (OKTAS) SR-SS CEILOMETER	SR-SS SATELLITE	MN-MN CEILOMETER	MN-MN SATELLITE	VISIBILITY (MILES) MINIMUM	VISIBILITY (MILES) MAXIMUM	RESERVED
01							10.00	10.00	
02							10.00	10.00	
03							8.00	10.00	
04							4.00	10.00	
05							4.00	10.00	
06							10.00	10.00	
07							10.00	10.00	
08							10.00	10.00	
09							9.00	10.00	
10							5.00	10.00	
11							1.25	10.00	
12							3.00	10.00	
13							10.00	10.00	
14							10.00	10.00	
15							10.00	10.00	
16							10.00	10.00	
17							2.00	10.00	
18							2.00	9.00	
19							3.00	10.00	
20							7.00	10.00	
21							10.00	10.00	
22							10.00	10.00	
23							4.00	10.00	
24							3.00	10.00	
25							10.00	10.00	
26							10.00	10.00	
27							10.00	10.00	
28							4.00	10.00	
MONTHLY AVGS							7.12	9.96	

SUNSHINE (MINUTES)
Total: Possible:
Percent Possible:

NUMBER OF DAYS WITH:

SKY CONDITION			
CLR	PTLY CLDY	CLOUDY	MISSING
			28

MINIMUM VISIBILITY (MILES)		
<=0.25	<=3.0	>=7.0
0	6	17

PAGE 3

OBSERVATIONS AT 3-HOURLY INTERVALS

NEW YORK C.PARK, NY

FEBRUARY 1998 NYC WBAN # 94728

HOUR (LST)			SATELLITE		VISIBILITY (MILES)	WEATHER	TEMPERATURE °F			RELATIVE HUMIDITY (PCT)	WIND		PRESSURE (INCHES,HG)	
	SKY COVER	CEILING 100'S OF FT	OBSERVATION TIME (LST)	EFF CLD AMT Oktas			DRY BULB	DEW POINT	WET BULB		SPEED (MPH)	DIRECTION TENS OF DEG	STATION	SEA LEVEL
					SUNRISE: 0706		FEB 01			SUNSET: 1713				
01	CLR	NC			10.00		33	19	28	56	0	00	30.04	30.11
04	CLR	NC			10.00		32	18	27	56	6	VR	30.08	30.15
07	CLR	NC			10.00		31	20	27	64	5	VR	30.12	30.19
10	CLR	NC			10.00		36	22	31	57	6	VR	30.16	30.23
13	CLR	NC			10.00		43	20	35	40	5	VR	30.13	30.19
16	CLR	NC			10.00		45	19	35	35	0	00	30.15	30.22
19	CLR	NC			10.00		40	27	35	60	5	VR	30.18	30.25
22	CLR	NC			10.00		39	28	35	65	0	00	30.17	30.24
					SUNRISE: 0705		FEB 02			SUNSET: 1715				
01	CLR	NC			10.00		38	23	32	55	0	00	30.17	30.23
04	CLR	NC			10.00		36	27	33	70	0	00	30.17	30.24
07	CLR	NC			10.00		37	29	34	73	6	26	30.19	30.26
10	CLR	NC			10.00		43	24	36	47	3	VR	30.20	30.27
13	CLR	NC			10.00		48	24	39	39	3	VR	30.14	30.20
16	CLR	NC			10.00		46	28	39	50	7	17	30.13	30.19
19	CLR	NC			10.00		43	32	38	65	6	VR	30.13	30.20
22	CLR	NC			10.00		44	34	40	68	6	VR	30.11	30.18
					SUNRISE: 0704		FEB 03			SUNSET: 1716				
01	CLR	NC			10.00		43	33	39	68	9	26	30.09	30.16
04	BKN	100			10.00		42	34	39	73	3	VR	30.08	30.15
07	SCT	NC			10.00		42	32	38	68	3	VR	30.07	30.13
10	CLR	NC			8.00		47	32	41	56	3	VR	30.06	30.12
13	SCT	NC			10.00		49	29	41	46	3	VR	30.07	30.14
16	CLR	NC			10.00		46	29	39	51	7	VR	30.02	30.08
19	OVC	065			10.00		44	30	38	58	5	VR	30.06	30.12
22	CLR	NC			10.00		41	24	35	51	10	05	30.06	30.12
					SUNRISE: 0703		FEB 04			SUNSET: 1717				
01	CLR	NC			10.00		38	26	33	62	14	06	29.99	30.06
04	OVC	100			10.00		38	25	33	60	10	05	29.97	30.03
07	OVC	110			10.00		39	25	34	57	14	07	29.96	30.03
10	CLR	NC			10.00		40	26	35	58	16	06	29.92	29.99
13	CLR	NC			10.00		42	27	36	55	15	09	29.83	29.90
16	CLR	NC			10.00		41	28	36	60	22	07	29.76	29.82
19	OVC	049			8.00	-RA	38	29	34	70	13	09	29.74	29.80
22	OVC	014			6.00	-RA	36	31	34	82	24	07	29.68	29.75
					SUNRISE: 0702		FEB 05			SUNSET: 1718				
01	OVC	014			4.00	RA BR	35	31	33	85	23	06	29.60	29.66
04	QVC	014			5.00	-RA BR	34	31	33	89	25	07	29.53	29.60
07	OVC	016			7.00	-RA	34	32	33	92	16	07	29.52	29.59
10	OVC	018			4.00	RA BR	35	31	33	85	20	06	29.49	29.56
13	OVC	018			5.00	RA BR	35	31	33	85	17	07	29.47	29.54
16	OVC	028			7.00	-RA	36	30	34	79	9	05	29.50	29.57
19	OVC	030			10.00	-RA	35	29	33	78	15	06	29.56	29.63
22	OVC	032			10.00		35	22	30	59	14	03	29.60	29.67
					SUNRISE: 0701		FEB 06			SUNSET: 1719				
01	OVC	032			10.00	UP	34	15	28	46	12	05	29.64	29.71
04	FEW	NC			10.00		33	13	27	43	9	06	29.66	29.72
07	CLR	NC			10.00		32	10	25	40	13	02	29.71	29.78
10	CLR	NC			10.00		37	11	29	34	12	04	29.81	29.88
13	CLR	NC			10.00		42	12	32	29	7	VR	29.76	29.83
16	CLR	NC			10.00		42	11	32	28	3	VR	29.82	29.88
19	CLR	NC			10.00		41	12	31	30	6	02	29.85	29.92
22	CLR	NC			10.00		37	12	29	36	6	04	29.88	29.95

HOUR (LST)			SATELLITE		VISIBILITY (MILES)	WEATHER	TEMPERATURE °F			RELATIVE HUMIDITY (PCT)	WIND		PRESSURE (INCHES,HG)	
	SKY COVER	CEILING 100'S OF FT	OBSERVATION TIME (LST)	EFF CLD AMT Oktas			DRY BULB	DEW POINT	WET BULB		SPEED (MPH)	DIRECTION TENS OF DEG	STATION	SEA LEVEL
					SUNRISE: 0660		FEB 07			SUNSET: 1721				
01	CLR	NC			10.00		35	14	28	42	5	VR	29.93	30.00
04	CLR	NC			10.00		35	15	29	44	6	VR	29.91	29.97
07	CLR	NC			10.00		32	13	26	45	6	03	29.95	30.01
10	CLR	NC			10.00		36	15	29	42	13	07	29.98	30.05
13	CLR	NC			10.00		41	24	35	51	15	08	29.95	30.01
16	CLR	NC			10.00		40	22	33	49	14	08	29.92	29.98
19	CLR	NC			10.00		38	26	33	62	12	10	29.91	29.98
22	CLR	NC			10.00		37	27	33	67	10	07	29.92	29.98
					SUNRISE: 0659		FEB 08			SUNSET: 1722				
01	CLR	NC			10.00		34	21	29	59	9	07	29.89	29.96
04	CLR	NC			10.00		32	22	28	66	15	07	29.87	29.94
07	CLR	NC			10.00		30	21	27	69	21	07	29.91	29.98
10	OVC	023			10.00		31	20	27	64	14	06	29.96	30.03
13	CLR	NC			10.00		37	22	32	54	8	12	29.92	29.98
16	CLR	NC			10.00		40	22	33	49	3	13	29.91	29.98
19	CLR	NC			10.00		38	21	32	51	7	08	29.95	30.02
22	CLR	NC			10.00		35	25	31	67	6	VR	29.99	30.06
					SUNRISE: 0657		FEB 09			SUNSET: 1723				
01	FEW	NC			10.00		33	25	30	72	8	07	30.01	30.08
04	CLR	NC			10.00		31	23	28	72	6	06	30.01	30.08
07	CLR	NC			10.00		30	22	27	72	6	06	30.05	30.11
10	CLR	NC			10.00		35	22	30	59	5	07	30.09	30.15
13	CLR	NC			10.00		43	19	34	38	5	32	30.04	30.11
16	CLR	NC			10.00		48	20	37	33	3	VR	30.01	30.08
19	CLR	NC			10.00		43	28	37	56	0	00	30.04	30.11
22	CLR	NC			10.00		42	27	36	55	3	VR	30.06	30.12
					SUNRISE: 0656		FEB 10			SUNSET: 1724				
01	CLR	NC			10.00		41	25	35	53	5	30	30.07	30.14
04	CLR	NC			10.00		37	28	34	70	0	00	30.10	30.16
07	CLR	NC			9.00		37	27	33	67	3	04	30.14	30.20
10	CLR	NC			10.00		42	22	35	45	6	09	30.18	30.24
13	CLR	NC			10.00		49	28	40	45	6	VR	30.15	30.22
16	CLR	NC			10.00		47	27	39	46	6	13	30.13	30.20
19	CLR	NC			8.00		43	30	38	60	9	17	30.17	30.23
22	CLR	NC			6.00	HZ	42	31	38	65	6	17	30.17	30.24
					SUNRISE: 0655		FEB 11			SUNSET: 1726				
01	CLR	NC			8.00		41	31	37	67	0	00	30.13	30.20
04	CLR	NC			10.00		40	33	37	77	3	VR	30.13	30.20
07	CLR	NC			3.00	BR	37	34	36	89	3	02	30.14	30.20
10	BKN	010			2.50	BR	40	36	38	86	0	00	30.13	30.19
13	SCT	NC			10.00		49	35	43	59	6	VR	30.05	30.11
16	BKN	055			10.00		46	37	42	71	9	08	29.96	30.03
19	OVC	009			10.00		48	44	46	86	9	17	29.88	29.95
22	OVC	003			3.00	RA	49	28	40	45	8	15	29.74	29.80
					SUNRISE: 0654		FEB 12			SUNSET: 1727				
01	OVC	004			3.00	RA	50	28	41	43	8	19	29.58	29.65
04	OVC	008			10.00		53	29	43	40	7	VR	29.44	29.51
07	OVC	010			3.00	RA	51	24	40	35	6	20	29.37	29.44
10	OVC	023			10.00		53	22	40	30	10	27	29.36	29.43
13	OVC	032			10.00		51	28	41	41	8	31	29.34	29.41
16	OVC	050			10.00		50	36	44	59	14	30	29.39	29.46
19	BKN	039			10.00		49	34	42	57	14	30	29.47	29.54
22	BKN	055			10.00		45	27	38	49	18	30	29.55	29.62

PUBLISHED BY: NCDC, ASHEVILLE, NC.

PAGE 4

OBSERVATIONS AT 3–HOURLY INTERVALS

NEW YORK C.PARK, NY
FEBRUARY 1998 NYC WBAN # 94728

HOUR (LST)	SKY COVER	CEILING 100'S OF FT	SATELLITE OBSERVATION TIME (LST)	SATELLITE EFF CLD AMT Oktas	VISIBILITY (MILES)	WEATHER	TEMPERATURE °F DRY BULB	DEW POINT	WET BULB	RELATIVE HUMIDITY (PCT)	WIND SPEED (MPH)	WIND DIRECTION TENS OF DEG	PRESSURE (INCHES,HG) STATION	SEA LEVEL
					SUNRISE: 0652		FEB 13		SUNSET: 1728					
01	OVC	043			10.00		43	26	36	51	12	30	29.63	29.70
04	OVC	039			10.00		42	27	36	55	8	32	29.70	29.77
07	BKN	037			10.00		38	24	33	57	7	VR	29.80	29.87
10	FEW	NC			10.00		40	24	34	53	9	30	29.87	29.93
13	CLR	NC			10.00		44	22	36	41	13	32	29.84	29.91
16	CLR	NC			10.00		42	22	35	45	13	33	29.84	29.91
19	CLR	NC			10.00		38	20	32	48	8	32	29.88	29.95
22	CLR	NC			10.00		34	18	29	52	6	32	29.93	29.99
					SUNRISE: 0651		FEB 14		SUNSET: 1729					
01	CLR	NC			10.00		31	14	26	49	6	VR	29.93	29.99
04	CLR	NC			10.00		28	11	23	49	3	VR	29.94	30.01
07	CLR	NC					24	8	20	50	8	06	29.99	30.06
10	CLR	NC			10.00		26	7	21	44	12	04	30.06	30.12
13	CLR	NC			10.00		34	5	26	29	6	VR	30.05	30.12
16	CLR	NC			10.00		36	1	26	23	10	31	30.03	30.10
19	CLR	NC			10.00		33	-1	24	23	10	32	30.11	30.18
22	CLR	NC			10.00		29	-3	21	25	12	02	30.17	30.24
					SUNRISE: 0650		FEB 15		SUNSET: 1730					
01	CLR	NC			10.00		25	-3	19	29	8	36	30.22	30.30
04	CLR	NC					21	-5	16	31	9	36	30.28	30.36
07	CLR	NC					18	2	14	49	5	VR	30.33	30.40
10	CLR	NC					20	0	15	41	3	VR	30.43	30.50
13	CLR	NC			10.00		29	-4	21	24	9	07	30.41	30.49
16	CLR	NC			10.00		32	-1	24	24	0	00	30.40	30.48
19	CLR	NC			10.00		31	-2	23	24	0	00	30.40	30.48
22	CLR	NC			10.00		30	7	24	38	3	07	30.42	30.50
					SUNRISE: 0649		FEB 16		SUNSET: 1732					
01	CLR	NC			10.00		28	8	23	43	3	30	30.43	30.51
04	CLR	NC			10.00		28	8	23	43	3	33	30.41	30.49
07	CLR	NC			10.00		28	12	23	51	5	08	30.45	30.53
10	CLR	NC			10.00		32	17	27	54	8	10	30.46	30.54
13	CLR	NC			10.00		36	13	29	39	6	VR	30.43	30.51
16	CLR	NC			10.00		37	18	31	46	8	20	30.41	30.48
19	CLR	NC			10.00		36	21	31	55	5	VR	30.42	30.49
22	OVC	026			10.00		36	23	31	59	7	13	30.40	30.48
					SUNRISE: 0647		FEB 17		SUNSET: 1733					
01	OVC	027			10.00		36	25	32	64	3	VR	30.34	30.42
04	OVC	029			10.00		37	27	33	67	10	08	30.29	30.36
07	BKN	120			10.00		37	29	34	73	16	08	30.24	30.32
10	BKN	013			10.00		39	34	37	82	16	08	30.21	30.29
13	FEW	NC			10.00		39	33	37	79	15	09	30.11	30.18
16	OVC	020			4.00	-RA BR	38	34	36	86	18	07	29.94	30.01
19	OVC	006			2.50	RA BR	38	38	38	100	14	11	29.86	29.93
22	OVC	004			2.00	RA BR	40	39	40	97	18	08	29.77	29.83
					SUNRISE: 0646		FEB 18		SUNSET: 1734					
01	OVC	004			2.00	RA BR	40	39	40	97	18	09	29.63	29.70
04	OVC	006			4.00	-RA	41	31	37	67	25	08	29.58	29.64
07	OVC	004			5.00	HZ	42	31	37	65	22	09	29.56	29.62
10	OVC	004			3.00	HZ	42	31	37	65	16	08	29.57	29.63
13	OVC	004			6.00	HZ	45	29	38	54	14	08	29.55	29.62
16	OVC	006			6.00	HZ	45	21	36	39	8	10	29.52	29.58
19	OVC	006			4.00	HZ	43	16	33	34	8	09	29.56	29.62
22	OVC	008			9.00		42	18	33	38	7	VR	29.56	29.63

HOUR (LST)	SKY COVER	CEILING 100'S OF FT	SATELLITE OBSERVATION TIME (LST)	SATELLITE EFF CLD AMT Oktas	VISIBILITY (MILES)	WEATHER	TEMPERATURE °F DRY BULB	DEW POINT	WET BULB	RELATIVE HUMIDITY (PCT)	WIND SPEED (MPH)	WIND DIRECTION TENS OF DEG	PRESSURE (INCHES,HG) STATION	SEA LEVEL
					SUNRISE: 0645		FEB 19		SUNSET: 1735					
01	OVC	004			4.00	-RA	40	21	33	47	5	VR	29.55	29.62
04	OVC	006			5.00	RA					0	00	29.56	
07	OVC	010			10.00						0	00	29.59	
10	OVC	010			4.00	HZ					5	32	29.60	
13	OVC	016			10.00						7	30	29.58	
16	OVC	029			10.00		50	42	46	74	5	VR	29.63	
19	OVC	037			10.00		50	41	46	71	13	30	29.67	
22	BKN	030			10.00		48	41	45	77	8	31	29.70	
					SUNRISE: 0643		FEB 20		SUNSET: 1736					
01	OVC	030			10.00		47	38	43	71	3	VR	29.71	
04	OVC	026			10.00		46	37	42	71	5	30	29.70	29.76
07	OVC	100			10.00		45	37	41	74	5	VR	29.68	29.75
10	BKN	100			10.00		48	36	43	63	0	00	29.67	29.73
13	CLR	NC			10.00		50	36	44	59	3	VR	29.57	29.64
16	OVC	026			7.00	-RA	46	41	44	83	7	VR	29.53	29.59
19	OVC	038			7.00	-RA	44	41	43	89	5	VR	29.54	29.60
22	OVC	045			10.00	-RA	43	40	42	89	5	VR	29.53	29.60
					SUNRISE: 0642		FEB 21		SUNSET: 1738					
01	OVC	110			10.00		43	36	40	76	10	30	29.53	29.60
04	OVC	031			10.00		43	29	37	58	8	29	29.56	29.62
07	OVC	033			10.00		43	29	37	58	10	30	29.60	29.67
10	OVC	034			10.00		43	29	37	58	14	31	29.65	29.71
13	OVC	042			10.00		44	27	37	51	12	32	29.63	29.70
16	CLR	NC			10.00		44	27	37	51	14	32	29.68	29.74
19	FEW	NC			10.00		42	28	36	58	12	33	29.78	29.85
22	CLR	NC			10.00		41	30	37	65	10	31	29.81	29.88
					SUNRISE: 0640		FEB 22		SUNSET: 1739					
01	OVC	029			10.00		42	29	37	60	8	32	29.87	29.94
04	OVC	029			10.00		41	30	37	65	12	32	29.90	29.97
07	BKN	029			10.00		41	29	36	62	8	32	29.96	30.02
10	CLR	NC			10.00		44	28	38	53	9	32	30.02	30.09
13	CLR	NC			10.00		48	27	39	44	6	VR	29.99	30.06
16	CLR	NC			10.00		50	25	40	38	5	VR	29.95	30.02
19	CLR	NC			10.00		48	25	39	41	3	VR	29.99	30.06
22	CLR	NC			10.00		43	27	37	53	0	00	30.03	30.09
					SUNRISE: 0639		FEB 23		SUNSET: 1740					
01	CLR	NC			10.00		42	24	35	49	9	06	30.00	30.06
04	BKN	110			10.00		41	24	35	51	12	09	29.98	30.04
07	CLR	NC			10.00		39	28	35	65	10	11	29.96	30.03
10	BKN	110			8.00		41	35	38	79	9	10	29.94	30.00
13	OVC	019			8.00		42	37	40	82	14	07	29.84	29.91
16	OVC	011			6.00	-RA BR	40	37	39	89	17	09	29.76	29.83
19	OVC	011			5.00	-RA BR	39	37	38	93	25	08	29.64	29.71
22	OVC	009			4.00	RA BR	40	38	39	93	24	07	29.51	29.57
					SUNRISE: 0637		FEB 24		SUNSET: 1741					
01	OVC	011			3.00	+RA BR	40	38	39	93	22	07	29.42	29.49
04	OVC	013			7.00	-RA	39	37	38	93	23	08	29.29	29.35
07	OVC	016			10.00		41	38	40	89	10	04	29.25	29.31
10	OVC	014			3.00	-RA BR	40	37	39	89	12	36	29.24	29.30
13	OVC	009			4.00	-RA BR	37	35	36	93	9	01	29.19	29.25
16	OVC	010			4.00	-RA BR	37	35	36	93	8	35	29.17	29.23
19	OVC	006			4.00	-RA BR	36	34	35	93	6	VR	29.21	29.28
22	OVC	010			10.00	UP	37	35	36	93	8	36	29.24	29.31

PUBLISHED BY: NCDC, ASHEVILLE, NC.

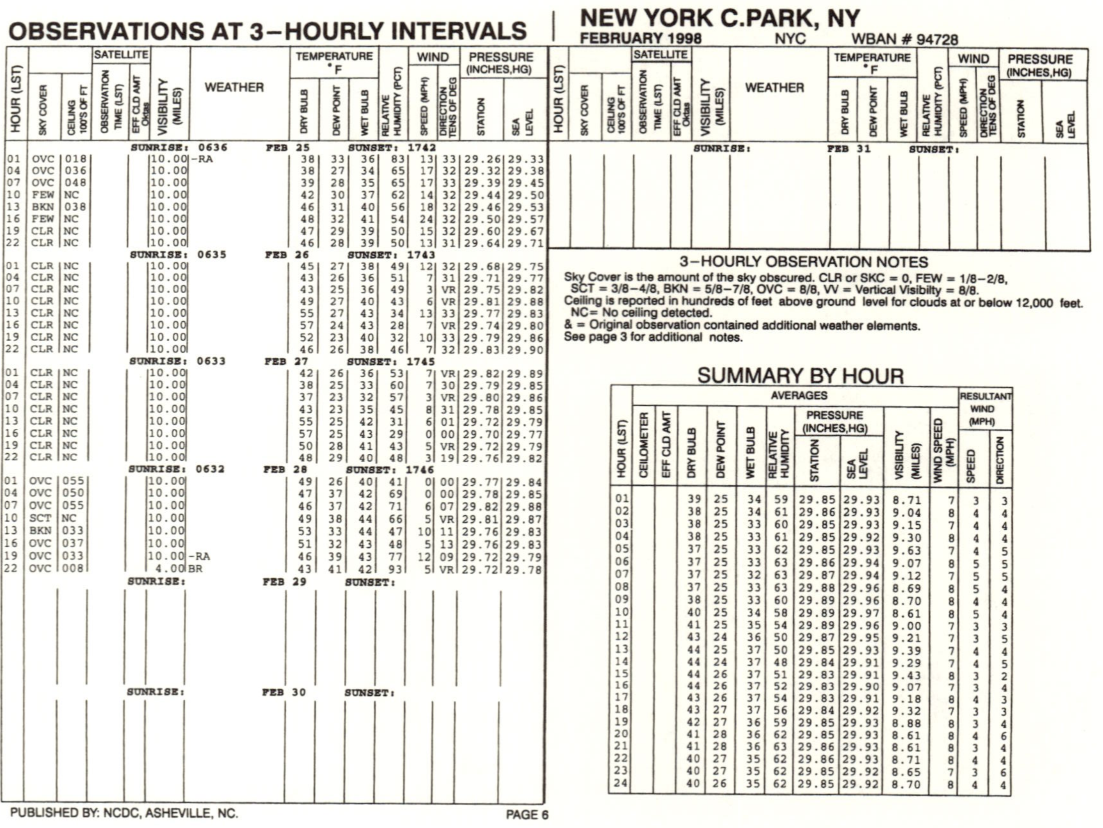

OBSERVATIONS AT 3-HOURLY INTERVALS

NEW YORK C.PARK, NY

FEBRUARY 1998 NYC WBAN # 94728

HOUR (LST)	SKY COVER	CEILING 100'S OF FT	SATELLITE OBSERVATION TIME (LST)	SATELLITE EFF CLD AMT Oktas	VISIBILITY (MILES)	WEATHER	TEMPERATURE °F DRY BULB	TEMPERATURE °F DEW POINT	TEMPERATURE °F WET BULB	RELATIVE HUMIDITY (PCT)	WIND SPEED (MPH)	WIND DIRECTION TENS OF DEG	PRESSURE (INCHES,HG) STATION	PRESSURE (INCHES,HG) SEA LEVEL
					SUNRISE: 0636		FEB 25		SUNSET: 1742					
01	OVC	018			10.00	-RA	38	33	36	83	13	33	29.26	29.33
04	OVC	036			10.00		38	27	34	65	17	32	29.32	29.38
07	OVC	048			10.00		39	28	35	65	17	33	29.39	29.45
10	FEW	NC			10.00		42	30	37	62	14	32	29.44	29.50
13	BKN	038			10.00		46	31	40	56	18	32	29.46	29.53
16	FEW	NC			10.00		48	32	41	54	24	32	29.50	29.57
19	CLR	NC			10.00		47	29	39	50	15	32	29.60	29.67
22	CLR	NC			10.00		46	28	39	50	13	31	29.64	29.71
					SUNRISE: 0635		FEB 26		SUNSET: 1743					
01	CLR	NC			10.00		45	27	38	49	12	32	29.68	29.75
04	CLR	NC			10.00		43	26	36	51	7	31	29.71	29.77
07	CLR	NC			10.00		43	25	36	49	3	VR	29.75	29.82
10	CLR	NC			10.00		49	27	40	43	6	VR	29.81	29.88
13	CLR	NC			10.00		55	27	43	34	13	33	29.77	29.83
16	CLR	NC			10.00		57	24	43	28	7	VR	29.74	29.80
19	CLR	NC			10.00		52	23	40	32	10	33	29.79	29.86
22	CLR	NC			10.00		46	26	38	46	7	32	29.83	29.90
					SUNRISE: 0633		FEB 27		SUNSET: 1745					
01	CLR	NC			10.00		42	26	36	53	7	VR	29.82	29.89
04	CLR	NC			10.00		38	25	33	60	7	30	29.79	29.85
07	CLR	NC			10.00		37	23	32	57	3	VR	29.80	29.86
10	CLR	NC			10.00		43	23	35	45	8	31	29.78	29.85
13	CLR	NC			10.00		55	25	42	31	6	01	29.72	29.79
16	CLR	NC			10.00		57	25	43	29	0	00	29.70	29.77
19	CLR	NC			10.00		50	28	41	43	5	VR	29.72	29.79
22	CLR	NC			10.00		48	29	40	48	3	19	29.76	29.82
					SUNRISE: 0632		FEB 28		SUNSET: 1746					
01	OVC	055			10.00		49	26	40	41	0	00	29.77	29.84
04	OVC	050			10.00		47	37	42	69	0	00	29.78	29.85
07	OVC	055			10.00		46	37	42	71	6	07	29.82	29.88
10	SCT	NC			10.00		49	38	44	66	5	VR	29.81	29.87
13	BKN	033			10.00		53	33	44	47	10	11	29.76	29.83
16	OVC	037			10.00		51	32	43	48	5	13	29.76	29.83
19	OVC	033			10.00	-RA	46	39	43	77	12	09	29.72	29.79
22	OVC	008			4.00	BR	43	41	42	93	5	VR	29.72	29.78
					SUNRISE:		FEB 29		SUNSET:					
					SUNRISE:		FEB 30		SUNSET:					
					SUNRISE:		FEB 31		SUNSET:					

3-HOURLY OBSERVATION NOTES

Sky Cover is the amount of the sky obscured. CLR or SKC = 0, FEW = 1/8–2/8,
SCT = 3/8–4/8, BKN = 5/8–7/8, OVC = 8/8, VV = Vertical Visibilty = 8/8.
Ceiling is reported in hundreds of feet above ground level for clouds at or below 12,000 feet.
NC= No ceiling detected.
& = Original observation contained additional weather elements.
See page 3 for additional notes.

SUMMARY BY HOUR

HOUR (LST)	AVERAGES CEILOMETER	EFF CLD AMT	DRY BULB	DEW POINT	WET BULB	RELATIVE HUMIDITY	PRESSURE (INCHES,HG) STATION	PRESSURE (INCHES,HG) SEA LEVEL	VISIBILITY (MILES)	WIND SPEED (MPH)	RESULTANT WIND (MPH) SPEED	RESULTANT WIND (MPH) DIRECTION
01			39	25	34	59	29.85	29.93	8.71	7	3	3
02			38	25	34	61	29.86	29.93	9.04	8	4	4
03			38	25	33	60	29.85	29.93	9.15	7	4	4
04			38	25	33	61	29.85	29.92	9.30	8	4	4
05			37	25	33	62	29.85	29.93	9.63	7	4	5
06			37	25	33	63	29.86	29.94	9.07	8	5	5
07			37	25	32	63	29.87	29.94	9.12	7	5	5
08			37	25	33	63	29.88	29.96	8.69	8	5	4
09			38	25	33	60	29.89	29.96	8.70	8	4	4
10			40	25	34	58	29.89	29.97	8.61	8	5	4
11			41	25	35	54	29.89	29.96	9.00	7	3	3
12			43	24	36	50	29.87	29.95	9.21	7	3	5
13			44	25	37	50	29.85	29.93	9.39	7	4	4
14			44	24	37	48	29.84	29.91	9.29	7	4	5
15			44	26	37	51	29.83	29.91	9.43	8	3	2
16			44	26	37	52	29.83	29.90	9.07	7	3	4
17			43	26	37	54	29.83	29.91	9.18	8	4	3
18			43	27	37	56	29.84	29.92	9.32	7	3	3
19			42	27	36	59	29.85	29.93	8.88	8	3	4
20			41	28	36	62	29.85	29.93	8.61	8	4	6
21			41	28	36	63	29.86	29.93	8.61	8	3	4
22			40	27	35	62	29.86	29.93	8.71	8	4	4
23			40	27	35	62	29.85	29.92	8.65	7	3	6
24			40	26	35	62	29.85	29.92	8.70	8	4	4

PUBLISHED BY: NCDC, ASHEVILLE, NC. PAGE 6

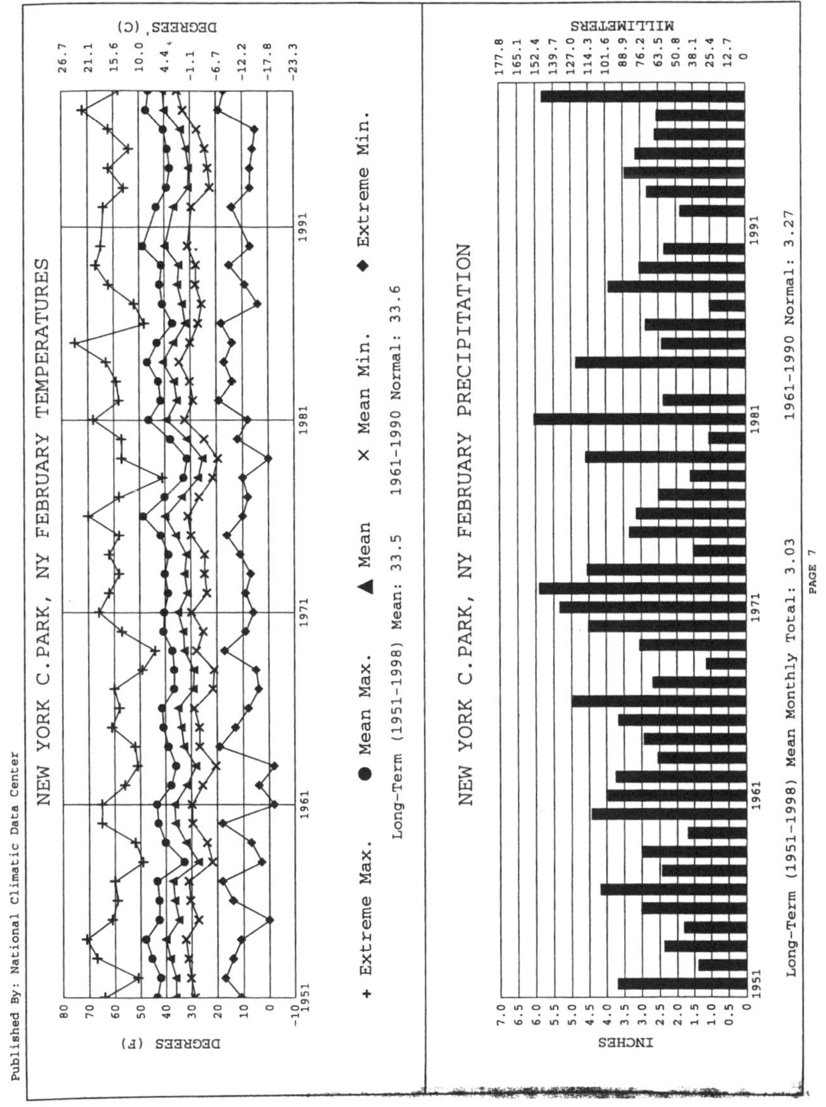
Published By: National Climatic Data Center
NEW YORK C.PARK, NY FEBRUARY TEMPERATURES
DEGREES (F)
DEGREES (C)
+ Extreme Max.
● Mean Max.
▲ Mean
× Mean Min.
◆ Extreme Min.
Long-Term (1951-1998) Mean: 33.5
1961-1990 Normal: 33.6
NEW YORK C.PARK, NY FEBRUARY PRECIPITATION
INCHES
MILLIMETERS
Long-Term (1951-1998) Mean Monthly Total: 3.03
1961-1990 Normal: 3.27
PAGE 7

Demonstrative Evidence 16

Demonstrative evidence is "evidence addressed directly to the senses without intervention of testimony."[1] In other words, the jury can see the evidence for what it is, e.g., a photograph of the scene of the accident, although a witness's testimony may be necessary to identify, explain, or introduce the evidence. The trial court has the authority to compel the production of demonstrative evidence, such as photographs, records, or papers that are present in the courtroom.[2] This chapter will discuss the demonstrative evidence used most often in actions for negligence: photographs, movies and recordings, diagrams and models, x-rays and blood samples, premises, and hospital and repair bills.

16.1 PHOTOGRAPHS

16.1.1 The General Rule

The general rule is that admitting photographs into evidence rests in the sound discretion of the trial court.[3] So long as the photograph is relevant to the issue of liability or damages and accurately reflects the condition of the scene

1. BLACK'S LAW DICTIONARY 419 (4th ed. 1968).
2. Bloodgood v. Lynch, 293 N.Y. 308, 56 N.E. 718 (1944).
3. Markey v. Eiseman, 114 A.D.2d 887, 495 N.Y.S.2d 61 (2d Dep't 1985); Wesler v. Kassl, 109 A.D.2d 740, 485 N.Y.S.2d 844 (2d Dep't 1985); People v. Winchell, 98 A.D.2d 838, 470 N.Y.S.2d 835 (3d Dep't 1983).

at the time of the incident or accurately reflects the plaintiff's injuries, then the court should admit the photograph for the jury's consideration.[4] Anyone who is familiar with the scene at the time of the incident may testify that the photograph is an accurate depiction;[5] this witness need not be the photographer. However, if no one testifies that the photograph accurately reflects the scene or product at the relevant time, the photograph is not admissible.[6] For example, if the photograph purports to show the positions of the automobiles after the collision, there must be preliminary testimony that the automobiles were not moved before the photograph was taken.[7] Of course, the photograph is inadmissible if the witnesses testify that it is not a fair representation.[8]

Once admitted into evidence, the photograph may be the basis for expert testimony like any other evidence.[9] There are situations in which the setting or occurrence cannot be duplicated, and, in those situations, a photograph may be the best evidence of the condition at the crucial time.[10]

---

4. FED. R. EVID. 901, 403 (the general exclusionary rule); see Busch, *Photographic Evidence*, 4 DEPAUL L. REV. 195 (1955).
5. Archer v. New York, N.Y. & H. R.R., 106 N.Y. 589 (1887); Annot., *Authentication or Verification of Photograph as Basis for Introduction in Evidence*, 9 A.L.R.2D 899 (1950).
6. Keefner v. City of Albany, 77 A.D.2d 747, 430 N.Y.S.2d 877 (3d Dep't 1980). For a decision excluding the photograph of a product because the photograph was not taken at a relevant time, *see* Saratoga Spa & Bath, Inc. v. Beeche Systems Corp., 230 A.D.2d 326 (3d Dep't 1997).
7. Roberson v. Keogh, 66 A.D.2d 816, 411 N.Y.S.2d 370 (2d Dep't 1978).
8. People v. Tortorice, 142 A.D.2d 916 (3d Dep't 1988).
9. Markey v. Eiseman, 114 A.D.2d 887, 495 N.Y.S.2d 61 (2d Dep't 1985); Bolm v. Triumph Corp., 71 A.D.2d 429, 422 N.Y.S.2d 969 (4th Dep't), *aff'd*, 33 N.Y.2d 151 (1974).
10. Bolm v. Triumph Corp., 71 A.D.2d 429, 422 N.Y.S.2d 969 (4th Dep't 1979).

16.1.2 Posed Photographs of the Scene

Although posed photographs are generally not admissible, some such photographs are.[11] Thus, one foreign court admitted a photograph of the scene of a highway accident, which photograph showed a witness standing on the road and pointing to certain marks on the roadway, because the only purpose of the witness's presence in the picture was to draw attention to fixed marks that were present immediately after the accident.[12] Sometimes a map marked by a witness during the witness's testimony is a more lucid alternative.[13]

16.1.3 Photographs of Injuries

The trial court has the discretion to admit photographs of the plaintiff's injuries, even if the injuries are unsightly, when the plaintiff offers the photographs on the issue of damages and the photographs are relevant to the jury's understanding of the plaintiff's injuries.[14] In other words, gruesome photographs are not necessarily inadmissible.[15] Hence, the court properly admitted color photographs of the plaintiff lying on a Stryker frame with Crutchfield tongs attached to his scalp.[16] Even though the plaintiff's scars are

---

11. Annot., *Admissibility of Posed Photograph Based on Recollection of Position of Persons or Moveable Objects*, 19 A.L.R.2D (1951).
12. Square Deal Cartage Co. v. Smith's Adm'r, 307 Ky. 135, 210 S.W.2d 340 (1948).
13. *See* section 16.3 *infra.*
14. Gallo v. Supermarkets Gen. Corp., 112 A.D.2d 345, 491 N.Y.S.2d 796 (2d Dep't 1985); Caprara v. Chrysler Corp., 71 A.D.2d 515, 423 N.Y.S.2d 694 (3d Dep't 1979), *aff'd*, 52 N.Y.2d 114, 417 N.E.2d 545, 436 N.Y.S.2d 251 (1981); Note, *Admission of Gruesome Photograph in Homicide Prosecution*, 16 CREIGHTON L. REV. 73 (1982).
15. Knox v. City of Granite Falls, 245 Minn. 11, 19, 72 N.W.2d 67, 73 (1955). In fact, photographs of the plaintiff showing his lacerations and sutures and taken while the plaintiff was still in the hospital were held admissible in New v. Cortright, 32 A.D.2d 576, 299 N.Y.S.2d 43 (3d Dep't 1969). *See* Gomaco Corp. v. Faith, 550 So. 2d 482 (Fla. App. 1989).
16. Caprara v. Chrysler Corp., 71 A.D.2d 515, 423 N.Y.S.2d 694 (3d Dep't 1979), *aff'd*, 52 N.Y.2d 114, 417 N.E.2d 545, 436 N.Y.S.2d 251 (1981).

obvious to the jury, the plaintiff may introduce the photographs of the injuries so that the appellate court can better understand their nature[17] or so that the jury can assess the plaintiff's pain and suffering.[18] Courts have admitted color slides of a plaintiff's injuries as well as black-and-white photographs.[19]

The court of appeals has ruled, however, that it was prejudicial to admit a photograph of the decedent in an action for wrongful death.[20]

16.1.4 Photographs to Prove Notice

As we discussed in chapter 6, photographs are admissible to prove that the defendant had constructive notice of a defective or dangerous condition.[21] If a witness at the deposition marked a photograph to indicate the place at which the accident occurred, that photograph is admissible at the trial, assuming the party's attorney laid a proper foundation for the photograph at the deposition.[22]

---

17. Carlisle v. County of Nassau, 64 A.D.2d 15, 408 N.Y.S.2d 114 (2d Dep't 1978).
18. Krueger v. Frisenda, 218 A.D.2d 685 (2d Dep't 1995).
19. Annot., *Admissibility in Evidence of Colored Photographs*, 53 A.L.R.2D 1102 (1978).
20. Smith v. Lehigh Valley R.R., 177 N.Y. 379, 384, 69 N.E. 729, 730 (1904), and Allen v. Stokes, 260 N.Y. 600 (1940); Annot., *Admissibility in Wrongful Death Action, of Photograph of Decedent Made in Her Lifetime*, 74 A.L.R. 928 (1960). *See also* Annot., *Admissibility of Photograph of Corpse in Prosecution for Homicide or Civil Action for Causing Death*, 73 A.L.R.2D 769 (1960). However, in Mayes v. County of Nassau, 31 A.D.2d 638, 295 N.Y.S.2d 989 (2d Dep't 1968), the appellate court held that although the trial court should not have admitted the photograph of the deceased plaintiff, the error was not prejudicial as to require an unconditional reversal.
21. *See also* Taylor v. New York City Transit Auth., 48 N.Y.2d 903, 400 N.E.2d 1340, 424 N.Y.S.2d 888 (1976); Batton v. Agradgon, 43 N.Y.2d 898, 374 N.E.2d 611, 403 N.Y.S.2d 717 (1973), and Karten v. City of New York, 109 A.D.2d 126 (1st Dep't 1985). Although these cases pre-date written notice ordinances, the means of proving constructive notice are still appropriate against private defendants and for other kinds of accidents.
22. Roach v. City of Albany, 282 A.D. 807, 122 N.Y.S.2d 437 (3d Dep't 1955).

If, between the time of the accident and the taking of the photograph, there have been minor changes in the condition of the premises that do not affect any important issue, the trial court should admit the photograph into evidence.[23] However, if the change was substantial[24] or if repairs have been made, the court should not admit the photograph. The reason in the latter case is that an opposing party may prove subsequent repairs only if control of the premises is an issue.[25] For example, if the exterior staircase had no handrail at the time of the accident, and that fact underlines the plaintiff's claim of negligence, it would be prejudicial to the

---

23. FED. R. EVID. 407; Amsler v. City of N.Y., 172 A.D. 63, 58 N.Y.S. 219 (1st Dep't 1916). *See also* Robertson v. Giangrasso, 7 A.D.2d 733, 735, 180 N.Y.S.2d 627, 628 (2d Dep't 1958), which held that "it was error to exclude the testimony proffered by appellant as to the condition of respondents' vehicle and the photograph taken *one-half hour after the accident* away from the scene thereof." (Emphasis added.) The court cited Simon v. Ora Realty Corp., 1 N.Y.2d 388, 393, 135 N.E.2d 580, 582, 153 N.Y.S.2d 39, 42 (1956) ("the trial court should have permitted the introduction of evidence of the condition of the ash can *on the day following the accident* since, without proof to the contrary it was reasonable to assume that its then condition was substantially the same as at the time in question." (Emphasis added.) *See also* Peil v. Reinhart, 127 N.Y. 381, 385, 27 N.E. 1077, 1078 (1891) ("[T]here was no error in the reception of the evidence of the condition of the stair carpet the morning following the injury."); Coffin v. Cunningham, 11 A.D.2d 1082, 206 N.Y.S.2d 353 (4th Dep't 1960) (a witness who had arrived at the scene of an accident shortly after it had occurred could properly testify to the fire marks that appeared in newly fallen snow and led to a vehicle involved in the accident).
24. In Dugan v. Dieber, 32 A.D.2d 815, 302 N.Y.S.2d 423 (2d Dep't 1969), the appellate court held that it was prejudicial to the plaintiff to admit photographs taken of a street where apartment houses had replaced private houses and that showed different parking conditions with cars not parked close together. *But see* Saporito v. City of N.Y., 14 N.Y.2d 474, 202 N.E.2d 369, 253 N.Y.S.2d 985 (1964), in which the court of appeals held that it was error to exclude the defendants' offer of photographs of the condition of the roadway when the plaintiff claimed that there had been a hole in the roadway, for "[i]t did not impair the admissibility of these photographs that they showed the building abutting the street, or the presence of rubbish or other debris on the sidewalk, if, as was testified by several witnesses, they correctly showed the condition of the pavement 15 feet out into the street."
25. Scudero v. Campbell, 288 N.Y. 328, 43 N.E.2d 66 (1942); Feinstein v. New York City Transit Auth., 17 Misc. 2d 45, 190 N.Y.S.2d 304 (2d Dep't 1958) (evidence that a subway platform had been sanded after the accident was not admissible).

defendant to admit a photograph that was taken months later and that shows a handrail.

Of course, the parties may dispute whether a particular photograph accurately represents the condition of the scene at the time of the incident, and both may introduce photographs. Thus, in an action against a county for the death of a passenger in an automobile that had gone over a precipitous embankment into a river, the court of appeals held that the trial court had properly permitted the plaintiff to show that the guardrails had not been installed at the time of the accident because the defendant had introduced, as a fair representation of the conditions at the time of the accident, a photograph of the roadway showing that there had been guardrails.[26]

Example 16-1, at the end of the chapter, is the paragraph demanding that the opposing party produce any relevant photograph. And examples 16-1A, 16-1B, and 16-1C are, respectively, a posed photograph of the scene of an auto accident, a photograph of the plaintiff's injuries, and a photograph establishing notice of a dangerous condition.

26. Huston v. City of Chenango, 253 A.D. 56, 1 N.Y.S.2d 252 (3d Dep't 1934), *aff'd*, 278 N.Y. 646, 16 N.E.2d 301 (1938).

16.2 MOVIES, VIDEOTAPES, AND TAPE RECORDINGS

16.2.1 Admissibility

Motion pictures or videotapes are admissible only if they are relevant and only if they are not cumulative, sensational, or prejudicial.[27] Thus, a motion picture of an allegedly injured plaintiff working around the house or a "day-in-the-life" film of an injured party might be relevant, but the film must be accurate, and the person who made the film must testify to the facts surrounding the film. In other words, the rule for introducing films differs from the rule for introducing still photographs since any person with knowledge of the scene may testify that the photograph is an accurate representation. He need not be the photographer, but the witness who introduces moving pictures must have participated in the filming.

A good example of how a court evaluates the admissibility of a movie or videotape is *Mechanick v. Conradi,*[28] in which the Appellate Division, Third Department, upheld the trial court's refusal to admit a videotape by which the plaintiff intended to show the sighting distances at the scene of the accident between his motorcycle and the defendant's vehicle. The appellate court observed that admitting such a videotape lies in the discretion of the trial court, de-

---

27. Boyarsky v. G.A. Zinnerman Corp., 240 A.D. 361, 270 N.Y.S. 134 (1st Dep't 1934); Gibson v. Gunn, 206 A.D. 464, 202 N.Y.S. 19 (1st Dep't 1923); Annot., *Use of Motion Pictures as Evidence*, 62 A.L.R.2D 686 (1958). On authentication, see People v. Turnstall, 97 A.D.2d 523, 468 N.Y.S.2d 32 (2d Dep't 1983); Peters v. Wiles, *Videotaping of Surgery for Use as Demonstrative Evidence in Medical Malpractice Litigation*, 16 DUQUESNE L. REV. 360 (1978); Wells, *Motion Pictures in Evidence*, 8 BROOKLYN L. REV. 290 (1939); *see also* Repple v. Barnes Hosp., 778 S.W.2d 819 (Mo. App. 1989); Annot., *Authentication or Verification of Moving Pictures as Basis for Introduction in Evidence*, 9 A.L.R.2D 921 (1950).
28. Mechanick v. Conradi, 139 A.D.2d 857, 527 N.Y.S.2d 586 (3d Dep't 1988).

pends on the circumstances of the case, and requires that the videotape not exaggerate any feature the party seeks to prove. The court then pointed out the videotape's deficiencies, to wit:

> [T]he videotape depicted a full-size van heading south on Route 147 instead of a motorcycle. It presented a north-bound view of what defendant would have seen but never shows what plaintiff would have seen while traveling south. Moreover, the videotape could have unfairly misled the jury since the van was clearly more visible than the motorcycle. Additionally, large red cones were placed on the side of the road as visual reference markers which were obviously not there at the time of the accident. The use of a telephoto lens also enhanced defendant's alleged sight distance. Finally, the van was operated at speeds no greater than 55 miles per hour, which, while consistent with plaintiff's claim that he was not speeding, contradicted the trooper's testimony that plaintiff was speeding.

Therefore, the trial court had properly refused to admit the videotape.

Audiotapes are also admissible, but they are admitted less often than movies or videotapes because it would be a rare instance in which an audiotape could depict the accident, the scene, or an injury. However, if authenticated as accurate, a tape recording of a person speaking may be admissible to establish an admission against interest.[29] In addition, tapes of 911 calls may be admissible as excited utterances[30] or present-sense impressions. (See chapter 17.)

---

29. Tepper v. Tannenbaum, 65 A.D.2d 359, 411 N.Y.S.2d 588 (1st Dep't 1978).
30. People v. Lewis, 635 N.Y.S.2d 872 (4th Dep't 1995).

16.2.2 Discovery

The rule in New York is that the plaintiff is entitled to discovery of all surveillance films or videotapes made of the plaintiff for the defendant and of redacted copies of the defense attorney's memoranda about the tapes. However, the defendant need not produce the tapes and the memoranda until after he or she has taken the plaintiff's deposition, and, if the defendant does not introduce the surveillance tapes at the trial, the plaintiff's attorney may not even comment on this choice.

According to one commentator in 1993, "the use of videotape evidence has grown dramatically over the last 10 years as the cost associated with its production has dropped and as more companies have become willing and able to perform surveillance."[31] One result of the popularity of this form of investigation was that every appellate division was required to rule on the discovery of these tapes, but the four departments formulated three different rules.[32] Fortunately, the court of appeals heard two companion cases from the Fourth Department. Thus, in *DiMichel v. South Buffalo Railway Co.* and *Poole v. Consolidated Rail Corporation,*[33] the court held,

> [W]e agree . . . that surveillance films should be treated as material prepared in anticipation of litigation, and as such, are subject to a qualified privilege that can be overcome only by a factual showing of substantial need and undue hardship.
>
> That the plaintiffs in both these cases have a substantial need to view surveillance films before trial is manifest.[34]

---

31. James P. Connors, *Assault on an Effective Way to Expose Fraud,* N.Y.L.J., Dec. 1, 1993, at 2.
32. Marte v. W. O. Hickok Manufacturing Co., 154 A.D.2d 173 (1st Dep't 1990); Careccia v. Enstrom, 174 A.D.2d 48 (3d Dep't 1992); Kane v. Her-Pet Refrigeration, 181 A.D.2d 257 (2d Dep't 1992); and DiMichel v. South Buffalo Railway Co., 178 A.D.2d 914 (4th Dep't 1991).
33. DiMichel v. South Buffalo Railway Co., 80 N.Y.2d 184, 590 N.Y.S.2d 1 (1992).
34. *Id.* at 196.

In other words, any plaintiff's need for the films overcomes the defendant's privilege almost ipso facto.

The legislature codified the central holding of *DiMichel* in C.P.L.R. section 3101(i): " . . . , there shall be full disclosure of any films, photographs, video tapes or audio tapes, including transcripts or memoranda thereof, involving a person referred to in paragraph one of subdivision (a) of this section. There shall be disclosure of all portions of such material, including out-takes, rather than only those portions a party intends to use." C.P.L.R. section 3101(a)(1) enumerated a party or the officer, director, member, agent, or employee of a party.

However, the attorney still must refer to the court's opinion in *DiMichel* for other elements of the court's decision, and the attorney should remember that the court was concerned to protect each party from dishonesty by the other. Thus, although the court decided that the possibility of the defendant's manipulating the tape required that the plaintiff receive a copy before the trial, the possibility of the plaintiff's altering his testimony required that the defendant be allowed to withhold that copy until after he had taken the plaintiff's deposition.[35] Moreover, if the defendant produces the surveillance film but decides not to use it at the trial, then the plaintiff's attorney may not even comment on this choice.[36] Most commentators have interpreted this prohibition as implying a fortiori that the plaintiff may not introduce the surveillance film as part of his or her direct case,[37] but one court has allowed the plaintiff to introduce the defendant's surveillance films during the damage phase.[38]

---

35. *Id.* at 197. This was the position of the Appellate Division, First Department, in Marte v. W.O. Hickok Manufacturing, 154 A.D.2d 173 (___) and in Rodgers v. City of New York, N.Y.L.J., June 11, 1992, at 24.
36. *DiMichel, supra* at 199.
37. For example, Susan C. Roney and Laurie Styka Bloom, letter to ed., N.Y.L.J., Oct. 28, 1993, at 2.
38. Baird v. Campbell, N.Y.L.J., Oct. 30, 1992, at 34 (Sup. Ct. Queens).

16.3 DIAGRAMS, MODELS, ANATOMICAL EXHIBITS, AND DEMONSTRATIONS

The trial court has considerable latitude to admit diagrams, models, etc.,[39] and a map, diagram, or model that has been properly authenticated is clearly admissible.[40] A diagram or survey need not have been made by a surveyor or have been drawn to scale. Anyone, e.g., an investigator, may have drawn the diagram, and it becomes admissible when the witness testifies regarding how the area was measured and certifies the diagram's accuracy.[41] For example, in an action for wrongful death due to the collapse of a temporary bridge, the plaintiff produced what he claimed was a model of the bridge. The plaintiff called a witness who testified that he had constructed the model and who detailed the construction. Another witness testified that the model correctly represented the bridge at the time of the accident. The trial court then admitted the model into evidence although the defendant disputed the model's accuracy.[42]

The trial court has the discretion to permit a party's attorney to use anatomical charts or models of parts of the body.[43] It is proper for the attorney to use a skull to explain to the jury the nature of the injuries to the plaintiff's eye.[44]

---

39. *See* Ladd, *Demonstrative Evidence and Expert Opinion*, 1956 WASH. U. L.Q. 1; Article, *Charts, Graphs and Mini Summations*, 16 LITIG. 1, at 21 (Fall 1989).
40. Clegg v. Metropolitan St. Ry., 1 A.D. 207, 37 N.Y.S. 130 (2d Dep't 1896), *aff'd*, 159 N.Y. 550, 54 N.E.2d 1089 (1899).
41. Annot., *Evidence: Use and Admissibility of Maps, Plats, and Other Drawings to Illustrate or Express Testimony*, 9 A.L.R.2D 1044 (1950); Annot., *Admissibility in Evidence, in Automobile Negligence Action, of Charts Showing Braking Distance, Reaction Times, Etc.*, 9 A.L.R.3D 976 (1966).
42. Coolidge v. City of N.Y., 99 A.D. 175, 90 N.Y.S. 1078 (1st Dep't 1904), *aff'd*, 185 N.Y. 529, 77 N.E. 1192 (1906). *See* Annot., *Propriety, in Trial of Civil Action, of Use of Model of Object or Instrumentality or of Site or Premises, Involved in the Accident or Incident*, 69 A.L.R.2D 424 (1960).
43. Dietz v. Aronson, 244 A.D. 746, 299 N.Y.S.2d 66 (2d Dep't 1935).
44. McNair v. Manhattan Ry., 51 Hun. 644, 4 N.Y.S. 310 (Gen. Term 2d Dep't 1889), *aff'd*, 123 N.Y. 664, 26 N.E. 750 (1890).

In such a case, *McNaier v. Manhattan Railway Co.*, the appellate court wrote:

> The objection of defendant to the use of a skull to explain to the jury the nature of plaintiff's injuries is not well taken, nor was the objection to the exhibition of the surgical instruments, by which the operation was performed, valid . . . . To suppose that the sight of a skull and the instruments, used, as they were, to explain the injury and the operation necessary to relieve it, should have "inflamed the passion of the jury" is quite unreasonable.[45]

The party's attorney or witness may draw the chart or diagram, and the trial court has the discretion to permit the use of a blackboard.[46] The court may even admit an object as an illustration of missing tangible evidence rather than as a scale model, e.g., a baseball bat similar to the one with which the defendant supposedly murdered his victim.[46.1]

A party's attorney may even arrange a demonstration. Hence, in *Uss v. Town of Oyster Bay*,[47] the court of appeals held that the trial court should have permitted a demonstration, although the circumstances were not identical to those of the accident, because the opposing party had an unrestricted right to cross-examine the person performing the demonstration. However, in *DiSanto v. County of Westchester*,[48] a slip and fall case, the trial court properly refused to

---

45. *Id.* at 645, 4 N.Y.S. at 311; *see* Annot., *Propriety in Trial of Civil Action, Use of Skeleton or Model of Human Body or Part*, 58 A.L.R.2D 689 (1958).

46. McKay v. Lasher, 121 N.Y. 477, 483, 24 N.E. 711, 712 (1890); *see also* Haley v. Hockey, 199 Misc. 512, 103 N.Y.S.2d 717 (Sup. Ct. 1950) (it was proper to place figures on a blackboard during the plaintiff's summation). *See* Annot., *Counsel's Use in Trial of Personal Injury or Wrongful Death Case of Blackboard, Chart, Diagram or Placard, Not Introduced in Evidence Relating to Damages*, 86 A.L.R.2D 239 (1962).

46.1. People v. Langley, 232 A.D.2d 427 (2d Dep't 1996), *appeal denied*, 89 N.Y.2d 865 (1996).

47. Uss v. Town of Oyster Bay, 37 N.Y.2d 639, 399 N.E.2d 147, 376 N.Y.S.2d 449 (1975).

48. DiSanto v. County of Westchester, 210 A.D.2d 628 (3d Dep't 1994).

let the plaintiffs demonstrate that fuel and water do not mix and that fuel floats thereby creating a slippery condition. The plaintiff could not prove that this demonstration would replicate the conditions at the scene of the accident.

Example 16-2 is a map of a county park.[49] Assume that an equestrian organization held a point-to-point contest on the same Sunday that an orienteering club held an orienteering contest and that a rider trampled an orienteer. A witness, such as an employee of the park, could testify to the accuracy of the map and then mark on this copy the sign saying "No Horses Beyond This Point" and the spot of the accident.

16.4 X-RAYS AND BLOOD SAMPLES

16.4.1 X-Rays

A medical test can result in demonstrative evidence when the test produces an object, such as an x-ray negative.

C.P.L.R. rule 4532-a establishes three requirements for admitting x-rays into evidence in an action for personal injury. First, the name of the injured party, the date, an identifying number, and the name and address of the supervising physician must be inscribed photographically on the x-ray. Second, at least ten days before the trial, the attorney for the party offering the x-ray must serve on the opposing party's attorney a notice of intention to offer the x-ray into evidence and the availability of the x-ray for inspection. Third, an affidavit from the supervising physician must accompany the notice and attest both to the inscribed information and that the physician would so testify.

---

49. The map is provided by the courtesy of John Pekarik, the president of the Long Island Orienteering Club.

Note that the attorney's compliance with this section must be strict and literal, or the trial court will not admit the x-ray unless it qualifies for admission under C.P.L.R. rule 4518, the business record exception.[50] Judge Joseph McLaughlin, in his commentary to C.P.L.R. rule 4532-a,[51] states that the section has a flaw in it that allows a party to introduce x-rays without calling a physician to interpret them. While that technically may be true, the trial court has the discretion to rule that the jury cannot interpret the x-ray and that the plaintiff's failure to call a physician to do so will result in nonsuiting the complaint.

16.4.2 Blood Samples

When relevant, e.g., when the blood alcohol level of a party is in issue, the results of a blood test are admissible. Generally, the person who performed the test must testify regarding the test performed, the results it produced, and what they mean. However, the technician's supervisor may testify instead.[52] Another problem with such evidence has always been that the party offering it had to establish the chain of custody of the blood sample to the smallest detail: any lapse or mistake usually meant that the test's results were not admissible.[53] In *Timmons v. Hecker,*[54] however, the Appellate Division, Second Department, held, "any purported deficiencies in the chain of custody relating to blood samples taken from the deceased . . . went to the weight and not the

---

50. Galuska v. Arbaiza, 106 A.D.2d 543, 482 N.Y.S.2d 846 (2d Dep't 1984).

51. 7B McKinney's C.P.L.R. §§ 3401-5100 Supp. Pamphlet 420 (1987).

52. Amaro v. City of N.Y., 40 N.Y.2d 30, 351 N.E.2d 665, 386 N.Y.S.2d 19 (1976). Note that the chain of custody of a photograph or a tape recording is not so important because such an item has its own identifiable characteristics whereas one sample of blood or drugs looks much like another. People v. Arena, 65 A.D.2d 182 (4th Dep't 1978).

53. For a DNA test, see Pepole v. Vega, 255 A.D.2d 890, 639 N.Y.S.2d 511 (3d Dep't 1996); for a test on suspected narcotics, see People v. Torres, 213 A.D.2d 797, 632 N.Y.S.2d 645 (3d Dep't 1995), *appeal denied*, 86 N.Y.2d 784 (1995).

54. Timmons v. Hecker, 110 A.D.2d 762, 488 N.Y.S.2d 49 (2d Dep't 1985).

admissibility of the resulting report." Then the pendulum swung back. In *North v. Travelers' Insurance Co.*, the Appellate Division, Fourth Department, denied the defendant's motion for summary judgment because there was no evidence regarding how the plaintiff's blood sample was obtained, handled, or analyzed.[55]

The results of a test for blood alcohol are admissible in an action for personal injuries even if the person tested was not convicted of drunken driving and even if he did not consent to the test, as long as the test was performed legally and properly.[56]

Example 16-3 consists of the results of common blood tests. Note that, in accordance with a recent trend, the form includes the normal range next to the result of each test.

16.5 INSPECTION OF THE PREMISES

C.P.L.R. section 4110-c provides for the jury's inspection of premises. If the trial court decides that viewing the place where the accident or its cause occurred, the place where the injuries were sustained, or other relevant premises will help the jury to determine a material factual issue, then the court has the discretion to order the jury conducted to that place before the summations. The court may be present during the inspection, and the parties and their attorneys have a right to be present, but an official appointed by the court must keep the jurors together. The sole purpose of the inspection is to permit the jury to observe the place or premises, and neither the court, the parties, their attorneys, nor the jurors themselves may discuss the case.

The attorney should remember that whether to permit an inspection of the premises is discretionary with the court.[57] That a juror visited the scene of the accident is not inherent-

55. North v. Travelers' Insurance Co., 218 A.D.2d 901 (3d Dep't 1995).
56. Fafinski v. Reliance Ins. Co., 106 A.D.2d 88, 484 N.Y.S.2d 729 (4th Dep't 1985).
57. Cole v. Lawas, 97 A.D.2d 912, 470 N.Y.S.2d 747 (3d Dep't 1983).

ly prejudicial,[58] but the court must assure itself that this improper act will not affect the jury's deliberation. If the juror's visit will affect the deliberations, then the trial court must grant a mistrial.

16.6 HOSPITAL AND REPAIR BILLS

Two statutory provisions govern using bills as evidence. One provision applies to hospital bills; the other applies to all repairs and services, including medical care, but only up to the amount of $1,500.

The provision governing hospital bills is C.P.L.R. rule 4518(b), which states that a hospital bill is admissible and is prima facie evidence of the facts contained therein provided that the bill bears a certification that it is correct, that each of the items was supplied necessarily, and that the amount charged was reasonable. There is no monetary limit.

The provision governing bills for repairs and services is C.P.L.R. rule 4533-a. This rule provides that a party may introduce an itemized bill, receipted or marked paid, for repairs or services not exceeding $2,000. Such a bill is prima facie evidence of the reasonable value and necessity for the repairs provided that the business that made the repairs certifies the bill and includes a verified statement that no part of the payment will be refunded to the debtor and that the charges are the customary ones. In addition, the party offering the bill in evidence must, at least ten days before the trial, serve on the other parties a notice of intention accompanied by a true copy of the bill. Finally, only one such bill from the same provider to the same customer may be introduced in one action.

Since C.P.L.R. rule 4533-a applies to services as well as repairs, the court of appeals has construed the rule to govern medical bills as well as bills for repairs to property.[59] The

58. Alford v. Sventek, 53 N.Y.2d 743, 421 N.E.2d 831, 439 N.Y.S.2d 339 (1981).

59. River v. State, 115 Misc. 2d 523, 454 N.Y.S.2d 408 (Ct. Cl. 1982).

bill constitutes prima facie evidence of the facts it contains, creates a true presumption, and must be rebutted by evidence to the contrary, or the trial court must find that the amount of the bill is binding on the opposing party. However, a medical bill cannot establish that the defendant's negligence was the proximate cause of the plaintiff's injury.[60]

Example 16-4 is a sample of a certified hospital bill.

60. *Id.*

EXAMPLE 16-1: DEMAND FOR PHOTOGRAPH

2. Demand is hereby made that you produce for inspection and photocopying any and all photographs in your possession or in the custody or control of any party that you represent, depicting the location which is the subject of this occurrence, the location where the accident occurred, or depicting the plaintiff or the plaintiff's physical condition, injuries, disability, or any lack thereof, for inspection and photocopying. Please take notice that an application will be made at trial to preclude any photographs not produced in response to this demand.

EXAMPLE 16-1A: STAGED PHOTO OF SCENE OF ACCIDENT

EXAMPLE 16-1B: PHOTOGRAPH OF PATIENT'S INJURIES

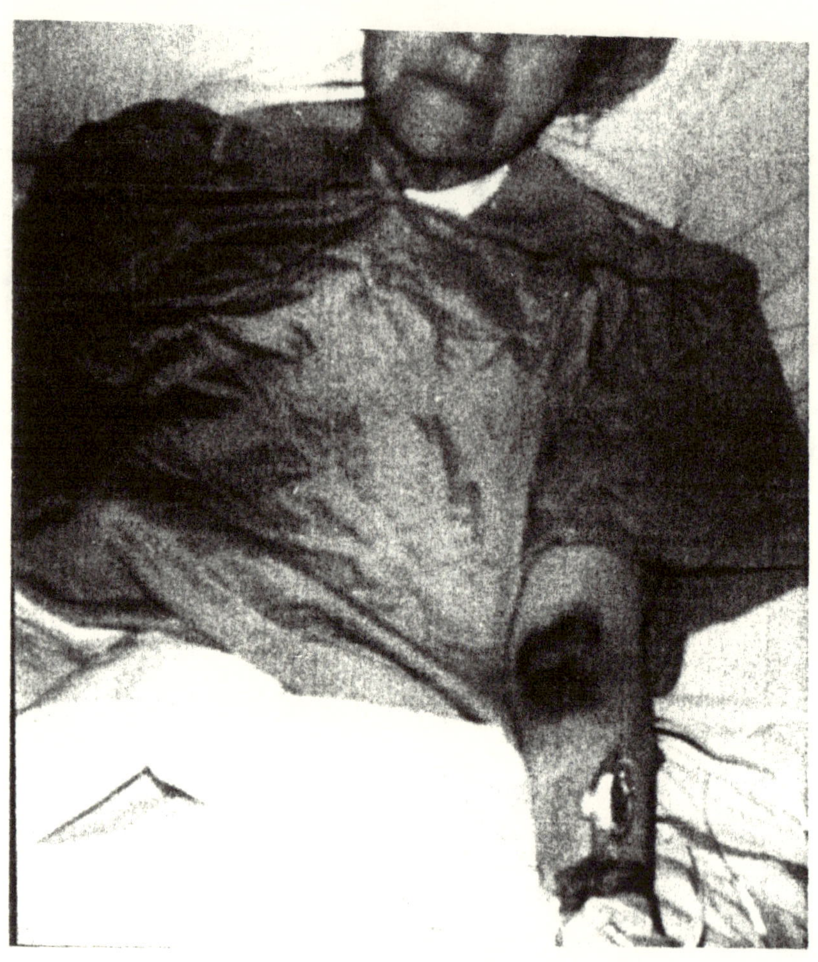

EXAMPLE 16-1C: PHOTOGRAPH ESTABLISHING NOTICE

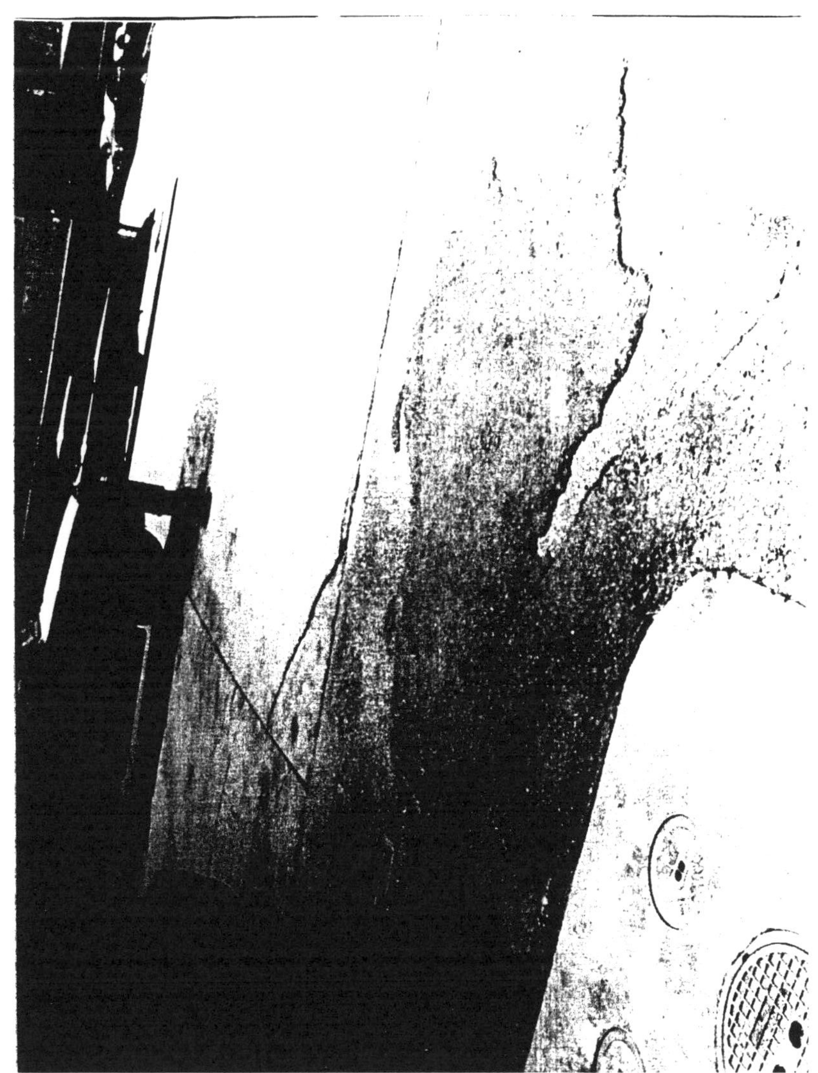

EXAMPLE 16-2: MAP

Orienteering

involves the mind and the body. With the aid of a map and compass, you find your way on foot across the countryside from check point to check point. Your imagination and skills choose the best route. The course has orange and white markers (check points or controls) at the locations designated on your map. You visit each control in sequence and punch a score card. Each punch perforates your card with a different design verifying your visit.

Orienteering courses are usually set in a pleasant forest environment and you set your own pace. You can treat orienteering as a highly competitive race of navigational skill and physical speed or as a hike through the woods with the added fun of finding the orange and white controls. Orienteering can be enjoyed by everyone. Meet organizers generally set short courses for new orienteers and longer, more complicated courses for experienced orienteers. At large meets there are over 35 categories based upon age, sex and skill level. These categories for males and females are broken down into age groups from under 12 to over 55 years of age spread over 6 different courses of various lengths and levels of difficulty. You orienteer on a course comparable to your experience and fitness. Course lengths range from under 3 to over 12 KM in length.

Orienteering is usually an individual effort but it is also common to see groups or families hiking around an orienteering course together. Orienteering lends itself to many variations and can be done from a canoe, on skis, on horseback, or on a bicycle. the skills learned can be used by hunters, hikers, and backpackers. Fitness and experiencing the outdoors come naturally with this sport.

Long Island Orienteering Club

62 KNOLLWOOD DRIVE, CARLE PLACE, N.Y. 11514
Affiliate Member of United States Orienteering Federation ©

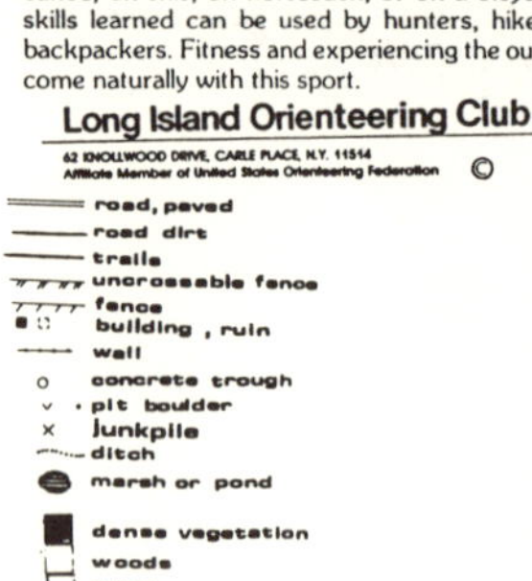

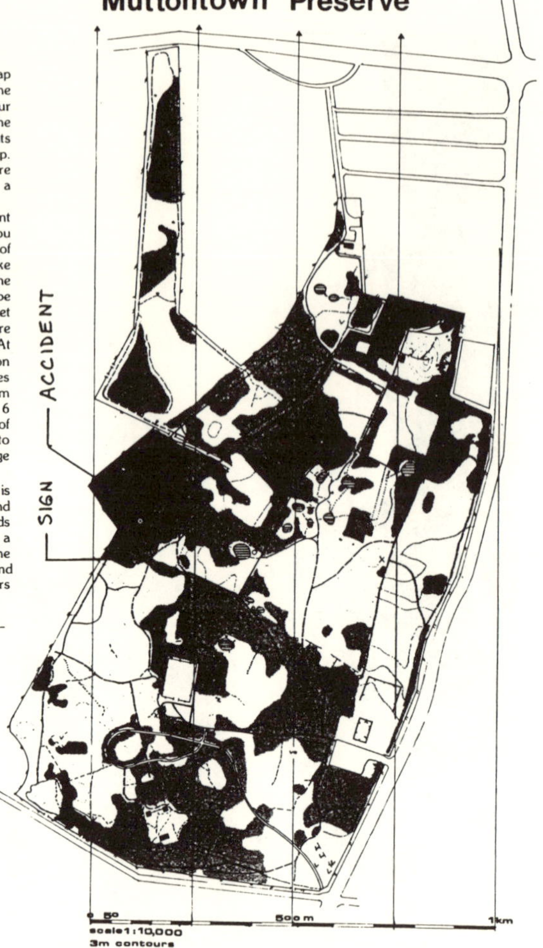

EXAMPLE 16-3: RESULTS OF BLOOD TESTS

MEDICAL DIRECTOR
708 993 1500
800 597 8026

National Health Laboratories Incorporated
LABORATORY REPORT
"Quality Results Through Exceptional People"

ELMHURST, IL 60126
CLIA #14D0703742
CAP #44212-01

DATE REPORTED	DATE RECEIVED	PATIENT NAME – I.D.	PHONE	AGE	SEX
15-SEP-95	15-SEP-95	MCMULLEN, KEVIN		48	M

DATE COLLECTED	TIME COLLECTED	HOSPITAL I.D.	REQUISITION NO.	ACCESSION NO.
14-SEP-95	6:00 AM		A07340751	4383450-5

CLIENT NAME/ADDRESS		TEST REQUESTED
P.H.S.	87614-4	PROFILE [illegible]-4.
HEALTH UNIT RM 2010	[SL]	
9700 PAGE BLVD	[90]	
SAINT LOUIS, MO 63121	9031-56505.002	

PHYSICIAN	VOLUME	FASTING	PATIENT SS#	COMMENTS
		YES		

TEST NAME	RESULT	UNITS	REFERENCE RANGE
GLUCOSE, PLASMA OR SERUM:			
GLUCOSE	82	MG/DL	65 - 115
CORONARY RISK PROFILE I:			
CHOLESTEROL	173	MG/DL	DESIRABLE: <200
TRIGLYCERIDES	57	MG/DL	30 - 150
HDL-CHOLESTEROL	43	MG/DL	30 - 75
CHOL/HDL RATIO	4.0		AV:4.2-7.3
LDL (CALCULATED)	119	MG/DL	< 130
LDL/HDL RATIO	2.8		< 3.1
VLDL (CALCULATED)	11	MG/DL	< 39
RISK FACTOR	< 1		=< 1

EXAMPLE 16-4: CERTIFIED HOSPITAL BILL

MED CTR
BLVD
, NY 11421

215

:EN 21 F / / / /

1 30 B23

DRIVE
NY 11

ᴙY OF CHARGES				
C U 9DAYS@	1300.00	11700.00	11700.00
E.R. VISIT	236	65.00	65.00
LAB/MICRO	421	5989.00	5989.00
CYTO PATHOLOGY	423	88.00	88.00
VASCULAR LAB	119	170.00	170.00
BLOOD PROCESS	426	625.00	625.00
RADIOLOGY	432	3960.00	3960.00
CAT SCAN	434	290.00	290.00
ULTRA DIAG	127	373.00	373.00
EKG	429	280.00	280.00
EEG	446	70.00	70.00
PHARMACY	415	2502.55	2502.55
RESP/PULMONARY	442	2145.00	2145.00

SUB-TOTAL OF CHARGES 28257.55 28257.55

9/22/

DRG

Covered by Blue Cross at B/C rates

$3641.85

Bal. — 0 —

...O HEREBY CERTIFY THAT THE SAID BILL IS TRU... AND CORRECT, THAT EACH OF THE ITEM... SHOWN THEREON WAS NECESSARILY FURNISHE... OR SUPPLIED AND THAT THE AMOUNT OF TH... CHARGES THEREFOR IS THE FAIR AND REASON... ABLE VALUE THEREOF.

****BENEFITS ARE ASSIGNED TO THE HOSPITAL****

T O T A L S 28257.55 28257.55

Medical Records Dept.

PAY THIS AMOUNT 0

MED CTR
, NY

THE SUBSTITUTES FOR TESTIMONY IV

The ordinary method of proving a fact is to present the oral testimony of a witness who observed the fact. Sometimes, however, that method is cumbersome, or the witness is unavailable. Therefore, the law allows a party's attorney to employ other kinds of evidence in certain limited circumstances. The chapters in Part Four explain these other kinds of evidence in the order of their increasing remoteness from the ordinary method. Hence, Chapter 17 explains the exceptions to the hearsay rule, i.e., testimony by one witness about a matter that someone else observed. Chapter 18 explains the use of depositions, i.e., a record of the witness's testimony at the examination before trial, and Chapter 19 explains judicial notice, i.e., the court's acceptance of a well-known fact without evidence. Chapter 20 explains res ipsa loquitur, which is not evidence at all but a rule that allows the jury to draw an inference of negligence from circumstantial evidence. Finally, Chapter 21 explains the use of presumptions, including the burden of proof.

Hearsay 17

17.1 THE HEARSAY RULE

Hearsay is evidence of something said outside of the courtroom that is offered for the truth of the matter contained therein. Hearsay is what the witness heard another say happened rather than what the witness actually observed.[1] For example, a witness may testify to first-hand knowledge of an accident that the witness saw, but the witness may not testify that "a passenger in the defendant's car told me that the defendant ran the red light." Even a witness who is a policeman may not so testify;[2] if the plaintiff wants the passenger's observation in evidence, then the plaintiff must call the passenger as a witness.

There are, however, numerous exceptions to the hearsay rule, and those exceptions enable the courts to operate in a practical manner. This chapter discusses several of those exceptions, including business records, official certificates, admissions against interest, res gestae, and declarations by witnesses who are unavailable.

It is crucial to remember that testimony is hearsay only if the party offering the testimony offers the statement for its

---

1. FED. R. EVID. 801(c), 802.
2. Flynn v. Manhattan & Bronx Surface Transit Operating Auth., 94 A.D.2d 617, 462 N.Y.S.2d 17 (1st Dep't 1983), *aff'd,* 61 N.Y.2d 769, 461 N.E.2d 291, 473 N.Y.S.2d 154 (1984). Similarly, a friend of the decedent's cannot testify that the decedent complained to him of chest pains following a stress test administered by the doctor. Rosenberg v. Equitable Life Assurance Soc'y, 148 A.D.2d 337, 538 N.Y.S.2d 551 (1st Dep't 1989).

truth. If the party offers the out-of-court statement for some other purpose, e.g., to show the plaintiff's state of mind, then the hearsay rule does not bar the testimony. Unless there is a relevant exception to the hearsay rule, out-of-court statements may not be admitted for the truth of the matter contained therein.[3] Thus, the Appellate Division, First Department, held that a trial court erred by admitting pages from the *Physician's Desk Reference* in an action for medical malpractice based on the misuse of a drug.[4] Similarly, in *Boucheron v. Tilley,*[5] the Appellate Division, Fourth Department, held that the trial court did not err by excluding the manufacturer's package insert, which the FDA had approved and which explained the use of the drug Butazolidin. In *Cummings v. Fondak,*[6] the Appellate Term, First Department, held that in an action for medical malpractice based upon the dye-light treatment of a patient for herpes, the trial court erred by allowing the plaintiff to introduce magazine articles which supported the plaintiff's position that the treatment had increased his risk of developing cancer.

Even an ancient rule of law like hearsay continues to develop, however. For example, the Appellate Division, Second Department, has held that a statement that is hearsay may be admissible if the person who made the statement is present in the courtroom and subject to cross-examination.[7] The courts have not explained this new exception so, if it exists, it is still undefined.

---

3. People v. Ortiz, 119 Misc. 2d 572, 463 N.Y.S.2d 713 (Sup. Ct. 1983).
4. Rosario v. New York City Health & Hosps. Corp., 87 A.D.2d 211, 450 N.Y.S.2d 805 (1st Dep't 1982). *See also* Nicolla v. Fasulo, 161 A.D.2d 966 (3d Dep't 1990): the trial court erred by allowing the defendant to read from the P.D.R., but the error did not justify a reversal because several witnesses already had referred to the P.D.R.'s contents and because both parties had called the defendant as an expert witness.
5. Boucheron v. Tilley, 87 A.D.2d 983, 450 N.Y.S.2d 110 (4th Dep't 1982).
6. Cummings v. Fondak, 122 Misc. 2d 913, 474 N.Y.S.2d 356 (App. Term 1st Dep't 1983).
7. Vincent v. Thompson, 50 A.D.2d 22, 377 N.Y.S.2d 118 (2d Dep't 1975).

The following sections of this chapter explain the important exceptions to the hearsay rule.

17.2 RECORDS KEPT IN THE ORDINARY COURSE OF BUSINESS

17.2.1 The General Rule

Both by common law[8] and by statute,[9] records kept in the ordinary course of business are admissible as an exception to the hearsay rule. Such records might be police or accident reports, reports by governmental agencies, hospital records, or a doctor's records.

In New York, the statutory provision is C.P.L.R. section 4518(a), which provides that any writing made as a memorandum of any event is admissible to prove that event if the judge finds, first, that the record was made in the regular course of business; second, that the regular course of the business was to make the record; and third, that the record was made within a reasonable time after the event. The term "business" also includes a profession, occupation, and calling of every kind. All other circumstances surrounding the making of the record, including the entrant's lack of personal knowledge, are themselves admissible to affect the record's weight but not its admissibility.[10]

Other subdivisions of the same section authorize parties to introduce hospital bills, hospital records, laboratory reports, the medical records of a department or bureau of a municipal corporation or of the state, the books, papers, or

8. Leland v. Cameron, 31 N.Y. 115 (1865).
9. FED. R. EVID. 801(6)-(11).
10. Such records are admissible in the federal courts under the Federal Business Records Act, 28 U.S.C. § 1732 (Supp. 1980), the language of which is almost identical to C.P.L.R. rule 4518(a); *see also* Annot., *Verification and Authentication of Slips, Tickets, Bills, Invoices, Etc., Made in Regular Course of Business Under the Uniform Business Records as Evidence Act or Under Similar "Model Acts,"* 21 A.L.R.2D 773 (1952).

other things of a library or of a department or bureau of a municipality or the state, the results of a blood genetic marker or DNA test administered pursuant to sections 418 and 532 of the Family Court Act, and the records of support payments maintained by the department of social services.[11]

In order to comply with the best-evidence rule, the party must produce the record itself. In addition, the record must meet the statutory tests because the record's failure to meet any of the criteria will cause the trial court to exclude it.[12] (Remember that reproductions from optical disks now satisfy the best-evidence rule.[13])

Although the attorney deals with many kinds of business records, the most common ones in actions for negligence are accident reports (such as police reports, aided cards, and MV-104's) and hospital records. Note that such reports are not invariably admissible.

17.2.2 Police and Accident Reports

Any discussion of the admissibility of police reports must begin with *Johnson v. Lutz,*[14] in which the court of appeals clarified the standard for the admissibility of police accident reports. Such reports are inadmissible if they are themselves based on hearsay. The court ruled that the report in the case before the court was inadmissible and explained:

> The memorandum in question was not made in the regular course of any business, profession, occupation or calling. The policeman who made it was not present at the time of the accident. The memorandum was made from hearsay statements

11. C.P.L.R. section 4518(b)-(f). *See also* C.P.L.R. sections 2306 and 2307, Family Court Act sections 418 and 532, and Social Services Law, Title 6A, article 3.
12. O'Connor v. Incorporated Village of Jefferson, 104 A.D.2d 861, 480 N.Y.S.2d 376 (2d Dep't 1984).
13. C.P.L.R. rule 4539(b).
14. Johnson v. Lutz, 253 N.Y. 124, 170 N.E. 517 (1939). *See also* Rubin v. O'Donnell, 37 A.D.2d 858 (2d Dep't 1971).

> of third persons who happened to be present at the scene of the accident when he arrived. It does not appear whether they saw the accident and stated to him what they knew, or stated what some other persons had told them.[15]

The court construed the statute as

> [permitting] a writing or record, made in the regular course of business, to be received in the evidence without the necessity of calling as witnesses all of the persons who had any part in making it, provided the record was made as part of the duty of the person making it, or on information imparted by persons who were under a duty to impart such information.

Thus, under the *Johnson* rule, an accident report is inadmissible if based upon information obtained from third parties who were not under a business duty to inform the police of what had happened.[16] Similarly, a 911 call made by someone else on behalf of a pregnant woman did not qualify as a business record.[17]

Twenty-nine years after *Johnson*, in *Kelly v. Wasserman,*[18] a case that did not involve a police report, the court of appeals made the complementary ruling, to wit, a business record is admissible if the person who made it was under a business duty to make the report. Thereafter, in *Toll v. State*

15. *Id.* at 127-28.
16. Conners v. Duck's Cesspool Serv. Ltd., 144 A.D.2d 329, 533 N.Y.S.2d 942 (2d Dep't 1988); People v. Dyer, 128 A.D.2d 719, 513 N.Y.S.2d 211 (1987); Murray v. Donlon, 77 A.D.2d 337, 433 N.Y.S.2d 184 (2d Dep't 1980); Hayes v. State, 50 A.D.2d 693, 376 N.Y.S.2d 647 (3d Dep't 1975), *aff'd*, 40 N.Y.2d 1044, 360 N.E.2d 959, 392 N.Y.S.2d 282 (1976). For recent and contrasting cases, *see* Hatton v. Gassler, 219 A.D.2d 697 (2d Dep't 1995) (police report inadmissible) and Lopez v. Ford Motor Credit Co., 238 A.D.2d 211 (1st Dep't 1997).
17. Canty v. New York City Health and Hospitals Corporation, 158 A.D.2d 271 (1st Dep't 1990).
18. Kelly v. Wasserman, 5 N.Y.2d 425, 158 N.E.2d 241, 185 N.Y.S.2d 538 (1959). The court of appeals relied on *Kelly* when deciding People v. Cratsley, 86 N.Y.2d 81 (1995). In *Cratsley*, the report of the complainant's I.Q. test was admissible in a prosecution for rape because the informant reported the results pursuant to his duty and in the regular course of his business. *See also* Chemical Leaman Tank Lines, Inc. v. Stevens, 21 A.D.2d 556 (3d Dep't 1964). By contrast, the exculpatory version by one driver in a three-car accident was inadmissible as part of the police report. Mahon v. Giordano, 30 A.D.2d 792 (1st Dep't 1968).

of New York, the Appellate Division, Third Department, merged *Johnson* and *Kelly* to forge the rule that the courts still follow:

> Subdivision (a) of C.P.L.R. 4518 permits a police report to be admitted as proof of the facts recorded therein if (1) the entrant of those facts was a witness, or (2) the person giving the entrant the information was under a business duty to relate the facts to the entrant.[19]

The court of appeals has confirmed this rule and has explained how the proponent of a business record should methodically establish its admissibility:

> To constitute a business record exception to the hearsay rule, the proponent of the record must first demonstrate that it was within the scope of the entrant's business duty to record the act, transaction or occurrence sought to be admitted. But this satisfies only half the test. In addition, each participant in the chain producing the record, from the initial declarant to the final entrant, must be acting within the course of regular business conduct or the declaration must meet the test of some other hearsay exception. . . . Thus, not only must the entrant be under a business duty to record the event, but the informant must be under a contemporaneous business duty to report the occurrence to the entrant as well. . . .[20]

Therefore, for example, a police report is inadmissible in an action for assault and battery to prove who punched whom,[21] but a foster mother may have a duty to report evidence of child abuse, and thus, the record of her report may be admissible.[22]

---

19. Toll v. State, 32 A.D.2d 47, 299 N.Y.S.2d 589 (3d Dep't 1969).
20. *In re* Leon R.R., 48 N.Y.2d 117, 397 N.E.2d 374, 421 N.Y.S.2d 863 (1979); *see* Murray v. Donlon, 77 A.D.2d 337, 433 N.Y.S.2d 184 (2d Dep't 1980), for a thorough analysis of this rule and its history.
21. Donohue v. Losito, 141 A.D.2d 691 (2d Dep't 1988).
22. Matter of the Department of Social Services v. Waleska M., 195 A.D.2d 507 (2d Dep't 1993).

The Appellate Division, Second Department, applied this rule in *Murray v. Donlon.*[23] The appellate court ruled that the trial court should have excluded the police report because the report was based upon interviews with witnesses who could not be identified and could have included the parties. In particular, it was unclear who was the source of the information that the defendant's car was speeding. The policeman could not say whether that information had come from the plaintiff (in which case it would not be admissible), from the defendant (in which case it would be admissible as an admission), or from a witness. Therefore, the trial court should not have admitted the report into evidence. The appellate court also noted that the opinion expressed in the accident report (that the causes of the accident were the defendant's speeding and his failure to yield the right of way) was inadmissible.

> Since the officer had not witnessed the accident his opinion as to its cause had to be based on postincident expert analysis of observable physical evidence. [Yet there] was no proof of analysis of that type, or of the officer's qualifications to conduct one. Moreover, there was no proof that he was qualified to render an opinion based on such an analysis . . . Thus, to the extent that the accident report contained unqualified opinion evidence by Police Officer Colan, the report was inadmissible. . . .[24]

At this point, clarity requires us to summarize several corollaries. First, if the police officer prepares the police report or aided card from his or her own investigation, the cars had not been moved prior to this investigation, and there are no hearsay statements in the report, then the re-

---

23. Murray v. Donlon, 77 A.D.2d 337, 345, 433 N.Y.S.2d 184, 190 (2d Dep't 1980).
24. *Id.* at 347, 433 N.Y.S.2d at 192. In Skiller v. Short, 35 N.Y.S.2d 68 (City Ct. 1942), the court ruled that this is a question of fact for the jury and that the policeman's opinion is not admissible.

port is admissible[25] including the diagrams the police officer drew from his or her own observation.[26]

Second, if the police officer reconstructs the accident from skid marks and measurements, and he or she is an expert in reconstructing traffic accidents, then the officer's diagram of the course of the accident is admissible.[27] Even if the police officer is not an expert, the police report is admissible to show the skid marks[28] and the list of the witnesses the police officer enumerated thereon.[29]

Third, if the police report contains a statement by a bystander of a self-serving declaration by a party, that part of the report is not admissible,[30] but a party's admissions

---

25. Williams v. Alexander, 309 N.Y. 283, 129 N.E.2d 417 (1955); D'Arienzo v. Manderville, 106 A.D.2d 686, 484 N.Y.S.2d 171 (3d Dep't 1984); Auer v. Bienstock, 104 A.D.2d 350, 478 N.Y.S.2d 681 (2d Dep't 1984); Cornier v. Spagna, 101 A.D.2d 140, 475 N.Y.S.2d 7 (1st Dep't 1984); Quaglio v. Tomaselli, 99 A.D.2d 487, 470 N.Y.S.2d 427 (2d Dep't 1984); Utica Mut. Ins. Co. v. Cilento, 97 A.D.2d 422, 467 N.Y.S.2d 259 (2d Dep't 1983); Annot., *Admissibility of Report of Police or Other Public Officer or Employee, or Portions of Report, as to Cause of Responsibility for Accident, Injury to Person, or Damage to Property*, 69 A.L.R.2D 1148 (1960).
26. Quaglio v. Tomaselli, 99 A.D.2d 487, 420 N.Y.S.2d 427 (2d Dep't 1984); Campbell v. Manhattan & Bronx Surface Transit Operating Auth., 81 A.D.2d 529, 438 N.Y.S.2d 87 (1st Dep't 1981); Heiney v. Pattillo, 76 A.D.2d 855, 428 N.Y.S.2d 513 (2d Dep't 19870); Lee v. Decarr, 36 A.D.2d 554, 317 N.Y.S.2d 225 (3d Dep't 1971).
27. Campbell v. Manhattan & Bronx Surface Transit Operating Auth., 81 A.D.2d 529, 438 N.Y.S.2d 87 (1st Dep't 1981).
28. In Dugan v. Dieber, 32 A.D.2d 815, 302 N.Y.S.2d 423 (2d Dep't 1969), the appellate court held that skidmarks are pertinent as bearing on the speed of the defendant's automobile and that the trial court erred by charging the jury "that the only evidence in the case on speed was that the defendant was traveling at about 15 miles per hour and that evidenceof 'skidmarks' in and of itself is no indication of speed of vehicle." *See* Schaffner v. Rockmacher, 38 A.D.2d 835, 329 N.Y.S.2d 630 (2d Dep't 1972), in which the appellate court held that the trial court erred by excluding the policeman's diagram of the position of the infant plaintiff, the automobile, and the skidmarks when the proper foundation had been laid. *But see* Driscoll v. New York City Transit Auth., 53 A.D.2d 391, 395, 385 N.Y.S.2d 540, 543-44 (1st Dep't 1976), in which the appellate court held that the trial court had erred by admitting the police diagram showing the location of the infant plaintiff although the police officer had not witnessed the accident and no prior foundation had been laid.
29. Leonick v. City of N.Y., 120 A.D.2d 573, 502 N.Y.S.2d 60 (2d Dep't 1986).
30. Quaglio v. Tomaselli, 99 A.D.2d 487, 470 N.Y.S.2d 427 (2d Dep't 1984); Utica Mut. Ins. Co. v. Cilento, 97 A.D.2d 422, 467 N.Y.S.2d 259 (2d Dep't 1983).

against that party's interest are admissible.[31] Similarly, a party's admissions in an MV-104 are admissible unless the police officer has testified in accordance with the MV-104 and the trial court decides that the documentary evidence is merely cumulative.[32]

Fourth and finally, if the original police report has been lost, but the police officer reconstructs the report from notes and from memory, then the new police report is admissible.[33] This assumes, of course, that the original report would have been admissible.

Remember that we are discussing introducing the police officer's written report. By contrast, if a police officer is an expert in reconstructing accidents, the officer may testify regarding the point of impact based on his or her own observations although the officer did not see the accident.[34]

A sample of an accident report appears in chapter 1; example 17-1, at the end of the chapter, is a sample of a crime and incident report. Example 17-2 is an ambulance report.

17.2.3 Reports of Governmental Agencies

The category of business records includes the reports of governmental agencies, such as the department of buildings and the fire department.[35] Of course, those portions of the report based on hearsay and not on the personal findings of the author are inadmissible. Nevertheless, if properly based,

31. Ferrara v. Poranski, 88 A.D.2d 904, 450 N.Y.S.2d 596 (2d Dep't 1982).
32. Dempsey v. National Car Rental, 87 A.D.2d 835, 449 N.Y.S.2d 270 (2d Dep't 1982); Heniey v. Pattillo, 76 A.D.2d 855, 428 N.Y.S.2d 513 (2d Dep't 1980).
33. D'Arienzo v. Manderville, 106 A.D.2d 686, 484 N.Y.S.2d 171 (3d Dep't 1984).
34. Horton v. Smith, 71 A.D.2d 748 (3d Dep't 1979).
35. *See* FED. R. EVID. 803(8); Miller, *Availability and Use of Non-Public Government Records and Reports in Civil Litigation*, 9 SYRACUSE L. REV. 163 (1958); Annot., *Admissibility in Evidence on Issue of Negligence of Codes or Standards of Safety Issued by Governmental Body or by Voluntary Association*, 58 A.L.R.2D 148 (1974); Annot., *Municipal Corporation's Safety Rule and Regulation as Admissible in Evidence in Action by Private Party Against Municipal Corporation or Its Officers or Employees for Negligent Operation of Vehicle*, 82 A.L.R.3D 1285 (1978).

the conclusion of a report of the fire department, stating that inflammable rags caused the fire, or the conclusion of the department of buildings that a defective drum cable caused the elevator to fall is admissible on the same theory that a doctor's conclusions in a hospital record are admitted, i.e., that the inspector, if called as a witness, would be permitted to give his or her opinion of the cause.[36] The court will evaluate the report to determine whether sufficient care went into the preparation of the report to make it probative. Consequently, in a doctor's action for improper suspension, the trial court admitted a lengthy report on the doctor's competence,[37] but, in an action against the Metropolitan Transit Authority, another trial court excluded a report about the causes of an accident at a railroad crossing.[38]

17.2.4 Hospital Records

Hospital records are generally business records within the meaning of the exception to the hearsay rule, but applying the exception to hospital records involves more technical considerations and, therefore, exceptions to the exception.

17.2.4.1 The Statutory Rule

C.P.L.R. section 4518(c) provides that hospital records subpoenaed to court under C.P.L.R. section 2306 are admissible pursuant to the business records exception and are prima facie evidence of the facts contained therein provided

---

36. People v. Lederle, 206 Misc. 244, 132 N.Y.S.2d 693 (Spec. Sess. 1954), *aff'd*, 285 A.D. 974, 139 N.Y.S.2d 915 (2d Dep't 1955), *aff'd*, 309 N.Y. 866 (1955). C.P.L.R. rule 4520 ("the certificate or affidavit [of a public officer] so filed or deposited is prima facie evidence of the facts stated"). *See also* Annot., 69 A.L.R.2D 1148 (1960).

37. Bogdan v. Peekskill Community Hosp., 624 N.Y.S.2d 478 (Sup. Ct. Westchester 1996).

38. Kaiser v. Metropolitan Transit Authority, N.Y.L.J., Sep. 13, 1996, at 25 (Sup. Ct. Suffolk).

the records bear a certification or authentication by the head of the hospital, by an employee delegated for that purpose, or by a physician. Consequently, hospital records that are material and relevant are admissible whether subpoenaed to court or procured by a telephone call to the hospital's department of records.[39] A patient's x-rays are also admissible pursuant to C.P.L.R. section 4518, and a patient need not comply with the notice requirements of C.P.L.R. section 4532-a to protect that admissibility.[40]

17.2.4.2 The Distinction Between Actions for Negligence and Those for Medical Malpractice

In actions for both negligence and medical malpractice, the admissibility of the plaintiff's hospital records is subject to the general criterion of relevance. However, the history portion of the record is more likely to be relevant in an action for medical malpractice since that portion contains some of the information that was available to the defendant physician. In fact, in an action for medical malpractice, the plaintiff's entire medical record is usually admissible.[41] In an action for negligence, by contrast, the plaintiff's entire hospital record is not admissible because it may contain matter that is irrelevant, superfluous, or an ultimate question of fact for the jury.[42] Consequently, in an action for negligence, the history portion of the hospital record is admissible only if it is clearly relevant to the care and treat-

39. Joyce v. Kowalcowski, 80 A.D.2d 27, 437 N.Y.S.2d 809 (4th Dep't 1981).

40. Hoffman v. City of N.Y., 141 Misc. 2d 893 (Sup. Ct. Kings 1988); C.P.L.R. rule 4532-a: "Nothing contained in this section, however, shall prohibit the admissibility of an x-ray in evidence in a personal injury action where otherwise admissible."

41. *Cf.* Boucheron v. Tilley, 87 A.D.2d 983, 450 N.Y.S.2d 110 (4th Dep't 1982).

42. Meiselman v. Crown Heights Hosp., 185 N.Y. 389, 34 N.E.2d 367 (1941); Diamond v. Archer, 78 A.D.2d 546, 432 N.Y.S.2d 34 (2d Dep't 1980); FED. R. EVID. 803(3), 804(4), 804(b).

ment of the patient.[43] "[I]n some instances, perhaps the patient's explanation as to how he was hurt may be helpful to an understanding of the medical aspects of his case. It might, for instance, assist the doctors if they were to know that the injured man had been struck by an automobile."[44] For example, in *People v. Singleton*,[45] the Appellate Division, Second Department, ruled that the history, "hit in the face," in a hospital record was relevant to the doctor's diagnosis and treatment of the plaintiff's injuries and was, therefore, admissible. However, the trial court will not admit that part of the history which goes beyond what was necessary for treatment, e.g., that the patient was hit by an auto that ran a red light.

The history portion of the plaintiff's hospital record is admissible more readily in an action for medical malpractice because the history constituted notice to the treating physician. For example, in *Segreti v. Putnam Community Hospital,*[46] the plaintiff's intestate allegedly died as a result of the defendant physician's failure to treat the decedent for coronary insufficiency. The trial court dismissed the plaintiff's claim against the defendant hospital, but the Appellate Division, Second Department, reversed that decision, noting that the trial court had erred in refusing to admit the history portion of the records from the decedent's two prior admissions to the hospital during which he was treated for cardiac problems. The appellate court held, "The redacted portions

43. Passino v. De Rosa, 199 A.D.2d 1017 (4th Dep't 1993); the cause of the plaintiff's fall was irrelevant. *See also* Williams v. Alexander, 309 N.Y. 283, 129 N.E.2d 417 (1955); People v. Jackson, 124 A.D.2d 975, 509 N.Y.S.2d 230 (4th Dep't 1986); Edelman v. City of N.Y., 80 A.D.2d 506, 435 N.Y.S.2d 603 (2d Dep't 1981); Woods v. Mahbern Realty Corp., 5 A.D.2d 411, 172 N.Y.S.2d 503 (1st Dep't 1958); Annot., *Admissibility of Hospital Record Relating to Cause or Circumstances of Accident or Incident in Which Patient Sustained Injury*, 44 A.L.R.2D 553 (1955).

44. Williams v. Alexander, 309 N.Y. 283, 129 N.E.2d 417, 419 (1955).

45. People v. Singleton, 140 A.D.2d 388, 527 N.Y.S.2d 867 (2d Dep't 1988).

46. Segreti v. Putnam Community Hosp., 88 A.D.2d 590, 449 N.Y.S.2d 785 (2d Dep't 1982).

of the hospital record were clearly relevant to the issue of whether defendant Chang was on notice that Segreti had a coronary condition and were improperly excluded from the jury's consideration."[47]

17.2.4.3 An Admission Against Interest

Before one party may introduce the other party's purported admission against interest, the first party must establish that the second party actually made the admission. Thus, even if an entry in the plaintiff's hospital records is adverse to his or her position, the entry is not admissible as an admission against interest unless the person who made the entry testifies that the plaintiff made the statement[48] or unless the record clearly contains a quotation from the plaintiff.[49] For example, in *McDermott v. Baker*,[50] the trial court admitted the hospital record including the patient's admission regarding the manner of the accident after the doctor who had completed the form testified that he would not have recorded the statement unless the patient herself had made it.

47. *Id.* at 592, 449 N.Y.S.2d at 787.
48. Gunn v. City of N.Y., 104 A.D.2d 848, 480 N.Y.S.2d 365 (2d Dep't 1984); Edelman v. City of N.Y., 80 A.D.2d 506,435 N.Y.S.2d 603 (2d Dep't 1981); Fischer v. City of N.Y., 207 Misc. 628, 138 N.Y.S.2d 754 (Sup. Ct. 1955); *see also* Shaughnessy v. City of N.Y., 7 A.D.2d 734, 180 N.Y.S.2d 621 (2d Dep't 1958); *but see* Guadino v. New York City Housing Auth., 23 A.D.2d 838, 259 N.Y.S.2d 478 (1st Dep't 1965), in which the court held that it is not proper to admit the history given to an intern through a Spanish interpreter, for even if the intern testified to what the interpreter said, the intern's testimony is hearsay. In Ehrlich v. Marra, 32 A.D.2d 638, 300 N.Y.S.2d 81 (2d Dep't 1969), the appellate court held that the trial court had erred by permitting the defendant to introduce the history in the hospital record of the infant plaintiff (four years and ten months old), which history gave the father or mother's version of the accident although neither saw it. Barzaghi v. Maislin Transp., 115 A.D.2d 679, 497 N.Y.S.2d 131 (2d Dep't 1985), is a more important case because the witness testified that she took down the history on the chart as the patient gave it to her, but she did not recall the patient. Nevertheless, the history was admissible due to her testimony of her practice and procedure.
49. Cotter v. Mercedes Benz, 108 A.D.2d 173, 488 N.Y.S.2d 390 (1st Dep't 1985).
50. McDermott v. Baker, 20 A.D.2d 546 (2d Dep't 1963).

Sometimes the party offering the admission in evidence fails to carry the burden of proving that the other party made the admission. For example, in *Castro v. Leeds,*[51] the Appellate Division, Second Department, discussed the trial court's error in admitting that part of the hospital record in which the plaintiff was reported to have described how the explosion occurred:

> Ordinarily such a statement can be introduced as an admission, but the nurse who recorded it could not say with certainty whether it came from Mrs. Castro or one of several other individuals who were present in the emergency room during her treatment. Since the origin of the statement is unclear, the proponent of the admission of the hospital records into evidence failed to establish that they contained an admission by Mrs. Castro, and they should not have been received in evidence . . . .

17.2.5 Consumption of Alcohol as Reported in a Hospital Record

Whether a statement concerning alcohol contained in a hospital record is admissible depends on whether the statement was based either on the entrant's own observation or on the patient's admission. Thus, a nurse's notes, which stated that the patient was "apparently intoxicated" were admissible because they were the result of her own observations,[52] but in another case, the court excluded a portion of the hospital record that stated, "evidently after a day of beer and wine drinking, he was somehow involved in an auto accident" because the statement obviously was not based on the en-

51. Castro v. Alden Leeds, Inc., 144 A.D.2d 613, 535 N.Y.S.2d 73 (2d Dep't 1988).

52. Tyson v. Bittner, 3 A.D.2d 861, 161 N.Y.S.2d 710 (2d Dep't 1957); *see also* Campbell v. Manhattan & Bronx Surface Transit Operating Auth., 81 A.D.2d 529, 438 N.Y.S.2d 87 (1st Dep't 1981); Miller v. City of N.Y., 286 A.D. 1033, 145 N.Y.S.2d 295 (2d Dep't 1955); Annot., *Admissibility of Hospital Record Relating to Intoxication or Sobriety of Patient,* 38 A.L.R.2D 778 (1954).

trant's own observation.[53] Similarly, the court excluded a statement in the hospital record that the plaintiff had been intoxicated at the time of the accident because the information was obtained from a third person.[54] By contrast, the Appellate Division, Second Department, held that the trial court had erred by excluding an entry in the hospital record that stated, "admits to heavy drinking, over a pint of whiskey a day."[55] In this case, the plaintiff had provided the information directly to the entrant. The same appellate court ruled that the trial court had erred by admitting from the history portion of a hospital record the statement by the father of the defendant's driver that his son "had a few beers" although the father had not seen his son all day. The appellate court also held that it was improper to allow the son's companion to testify that he had seen the son drinking in the past.

Sometimes, the notation regarding intoxication is admissible from one medical record but not another depending upon how the notation is phrased. Thus, in *Mercedes v. Amusements of America,*[56] a case in which the plaintiff was injured when he was thrown from a ride in an amusement park, the trial court correctly admitted the notation from the ambulance record that the plaintiff had alcohol on his breath, but the court erroneously admitted the notation from the hospital record that the plaintiff was intoxicated.

---

53. Roberto v. Nielson, 262 A.D. 1035, 30 N.Y.S.2d 334 (2d Dep't 1941), *aff'd*, 288 N.Y. 581 (1942).
54. Geroeami v. Fancy Fruit & Produce Corp., 249 A.D. 221, 291 N.Y.S. 837 (1st Dep't 1936).
55. Shaughnessy v. City of N.Y., 7 A.D.2d 734, 180 N.Y.S.2d 621 (2d Dep't 1958); *but see* Ward v. Thisleton, 32 A.D.2d 846, 302 N.Y.S.2d 339 (2d Dep't 1969), which held that an entry of "drunk" on a "Radiographic Request Card" of a hospital record, with no indication of who wrote it, was inadmissible. *See also* David v. Granger, 35 A.D.2d 636, 312 N.Y.S.2d 963 (3d Dep't 1970), which held that proof of a blood alcohol test was not admissible as evidence of the proximate cause of the accident because the driver was dead and because it would entail an inference on an inference.
56. Mercedes v. Amusements of America, 160 A.D.2d 630 (1st Dep't 1990).

The attorney who tries actions for personal injury or medical malpractice should become familiar with the forms used for hospital and medical records. In fact, the attorney should collect standard sets of such forms and should seek a course in nursing documentation. The attorney who is familiar with such forms will be better able to use the results of discovery, and the attorney who has collected standard sets of forms will notice that a particular form is missing from the records produced during discovery.[56.1] Some parties will suppress damaging documents, but, even if the party and his attorney are honest, hospital records pass through so many hands that parts may genuinely be lost. A missing form also may mean that the medical personnel never performed a particular test or examination. Assuming that the records are complete, the attorney and his or her expert should examine the documents to evaluate the injury and the legal claim. The attorney who tries cases for personal injuries must be alert to the possibility that medical malpractice exacerbated the injury and examine the records for clues to pre-existing conditions and dangerous medications.

We have reproduced three documents[57] at the end of the chapter for the reader's information. The first document (example 17-3) consists of the instructions to the nurse for completing the hospital's admission form. The second document (example 17-4) is a completed admission form for an adult (there are also pediatric and neonatal forms), and the third (example 17-5) is a specialty overprint for the same form. This particular overprint deals primarily with intoxication.

56.1. For an interesting example of missing forms, see the sample summation reproduced in chapter 9.

57. These forms were extracted from the Outcome-Oriented Nursing Documentation System (OONDS) of the U.S. Air Force courtesy of Maj. Diane Proctor, formerly the chief of the office of continuing education, Walson Hospital, Fort Dix.

17.2.6 The Doctor's Records

17.2.6.1 The Records of the Treating Physician

The office records of a physician, whether he or she is the defendant in an action for medical malpractice or treated the plaintiff in an action for negligence, are admissible as business records provided that the party offering them calls as a witness someone with personal knowledge of the physician's business practices and procedures.[58] That witness may be the physician's nurse, his or her secretary,[59] or the physician. Thus, the attorney need not call the physician to lay the foundation for the physician's own office records.[60] However, if the witness cannot explain a notation in the office records, and the note is susceptible to several explanations, the trial court will not admit that notation into evidence.[61] Finally, if the physician is deceased, the physician's office records are still admissible provided that some witness can lay the foundation.[62]

17.2.6.2 The Testimony of Examining and Treating Physicians

When a physician who was not the treating physician examines the plaintiff solely to testify at the trial, the party employing the physician must comply with the rules for exchanging medical reports.[63] The physician then may testify

58. Hefte v. Bellin, 137 A.D.2d 406, 524 N.Y.S.2d 42 (1st Dep't 1988).
59. McClure v. Baier's Automotive Serv., 126 A.D.2d 610, 511 N.Y.S.2d 50 (2d Dep't 1987).
60. Napolitano v. Branks, 141 A.D.2d 705, 529 N.Y.S.2d 824 (2d Dep't 1988).
61. Wilson v. Bodian, 130 A.D.2d 221, 519 N.Y.S.2d 126 (2d Dep't 1987). On the admissibility of office records generally, see Article, *Hearsay Problems in the Use of Medical Evidence,* N.Y.L.J., Dec. 24, 1986, at 1, col. 2; Lipsig, *Admissibility of Doctor's Office Records,* N.Y.L.J., Dec. 4, 1987, at 1, col. 1; Martin, *Medical Office Records, N.Y.S.*, N.Y.L.J., Jan. 8, 1988, at 1, col. 1.
62. *In re* Katz, 230 A.D. 172, 243 N.Y.S. 96 (1st Dep't 1930); FED. R. EVID. 803(3), 803(5).
63. *See* chapter 13.

concerning the physician's examination of the plaintiff and may even refer to the medical records and testimony that are in evidence to support his or her opinion,[64] but may not base this opinion upon any medical reports that are not in evidence.[65] In addition, the examining physician may not testify concerning the plaintiff's medical history or subjective complaints as related to the physician by the patient.[66] For example, the trial court should not have allowed the examining physician to testify that the plaintiff told him that she still had headaches and easily became fatigued.[67]

By contrast, the treating physician may testify concerning the patient's expressions of current pain and suffering to the physician.[68] These expressions are part of the res gestae, and the law considers them reliable because a patient has little reason to speak untruthfully when consulting a physician for treatment. Moreover, the treating physician may testify concerning the physician's own treatment of the plaintiff and the medical history the plaintiff provided insofar as this history was relevant to the treatment. The plaintiff's statement, "I was hit by a car while crossing the street, thrown twenty feet, and landed on my back," was relevant. The plaintiff's claim that he was in the crosswalk when hit was irrelevant and, therefore, inadmissible.

---

64. Fox v. Raferty, 45 A.D.2d 723, 356 N.Y.S.2d 341 (2d Dep't 1974).

65. *Id.*

66. Davidson v. Cornell, 132 N.Y. 228 (1892); Lessin v. Direct Delivery Serv., 10 A.D.2d 624, 196 N.Y.S.2d 751 (1st Dep't 1960); Maucere v. Munson, 6 A.D.2d 892, 177 N.Y.S.2d 443 (2d Dep't 1958).

67. Christastie v. Elmira Water, Light and Railroad Co., 202 A.D. 270 (3d Dep't 1922). *See also* Belter v. Winkle, 234 A.D. 886 (2d Dep't 1931).

68. Maucere v. Munson, 6 A.D.2d 892, 177 N.Y.S.2d 443 (2d Dep't 1958).

17.3 OFFICIAL CERTIFICATES AS BUSINESS RECORDS

Official certificates are admissible pursuant to the business records exception to the hearsay rule, but official certificates are more persuasive than other business records because official certificates are prima facie evidence of their own contents.

17.3.1 A Death Certificate

In New York, a death certificate is admissible not only to prove the fact of death but also to show the cause of death. There is no problem of privilege and waiver because the certificate is a public document.[69] Thus, in *Regan v. National Postal Transportation Association*,[70] an action for death benefits due on an insurance policy, the trial court admitted the death certificate to prove that the cause of death was "suffocation due to a foreign body in the pharynx." Similarly, in *Scott v. Empire State Degree of Honor*,[71] the Appellate Division, Fourth Department, held that a death certificate that gave the primary cause of death as "[s]hock and hemorrhage following gunshot wound in left chest" and the second cause as "suicide" was admissible and was presumptive evidence that the insured's death was self-inflicted.

The attorney may be aware that the New York City Sanitary Code requires that, in addition to the death certificate, the physician must file a confidential medical report. This report, however, is not "subject to subpoena or open to in-

---

69. Ellenberger v. Pena, 88 A.D.2d 373, 453 N.Y.S.2d 436 (2d Dep't 1982).
70. Regan v. National Postal Transp. Ass'n, 53 Misc. 2d 901, 280 N.Y.S.2d 319 (Civ. Ct. 1967). *See* FED. R. EVID. 803(9); N.Y. PUB. HEALTH LAW § 4103; Gioia v. State, 22 A.D.2d 181, 254 N.Y.S.2d 384 (4th Dep't 1964); Brownrigg v. Boston & A. R.R., 8 A.D.2d 140, 142, 185 N.Y.S.2d 977, 979 (1st Dep't 1959).
71. Scott v. Empire State Degree of Honor, 204 A.D. 530, 198 N.Y.S. 538 (4th Dep't 1923).

spection for any reason whatsoever, except for scientific purposes,"[72] and the Department of Health must refuse to produce the confidential medical report in response to a subpoena.[73]

Example 17-6 is a sample of a certified death certificate.

17.3.2 An Autopsy Report

Although the physician's confidential medical report is unavailable, the medical examiner's report is admissible in evidence in toto. Hence, in *People v. Morris,*[74] the Appellate Division, Second Department, ruled, "It was also serious error for the trial court to exclude the history portion of the autopsy . . . . Furthermore, an autopsy report is admissible in evidence as a provable document."[75]

The medical examiner's report usually contains the following subdivisions: history, anatomical findings, anatomical diagnosis, and cause of death. For example, the history may include "the deceased was struck by an automobile while he was crossing the street." The anatomical findings contain a detailed breakdown of both the normal and the abnormal findings at the autopsy. The anatomical diagnosis may be "fracture of base of skull, laceration of the brain, ruptured spleen, generalized arteriosclerosis, and enlargement of the heart." Concomitantly, the cause of death may be "fracture of base of skull, lacerated brain, and rupture of spleen."[76] The entire report, including the history of the accident, is admissible, but the history should not include extraneous matters.

---

72. N.Y.C. Sanitary Code § 33 (1980).
73. *In re* Bakers Mut. Ins. Co., 301 N.Y. 21, 92 N.E. 49 (1950).
74. People v. Morris, 42 A.D.2d 968, 347 N.Y.S.2d 975 (2d Dep't 1973), *aff'd,* 36 N.Y.2d 877, 334 N.E.2d 10, 372 N.Y.S.2d 210 (1975).
75. *Id.* 42 A.D.2d at 968-69, 347 N.Y.S.2d at 976; *see* FED. R. EVID. 803(8); People v. Courtner, 40 Misc. 2d 541, 243 N.Y.S.2d 457 (Sup. Ct. 1963).
76. In Walter v. State, 125 Misc. 2d 604, 479 N.Y.S.2d 964 (Ct. Cl. 1984), the court held that the cause of death listed in the autopsy report is admissible.

Example 17-7 is a sample of an autopsy report. The subject died of a heart attack after an emergency Cesarean section.

17.3.3 A Marriage Certificate

A marriage certificate is admissible and is prima facie proof of its own contents. C.P.L.R. section 4526 provides, "An original certificate of a marriage made by the person by whom it was solemnized within the state, or the original entry thereof made pursuant to law in the office of the clerk of a city or a town within the state, is prima facie evidence of the marriage."

A claimant may use a marriage certificate to establish his status as a distributee in an action for wrongful death or as a beneficiary of the estate in a surviving action for personal injury. (Note that a relative other than a spouse may use a marriage certificate as one item in the chain of proof establishing his connection.)

Example 17-8 is a sample of a marriage certificate.

17.3.4. A Weather Report

An official weather report is another official certificate that is admissible and prima facie evidence. C.P.L.R. section 4528 provides, "Any record of the observations of the weather, taken under the direction of the United States weather bureau, is prima facie evidence of the facts stated."[77] The party's attorney may use that report either to establish the conditions on the day of the accident or to contradict or impeach a witness by showing that the witness's testimony was inaccurate. A party might also use the certified weather report to show how much time was available to rectify a condition, e.g., ice on the sidewalk.

---

77. Annot., *Weather Reports and Records as Evidence*, 34 A.L.R.2D 1249 (1954); Annot., *Admissibility of Non-Expert Testimony as to Weather Conditions*, 56 A.L.R.3D 575 (1974). For a sample of an official weather report, see example 15-8.

17.4 ADMISSIONS AGAINST INTEREST

17.4.1 The Rule

The trial court may admit into evidence a party's admission against interest as evidence-in-chief.[78] In other words, one party may use the opposing party's admission to establish the first party's direct case through the testimony of a witness who heard the admission, or the first party may use the admission as a basis for cross-examining the opposing party. For example, if the defendant, when testifying, denies making the admission, then the plaintiff may prove the admission, and the trial court will not bar the proof as collateral. Of course, the admission would also be a prior inconsistent statement, which the plaintiff's attorney could use to impeach the defendant, and the admission may have been embodied in a document.

A party's admission is admissible even if made pursuant to what someone told him or her rather than through personal observation. Thus, in *Brusca v. El Al Airlines,*[79] the Appellate Division, Second Department, wrote, "The fact that a particular admission is apparently not based on personal knowledge of the occurrence described, but rather only upon information gleaned from others, is no bar to its admission into evidence."[80] However, an admission is not a stipulation. Therefore, an admission does not estop a party from explaining the circumstances of the admission in order to undermine its weight.

---

78. Reed v. McCord, 160 N.Y. 330, 54 N.E. 737 (1899); Cotter v. Mercedes Benz, 108 A.D.2d 173, 488 N.Y.S.2d 390 (1st Dep't 1985); FED. R. EVID. 801(d)(2). Note that an infant's admission is admissible against him even if the infant cannot take an oath. W. RICHARDSON, EVIDENCE § 229 (10th ed. 1973) [hereinafter cited as RICHARDSON, EVIDENCE].

79. Brusca v. El Al Airlines, 75 A.D.2d 798 (2d Dep't 1980).

80. *Id.* at 800.

17.4.2 Admissions in Automobile Accidents

Automobile accidents provide a good example of the tactical considerations involved in utilizing the admission against interest. For example, if the plaintiff knows that the driver of an automobile made an admission, the plaintiff should name that driver as a defendant since the plaintiff may use the admission only against the party who made it and not against a defendant who bears only vicarious liability.[81] Once the plaintiff has established the driver's liability, the owner's vicarious liability will follow as a matter of law.

The attorney should also remember that, although a traffic infraction is not a crime, a plea of guilty to a relevant infraction is an admission against interest and admissible in the civil action arising from the same incident.[82] Therefore, the plaintiff's attorney should examine the police report to see if the police issued a ticket to the defendant. The attorney should then ascertain how the defendant pleaded to that ticket. In addition, if the defendant made an admission to the police officer, and the officer recorded the admission in the report or MV-104, then a certified copy of that document is admissible to prove the admission.[83]

Interestingly, the trial court should exclude a conviction for a traffic infraction since the result of such a summary proceeding is too untrustworthy to establish the defendant's negligence.[84] Hence, a plea of guilty is admissible, but a conviction is not.

---

81. Basile v. Huntington Fuel Corp., 60 A.D.2d 616, 404 N.Y.S.2d 140 (2d Dep't 1977).
82. Ando v. Woodberry, 8 N.Y.2d 165, 168, 168 N.E.2d 520, 522, 203 N.Y.S.2d 74, 76 (1960), *overruling* Walther v. News Syndicate Co., 276 A.D. 169, 176, 93 N.Y.S.2d 537, 544-45 (1st Dep't 1949). *See* Annot., *Nolo Contendere on Non Vult Plea as Admission of Guilty in Civil Proceedings*, 89 A.L.R.2D 600 (1963); Annot. *Admissibility as Against Interest, in Criminal Case of Declaration of Commission of Criminal Act*, 92 A.L.R.3D 1164 (1979).
83. Epstein v. Cohen, 288 N.Y. 307, 43 N.E.2d 56 (1942); Carter v. Castle Elec. Contracting Corp., 26 A.D.2d 83, 271 N.Y.S.2d 51 (2d Dep't 1966).
84. Montalvo v. Morales, 18 A.D.2d 20 (2d Dep't 1963).

17.4.3 Admissions by Agents

Some employees are empowered to make admissions on behalf of their employers. In particular, an employee who is an officer or a manager can, by his or her statements, make admissions against interest binding the employer.[85] Other employees may not.[85.1] The rule is that speaking for the employer must be within the scope of the employee's duties and that the employee must be performing his or her duties when making the admission.[86]

A few examples should clarify the distinction. In *Cook v. Great Atlantic & Pacific Tea Co.*,[87] the plaintiff had slipped on some cream cheese on the floor of the defendant's store. In order to prove notice, the plaintiff testified that after she fell, the defendant's' employee helped her up and said, "I told someone to clean it up." The Appellate Division, Fourth Department, however, held that that statement was not admissible either as an admission or as res gestae. The court of appeals reached a similar decision in *Golden v.*

---

85. *See* Spett v. President Monroe Bldg. & Mfg. Corp., 19 N.Y.2d 203, 206, 225 N.E.2d 527, 529, 278 N.Y.S.2d 826, 829 (1967) (the court of appeals held it was error to exclude "alleged admission of responsibility for placement of the skid" [a platform on runners] made by the husband of the defendant and the "general foreman" of the printing business). *See also* Testa v. Federated Dep't Stores, Inc., 118 A.D.2d 696, 499 N.Y.S.2d 973 (2d Dep't 1986); Cianci v. Board of Educ., 18 A.D.2d 930, 238 N.Y.S.2d 547 (2d Dep't 1963) (the appellate court held that it was an error to exclude plaintiff's offer of a report of the accident to the board of education by its director of health and physical education, even though the director had no personal knowledge of the accident, for "[a]n employer is bound by the contents of a report made by an authorized agent; and to the extent it contains any inconsistent or contradictory statements it is admissible as a party's declaration against interest, despite the agent's lack of personal knowledge"); Annot., *Admissibility, in Action Against Proprietor of Store, Office, or Similar Business Premises for Injury from Fall on Floor Made Slippery by Tracked-In or Spilled Water, Mud, Snow or the Like, or Statement of Defendant's Employee to Show Notice*, 62 A.L.R.2D 45 (1959); Annot., 23 A.L.R.2D 1360 (1952).

85.1. Lowen v. Great Atlantic & Pacific Tea Co., Inc., 223 A.D.2d 534 (2d Dep't 1996).

86. Niesig v. Team, 149 A.D.2d 94 (2d Dep't 1989).

87. Cook v. Great Atl. & Pac. Tea Co., 244 A.D. 63, 278 N.Y.S. 777 (4th Dep't 1934), *aff'd,* 268 N.Y. 599, 198 N.Y. 423 (1935).

Horn & Hardart,[88] and *Williams v. Waldbaums Supermarkets, Inc.*[88.1] However, the plaintiff in *Bransfield v. Grand Union Co.*[89] was luckier. This plaintiff claimed she had slipped on a broken egg in the defendant's supermarket. The plaintiff testified that she had slipped on a "sticky spot" about twelve inches wide, and the trial court permitted her to testify that, a few minutes after her fall, the manager came up the aisle and said to a clerk standing nearby, "I thought I told you to clean that up." The clerk replied, "I did clean it," and the manager then "took a mop and cleaned it all up where it was wet when I fell." The court of appeals held that this testimony constituted proper proof of notice.

Recently, in *Badr v. Hogan,*[90] the Appellate Division, Second Department, broadened this notion of an admission by an agent to include the statements by the parents of an infant party. The court held that the defendant could introduce the out-of-court statement by the infant's father, who was not a party, to establish that the plaintiff fell out of bed thereby refuting the child's version of the accident. However, the same court has ruled in *Sujak v. Buono,* a dog bite case, that the plaintiff's estranged husband was not her agent for admitting that he liked the dog.[90.1]

17.4.4 Special Instances that May Constitute Admissions Against Interest

17.4.4.1 Pleadings and Auxiliary Documents

An admission contained in a pleading is, of course, admissible against the party who served the pleading.[91] Al-

---

88. Golden v. Horn & Hardart, 244 A.D. 92, 278 N.Y.S. 385 (1st Dep't 1935), *aff'd,* 270 N.Y. 544 (1936).

88.1. Williams v. Waldbaums Supermarkets, Inc., 236 A.D.2d 605 (2d Dep't 1997).

89. Bransfield v. Grand Union Co., 17 N.Y.2d 474, 214 N.E.2d 161, 266 N.Y.S.2d 981 (1965).

90. Bader v. Hogan, N.Y.L.J., Oct. 10, 1989 (2d Dep't 1989).

90.1. Sujak v. Buono, 238 A.D.2d 405 (2d Dep't 1997).

91. Brisbane v. City of N.Y., 6 A.D.2d 882, 177 N.Y.S.2d 606 (2d Dep't 1958); Anot., *Admissibility of Pleading as Evidence Against Pleader, on Behalf of Strang-*

though the bill of particulars is not a pleading, the case law is plentiful that a party may not prove anything that he or she did not include in the bill.[92] A party's deposition is not a pleading either, but one party may use the opposing party's deposition as an admission against interest if the document contains such a statement.[93] In addition, a party may use as evidence-in-chief the admissions contained in the depositions of the opposing party's officers and the opposing party's employees called to the stand by their employer.

The pleading containing the admission need not even be one from the same action. For example, in *Pitt v. Brough,*[94] the Appellate Division, Third Department, ruled that the defendant could introduce a complaint the plaintiff had served against a different defendant and in which the plaintiff had alleged injuries similar to the ones he was alleging against the defendant in the instant case.

17.4.4.2 Conduct

Conduct may constitute an admission against interest. For example, a driver's conduct was tantamount to an admission of liability when he fled the scene of the accident and then committed perjury to explain his actions.[95] Although fleeing the scene may appear to be only circumstantial evidence, the courts treat such conduct as an admission.

---

er to Proceedings in Which Pleading Was Filed, 63 A.L.R.2D 412 (1959). *See also* FED. R. EVID. 803(24); Annot., *Admissibility in Evidence of Withdrawn, Superseded, Amended, or Abandoned Pleading as Containing Admissions Against Interest,* 52 A.L.R.2D 516 (1957).

92. *See* chapter 2.

93. C.P.L.R. rule 3117.

94. Pitt v. Brough, 132 A.D.2d 836, 517 N.Y.S.2d 623 (3d Dep't 1987).

95. Garippa v. Wisotsky, 280 A.D. 807, 113 N.Y.S.2d 772 (2d Dep't 1952), *aff'd*, 305 N.Y. 571, 111 N.Y.2d 443 (1953); *see also* Ryan v. Dwyer, 33 A.D.2d 878, 307 N.Y.S.2d 565 (4th Dep't 1969); FED. R. EVID. 801(a)(2).

17.4.5 Special Instances That Do Not Constitute Admissions Against Interest

17.4.5.1 Silence

The courts of New York do not consider it to be an admission against interest for the defendant to remain silent when someone has asserted in the defendant's presence that he or she was at fault.[96] The defendant's failure to rebut the allegations is not tantamount to agreement although, depending upon the facts, the silence might be circumstantial evidence.

17.4.5.2 Negotiations for a Settlement

A party's participating in negotiations aimed at a settlement does not constitute an admission of fault.[97] Therefore, the defendant's offer to pay the plaintiff's medical or hospital expenses or lost wages is not admissible,[98] and the plaintiff may not show that the defendant has compromised the action of another plaintiff injured in the same accident.[99]

---

96. Lichtenstein v. Gascio, 274 A.D. 309, 83 N.Y.S.2d 195 (1st Dep't 1948); Dougherty v. City of N.Y., 267 A.D. 828, 45 N.Y.S.2d 808 (2d Dep't 1944), *aff'd*, 295 N.Y. 786, 66 N.E.2d 199 (1946); Annot., *Admissibility of Evidence of Party's Silence, as Implied or Tacit Admission, When a Statement Is Made by Another in His Presence, Regarding Circumstances of an Accident*, 70 A.L.R.2D 1099 (1960); *see* FED. R. EVID. 801(a)(2).
97. Admissions against interest contained in a letter from the plaintiff's lawyer to the defendant's lawyer requesting the settlement of the case are admissible against plaintiff at trial. Bellino v. Bellino Constr. Co., 75 A.D.2d 630, 427 N.Y.S.2d 303 (2d Dep't 1980). *See* FED. R. EVID. 408, 409; Bell, *Admissions Arising Out of Compromise: Are They Relevant?*, 31 TEX. L. REV. 239 (1953). *See also* Bigelow-Sanford, Inc. v. Specialized Floors of Rochester, Inc., 77 A.D.2d 464 (4th Dep't 1980).
98. Grogan v. Dooley, 211 N.Y. 30, 105 N.E. 135 (1914); Annot., *Admissibility of Evidence to Show Payment, or Offer or Promise of Payment of Medical, Hospital, and Similar Expenses of an Injured Party by the Opposing Party*, 20 A.L.R.2D 291 (1951), 65 A.L.R.3D 932 (1975); FED. R. EVID. 409.

However, if the other person testifies for the defendant, the plaintiff's attorney may cross-examine the witness about whether the witness has settled the witness's claim against the defendant.[100] Similarly, C.P.L.R. rule 4533-b forbids the defendant to inform the jury that the plaintiff has settled with another defendant, but the defendant may prove the settlement to the court, which will deduct any appropriate amount from the jury's award.[101] Finally, since New York has adopted no-fault automobile insurance, the plaintiff may not prove that the defendant paid first-party benefits under the no-fault scheme.[102]

17.5 RES GESTAE

Res gestae, which means "the things that have been done," is a grab-bag of exceptions to the hearsay rule that allow the introduction of various declarations on the grounds that they were part of some event. In New York, the term res gestae encompasses four exceptions:

1. Excited utterances
2. Declarations of present bodily condition
3. Declarations of present sense impression
4. Declarations of present mental state[103]

---

99. Fitzgerald v. Ladabouch, 252 A.D. 912, 299 N.Y.S. 880 (3d Dep't 1937), *aff'd*, 277 N.Y. 669, 14 N.E.2d 212 (1938); Cochrane v. Fahey, 245 A.D. 41, 280 N.Y.S. 622 (4th Dep't 1935); Annot., *Admissibility of Evidence That Defendant in Negligence Action Has Paid Third Persons on Claims Arising from the Same Transaction or Incident as Plaintiff's Claim*, 20 A.L.R.2D 304 (1951).

100. Kett v. Murring, 260 N.Y. 586, 184 N.E. 104 (1932).

101. Ammerman v. Utilities Oil Corp., 222 A.D. 481, 226 N.Y.S. 673 (1st Dep't 1928); *see also* N.Y. GEN. OBLIG. LAW § 15-108, dealing with the effects of settlement with codefendant tortfeasors on the remaining tortfeasors' share of the liability.

102. Dermatossian v. New York City Transit Authority, 67 N.Y.2d 219 (1986).

103. Loschiavo v. Port Auth., 86 A.D.2d 624, 446 N.Y.S.2d 358 (2d Dep't 1982), *aff'd*, 58 N.Y.2d 1040 (1983); E. FISCH, NEW YORK EVIDENCE §§ 995, 997, 1000 (2d ed. 1977); *cf.* Proposed Code of Evidence for State of N.Y. § 803(1-4).

We can further divide those four exceptions into three true exceptions and one apparent exception, i.e., testimony that is not really an exception but merely a correct application of the hearsay rule.

17.5.1 The True Exceptions

17.5.1.1 Excited Utterances

The excited utterance is the essential notion of res gestae. The court of appeals explained the exception in *People v. Caviness*:

> Spontaneous declarations, frequently referred to with some inexactitude as res gestae declarations . . . form an exception to the hearsay rule. It is established that spontaneous declarations made by a participant while he is under the stress of nervous excitement resulting from an injury or other startling event, while his reflective powers are stilled and during the brief period when considerations of self interest could not have been fully brought to bear by reasoned reflection and deliberation, are admissible as true exceptions to the hearsay rule.[104]

A fortiori, if the declaration was made by a bystander who witnessed the event rather than by a participant, the declaration is admissible.[105] Should a party have produced an excit-

104. People v. Caviness, 38 N.Y.23d 227, 230-231, 342 N.E.2d 496, 498, 379 N.Y.S.2d 695, 698-99 (1975); Swenson v. New York, Albany Despatch Co., 309 N.Y. 497, 131 N.E.2d 902 (1956); Flynn v. Manhattan & Bronx Surface Transit Operating Auth., 94 A.D.2d 617, 462 N.Y.S.2d 17 (1st Dep't 1983), *aff'd,* 61 N.Y.2d 769, 461 N.E.2d 291, 473 N.Y.S.2d 154 (1984); Loschiavo v. Port Auth., 86 A.D.2d 624, 446 N.Y.S.2d 358 (2d Dep't 1982); Annot., *Admissibility as Res Gestate of Statement or Exclamations Relating to Cause of, or Responsibility for, Motor Vehicle Accident,* 53 A.L.R.2D 1245 (1957). They must, of course, be competent and relevant. *See* Slough, *Res Gestae*, 2 KAN. L. REV. 41, 121, 246 (1953-54); FED. R. EVID. 803(1), 803(2).

105. People v. Caviness, 38 N.Y.2d 227, 231-32, 342 N.E.2d 496, 499, 379 N.Y.S.2d 695, 699 (1975).

ed utterance that is also adverse to the party's interests, the statement is also admissible on that ground.[106]

> While one is engaged in an act, and the intention with which he is acting is a proper subject of inquiry, his declarations, made at the time, may be given in evidence to characterize the act.[107]

Of course, the statement must have been spontaneous and contemporary with the event.[108] In order for a statement to qualify as an excited utterance, the declarant must have been under the stress of the excitement caused by an external event, and this stress must have been sufficient to suppress the declarant's reflective faculties thereby precluding that deliberation which might lead him or her to be untruthful.[109] For example, in *Flynn v. MABSTOA*,[110] a bus hit a bicycle rider, causing him serious injuries. The police officer testified that he had investigated the accident and talked with the bus

---

106. Flynn v. Manhattan & Bronx Surface Transit Operating Auth., 94 A.D.2d 617, 462 N.Y.S.2d 17 (1st Dep't 1983), *aff'd*, 61 N.Y.2d 769, 461 N.E.2d 291, 473 N.Y.S.2d 154 (1984); Zavlich v. Thompkins Square Holding Co., 10 A.D.2d 492, 200 N.Y.S.2d 550 (1st Dep't 1960).

107. Whitaker v. Eighth Avenue Rail Road Co., 51 N.Y. 295, 299 (1873).

108. In Luby v. Hudson River R.R., 17 N.Y. 131 (1858), the court of appeals held that the trial court had erred by permitting a police officer to testify that immediately after the accident the driver of the car stated that his brakes did not work. The court said: "The alleged wrong was complete, and the driver, when he made the statement, was only endeavoring to account what he had done."

109. People v. Brown, 70 N.Y.2d 513, 517 N.E.2d 515, 522 N.Y.S.2d 837 (1987); Deutsch v. Horizon Leasing Corp., 145 A.D.2d 405, 535 N.Y.S.2d 383 (2d Dep't 1988), and People v. Norton, 164 A.D.2d 343 (1st Dep't 1999). For an example of a statement that failed to quality as an excited utterance, see Lieb v. County of Westchester, 176 A.D.2d 704 (2d Dep't 1991): A bus driver talked to the passengers after the accident, claimed that a brown car had cut him off, and asked the passengers to back him up so he would not lose his job. The driver had time for reflection before he claimed someone had cut him off. In People v. Miklejohn, 184 A.D.2d 735 (2d Dep't 1992), the trial court should have admitted as an excited utterance the deceased victim's statement that he could not identify his assailant. He had known the defendant for fifteen years.

110. Flynn v. Manhattan & Bronx Surface Transit Operating Auth., 94 A.D.2d 617, 462 N.Y.S.2d 17 (1st Dep't 1983), *aff'd*, 61 N.Y.2d 769, 461 N.E.2d 291, 473 N.Y.S.2d 154 (1984).

driver. Shortly after the accident, a passenger told the driver that he had hit someone on a bike, and the driver related this to the policeman. Another passenger testified that a passenger behind her had yelled, "Stop, you hit someone." The plaintiff, who was on the ground, told a passerby, "The bus, it hit me. I think I broke my arm." The defendant denied that the bus had hit the plaintiff but introduced no witnesses at the trial; instead, the defendant relied on the police report.

The Appellate Division, First Department, held,

1. The plaintiff may establish the defendant's liability through circumstantial evidence.[111]
2. Although the plaintiff could produce no witness who saw the bus hit the plaintiff, the circumstantial evidence of the defendant's liability was strong, convincing, and uncontroverted.
3. Since the plaintiff had amnesia regarding the accident, a lesser burden of proof applied to his action.
4. The statements from the plaintiff and the passengers were admissible as spontaneous declarations.[112]
5. The bus driver's statement to the policeman regarding what the driver had been told by a passenger was also admissible as an admission against interest.

The traditional method of introducing an excited utterance is to call as a witness someone who heard the utterance. The person who spoke the utterance also might testify. However, an excited utterance now might have been recorded on audio tape. (A witness still must testify regarding the making of the tape.) For example, in *People v. Sanchez,*[113] the trial court properly admitted as excited utterances the audio tape of radio transmissions by police officers at the scene of a shooting.

111. *Id.* 94 A.D.2d at 618, 462 N.Y.S.2d at 18.

112. Kelner, *Res Gestate and Spontaneous Declarations*, N.Y.L.J., Sept. 14, 1983, at 1, col. 1.

113. People v. Sanchez, 216 A.D.2d 207 (1st Dep't 1995).

17.5.1.2 Declarations of Present Bodily Condition

The exception for declarations of present bodily condition resembles the exception for excited utterances but allows testimony of utterances made after the event. In New York, a nonmedical witness may testify to the complaints of pain that the plaintiff made immediately after the accident. "Screaming, or some similar exclamation, is the natural language of pain in all men, and in all animals as well. It usually, and almost invariably, accompanies intense pain; and hence, such exclamations have always been received as competent evidence, tending to show suffering."[114]

Declarations of present bodily condition made some time after the accident are not admissible unless the plaintiff made them to a physician for the purpose of treatment.[115] However, if the injured person has died, the courts permit his or her personal representative to establish the decedent's complaint of present bodily pain to someone other than a doctor.[116] Furthermore, testimony regarding the plaintiff's "groans and screams" is always admissible even if uttered after the accident, as distinguished from the plaintiff's complaints of pain[117] made later when being examined by an expert witness.

17.5.1.3 Declarations of Present Sense Impression

The exception from the hearsay rule for a present sense impression is the excited utterance without the excitement. The exception might also be called the 911 rule. In the archtypical case, the declarant telephones 911 then describes a burglary in progress; the prosecutor or the plaintiff subsequently seeks to introduce the tape of the 911 call as evidence of the events described. In the seminal cases of

114. FED. R. EVID. 803(3).

115. Roche v. Brooklyn C.& N. R.R., 105 N.Y. 294, 11 N.E. 630 (1887).

116. Tromblee v. North Am. Accident Ins. Co., 173 A.D. 174, 158 N.Y.S. 1014 (2d Dep't), *aff'd*, 226 N.Y. 615, 123 N.E. 892 (1916).

117. RICHARDSON, EVIDENCE § 287.

People v. Luke[118] and *People v. Brown,*[119] the declarant called 911 and described such a burglary. The difference between the cases was that the declarant in *Luke* identified herself while the declarant in *Brown* did not. In *People v. Buie,*[120] the declarant chased the burglar out of the house and down the street while talking to the 911 operator on his cellular telephone.

As a rule of law, the present sense impression requires that the declarant describe events that he or she is actually and simultaneously observing and that there be some corroboration of the events described by the declarant.[121] This corroboration need not be another eyewitness; for example, physical evidence could provide the corroboration.[122] Moreover, the exception does not require that the declarant be unavailable to testify.[123]

The court of appeals adopted the exception for a present sense impression in *People v. Brown,*[124] and nearly all of the cases involving such an offer have been criminal ones.[125] In some of these cases, the declaration probably would have been admissible as an excited utterance. However, the courts frequently reject offers of a present sense impression because the declaration was not truly simultaneous,[126] because there was no cor-

118. People v. Luke, 136 Misc. 2d 733, 519 N.Y.S.2d 316 (Sup. Ct. Bronx 1987), *aff'd sub nom.* People v. Duke, 147 A.D.2d 989, 538 N.Y.S.2d 886 (1st Dep't 1989).
119. People v. Brown, 80 N.Y.2d 729, 594 N.Y.S.2d 696 (1993).
120. People v. Buie, 86 N.Y.2d 501, 634 N.Y.S.2d 415 (1995).
121. *Id.*
122. People v. Luke, *supra* at 739.
123. People v. Buie, 86 N.Y.2d 501 (1995); People v. Farrell, 646 N.Y.S.2d 124 (2d Dep't 1996); People v. Hughes, 645 N.Y.S.2d 493 (2d Dep't 1996), and People v. Cook, 159 Misc. 2d 430, 603 N.Y.S.2d 979 (Sup. Ct. King, 1993).
124. People v. Brown, 80 N.Y.2d 729, 594 N.Y.S.2d 696 (1993).
125. The most significant civil case is Taft v. New York City Transit Authority, 193 A.D.2d 503, 597 N.Y.S.2d 374 (1st Dep't 1993). Query: shouldn't the declarant's statement after the victim fell under a subway train have been admissible as an excited utterance?
126. Griggs v. Children's Hosp., Inc., 193 A.D.2d 1060, 599 N.Y.S.2d 197 (4th Dep't 1993); People v. Slaughter, 189 A.D.2d 157, 596 N.Y.S.2d 22 (1st Dep't 1993); People v. Dalton, 88 N.Y.2d 561 (1996), and People v. Atkinson companion case to *Dalton.*

roboration,[127] or because the declarant was not the observer.[128] Nevertheless, if the declaration is otherwise admissible, the declaration remains admissible even if the declarant testifies at the trial.[129] In other words, the present sense impression does not constitute impermissible bolstering. Finally, defendants have begun to invoke the rule in criminal cases. For example, in *People v. Semple*, the defendant successfully sought to introduce the tape recording of the radio calls between the policemen in their patrol car and their headquarters.[129.1]

17.5.2 The Apparent Exception

The following exception to the hearsay rule is only an apparent one because the party offers the declaration not for the truth of its contents but as evidence of someone's state of mind. Hence, the rule is not an exception to the hearsay rule but merely an application of it.

17.5.2.1 Declarations of Present Mental State

A person's declaration of his own mental state is admissible despite the hearsay rule because the declaration is admissible solely to convey the person's state of mind when that person was doing something. For example, when drafting a will, the testator might say that he is giving his son nothing because his son had been cruel to him. If the son later sues to overturn the will, the testator's statement will be admissible, not for its truth, but to establish the testator's intention.[130] Note that the declaration must reflect the

127. People v. Vasquez, 88 N.Y.2d 561 (1996); People v. Watson, 100 A.D.2d 452, 474 N.Y.S.2d 978 (2d Dep't 1984), and Berger v. City of New York, 157 Misc. 2d 521, 597 N.Y.S.2d 555 (Sup. Ct. N.Y. 1993). The interesting point in *Vasquez* is that the supposed corroboration differed from the declarant's version in that the two versions had the culprit running in different directions.

128. People v. Adkinson, 88 N.Y.2d 561 (1996).

129. People v. Buie, 86 N.Y.2d 501, 634 N.Y.S.2d 415 (1995), and People v. Victor, 161 Misc. 2d 212, 613 N.Y.S.2d 567 (Sup. Ct. Kings 1994).

129.1. People v. Semple, 174 Misc.2d 879, 881-83 (Sup. Ct. Kings 1997).

130. Note, *The State of Mind Exception to the Hearsay Rule*, 16 WAKE FOREST LAW REV. 431 (1979).

declarant's present intention and may not refer to an event in the past (e.g., "I did not do it because . . .").[131]

When the act of a party may be given in evidence, his declarations, made at the time, calculated to elucidate and explain the character and quality of the act, so connected with it as to constitute one transaction, and so as to derive credit from the act itself, are admissible in evidence.[132] In the example above, the testator's statement about his son was part of the declarant's present intention. It is admissible not for its truth, i.e., that the son was cruel to his father, but to establish the father's intent when he made his will.

A typical example of the exception was provided by the decision of the Appellate Division, Second Department, in *Garsten v. MacMurray,*[133] in which the plaintiff sought to establish his state of mind when he completed the accident report in order to undermine his admission on that form. The appellate court noted that the trial court had erred in precluding the plaintiff from eliciting certain testimony, which he alleged proved his state of mind:

> Garsten sought to explain why he had stated on a form he filled out soon after the automobile accident that the car he was driving "skidded on an oil slick." He would have testified that his wife heard a report on the radio that an oil slick was involved and that she had told this to him. The testimony was offered to show that Garsten's belief that there was an oil slick was based not upon his observations during the accident but upon second-hand information. The appellants thereby sought to demonstrate Garsten's state of mind rather than the truth that there was any oil slick . . . . Hence, the proffered testimony would not have been hearsay and the court's ruling was erroneous.

131. Loschiavo v. Port Auth., 86 A.D.2d 624, 446 N.Y.S.2d 358 (2d Dep't 1982); *In re* Will of Engelken, 103 Misc. 2d 772, 426 N.Y.S.2d 894 (Surr. Ct. 1980); United States v. Harris, No. 83-1169 (2d Cir. 1983).

132. Lund v. Tyngsborough, 9 Cush. (Mass.) 36, 42.

133. Garsten v. MacMurray, 133 A.D.2d 442, 519 N.Y.S.2d 563 (2d Dep't 1987).

In other words, Garsten wanted to testify to his wife's declaration in order to show his own state of mind in order to undermine his own statement in the accident report, and the trial court should have let him. Note that the declarant's state of mind still must have been contemporaneous with the act of completing the form.

Sometimes the declaration is the act itself rather than just part of the act. In such a case, a person's declaration is admissible to prove his or her state of mind in order to prove the person's intention. For example, a person's declaration that he or she did not want to have his or her life prolonged by artificial means would be admissible in a relative's action to have the declarant's life support systems shut off.[134]

17.6 TESTIMONY AND DECLARATIONS FROM WITNESSES WHO ARE UNAVAILABLE

If a witness is unavailable at the time of the trial, a party may be able to substitute that witness's former testimony or declaration against interest for the witness's oral testimony. A decedent's dying declaration, however, is inadmissible in a civil action.

17.6.1 The Admission of Former Testimony

C.P.L.R. rule 4517 provides that, in a civil action, any party may introduce a witness's testimony from an earlier trial of the same subject matter between the same parties if the wit-

134. Eichner v. Dillon, 73 A.D.2d 431, 426 N.Y.S.2d 517 (2d Dep't 1980), *modified to execute order*, 52 N.Y.2d 363 (1981). In New York, there is no such thing as a living will. For the law of health care proxies and orders not to resuscitate, see Public Health Law sections 2803, 2960-2976, and 2980-2994.

ness is no longer available. The cause of the witness's unavailability may be a privilege, death, a physical or mental illness, absence from the jurisdiction of the court, the party's inability to locate the witness despite due diligence, or the dead man's statute.[135] Naturally, a party's personal representative is the same party, but the party offering the former testimony must not have procured the witness's absence. The ordinary method of introducing the former testimony is to have the stenographer read the notes into evidence, but any person who can read them accurately may do so if the stenographer is dead or incompetent.

This exception is actually broader than the statute indicates because the courts have allowed parties to introduce a witness's former testimony from actions regarding the same subject matter but not involving precisely the same parties because the proceeding was criminal or administrative. The key prerequisite is that the party against whom the former testimony will be introduced had the opportunity to cross-examine the witness. For example, in *Healy v. Rennert,*[136] the court of appeals held that the testimony of an out-of-state witness, whom the defendant's attorney had cross-examined in a magistrate's court proceeding in which the defendant was charged with a traffic infraction, was admissible in a civil action against the same defendant and arising from the same incident since "the issue was so clear-

---

135. The previous testimony of a deceased witness was admissible at common law. Fleury v. Edwards, 14 N.Y.2d 334 (1964). *See also* RICHARDSON, EVIDENCE § 268; FED. R. EVID. 804(b)(1), (d)(1), 613(a)&(b). In Cohen v. Long Island R.R., 154 A.D. 603, 139 N.Y.S. 887 (1st Dep't 1913), the plaintiff, as administratrix, sued for the death of her daughter. The defendant offered in evidence the testimony of a deceased flagman who had testified at the trial of a similar action brought by the plaintiff as the administratrix of her son, who had been killed in the same accident. The court, 154 A.D. at 605, 139 N.Y.S. at 889, admitted the testimony in evidence because "[t]he subject or lack of negligence of defendant's servant is the same in both actions. . . ." *See* Annot., *Identity of Subject Matter or of Issues as Condition of Admissibility in Civil Case of Testimony or Deposition in Former Proceeding of Witness Not Now Available*, 70 A.L.R.2D 494 (1960).

136. Healy v. Rennert, 9 N.Y.2d 202, 173 N.E.2d 777, 213 N.Y.S.2d 44 (1961).

ly identical that the cross-examination in both instances would normally cover the same field."[137] Similarly, a claimant's testimony before the comptroller of a municipality is admissible at the trial of his civil action if he is no longer living.[138] A motor vehicle hearing is a special proceeding so the testimony of the plaintiff's intestate at such a hearing, when the defendant's attorney had an opportunity to cross-examine him, is admissible in the civil action.[139]

The *Healy* case also clarifies the type of evidence necessary to establish that the witness is not a resident of New York. The court of appeals ruled that the trial court had erred by excluding a letter the witness had written from Arizona, letters sent to him in Arizona, a telephone conversation between the witness and the plaintiff in which the former had indicated that he had become a resident of Arizona, and a card from the files of the New York City Pension Bureau showing that the witness was living in Arizona.[140]

Finally, the party offering the testimony should arrange to have the stenographic notes of the testimony read to the jury and a transcript prepared, but he or she is not required to do so because the best-evidence rule is not applicable. Instead, the party may offer the oral testimony of anyone who heard the former testimony and can relate the substance of it.[141] Naturally, the stenographic record may be more persuasive, and the witness relating the former testimony is subject to cross-examination and impeachment.

---

137. *Id.* at 209, 173 N.E.2d at 783, 213 N.Y.S.2d at 50.

138. Rothman v. City of N.Y., 273 A.D. 780, 75 N.Y.S.2d 151 (2d Dep't 1947). Actually, under N.Y. Gen. Mun. Law § 50-h(4), either party may read into evidence the herding before the comptroller.

139. Fleury v. Edwards, 14 N.Y.2d 334, 200 N.E.2d 550, 251 N.Y.S.2d 647 (1964).

140. *See* Annot., *Nonaccessibility of Witness as Ground for Use in Civil Case of Testimony Given in Criminal Case*, 70 A.L.R.2D 1179 (1960).

141. RICHARDSON, EVIDENCE § 272.

17.6.2 The Admission of a Declaration Against the Interest Of a Non-Party

As distinguished from an admission against interest by a party and as an exception to the hearsay rule, a statement is admissible as a declaration against the interest of a declarant if:

1. The declarant is unavailable;
2. The statement, when made, was against the declarant's penal, pecuniary, or proprietary interest;
3. The declarant had personal knowledge of the facts when making the declaration; and
4. There exist sufficient indicia of the declaration's trustworthiness to ensure its reliability.[142]

For example, assume that after a collision between the plaintiff's and the defendant's automobiles, the plaintiff sued only the owner of the other automobile and not the driver, and that the driver has since died. May the plaintiff prove at the trial that the deceased driver told the police that the driver "never saw plaintiff's car before the accident?" The plaintiff may because the driver's statement was a declaration against interest when the driver made it.[143]

The fourth criterion, sufficient indicia of trustworthiness, is often the focus of dispute between the attorneys for the parties. Remember that it is incorrect to call the declarant a

142. FED. R. EVID. 804(b)(3), 804(a)(1); People v. Brown, 26 N.Y.2d 88, 308 N.Y.S.2d 825 (1970); Ellis v. Allstate Ins. Co., 97 A.D.2d 970, 468 N.Y.S.2d 776 (4th Dep't 1966); Basile v. Huntington Fuel Corp., 60 A.D.2d 616, 400 N.Y.S.2d 150 (2d Dep't 1977). *See also* People v. Smith, 195 A.D.2d 112 (1st Dep't 1994). *Brown* enlarged the scope of the declaration against interest to include penal interest as well as pecuniary and proprietary interests.

143. Ellwanger v. Whiteford, 15 A.D.2d 298, 225 N.Y.S.2d 734 (1st Dep't 1966); Halvorsen v. Moon & Kerr Lumber Co., 87 Minn. 18, 91 N.W. 28 (1902); *see also* Jefferson, *Declarations Against Interest: An Exception to the Hearsay Rule*, 58 HARV. L. REV. 1 (1944).

witness since this exception allows someone else to testify to the declarant's out-of-court statement for the truth of its contents and without affording the opposing party's attorney an opportunity to cross-examine the declarant. The result of these limitations is that any doubt about the declaration's trustworthiness may lead the trial court to exclude the declaration. As the court of appeals explained in *People v. Shortridge:*

> [C]ertain considerations may be fatal to the reliability of a declaration and thereby render the out of court statement inadmissible.
>
> These considerations include the declarant's motivation — e.g., whether the statement was designed to exculpate a loved one or inculpate an enemy. Important also is the declarant's personality — e.g., whether he suffers psychological or emotional instability or whether he is a chronic or pathological liar. Additionally, the declarant's spontaneity or hesitancy, promptness or tardiness in making the statement may shed light on its authenticity. Likewise, the internal consistency and coherence of the declaration, or its lack thereof, may reflect on its bona fides. Most critical in some cases, is the availability of supporting evidence — that is, some proof, independent of the declaration itself, which tends to confirm the truth of the facts asserted therein.
>
> * * *
>
> While these and other relevant considerations should all be weighed, whenever applicable, by the trial court in the exercise of its sound discretion, the presence of a strong motivation to fabricate or the absence of supporting evidence can, without more, be sufficient to render a declaration inadmissible as a matter of law.[144]

Doubts about the witness reporting the declaration may also cause the trial court to exclude an admission against interest. For example, in *People v. McGovern,*[145] a prosecution

144. People v. Shortridge, 65 N.Y.2d 309, 312-13, 480 N.Y.2d 1080, 491 N.Y.S.2d 298, 299-300 (1985).

145. People v. McGovern, 158 A.D.2d 551 (2d Dep't 1990).

for robbery, the court properly refused to allow the defendant's mother to testify that her younger son had admitted being the culprit, i.e., that the son being tried was innocent.

17.6.3 A Dying Declaration Is Inadmissible

In order for a statement to be admissible as a dying declaration, it must appear that:

1. The declarant was in extremis;
2. The declarant was under a sense of impending death without any hope of recovery; and
3. The declarant, if living, would be competent to testify.[146]

Unfortunately, this exception to the hearsay rule is not available in civil actions. Dying declarations are admissible only in criminal actions for homicide and only when the defendant is charged with the declarant's death and when the circumstances of that death are the subject of the declaration.[147]

146. People v. Nieves, 108 A.D.2d 165, 488 N.Y.S.2d 654 (1st Dep't 1985); RICHARDSON, EVIDENCE § 307.

147. People v. Becker, 215 N.Y. 126, 109 N.E. 127 (1915). In People v. Nieves, 108 A.D.2d 165, 468 N.Y.S.2d 654 (1st Dep't 1985), the appellate court underscored the necessity that the utterant be in extremis with no hope of recovery.

EXAMPLE 17-1: CRIME AND INCIDENT REPORT

HEALTH AND HOSPITALS CORPORATION
HOSPITAL POLICE
CRIME AND INCIDENT REPORT

Pct. Occurrence: 98
NYPD Compl. #: 987
Boro: NEW YORK
Control #: 7-56
Headquarters File #:

Military Time and Date of This Report: Time 920, Date 1/12/88
Occurrence On or From: Time 1030, Date 1/07/88, Day Of Week SUN
Occurrence Through: Time, Date

Person Reporting: P.O. JOHN DOE
Position/Relationship: HOSP.POLICE OFF.
Address, City, State, Apt. #: GENERAL HOSPITAL
Home Telephone:
Business Telephone: 212-567-4444

Victim's Name: P.S.N.Y.
Address, City, State, Apt. #:
Home Telephone:
Business Telephone:

Victim: ☐ Male ☐ Female ☐ Corporation ☒ State
Age:
Victim's Race: ☐ White ☐ Oriental ☐ Black ☐ Hispanic ☐ American Indian ☐ Other
Can Identify? ☐ No — If YES, answer below ☐ Patient ☐ Employee ☐ Visitor ☐ Other:
Will Prosecute? ☐ Yes ☐ No
How Was Complaint Received? ☐ Radio ☐ Phone ☐ Walk-in ☐ Pick-up

Offense(s) or Incident(s): BURGLARY 3
Was Entry Forced? ☐ Yes ☒ No ☐ Attempted
Weapon: ☐ Used ☐ Possessed
Type:

Address/Location of Occurrence: 230 11th Ave., NY, NY 100
Location (Be Specific): Laundry/Supply Room 3rd Floor
Post: B
Visible by Patrol Assigned: ☒ Yes ☐ No

Pct. of Arrest: 98
Arrest Number(s): 980
Type of Evidence: Medical Supplies
NYPD Property Voucher #: D-23899
Court Docket #:

PROPERTY INFORMATION ☐ Lost ☐ Stolen ☐ Corporation ☐ Patient ☐ Employee ☐ Visitor
If Corporation property, was item marked for identification? ☐ Yes ☐ No

PROPERTY INFORMATION (Itemized)				PROPERTY SUMMARY	VALUE STOLEN	VALUE REC'D
Quantity	Article	Description, Model & Serial #	Item Value	CORPORATE PROPERTY		
				Typewriter		
				Currency		
				Calculator		
				Radio/Walkie Talkie		
				Other Hospital Equipment		
				Other Office Equipment		
				Vehicle		
				Miscellaneous		
				OTHER THAN CORP. PROPERTY		
				Currency		
				Auto		
				Jewelery		
				Furs, Clothing		
				TV's, Radios, Cameras		
				Miscellaneous		
				WEAPONS		
				Firearms		
				Other		

ARRESTED PERSONS INFORMATION (Include persons wanted)

Name, Last, First MI	Wanted	Arrested	Address, City, State, Apt. #	Home Telephone	Business Telephone
Roe, Peter		X	89 Manhattan Ave, NY, NY	212 897-0980	

No.	Sex	Race	Age	Date of Birth	Height	Weight	Hair Color	Clothing	Wanted Alarm
1	M	B	30	1/4/50	5'6"	130	blk	Red Sweatshirt	

DETAILS, INCLUDE WITNESS AND ADDITIONAL ARRESTS AND VICTIMS

AT T/P/O DEFT DID ENTER AND REMAIN UNLAWFULLY IN THE LAUNDRY ROOM AT GENERAL HOSPITAL. DEFT WAS FOUND TO BE IN POSS OF Medical Supplies (Hypd-Needles) AND A STETHOSCOPE

CASE CLOSED BY ARREST:

REF.

EXAMPLE 17-2: AMBULANCE REPORT

Prehospital Care Report 3-2186611

DATE OF CALL: 2/03/92 | RUN NO. | AGENCY CODE: 08133 | VEH. ID. 1-32

Agency Name: Copiague F.D.
Call Location: 25 E Granada
CHECK ONE: ☒ Residence ☐ Health Facility ☐ Farm ☐ Indus. Facility ☐ Other Work Loc. ☐ Roadway ☐ Recreational ☐ Other
Dispatch Information: A/F chest pains

MILEAGE: END / BEGIN / TOTAL

USE MILITARY TIMES: CALL REC'D 2330 | ENROUTE 2332 | ARRIVED AT SCENE 2340 | FROM SCENE 2353 | AT DESTIN 0000 | IN SERVICE 0012 | IN QUARTERS

AGE 34 | DOB 01/26/58 | SEX: M ☐ F ☒

CALL TYPE AS REC'D: ☒ Emergency ☐ Non-Emergency ☐ Stand-by

COMPLETE FOR TRANSFERS ONLY: Transferred from ☐ No Previous PCR ☐ Unknown if Previous PCR; Previous PCR Number

CARE IN PROGRESS ON ARRIVAL: ☒ None ☐ Citizen ☐ PD/FD/Other First Responder ☐ Other EMS

MECHANISM OF INJURY: ☐ MVA (complete seat belt section) ☐ Struck by vehicle ☐ Fall of ___ feet ☐ Unarmed assault ☐ GSW ☐ Knife ☐ Machinery ☐ Extrication required ___ minutes | Seat belt used? N/A ☐ Yes ☐ No ☐ Unknown | Seat Belt Use Reported By ☐ Crew ☐ Patient ☐ Police ☐ Other

CHIEF COMPLAINT: Pt st "My chest hurts."

SUBJECTIVE ASSESSMENT: pt found lying on bed C/O substernal chest pain radiating to (R) arm

PRESENTING PROBLEM (If more than one checked, circle primary): ☐ Airway Obstruction ☐ Respiratory Arrest ☐ Respiratory Distress ☒ Cardiac Related (Potential) ☐ Cardiac Arrest ☐ Allergic Reaction ☐ Syncope ☐ Stroke/CVA ☐ General Illness/Malaise ☐ Gastro-Intestinal Distress ☐ Diabetic Related (Potential) ☒ Pain (chest) (R) arm ☐ Unconscious/Unresp. ☐ Seizure ☐ Behavioral Disorder ☐ Substance Abuse (Potential) ☐ Poisoning (Accidental) ☐ Shock ☐ Head Injury ☐ Spinal Injury ☐ Fracture/Dislocation ☐ Amputation ☐ Other ☐ Major Trauma ☐ Trauma-Blunt ☐ Trauma-Penetrating ☐ Soft Tissue Injury ☐ Bleeding/Hemorrhage ☐ OB/GYN ☐ Burns Environmental ☐ Heat ☐ Cold ☐ Hazardous Material ☐ Obvious Death

PAST MEDICAL HISTORY: ☐ None ☒ Allergy to UNK ☐ Hypertension ☐ Seizures ☐ COPD ☒ Other (List) Lupus ☐ Stroke ☐ Diabetes ☐ Cardiac ☐ Asthma
Current Medications (List): Atabrine 100 mg

VITAL SIGNS	TIME	RESP	PULSE	B.P.	LEVEL OF CONSCIOUSNESS	GCS	PUPILS	SKIN
	2344	Rate: 24, Labored	Rate: 88, Regular	140/100	Alert	15	Normal (R, L)	Warm, Moist
		Rate:	Rate:					
		Rate:	Rate:					

OBJECTIVE PHYSICAL ASSESSMENT: 34 y/o F pt st that she has chest pain radiating to her (R) arm x approx 25 min. prior to our arrival. pt put on 15 LPM of O2 via NRB w/ no relief. pt hx of lupus. Pt transported

COMMENTS: s̄ further incident. pt st. a "pressure like" pain at chest rad. (R) arm.

TREATMENT GIVEN
☒ Moved to ambulance on stretcher/backboard
☒ Moved to ambulance on stair chair
☐ Walked to ambulance
☒ Airway Cleared
☐ Oral/Nasal Airway
☐ Esophageal Obturator Airway/Esophageal Gastric Tube Airway (EOA/EGTA)
☐ EndoTracheal Tube (E/T)
☒ Oxygen Administered @ 15 L.P.M., Method NRB
☐ Suction Used
☐ Artificial Ventilation Method
☐ C.P.R. in progress on arrival by: ☐ Citizen ☐ PD/FD/Other First Responder ☐ Other
☐ C.P.R. Started @ Time | Time from Arrest Until C.P.R. ___ Minutes
☐ EKG Monitored (Attach Tracing) [Rhythm(s)]
☐ Defibrillation/Cardioversion No. Times ☐ Manual ☐ Semi-automatic
☐ Medication Administered (Use Continuation Form)
☐ IV Established Fluid ___ Cath. Gauge
☐ Mast Inflated @ Time
☐ Bleeding/Hemorrhage Controlled (Method Used:)
☐ Spinal Immobilization Neck and Back
☐ Limb Immobilized by ☐ Fixation ☐ Traction
☐ (Heat) or (Cold) Applied
☐ Vomiting Induced @ Time ___ Method
☐ Restraints Applied, Type
☐ Baby Delivered @ Time ___ In County ☐ Alive ☐ Stillborn ☐ Male ☐ Female
☐ Transported in Trendelenburg position
☐ Transported in left lateral recumbent position
☒ Transported with head elevated
☒ Other U-SPEA, PE FRAXIN

DISPOSITION (See list): BMH | DISP. CODE 512 | CONTINUATION FORM USED

CREW: IN CHARGE Espinal ☒ EMT # 156739 | DRIVER'S NAME Ganz ☒ EMT # 1300157 | NAME Debragh ☒ EMT # 176221 | NAME Simmons

AGENCY COPY/WHITE RESEARCH COPY/YELLOW HOSPITAL PATIENT RECORD COPY/PINK

EMS 100 (11/86) DOH 3283 (1-92)

EXAMPLE 17-3: INSTRUCTIONS FOR ADMISSION ASSESSMENT FORM

17

SGHN OI 168-6, Atch 1, 1 Apr 90

INSTRUCTIONS
ADMISSION ASSESSMENT FORM

AF FORM 3241, 3244, 3247

1. Must be completed within 8 hours after admission; note date and time of admission.

2. Reason for admission - Must include the Patient's statement of why he/she was admitted.

3. Request for Chaplain - Circle appropriate response; if yes, write in denomination and/or name of chaplain contacted. Optional unless pertinent to hospitilization.

4. Vital signs, height, weight, allergies - Include T, P, R, B/P, Ht and Wt. Check whether height and weight were stated or if patient was actually weighed. Write specific names of food/drugs to which patient states he/she is allergic. Indicate patient's response. If patient denies drug allergies, indicate this with "NKDA".

5. MD notified/time - write name of MD notified and time (JCAHO standard).

6. Unit rules - Check yes or no. Actual documentation of teaching is maintained on AF FORM 3256, Pt/Family Teaching Flow Sheet. If no is checked, reason why rules were not explained must be indicated.

7. Signature - for Admission note - in addition to RN, may be 902 or LVN, but must be countersigned by RN.

8. MD saw patient/time - write name and time MD saw patient (IAW AFR 168-4). Rn initials entry.

9. Impact of Previous Hospitalization - Include brief description of how pt/family coped with previous hospitalization(s); include information about any problems they had, fears that developed, and/or other family member hospitalizations if pertinent to this admission (ex. pt admitted for BX to R/O malignancy and other family member was once admitted for similar reason). Do Not limit information to dates and DX's of previous hospitalizations.

10. Social & Family history/support systems/living arrangements/occupation - Include a brief description of social history pertinent to patient's illness and extent to which family and life style may be impacted by that illness. For example, will a post-MI patient be returning to a third floor walk-up apartment where he/she lives alone; does a patient admitted for extended hospitalization have child-care arrangements for only one week; is a family member here with the patient; etc. Occupation is self-explanatory. Include "Pt on PRP" if appropriate. For example, it may be important to know that a patient is a wing Commander who might need phone access during hospital stay, or that the patient admitted for abdominal surgery has a job requiring heavy lifting and will need sufficient convalescent leave post discharge.

11. Nursing assessment of patient - Must be completed by RN - check options and complete brief narrative as necessary. Discussion under each system should reflect physical, functional, psychosocial, and patient/family educational needs. Write, as appropriate, if "pt (or family member) denies problems" or if "Pt demonstrates no problems at present". Use of N/A provides little informational about patient assessment/status. "0" and "-" are not acceptable. Note that **Skin Assessment** should be included with the MusculoSkeletal/Intergumentary Systems on side two. The nurse must state specifically that skin problems were or were not present.

12. Present Medications - As stated by the patient/family. Include any regularly taken over-the-counter meds, as these may have a synergistic / antagonistic effect on other meds. All portions of this section must be completed (i.e. name, dose, last dose, and patient's stated reason for taking the medication) to the extent of the pt/family member's knowledge. The purpose is to identify knowledge deficit regarding medications.

13. Disposition of Meds - state whether meds were sent home or kept on unit; whether patient will self-medicate.

14. ADL needs - this section incorporates functional assessment data noted earlier under each system. Include aspects of self-care with which patient may require assistance(ex. prosthesis, walker, dentures) and initiate Pt Care Plan Problem #2. Any entry made here should also be considered in discharge planning and possible initiation of Pt Care Plan problem #11. Put **SELF** in the space if patient is totally self care.

15. Discharge planning assessment - list the type of instructions/equipment /other assistance the patient/family will need prior to discharge for effective home care management. Consider initiation of Pt Care Plan #2 and #11 as actual or potential patient problems. This information must be consistent with data written under other sections.

16. Specialty overprint - optional according to unit facility needs.

EXAMPLE 17-4: ADULT ADMISSIONS NOTE

ADULT ADMISSION NOTE

DATE 25 Nov. 89 TIME 1600

REASON FOR ADMISSION (from patient): Patient feared heart attack. Abdominal pain, nausea and vomiting. "It hurts so bad I can hardly breathe."

REQUEST CHAPLIN: YES [ ] NO [X]

MODE OF ARRIVAL: AMBULATORY [ ] WHEELCHAIR [X] STRETCHER [ ]

FROM

VITAL SIGNS: TEMPERATURE 99.7 | PULSE 95 | RESPIRATION 24 | BLOOD PRESSURE 150/85 | HT STATED — ACTUAL 63 | WT STATED — ACTUAL 185

ALLERGIES: Aspirin

TIME: 1615 DR. NOTIFIED OF PATIENT'S ADMISSION (Name): Thomas Principe

TIME: 1632 DR. SAW PATIENT (Name): Thomas Principe — RN INITIALS: RM

UNIT RULES (Fire, Safety, Unit orientation, Valuables etc.) EXPLAINED: YES [ ] NO [X] (Reason) too upset

SIGNATURE: Kevin McMullen — DATE 25 Nov. 89 TIME 1730

NURSING ASSESSMENT/HISTORY (TO BE FILLED OUT BY AN RN)

CHECK APPROPRIATE BOX — ELABORATE AS NECESSARY — INITIAL AT END OF STATEMENT

INFORMATION GIVEN BY: Leroy Brown-husband

IMPACT OF PREVIOUS HOSPITALIZATION(S) (Example — Coping patterns, Concerns affecting this hospitalization): Two previous hospitalizations for uneventful term vaginal deliveries. Hospitalized five years ago for adult onset diabetes mellitus.

SOCIAL & FAMILY HISTORY/SUPPORT SYSTEM/LIVING ARRANGEMENTS/OCCUPATION: Married to unemployed but retired AF E7. Two teenaged sons. Job with stockbroker hectic and entails long hours.

MENTAL STATUS: ALERT [ ] CONFUSED [ ] UNRESPONSIVE [ ] LETHARGIC [ ] DEPRESSED [ ] ANXIOUS [X] COOPERATIVE [ ]

HEENT: GLAUCOMA [ ] CATARACTS [ ] BLIND [ ] GLASSES [X] CONTACT LENS [ ] HEARING LOSS [ ] NOSE BLEED [ ] DYSPHAGIA [ ] DENTURES [ ]

RESPIRATORY: PAIN [X] DYSPNEA [ ] WHEEZING [ ] ORTHOPNEA [ ] PRODUCTIVE COUGH [ ] NONPRODUCTIVE COUGH [ ] SMOKER [ ]

CIRC.: EDEMA [ ] NUMBNESS [ ] SYNCOPE [ ] ANEMIA [ ] BRUISING [ ] CHEST PAIN [ ] PALPITATIONS [ ] HYPERTENSION [ ] MURMUR [ ] PHLEBITIS [ ] LEG PAIN [ ] sweating.

GI: ABDOMINAL DISTENSION [ ] NAUSEA [X] VOMITING [X] DYSPHAGIA [ ] ULCERS [ ] CONSTIPATION [ ] DIARRHEA [ ] INCONTINENCE [ ] OSTOMY [ ] BLOOD [ ] LAXATIVES [ ] HEMORRHOIDS [ ] ETOH [ ]

GU: INCONTINENCE [ ] NOCTURIA [ ] STONES [ ] UTI [X] PROSTATE PROBLEMS [ ] OSTOMY [ ] FREQUENCY [ ] BURNING [ ] BLOOD [ ] FOLEY [ ] History of UTI twice a year.

Patient's name stamped here.

ENDOCRINE | TREMOR | GOITER | X DIABETES | MOOD SWINGS | MENSTRUAL PROBLEMS | WEIGHT CHANGES

NEUROLOGICAL | SEIZURES | PARALYSIS | X NUMBNESS | WEAKNESS | DIZZINESS | TREMORS | HEADACHE | HEAD INJURY | LOSS OF CONSCIOUSNESS
FAINTING | TINGLING | GAIT PROBLEMS

Hands and feet since onset of diabetes.

MUSCULOSKELETAL INTEGUMENTARY | DEFORMITIES | PAIN | STIFFNESS | CONTRACTURES | HISTORY OF FRACTURES | JOINT REPLACEMENT(S)

PRESENT MEDICATIONS

AS STATED BY: PATIENT X FAMILY

NAME	DOSE FREQUENCY	LAST DOSE	DISP	PURPOSE	NAME	DOSE FREQUENCY	LAST DOSE	DISP	PURPOSE
DIABINASE	BID	AM	FAM: ABC-pharmacy chain	control diabetes					

ADL NEEDS X | SPECIAL DIET (State) ADA diet | ASSISTANCE WITH (State)

DISCHANGE PLANNING ASSESSMENT (Example: Impaired physical and or mental status, Needs equipment, Behavior problem, Terminal Status, Financial concerns, Visiting nurse, Social work consult, Extended care)

may need social services support to afford to take time off from work.

RN SIGNATURE Kevin McMullen | DATE 25 Nov 89 | TIME 1815

SPECIALTY OVERPRINTS

Form 3241, MAR 89 (Reverse)

EXAMPLE 17-5: SPECIALTY OVERPRINT

ENDOCRINE: | TREMOR | GOITER | DIABETES | MOOD SWINGS | MENSTRUAL PROBLEMS | WEIGHT CHANGES

NEUROLOGICAL: | SEIZURES | PARALYSIS | NUMBNESS | WEAKNESS | DIZZINESS | TREMORS | HEADACHE | HEAD INJURY | LOSS OF CONSCIOUSNESS
| FAINTING | TINGLING | GAIT PROBLEMS

MUSCULOSKELETAL/INTEGUMENTARY: | DEFORMITIES | PAIN | STIFFNESS | CONTRACTURES | HISTORY OF FRACTURES | JOINT REPLACEMENT(S)

PRESENT MEDICATIONS — AS STATED BY: PATIENT | FAMILY

NAME	DOSE FREQUENCY	LAST DOSE	DISP	PURPOSE	NAME	DOSE FREQUENCY	LAST DOSE	DISP	PURPOSE

ADL NEEDS. | SPECIAL DIET (State) | ASSISTANCE WITH (State)

DISCHARGE PLANNING ASSESSMENT (Example--Impaired physical and or mental status. Needs equipment. Behavior problem. Terminal Status. Financial concerns. Visiting nurse. Social work consult. Extended care)

RN SIGNATURE | DATE | TIME

SPECIALTY OVERPRINTS

1. Appearance: ______
2. Behavior: ______
3. Characteristics of Speech: ______
4. Mood: ______
5. Affect: ______
6. Thought Content: ______
7. Orientation: ______
8. Memory- Short term: ______
   Long term: ______
9. Judgement: ______
10. Insight: ______
11. Other Comments: ______

HPI: ______

Suicidal Ideation: YES/NO Homicidal Ideation: YES/NO Concerning Who? ______
PRP: YES/NO Security Clearance: YES/NO Level of Clearance: ______
Recent Sleeping Habits: ______ Recent Eating Habits & Weight Loss: ______
Degree of Involvement with: (1) Drugs: ______ (
(2) Alcohol ______ (3) Tobacco ______
Date of Last Drink: ______ Amount of ETOH last consumed: ______
Evidence of DT's: ______ History of DT's: ______

Command Directed or Volunteer for ARC (Please Circle One)

Nursing Assessment/Diagnosis: ______

12. The patient relates the following: (Circle No More Than Two)
    a. I have had an IPPD test.
    b. I have NOT had an IPPD test within the past year.
    c. I am ALLERGIC to the IPPD test.
    d. I have had a POSITIVE IPPD test in the past.

AF Form 3241, MAR 89 (Reverse)

16

EXAMPLE 17-6: DEATH CERTIFICATE

VITAL RECORDS
DEPARTMENT OF HEALTH

DATE FILED 11:40 20-May 92

CERTIFICATE OF DEATH Certificate No. 92-0275-2

1. NAME OF DECEASED (Type or Print) John (First Name) (Middle Name) Smith (Last Name)

MEDICAL CERTIFICATE OF DEATH *(To be filled in by the Physician)*

2. PLACE OF DEATH — 2a. NEW YORK CITY BOROUGH: New York — 2b. Name of hospital or other facility if not facility, street address: General Hospital — 2c. If in Hospital or Other Facility (Check) 1 ☐ DOA 3 ☐ Outpatient 2 ☐ Emerg. 4 ☑ Inpatient — 2d. If Inpatient, date of current admission: Month 3 Day 18 Year 92

3a. Date and Hour of Death (Month) May (Day) 15 (Year) 92 — 3b. HOUR 7:15 ☑ AM ☐ PM — 4. SEX MALE — 5. APPROXIMATE AGE 39

6. I HEREBY CERTIFY THAT: *(Check One)*

☐ I attended the deceased ☑ A staff physician of this institution attended the deceased

☐ Dr. ______ attended the deceased

from 3/18 1992 to 5/15 1992 and last saw him alive at 7:00 AM

on 5/15 1992. I further certify that traumatic injury or poisoning DID NOT play any part in causing death, and that death did not occur in any unusual manner and was due entirely to NATURAL CAUSES.

*See first instruction on reverse of certificate.

Witness my hand this 5 day of 15 19 92 Signature ______ D.O. M.D.

Name of Physician Dr. Doe (Type or Print) Address 320 - 11th Street NY, NY 110

PERSONAL PARTICULARS *(To be filled in by Funeral Director)*

7. Usual Residence a. State N.Y. — 7b. County NY — 7c. City, Town, or Location New York — 7d. Street & House No. Zip Apt. No. 23 West 42 St. 100 — 7e. Inside City Limits of 7c ☑ Yes ☐ No

8. Served in U.S. Armed Forces No 0 ☑ Yes 1 ☐ Specify years From To — 9. Marital Status (Check One) 1 ☐ Never Married 2 ☐ Widowed 3 ☑ Married or separated 4 ☐ Divorced — 10. Name of Surviving Spouse (If wife, give maiden name) Jane Smith (nee Jones)

11. Date of birth of Decedent (Month) (Day) (Year) April 4, 1953 — 12. Age at last birthday 39 — If under 1 Year mos. days — If less than 1 Day hours min. — 13. Social Security No. 000-33-8902

14a. Usual Occupation (Kind of work done during most of working lifetime, do not enter retired) Salesman — 14b. Kind of Business Auto Sales

15. Birthplace (City & State or Foreign Country) Brooklyn, NY — 16. Education (Check only one) 0-11 ☐ 1 12 ☐ 2 13-15 ☐ 3 16 ☑ 4 17+ ☐ 5 — 17. Other name(s) by which decedent was known

18. NAME OF FATHER OF DECEDENT Edward Smith — 19. MAIDEN NAME OF MOTHER OF DECEDENT Roe

20a. NAME OF INFORMANT Jane Smith — 20b. RELATIONSHIP TO DECEASED wife — 20c. ADDRESS (City) (State) (Zip) 23 West 42 St. New York, New York 100

21a. NAME OF CEMETERY OR CREMATORY Rose Rest — 21b. LOCATION (City, Town, State and Country) Hillside, New York — 21c. DATE OF BURIAL OR CREMATION May 19, 1992

22a. FUNERAL DIRECTOR Martin Greenwood — 22b. ADDRESS 8990 Hillside Road, Hillside

BUREAU OF VITAL RECORDS DEPARTMENT OF HEALTH THE CITY OF NEW YORK

VR15 (1/88)

This is to certify that the foregoing is a true copy of a record on file in the Department of Health. The Department of Health does not certify to the truth of the statements made thereon, as no inquiry as to the facts has been provided by law.

DEATH TRANSCRIPT

IRENE A SCANLON
CITY REGISTRAR

DEPARTMENT OF HEALTH THE CITY OF NEW YORK

Do Not accept this transcript unless it bears the raised seal of the Department of Health. The reproduction or alteration of this transcript is prohibited by Section 3.21 of the New York City Health Code.

BUREAU OF VITAL RECORDS DEPARTMENT OF HEALTH THE CITY OF NEW YORK

DATE ISSUED MAY 1992 DOCUMENT NO. A 602889

EXAMPLE 17-7: REPORT OF AUTOPSY

OFFICE OF THE MEDICAL EXAMINER

COUNTY OF NASSAU

Case No.

REPORT OF AUTOPSY

,M.D., in the presence of ,M.D.

eby certify that I have performed an autopsy on the body of

May , 19 at 11:10 A.M. and said autopsy revealed as follows:

CAUSE OF DEATH: Pending toxicological and microscopic examinations.

/ / FINAL DIAGNOSIS: Acute and Chronic Fibrosing Interstitial Myocarditis;
Status Post Emergency Caesarian Section.

NASSAU COUNTY MEDICAL EXAMINER'S OFFICE — NAME:

VITREOUS CHEMISTRY REQUEST: — ME #:

AGE: — SEX: female

DRAWN BY: ______ TIME: 10^50 AM DATE: 5- -

REC'D BY: ______ TIME: ______ DATE: ______

SODIUM 145 Meq/1

POTASSIUM 7.1 Meq/1

SUGAR 118 mg/dl

UREA NITROGEN 10 mg/dl

CREATININE 0.3 mg/dl

LACTIC ACID ______

CHLORIDE 130 Meq/dl

OTHERS: ______

______

______

______ MAY 19

CHIEF TOXICOLOGIST — DATE

______ ______

PATHOLOGIST — DATE

MAY 11 59

RECEIVED

MEDICAL EXAMINER'S OFFICE

OF NASSAU COUNTY, N. Y.

TOXICOLOGY REPORT

Date May , 19

Tox Case #

M.E. Case #

On 11

Examine for General Unknown

Organs Submitted Blood, Brain, Liver, Kidney, Stomach Contents (20oz), Abdominal Fat.

Organs Used Blood, Brain, Liver, Kidney, Stomach Contents (4oz).

Poisonous Gases: CARBON MONOXIDE: 0.5% Hemoglobin Saturation

Volatile Compounds: ABSENT

Acidic & Neutral Compounds: ABSENT

Amphoterics Compounds: KETAMINE ~~present~~ in Brain, Stomach (estimated 300 mgs recovered) and Liver; 1.0 mg/kg in Liver.

OTHERS: Absent

Metallic Poisons: ABSENT

Additional Findings:

S/

63 5M-3/83

OFFICE OF THE MEDICAL EXAMINER

COUNTY OF NASSAU

________________ - 1A - Case No.

ANATOMICAL SUMMARY

GENERAL:	Status post Caesarean section.
SEROUS CAVITIES:	Hemoperitoneum.
HEART:	Unremarkable.
LUNGS:	Congestion and partial atelectasis.
GASTROINTESTINAL TRACT:	Unremarkable.
LIVER:	Hepatomegaly. Congestion.
PANCREAS:	Unremarkable.
SPLEEN:	Unremarkable.
KIDNEYS:	Congestion. Focal hemorrhages in the pelvic mucosa.
URINARY BLADDER:	Submucosal hemorrhages.
UTERUS:	Unremarkable post partum appearance. Status post Caesarean section.
OVARIES:	Unremarkable.
ADRENALS:	Unremarkable.
THYROID:	Unremarkable.
MUSCULO-SKELETAL SYSTEM:	Unremarkable.
BRAIN:	Unremarkable.

OFFICE OF THE MEDICAL EXAMINER

COUNTY OF NASSAU

________________ -2- Case No.

EXTERNAL EXAMINATION:

The body is that of a normally-developed, well-nourished, female appearing the stated age of 35 years, measuring 5 feet 0 inches in length with a scale weight of 208 pounds. Rigor mortis is mild. Livor mortis is posterior. The head is normocephalic and without evident trauma. The hair is brown in color and long. The irides are brown. The sclerae and conjunctivae are pale. No petechial hemorrhages are noted. The ears are unremarkable. The nose is intact and patent. The lips show no evident injury. The teeth are natural. The oral cavity is unremarkable. The neck is symmetrical and without evident trauma. The chest is symmetrical and without evident injury. The breasts are pendulous and without palpable masses. The abdomen is protuberant with multiple abdominal striae and a surgical scar in the right upper quadrant. Below the umbilicus is an unhealed midline surgical incision approximated with metal staples. The external genitalia are those of a normal adult female. The vagina contains a small amount of clotted blood.

The lower and upper extremities are symmetrical and without injury. The back is unremarkable.

INTERNAL EXAMINATION:

The body is opened with the usual Y-shaped incision.

SEROUS CAVITIES:

The pleural cavities are free from fluid, blood or adhesions. The pericardial cavity contains the usual amount of fluid. The diaphragm is intact. The peritoneal cavity contains approximately 1800 cc. of liquid blood.

CARDIOVASCULAR SYSTEM:

The heart weighs 430 grams. The epicardial chambers are free from thrombi and are intact. The valves are patent and the cusps and leaflets are normal in appearance. The atrial and ventricular septae are intact. The endocardium is smooth. The myocardium is brown in color and without evident fibrosis. The coronary ostia and coronary arteries are widely patent.

The aorta is patent and intact with mild atherosclerotic streaking. The superior and inferior vena cavae are intact.

OFFICE OF THE MEDICAL EXAMINER

COUNTY OF NASSAU

_________________ -3- Case No.

RESPIRATORY SYSTEM:

The right lung weighs 400 grams. The left lung weighs 330 grams. The pleural surfaces are smooth and shiny. The lungs are partially atelectatic and congested. The bronchial and vascular trees are normal in calibre, patent and intact.

NECK ORGANS:

The endotracheal tube is present in its correct position. The larynx and trachea are patent and intact. The mucosa shows focal submucosal hemorrhages without appreciable edema. The strap muscles show hemorrhages with therapeutic needle punctures. The thyroid gland is normal in size, shape and appearance.

GASTROINTESTINAL SYSTEM:

The esophagus is patent and the mucosa is grey and smooth. The stomach is usual in size and shape and contains a moderate amount of partly digested food. The mucosa shows autolytic changes. The small and large intestines appear normal.

HEPATO-BILIARY SYSTEM:

The liver weighs 2300 grams. The capsule is smooth and intact. The parenchyma is light brown in color and congested.

The gallbladder is not present.

PANCREAS:

The pancreas is normal in size and shape and appearance.

URINARY SYSTEM:

The right kidney weighs 120 grams. The left kidney weighs 130 grams. The capsules strip easily revealing smooth brown cortical surfaces. Cross sections reveal congestion and multifocal hemorrhages in the mucosa of the pelves. The ureters are patent and intact. The urinary bladder does not contain urine and the mucosa shows focal submucosal hemorrhage secondary to a Foley catheter placement.

GENITAL ORGANS:

The uterus measures approximately 18 x 15 x 5 cm. in maximum dimension. The lower anterior uterine wall shows a transverse unhealed surgical incision which is sutured and grossly intact. The cervical os is markedly patulous. The myometrium is boggy and otherwise unremarkable. The endometrial cavity is remarkable for a moderate amount of adherent blood clot. Placental fragments are not identified. The Fallopian tubes and ovaries are normal in appearance.

OFFICE OF THE MEDICAL EXAMINER

COUNTY OF NASSAU

________ -4- Case No.

RETICULO-ENDOTHELIAL SYSTEM;

The spleen weighs 120 grams. The capsule is smooth and intact. The parenchyma is unremarkable. A small unremarkable accessory spleen is noted.

The lymph nodes in the chest and abdomen are unremarkable.

The vertebral bone marrow is brown in color and firm.

ADRENALS:

The adrenals are normal in size, shape and appearance.

MUSCULO-SKELETAL SYSTEM:

The muscular and skeletal systems are unremarkable.

HEAD AND CRANIAL CONTENTS:

The scalp is incised and reflected. There is no evident injury. The dura mater is grey and smooth. There are no epidural or subdural hematomas. The brain weighs 1300 grams. There are no subarachnoid hemorrhages. The cerebral hemispheres, brain stem and cerebellum are symmetrical. The vessels of the Circle of Willis are patent and intact. Multiple cross sections do not reveal hemorrhage, necrosis or tumor. The ventricles are unremarkable.

The pituitary gland is normal in size, shape and appearance.

COUNTY OF NASSAU

- 5 - CASE NO:

MICROSCOPIC EXAMINATION

HEART:	Focal acute interstitial myocarditis with eosinophiles. Multifocal chronic fibrosing myocarditis. Focal fatty infiltration.
RONARIES:	Patent.
LUNGS:	Intra-alveolar and perivascular edema.
LARYNX:	Mild chronic inflammation. Focal acute intramuscular hemorrhage.
LIVER:	Within normal limits.
SPLEEN:	Within normal limits.
PANCREAS:	Early autolytic change.
KIDNEYS:	Acute passive congestion. Autolytic changes of tubular epithelium.
UTERUS:	Hyperplasia of smooth muscle. Giant cells consistent with trophoblast, focal necrosis, acute inflammation and acute hemorrhage- consistent with implantation site.
OVARIES:	Within normal limits.
BONE MARROW:	Normocellular.
ADRENASL:	Within normal limits.
THYROID:	Within normal limits.
PITUITARY GLAND:	Within normal limits.
BRAIN:	Within normal limits.

PATHOLOGIST

HIEF MEDICAL EXAMINER

EXAMPLE 17-8: CERTIFICATE OF MARRIAGE REGISTRATION

1983 STATEN ISLAND INDEX

A

THE CITY OF NEW YORK
OFFICE OF THE CITY CLERK
MARRIAGE LICENSE BUREAU-BOROUGH OF STATEN ISLAND

№ 0

Certificate of Marriage Registration

This Is To Certify That Ago Richard

residing at 61 3rd Avenue, Brooklyn, New York born October , 19

at New York, New York and Marie Vit

residing at 321 2nd Street, Brooklyn, New York born October , 19

at Bari, Italy

Were Married

on June , 19 at Brooklyn, New York

as shown by the duly registered license and certificate of marriage of said persons on file in this office.

CERTIFIED THIS DATE AT THE
CITY CLERK'S OFFICE, STATEN ISLAND, N.Y.

June , 19

FACSIMILE SIGNATURE AND SEAL
ARE PRINTED PURSUANT TO SECTION 11-A,
DOMESTIC RELATIONS LAW OF NEW YORK
(SEE REVERSE SIDE FOR EXTRACT OF LAW)

David N. Dinkins
City Clerk of the City of New York

RF 226 (REV 8/80)

Depositions 18

18.1 INTRODUCTION

C.P.L.R. section 3117 governs the use of depositions during a trial. The normal manner of introducing a witness's testimony is to call the witness to the stand and to have him or her testify orally in the presence of the jury. Nevertheless, a witness's deposition from the examination before trial is sometimes admissible pursuant to the specific rules in the C.P.L.R. and so far as otherwise permissible under the rules of evidence. In other words, the party seeking to introduce a deposition during a trial must meet the requirements of the C.P.L.R. and of an exception to the hearsay rule. The C.P.L.R. refers to these latter rules only obtusely; thus, the introductory sentence to section 3117(a) reads,

> At the trial . . . , any part or all of a deposition, so far as admissible under the rules of evidence, may be used in accordance with the following provisions: . . . .

18.1.1 The Trial Court's Authority

Although C.P.L.R. section 3117 specifies how a party may use a deposition during the trial, the trial court retains the right to control the orderly and fair introduction of the deposition.[1] In particular, the court has the inherent right to rule that a party's attorney may not have a deposition read into evidence at a certain point in the trial if the court de-

1. Feldsberg v. Nitschke, 49 N.Y.2d 636, 404 N.E.2d 1293, 427 N.Y.S.2d 751 (1980).

cides that the attorney is using the deposition in a prejudicial manner. As the court of appeals explained in *Feldsberg v. Nitschke*:

> A trial court is not without power to ensure the orderly and fair administration of justice merely because a particular item of evidence is technically admissible. Although there exist general rules for the conduct of trials, deviation from these rules may be necessary to fit the circumstances of a particular case. Indeed, the power to permit deviation is an integral part of the Trial Judge's function. The court often has before it complex litigation and is duty bound to assure fairness and avoid unnecessarily protracted or confusing presentation of evidence. This power to control the case necessarily is of a discretionary nature, and its exercise is not reviewable save for a clear abuse of discretion . . . .[2]

18.1.2 The Creation of the Deposition

The parties create depositions by conducting an examination before trial at which each party has a right to be represented and to question the witnesses and at which a stenographer makes a verbatim record. The notary (usually the stenographer) records in the deposition all the objections to the notary or the stenographer, to the manner of taking the deposition, the testimony presented, the conduct of any person, or anything else about the proceedings. However, the examination should proceed without unreasonable adjournment.[3] Bother the judge assigned to the case for a ruling only as a last resort. Meanwhile,

> Examination and cross-examination of deponents shall proceed as permitted in the trial of actions in open court. When the deposition of a party is taken at the instance of an adverse

2. *Id.* at 643. 404 N.E.2d at 1298, 427 N.Y.S.2d at 754.
3. C.P.L.R. 3113(b).

> party, the deponent may be cross-examined by his own attorney. [However] Cross-examination need not be limited to the subject matter of the examination in chief.[4]

In other words, the order of the examinations is the reverse of that typical of a trial, unless the plaintiff calls the defendant as the plaintiff's witness at the trial.

The stenographer then transcribes each witness's deposition, and the deposition is sent to the witness to read, correct, and sign. C.P.L.R. rule 3116 formerly provided that the witness must correct the deposition and include a statement of any reasons for the corrections. Despite this rule, the trial court had the discretion to use a deposition although the witness corrected it but failed to include the reasons.[5] Moreover, if the witness refused to sign the deposition, its introduction into evidence was harmless error.[6] Finally, the legislature has amended C.P.L.R. 3116(a) to allow the witness sixty days to correct, sign, and return his deposition. After that, the deposition is admissible without his signature, and the witness may not subsequently revise the deposition. Example 18-1, found at the end of the chapter, is a simple form for helping the deponent to make the corrections.

In addition, the notary should annex to the deposition any documentary evidence or exhibits marked for identification and deliver them to the court with the transcript of the deposition. However, if the party producing the document or exhibit so requests, the notary shall mark the item for identification, allow each party to inspect or copy it, and then return the item to the party producing it.[7]

---

4. C.P.L.R. 3113(c).
5. Roberts v. Ausable Chasm Co., 47 A.D.2d 979, 367 N.Y.S.2d 120 (3d Dep't 1975); *In re* Estate of Kurtz, N.Y.L.J., Feb. 5, 1986 (Sur. Ct. 1986).
6. Hahn v. City of Niagara Falls, 143 A.D.2d 517, 533 N.Y.S.2d 62 (4th Dep't 1988); American Tel. & Tel. Co. v. Lincoln Indus. Enters., 122 A.D.2d 925, 506 N.Y.S.2d 90 (2d Dep't 1986).
7. C.P.L.R. 3116(c).

18.1.3 The Substitution of Parties or Actions

C.P.L.R. section 3117(c) provides, "substitution of parties does not affect the right to use depositions previously taken," so a change in a nominal party, e.g., the commissioner of the city's department of highways, will not affect any party's right to use a deposition. Moreover, the parties may use in one action all of the depositions taken in a prior action if three conditions are met:

1. The subject matter is the same;
2. The prior action was brought in a state or federal court in the United States; and
3. The parties are either the same ones or their representatives or successors in interest.[8]

Naturally, the deposition must also meet the other requirements imposed by C.P.L.R. section 3117(a) and the rules of evidence. Example 18-1A consists of the notice of motion and the accompanying affirmation to substitute two executrices for the original plaintiff.

18.2 THE SPECIFIC RULES ALLOWING A PARTY TO INTRODUCE A DEPOSITION

C.P.L.R. section 3117(a) contains four rules authorizing a party to introduce a deposition in specific situations during a trial. These rules allow a party's attorney to use a deposition:

1. To impeach a witness by means of a prior inconsistent statement;

---

8. C.P.L.R. 3117(c).

2. To any purpose, e.g., to establish an admission against interest, when another party made the deposition;
3. To substitute the deposition for a witness's oral testimony when the witness is unavailable; and
4. To substitute the deposition for the oral testimony of a witness who is authorized to practice medicine.

18.2.1 Impeaching a Witness

C.P.L.R. section 3117(a) provides, "any deposition may be used by any party for the purpose of contradicting or impeaching the testimony of the deponent as a witness." Thus, a party's attorney may use the witness's deposition to impeach either his or her client's own witness or the opposing party's witness if the deposition qualifies as a prior inconsistent statement. Although the statute does not say so, the attorney may also use the deposition to rehabilitate a witness whom the opposing attorney has accused of a recent fabrication.

18.2.2 An Admission Against Interest

The former version of C.P.L.R. section 3117(a)(2) provided that one party could use an opposing party's prior statement in a deposition as evidence in chief if the statement constituted an admission against interest. This section is now broader and reads:

> The deposition testimony of a party or of any person who was a party when the testimony was given or of any person who at the time the testimony was given was an officer, director, member, employee or managing or authorized agent of a party, may be used for any purpose by any party who was adversely interested when the deposition testimony was given or who is adversely interested when the deposition testimony is offered in evidence...

Thus, effective January 1, 1997, C.P.L.R. 3117(a)(2) allows any party to use the deposition of a former party for any purpose so long as the proponent and the deponent had adverse interests either at the date of the examination or at the date of the trial. This amendment will help the parties to cope with the complications created by the combination of the comparative negligence rule and section 15-108 of the General Obligations Law, which section allows a plaintiff to settle his or her claim against one tortfeasor without thereby releasing the others. At the trial, the plaintiff's interest is to magnify the fault attributable to the remaining defendants while the defendant's interest is to magnify the fault attributable to the discharged tortfeasor. Allowing both remaining parties to use the discharged party's deposition as evidence in chief may assist the jury in allocating the comparative fault. For example, a plaintiff could sue two defendants, take depositions of both, settle with one, then use the former defendant's deposition against the remaining defendant at the trial. However, the remaining defendant could retaliate by reading other parts of the former defendant's deposition and by reading the plaintiff's deposition.

The utility of another amendment is obscure. Effective January 1, 1997, C.P.L.R. 3117(a)(2) allows a party to use the deposition of the employee of another party for the same purpose as the proponent could use the employer's deposition. Remember, however, that the provisions of C.P.L.R. 3117(a)(2) remain subject to the law of evidence and that every employee is not authorized to make any admission on behalf of his or her employer. Until now, section 3117(a)(2) applied to the officers of a party because they represented the entity. However, the statute did not authorize a party to use the deposition of an opposing party's employee as freely as an officer's because an employee does not represent the entity for the purpose of making admissions. Specifically, one party might use the deposition of the opposing party's employee for any purpose only if the employer had called the employee to the stand during the trial, thereby presenting the employee as knowledgeable and credible. Thus, if the employer called the employee to the stand, then the opposing party might use the employee's deposition as an admission against the employer's interest, i.e., as evidence-in-chief, but if the opposing party called the employee to the stand, then that party might use the deposition only to impeach the witness. This was the holding of the Appellate Division, Second Department, in *Rodriguez v. Board of Education.*[9]

In *Rodriguez,* the plaintiff had called the defendant's employee to the stand and had sought to use the employee's deposition as evidence-in-chief. The appellate court ruled that this was impermissible:

> The only uncorrected error was in allowing plaintiffs, as part of their case-in-chief, to read into the record that statement made by Beverely Kolstein during her examination before trial. The deposition of a party's employee may be used for any purpose at trial by any adversely interested party so long as the party employer produced the employee . . . . However, if any party other than the employer has called the employee as a witness, neither that party nor any other may use the employee's deposition under that provision. . . .[10]

The appellate court did not reverse the judgment, however, because the statement from the deposition was brief and merely repeated the witness's testimony at the trial.

According to *Rodriguez,* the plaintiff may use the deposition of the defendants' employee as evidence-in-chief if the employee is unavailable to testify. Of course, if the defendant's employee is a person authorized to practice medicine, then the plaintiff need not show either that the witness is unavailable or that there are special circumstances.[11]

---

9. Rodriguez v. Board of Educ., 104 A.D.2d 978, 480 N.Y.S.2d 901 (2d Dep't 1984).
10. *Id.* at 980, 480 N.Y.S.2d at 903.
11. C.P.L.R. rule 3117(a)(4).

18.2.3 Substituting the Deposition for an Unavailable Witness

C.P.L.R. section 3117(a)(3) provides, "the deposition of any person may be used by any party for any purpose against any other party who was present or represented at the taking of the deposition or who had the notice required under these rules, provided the court finds" any one of five conditions that constitute the witness being unavailable in some sense. These five conditions are:

1. That the witness is dead;
2. That the witness is outside the state or more than one hundred miles from the place of the trial unless the party offering the deposition has procured the witness's absence;
3. That the witness is unable to testify because of age, illness, infirmity, or imprisonment;
4. That the party's diligent efforts have been unable to procure the witness's attendance; or
5. That exceptional circumstances and the interests of justice make using the deposition desirable despite the preference for oral testimony.

If a party can satisfy one of these conditions, then he may use the absent witness's deposition as evidence-in-chief. The party may not, of course, use the deposition to impeach a witness since the deponent is absent.

Note that C.P.L.R. section 3117(a)(3)(iv) provides that a party may introduce a witness's deposition if the party offering the deposition was unable to procure the attendance of the witness by diligent efforts. Therefore, in *Miller v. Daub,*[12]

12. Miller v. Daub, 128 Misc. 2d 1060, 492 N.Y.S.2d 703 (Civ. Ct. 1985). In Daugherty v. City of N.Y., 137 A.D.2d 441, 524 N.Y.S.2d 703 (1st Dep't 1988), the court found that counsel's efforts to procure the attendance of the witness did not amount to due diligence.

the trial court held that the service of a subpoena and the witness's failure to appear did not constitute diligent efforts. The party must do more, e.g., obtain a bench warrant for the witness, before being entitled to substitute the deposition for the witness's oral testimony.

18.2.4 Substituting the Deposition for the Oral Testimony of Someone Authorized to Practice Medicine

C.P.L.R. section 3117(a)(4) provides, "the deposition of a person authorized to practice medicine may be used by any party without the necessity of showing unavailability or special circumstances, subject to the right of any party to move pursuant to section 3103 to prevent abuse." In other words, a party may offer a physician's deposition as a substitute for the physician's testimony and as evidence-in-chief — even if the witness is legally available to testify. This provision complements C.P.L.R. section 3103(d), which authorizes taking the depositions of expert medical witnesses in actions for medical malpractice by the mutual consent of the parties. Thus, a party's attorney may chose to examine a medical expert at the examination before trial rather than at the trial itself. The attorney should remember, however, that the examination and cross-examination conducted in front of the jury have more influence on the jury than does any deposition. Of course, the creation of the experts' depositions may lead the parties to settle the case.

In *Cruz v. City of New York,*[13] the trial court allowed the plaintiff to introduce the deposition of a physician who was not a party but who was employed by a hospital that is a part of the city's health and hospitals corporation, the defendant. The court allowed the plaintiff to introduce the physician's answers to questions that required him to testify as an

---

13. Cruz v. City of N.Y., 135 Misc. 2d 393, 515 N.Y.S.2d 398 (Sup. Ct. N.Y. 1987).

expert. The result was undoubtedly correct, but the court strained to analogize the nonparty physician to a party. The correct ground simply would have been that the witness was authorized to practice medicine.

In *Hardter v. Semel,* the Appellate Division, Fourth Department, held that the plaintiff could force the partner of the defendant-doctor to answer questions at the examination beyond those concerning the deponent's care of the plaintiff's decedent while covering for the defendant. Specifically, the plaintiff could require the deponent to give his expert opinion regarding the fluid culture test, communicating with a partner about the latter's patient, and the circumstances of his own care and treatment of the decedent. The court's rationale was that one partner is the other's employee for the purposes of the pretrial examination.[14] Either party will be able to substitute Dr. Semel's deposition for his live testimony at the trial.

18.3 THE EFFECTS OF USING A DEPOSITION

18.3.1 Adopting the Deponent as the Party's Witness

The rule governing whether a party makes a witness his own by introducing the witness's deposition, C.P.L.R. section 3117(d), contains exceptions to the exceptions. Fortunately, the basis of the rule is common sense. First, a party does not adopt a witness for any purpose either by taking the witness's deposition or by using the witness's deposition to contradict or impeach the witness. Second, a party does adopt a witness by using the witness's deposition for any other purpose. In other words, a party adopts a witness if the party uses the witness's deposition as evidence-in-chief. Third, however, the second rule is inapplicable, i.e., the party may use the deposition as evidence-in-chief without mak-

14. Hardter v. Semel, 197 A.D.2d 846 (4th Dep't 1993).

ing the witness his or her own, if the witness is an adverse party, an officer of an adverse party, or an employee called by an adverse party who is the witness's employer. In that case, a useful deposition would constitute an admission against interest. Of course, introducing the deposition of a witness who is simply unavailable would constitute adopting the witness. Fourth, even if the party does adopt the deponent as that party's witness by introducing the witness's deposition as evidence-in-chief, the party is not bound by every statement in the deposition for, according to C.P.L.R. section 3117(d), "[a]t trial, any party may rebut any relevant evidence contained in a deposition, whether introduced by him or by any other party."

18.3.2 Reading Only Part of a Deposition

A party is permitted to read only part of a deposition into evidence, but he or she cannot thereby preclude another party from reading other parts of the deposition. C.P.L.R. section 3117(b) provides, "[i]f only part of a deposition is read at the trial by a party, any other party may read any other part of the deposition which ought in fairness to be considered in connection with the part read."

As noted above, the trial court has the discretion to control the use of depositions. However, the Appellate Division, Third Department, has ruled that it is reversible error for the trial court to allow one party to read part of the adverse party's deposition into evidence but to refuse to allow the second party to read additional parts of the deposition on the ground that the deposition is merely a self-serving declaration to bolster the party's testimony as a witness. The appellate court wrote:

> We hold that this ruling contravenes C.P.L.R. 3117 (subd.[b]), which entitles a party to introduce into evidence his deposition taken before trial to correct a false impression that reading only a part of the statement may give. Such evidence is not present to bolster a witness's testimony but rather simply to remedy any misimpression resulting from a selective reading of a deposition.[15]

As a procedural matter, however, the opposing party does not have the right to read the additional portions of the deposition immediately. The opposing party must wait until it is his or her turn to present evidence. There is no inherent right to read the additional part as soon as the initial reading has been completed.[16]

Example 18-2, found at the end of the chapter, is the transcript from a trial in which the plaintiff's attorney read part of an expert's deposition to the jury. This transcript includes the judge's explanation to the jury and the beginning of the deposition.

---

15. Hallock v. State, 98 A.D.2d 856, 857, 470 N.Y.S.,2d 844, 845 (3d Dep't 1983), *rev'd on other grounds*, 64 N.Y.2d 224 (1984).
16. Villa v. Vetuskey, 50 A.D.2d 1093, 376 N.Y.S.2d 359 (4th Dep't 1975).

EXAMPLE 18-1: CORRECTION SHEET

CORRECTION SHEET

STATE OF NEW YORK)
ss: CASE NAME:

COUNTY OF)

___________________, being duly sworn, deposes and says: the following are corrections made to my transcript of the 50H Hearing held on at

PAGE _______, LINE_____ SHOULD READ:_______________________________
____

PAGE _______, LINE_____ SHOULD READ:_______________________________
____

PAGE _______, LINE_____ SHOULD READ:_______________________________
____

PAGE _______, LINE_____ SHOULD READ:_______________________________
____

PAGE _______, LINE_____ SHOULD READ:_______________________________
____

PAGE _______, LINE_____ SHOULD READ:_______________________________
____

PAGE _______, LINE_____ SHOULD READ:_______________________________
____

PAGE _______, LINE_____ SHOULD READ:_______________________________
____

PAGE _______, LINE_____ SHOULD READ:_______________________________
____

PAGE _______, LINE_____ SHOULD READ:_______________________________
____

PAGE _______, LINE_____ SHOULD READ:_______________________________
____

PAGE _______, LINE_____ SHOULD READ:_______________________________
____

PAGE _______, LINE_____ SHOULD READ:_______________________________
____

PAGE _______, LINE_____ SHOULD READ:_______________________________
____

X_______________________________

Subscribed and sworn to before me
this day of 199

____
NOTARY PUBLIC

EXAMPLE 18-1A: MOTION TO SUBSTITUTE PARTY

SUPREME COURT OF THE STATE OF NEW YORK
COUNTY OF NEW YORK
--X

Plaintiff, **NOTICE OF MOTION**

-against- **Index No.**

Defendants.
--X

Motion By:	KRAMER, DILLOF, TESSEL, DUFFY & MOORE Attorneys for Plaintiffs
Date, Time and Place of Hearing:	October 17, 1995, 9:30 a.m., MSO, Room 119, Supreme Court, County of New York, 60 Centre Street, New York, New York.
Supporting Papers:	Affirmation of
Relief Requested:	Order pursuant to CPLR §3025(b), granting plaintiff leave to amend the Complaint to add a cause of action for wrongful death, and an Order substituting as Co-Executrixes of the Estate of in the place of , now deceased, and and Order amending the title of this action to henceforth reflect same and an Order pursuant to CPLR §2004, §2005 and §3406(1), granting plaintiff leave to file a late Notice of Medical Malpractice Action and for such other and further relief as to this Court may seem just and proper, and and Order pursuant to CPLR § 3124 and § 3126 striking defendants and affirmative defenses that this action is barred by the applicable Statute of Limitations.

Answering affidavits, if any, are required to be served at least twelve days prior to the return date of this motion.

Dated: New York, New York
September 21, 1995

Yours, etc.,

KRAMER, DILLOF, TESSEL, DUFFY & MOORE
Attorneys for Plaintiffs
233 Broadway
New York, New York 10279
(212) 267-4177

TO:

KESSLER & WIDOWSKI, ESQ.
113-115 University Place
8th Floor
New York, New York 10003-4257

KOPFF, NARDELLI & DOPF
Attorneys for Defendants
440 Ninth Avenue
New York, New York 10001.

SUPREME COURT OF THE STATE OF NEW YORK
COUNTY OF NEW YORK

____X

Plaintiff, **AFFIRMATION**

-against- **Index No.**

Defendants.

____X

---------------, an attorney duly admitted to practice law before the Courts of the State of New York, and an associate with the law firm of **KRAMER, DILLOF, TESSEL, DUFFY & MOORE, ESQS.**, attorneys for plaintiffs herein, hereby affirms the following to be true under the penalties of perjury:

I am fully familiar with the facts and circumstances underlying the above-captioned cause of action by virtue of a file maintained in our office.

This affirmation is submitted in support of the Motion for an Order pursuant to CPLR §3025(b), granting plaintiff leave to amend the Complaint to add a cause of action for wrongful death, an Order substituting ______________, as Co-Executrixes of the Estate of ________________, in the place of ________________, now deceased, an Order amending the title of this action to henceforth reflect same and for an Order pursuant to CPLR §2004, §2005 and §3406(1), granting plaintiff leave to file a late Notice of Medical Malpractice Action and for such other and further relief as this Court may deem just and proper.

PRELIMINARY STATEMENT

This is an action sounding in medical malpractice. Plaintiff alleges that the defendants failed to timely and properly diagnosis and treat **plaintiff's** cancer of the left breast. As a result of the defendants' failure to properly diagnose and treat the plaintiff's breast cancer said cancer was allowed to metastasize to her lymph nodes. As a result of this metastasis **plaintiff** was required to undergo chemotherapy and radiation therapy. These therapies compromised **plaintiff's** immune system which resulted in her contracting pneumonia and ultimately dying.

This action was commenced by service of a Summons and Complaint upon defendant __________________ on or about March 25, 1993 and upon defendant _________ on or about April 24, 1993. (Please see complaints as to defendants ___________________ and _________________ annexed hereto as **Exhibit "A"**.) The defendants then answered on or about April 14, 1993 and May 14, 1993 respectively. (Please see answers as to defendants _________ and _________ annexed hereto as **Exhibit "B"**.) On or about April 8, 1994, Bills of Particulars as to defendant ______________ were served along with various authorizations. (Please see Verified Bills of Particulars as to defendant _____________ annexed hereto as **Exhibit "C"**.) This office was in the process of preparing the Bills of Particulars as to defendant _____________ in July of 1994, when counsel was informed that **plaintiff** had passed away on July 15, 1994. In November of 1994, this office also provided counsel for defendant ____________ with authorizations for **plaintiff**'s prior treating physicians.

POINT I

PLAINTIFF SHOULD BE GRANTED LEAVE TO AMEND THE CAPTION FOR THIS ACTION SO AS TO SUBSTITUTE THE CO-EXECUTRIXES OF THE DECEDENT PLAINTIFF IN THE DECEDENT PLAINTIFF'S STEAD

As previously stated, plaintiff, **plaintiff** died on July 15, 1994 at Memorial Sloan Kettering Hospital. By Order of the Surrogate's Court of New York County dated August 17, 1994 Letters Testamentary were granted to her daughters, __________.. Annexed hereto as **Exhibit "D"** collectively are a copy of the Death Certificate and the Letters Testamentary. Since the plaintiff has died, we respectfully request the Court make and enter an Order substituting ____________________ in place and stead of **plaintiff** amending the title of this action to therefore henceforth read:

SUPREME COURT OF THE STATE OF NEW YORK
COUNTY OF NEW YORK
---X
_____ as Administratix of the Estate
of _________, deceased. **Plaintiffs,**

-against-

Defendants.
--X

EXAMPLE 18-2: READING OF A DEPOSITION

673

Feldman - by Plaintiffs - Voir Dire

MS. LIVINGSTON: I object.

I agree with the Court.

THE COURT: Sustained.

Q Well, did you serve Dr. Clare in this case?

MS. LIVINGSTON: Objection.

THE COURT: Sustained.

MR. GREENFIELD: I have no further questions.

MS. LIVINGSTON: I have nothing further.

THE COURT: I'm sorry?

MS. LIVINGSTON: I have nothing further.

THE COURT: Okay.

Thank you, Mr. Feldman.

MS. LIVINGSTON: Thank you, Mr. Feldman.

THE WITNESS: Thank you.

MS. LIVINGSTON: May I, your Honor -- Judge, at this time, I would like to read some portions of the deposition of Dr. O'Neill, if I may.

It's the deposition of Mary

JAMES V. ALLOCCA, C.S.R. - OFFICIAL REPORTER

EBT - O'Neill

Margaret O'Neill, M.D., taken -- date, September 15, 1992, time, 10:15 a.m.

THE COURT: Do I have that deposition?

MS. LIVINGSTON: Yes, you do, your Honor.

Or, I should say, it was provided.

THE COURT: I have Ms. Rosario, but -- oh, wait. There it is.

MS. LIVINGSTON: Appearances for the plaintiff, Kramer, Dillof, Tessel Duffy & Moore, by Jesse S. Waldinger; for the defendants, McAloon & Friedman & Mandell by Brendan Lantier.

THE COURT: I don't think I explained to them about examinations before trial. Before you start reading, let me just do that.

An examination before trial is a sworn statement that was taken outside of court in preparation for the trial.

And, I know Ms. Livingston mentioned to you during her opening statement that Dr. O'Neill is now in

EBT - O'Neill

California -- is it California?

MS. LIVINGSTON: Yes, your Honor.

THE COURT: -- and, therefore, could not be served to come to testify.

So, her sworn statement is to be considered by you as testimony at this trial. And, I wanted to explain that to you before you heard it read to you.

And, I think that lawyers understand, one hopes that lawyers understand, that testimony that's read is not quite as interesting as having a real, live witness.

So, hopefully, it won't take that long.

MS. LIVINGSTON: I tried to cut it down as much as possible, being acutely aware of that, or painfully aware of that, Judge.

Thank you.

↓ START

Beginning on page 4, "Examination by Mr. Waldinger:

"QUESTION: Could you state your name and address, please?

JAMES V. ALLOCCA, C.S.R. - OFFICIAL REPORTER

EBT - O'Neill

"ANSWER:" -- Well, "Mary Margaret O'Neill. Business address.

"QUESTION: Sure.

"ANSWER: 105 North Bascom, Suite 202, San Jose, California, 95128.

"QUESTION: Are you licensed to practice medicine in the State of California?

"ANSWER: Yes.

"QUESTION: When were you licensed?

"ANSWER: 1990.

"QUESTION: Are you licensed anywhere else?

"ANSWER: New York City.

"QUESTION: New York City.

"When were you licensed in New York State?

"ANSWER: 1987.

"QUESTION: Where did you go to medical school?

"ANSWER: Creighton University.

"QUESTION: When did you graduate?

"ANSWER: 12/" --

MR. GREENFIELD: There's

JAMES V. ALLOCCA, C.S.R. - OFFICIAL REPORTER

Judicial Notice 19

19.1 INTRODUCTION

Judicial notice is a shortcut to establishing a law or a fact. Specifically, judicial notice is

> [t]he act by which a court, in conducting a trial, or framing its decision, will, of its own motion [or on the motion of a party] and without the production of evidence, recognize the existence and truth of certain facts, having a bearing on the controversy at bar, which, from their nature, are not properly the subject of testimony, or which are universally regarded as established by common notoriety, e.g., the laws of the state, international law, historical events, the constitution and course of nature, main geographical features, etc.[1] (interpolation added.)

A court that takes judicial notice of a law or a fact expedites the trial because the court relieves the parties of the obligation to prove the law or the fact. For example, a court will take judicial notice of the laws of mathematics since it would lengthen and complicate the trial to force the parties to prove that one plus one equals two. Statute controls judicial notice of the law, but common law controls judicial notice of facts.

The trial court's having taken judicial notice is not the end of the matter, for C.P.L.R. section 4511(c) provides that the court must charge the jury that the court has taken judicial notice of a law or fact and that the finding or the result-

1. BLACK'S LAW DICTIONARY 986 (4th ed. 1968).

ing charge are appealable.[2] Moreover, the court of appeals ruled in *Green v. Downs*[3] that a trial court which has taken judicial notice of a law must charge the jury by reading the law. In other words, when the determination of the case depends upon an evaluation of the parties' actions under the law, the court should read the law to the jury rather than paraphrase it.

19.2 JUDICIAL NOTICE OF THE LAW

Although no statute expressly states that a court must take judicial notice of the laws of New York, the courts deem that duty to be obvious.[4]

19.2.1 The Statutory Scheme

C.P.L.R. section 4511 divides the trial court's judicial notice of laws into three parts:

1. Those laws of which the court must take judicial notice even without a request from a party;
2. Those laws of which the court may take judicial notice without a request from a party; and
3. Those laws of which the court must take judicial notice pursuant to the request of a party.

First, even without a request from a party, the trial court must take judicial notice of the common law, constitutions,

---

2. C.P.L.R. § 4511(c): "Determination by court; review as matter of law. Whether a matter is judicially noticed or proof is taken, every matter specified in this section shall be determined by the judge or referee, and included in his findings or charged to the jury. Such findings or charge shall be subject to review on appeal as a finding or charge on a matter of law."
3. Green v. Downs, 27 N.Y.2d 205, 265 N.E.2d 68, 316 N.Y.S.2d 221 (1970).
4. People v. Herkimer, 4 Cow. (N.Y.) 345 (1825); Souveran Fabrics Corp. v. Virginia Fibre Corp., 32 A.D.2d 753, 301 N.Y.S.2d 273 (1st Dep't 1969).

public statutes, official compilations of regulations, local laws, and county acts of the federal government and of every state and territory.[5] However, the court need not take judicial notice of the regulations governing the organization or internal management of a governmental agency.

Second, without a request from a party, the trial court may take judicial notice of the private acts and resolutions of Congress and the state legislatures, the ordinances of agencies and political subdivisions, and the laws of foreign countries or their political subdivisions.[6]

Third, the trial court must take judicial notice of the items listed in the second division if a party so requests, furnishes the court with sufficient information to do so, and gives the adverse party notice. "Notice shall be given in the pleadings or prior to the presentation of any evidence at the trial, but a court may require or permit other notice."[7]

19.2.2 Pleading the Foreign Law in a Timely Manner

The trial court's duty to take judicial notice of foreign law is a different issue from whether the foreign law governs the action at trial. The attorney's failure to plead that the court should take judicial notice of one of the items specified by C.P.L.R. section 4511 does not preclude the court from taking judicial notice of that law,[8] but the attorney must apprise the court of the attorney's desire to have the court decide the action or a particular issue in accordance with the laws of a foreign country or a sister state.[9] In other

---

5. C.P.L.R.§ 4511(a).
6. C.P.L.R.§ 4511(b).
7. *Id.*
8. Cousins v. Instrument Flyers, Inc., 44 N.Y.2d 698, 376 N.E.2d 914, 405 N.Y.S.2d 441 (1978).
9. Annot., *Foreign Law Pleading and Proof of Law of Foreign Country,* 75 A.L.R.3d 177 (1977).

words, the courts' obligation to take judicial notice of the law of New Jersey does not mean that the court must apply that law without a timely request from an attorney for a party. Should the attorney fail to apprise the court until a time the court deems to be too late in the proceeding, the court may apply the law of New York.[10] For the court's duty to take judicial notice of foreign law to arise, the foreign law must be relevant to the action.

19.2.3 Evidence of the Law

While a court's taking evidence in order to decide whether to take judicial notice may seem to violate the notion of judicial notice, the trial court knows the foreign law only constructively and needs an authoritative source of it. Moreover, the presentation of this evidence is usually pro forma, for the C.P.L.R. provides:

> [A] printed copy of a statute or other written law . . . contained in a book or publication, purporting to have been published by a government or commonly admitted as evidence of the existing law in the jurisdiction where it is in force, is prima facie evidence of such law and the unwritten common law of a jurisdiction may be proved by witnesses or printed reports of cases of the courts of the jurisdiction.[11]

In addition, the court may consider any relevant testimony, document, information, or argument when deciding whether to take judicial notice of a law.[12]

If the law is difficult to ascertain, the court may move beyond judicial notice while still employing that term, and we may make a similar observation about the notice that one

10. Gevinson v. Kirkeby-Natus Corp., 26 A.D.2d 71, 270 N.Y.S.2d 989 (1st Dep't 1966).
11. C.P.L.R. § 4511(d).
12. *Id.*

party must give another. In *Gevinson v. Kirkeby-Natus Corp.*,[13] the Appellate Division, First Department, was faced with a case in which the defendant had asked the plaintiff to set forth the statutes and cases (with their official citations) upon which the plaintiff intended to rely at the trial. The court held that the defendant was not entitled to such a list. The trial court was required to take judicial notice of the law of Texas since that law governed the cause of action, but the plaintiff was not required to do the defendant's research. Nevertheless, the appellate court observed:

> It should be obvious that in a proper case, even one involving sister-State law, a court, in its discretion, may require an adversary to disclose the bases of his claim, if the bases in the statute and decisional law of another State are difficult of ascertainment, for whatever the reason, by the usual legal research techniques, or, more important, if it is unclear whether the litigant is relying at all on nonforum law (e.g., a guest statute of another State). This requirement may, perhaps, be imposed in a particularization, or better yet, in one of the truly discovery or other pretrial procedures available to a litigant.
>
> * * *
>
> If, however, a litigant should succeed in concealing the bases of his claim resting on sister-State law to the obvious prejudice of his adversary, a court in a proper case would have ample remedies. Even if the disclosure should not arise until the trial, the court would be justified, in aid of its own obligation, to give judicial notice as well to assist the adversary, to grant a continuance, impose conditions and, in a permissible case, withhold costs.[14]

---

13. Gevinson v. Kirkeby-Natus Corp., 26 A.D.2d 71, 270 N.Y.S.2d 989 (1st Dep't 1966).
14. *Id.* at 76, 270 N.Y.S.2d at 922; *cited as authority by* the Appellate Division, Second Department, in Government Employees Insurance Co. v. Sheerin, 65 A.D.2d 10, 15 (2d Dep't 1978).

19.3 JUDICIAL NOTICE OF FACTS

19.3.1 The Common Law Rule

A party's attorney must request that the court take judicial notice of a fact,[15] e.g., that February 15, 1993 was a public holiday[16] or that the state was experiencing a fiscal crisis.[17] Nevertheless, a trial court should take judicial notice of all relevant facts that are matters of common knowledge, well-established, and authoritatively settled, not doubtful or uncertain.[18] The court may even take judicial notice of a fact within the judge's personal knowledge that the judge acquired in an unrelated case.[19] However, the court should not take judicial notice of a disputed fact from that other case,[19.1] and conversely, the court is not generally required to take judicial notice of facts[19.2] other than the obvious ones, such as dates. Finally, the court should inform the attorneys of its intent to take judicial notice.

19.3.2 Examples of the Proper Judicial Notice of a Fact

The following items are seventeen cases, arranged by subject, in which the trial court properly took judicial notice of a fact.

---

15. Walter v. Stafford, 14 A.D. 310, 43 N.Y.S. 1049 (1st Dep't 1899), *aff'd,* 162 N.Y. 558, 57 N.E. 92 (1900). But a trial or appellate court may take judicial notice of a fact that is so obvious it would be a failure of discretion not to do so. Hunter v. New York O.&W. Ry., 116 N.Y. 615, 23 N.E. 9 (1899); Cooper v. Morin, 91 Misc. 2d 302, 398 N.Y.S.2d 36 (Sup. Ct. 1977), *modified on other grounds,* 64 A.D.2d 130, 409 N.Y.S.2d 30 (4th Dep't 1978), *modified on other grounds,* 49 N.Y.2d 69, 399 N.E.2d 1188, 424 N.Y.S.2d 168 (1979).
16. Matter of Persing v. Coughlin, 214 A.D.2d 145 (4th Dep't 1995).
17. Rivera v. State of New York, 205 A.D.2d 605 (2d Dep't 1994).
18. Wertling v. Manufacturers Hanover Trust Co., 118 Misc. 2d 722, 461 N.Y.S.2d 157 (Sup. Ct. 1983).
19. Sam & Mary Hous. Corp. v. Jo/Sal Mkt. Corp., 100 A.D.2d 901, 474 N.Y.S.2d 786 (2d Dep't 1984).

19.1. Dallas v. W.R. Grace and Co., 225 A.D.2d 319 (1st Dep't 1996).

19.2. Sorrel v. Iacobucci, 221 A.D.2d 852 (3d Dep't 1995)(court need not take judicial notice that German Shepherd dogs are vicious).

19.3.2.1 Transportation

19.3.2.1.1 Pedestrians

1. The ordinary walking speed of pedestrians is two and one-half to three miles an hour.[20]

19.3.2.1.2 Common Carriers

2. A particular railroad suffered from persistent and lengthy delays, a lack of heating in subfreezing weather, filth, overcrowding, and noxious odors within its vintage coaches.[21]

19.3.2.1.3 Motor Vehicles

3. After ten minutes to one-half hour, the water or coolant in the radiator of an overheated car will cool down so that the cap may be removed safely.[22]
4. An automobile may swerve suddenly and go off the road due to many causes and not merely due to the driver's lack of care in operating the automobile.[23] (However, the plaintiff who was a passenger no longer has the burden of eliminating those causes other than the driver's negligence.[24])
5. Radar devices are reliable, but a particular new radar device may not be.

---

20. Wood v. Woodlawn Improvement Ass'n, 215 A.D. 628, 214 N.Y.S. 398 (3d Dep't 1926), *aff'd,* 247 N.Y. 598, 161 N.E. 197 (1928).
21. Dominianni v. Consolidated Rail Corp., 110 Misc. 2d 929, 443 N.Y.S.2d 334 (Sup. Ct. 1981).
22. Myers v. Fir Cab Corp., 100 A.D.2d 29, 473 N.Y.S.2d 413 (1st Dep't 1984), *rev'd on other grounds,* 64 N.Y.2d 806, 476 N.E.2d 321, 486 N.Y.S.2d 922 (1985).
23. Galbraith v. Busch, 267 N.Y. 230, 196 N.E. 36 (1935).
24. Pfaffenbach v. White Plains Express Corp., 17 N.Y.2d 132 (1966).

19.3.2.2 Medical Phenomena

6. An infant born alive but weighing five and one-half pounds or less may be premature.[25]
7. Many people have low blood pressure and poor circulation.[26]
8. Hardening of the arteries may exist for years without causing serious effects.[27]

19.3.2.3 Geographical and Astronomical Phenomena

9. The locations of streets and of towns.[28]
10. The times of the rising and setting of the sun and the moon.[29]
11. The computation of time and the day of the week upon which a certain day of the month falls.[30]

19.3.2.4 "Slip-and-Fall" Cases

12. Tile floors are slippery, and such a condition in a bathhouse is a necessary incident to using the bath.[31]

---

25. Moreover, the hospital record is admissible to confirm that the baby was premature. Patricia A. v. Philip De G., 97 A.D.2d 760, 468 N.Y.S.2d 390 (2d Dep't 1983), *remanded* 59 N.Y.2d 137 (1983).
26. Owen v. Rochester-Penfield Bus Co., 304 N.Y. 457, 108 N.E.2d 606 (1952). *See* Annot., *Judicial Notice of Diseases or Similar Conditions Adversely Affecting Human Beings,* 72 A.L.R.2D 554 (1960).
27. McGrail v. Equitable Life Assurance Soc'y, 292 N.Y. 419, 55 N.E.2d 483 (1944).
28. People v. Myles, 107 Misc. 2d 960, 436 N.Y.S.2d 134 (Sup. Ct. 1981); Salamon v. Knonklijke Luchtvaat Maatschappij, N.V., 198 Misc. 780, 100 N.Y.S.2d 702 (Sup. Ct. 1950); Annot., *Judicial Notice as to Location of Street Address Within Particular Political Subdivision,* 86 A.L.R.3D 484 (1978).
29. Montes v. Metropolitan St. Ry., 77 A.D. 493, 78 N.Y.S. 1059 (2d Dep't 1902).
30. Cohn v. Kahn, 14 Misc. 255, 35 N.Y.S. 829 (City. Ct. 1895).
31. Conroy v. Saratoga Springs Auth., 259 A.D.365, 19 N.Y.S.2d 538 (3d Dep't), *aff'd,* 284 N.Y. 723, 31 N.E.2d 197 (1940). For wet areas around swimming pools, *see* Beck v. Broad Channel Bathing Park, 255 N.Y. 641 (1931), *and* Sciarello v. Coast Holding Co., 242 A.D. 802, *aff'd* 267 N.Y. 585 (1935).

13. Snow and ice can be removed from the sidewalks although the temperature is below freezing.[32]
14. Proof that a rotted and rusted condition existed at the time of the accident creates an inference that the condition had existed for some time before the accident and, thus, is evidence of notice.[33]

19.3.2.5 Infants

15. A body of water is an attractive spot to children, as well as to adults, and especially during hot weather.[34]
16. A contractor who piles beams on the street should be aware of the proclivity of children to be drawn to such objects.[35] (However, this foreseeability does not, ipso facto, impose liability.[36])
17. An infant lacks an adult's knowledge of the probable consequences of his or her acts or omissions, and an infant is unable to make an effective use of such knowledge as he or she has.[37]

---

32. Rosenberg v. City of N.Y., 256 A.D. 927, 9 N.Y.S.2d 653 (2d Dep't), *aff'd,* 280 N.Y. 815, 21 N.E.2d 877 (1939). *See also* Thiel v. City of New York, 256 A.D. 929 (1939).
33. LaScalea v. Woolsey Holding Corp., 14 A.D.2d 912, 221 N.Y.S.2d 551 (2d Dep't 1961); Schmidt v. New York Tel. Co., 258 A.D. 767, 14 N.Y.S.2d 708 (3d Dep't 1939); Weingard v. Putnam Theatrical Corp., 225 A.D. 808, 232 N.Y.S. 296 (2d Dep't 1929).
34. Cunningham v. Niagara Falls, 242 A.D. 39, 272 N.Y.S. 720 (4th Dep't 1934), *aff'd on other grounds,* 269 N.Y. 644 (1936).
35. Boylhart v. DiMarco, 270 N.Y. 217, 200 N.E. 793 (1936).
36. The defendant in Boylhart was liable because the beams had a tendency to roll, but a defendant who created a stable pile of rocks was not liable when a child climbed the pile and fell. Schiff v. John Arborio, Inc., 12 A.D.2d 680 (3d Dep't 1960).
37. Locklin v. Fisher, 264 A.D. 452, 36 N.Y.S.2d 162 (3d Dep't 1942).

19.3.3 An Example of an Improper Taking of Judicial Notice

In *Murray v. Donlon,*[38] the trial court took judicial notice of the fact that "an automobile equipped with good brakes and traveling 10-12 miles per hour can be stopped in considerably less than 15 feet." The Appellate Division, Second Department, held that the finding was erroneous. The appellate court quoted with approval an opinion[39] of the Supreme Court of Connecticut to the effect that, in such matters, expert testimony is superior to judicial notice as a method of finding facts. The foreign court wrote:

> The better practice is to have opinion testimony of an expert as to the speed of a motor vehicle based on skid marks and other physical facts proven on the trial of each particular case. . . . When a witness testifies, his testimony can be challenged and the trier can pass on his credibility and determine what weight should be given to the evidence. This is not true when an act is established by judicial notice.[40]

Even statistical charts are inferior to expert testimony concerning the actual conditions of the accident.

The Appellate Division, Second Department, applied this view to the case before it and decided that the trial court had improperly taken judicial notice of the distance necessary to stop the automobile. "In fact, on this record, there appears to be no basis for the stopping distance recognized by the trial court. Moreover, it was not clearly indicated to the jury that it was an average distance for automobiles operating under favorable conditions."[41]

---

38. Murray v. Donlon, 77 A.D.2d 337, 433 N.Y.S.2d 184 (2d Dep't 1980).
39. Thomas v. Commerford, 168 Conn. 64.
40. *Id.* at 69.
41. Murray v. Donlon, 77 A.D.2d 337, 351-52, 433 N.Y.S.2d 184, 190 (2d Dep't 1980).

Res Ipsa Loquitur 20

20.1 THE RULE

20.1.1 The General Statement

Res ipsa loquitur, referred to as res ipsa, is a rule of evidence meaning "the thing speaks for itself."[1] In addition to being a rule of evidence, res ipsa is a rule of substantive law in that it permits an inference of negligence and makes out a prima facie case if the trial court finds that the plaintiff has met the criteria for submitting the inference to the jury. Res ipsa is, therefore, an important evidentiary tool in the trial of actions for negligence.

In New York, the plaintiff may submit a cause of action to the jury with an appropriate charge on res ipsa if the plaintiff has established the following three propositions:

1. The event which caused the plaintiff's injury would not ordinarily have occurred in the absence of someone's negligence;
2. The event was caused by an instrumentality within the defendant's exclusive control;[2] and

---

1. The earliest reported cases dealing with this new evidentiary principle are Scott v. London & St. Katherine Docks Co., 3 H&C 596, 159 Eng. Rep. 665 (1885); Byrne v. Boadle, 2 H&C 722, 159 Eng. Rep. 199 (1886).
2. The control need not be exclusive in one person; it may be shared by two or more people. Corcoran v. Banner Supermarkets, Inc., 19 N.Y.2d 425, 227 N.E.2d 304, 280 N.Y.S.2d 385 (1967) (the court found shared or dual control of two buildings because the board that fell on the passing plaintiff was perched between the two buildings and either owner [or both] could be found liable); Schroeder v. City & County Sav. Bank, 293 N.Y. 370 (1944); Annot., *Applicability of Res Ipsa Loquitur*

3. The event was not due to the plaintiff's voluntary act or contributory negligence.[3]

Occasionally, a court will add a fourth criterion: "(4) evidence as to the true explanation of the event must be more readily accessible to the defendant than the plaintiff."[4] However, this is a minority view unless the second criterion implies the fourth one.

Once the plaintiff has established these essential conditions, the "plaintiff having first established the nature of the instrumentality which allegedly occasioned the injury and its identity with the defendant, ... the jury may be charged on res ipsa loquitur."[5]

The courts' traditional view is that res ipsa does not create a presumption of negligence which the defendant must rebut; instead, res ipsa permits an inference of negligence which leaves the burden of proof on the plaintiff[6] and which the defendant may, but need not, counter with opposing evi-

---

in Case of Multiple Defendants, 38 A.L.R.2D 905 (1954), Butti v. Rollins, 133 A.D.2d 205 (2d Dep't 1987); Sullivan v. Isadore Rosen & Sons, Inc., 36 A.D.2d 809 (1st Dep't 1971); Moeller v. Pearl, 78 A.D.2d 540 (2d Dep't 1980); Ciciarelli v. Ames Department Stores, Inc., 162 A.D.2d 996 (4th Dep't 1990); Jungjohann v. Hotel Buffalo, 5 A.D.2d 496 (4th Dep't 1958), and Bauer v. Harris Intertype Corporation, 35 A.D.2d 426 (3d Dep't 1970).

3. Corcoran v. Banner Supermarkets, 19 N.Y.2d 425, 227 N.E.2d 304, 280 N.Y.S.2d 385 (1967); Pollock v. Rapid Indus. Plastics Co., 113 A.D.2d 520, 497 N.Y.S.2d 45 (2d Dep't 1986); Weeden v. Armor Elevator Co., 97 A.D.2d 197, 468 N.Y.S.2d 898 (2d Dep't 1983); Moeller v. Pearl, 78 A.D.2d 540, 432 N.Y.S.2d 96 (2d Dep't 1980); Pipers v. Rosenow, 39 A.D.2d 240, 333 N.Y.S.2d 480 (2d Dep't 1972); Duke v. Duane Broad Co., 181 A.D.2d 589 (1st Dep't 1992).
4. Fogal v. Genessee Hospital, 41 A.D.2d 468, 474, 345 N.Y.S.2d 989 (4th Dep't 1973).
5. Weeden v. Armor Elevator Co., 97 A.D.2d 197, 203, 468 N.Y.S.2d 898, 901 (2d Dep't 1983); *see also* Fogal v. Genessee Hosp., 41 A.D.2d 468, 345 N.Y.S.2d 989 (4th Dep't 1973).
6. George Foltis, Inc. v. City of N.Y., 287 N.Y. 108, 38 N.E.2d 455 (1941); Weeden v. Armor Elevator Co., 97 A.D.2d 197, 468 N.Y.S.2d 898 (2d Dep't 1983). Hatch v. King, 33 A.D.2d 879 (4th Dep't 1969), and Davis v. Goldsmith, 19 A.D.2d 514 (1st Dep't 1963).

dence.[7] Res ipsa merely permits an inference of negligence, i.e., the inference that an unusual occurrence resulted from negligence.[8] Even if the defendant offers no evidence, the jury still must decide whether the plaintiff's evidence has established the defendant's liability.[9] The defendant may, of course, come forward with an explanation, thereby rebutting the inference,[10] and if the rebuttal is successful, the plaintiff must overcome it with evidence or lose.[11] It is, in fact, a rare case in which the plaintiff would be entitled to a directed verdict because the prima facie case was so convincing that the inference arising from res ipsa was inescapable if not rebutted by other evidence,[12] and it is rare that a defendant would be entitled to a directed verdict because the rebuttal evidence was so overwhelming that it prevented any reasonable inference of negligence. Most commonly, the evidence allowing the inference and the rebuttal evidence combine to create a question of fact for the jury.[13]

The traditional view is, of course, nonsensical. If the invocation of res ipsa were sufficient to create a prima facie case, then ipso facto the burden of rebuttal must have shifted to the defendant. That is what stating a prima facie case entails.[14] Courts sometimes imply this view. For example,

---

7. Bauman v. Long Island R.R., 110 A.D.2d 739, 487 N.Y.S.2d 833 (2d Dep't 1985); Weeden v. Armor Elevator Co., 97 A.D.2d 197, 468 N.Y.S.2d 898 (2d Dep't 1983).
8. Shapiro v. Art Craft Strauss Sign Corp., 39 A.D.2d 696, 332 N.Y.S.2d 588 (1st Dep't 1972); Parsons v. State, 31 A.D.2d 596, 295 N.Y.S.2d 383 (3d Dep't 1968).
9. Chisholm v. Mobil Oil Corp., 45 A.D. 2d 776, 356 N.Y.S.2d 699 (3d Dep't 1974), and LoPiccolo v. Knight of Rest Products Corporation, 7 A.D.2d 369 (1st Dep't 1959).
10. Parsons v. State, 31 A.D.2d 596, 295 N.Y.S.2d 383 (3d Dep't 1968).
11. Plumb v. Richmond Light & R.R. Co., 233 N.Y. 285, 135 N.E.2d 504 (1922).
12. George Foltis, Inc. v. City of N.Y., 287 N.Y. 108, 38 N.E.2d 455 (1941); Horowitz v. Kevah Konner, Inc., 67 A.D.2d 38, 414 N.Y.S.2d 540 (1st Dep't 1979); Myers v. Fir Cab Corp., 100 A.D.2d 29 (1st Dep't 1984); *see* Annot., *Res Ipsa Loquitur as a Ground for Direction of Verdict in Favor of Plaintiff,* 97 A.L.R.2D 522 (1964).
13. Weeden v. Armor Elevator Co., 97 A.D.2d 197, 204-05, 468 N.Y.S.2d 898, 904 (2d Dep't 1983).

in *Ciciarelli v. Ames Department Stores, Inc.,* the Appellate Division, Fourth Department, held, "The unexplained fall of the TV tray required the defendant to come forward with an explanation as to its cause . . . . This it failed to do."[15] In other words, the defendant was not free to rely on the presumption against negligence and to decline to present a rebuttal.

The coherent explanation should begin with the observation that the plaintiff must present a prima facie case as his or her first step in carrying the burden of proof. When the plaintiff has presented such a case, the burden of rebuttal shifts to the defendant. Meanwhile, to establish a prima facie case, the plaintiff may use any permissible means, and one such means is res ipsa loquitur if the plaintiff can meet the three criteria. The court must decide whether the plaintiff has met those criteria: usually, the question arises when the defendant moves to dismiss the complaint at the end of the plaintiff's case or when the plaintiff asks the court to charge the jury on res ipsa. Assuming that the plaintiff has met the three criteria, the jury will decide which party has met its burden of persuasion, i.e., whether the plaintiff has

---

14. BLACK'S LAW DICTIONARY 1353 (4th ed. 1968): "A litigating party is said to have a *prima facie* case when the evidence in his favor is sufficiently strong for his opponent to be called on to answer it. A *prima facie* case, then, is one which is established by sufficient evidence, and can be overthrown only by rebutting evidence adduced on the other side." (Citing Motzley v. Whitley.) As the use of Latin implies, the complementary notions of a prima facie case and the burden of rebuttal re philosophical (i.e., logical) requirements and entered the common law from classical rhetoric and Roman law. Modern rhetoricians have preserved these fundamental notions. For example, *see* AUSTIN J. FREELEY, ARGUMENTATION AND DEBATE, 8th ed. (Balmont, Cal.: Wadsworth Pub'g Co., 1993), pp. 194, 272-3; WAYNE N. THOMPSON, MODERN ARGUMENTATION AND DEBATE (New York: Harper & Row, Pubrs., 1971), pp. 10-11; LUTHER W. COURTNEY AND GLENN R. CAPP, PRACTICAL DEBATING (New York: J.B. Lippincott Co., 1949), pp. 20, 23; ROY V. WOOD, STRATEGIC DEBATE 2nd ed (Skokie, Ill.: Natl. Textbook Co., 1972), pp. 15-17; MARIDELL FRYAR & DAVID A. THOMAS, BASIC DEBATE (Skokie, Ill.: Natl. Textbook Co., 1979), pp. 55-7, and DONALD W. KLOPF AND JAMES C. MCCROSKEY, THE ELEMENTS OF DEBATE (New York: Arco, 1969), pp. 16-18.
15. Ciciarelli v. Ames Department Stores, Inc., 162 A.D.2d 996 at 997 (4th Dep't 1990).

met the burden of proof or the defendant has met the burden of rebuttal. However, even if the plaintiff has met the three criteria allowing the inference, he or she has not necessarily presented a prima facie case. Thus, we may understand the words of the Appellate Division, First Department, in *Lo Piccolo v. Knight of Rest Products Corporation*:

> the doctrine of *res ipsa loquitur* classifies as simply another species of circumstantial evidence. As such, the permissible inferences and the procedural consequences relate to the nature and quality of the evidence offered by plaintiff to sustain the inference of negligence.[16]

The circumstances are the factual bases of the three criteria, e.g., that the accident would not ordinarily have occurred in the absence of negligence.

We also may understand the holding of the Appellate Division, Third Department, in *Bauer v. Harris Intertype Corporation*, that reliance on res ipsa will not refute a prima facie defense.[17] This is another way of saying that a prima facie defense meets the defendant's burden of rebuttal and shifts the burden of rebuttal back to the plaintiff.

Consequently, res ipsa is permissible circumstantial evidence which may or may not give rise to a prima facie case. If it does, the jury will decide whether the defendant's arguments or evidence refused the inference and, therefore, the case. When a court writes, "there is no burden of rebuttal, albeit a prima facie case is made out . . .",[18] the court is uttering an absurdity. What the court really means is that the court is reluctant to direct a verdict in a case in which an inference from res ipsa is available to the jury. This is sim-

16. Lo Piccolo v. Knight of Rest Products Corporation, 7 A.D.2d 369, 374 (1st Dep't 1959).
17. Bauer v. Harris Intertype Corporation, 35 A.D.2d 426 (3d Dep't 1970).
18. Davis v. Goldsmith, 19 A.D.2d 514 (1st Dep't 1963).

ply an instance of the court giving the plaintiff the benefit of the doubt on the question of a prima facie case. The courts prefer to rule against the plaintiff by finding that the plaintiff has failed to meet one of the criteria, e.g., by failing to establish the defendant's exclusive control of the instrumentality.

20.1.2 Res Ipsa in the Alternative

The plaintiff need not plead a cause of action for res ipsa since it is not a cause of action, nor need res ipsa be alleged in the bill of particulars. Moreover, the plaintiff's specific allegations of negligence do not bar him or her from employing res ipsa if the facts warrant its application.[19] In other words, the plaintiff's presenting evidence of negligence does not prevent the trial court from instructing the jury on res ipsa loquitur.[20] As the Appellate Division, Second Department, noted in *Weeden v. Armor Elevator Co.*,

> Indeed the majority view, and that of our Court of Appeals, is that the introduction at trial by a plaintiff of specific evidence of a defendant's negligence will not preclude invocation of res ipsa loquitur unless the proof so adduced "actually refutes or negates the inference which might otherwise have been drawn from application of that doctrine" (*Abbott v. Page Airways*, 23 N.Y.2d 502, 511). As former Chief Judge Fuld observed in *Abbott*, (*supra*. p. 512): "It is clear that there can be no logical or reasonable basis for requiring a plaintiff to choose between res ipsa and specific evidence of negligence or for precluding him from relying on res ipsa principles once evidence of negligence [has] been introduced, unless the two alternate modes of proof are fundamentally or inherently inconsistent."[21]

---

19. Weeden v. Armor Elevator Co., 97 A.D.2d 197 at 204-05, 468 N.Y.S.2d at 902; Silberman v. Lazarowitz, 130 A.D.2d 736, 515 N.Y.S.2d 837 (2d Dep't 1987); Fogal v. Genessee Hosp., 41 A.D.2d 468, 345 N.Y.S.2d 989 (4th Dep't 1973).
20. Silberman v. Lazarowitz, 130 A.D.2d 736, 515 N.Y.S.2d 837 (2d Dep't 1987).

The plaintiff took advantage of this rule in *Kerber v. Sarles*.[22] He awoke from an operation to correct his hammertoes to find his front teeth missing. At the trial, the plaintiff both invoked res ipsa and presented expert testimony that his injury was probably the result of inordinate pressure applied by the anesthetist.

20.2 THE APPLICATION OF RES IPSA LOQUITUR TO THE ISSUES OF PARTICULAR KINDS OF CASES

Establishing res ipsa loquitur requires all three elements, but which element is the most disputed depends upon the nature of the case.

20.2.1 The First Element: Characterization of the Event in an Action for Medical Malpractice

The application of res ipsa loquitur to an action for medical malpractice usually focuses on the first element. Control of the instrumentality is not an issue; instead, the disputed issue is whether the plaintiff's injury would have occurred in the absence of negligence. As the Appellate Division, Third Department, observed in *Schoch v. Dougherty*,[23] "In a medical malpractice case, the doctrine may apply where an inference exonerating the physician is improbable as a matter of fact.'. . . Such an inference is permissible where com-

---

21. Weedon v. Armor Elevator Co., 97 A.D.2d 197, 202, 468 N.Y.S.2d 898, 902 (2d Dep't 1983).
22. Kerber v. Sarles, 151 A.D.2d 1031 (4th Dep't 1989).
23. Schoch v. Dougherty, 122 A.D.2d 467, 504 N.Y.S.2d 855 (3d Dep't 1986). Another example is Frasier v. McIlduff, 161 A.D.2d 856 (3d Dep't 1999), in which the defendants performed heart surgery on the plaintiff four days after she had had an abortion.

mon knowledge indicates that an injury was occasioned by negligence . . . ."

However, the appellate court held that the plaintiff in *Schoch* had not established the first element of res ipsa because the particular facts required expert testimony.

> [T]he injury here did not occur in an area remote from the operative site, but occurred during an intricate part of the surgical procedure when the nerve was retracted to allow access to the polliteal area. Whether the resulting injury constituted a deviation from accepted medical practice is surely not a matter within the competence of laymen to evaluate, but necessitated expert testimony to establish a prima facie case. . . . Moreover, Dougherty's testimony indicated that plaintiff's obesity and/or the tautness of the nerve may have precipitated the injury rather than any error on the part of defendants. It follows that a res ipsa loquitur charge was not warranted.

In other words, the defendant in *Schoch* came forward with an explanation that rebutted the inference so the burden of rebuttal shifted to the plaintiff, who needed to present expert testimony to meet that burden.

20.2.2 The Second Element: Exclusive Control in an Action for Negligence

Innumerable cases deal with the issue of the defendant's exclusive control of the instrumentality that caused the plaintiff's injury.[24] One device which the courts have used to find exclusivity of control is to aggregate the defendants so that they have exclusive control among them. Thus, in *Corcoran*

---

24. Corcoran v. Banner Supermarkets, 19 N.Y.2d 425, 227 N.E.2d 304, 280 N.Y.S.2d 385 (1967); Quinn v. State, 61 A.D.2d 850, 401 N.Y.S.2d 926 (3d Dep't 1978); Chisholm v. Mobil Oil Corp., 45 A.D.2d 776, 356 N.Y.S.2d 699 (3d Dep't 1974); Cameron v. H.C. Bohack Co., 27 A.D.2d 362, 280 N.Y.S.2d 583 (2d Dep't 1967); Scimeca v. New York City Transit Authority, 39 A.D.2d 596 (2d Dep't 1972);

v. Banner Supermarkets,[25] the court of appeals ruled that the plaintiff had demonstrated the defendants' exclusive control of the board that fell from a space between the two abutting stores and injured the plaintiff. The appellate court held that both stores had control of the board and that the plaintiff did not need to prove which defendant was truly responsible for the board's presence and fall: "This shared or dual duty with respect to the board permits the application of res ipsa loquitur against either or both owners. Accordingly, in the first trial of this action it was not improper for the court to apply res ipsa loquitur against the owner defendant."

Some courts have aggregated defendants even in medical malpractice cases. For example, in *Ybarra v. Spangard,*[26] the plaintiff sued the surgeon, several nurses, the anesthetist, and the hospital for injuries to his neck that he apparently sustained during an operation for an abdominal ailment. The California Supreme Court applied res ipsa loquitur against all of the defendants although some of them clearly had not had exclusive control of the treatment of the patient.

The issue of exclusivity of control often arises in actions against common carriers, and the carrier may win the issue. For example, in *Dermatossian v. New York City Transit Authority,*[27] the court of appeals ruled that the plaintiff had not shown that the defendant had had exclusive control of a hand grab-bar in a bus because other passengers might have damaged the grab-bar before the plaintiff got on the bus.

Morales v. Foodway, Inc., 186 A.D.2d 407 (1st Dep't 1992); Raimondi v. New York Racing Association, 213 A.D.2d 708 (2d Dep't 1995); Camillo v. Geer, 185 A.D.2d 192 (1st Dep't 1992), and Ladd v. Hudson Valley Ambulance Service, 142 A.D.2d 17 (3d Dep't 1988).

25. Corcoran v. Banner Supermarkets, 19 N.Y.2d 425, 227 N.E.2d 304, 280 N.Y.S.2d 385 (1967).
26. Ybarra v. Spangard, 25 Cal. 2d 486 (1944).
27. Dermatossian v. New York City Transit Auth., 67 N.Y.2d 219, 501 N.Y.S.2d 784 (1986).

(The plaintiff was injured when he stood up because the grab-bar was sticking straight down rather than being angled in the usual way.) Similarly, in *Ebanks v. New York City Transit Authority,* the court of appeals held that the plaintiff had failed to prove the defendant's exclusive control over a public escalator.[28] The plaintiff had been thrown to the ground when her galoshes got stuck between the escalator and the side panel. the Appellate Division, First Department, affirmed the jury's verdict for the plaintiff, but the Court of Appeals reversed the judgment, dismissed the complaint, and wrote:

> The proof did not adequately refute the possibility that the escalator — located in a subway station used by approximately 10,000 persons weekly — had been damaged by a member of the public either through an act of vandalism or, as defendant's witness suggested, by permitting an object such as a hand truck to become caught in the space between the step and the sidewall. Plaintiff did not establish that the likelihood of such occurrences was so reduced "'that the greater probability lies at defendant's door.'"[29]

20.2.3 The Third Element: The Plaintiff's Voluntary Act Did Not Cause the Event

The plaintiff may have committed a voluntary act that precipitated the accident, but that act will not prevent the plaintiff from employing res ipsa loquitur unless the act

---

28. Ebanks v. New York City Transit Auth., 70 N.Y.2d 621, 518 N.Y.S.2d 776 (1987), *rev'g* 118 A.D.2d 363, 504 N.Y.S.2d 640 (1st Dep't 1986). *See also* DiSanto v. County of Westchester, 210 A.D.2d 628 (3d Dep't 1994); Farrell v. Stafford Machinery Corp., 205 A.D.2d 951 (3d Dep't 1994); Wen-Yu Chang v. F.W. Woolworth, 196 A.D.2d 708 (1st Dep't 1993), *and* Nesbit v. New York City Transit Authority, 170 A.D.2d 92 (1st Dep't 1991).
29. Ebanks v. New York City Transit Authority, 70 N.Y.2d 621 at 623, 518 N.Y.S.2d 776 at 777 (1987).

contained an element of fault. Thus, in *Kane v. Ten Eyck Co.,*[30] the trial court observed:

> The act of the injured party which sets in motion the instrument of injury must not be confused with an act of the injured party by which, sharing responsibility in some way with the defendant for the creation or maintenance of the dangerous condition, he is deemed also to share the negligence.[31]

The case before the court involved a guest in a hotel who turned on a water faucet and was scalded by the boiling water that came out. The plaintiff was not precluded from employing res ipsa by his having turned on the water. The court cited similar cases in which a plaintiff had pressed an elevator button and fallen into the shaft,[32] operated a dumbwaiter that had defective ropes,[33] and opened a window on which the sash chain was broken.[34] In other words, the plaintiff's faultless act does not become negligent because the act is the occasion for the injury caused by the defendant's negligence.

Some courts have gone further and have restricted the kind of act which will negate the third criterion to acts which impair the defendant's exclusive control of the instrumentality. As the Appellate Division, First Department, said in *Ebanks,*

> on that third aspect the first focus must be upon *what* kind of "voluntary action or contribution on the part of the plaintiff" will prevent his reliance upon the res ipsa doctrine. Comparison of the result reached in four elevator cases . . . indicates that the kind of "voluntary action" by the plaintiff sufficient to negate the applicability of res ipsa must be his negligent in-

30. Kane v. Ten Eyck Co., 10 Misc. 2d 398, 175 N.Y.S.2d 88 (Sup. Ct. 1943), *aff'd successively in* 267 A.D. 789 (3d Dep't 1943) and 292 N.Y. 701 (1944); for an identical case, *see* Jungjohann v. Hotel Buffalo, 5 A.D.2d 496 (4th Dep't 1958).
31. *Kane, supra* at 400-1, 175 N.Y.S.2d at 91-2.
32. Gustavson v. Thomas, 227 A.D. 303, 237 N.Y.S.2d 479.
33. Maslenka v. Brady, 188 A.D. 661, 176 N.Y.S.2d 842 (2d Dep't 1919).
34. Monahan v. National Realty Co., 4 Ga. App. 680.

terference with, intrusion upon, or invasion of control of the instrumentality causing the injury.[35] (Citations omitted.)

The plaintiff had placed his foot between the moving steps and the side panels of the escalator. There was a vigorous dissent, and this approach is controversial.

20.3 REPRESENTATIVE CASES INVOLVING RES IPSA LOQUITUR

The following cases are representative of the situations in which a plaintiff might employ res ipsa loquitur to establish a cause of action. The cases are divided between negligence and medical malpractice.

20.3.1 Negligence

20.3.1.1 Transportation

20.3.1.1.1 Motor Vehicles

1. *Carter v. Castle Electric Contracting Corp.*[36] Res ipsa was available to a plaintiff who was sitting in a stationary car that was hit in the rear by the defendant's car.
2. *Markel v. Spencer & Ford Co.*[37] Res ipsa was available to a plaintiff who, while operating a new automobile that had been delivered to him only three days before,

35. Ebanks v. New York City Transit Authority, 118 A.D.2d 363 at 366 (1st Dep't 1986).
36. Carter v. Castle Elec. Contracting Corp., 26 A.D.2d 83, 271 N.Y.S.2d 851 (2d Dep't 1966). For a similar case, see Hatch v. King, 33 A.D.2d 879 (4th Dep't 1969).
37. Markel v. Spencer & Ford Co., 5 A.D.2d 400, 171 N.Y.S.2d 770 (4th Dep't 1958), *aff'd*, 5 N.Y.2d 958, 184 N.Y.S.2d 835 (1959). For a similar case, see Guagliardo v. Ford Motor Co., 7 A.D.2d 472 (4th Dep't 1959).

applied the brakes, which had previously worked properly. The foot pedal touched the floor, but the brakes did not hold. At the time, the plaintiff felt something fall past his leg, and that object turned out to be a brake bolt. The appellate court held that the jury could have inferred the defendants' negligence and that the plaintiff need not have adduced evidence establishing the precise cause of the accident.

3. *LoPiccolo v. Knight of Rest Products Corporation.*[38] Two trucks collided head-on in an outside lane on a bridge on a rainy day. Although the plaintiff invoked res ipsa, and the defendant presented no evidence, the trial court erred in setting aside the verdict for the defendant.

20.3.1.1.2 Common Carriers

4. *Horowitz v. Kevah Konner, Inc.*[39] Horowitz underscores that a common carrier must present a reasonable explanation of how and why the accident occurred when the defendant's driver left the roadway and crashed under circumstances that are not otherwise explained. The driver must explain the accident or be cast in liability.[40]

---

38. LoPiccolo v. Knight of Rest Products Corporation, 7 A.D.2d 369 (1st Dep't 1959).
39. Horowitz v. Kevah Konner, Inc., 67 A.D.2d 38, 414 N.Y.S.2d 540 (2d Dep't 1979).
40. *Id.* at 40, 414 N.Y.S.2d at 542 (citing Pfafferback v. White Plains Express Corp., 17 N.Y. 132, 135, 216 N.E.2d 324, 269 N.Y.S.2d 115 (1966)); *see also* Cebula v. Bonime, 92 A.D.2d 856, 459 N.Y.S.2d 847 (2d Dep't 1983); Annot., *Application of Res Ipsa Loquitur Doctrine Where Motor Vehicle Turns Over on Highway,* 79 A.L.R.2D 211 (1961); Annot., *Applicability of Res Ipsa Loquitur Doctrine Where Motor Vehicle Stops on Highway,* 79 A.L.R.2D 153 (1961); Annot., *Applicability of Res Ipsa Loquitur Doctrine Where Motor Vehicle Leaves Road,* 79 A.L.R.2D 6 (1961).

5. *Towne v. City of New York.*[41] Res ipsa was available when a subway door closed on the plaintiff, thereby causing her injury.

20.3.1.1.3 Elevators

6. *Weeden v. Armor Elevator Co.*[42] Res ipsa was available to a plaintiff who was injured when an elevator jerked up and down suddenly, forcing the plaintiff to bounce around within the cab. The defendant was the maintenance company, which had an exclusive contract to inspect and maintain the elevator.
7. *Mallor v. Wolk Properties, Inc.*[43] Res ipsa was available to a plaintiff who was injured by the elevator's sudden and high-speed drop.
8. *Sullivan v. Isadore Rosen & Sons, Inc.*[44] Res ipsa was unavailable to the plaintiff because "There is no proof that Otis Elevator Company was in possession or control of the elevator at the time of the claimed accident."[45]

---

41. Towne v. City of N.Y., 278 A.D. 833, 104 N.Y.S.2d 190 (2d Dep't 1951); *see* Annot., *Applicability of Res Ipsa Loquitur Doctrine Where Injury Results from Prospective Passenger's Contact with Open Door of Carrier's Motor Vehicle,* 71 A.L.R.2D 376 (1969); Annot., *Application of Res Ipsa Loquitur Doctrine in Action Against Carrier by Motorbus for Injury to Person Boarding Bus,* 93 A.L.R.2D 250 (1964).
42. Weedon v. Armor Elevator Co., 97 A.D.2d 197, 202, 468 N.Y.S.2d 898, 902 (2d Dep't 1983). *See* Annot., *Applicability of Res Ipsa Loquitur in Action in Connection with Automatic Elevators,* 6 A.L.R.2D 339 (1949); Annot., *Applicability of Res Ipsa Loquitur Doctrine in Non-Automatic Elevator Cases,* 56 A.L.R.2D 1059 (1957). *See also* Sirigiano v. Otis Elevator Co., 118 A.D.2d 920, 499 N.Y.S.2d 486 (3d Dep't 1986); Burgess v. Otis Elevator Co., 114 A.D.2d 784, 495 N.Y.S.2d 376 (1st Dep't 1985), *aff'd,* 69 N.Y.2d 623 (1986).
43. Mallor v. Wolk Properties, Inc., 63 Misc. 2d 187, 311 N.Y.S.2d 735 (Sup. Ct.).
44. Sullivan v. Isadore Rosen & Sons, Inc., 36 A.D.2d 809 (1st Dep't 1971).
45. *Id.* at 809. For a similar case, *see* Koch v. Otis Elevator Co., 10 A.D.2d 464 (1st Dep't 1960).

9. *Duke v. Duane Broad Co.*[46] The plaintiffs were injured when the elevator dropped six stories then the governor stopped it. The trial court dismissed the complaint, but the appellate court reinstated it and wrote, "Nor is there any contention that plaintiffs were contributorily at fault."[47]

20.3.1.1.4 Escalators

10. *Ciampi v. Sears.*[48] Res ipsa was not available to an infant who caught his toe in an escalator that was going down because no one was available to testify regarding what the infant was doing when his toe got caught. The court explained,

> Research disclosed that [in] those cases where it has been held that the doctrine of res ipsa loquitur was applicable there was some external, sudden force or movement of an instrumentality within the exclusive control of the defendant justifying an inference of negligence. . . .

11. *Enselein v. Hudson & Manhattan Railroad Co.*[49] Res ipsa was available when a sudden lurch by a moving escalator caused the plaintiff's injuries.
12. *Wen-Yu Chang v. F.W. Woolworth.*[50] A three and one-half year old girl caught her leg between the moving stairs and the side panel. The trial court refused to charge the jury on res ipsa, but the appellate court ordered a new trial. The defendants' control was exclu-

---

46. Duke v. Duane Broad Co., 181 A.D.2d 589 (1st Dep't 1992).
47. *Id.* at 591. *See also* Burgess v. Otis Elevator Co., 114 A.D. 784 (1st Dep't 1985), *aff'd*, 69 N.Y.2d 623 (1986): the plaintiff had no control over the misleveling of the elevator.
48. *See also* Birdsall v. Montgomery Ward & Co., 109 A.D.2d 969, 486 N.Y.S.2d 461 (3d Dep't 1985), *aff'd,* 65 N.Y.2d 913 (1985); Stafford v. Sibley, Lindsay & Curr Co., 280 A.D. 495, 114 N.Y.S.2d 177 (4th Dep't 1952); Annot., *Application of Res Ipsa Loquitur to Injuries Suffered in Connection with the Use of an Escalator,* 66 A.L.R.2D 507 (1959).
49. Enslein v. Hudson & Manhattan R.R. Co., 6 N.Y.2d 723, 185 N.Y.S.2d 810 (1960).
50. Wen-Yu Chang v. F.W. Woolworth, 196 A.D.2d 708 (1st Dep't 1993).

sive enough because (1) the gap between the stairs and the panels was smaller than in other cases, (2) there was no testimony regarding vandalism, and (3) Westinghouse had inspected the escalator a few hours before the accident.

20.3.1.1.5 Chair Lifts

13. *Alberti v. State of New York.*[51] Res ipsa was available to a plaintiff who was riding in a chair lift at a ski resort when he was thrown to the ground because the bolt holding the chair broke.

20.3.1.2 Falling Objects

14. *Shapiro v. Art Craft Strauss Sign Co.*[52] Res ipsa was available when a sign fell from the defendant's building and struck the plaintiff.
15. *Bauman v. Long Island Rail Road.*[53] Res ipsa was available when an arm of a railroad crossing gate broke off its hinges and fell on the plaintiff while she was walking across the track.
16. *Walches v. State of New York.*[54] Res ipsa was available when a filing cabinet fell on the plaintiff, who was in

---

51. Alberti v. State, 80 Misc. 2d 105, 362 N.Y.S.2d 341 (Ct. Cl. 1974), *aff'd*, 51 A.D.2d 611, 378 N.Y.S.2d 125 (3d Dep't 1976).
52. Shapiro v. Art Craft Strauss Sign Corp., 39 A.D.2d 696, 332 N.Y.S.2d 588 (1st Dep't 1972).
53. Bauman v. Long Island R.R., 110 A.D.2d 739, 487 N.Y.S.2d 833 (2d Dep't 1985); Weiss v. Brooklyn Edison Co., 253 A.D. 746, 300 N.Y.S. 756 (2d Dep't 1937). *See* Annot., *Application of Doctrine of Res Ipsa Loquitur in Action for Injury to Person in Street by Glass Falling from Window, Door, or Wall,* 81 A.L.R.2D 897 (1962); Annot., *Application of Res Ipsa Loquitur Rule in Action Against Electric Power, Telephone, or Telegraph Company for Personal Injury from Fall of Pole,* 97 A.L.R.2D 674 (1964); Annot., *Application of Res ipsa Loquitur Doctrine in Action Against Owner or Occupant of Building for Personal Injury or Death of Person in Street Resulting from Object Falling or Thrown from Building,* 97 A.L.R.2D 1444 (1964).
54. Walches v. State, 34 Misc. 2d 199, 228 N.Y.S.2d 342 (Ct. Cl. 1962).

the defendant company's office being interviewed for a job.

17. *Camillo v. Geer.*[55] A pedestrian was injured by falling concrete when a crane collapsed and damaged a building. The trial court correctly rejected the request of the manufacturer of a component part to charge res ipsa against another defendant because there was evidence that the manufacturer's part failed and caused the accident.
18. *Scimeca v. New York City Transit Authority.*[56] While the plaintiff was driving under an elevated subway, a train passed overhead, then a piece of steel fell through his windshield. The trial court dismissed the complaint after the plaintiff's case, but the appellate court ordered a new trial with the direction to allow additional testimony in the interest of justice.

20.3.1.3 Slip and Fall

19. *Bauer v. Harris Intertype Corporation.*[57] Res ipsa was not available to a window washer who claimed he slipped on oil which had dripped from a new catwalk because the defendant's affidavit established that it had finished the installation sixteen days before the accident and had not used oil.
20. *Morales v. Foodway, Inc.*[58] Res ipsa was not available to a customer who slipped on a tomato because another customer might have dropped it.

55. Camillo v. Geer, 185 A.D.2d 192 (1st Dep't 1992).
56. Scimeca v. New York City Transit Authority, 39 A.D.2d 596 (2d Dep't 1972). For a similar case, *see* Nesbit v. New York City Transit Authority, 170 A.D.2d 92 (1st Dep't 1991): a pedestrian was hit by a safety chain from an elevated subway train. Res ipsa was available because even the defendant's witnesses admitted that a third party could not have dislodged the chain.
57. Bauer v. Harris Intertype Corp., 35 A.D.2d 426 (3d Dep't 1970).
58. Morales v. Foodways, Inc., 186 A.D.2d 407 (1st Dep't 1992).

21. *DiSanto v. County of Westchester.*[59] Res ipsa was unavailable to a passenger who fell on the tarmac at an airport because the plaintiff's evidence regarding the cause of her fall was inconclusive.

20.3.1.4 Miscellany

20.3.1.4.1 Hot Water

22. *Mikel v. Flatbush General Hospital.*[60] Res ipsa was available in an action against a hospital by a patient who was scalded in the shower by water that had been heated higher than was proper.
23. *Myers v. Fir Cab Corporation.*[61] When a taxicab's engine overheated, the driver removed the cap from the radiator. The hot spray of steam and water scalded a pedestrian who was walking past the car. Res ipsa did not justify a summary judgment for the plaintiff.

20.3.1.4.2 Exploding Bottles

24. *Cameron v. H.C. Bohack Co.*[62] Res ipsa was available to a customer in a supermarket who was injured by an exploding bottle.

---

59. DiSanto v. County of Westchester, 210 A.D.2d 628 (3d Dep't 1994).
60. Mikel v. Flatbush Gen. Hosp., 49 A.D.2d 581, 370 N.Y.S.2d 162 (2d Dep't 975).
61. Myers v. Fir Cab Corporation, 100 A.D.2d 29 (1st Dep't 1984).
62. Cameron v. H.C. Bohack Co., 27 A.D.2d 362, 280 N.Y.S.2d 583 (2d Dep't 1967); Day v. Grand Union Co., 280 A.D. 253, 113 N.Y.S.2d 436 (3d Dep't 1952), *aff'd*, 304 N.Y. 821 (1952); *see also* Trembley v. Coca-Cola Bottling Co., 285 A.D. 539, 138 N.Y.S.2d 332 (3d Dep't 1955); Annot., *Presumption of Prima Facie Case of Negligence Based on Presence of Foreign Substance in Food in Can or Other Sealed Container,* 52 A.L.R.2D 159 (1957); Annot., *Presumption of Prima Facie Case of Negligence Based on Presence of Foreign Substance in Bottled or Canned Beverage,* 52 A.L.R.2D 117 (1957); Annot., *Application of Res Ipsa Loquitur Doctrine in Action Against Manufacturer or Seller of Container or Other Packaging Material for Injury Caused Thereby,* 81 A.L.R.2D 356 (1962).

25. *DeSimone v. Inserra Supermarkets, Inc.*[63] Res ipsa was unavailable to a plaintiff who claimed that a bottle exploded in her hand.

> Here, the trial evidence establishes that the juice bottle broke when plaintiff removed it from the store shelf and did not, as characterized by the plaintiff explode. As such, defendant's negligence was no more likely a causative agent than plaintiff's own conduct. . . . Additionally, the element of exclusive control is lacking . . . because any number of other customers had access to the bottle in the hours between the 7:00 a.m. store opening and the 3:00 p.m. incident.[64]

20.3.1.4.3 Windows

26. *Kaplan v. City University of New York.*[65] Res ipsa was available to a plaintiff who lifted a window and had it fall back down on his fingers.[66]

20.3.1.4.4 Swimming

27. *Dvong v. City University of New York.*[67] Res ipsa was available in a case in which a beginning swimmer drowned after his first swimming class and in which the defendant university could not adequately explain how or why the death occurred.

20.3.1.4.5 Faucets

28. *Jungjohann v. Hotel Buffalo.*[68] Res ipsa was available to a guest in a hotel who turned the faucet in the shower. The faucet broke and cut his hand.

---

63. DeSimone v. Inserra Supermarkets, Inc., 207 A.D.2d 615 (3d Dep't 1994).
64. *Id.* at 616.
65. Kaplan v. City Univ., N.Y.L.J., Mar. 9, 1985 (Ct. Cl. 1985).
66. *See also* Nikisch v. Madison 34th St. Corp., 295 N.Y. 833, 66 N.E.2d 850 (1946) (res ipsa applied when plaintiff lifted window shade and roller fell on her head).
67. Dvong v. City Univ., N.Y.L.J., Feb. 9, 1988 (Ct. Cl. 1988).
68. Jungjohann v. Hotel Buffalo, 5 A.D.2d 496 (4th Dep't 1958). For a similar case, *see* Kane v. Ten Eyck Co., 10 Misc. 2d 398, 175 N.Y.S.2d 88 (Sup. Ct. 1943), *aff'd,* 267 A.D. 789 (3d Dep't 1943) and 292 N.Y. 701 (1944).

20.3.1.4.6 Leaks

29. *Union Novelty Co., Inc. v. Elias Associates.*[69] Res ipsa was available when water accumulated on the roof from a watertank exclusively maintained by the defendant. Water leaked into the plaintiff's premises.

20.3.2 Medical Malpractice

20.3.2.1 Foreign Objects

30. *Gravitt v. Newman.*[70] Res ipsa was available against both the hospital and the attending surgeon after a surgical instrument broke off inside the patient during surgery.
31. *Anderson v. Sandberg.*[71] Res ipsa was available in a suit against a hospital after a piece of equipment broke during surgery and lodged within the plaintiff's body.
32. *Prooth v. Walsh.*[72] Res ipsa was available when a foreign object was left inside a patient during surgery.

32A. *Kambat v. St. Francis Hospital.*[72.1] Res ipsa was available when the surgeon left an 18-by-18-inch laperotomy pad inside the patient.

20.3.2.2 Related Injuries

33. *Gorka v. Highland Hospital.*[73] Res ipsa was available in an action by the plaintiff for injuries she sustained in an operating room when a fire erupted in the operative field while the defendant was performing a cauterization procedure upon a laceration near the plaintiff's eye.

---

69. Union Novelty Co., Inc. v. Elias Associates, 12 A.D.2d 761 (1st Dep't 961).
70. Gravitt v. Newman, 114 A.D.2d 1000, 498 N.Y.S.2d 620 (2d Dep't 1985).
71. Anderson v. Sanberg, 338 A.2d 1 (1975); *see also* Gravitt v. Newman, 114 A.D.2d 1000, 498 N.Y.S.2d 620 (2d Dep't 1985).
72. Prooth v. Walsh, 105 Misc. 2d 603, 432 N.Y.S.2d 666 (Sup. Ct. 1980).

72.1. Kambat v. St. Francis Hospital, 89 N.Y.2d 489 (1997).

73. Gorka v. Highland Hosp., 132 Misc. 2d 783, 505 N.Y.S.2d 595 (Sup. Ct. 1986).

34. *Mack v. Lydia E. Hall Hospital.*[74] Res ipsa was available when the plaintiff was burned by a grounding pad during electrocoagulation surgery.
35. *Pipers v. Rosenow.*[75] Res ipsa was not available in an action for medical malpractice after the plaintiff sustained an injury to his arm following the insertion of a needle and the withdrawal of blood for laboratory examination.

20.3.2.3 Unrelated Injuries

36. *Kerber v. Sarles.*[76] Res ipsa was available after the plaintiff underwent surgery for a hammer toe, but awoke to find her two front teeth missing.
37. *Pliss v. 83rd Foundation, Inc.*[77] Res ipsa was available to a person who suffered a burn to a part of his body unrelated to the surgery.

20.3.2.4 Childbirth

38. *Abbott v. New Rochelle Hospital Medical Center.*[78] Res ipsa was not available to a child who was born with a neurological injury to the brachial plexus (Erb's Palsy).

20.3.2.5 Personal Injury in a Medical Facility

39. *Ladd v. Hudson Valley Ambulance Service.*[79] Res ipsa was available to a patient who was injured in a hospital when he was placed on a gurney which collapsed. He was to be transported to another medical facility.

---

74. Mack v. Lydia E. Hall Hosp., 121 A.D.2d 431, 503 N.Y.S.2d 131 (2d Dep't 1986).
75. Pipers v. Rosenow, 39 A.D.2d 240, 333 N.Y.S.2d 480 (2d Dep't 1972).
76. Kerber v. Sarles, 151 A.D.2d 1031, 542 N.Y.S.2d 94 (4th Dep't 1989).
77. Pliss v. 83rd Found, Inc., 69 N.Y.S.2d 727 (City Ct. 1947); *see* Annot., *Hospital's Liability Under Doctrine of Res Ipsa Loquitur for Injury to Patient from Heat Lamp or Pad or Hot Water Bottle,* 72 A.L.R.2D 408 (1960).
78. Abbott v. New Rochelle Hosp. Medical Center, 141 A.D.2d 589, 529 N.Y.S.2d 352 (2d Dep't 1988).
79. Ladd v. Hudson Valley Ambulance Service, 142 A.D.2d 17 (3d Dep't 1988).

40. *Payette v. Rockefeller University.*[80] Res ipsa is available either in an action for personal injury or medical malpractice. The plaintiff's claim for negligent prescription of dietary regimen in a research project was a claim for personal injury and was governed by that statute of limitations.

20.4 BUILDING A CASE FOR RES IPSA LOQUITUR

The attorney who believes that a client's causes of action might invoke the inference of res ipsa loquitur must prepare to establish all three of the elements upon which the inference depends. The attorney must also prepare to present a clear chain of reasoning between the facts and any element in dispute. Naturally, the attorney for the defendant must foresee such a strategy and be prepared to dispute it.

20.4.1 Establishing Three Elements of Res Ipsa Loquitur

The Appellate Division, First Department, has provided an excellent analysis of res ipsa in *Burgess v. Otis Elevator Co.*[81] *Burgess* involved an elevator that stopped and opened out of alignment, or level, with the floor, thereby injuring the plaintiff. The trial court charged the jury on res ipsa loquitur; the jury returned a verdict for the plaintiff, and the appellate court affirmed the judgment. The appellate court began by positing the three elements and then considered each in turn, as established by the plaintiff.

---

80. Payette v. Rockefeller University, 220 A.D.2d 69 (1st Dep't 1996). However, the same appellate division has ruled that the proper cause of action is medical malpractice when the physician mixes up the patients' files and erroneously informs one of them that he is HIV-positive. Harvey v. Cramer, 235 A.D.2d 315 (1st Dep't 1997).

81. Burgess v. Otis Elevator Co., 114 A.D.2d 784, 495 N.Y.S.2d 376 (1st Dep't 1985), *aff'd,* 69 N.Y.2d 623, 503 N.E.2d 692, 511 N.Y.S.2d 227 (1986).

First, the plaintiff had presented testimony that the degree of misleveling would not ordinarily have occurred in the absence of negligence for the misleveling was beyond the acceptable tolerance, and the "malfunction was probably due to a serious defective condition, ordinarily discoverable upon reasonable inspection. . . ."

Second, the plaintiff had established the defendant's exclusive control by showing that the building's owner had relied "upon defendant's expertise to inspect and maintain the intricate devices of the elevator in reasonably safe operating condition, pursuant to the service agreement." The appellate court observed, "'Exclusivity' is a relative term, not an absolute. 'The logical basis for [the control] requirement is simply that it must appear that the negligence of which the thing speaks is probably that of defendant and not of another.'"

Third, the plaintiff had established that he had not caused or contributed to the event by his own voluntary act simply by observing that a passenger had no control over the leveling of an elevator The defendant's greater access to information reinforced the three conclusions. (Remember that some courts consider this greater access to be a fourth criterion.)

20.4.2 Reasoning from an Inference upon an Inference

The Appellate Division, Second Department, decided *Pollock v. Rapid Industrial Plastics Co.*,[82] which explained how to build a chain of reasoning to reach the ultimate inference allowed by res ipsa.

In *Pollock*, the plaintiff was severely injured when he was hit by a tire that was traveling by itself at a high rate of speed down the Bruckner Expressway. The plaintiff had got

82. Pollock v. Rapid Indus. Plastics Co., 113 A.D.2d 520, 497 N.Y.S.2d 45 (2d Dep't 1985).

out of his car at an entrance ramp after locking bumpers with the car in front of him when the tire hit him. Stapled to the tire was a tag that said, "Rapid Plastics 57-022," and there was evidence that the General Tire Service had repaired a tire for Rapid Plastics, delivered it to the latter about a week before the accident, and tagged it like the one found at the accident. There was no other evidence of a connection between the defendant, Rapid Plastics, and the tire that rolled down the highway. The trial court refused to apply res ipsa against Rapid Plastics because the plaintiff had failed to prove that the defendant had had exclusive control of the tire at the time of the accident. In particular, the trial court held that permitting the jury to apply res ipsa in this case would have required an inference upon an inference.

The Appellate Division, Second Department, reversed the judgment and held:

> [T]here is no rule of evidence which prohibits placing an inference upon an inference, for in "innumerable instances inferences are built upon inferences.". . .
>
> The rule in this State is "that an *inference* may be based on inference, but that inference may not be based on conjecture, nor conjecture upon inference to prove a fact or to serve as the basis for an ultimate conclusion.
>
> * * *
>
> Clearly, an inference can be based upon a fact which is itself based upon circumstantial evidence . . . if the first inference is a reasonably probable one, it may be used as a basis for a succeeding inference." . . . In addition, "[c]ircumstantial evidence may, of course, be sufficient to sustain a finding of negligence. All that is involved. . . is a series of natural and logical inferences from the facts proven.". . .[83]

83. *Id.* at 525, 497 N.Y.S.2d at 49-50.

The appellate court then found justifiable the ultimate inference that the defendant, the Rapid Plastics Co., had had exclusive control of the tire that injured the plaintiff. In the court's view, that ultimate inference rested on a chain of reliable prior inferences, to wit:

1. The tag establishes that the General Tire Service repaired the tire and delivered it to Rapid Plastics one week before the accident, November 24, 1975.
2. The invoice establishes that Rapid Plastics owned and controlled the tire on November 24, 1975.
   - Rapid Plastics acknowledged receipt of possession.
   - Possession of tangible property creates a presumption of ownership.
3. Ownership is presumed to continue, and the defendant adduced no evidence to rebut this presumption.
4. The defendant's ownership of the tire creates the presumption that the tire was being used for its benefit.
5. Therefore, the defendant exercised exclusive possession and control of the tire on the date of the accident, December 1, 1975.
   - In the absence of evidence, only speculation could generate a different conclusion.[84]

The *Pollock* case shows the lengths to which a court may go to infer exclusive control when the pieces of the puzzle otherwise fit.

20.4.3 Requesting a Charge of Res Ipsa Loquitur

The plaintiff will waste his effort establishing the three necessary conditions for involving res ipsa unless he or she asks the court to instruct the jury that it may draw the inference that the defendant was negligent. Naturally, the Pat-

84. *Id.*

tern Jury Instructions include a generic charge,[85] reproduced as example 20-1, but the plaintiff should propose a form of the charge adapted to the specific case. In composing this charge, the attorney should consult the official comment.

85. PJI 2:65. RES IPSA LOQUITUR, PATTERN JURY INSTRUCTIONS, Vol. 1, Second Ed., 1995, 1996 Supp., Off. of Ct. Ad., p. 164.

EXAMPLE 20-1: CHARGE TO THE JURY ON RES IPSA LOQUITUR

Plaintiff must prove by the preponderance of the evidence that the defendant was negligent. Plaintiff may do this by circumstantial evidence, that is, by proving facts and circumstances from which negligence may be reasonably inferred. If the instrumentality causing the injury was in the exclusive control of defendant, and if the circumstances surrounding the happening of the accident were of such a nature that in the ordinary course of events it would not have occurred if the person having control of the instrumentality had used reasonable care under the circumstances, the law permits, but does not require, you to infer negligence from the happening of the accident.

The requirement of exclusive control is not rigid. It implies control by defendant of such kind that the probability that the accident was caused by someone else is so remote that it is fair to permit an inference that defendant was negligent.

Thus, if you find by a preponderance of the evidence that the instrumentality causing the injury was, at the time of the injury, in the exclusive control of defendant, and that the circumstances of the accident were such that in the ordinary course of events it would not have occurred if reasonable care had been used by the defendant, then you may infer that defendant was negligent. However, if taking into consideration all of the evidence in the case you conclude that the accident was not due to any negligence on defendant's part, the you will find for defendant (on this issue).

Presumptions 21

Presumptions are another substitute for testimony. Therefore, in this chapter, we will discuss presumptions and related matters. We must begin with a discussion of the burden of proof because this burden and presumptions are complementary notions and because the burden of proof is the more fundamental notion. We will then discuss presumptions.

Unfortunately, presumptions are an important subject on which it is difficult to say anything definitive. The New York County Lawyers' Association once presented a panel discussion on presumptions. The panel consisted of experienced practitioners and judges, and each panelist presented a scheme organizing the subject. However, everyone's scheme was different; for example, the panelists disagreed over whether the presumption itself disappears once the opposing party presents some contrary evidence. Therefore, we must approach this subject in an orderly fashion. Order is not itself logic, but order is necessary for the consistent application of logic and of the rules of law. Hence, for example, we examine the cause of action before the affirmative defense and the pleadings before the evidence. In this chapter, we will examine the burden of proof before the presumptions and the true presumptions before the secondary meanings of presumption.

21.1 THE BURDEN OF PROOF: THE GRAND PRESUMPTION

21.1.1 The Definition

In a civil case, the burden of proof, also known as the burden of persuasion, is the obligation of the plaintiff to establish the elements of his cause of action and to maintain them by a fair preponderance of the evidence.[1] The defendant, in turn, will have the burden of proof on any affirmative defense he asserts.[2] Thus, the defendant can win either because the plaintiff has failed to meet his burden of proof or because the defendant has met his. From the point of view of the party who does not bear this burden, the burden of proof is really the grand presumption.

The notion of a burden of proof is an example of the intertwining of the history of law with the history of rhetoric. The Greeks of the classical age developed rhetoric as a response to their legal system: trials were public events held

---

1. Hornbooks and judicial opinions usually fail to distinguish clearly between these two elements of the burden of proof. The plaintiff must end the trial with a preponderance of evidence over the defendant, but the plaintiff also must establish all the elements of his cause of action by presenting arguments and evidence sufficient to persuade a reasonable man. In other words, the plaintiff could present the preponderance of the evidence and still lose if that evidence were otherwise insufficient. As a necessary step in bearing his burden of proof, the plaintiff must present a prima facie case by the end of his direct case. In other words, for the trial to proceed, the plaintiff must present a case which would persuade a reasonable man in the absence of a rebuttal. Thus, the plaintiff's direct case must have survived cross-examination. After the defendant's case, any rebuttal witnesses, and the closing arguments, the jury will decide whether the plaintiff has established all the elements of his cause of action despite the defendant's rebuttal and by the preponderance of the evidence. For the plaintiff's duty to plead and prove the elements of his cause of action, see Farmers' Loan and Trust Co. v. Siefke, 144 N.Y. 354 (1895). For the plaintiff's need to produce a preponderance of the evidence, see Roberge v. Bonner, 185 N.Y. 265 (1906); Ward v. New York Life Insurance Co., 225 N.Y. 314 (1919); Rinaldi and Sons, Inc. v. Wells Fargo Alarm Service, Inc., 39 N.Y.2d 191 (1976); Jarrett v. Madifari, 67 A.D.2d 396 (1st Dept. 1979).
2. Farmers' Loan and Trust Co. v. Siefke, 144 N.Y. 354, 358-59 (1895).

before hundreds of jurors, and each litigant had to deliver his own speeches.[3] There were no professional lawyers, but there were ghostwriters. The burden of proof was a logical and practical device for dealing with uncertainty, to wit: the unreliability of the evidence and the lack of omniscience of the jurors. The gods would not need a burden of proof, but mortals did. In the face of uncertainty, therefore, the law must require one party to prove his case so far as that is humanly possible. In other words, the party with the presumption would win if the party with the burden of proof failed to carry his burden. The more general rhetorical notion is that he who asserts must prove,[4] and this notion applies even to individual facts, e.g., that A struck B with his automobile or that C did not report to the hospital until 12:30 p.m. Thus, *Black's Law Dictionary* defines burden of proof as "the necessity or duty of affirmatively proving a fact or facts in dispute on an issue raised between the parties in a cause."[5] Both attorneys and rhetoricians also use the term "burden of proof" as we have used it here, to wit: the obligation of a party to establish the elements of his cause of action or affirmative defense despite the attempts of the opposing party to rebut them.

21.1.2 Rhetorical Basis for the Burden of Proof

The notion of a burden of proof is deceptively simple. It can be illuminated by briefly discussing the rhetorical basis for the burden of proof and then (in the following section) how the law has adapted rhetoric to the needs of the specialized debate called the trial.

---

3. S.C. Todd, The Shape of Athenian Law 127-30 (1993).
4. George McCoy Musgrave, Competitive Debate: Rules and Techniques 18-20 (3d ed. 1957).
5. Black's Law Dictionary 246 (rev'd 4th ed. 1968).

Rhetoricians[6] have elaborated the notion of the burden of proof into a comprehensive scheme.[7] We will content ourselves with nine pertinent points. First, the party seeking a change in the status quo bears the burden of proof, and imposing damages on the defendant is a change in the status quo. Second, the opposing party, i.e., the negative in a debate or the defendant in a trial, has the benefit of a presumption in his favor. This presumption is merely a complementary way of saying that the affirmative or the plaintiff has the burden of proof. Third, in his direct case, the affirmative or the plaintiff must present a prima facie case, i.e., a case which would persuade a reasonable man if there were no rebuttal. Fourth, if the affirmative or the plaintiff does present a prima facie case, then the burden of rebuttal shifts to the negative or the defendant. In other words, the defendant must rebut the prima facie case, or the audience (the judge or the jury) logically will vote for the plaintiff. Fifth, the negative or the defendant must rebut the prima facie case with arguments and, perhaps, evidence. The advocate generates proof by applying arguments to the evidence, but this evidence may be the opposing advocate's evidence or the lack thereof. Hence, rebutting the affirmative's or the plaintiff's prima facie case does not, ipso facto, require the negative or the defendant to introduce evidence. (As a practical matter, of course, the negative or the defendant usually does introduce evidence). And sixth, if the negative or the defendant succeeds in rebutting the affirmative's or the plaintiff's prima facie case, then the burden of rebut-

---

6. Rhetoric, per Aristotle, is the discovery of all available means of persuasion. A rhetorician is a scholar or teacher of rhetoric whereas a rhetor is a practitioner of rhetoric, i.e., a speaker. Naturally, one person may perform both functions.
7. There are many books on rhetoric. Some good ones are EDWARD P.J. CORBETT, CLASSICAL RHETORIC FOR THE MODERN STUDENT (1965); WILLIAM NORWOOD BRIGANCE, SPEECH: ITS TECHNIQUES AND DISCIPLINES IN A FREE SOCIETY (2d ed. 1961); AUSTIN J. FREELEY, ARGUMENTATION AND DEBATE: CRITICAL THINKING FOR REASONED DECISION MAKING (8th ed. 1993); W. WARD FEARNSIDE & WILLIAM B. HOLTHER, FALLACY : THE COUNTERFEIT OF ARGUMENT (1959).

tal shifts back to the affirmative or the plaintiff. In fact, in the course of the debate or the trial, the burden of rebuttal may shift several times.

Assume that the debate or the trial is now over. The seventh observation is that the burden of proof remains with the affirmative or the plaintiff throughout the proceeding. Therefore, eighth, at the end of the proceeding, the judge (i.e., the audience, the trial judge, or the jury) will decide whether the affirmative or the plaintiff has carried his burden of proof based on the totality of the arguments and the evidence presented by both sides. If the burden of rebuttal rests on the affirmative or the plaintiff, then the negative or the defendant wins, but if the burden of rebuttal rests on the negative or the defendant, then the affirmative or the plaintiff wins. Finally, ninth, merely presenting the preponderance of the evidence is insufficient to carry the burden of proof. Instead, the affirmative or the plaintiff must win all the necessary issues. In a debate, the affirmative must win all the stock issues including defeating the negative's attacks on the affirmative's plan. In a trial, the plaintiff must establish all the elements of his cause of action and defeat any affirmative defenses. If a mere preponderance of the evidence were sufficient, the plaintiff could win his lawsuit without presenting a prima facie case. Moreover, a motion for a directed verdict at the end of the plaintiff's direct case would be nonsensical: only the plaintiff has presented evidence so he must have the preponderance. Of course, at the end of the trial, the plaintiff cannot win without the preponderance of the evidence, but he still must have established all the elements of his cause of action.

21.1.3 Adaptations by the Law

The law has made several adaptations in the practice of rhetoric to accommodate the special nature of the trial (which is an exercise in forensic oratory, i.e., speeches disputing factual violations of rules). We will examine eight such adaptations.

First, every trial is a debate about a proposition of fact. Debates about policy, value, and fact are possible.[8] Academic and political debates are often about proposition of policy, e.g., "resolved, that NATO should intervene in Kosovo." However, a trial is always a debate about a proposition of fact: one party always accuses the other of already having committed some act, e.g., "resolved, that the defendant injured the plaintiff by an act of medical malpractice." This proposition constitutes the top of the pyramid of justification.[9]

Second, the law restricts the *topoi* which trial attorneys may use.[10] More specifically, the law limits the aids to invention to the elements of the cause of action or affirmative defense and the forms of admissible evidence. By contrast, someone advocating that NATO intervene in Kosovo may employ any reason he deems sufficient.

Third, the law imposes on the advocates rules of evidence as distinguished from logical tests of evidence. However, the law imposes these rules of evidence, i.e., rules governing the admissibility and use of evidence, in aid of the logical tests. The ancient view of the common law is that jurors are not too bright so the law withholds from jurors evidence which the law believes will inflame or mislead them, e.g., pictures

---

8. GEORGE W. FLUHARTY & HAROLD R. ROSS, PUBLIC SPEAKING (1966); FREELEY, *supra* note 7, at 46-49.
9. Kevin P. Mc Mullen, Essay Writing Clinic Workbook (New York: Marino Bar Review Course, 1978), p. 12.
10. CORBETT, *supra* note 7, at 136-39.

of the plaintiff in his coffin[11] or hearsay for which there is no exception.

Fourth, the law has adopted formal affirmative defenses, i.e., certain counterarguments which will defeat the plaintiff's cause of action even if he has established all the elements of it.[12]

The fifth adaptation is that the law separates the speeches by the advocates from the introduction of the evidence to support the arguments the advocates make in those speeches. This format goes back at least to the Athenians, who allowed each party to make opening and closing arguments but who provided a clerk to read the affidavits of the witnesses between the two sets of speeches.[13] Today, the party's attorneys question the witnesses in person before the jury. In an academic or political debate, by contrast, each advocate integrates his evidence into each speech by quotation or paraphrase.

The sixth adaptation was unknown to the Athenians: the attorneys now cross-examine one another's witnesses.

The seventh adaptation results form the fifth and sixth ones but requires more explanation, to wit: a trial lacks the obvious and constant shifting of the burden of rebuttal exhibited by academic debate. In a debate, each side delivers two constructive speeches and two rebuttals. Thus, there are eight alternating speeches with the affirmative beginning the constructive speeches and the negative beginning the rebuttals.[14] Moreover, each speaker integrates evidence into each of his speeches. Thus, the audience or critic-judge can follow the shifting of the burden of rebuttal on each issue at the end of each speech. In a trial, by contrast, the judge evaluates the status of the burden of rebuttal when he rules on motions for a directed verdict at the end of the plaintiff's di-

---

11. Allen v. Stokes, 260 A.D. 600 (1940).
12. BLACK'S LAW DICTIONARY, *supra* note 5, at 82.
13. TODD, *supra* note 3, at 127-30.
14. MUSGRAVE, *supra* note 4, at 45-47.

rect case and at the end of the evidence.[15] The academic format is a better tool for exposing fallacies in the opposing cases, but the trial attorney can adapt to his format successfully if he understands what is transpiring in the minds of the jurors.

The juror will begin evaluating the opposing parties' cases during the selection of the jury. He will then decide tentatively whether the plaintiff's attorney has delivered a persuasive opening statement (or at least a lucid one) and then whether the defendant's attorney has cast doubt on the claim in his opening. During the plaintiff's direct case, an alert juror will mentally test the plaintiff's witnesses and the arguments implied by their testimony, and he will evaluate the defendant's implied refutation during the cross-examination. At the end of the plaintiff's direct case, the juror should ask himself whether the plaintiff has presented a prima facie case. During the defendant's direct case and any rebuttal testimony, the juror should decide whether the burden of rebuttal has shifted and why. By the end of the testimony, the alert juror should know the issues that the attorneys need to address in their summations in order to persuade him,[16] and, at the end of the defendant's summation, the juror should have decided whether the burden of rebuttal has shifted to the plaintiff. Finally, the juror should listen carefully to the judge's charge to detect any guidance that would change the juror's opinion, e.g., who has the burden of proof on contributory negligence.

This advice seems contrary to the injunctions judges issue to jurors. Nominally, it is, but a juror—especially one sitting through a long trial—cannot reach an intelligent verdict unless he constantly evaluates what he is hearing. When a judge warns the jurors before a recess not to form any con-

---

15. N.Y. C.P.L.R. 4401.

16. Part of the trial attorney's skill consists in perceiving the weaknesses of his own case, the weaknesses in his own presentation of his case, and the reactions of the jurors during the trial.

clusions, he means that the jurors should not form any final conclusion but should keep open minds. The jury in O.J. Simpson's criminal trial has been criticized for the wrong reason. The quick verdict meant that the jury had been paying attention. That verdict was also a warning for the trial attorney: Do not think that you can try the case de novo in the summation! The jurors have been evaluating your case since your first explanation during the selection of the jury. Make sense of your case from the beginning.

This warning brings us to our eighth and final adaptation: although the law permits the trial attorney to deliver only one frankly argumentative speech (his summation), the attorney may present his client's case to the jury on every occasion from the selection to the charge. He need only act skillfully to avoid contravening any rule. Thus, even New York's new uniform rules for conducting the voir dire allow the attorney to state his client's contentions.[17] The opening statement, although nominally expository, is a disguised argumentative speech because an outline of the testimony makes sense only in the context of the cause of action. The attorney's direct examination of his own witnesses may not be frankly argumentative, but the examination must elicit testimony of obvious relevance, and the cross-examination should be pointed. The rebuttal witnesses should answer the questions which the opponent's cross-examination or direct witness probably raised in the minds of the jurors. The attorney's summation is a frankly argumentative speech, but the debate does not end there. The judge delivers the charge to the jury, but the attorney provides the judge with proposed charges and argues for them in a conference with the judge and opposing counsel.[18]

In summary, the plaintiff in a civil case has the burden of proving his case by establishing all the elements of his cause of action and by maintaining them by a fair prepon-

---

17. Uniform Civil Rule 202.33, Appendix E, subdivision A (4).
18. N.Y. C.P.L.R. 4 110-b. See section 8.2 of this book.

derance of the evidence against the defendant's rebuttal. Once the plaintiff has presented a prima facie case, the defendant has the burden of rebuttal, and the defendant also bears the burden of proof for any affirmative defense he asserts. The burden of rebuttal may shift several times during the trial, but the burden of proof always remains on the plaintiff to establish his cause of action. Having examined that grand presumption, we will now examine more limited presumptions.

21.2 THE PRESUMPTIONS

Presumptions are like the tribbles in that old episode of *Star Trek*: you cannot tell their heads from their tails, but the critters keep multiplying.[19] Part of the problem is that the term "presumption" has several meanings. Hence, when an attorney uses the term, he may intend any of several different things. If we are to make sense of presumptions, use them effectively for our clients, and argue effectively when the we must be aware of these different meanings, and so the following discussion of definitions is fundamental.

21.2.1 Definitions

21.2.1.1 Definition of a True Presumption

The core meaning of the term "presumption" consists of what attorneys traditionally call a presumption of law and what scholars now call a true presumption. For example, *Black's Law Dictionary* defines a presumption of law as "a rule of law that courts and judges shall draw a particular inference from a fact, or from particular evidence, unless and

---

19. Perhaps slippery electric eels would make a fitter simile.

until the truth of such inference is disproved."[20] *Richardson on Evidence* agrees:

> A presumption may be defined as a rule of law "which requires that a particular inference must be drawn from an ascertained state of facts." The inference is mandatory once the basic fact . . . is established on the trial. This inference continues until it is overcome by sufficient evidence to the contrary.[21]

Other scholars have adopted essentially the same definition.[22]

Some observations about the foregoing definition: First, we have defined an evidentiary presumption rather than a presumption allocating the burden of proof. While the burden of proof and presumptions are complementary and while, therefore, one may speak properly of a presumption in favor of the adverse party,[23] we are using the term in a narrower sense. We mean that the introduction of some preliminary evidence has created a mandatory inference that some other fact is true; for example, one party might present evidence of his own office's invariable business practice in mailing notices in order to raise the presumption that the other party received the notice.[24]

---

20. BLACK'S LAW DICTIONARY, *supra* note 5, at 1349.
21. JEROME PRINCE, RICHARDSON ON EVIDENCE §54 (9th ed. 1964).
22. For example, see ROBERT A. BARKER & VINCENT C. ALEXANDER, EVIDENCE IN NEW YORK STATE AND FEDERAL COURTS 80 (1996) ("[T]he term 'presumption' refers to a rule of law that a particular inference must be drawn from particular facts unless the opponent, at minimum, introduces contrary evidence.") (citing Platt v. Elias, 186 N.Y. 374, 379 (1906)). *See also* MICHAEL M. MARTIN, ET AL, NEW YORK EVIDENCE HANDBOOK: RULES, THEORY, AND PRACTICE 71 (1997).
23. People *ex rel.* Wallington Apartments v. Miller, 288 N.Y. 31 (1942).
24. Gardam and Sons v. Batterson, 198 N.Y. 175 (1910); Oregon Steam Ship Co. v. Otis, 100 N.Y. 446 (1885); Nassau Insurance Co. v. Murray, 46 N.Y.2d 828 (1978); Bossuk v. Steinberg, 58 N.Y.2d 916 (1983); Gonzalez v. Ross, 47 N.Y.2d 922 (1979); Law v. Benedict, 197 A.D.2d 808 (3d Dept. 1993); Lumbermens' Mutual Casualty Co. v. Collins, 135 A.D.2d 373 (1st Dept. 1987).

Further, the presumption is not itself evidence but is a substitute for evidence.[25] In other words, a party proves one fact in order to raise a presumption of another fact; for example, the plaintiff in an action for medical malpractice might prove that the defendant physician was unlicensed in order to raise a presumption that the physician's conduct was negligent.[26]

The reasoning underlying a true presumption is a conditional syllogism.[27]

> If A is true, then B is true.
>
> A is true.
>
> Therefore, B is true.

In a lawsuit, the conditional syllogism might be this one:

> If Jones has possession of the currency, then Jones has title to the currency.
>
> Jones has possession of the currency.
>
> Therefore, Jones has title to the currency.

The party intending to rely on the presumption must present evidence or take note of admitted facts that will support the minor premise and justify the conclusion.

Turning to the weight of the presumptions, note that the true presumption is not conclusive. There are, of course, rules of law which attorneys traditionally have called conclusive presumptions.[28] There are a few such rules, e.g., that a child under seven years of age cannot commit a crime[29] or that a written contract incorporates all the terms of the con-

---

25. BLACK'S LAW DICTIONARY, *supra* note 5, at 1350: "Presumptions are not 'evidence.'" "A presumption is a substitute for evidence . . . but is not itself evidence . . . It is a rule about the duty of producing evidence. . . . Presumptions will serve in the place of 'evidence' . . . until overcome by competent evidence to contrary."
26. N.Y. C.P.L.R. 4504 (d).
27. There are three kinds of syllogisms: categorical, conditional, and disjunctive. *See* FREELEY, *supra* note 7, 143-48.
28. BLACK'S LAW DICTIONARY, *supra* note 5, at 1349 col. 2.
29. RICHARDSON, *supra* note 21, p.34, §56.

tract.[30] However, such a presumption is really a rule of substantive law, not a rule of evidence.[31] Thus, all true presumptions are rebuttable, but different presumptions have different strengths. The presumption of title from possession is a weak presumption;[32] there is a stronger or ordinary presumption of negligence against a bailee who failed to return the goods,[33] but the presumption against suicide is very strong.[34]

Either the common law or a statute may create a presumption. For example, the presumption against suicide is a rule of the common law, but the rule imputing negligence to an unlicensed physician is a creature of statute.[35]

A final observation refers to the continuing effect of the presumption. The presumption should not disappear from the case once the adverse party has presented contrary evidence. Instead, the jury should weigh the evidence against the presumption to determine whether the adverse party has met his burden of rebuttal. Unfortunately, the courts of New York have not taken a consistent position on this question.[36] Therefore, the proper approach by the trial attorney is caution: he must research the cases on the particular presumption with which he is concerned, and he must be prepared

---

30. Cordua v. Guggenheim, 274 N.Y. 51 (1937).
31. RICHARDSON, *supra* note 21, p.34, §56. *See* Klin Co. v. New York Rapid Transit Corp., 271 N.Y. 376 (1936); People v. Nemadi, 140 Misc. 2d 712 (N.Y. Crim. Ct. 1988).
32. RICHARDSON, *supra* note 21, at 50-51 (citing Rawley v. Brown, 71 N.Y. 85 (1877)). *See* Benjamin v. Benjamin, 106 A.D.2d 599 (2d Dept. 1984), *aff'd*, 65 N.Y.2d 756 (1985).
33. Hogan v. O'Brien, 212 A.D. 193 (3d Dept. 1925); ICC Metals, Inc. v. Municipal Warehouse Company, 50 N.Y.2d 657 (1980); Art Masters Associates, Ltd. v. United Parcel Service, 77 N.Y.2d 200 (1990), Claflin v. Meyer, 75 N.Y. 260 (1878); Stewart v. Stone, 127 N.Y. 500 (1891); Goldstein v. Pullman Co., 220 N.Y. 549 (1917).
34. Schelberger v. Eastern Savings Bank, 60 N.Y.2d 506 (1983); Wellisch v. John Hancock Mutual Life Insurance Co., 293 N.Y. 178 (1944); Begley v. Prudential Insurance Co. of America, 1 N.Y.2d 530 (1956).
35. N.Y. C.P.L.R. 4504 (d).
36. *See* section 21.2.3.2.

to confront opponents and judges who disagree with him. The attorney also should be prepared to present additional evidence to support the same conclusion as the presumption; thus, the attorney for the plaintiff in an action for medical malpractice would introduce the fact that the defendant physician was unlicensed in order to raise the presumption that the defendant was negligent, but then the attorney would present expert testimony to establish the specific malpractice.

21.2.1.2 Other Meanings of Presumption

Besides using the term "presumption" to refer to a true presumption as defined above, lawyers use it with secondary or analogical meanings. Four of those meanings are discussed below: (1) a reliance on the burden of proof, (2) the rule of substantive law called a conclusive presumption, (3) the preferred inference called a presumption of fact, and (4) the argument from the circumstances of the case. Each of these analogical meanings is valid and useful; they are just not what we mean by a true presumption, and, in order to practice law effectively, the attorney must understand the concept he is employing.

Our first analogical meaning of presumption is the reliance on the burden of proof. As noted at the beginning of this chapter, if one party has the burden of proof on an issue, then the opposing party has the presumption in his favor. Moreover, the burden of proof may refer to the entire cause of action, e.g., the negligent infliction of a personal injury, or a particular fact asserted, e.g., that the driver entered the intersection against a red light. Hence, the plaintiff does not meet his burden of proof on his cause of action by asserting that the defendant ran the red light: the plaintiff must present evidence, such as the testimony of an eyewitness, to prove this narrower assertion. Remember, however, that "the party who has the burden of proof upon an issue may be aided in establishing his claim or defense by the operation of a presumption. . . ."[37]

A second analogical meaning of presumption is the conclusive presumption. Such a presumption is a substantive rule of law, not a rule of evidence, but such a rule would exclude evidence. For example, the rule that the written contract embodies the entire agreement between the parties would preclude evidence of oral terms as irrelevant.[38] More generally, a parol evidence rule is a necessary corollary of any statute of frauds, and a rule of prescription excluding challenges to title is another example of a conclusive presumption.

The third analogical meaning of presumption is the presumption of fact or the preferred inference. Calling the preferred inference a presumption of fact has probably confused generations of law students for, as Richardson wrote, "a presumption of fact is no presumption at all. It is a term used to describe a logical inference which the trier of the facts is authorized, but not required, to draw from the evidence in the case."[39] Nevertheless, attorneys and courts have persisted in calling such rules presumptions. We have described these rules as preferred inferences rather than just permissible ones because the law intends that the court alert the jury to the rule and because the ethic underlying the rule (every proposition of policy entails a proposition of value) is that the inference usually is justified but that the jury should consider all the evidence. Thus, the presumption of fact is an aid to the jury's untutored use of logic. Examples of the preferred inference are that a man intends the natural consequences of his acts[40] and that a party who de-

37. 57 NEW YORK JURISPRUDENCE 2D §97.

38. Cordua v. Guggenheim, 274 N.Y. 51 (1937); Di Baggio v. Provident Life and Casualty Co., 188 A.D.2d 510 (2d Dept. 1992); Summit Lake Associates v. Johnson, 158 A.D.2d 764 (3d Dept. 1990).

39. RICHARDSON, *supra* note 21, §55, p. 33 (citing Justice v. Lang, 52 N.Y. 323, 328).

40. Roberts & Co. v. Buckley, 145 N.Y. 215, 231 (1895).

stroys or fabricates evidence does so because the weight of evidence is against him.[41]

Preferred inferences have five characteristics in common. First, the preferred inference is not mandatory: the jury may refuse to draw it.[42] Second, the preferred inference is, like the presumption of law, based on evidence but is not itself evidence. However, third, the preferred inference, unlike the true presumption, is not a substitute for evidence.[43] In other words, the jury may not find in favor of the plaintiff merely because the defendant has fabricated evidence. Instead, the jury may construe the plaintiff's own evidence as favorably as possible. (Note that even res ipsa loquitur is not a substitute for all evidence but a substitute merely for expert testimony.) Fourth, the question of the preferred inference disappearing from the case does not arise. The inference becomes permissible once the evidence establishes the basis for it, e.g., spoliation; then the jury is free to apply the inference in weighing the evidence. But finally, fifth, the preferred inference may not be what the attorney really needs to prove. For example, the plaintiff's attorney is not trying to prove that the defendant discarded parts of the wrecked car but that the defendant's negligence caused the accident, and the attorney must have independent evidence of that.

Finally, a fourth analogical meaning of presumption (and furthest from the core meaning of the term) is the argument from the circumstances of the case. Attorneys typically confuse this phenomenon with the presumption of fact.[44] However, rather than being a rule of law, this phenomenon is

---

41. 57 NEW YORK JURISPRUDENCE 2D §131; Cruikshank v. Gordon, 118 N.Y. 178, 187 (1890); Nowack v. Metropolitan Street Railway Co., 166 N.Y. 433 (1901).
42. Platt v. Elias, 186 N.Y. 374 (1906).
43. RICHARDSON, *supra* note 21, §93, p. 67 ("As the court noted in Laffin v. Ryan, 4 App. Div. 2d 21, 26, 27 . . . the inference 'cannot supply a deficiency in the other party's case nor can it be regarded as proof of any essential fact'; 'the inference relates only to contradicting or corroborating evidence which is already in the case.'").
44. For example, BLACK'S LAW DICTIONARY, *supra* note 5, at 1349 col.1.

simply argument by deduction. Thus, the argument differs from a true presumption in that the jury is free to reject the argument, but the argument also differs from the presumption of fact in that the law does not encourage the inference. A hypothetical example may be illustrative.

Assume that the father of a twelve-year-old equestrienne hires an experienced horsewoman to accompany his daughter to a horse show as a coach and to transport the horses. After the show, the horsewoman loads Johnny Smoke into the horse van by sending him up the ramp which also serves as the side door of the van. After Johnny Smoke enters the van but before he is secured in a stall, the horsewoman raises the ramp to close the door while she stands directly behind the ramp. Unfortunately, Johnny Smoke backs up, steps on the ramp, and brings his weight and the ramp down on top of the horsewoman, who is injured. Subsequently, the horsewoman sues the equestrienne's father on the grounds that he owned the horse and the van and that he had hired her. She claims that the father should have warned her that the horse had a proclivity for backing up. At the trial, however, the defendant presents expert testimony that all horses tend to back up in such circumstances and that anyone experienced with horses knows that you move to the side of the ramp when you raise it precisely to avoid such an accident. The defendant's attorney or the appellate court might make the following argument.

> MR. HOGAN. An experienced horsewoman is presumed to know how horses behave. Specifically, the plaintiff, who is an experienced horsewoman, is presumed to have known that horses back up and that she should not have stood behind the ramp while raising it. The defendant hired the plaintiff to accompany his daughter to the horse show precisely because the plaintiff was an experienced horsewoman and could handle the horses safely. Johnny Smoke had no unusual proclivities, and the plaintiff knew how horses behave. Therefore, the plaintiff's negligence, not the defendant's, caused the plaintiff's injuries.

Clearly, this statement is not an example of a presumption of fact, i.e., a preferred inference offered by the law to the jury, but an example of arguing from the circumstances of the case. The attorney is using the term, presumption, in the sense of a deduction. However, this argument does share with the other kinds of presumption the form of a conditional syllogism, to wit:

> If the plaintiff was an experienced horsewoman, then she knew not to stand behind the ramp.
>
> The plaintiff was an experienced horsewoman. Therefore, the plaintiff knew not to stand behind the ramp.

21.2.2 Sample Presumptions for Actions in Negligence

This text cannot provide an exhaustive catalogue of presumptions, but a sample of those presumptions relevant to an action for negligence may be illuminating. For this purpose, we will divide the samples between the presumptions arising from the incident and the presumptions arising from the proceedings.

21.2.2.1 Presumptions Arising from the Incident

The first two presumptions listed below are conclusive presumptions.

(1) First, a common carrier owes a high degree of care to its passengers.[45] This duty is sometimes said to raise a presumption of negligence on the part of the carrier,[46] but this rule is really a substantive rule of law.

(2) Second, by statute, if two people have died simultaneously, then the estate or insurance proceeds of each shall

45. Middleton v. Whitridge, 213 N.Y. 499 (1915).

46. RICHARDSON, *supra* note 21, §93, p. 68.

be distributed as if he had survived the other.[47] In other words, each is presumed to have been the survivor as a rule of substantive law.

(3) The third sample is a mere presumption of fact: a man is presumed to intend the natural and probable consequences of his acts.[48] This rule is a merely permissible inference,[49] and the more specific arguments in the case usually obscure it.

The remaining six samples are all true presumptions.

(4) Fourth, possession of tangible property raises a weak presumption of ownership.[50]

(5) Fifth, the law presumes that the bailee was negligent if he failed to return the chattel or returned it in a damaged condition.[51] In fact, a bailment provides an especially good example of how a true presumption works. The bailor has the burden of proving the bailee's negligence. Once the bailor proves, however, that he delivered the chattel to the bailee and in good condition[52] and that the bailee failed to return it or returned it damaged, then the law raises a mandatory but rebuttable presumption that the bailee was negligent. The bailor can use this presumption to meet his burden of proof, but, if the bailee rebuts the presumption of negligence, then the burden of rebuttal shifts back to the plaintiff, who retains the burden of proof.[53]

---

47. N.Y. EST. POWERS & TRUSTS LAW 2-1.6 (a) and (d).
48. Roberts & Co. v. Buckley, 145 N.Y. 215, 231 (1895). Most of the cases on this subject arise from criminal trials.
49. RICHARDSON, *supra* note 21, §90, p.63.
50. Rawley v. Brown, 71 N.Y. 85 (1877); Benjamin v. Benjamin, 106 A.D.2d 599 (2d Dept. 1984), *aff'd*, 65 N.Y.2d 756 (1985).
51. Art Masters Associates, Ltd. v. United Parcel Service, 77 N.Y.2d 200, 207 (1990); Voorhis v. Consolidated Rail Corp., 60 N.Y.2d 878, 879 (1983); I.C.C. Metals, Inc. v. Municipal Warehouse Co., 50 N.Y.2d 657, 660 (1980); Hogan v. O'Brien, 212 A.D. 193, 194 (3d Dept. 1925); Claflin v. Meyer, 75 N.Y. 260 (1878).
52. Claflin v. Meyer, 75 N.Y. 260; Stewart v. Stone, 127 N.Y. 500; Goldstein v. Pullman Co., 220 NY. 549; Gerdau Co. v. Browne-Morton Stores, 1 A.D.2d 581 (1956), *aff'd*, 2 N.Y.2d 905 (1957); Aronette Manufactuing Co. v. Capital Piece Dye Works, 6 N.Y.2d 465 (1959).
53. *See* note 51.

(6) Another presumption referring to possession is that the driver of an automobile is presumed to be using the vehicle with the owner's permission. This is another good example of how a party uses a presumption. The injured plaintiff bears the burden of proof so he begins by proving the ownership of the vehicle. By statute in New York, the owner of an automobile is vicariously liable for the negligence of a driver who used the vehicle with the owner's permission;[54] in other words, there is a conclusive presumption. In order to establish this permission, moreover, the plaintiff may rely on the rebuttable presumption that the driver of a motor vehicle had the owner's permission.[55] This places the burden of rebuttal on the defendant owner to show that the driver was either a thief[56] or exceeded the scope of his permission.[57] The plaintiff even may rely on the strong presumption that the registered owner is the real owner,[58] but that party may rebut it.[59]

The latter three samples of true presumptions refer to actions leading to liability.

(7) By statute, that a driver hit a pedestrian in a crosswalk or collided with another vehicle in an intersection con-

---

54. N.Y. VEH. & TRAF. LAW § 388 (1).
55. Albouyeh v. Suffolk County, 62 N.Y.2d 681, 683 (1984); Barrett v. Mc Nulty, 27 N.Y.2d 928, 930 (1970); Leotta v. Plessinger, 8 N.Y.2d 449, 461 (1960); Comstock v. Beeman, 24 AD. 2d 931, 932 (3d Dept. 1965) *aff'd mem.* 18 N.Y.2d 772 (1966).
56. Albouyeh v. Suffolk County, 62 N.Y.2d 681, 683 (1984); Barrett v McNulty, 27 N.Y.2d 928, 930, (1970); Polsinelli v. Town of Rotterdam, 167 A.D.2d 579, 580 (3d Dept. 1990).
57. Walls v. Zuvic, 113 A.D.2d 936 (2d Dept. 1985).
58. N.Y. VEH. & TRAF. LAW § 2108 (c); Hartford Insurance Group v. Rubinshteyn, 66 N.Y.2d 732, 737 (1985); United Service Automobile Association v. Spyres, 28 N.Y.2d 631 (1971); Bornhurst v. Massachusetts Bonding and Insurance Co., 21 N.Y.2d 581, 585-86 (1968).
59. Guerriere v. Gray, 203 A.D.2d 324, 325 (2d Dept. 1994); Tabares v. Colin Service Systems, Inc., 197 A.D.2d 571 (2d Dept. 1993); State Farm Mutual Auto Insurance v. White, 175 A.D.2d 122, 123 (2d Dept. 1991); Corrigan v. Di Guardia, 166 A.D.2d 408, 409 (2d Dept. 1990); Leotta v. Plessinger, 8 N.Y.2d 449, 461 (1960).

trolled by a yield sign constitutes prima facie evidence that the driver failed to yield the right of way.[60]

(8) Also by statute, when a person not authorized to practice medicine does so and his acts are a proximate or contributing cause of injuries or death, then the defendant's unauthorized practice of medicine constitutes prima facie evidence of negligence in the resulting action for personal injuries or wrongful death.[61]

(9) Finally, the presumption against suicide and in favor of an accident is very strong. "Stated differently, the presumption is against suicide where one is found dead under such circumstances that the death might have resulted from accident."[62] The issue of suicide may arise either in an action for wrongful death against the alleged tortfeasor,[63] e.g., a subway system, or against an insurance company to collect the proceeds of a life insurance policy.[64] However, there is no such presumption against attempted suicide.[65]

---

60. N.Y. VEH. & TRAF. LAW § 1142 (b). *See* ROBERT A. BARKER & VINCENT C. ALEXANDER, EVIDENCE IN NEW YORK STATE AND FEDERAL COURTS 96 (1996) ("The apparent rule in civil cases is that prima facie evidence, as that term is used in a statute, generally shifts the burden of production. The opponent must therefore introduce evidence that is sufficient to support a finding of the non-existence of the facts to which the prima facie evidence gives rise.").

61. N.Y. C.P.L.R. 4504 (d). Article 131 of the Education Law regulates the practice of medicine. *See* N.Y. EDUC. LAW §§ 6520-6529.

62. 57 NEW YORK JURISPRUDENCE 2D §148 (citing Butterfield v. State, 118 Misc. 273 (1922), *rev'd on other grounds,* 205 A.D. 168, *aff'd,* 238 N.Y. 634).

63. Rinaldo v. New York City Transit Authority, 39 N.Y.2d 285, 287 (1976); Rooney v. S.A. Healey Co., 20 N.Y.2d 42, 45 n. (1967); Dubinsky v. Kofsky, 242 A.D. 342, 345 (3d Dept. 1934) rev'd on other grds, 266 N.Y. 631 (1935); Butterfield v. State, 118 Misc. 273, 275 (Ct. Cl. 1922). The issue also arises in suits for workmen's compensation. *See, e.g.,* Wiktorowicz v. Kimberly-Clark Corp., 99 A.D.2d 903, 904 (3d Dept. 1984); Bruning v. Sheffield Farms Co., 8 A.D.2d 241, 244 (3d Dept. 1959).

64. Schelberg v. Eastern Savings Bank, 60 N.Y.2d 506 (1983); Wellisch v. John Hancock Mutual Life Insurance Co., 293 N.Y. 178 (1944); Begley v. Prudential Insurance Co. of America, 1 N.Y.2d 530 (1956).

65. Rinaldo v. New York City Transit Authority, 39 N.Y.2d 285, 287-88 (1976).

21.2.2.2 Presumptions Arising from the Proceedings

(1), (2) The first two samples are a pair of presumptions regarding the mailing and receipt of notices. First, the post office is presumed to have delivered any letter that was properly stamped, addressed, and mailed.[66] Of course, the proponent must prove that he mailed the letter. He may do so directly by testimony and receipts,[67] or he may do so indirectly by proving a regular office practice sufficient to ensure that letters are always properly addressed and mailed.[68]

> [W]here the question is whether a letter was sent by mail at a certain time, in the absence of any evidence as to its being deposited with the post office authorities, proof of a course of business or of office practice, according to which it naturally would have been mailed, gives rise to a presumption that the letter had in fact been mailed. It is necessary to show, however, that the letter in question was placed in the usual office receptacle for outgoing mail and, in addition, to call as a witness the particular clerk whose duty it was to mail such letters and have him testify that he invariably mailed all letters found in the receptacle.[69]

Thus, the first presumption is that a letter properly mailed was received, and the second presumption is that a letter prepared according to an appropriate office procedure was mailed. Once the proponent has raised these presumptions, the alleged recipient cannot rebut them by the bare testimonial assertion that he did not receive the letter.[70] Instead, he

---

66. News Syndicate Co. v. Gatti PS Corp., 256 N.Y. 211 (1931); Rapoport v. Schneider, 29 N.Y.2d 396 (1972); Oregon Steam-Ship Co. v. Otis, 100 N.Y. 446 (1885).
67. All State Insurance Co. v. Patrylo, 144 A.D.2d 243, 246 (1st Dept. 1988).
68. Bossuk v. Steinberg, 58 N.Y.2d 916, 919 (1983); Gonzalez v. Ross, 47 N.Y.2d 922, 923 (1979); Nassau Insurance Co., v. Murray, 46 N.Y.2d 828, 829-30 (1978); Gardam and Son v. Batterson, 198 N.Y. 175, 178 (1910); Law v. Benedict, 197 A.D.2d 808, 810 (3d Dept. 1993); Lumbermens' Mutual Casualty Co. v. Collins, 135 A.D.2d 373, 375 (1st Dept. 1987).
69. RICHARDSON, *supra* note 21, §79, p.55.
70. European American Bank v. Abramoff, 201 A.D.2d 611, 612 (2d Dept. 1994).

must prove some office procedure of his own, e.g., logging all incoming mail, in order to rebut the presumption.[71]

The next three sample presumptions refer to interference with the evidence.

(3) Spoliation is the intentional destruction or mutilation of relevant evidence, and spoliation permits the jury to infer that the evidence was unfavorable to the culprit and, further, that his case is weak.[72] In a products liability case, when the physical evidence is indispensable for resolving the issues, a party's willful destruction of that evidence may justify the court in precluding evidence from that party on that issue or even in dismissing that party's pleading. Thus, in *Squitieri v. City of New York*, when the city destroyed the street sweeper that supposedly emitted toxic fumes, the court dismissed the city's third-party complaint against the manufacturer.[73] Spoliation may even work to the benefit of an innocent defendant against an innocent plaintiff. For example, in *Healey v. Firestone Tire & Rubber Co.*, the manufacturer of the tire rim assembly obtained the dismissal of the complaint against it because a co-defendant's destruction of the tire rims had fatally prejudiced the manufacturer's defense.[74] In such a case, however, the frustrated plaintiff may have a cause of action for the spoliation itself against the guilty party.[75]

(4) The presumption arising from the attempt to fabricate evidence is similar to the rule regarding spoliation: the jury may infer that the attempt indicates a weak case and con-

---

71. Jeraci v. Froelich, 129 A.D.2d 557, 558-9 (2d Dept. 1987); Vita v. Heller, 97 A.D.2d 464 (2d Dept. 1983).
72. Matter of Eno, 196 A.D. 131, 163 (1921); Armour v. Gaffey, 30 A.D. 121, 126 (1898), *aff'd*, 165 N.Y. 630 (1901); Noce v. Kaufman, 161 N.Y.S.2d 1 (1957).
73. Squitieri v. City of New York, 669 N.Y.S.2d 589 (1st Dept. 1998); *but see* Vaughan v. City of New York, 201 A.D.2d 556 (2d Dept. 1994).
74. Healy v. Firestone Tire & Rubber Co., 212 A.D.2d 351 (1st Dept. 1995).
75. *But see* Pharr v. Cortese, 147 Misc. 2d 1078 (1990). The common law borrowed the tort of spoliation from canon law, and the tort of spoliation meant the alteration of a document by a stranger to the transaction. BLACK'S LAW DICTIONARY, *supra* note 5, at 1573.

strue the proper evidence against the guilty party. (Once again, however, neither fabrication nor spoliation can serve as a substitute for all evidence from the innocent party.) The classic examples of fabrication are altering medical records[76] and bribing witnesses.[77]

(5) The consequences of refusing to produce documentary or physical evidence depend upon the importance of the evidence. Thus, the mere refusal to produce the document raises an adverse presumption of fact, i.e., an inference that the document would constitute evidence for the adverse party.[78] For example, in *Love v. New York Housing Authority*, the plaintiff was entitled to an adverse inference charge because the authority had failed to produce the record of complaints regarding the elevator on which the plaintiff was injured.[79] Such an inference is not, of course, a substitute for all evidence from the innocent party.[80] A true presumption arises if the document apparently would resolve the issue in dispute,[81] and, if the document would be conclusive, then only producing the document can rebut this presumption.[82]

The last two sample presumptions refer to the failure to present oral testimony.

(6) The sixth presumption is that a party's failure to testify to support his own case justifies an inference that he cannot do so honestly.

(7) The seventh presumption arises from a party's failure to call a witness within his control.[83] This latter inference

---

76. Pharr v. Cortese, 147 Misc. 2d 1078 (1990).

77. Lacs v. Jones Everard's Breweries, 170 N.Y. 444 (1902); Nowack v. Metropolitan Street Railway Co., 166 N.Y. 433 (1901); Nieves v. City of New York, 109 N.Y.S.2d 556, *aff'd*, 280 A.D. 972 (1952).

78. Feingold v. Walworth Brothers, Inc., 238 N.Y. 446 (1924).

79. Love v. New York Housing Authority, 674 N.Y.S.2d 750 (2d Dept. 1998).

80. Life and F. Ins. Co. v. Mechanic F. Inc. Co., 7 Wend 31 (____).

81. People *ex rel.* Woronoff v. Mallon, 222 N.Y. 456 (1918); Mullen v. J.J. Quinlan & Co., 195 N.Y. 109 (1909); Reehil v. Fraas, 129 A.D. 563 (1908), *rev'd on other grounds*, 197 N.Y. 64 (1909).

82. *Id.*

83. Robillard v. Robbins, 168 A.D.2d 803 (3d Dept. 1990) (strongest inference).

justifies a missing witness charge to the jury.[84] However, the witness must have relevant evidence, and his testimony must not be merely cumulative. Thus, even a party may lack evidence of his own knowledge, and a nonparty witness may be unavailable. Finally, either a party's[85] or a nonparty's[86] testimony may be merely cumulative.

The foregoing presumptions are only a small fraction of those presumptions lurking in the cases. Hence, the author urges the trial attorney to use his imagination and research skills to uncover any presumption relevant to his case.

21.2.3 Coping with Presumptions

In order to employ presumptions effectively the trial attorney must, first, grasp their use as rhetorical starting points, second, have presumptions consciously in mind, and third, prepare to accommodate contrary views.

21.2.3.1 Rhetorical Use of Presumptions

A presumption is not testimony. However, a presumption also is not evidence. At most, a presumption serves as a substitute for evidence, and many presumptions are only inferences. At the same time, the advocate may think of a presumption as a starting point. This observation is obvious for the presumption which consists of a reliance on the opponent's burden of proof, but any presumption or its evidentiary foundation may serve as a starting point in a chain of reasoning. For example, the plaintiff in an action arising out of an automobile accident might begin by introducing a certificate of registration to raise the presumption that one

---

84. Section 8.3.3.
85. Lepp v. Saks, 129 A.D.2d 681 (2d Dept. 1987) (refused).
86. Siegfried v. Siegfried, 123 A.D.2d 621 (2d Dept. 1986) (charge granted); Vaniglia v. Northgate Homes, Northgate Properties, Inc., 137 A.D.2d 806 (2d Dept. 1988), *app. den.* 72 N.Y.2d 806 (charge denied); Weinstein v. Daman, 132 A.D.2d 547 (2d Dept. 1987) *app. dis.* 70 N.Y.2d 872 (charge given erroneously).

defendant, named in the certificate, was the true owner of the motor vehicle; then the plaintiff might present eye witness testimony or testimony pursuant to an exception to the hearsay rule to raise the presumption that another defendant was driving the vehicle with the owner's permission. After presenting this evidence proving negligence, injuries, and damages, the plaintiff would rely on the permissive use statute to impose vicarious liability on the defendant owner as a conclusive presumption. In each of these instances, the law of evidence has provided a practical starting point for building the plaintiff's case.

Every advocate must analyze the audience to determine the means of persuasion, and this analysis should tell the advocate where in his chain of reasoning to begin his argument. Audiences are not uniformly intelligent, informed, and sympathetic, and no audience has unlimited time and attention. Therefore, the advocate must select his starting point in the chain of reasoning somewhere between the advocate's ultimate conclusion and Aquinas's five proofs for the existence of God. For example, a speaker advocating that NATO intervene in Kosovo would need to provide less background information to an audience that was familiar with national security affairs than to an audience which was not. Unfortunately, the uninformed audience might have no more time or patience for the speaker than the informed one does.

A jury is an audience, of course, and juries vary in quality, but the law uses such devices as standards of proof, rules of admissibility, and presumptions to minimize these differences and to encourage consistent and intelligent verdicts. In other words, by creating presumptions of fact, the law has encouraged the jury to draw particular conclusions, and, by creating true presumptions, the law has created starting points for the jury. The law does not ask the jury whether driving a motor vehicle should create a rebuttable presumption of having the owner's permission. Conclusive presumptions are even firmer starting points: the law is not interested in the jury's opinion of vicarious liability, so the reasoning underlying this rule is eliminated from the trial. The trial attorney litigating such a claim for personal injury must know his starting points so that he does not confuse the issues for the jury.

21.2.3.2 Integrating Presumptions with Trial Preparation

In order to employ or rebut presumptions effectively, the trial attorney must bring these rules consciously to mind. For example, when drafting his pleadings, the trial attorney outlines his own case as well as his opponent's, and he adds to the outline notations on the evidence. However, the attorney might find it useful to draft his first outline with notations of presumptions and then to add his notations of the evidence. After this, the attorney can make a flow sheet war-gaming the claims and responses to predict how the trial might develop. When the attorney identifies a presumption or evidence which is controversial, he can develop more evidence or draft a memorandum regarding the controversy.

Over time, the attorney should collect these outlines and memoranda in a loose-leaf binder for ready reference in future cases.[87] (Remember that specialization promotes efficiency.) Organize the memoranda by subject, i.e., the particular presumptions. You do not want to search for old files for a memorandum you know you wrote, and you certainly do not want to research and write a memorandum on the same presumption every time it appears in a case. Moreover, you cannot draft a memorandum overnight and try the case in the morning. Another advantage of compiling a

---

87. The author realizes that some readers have a visceral need to put everything on a computer. If that is how you work best, fine. As Jean Brodie would say, "For those who like that sort of thing, that is the sort of thing they like." Recognize the dangers, however. If you are run-over by a truck, and someone else must use your file in an emergency, he will find it much easier to use a loose-leaf binder than to go fishing in your computer. Moreover, a loose-leaf binder never crashed, and a disgruntled employee can sabotage your computer file without your realizing it for months.

loose-leaf binder of memoranda is that you will develop consistent views on the controversies regarding presumptions, and you do need consistent views. Otherwise, you might embarrass yourself by adopting conflicting views at different points of the same trial, e.g., on whether the presumption disappears after the adverse party introduces some contradictory evidence. Even if you adopt inconsistent views before the same judge during different trials, he will remember this and treat your views cautiously ever after.

21.2.4 Note on the Persistence Issue

The most consequential controversy regarding presumptions is between two schools of thought about their persistence. Specifically, does a presumption disappear from the case once the opposing party presents contradictory evidence, or does the presumption remain in the case to be weighed against the opposing evidence? This dispute reflects the real inconsistency in the judicial decisions and is associated with two scholars, Thayer and Morgan.

In 1898, J. Thayer advocated the position that the presumption itself should disappear from the case once the opponent has presented sufficient evidence to rebut the presumption in the absence of a counter-rebuttal, i.e., enough evidence to support a contrary finding.[88] In other words, the bubble bursts. The judge will not inform the jury of the presumption so the jury will not weigh the presumption against the contrary evidence. Instead, the original proponent must present evidence to refute the rebuttal although the jury may draw an inference from the facts which originally gave rise to the presumption.[89] For example, the jury may infer from the registra-

---

88. J. THAYER, A PRELIMINARY TREATISE ON EVIDENCE AT THE COMMON LAW (1898).

89. Hogan v. O'Brien, 212 A.D. 193, 195 (3d Dept. 1925). On the other hand, the rebuttal evidence may be so persuasive as to justify a directed verdict. O'Brien v. Equitable Life Assurance Society, 212 F. 2d 383, 387-89 (8th Cir. 1953) (inferences were insufficient).

tion certificate that one defendant did own the motor vehicle. Thus, the jury will decide the issue on the weight of the evidence.[90] The older cases in New York adopted Thayer's view.[91]

Two generations later, Professor Morgan espoused the contrary view that the court should inform the jury of the presumption, and that the jury should decide whether the contrary evidence actually rebutted it.[92] (The original proponent of course, may have introduced additional evidence anyway.)

New York has not adopted a consistent approach and followed either Thayer or Morgan. In other words, in some cases the presumption disappears but in other it persists. Some scholars claim to have found a pattern in this disorder, to wit that there are grades of presumptions, and, thus, whether the contrary evidence banishes a presumption depends upon the strength of the presumption.[93] The presumptions that survive a rebuttal include the presumptions against suicide,[94] in favor of the validity of marriages[95] and the legitimacy of children,[96] the presumption of permissive use of a

---

90. Fleming v. Ponziani, 24 N.Y.2d 105 (1969).

91. *Id.*

92. Morgan, *Instructing the Jury upon Presumptions and Burden of Proof*, 47 HARV. L. REV. 59, 82-83 (1933); Morgan & Maguire, *Looking Backward and Forward at Evidence*, 50 HARV. L. REV. 909, 913 (1937); Morgan, *Presumptions*, 12 WASH. L. REV. 255 (1937).

93. BARKER & ALEXANDER, *supra* note 60, at 93; MARTIN ET AL., *supra* note 22, at 75.

94. Schelberger v. Eastern Savings Bank, 60 N.Y.2d 506 (1983); Wellisch v. John Hancock Mutual Life Insurance Co., 293 N.Y. 178 (1944); 1 P.J.I.-Civil §1:63.2 and 2 P.J.I. 4:57.

95. Estate of Lowney, 152 A.D.2d 574, 575 (2d Dept. 1989); Esmond v. Thomas Lyons Bar & Grill, 26 A.D.2d 884 (3d Dept. 1966).

96. Jean P. v. Roger Warren J., 184 A.D.2d 1072 (4th Dept. 1992); Penny MM v. Bruce MM, 118 A.D.2d 979 (3d Dept. 1986).

motor vehicle,[97] the receipt of properly mailed letters,[98] and other presumptions when there is a question of the credibility of the witness.[99] In other cases, the presumption disappears if the evidence is substantial.[100] Finally, some presumptions, e.g., the validity of a release governed by the UCC, are so weak that contrary evidence destroys the presumption.[101] Another example is the presumption of ownership from possession alone.[102]

Whichever theory the trial attorney adopts, he must be prepared to cope with adversaries and judges who disagree with him. Thus, he must have ready his memoranda and additional evidence. If the attorney is the proponent of the presumption, but the judge is a Thayerite, the attorney must have evidence to meet the rebuttal, and if the attorney is the opponent, and the judge is a Morganite, the attorney must have sufficient evidence to outweigh the presumption.

---

97. Piwowarski v. Cornwell, 373 N.Y. 226, 229 (1937); Chaika v. Vandenberg, 252 N.Y. 101, 104-5 (1929).

98. Nassau Insurance Co. v. Murray, 46 N.Y.2d 828, 830 (1978); Engel v. Lichterman, 95 A.D.2d 536, 538 (2d Dept. 1983), *aff'd*, 62 N.Y.2d 943 (1984); Jonathan Woodner Co. v. Higgins, 179 A.D.2d 444 (1st Dept. 1992); T.J. Gulf, Inc. v. New York State Tax Commission, 124 A.D 2d 314, 315-6 (3d Dept 1986); European American Bank v. Abramoff, 201 A.D.2d 611, 612 (2d Dept. 1994). Actually rebutted in Vita v. Heller, 97 A.D.2d 464 (2d Dept. 1983); De Feo v. Merchant, 115 Misc. 2d 286, 289-90 (1982).

99. Bornhurst v. Massachusetts Bonding and Insurance Co., 21 N.Y.2d 581, 588 (1968).

100. *See, e.g.*, People v. Silver, 33 N.Y.2d 475, 481 (1974). *See also* Leotta v. Plessinger, 8 N.Y.2d 449, 461 (1960); St. Andrassy v. Mooney, 262 N.Y. 368 (1933) (regarding permissive use).

101. Fleming v. Ponziani, 24 N.Y.2d 105 (1969).

102. Rawley v. Brown, 71 N.Y. 85, 89 (1877).

Index

(References are to sections)

A

B

C

D

E

I

J

L

M

N

P

T

U

V

W

X

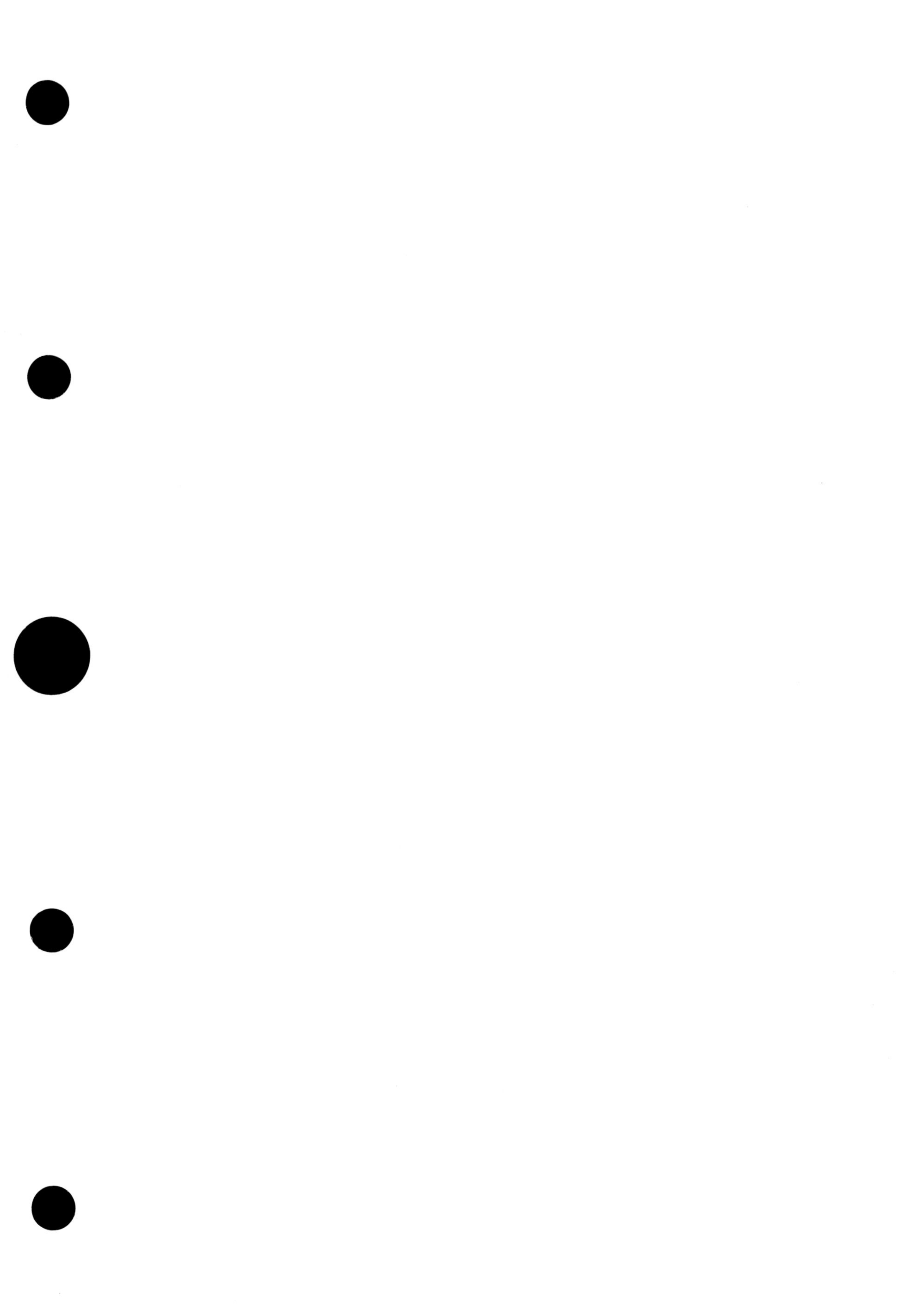